ADOLESCENTS

SECOND EDITION

Gary M. Ingersoll
Indiana University

PRENTICE HALL
Englewood Cliffs, New Jersey 07632

Library of Congress Cataloging-in-Publication Data

Ingersoll, Gary M.
   Adolescents / Gary M. Ingersoll. — 2nd ed.
     p. cm.
   Rev. ed. of: Adolescents in school and society. ©1982.
   Bibliography: p.
   Includes index.
   ISBN 0-13-008665-7
   1. Teenagers—United States.   I. Ingersoll, Gary M. Adolescents
in school and society.   II. Title.
HQ796.I454 1989
305.2'35—dc 19   88-34422
                                   CIP

Editorial/production supervision
  and Interior design: Robert C.Walters
Cover design: Ben Santora
Cover photo: Comstock, Inc./Skip Barrow
Manufacturing buyer: Ed O'Dougherty

 © 1989 by Prentice-Hall, Inc.
A Division of Simon & Schuster
Englewood Cliffs, New Jersey 07632

Printed in the United States of America
10 9 8 7 6 5 4 3 2

Prentice-Hall International (UK) Limited, *London*
Prentice-Hall of Australia Pty: Limited, *Sydney*
Prentice-Hall Canada Inc., *Toronto*
Prentice-Hall Hispanoamericana, S.A., *Mexico*
Prentice-Hall of India, Private Limited, *New Delhi*
Prentice-Hall of Japan, Inc., *Tokyo*
Prentice-Hall of Southeast Asia Pte. Ltd., *Singapore*
Editora Prentice-Hall do Brasil, Ltda, *Rio de Jeneiro*

To Helen

CONTENTS

1 ADOLESCENCE: DEVELOPING A NEW SENSE OF SELF   1

Defining Adolescence   2
Historical Views of Adolescence   4
   G. Stanley Hall, 4 / Storm and Stress, 5
Cross-Cultural Views of Adolescence   11
Theoretical Views of Adolescence   13
   Psychoanalytic Views, 14 / Behavioral Views, 17 / Cognitive Views, 19
Demographic Views of Adolescence   21
Developmental Goals   22
Self-Concept   27
Individual Differences 29
Summary   31

2 THE STUDY OF ADOLESCENTS IN LABORATORY AND NATURAL SETTINGS   32

Research Methods   22
   Experimental Research, 35 / Quasi-Experimental Research, 38 /
   Nonexperimental Research, 38 / Longitudinal and Cross-Sectional Research, 39 /
   Naturalistic Observation, 40 / Interviews, 43 / Observer Interference, 44
The Ethics of Research with Adolescents   46
Where to Begin   48
Summary   50

3 SELF-CONCEPT AND AFFECTIVE GROWTH 51

Erik Erikson 57
Measuring Self-Worth 62
Factors Affecting Self-Esteem 64
Self-Esteem and Social Adjustment 65
Shyness 65
Self-Worth and Achievement 69
The Locus of Control 70
Sex-Role Identity 72
Developing Self-Worth 74
Summary 75

4 PHYSICAL GROWTH AND DEVELOPMENT

Height, Weight and Proportionality 81
Changes in Females 83
Changes in Males 85
Sex Maturity Ratings 85
Psychological Correlates of Physical Growth 87
*Somatotypes, 88 / Early and Late Maturation, 89 / Physical Attractiveness, 91 /
Obesity, 92 / Anorexia Nervosa and Bulimia, 96 / Acne, 99*
Summary 101

5 DRUGS AND ALCOHOL 103

Drug Use and Abuse 107
Alcohol 110
Teenager's Drinking Patterns, 110 / Blood Alcohol Levels, 112
Marijuana 114
Tobacco 117
Depressants 118
Barbiturates and Sedative-Hypnotics, 118
Stimulants 119
Cocaine, 120 / Amphetamines, 120
Hallucinogens 122
LSD and PCP, 122
Inhalents 123
Heroin and Opiates 123
Drug and Alcohol Education 124
Summary

6   INTELLECTUAL GROWTH AND DEVELOPMENT   129

Tests of Intellectual Ability   130
The Binet Test, 130 / Group versus Individual Tests, 132 / Cultural Bias, 138 / Culture-Fair Tests, 138 / The Growth of Intelligence, 138 / Ethnic Differences, 140
Piaget's Theory of Cognitive Development   141
Stages of Development, 143
Individual Differences   149
Gifted Adolescents, 149 / Creativity, 150 / Mental Retardation, 155 / Mainstreaming, 156
Summary   157

7   ADOLESCENTS AND THE SCHOOLS   159

Achievement   161
Effective Schools   164
Teacher Roles   165
Students View Good Teaching, 166
Competency-Based Education   167
Restructuring the Schools   168
Middle Schools   170
Matching Environments   173
Academic Merit or Social Class   176
Dropouts   178
Summary   180

8   CHOOSING A VOCATION   182

Vocational Choice   185
Attitudes Toward Vocations, 185 / Sex Roles, 186 / Vocational Aptitudes, 188
Theories of Vocational Choice and Development   191
Ginsberg's Theory, 191 / Super's Theory, 193 / Holland's Theory, 194 / Some Limits on Vocational Theories, 196
Youth Employment and Unemployment   196
Entering the Job Market, 199 / Attitudes and Work, 200
Vocational Counseling   201
Summary   202

9   PARENTS AND ADOLESCENTS   204

Parenting Styles   207
Parenting Style and Personality Development, 210

The Generation Gap 212
Parent-Youth Conflict 213
The Struggle for Autonomy 214
Single Parent Families 216
Abusive Parents 219
Summary 224

10 FRIENDS AND PEERS 226

The Function of Peer Groups 228
The Structure of Peer Grups 231
The Formation of Peer Groups 233
Age and Peer Groups 234
Peers and Achievement 236
Adolescent Society 238
Social Cognition 240
Popularity and Social Competence 243
Summary

11 ADOLESCENT SEXUAL BEHAVIOR AND ATTITUDES 247

Masturbation 248
Dating 252
Sexual Attitudes 253
Premarital Coitus 254
Teenage Pregnancy 257
Controls over Conception, 260 / Controls over Gestation, 262 / Marriage, 263 / Delivery of the Baby, 264 / Keeping the Baby, 265
Homosexual Behavior 266
Sexually Transmitted Diseases 267
Syphilis, 268 / Gonorrhea, 269 / Chlamydia, 269 / Herpes Virus, Type II, 270 / AIDS, 270
Sex Education 271
Summary 273

12 DEVELOPING A VALUE SYSTEM 275

The Psychoanalytic View 276
The Social Learning (Behavioral) View 277
Modeling, 278 / Modeling and Television, 278
The Cognitive Developmental View 281
Stages of Moral Development, 284 / Universality of Moral Development, 287 / Moral Development and Moral Behavior, 288

Political Concepts   289
Adolescent Prejudice   290
Religion and Adolescents   292
*Identity Development, 293 / Intellectual Development, 294 /
Stages in Faith Development, 294 / Conversions, 298 / Cults, 299*
Summary   301

13   JUVENILE CRIME   303

Defining Delinquency   304
Types of Deinquents   309
Causes of Delinquency   310
Labelling   312
Status Offenses   313
School Vandalism and Violence   317
Gangs   318
Delinquents' Views   320
Juvenile Justice   321
Summary   323

14   MALADJUSTED ADOLESCENTS   324

Stress   326
Psychosomatic Disturbances   327
Conduct Disorders and Adjustment Reactions   329
Depression   330
Schizophrenia   332
Suicide   336
Counseling Adolescents   342
Assessing the Problem   343
Resistance to Treatment   345
Family Counseling   347
Confidentiality   348
Summary   349

15   CONCLUSION   351

The Physical Self   352
The Cognitive Self   352
The Social Self   353
Liking Our Selves   353

Is It Tougher Today? **354**

*Respect the Integrity of the Adolescent, 354 / Give A Damn, 355 /
Be Patient—Keep a Sense of Humor, 356 / Do As You Say, 356 /
Be Open and Honest, 356 / Be Gentle with Yourself, 357 /
Be Honest with Yourself, 357*

REFERENCES **359**

GLOSSARY **390**

INDEX OF NAMES **396**

INDEX OF KEY TERMS **402**

PREFACE

When I wrote the first edition of this text, I had as my primary focus the creation of a resource that would be of value more to the practitioner than to the theorist. The text was meant primarily for those who either expected to work with or who were currently working with adolescents and who wished to expand their knowledge in the area. As such I tried to present a basic core of information about adolescence and adolescents, drawn from contemporary research in psychology, sociology, education, medicine, and allied disciplines.

During the years since I wrote that first edition, I have continued to be involved in research in the area of adolescent development, particularly with young people who deal with diabetes and those who engage in behaviors that place them "at risk." As a result of that experience, I am convinced, more than ever, that the central task of the adolescent transition is the development of a positive sense of self-worth. Self-esteem or self-worth is a variable which is admittedly difficult to measure with reliability. Nonetheless, self-esteem pervades adolescents' adjustment to stress and change. If there was a particular shortfall in that earlier edition, I think it was in the lack of a strong affirmation of that effect. I have tried to correct that shortfall in this edition.

I assume a stance that adolescents are striving in psychological, social, and physical domains to gain a sense of who they are. As adults working with young people, we must help them accomplish the task of developing a positive sense of self-worth. In working with adolescents we must recognize that wide differences exist among young people and we cannot make global assumptions based solely on an individual's age or level of physical maturity. Finally, we must maintain a caring stance. Caring people, whether they are parents, teachers, counselors, pastors, or others, convey a sense to the individual adolescent that he or she is worthwhile.

Adolescents has been written at a level appropriate to the typical freshman or sophomore student. Insofar as possible, I have avoided using narrow jargon. In some intances, however, specific psychological or sociological language is needed to accurately describe a phenomenon. Where that occurs, I try to provide adequate definitions. These definitions are repeated in the glossary at the end of the text.

Also included in each chapter are a series of *Vignettes*. Their primary purpose is to improve the readers' level of understanding by offering nonacademic examples of adolescent behavior and development. Some of the vignettes are selected for their specific instructional value related to a current problem in adolescent development. Others are included for reader interest and humor. They should provide stimuli for additional classroom discussion.

Included in each chapter are selected photos. Like the vignettes the photos have been selected to depict specific or general processes in the adolescent transition. They offer bases for discussion and understanding. The book also includes a glossary and extensive reference list. The glossary defines terms from the text that the introductory student might find troublesome. The reference list contains bibliographic citations of sources cited in the text; it should also serve as a valuable resource for the student initiating a research study.

Instructors who used the previous edition of this text will notice a modest reorganization of the chapters. In large part that reorganization results from student feedback. An *Instructor's Guide* is available to assist professors in evaluating student achievement.

Creating a text is an effort that requires the aid and support of a variety of people. I would like to take this opportunity to thank a number of people who were instrumental in producing this text. First, I would like to thank Susan Willig at Prentice Hall who encouraged me to join the Prentice Hall "team" and Susan Finnemore who shepharded the manuscript though its development. Bob Walters expended considerable energy in earlier drafts to insure that the text was readable. I would also like to acknowledge the contributions of Stephen Hamilton and Stephan Wilson who reviewed early drafts of the manuscript and made useful suggestions for its improvement.

Mostly, I want to thank my wife Helen and my three children, Kristin, Rob, and John. During those times of stressful deadlines they were a source of support and love.

Gary M. Ingersoll

ADOLESCENCE: DEVELOPING A NEW SENSE OF SELF

Adolescence is a period of development that adults tend to view with a mixture of fear and fascination. Teachers, nurses, doctors, social workers, and so forth, seem to have reactions from one or another extreme. Either they see adolescents as exciting, enthusiastic, and fun to be with, or as a frightening mob of unruly, uncontrollable creatures who "ought to be put into deep freeze during the teen years." There does not seem to be much in the way of middle ground. Most professionals, it would seem, prefer to work with other age groups. Parents of preteen children will often describe their dread at the coming catastrophe to their family—their child is about to become a "teenager." Somewhere between the two extreme views lies an accurate picture of the period of life we call adolescence.

While there is a danger in viewing adolescence as a separate period of growth and development, there are also advantages. The major disadvantage is that viewing adolescence separately makes it appear overly different from other periods of growth. It segregates adolescence too much. However, adolescence is unique, not so much in the fact that it is a distinct period of growth and development, but in the types of tasks and expected events that are part of the process of becoming an adult. It is precisely those differences, and the ways in which young people who are adolescents respond to the tasks, that frightens many adults. Many professional practitioners avoid working with adolescents because they are neither children nor adults. The practitioners are unsure of how to relate to these young people. Practitioners are not the only ones who avoid adolescents. It would appear that social scientists have a similar aversion to the study of adolescents. You will find in your own studies that the proportion of research literature dealing with adolescents is small, compared to that dealing with, for example, infants and preschoolers.

Just what is adolescence? Or, what are adolescents? Is adolescence a period of life marked by storm and stress? Is it a period of naive, youthful idealism? Is it a period of rebellion? Or, is adolescence a little of all of the above? This textbook is about young people in the period of life that is called adolescence. My purpose in writing it is to acquaint you with the psychology of adolescence by dealing with various aspects of the process of moving from childhood to adulthood. I make no presumptions of presenting a unified "Theory of Adolescence." The field of study is itself too young to support that lofty goal. On the other hand, there are two theoretical themes that will dominate my comments in the chapters that follow. First, adolescence is a period of life in which a new sense of self is formed. This new sense of self is, in part, a result of the sense of oneself that the adolescent brings from childhood. It is also partly a result of where the young person sees himself or herself headed in the future. Our role in working with young people is thus one of aiding them in developing a positive sense of self. Second, adolescence is a period of development marked by significant qualitative shifts in the way young people conceive their psychological and social world. The manner in which adolescents are able to think about their world plays a major role in their ability to adjust to it, interact with it, and their sense of self. In the past, many sources have treated the ways in which people *think* about their world as distinctly different from their *feelings* about it. In recent years, however, more writers have become aware of the inter-connectedness of these two facets of personal development.

DEFINING ADOLESCENCE

How do we define adolescence? What is an adolescent? The answer to these questions is not as simple as you might initially think. The most common and obvious feature of the adolescent transition is a sudden spurt in physical and sexual development. At no other time since birth, does a person undergo such a rapid and monumental change. The physical and sexual transition is so profound that some writers, especially those with a medical orientation, have focused on it as the central element in a definition of adolescence. Although physical and sexual maturation are very important components of an adolescent's transition into adulthood, they are only part of the total process. The physical growth spurt must be viewed together with less obvious, but also important changes in intellectual ability, in new expectations for adultlike roles, in new interpersonal relationships, and in more mature social responsibilities. *Adolescence* is a period of personal development during which a young person must establish a sense of individual identity and feelings of self-worth which include an alteration of his or her body image, adaptation to more mature intellectual abilities, adjustment to society's demands for behavioral maturity, internalizing a personal value system , and preparing for adult roles.

Any definition of adolescence is certain to meet with some objections and the one offered here will not suit everyone. By looking at adolescence as a whole, for instance, it fails to warn that the nature of early adolescence differs in emphasis from middle adolescence, which in turn differs from later adolescence. At each level, within

Adolescence is a period not only of turbulence and soul-searching but also of great creativity and fun. (© Margaret Thompson)

adolescence, priorities change. The focus of young people's emerging sense of self changes with respect to which part of their self-concept they pay most attention.

If the general area of adolescent development has suffered from a lack of attention from researchers, early adolescence has been even more neglected (Lipsitz, 1977). During the early adolescent years young people make their first attempts to leave the dependent, secure role of a child and to establish themselves as unique individuals, independent of their parents. Early adolescence is marked by rapid physical growth and maturation. The focus of the adolescents' self-concepts are thus often on their physical self and their evaluation of their physical acceptability. Early adolescence is also a period of intense conformity to peers. "Getting along," not being different, and being accepted seem somehow pressing to the early adolescent. The worst possibility, from the view of the early adolescent, is to be seen by peers as "different."

Middle adolescence is marked by the emergence of new thinking skills. The intellectual world of the young person is suddenly greatly expanded. Although peers still play an important role in the life of middle-adolescents, they are increasingly self-directed. The middle-adolescent's energies are directed at preparing for adult roles and making preliminary decisions regarding vocational goals. Despite some delinquent behavior, middle adolescence is a period during which young people are oriented toward what is right and proper. They are developing a sense of behavioral maturity and learning to control their impulsiveness. During the middle-adolescent years young people focus on their acceptability by opposite sexed peers.

Late adolescence is marked by the final preparations for adult roles. Young people during this period attempt to crystallize their vocational goals and establish a sense of personal identity. Their need for peer approval is diminished, and they are largely independent of their parents. The shift to the adult stage of development is nearly completed. It may be a mistake however to conclude that all the outcomes of the adolescent transition are necessarily complete as we enter adulthood. As one friend puts it, "When I was an adolescent, I thought that when I got to be an adult I would have it all together. Now, I'm an adult and I sure don't have all the answers; I've got more questions."

Some writers (for example, Keniston, 1965) have even suggested that a period of postadolescent development, preceding formal acceptance of adult roles, be designated as "youth." The term *youth*, however, has traditionally had a broader connotation which includes young people who are still within the period that we refer to as adolescence. When the term youth is used in this text, it will be in reference to its more traditional referent to young people.

While it is certainly the case that adolescence is not singular, there are commonalities that pull the period together. Note too, that the proposed definition does not specify an age range. In common language we often talk about the "teen" years or about "teenagers." While much of the adolescent transition happens during the years of high school and college, there is no reason to assume that adolescence magically starts at 13 and ends at 20.

HISTORICAL VIEWS OF ADOLESCENCE

There is little question that adolescence, as we understand it now, is a relatively new concept. Before this century, few writers describe anything that would be seen as a distinctly "adolescent" period of development (Demos & Demos, 1969). Some early writers addressed to a vague sense of "youth." "Youth" was described alternately as a romanticized period of idealism where the highest of ideals were fostered, or as a period of rebellion and delinquency where morals were regularly violated.

G. Stanley Hall

The psychologist who is generally credited with establishing adolescence as a period of psychological and social development deserving separate study is G. Stanley Hall. Hall is also credited with initiating the child study movement in America. Hall, like many other social scientists at the turn of the twentieth century, was enamored of Charles Darwin's theory on the nature of evolution. Until the mid-nineteenth century, the dominant view of human behavior reflected the philosophical tradition of John Locke. Locke argued that humans were born with a "blank slate" and all behavior was learned. Darwin's theory of evolution and Herbert Spencer's elaboration with the notion of the "survival of the fittest," offered an alternate view. It was not long before a new breed of "Social Darwinists" were arguing that human social behavior followed the same "laws" of evolution. They argued, for example, that some people were poor, not because of any particular social evil, but as a selective genetic function which permitted the rich and powerful to emerge. Nations and races were also subject to the same evolutionary forces. Social Darwinism became something of an "academic rage."

Beyond his attraction to Social Darwinism, Hall appears to have been especially impressed with the writings of Ernst Haekel who proposed that as organisms develop they appear to repeat characteristics that mirror their evolutionary stages of development. Haekel referred to this process with the phrase "ontogeny recapitulates phylogeny." Hall felt that psychological development of children and adolescents proceeded in a "recapitulation" of the stages of development of society.

In his two-volume work with the forbidding title *Adolescence: Its Psychology and Its Relations to Physiology, Anthropology, Sociology, Sex, Crime, Religion, and Education* (1904), Hall depicted adolescence as a transitional period bridging the "savagery" of childhood with "civilized" adulthood. Since psychological development was presumed to parallel development of society, Hall saw adolescence as representative of the tumultuous history of humanity arriving at its current civilized state. Adolescence was described as "a new birth, for the higher and more completely human qualities are now born. . . . [Adolescence is] suggestive of some ancient period of storm and stress when old moorings were broken and a higher level attained. (p. 14)" Adolescents were seen as in a state of flux, alternating between periods of high enthusiasm and utter despair, between energy and lethargy, between altruism and self-centeredness. These radical shifts of necessity make adolescence a period of turmoil, of "storm and stress."

Storm and Stress

In one form or another, Hall's concept of "storm and stress" continues to be a popular conception of adolescence. Parents who seek advice about their adolescents often give a description of their offspring that is not unlike Hall's. One moment their adolescent is friendly and cooperative, and the next he or she is hostile and belligerent. Parents find that the child who was a docile, pleasant and helpful preadolescent now refuses to help around the house, will not listen to reason, is generally antagonistic and selfish, and seems to resent being part of the family.

The view presented by distraught parents is not very different from a description offered by Anna Freud (1966):

> Adolescents are excessively egoistic, regarding themselves as the center of the universe and the sole object of interest, and yet at no time in later life are they capable of so much self-sacrifice and devotion. They form the most passionate love relations, only to break them as abruptly as they began them. On the one hand, they throw themselves enthusiastically into the life of the community and, on the other, they have an over-powering longing for solitude. They oscillate between blind submission to some self-chosen leader and defiant rebellion against any and every authority. (pp. 137–138)

Anna Freud goes on to suggest that the period of adolescence is naturally "schizoid" and that the adolescents who should be of concern are those who show no signs of struggle.

Not all writers agree that adolescence is a tumultuous period. In his research, Bandura (1964) found that most young people with whom he had contact were *not* anxiety ridden and stressful. Bandura warned that the assumption of a tumultuous adolescence was a gross overstatement of fact. Also, if society presumes adolescence to be a period of radical tension, it runs the risk of creating a self-fulfilling prophecy. If parents, teachers, and other significant adults *expect* adolescents to be hostile, anxious, and emotionally variable and begin to worry if their teenagers are not, then adolescents, in order to conform to these expectations, may become hostile, anxious and emotionally variable. On the other hand, we must be careful not to run to the opposite conclusion—that is, that adolescence is a period of calm and serenity. Either view is misleading.

In an important set of studies by the Offers (Offer, 1969; Offer & Offer, 1975) a group of middle-class adolescent boys were followed longitudinally across their adolescent years. These boys were purposely selected to be not exceptional. That is, they were not suffering from chronic psychological problems. As the Offers followed these boys they found no unusual increase in anxiety or antisocial behavior. That is not to say that none of the boys experienced any problems. Some did and there was some rebellion against parental authority. Most of the young people, however, showed no major disruption. The Offers (1975) analyzed their data on the same of boys and found three groups which accounted for the great majority of their sample. The first group consisted of about a quarter of the boys. This group was marked by continuous growth with little evidence of emotional turmoil. They seemed to progress toward adult roles in a steady, positive fashion. The second group consisted of about one-third of the boys. These young people experienced some temporary disruptions in the smooth progression to adulthood. When faced with some trauma or upheaval they seemed thrown "off track" for a time. They were, however, ultimately able to muster their psychological resources and move forward. The third group, consisting of about one-fifth of the boys, more closely resembled the image of adolescence given by Hall. This group experienced a

Friends are very important during adolescence, especially in providing a sense of belonging.
(© Eric Kroll 1980/Taurus Photos)

tumultuous transition through adolescence. Normal problems seemed to escalate into major adjustment problems. They were not able to summon psychological resources to deal with conflict.

More recently, Offer (Offer, Ostrov & Howard, 1984) concluded that while a notable minority of normal adolescents report difficulty in coping with the struggles of adolescence, most do not. In their data, "The vast majority...function well, enjoy good relationships with their families and friends, and accept the values of the larger society. In addition, most report having adapted without undue conflict to the bodily changes and emerging sexuality brought on by puberty." (p. 12).

Other writers (Adelson, 1979; Oldham, 1976) have similarly concluded that adolescence is *not* characterized by storm and stress. Repeatedly, studies have shown that adolescence is not inherently any more stressful or tumultuous than any other period of life. Why, then, does the myth of a tumultuous adolescence persist. There are two probable reasons. First, psychologists and social workers who counsel adolescents are most likely to meet those who have adjustment problems. In a study of mental health professionals (Hartlage, Howard & Ostrov, 1984), most saw the typical "teenager" as confused, anxious, fearful, tense, and overly sensitive. The adolescents that counselors are apt to meet more closely resemble the third group in the Offer's study. The image of normally disturbed adolescents is reinforced and the counselors retain their stereotype. Second, as Oldham (1976) notes, many of our conceptions of adolescents are drawn from popular novels that we read. Stories such as *Catcher in the Rye, Ordinary People, Go Ask Alice,* and *The Outsiders* seem to reinforce our stereotype. This latter argument needs to be taken with some caution. Bleich (1980) points out that a variety of images of adolescents and adolescence are drawn from literature. Many of the images show young people dealing with stress in positive ways. The result, according to Bleich, is some young people read these novels and use the characters as models of how to deal with problems.

VIGNETTE 1–1
LETTERS FROM HOME

Magazines and newspapers often include cartoons or features that poke humor at the unwillingness of young people to write home to parents for anything other than financial support. What about letters from parents. Are they any better? The writer of this article would have us believe that letters from parents to their young offspring are similarly predictable. Oliver Wendell Holmes, looking back on advice given to him by his father in letters, categorized it as "twaddle." It is interesting to note that the advice from parents to their young students away from home doesn't seem to have changed very much over centuries. Indeed one letter from an Egyptian nobleman to his son three thousand years ago strangely resembles letters from home today.

Source: Linda Lewis, "Be Proud and Useful, Be Merry
and Wise," *Harvard Magazine* (January/February 1980):
38–44. Copyright © 1980 Harvard Magazine, Inc.
Reprinted by permission.

Dear Son,

If we waited for you to answer our previous letters, all communication would, presumably, cease. How are you enjoying your photography course? Your film course?

Your Origins of Jazz course? Do you honestly think this is what a college education is all about? What do you suppose you will be doing ten years from now? Ever read *The Odyssey* or *War and Peace?*

Naturally we worry about you. The few times we have seen you in the last year have been far from reassuring. It isn't just outward appearance (the tangled hair, the stubbly chin, the leather jacket, the mirrored sunglasses), but also your offhand attitude that dismisses our legitimate queries as meddlesome. We are bound to wonder at your choice of courses, your grades, your lack of a plan for a summer job, the example you seem to want to set for your sister and brother. The only reason we say all this is that we have your best interests at heart, and that...Etc., etc.

ALTERNATE VERSION A.

Dear Son,

Life is a bit dull without you. No one to push around or be pushed around by. I must say, you remind me of myself at your age—rebellious, tough-talking, badly organized, intolerant. I was really terrified of being on my own, didn't know what I would do or where I would fit in. I did a lot of stupid things.

If possible, don't hurt yourself by doing stupid things. Don't mess around with crazy kids. Don't spoil your chances to do what you want to do.

Please keep me in your heart, and please make me proud of you. If possible. At least be proud of yourself. Take it easy, son, Etc., etc.

ALTERNATE VERSION B.

Dear Son,

I beat your father at Scrabble last night. Thought you'd want to know. Cookies on the way. Press on!

Love,
Mother.

Which letter to send, that is the question; whether 'tis nobler in the mind to suffer the slings and arrows of outrageous children, or to take arms and by opposing and risk the fragile truce; whether to admonish, confess, or reassure; whether to go for short- or long-term results. It is hard to know what line to take. If one analyzed motives and probable effects too much, however, it is possible that no letter would be sent at all. And no cookies.

There is something about writing to a child away at school that brings out the worst in many of us. Approaching redundancy, needing to justify our parental existence, we re-enact scenes from our own childhood, play the parts our parents played, say things we said we'd never say.

There may be a certain dubious consolation in the realization that for many centuries parents have been writing letters to their absent children: letters whose petulant, anxious, reproving, improving tones scarcely change over time. Shining examples and purposeful blindness, self-interest and self-punishment, loving support and subtle under-cutting are woven into repeating patterns that document relations between parents and children. Mothers and fathers continue to urge young people to study seriously, to organize their time, to do the nastier jobs first, to improve their handwriting and spell-ing, to make friends with the right sort of people, to make the most of themselves. In literate societies, it seems an irresistible form.

Justice Oliver Wendell Holmes, writing to a friend, said he had discovered among his father's papers letters from his father's father "inculcating virtue in the same dull terms" that had been passed on to him. "If I had a son I wonder if I should yield to the temptation to twaddle in my turn." Bound to.

Instructive Examples of Ten Basic Twaddles

1. *Keep in touch.* . . . "Do write to me. You know that as long as I get letters from you I am cheerful about your safety." An anonymous Roman-Egyptian mother to her uncommunicative son.

"I certainly don't get all of those letters you keep telling me you write."

2. *Study hard.* . . . In the second century A.D. one Cornelios wrote to his son Hierax, who was away at school: "Take care you do not annoy anyone in the house, but study and devote yourself wholly to your books, and you will derive profit from them." . . .

3. *Honor thy God, Obey thy mother, Do thy duty, Etc., etc.* . . . On his seven-teenth birthday, Prince Edward Albert, who seemed destined never to satisfy his parents, Queen Victoria and the Prince Consort, received the usual spritely letter from them:

"Life is composed of duties, and in the due, punctual and cheerful perform-ance of them the true Christian, true soldier and true gentleman is recognized."

4. *Abhor vice and resist temptation/evil companions/gambling/smoking/ flattery/overindulgence, etc., etc., etc.* . . . .

Lorenzo de' Medici, writing to his son Giovanni upon his investiture as car-dinal at the remarkable age of sixteen, warned him against those who were jealous of him and would try, once he moved to that "sink of iniquity, Rome," to cause him to "slide into the same ditch into which they have themselves fallen, counting on success because of your youth."

"Darling Winston," Lady Churchill wrote to her fifteen-year-old son at Eton, "I hope you will try and not smoke. If only you knew how foolish and how silly you look doing it you wd give it up. . . ."

5. *Marry wisely.* . . . In the fourth century B.C. a young girl wrote to her mother to say she would not marry the boring man to whom she had been betrothed, but was prepared to insist upon a beautiful lad of her own choosing. Her mother wrote to her immediately:

"You are mad daughter, and entirely beside yourself. You need a dose of hellebore. . . Compose yourself and thrust from your mind this mischief. For, if your father should learn a word of this, he would without a moment's thought of hesitation throw you as food to the sea monsters." . . .

6. *Get ahead.* . . . Rose Kennedy, in a round-robin letter to her children, instructed them on some points of etiquette she thought they might have missed—the ritual of calling cards, for example. "I am just giving you these few hints," she wrote. "Perhaps if you follow them you will be more of a success socially."

7. *Keep well.* . . . Medicine, cod-liver oil, leeches, purges, fasts, "plain, nourishing food," steel braces for turned-in toes, periods of solitary confinement for the overactive, fresh air or changes of scene for the low in spirits, all have been recommended by well-meaning parents for the well-being of the young. Among the saddest of letters are those from parents to children suffering mental or emotional difficulties: James Joyce's to his dauther Lucia, Robert Frost's to his son Carol. Mark Twain, who should have known better, wrote uncomprehending, impatient, resentful, sometimes abusive letters to his daughters, one of whom was hypertense, one seriously depressed, and one an undiagnosed epileptic. . . .

8. *Think of me as your friend.* . . . "Do not think I mean to dictate as a parent," wrote Lord Chesterfield to his son. "I only mean to advise as a friend, and an indulgent one too. . . ."

9. *But remember who pays the bills and do not disappoint.* Having posed as a friend, Lord Chesterfield went on: "I do not, therefore, so much as hint to you how absolutely dependent you are on me—that you neither have nor can have a shilling in the world but from me; and that as I have no womanish weakness for your person, your merit must, and will be the only measure of my kindness. . . . When I reflect upon the prodigious quantity of manure that has been laid upon you, I expect you should produce more at eighteen than uncultivated soils do at eight and twenty. . . and I promise myself so much from you, that I dread the least disappointment.". . .

10. *Be happy, or, at any rate, don't be unhappy.* . . . When John Adams recommended "ice skating" to his son John Quincy, spending the winter in Holland, he meant him to appreciate it as a fine art and to "restrain that impetuous Ardour and violent Activity into which the Agitation of Spirits occasioned by this exercise is apt to hurry you, and which is inconsistent both with your Health and Pleasure. . . . Everything in Life should be done with Reflection, and Judgement, even the most insignificant Amusement. They should all be arranged in subordination, to the great Plan of Happiness and Utility. That you may attend early to this Maxim is the wish of your affectionate father.". . .

Any overgeneralization about adolescents and adolescent development is certain to meet with exceptions and qualifications. We, as practitioners, are dealing with a highly variable population. For some young people adolescence *will* be stressful and tumultuous. For others, it will be smooth and pleasant. Not all adolescents are the same. To impose a stereotype on young people because of their age may be as prejudicial as racism or sexism. As an adult working with young people, it will be your task to help them work through the demands of the adolescent transition and to help them adapt to whatever stresses they encounter which might jeopardize healthy maturation. If they experience upheaval, your role is to aid them in identifying and mustering those psychological and social resources they have available.

CROSS-CULTURAL VIEWS OF ADOLESCENCE

Several writers, especially anthropologists, rely upon evidence drawn from cross-cultural studies of development and conclude that adolescence is a phenomenon found primarily in western cultures. Those who hold this view point out that there are several socieites in which there is no discernible adolescence. At some point, usually around puberty, young people are no longer considered children and are given adult status. If adolescence does exist, it is not necessarily similar to western adolescence. Drawing on studies such as Margaret Mead's *Coming of Age in Samoa* (1928), for example, authors will emphasize that adolescence in some cultures is largely carefree and without stress. In cultures in which sexual constraints are few, adolescents do not seem to experience the same sexual anxieties that western teenagers feel. This does not mean that young people in such cultures do not experience *any* transitional anxiety, but rather, that if a culture does not emphasize an aspect of the transition to adulthood, anxiety in that area is lessened.

There are, however, some who examine the same evidence and conclude that indeed adolescence *is* a universal phenomenon (Ausubel, Montemayor & Svajian, 1977). In their view, some demarcation of adolescents as a separate group is characteristic of human societies everywhere. There is even some evidence of "adolescent" status among some species of primates, but it is a much shorter period than human adolescence. In western culture adolescence may extend to 10 years or more.

Perhaps the keystone of most anthropological studies of adolescence is the *initiation rite,* or the *"rites of passage."* In many cultures the transition from childhood to adulthood is marked by a specific test of manhood or womanhood. At some point in development, usually associated with puberty, young boys and girls are isolated from the community and readied for a test that will determine their suitability to be an adult member of the society. The ritual of initiation varies from culture to culture and may be relatively mild or quite severe. In more severe initiations, genital mutilation may occur. Several years ago an author observed several features that appeared common to many of the rites (Conklin, 1935). The young person is first isolated from the community and is often mocked and humilated. They may be forced to wear some clothing or mark that identifies them as an initiate and to eat indecent food. If physical injury or mutilation is a part of the initiation, the young person is not to show any signs of pain. For boys, the initiation often involves circumcision. If the young person passes the test he or she is then told the secrets of the tribe and then is inducted into the tribe as an adult member in a ceremony. Initiation rites for young girls in a remote tribe of northern South America, called the Maroni River Caribs, involve a variety of ritualistic elements (Brown, 1975, adapted from Kloos):

> When a girl first menstruates, she is confined to a special part of the house for eight days. She remains in seclusion particularly to avoid the spirits of the river and of the forest. These would be offended by her condition and they would cause her to sicken and die. The girl is dressed in old clothes in order to be unattractive to the spirits, and her diet is restricted rather severely. During these eight days, she is expected to spin cotton to be used in making a hammock for a member of her family. At the end of seclusion, an elderly couple noted for industry arrives at the home of the girl before sunrise. The girl is bathed. Then a small tuft of cotton is placed in the palm of her

hand, and fire is set to it. She must move the cotton rapidly from hand to hand to avoid getting burned. This ritual is done because her hands must always be busy. Next her hand is placed in a bowl of large, biting ants. She must not show pain. The ants are to remind her always to be industrious like the ant. Were a lazy person to attend this part of the ceremony, the girl would also become lazy. The girl is then dressed, painted and adorned with jewelry. Guests arrive and there is drinking, dancing and singing. When she has washed her hands in grated manioc, she is free once more to move about the village, to take her daily bath in the river, and to work in the household. (pp. 41–42)

Each element in the initiation rite has special symbolic and magical value to the members of the tribe, and each step of the process is followed rigidly since the elements of the ritual are tied closely to the values and needs of the community as a whole. As westerners, we might be prone to view these rituals as superstitious nonsense and to dismiss them with a patronizing snicker. To do so would be unfair. The religious and symbolic character of the rituals provide the young person with a sense of a personal link to the traditions of the tribe and all his or her ancestors.

In our culture there is no clearly defined point at which we can say a young man or woman is considered an adult. In the early days of American culture, a young man may have been indentured as an apprentice and a young girl trained in domestic roles so that they were moved from childhood to adulthood at the appropriate time (Kett, 1977) but that pattern no longer exists. It is tempting, as Conklin (1935) and Leemon (1972) have, to draw parallels between tribal initiation rites and those of many college fraternities and sororities. Leemon established a correspondence between periods of fraternal initiation rites and three stages in tribal rites of passage, that is, separation from others, transition rites into the group, and incorporation or formal acceptance into the group and instruction in the secrets and rituals of the group. While such parallels are tempting, they may be misleading since all that is achieved is acceptance into the social group, not acceptance into adult society. Whether such a rite would be of value in this culture is not the issue. Nor is the argument that western society has prolonged the transition from childhood to adulthood and thus *created* adolescence particularly relevant. To worry whether adolescence is a creation of western industrialization does little to benefit young people or to understanding the nature of their developmental transition. We exist in a culture in which the adolescent transition has become a reality. Our role is to identify those features of adult society which the adolescent much achieve in order to view oneself as an adult and to have society as a whole view the adolescent likewise.

The greatest advantages of cross-cultural studies of adolescence are to be gained not so much from studying rites of initiation but from increasing our awareness of differences in the socialization process from population to population within our own multifaceted culture. Any discussion of adolescent development must be tempered by the recognition that adolescence for a black youth in the Bedford-Stuyvesant section of Brooklyn is hardly the same as adolescence for a young white person in Shelbyville, Indiana. Neither of these young people share the same adolescence as an American Indian youth on a Hopi reservation in Arizona, an adolescent from an affluent suburb of Los

Angeles, or a Mexican-American for whom English is a second language. Any generalizations about adolescents must recognize that the form and structure of adolescence is not common to all and must be modified in light of our knowledge of the society in which a young person is raised.

THEORETICAL VIEWS OF ADOLESCENCE

There are three primary theoretical approaches to the study of adolescence that dominate writing in the area. The first, and the one with the longest continuous history, is the psychoanalytic view. *Psychoanalytic* (or sometimes neopsychoanalytic) theories draw directly or indirectly upon the writings of Sigmund Freud. The second dominant theme in adolescent psychological study is a behavioral view. *Behavioral* models draw on the early writings of psychologists such as E. L. Thorndike, John Watson, and B. F. Skinner. Writers with a behavioral focus operate under a presumption that behavior is learned and thus may be explained and predicted by an understanding of the stimuli that lead to the response. The third view, and the general theoretical view for much of this text, is the cognitive developmental view. The *cognitive developmental* position draws mainly on the writings of Jean Piaget but also builds on the writings of Heinz Werner, Lawrence Kohlberg, and others. From a cognitive developmental view one focuses on the thinking processes of the individual. Thinking processes display a pattern of changes over development through the life span. The manner in which a person thinks about his or her world influences the way in which he or she responds to it.

Why have a theoretical view at all? There are many who would argue that the area of adolescent psychology is not well enough defined to justify a "theory of adolescence." I agree. What is not proposed in this text is a theory of adolescence. Rather, adolescence will be viewed within a broader theoretical framework. On the other hand, a theory or a theoretical position allows a professional or a researcher to organize a broad range of information and to use the information effectively for decision making and problem solving. Theory provides a structure within which to organize the information and from which one may make intelligent guesses or hypotheses about new information. Not only does a theory organize information gained in the past, but a good theory also provides a model by which one can plan for the future. In some disciplines, theory can be stated in precise, narrow terms with little room for error. Unfortunately, social scientific theories do not achieve that degree of rigor. Our theories tend to be less precise and more prone to error. Nonetheless, our theories do offer considerable insight into human behavior.

The reader should be warned that while I focus on a cognitive developmental view, I draw on other theoretical viewpoints. In some cases, a behavioral view is simply more convincing and more useful. In a few instances, the psychoanalytic tradition offers useful insights. By and large however, the emerging sense of self as seen in this text is a reflection of the increasingly complex sense of one's world described in cognitive developmental writings.

Psychoanalytic Views

In classic psychoanalytic theory (for example, S. Freud, 1952, 1953) adolescence is dominated by a renewed struggle to control sexual impulses. Sigmund Freud's original formulation emphasized the development of an individual through a series of *psychosexual* stages starting at birth and continuing through adulthood. In infancy, sexual arousal is concentrated in the *oral* erogenous zone. The infant's primary source of pleasure and gratification occurs orally through sucking, biting, and eating. Satisfactory fulfillment of oral needs during infancy is seen as a prerequisite to adequate adult adjustment. Undergratification or overgratification of these needs may lead to a *fixation* in this stage; hence cigarette smoking, compulsive eating, or a need to talk constantly all would be seen as oral fixations.

At around one and one-half years, the toddler age, the focus of sexual excitement shifts and the child enters the second stage of development. During the toddler years, sexual gratification and stimulation are concentrated in the *anal* zone. The primary developmental task associated with the anal stage is toilet training. Children learn quickly that they have some control over their parents through their ability to release or hold back their excretions. Once again, undergratification or overgratification of sexual impulses at this stage may lead to fixations. Children who are fixated in the retentive character of the anal stage may, as adults, show anal-retentive characteristics, such as hoarding or unwillingness to cooperate with others. On the other hand, failure to control the expulsive character of the anal stage may lead to personality traits such as squandering of money and irresponsibility.

At about age three, the child moves into the *phallic* stage. Sexual gratification is now concentrated in the genital area. During this period masturbation is quite common and, according to Freud, the manner in which parents react to this early masturbation has an impact on the child's development of attitudes about his or her sexuality. Overreaction by parents leads the child to see his or her sexuality as "dirty" and repulsive.

Later in the phallic stage, the male child experiences what Freud described as the *Oedipal conflict*. In girls the comparable phenomenon is the *Electra conflict*. During this stage the young child develops incestuous desires for his or her opposite sexed parent. The boy desires his mother and wishes to replace his father. The boy may want to sleep in his mother's bed and tells the father "You sleep in my bed." The daughter of a friend once described her mother as "The woman who sleeps with my father." In each case, the child verbalizes feelings of jealousy toward the same sexed parent. Soon, however, the child recognizes that the parent has the capability of retribution. The boy begins to fear that the father may gain revenge by castration. In Freud's view, the young girl may decide that she has already been castrated and as a result develops *penis envy*. In order to avoid punishment or further retribution, the young child suppresses his or her incestuous desires and identifies with the same-sexed parent. The important outcome of the resolution of the Oedipal conflict is the emergence of a rudimentary sense of right and wrong, a conscience, or in Frued's terms a *Superego*. Until this point the child had had little in the way of internal controls over sexual impulses. The fear and guilt arising from these Oedipal feelings, however, establish initial control over the *Id*, the center of impulses, which previously had free reign.

Following the phallic stage, sexual impulses go into a *latency* period, in which they remain dormant until early adolescence. During this time the Superego increases in strength, and sexual drives are released through heightened physical activity. By and large, girls prefer to be with girls and boys with boys. Girls, however, usually show interest in boys earlier than boys do in girls.

At puberty the young person starts to move toward *adult genital* sexuality. At this point Oedipal conflicts are reawakened by the rapid increase in the output of sexual hormones. Increasingly, sexual drives are redirected away from parents and toward other members of the opposite sex. Freud felt that frustration of these heightened sexual drives, which is inherent in our society, leads to delinquent behavior and aggression. In an attempt to achieve balance between the sexual impulses of the Id and the overcontrol of the Superego, the individual develops an *Ego* which serves to moderate the opposing forces. The Ego is the center of personality. A strong Ego keeps the forces of the Id and Superego in appropriate balance. A weak Ego leads to the domination of one over the other.

The intricacies of psychoanalytic theory as it applies to adolescents was developed largely through the efforts of Freud's daughter Anna. In her view the renewed conflict from Oedipal impulses and increased sexual drives leads to anxiety, because the adolescent, unlike the small child, is expected to have control over such impulses.

Like her father, Anna Freud saw adolescence as a period of critical development of the Ego. In her writings (especially 1966) she describes the functions of defense mechanisms in the organization of a strong or weak personality. To maintain control, the adolescent draws upon a variety of defense mechanisms. During early adolescence, young people draw upon simple defenses such as *regression* in which they resort to behaviors that were acceptable when they were younger but that are no longer appropriate. Regression is a particularly frustrating maneuver to adults who typicaly respond by telling the adolescent to "Act your age," or "Grow up." On the other hand regression may be useful in creative thinking. The individual may try looking at a problem from the naive, uncluttered perspective of the child. Freud, in fact, once described creativity as "regression in the service of the Ego."

As adolescents mature, their mechanisms of defense also become more mature. The two most common forms of internalized control of these impulses are *intellectualization* and *asceticism*. With their improved cognitive skills, adolescents may try to justify gratification of their sexual desires through arguments for free love, new marital life styles, freedom of thought, and adoption of antiestablishment philosophy (A. Freud, 1966). On the other hand, adolescents may assume an ascetic stance using the same intellectual powers and may refuse themselves any form of sexual gratification. Asceticism may also include extreme religiosity and preoccupation with thinking about abstractions.

Two current writers in adolescent psychology with clear roots in Freudian theory are Jane Loevinger and Erik Erikson. While both have made significant alterations in "classic" psychoanalytic theory, the Freudian ancestry of their writings remains clear. Loevinger focuses on an elaborated set of stages of "Ego Development." These stages will be described in more detail later in the text, but the stages incorporate a broader intercorrelation of ego development with social and cognitive development.

Among those psychoanalytically oriented writers who are currently popular is Erik Erikson. Erikson, especially in his works *Identity and the Life Cycle* (1959) and

Part of the adolescent's preparation for adult roles is the establishment of caring relationships with members of the opposite sex. (© George W. Gardner)

Identity: Youth and Crisis (1968), shifts the focus of development from a set of *psychosexual* stages, to a set of eight *psychosocial* stages. The details of those eight stages will be described in more detail in Chapter 3, but the basic idea follows.

As noted in the previous section, Freud emphasized that the individual's motives are to satisfy basic sexual needs—first oral, then anal, and finally genital gratification. Failures to satisfy those early motives adequately, or oversatisfaction of them, leads to a fixation at an earlier stage of development. Erikson alters the focus from sexual conflict to social conflict. At each stage of life, from infancy to old age, the individual must work through a critical set of problems. Like Freud, however, Erikson feels that failure to resolve conflicts adequately at one stage of development interferes with adjustment at the next and later stages of life.

The primary crisis of adolescence—and the crisis that is at the heart of Erikson's theory—is the need to establish a personal sense of identity. The adolescent must accept himself or herself as a unique person, with strengths as well as weaknesses. The adolescent restructures his or her sense of self from childhood in anticipation of adult independence. The adolescent's new identity includes a personal assessment of his or her own sexuality and an understanding that one has control of one's own destiny. As adolescents become more aware that they control their own destinies, gaining self-control, accepting adult responsibilities, and forging a personal set of values and vocational goals follow.

The point at which the individual adolescent goes through the clarification of this identity is called the identity crisis. The term *identity crisis* has become highly popularized and, as with many overgeneralizations, misunderstood. Some assume that adolescents will inevitably go through a major turmoil in which they are concerned with the questions "Who am I?" or "What am I going to do with my life?" However, not all adolescents experience a crisis. Some never have the chance to ask the questions. Social or economic factors may interfere with the opportunity to seek out options. Some young people accept an intact, adult identity with little or no questioning. For example, a young boy may be convinced early that he will become a doctor because his father and grandfather were both doctors before him. He may consider no other alternative. In any case, whether an adolescent develops a sense of identity by himself or assumes an identity that is provided by others, a personal identity is necessary for moving into adulthood. Failure to establish a sense of identity interferes with life tasks that are part of adult personal development.

Behavioral Views

In the traditional behavioral view, an individual's behavior is seen as a result of learning. Learning is the result of reinforcement controlled by an outsider or coming from a beneficial (or hostile) environment. As such, behaviorism is not a theory of adolescence. Rather, it is a set of principles defining the learning process at all levels of human development. The focus in classical behaviorism was on the measurable (observable) behavior of the person. Little value was seen in the use of ambiguous, unnecessary terms like self-concept or motivation to succeed. The primary architect of behaviorism as we now know it was B. F. Skinner. His research refined the earlier work of such notable individuals as Ivan Pavlov, E. L. Thorndike, and John Watson. Skinner set the stage for subsequent refinements of behaviorism for social learning theorists (Dollard & Miller, 1950; Bandura, 1977).

Behavioral principles are fairly straightforward. Learning, and thus behavior, result from two processes. The first process, which resembles the "conditional" learning described by Pavlov, may be called *classical conditioning* (Hilgard & Bower, 1975). In classical conditioning, an *Unconditional Stimulus* (UCS) is linked to an *Unconditional Response* (UCR). If the UCS occurs in the presence of the individual, the UCR follows. Pain (UCS) causes the person to react with a reflexive pulling away (UCR) from the object causing the pain. Unless the person is ill, or is somehow not capable of registering the UCS, the UCR will follow unconditionally. If a neutral stimulus which does not elicit a withdrawal response is now "paired" with the UCS, it may begin to acquire some of the character of the UCS since it also leads to withdrawal. When this happens, the neutral stimulus is described as a *Conditional Stimulus* (CS) and the learned response is a *Conditional Response* (CR). Suppose you are walking down the street and suddenly hear a dog bark behind you. You think nothing of it but the dog quickly bites you (UCS = pain). You immediately respond by pulling your leg away (UCR) and probably saying something unpleasant. The next time you hear a dog bark close by (CS) you may feel fear (CR). Notice the CR is not exactly the same as the UCR. It is an approximation of the UCR. In classical Pavlovian theory, it is not necessary to experience the actual event for a human to develop a CR. Because we have the capability of communicating ideas by language, we can think of the possibility and thus generalize a CR from other experiences.

A second form of conditioning, the one most associated with B. F. Skinner, is called *Instrumental Conditioning* or *Operant Conditioning*. The primary behavioral principle in operant conditioning is fairly intuitive. A person learns to behave in a specified manner because the behavior is *reinforced*. Any behavior that is followed immediately by reinforcement will be likely to occur again, especially under similar circumstances. The teacher or coach who uses praise when a student or athlete performs well is using this basic principle. But reinforcement is not a reward in its usual sense. *Positive reinforcement* is similar to our typical idea of a reward. It is the presentation of something positive immediately following the desired behavior. *Negative reinforcement,* on the other hand, is the removal of something negative following the desired behavior. The result is the same. Removal of something unpleasant is positive. A key to the effective use of behavioral principles, especially during early phases of learning, is that the reinforcement is immediate and continuous. Delayed reinforcement will not work and may be associated with the wrong behavior. Reinforcement must occur frequently. Once a behavior is learned, reinforcement may occur less regularly. But early learning requires frequent and immediate attention.

Control of behavior is achieved through the control of reinforcers and reinforcement. In developing the desired behavior, the behavior modifier identifies appropriate reinforcers and applies them to the learner as he or she approaches some specified level of performance. In behavioral terms, a complex behavior is *shaped.* The trainer or teacher does not necessarily expect the final behavior immediately. Rather, the final behavior is achieved through gradual approximation and the linking together of several skills or behaviors. As the learner achieves one level of performance, the demands are increased modestly to be closer to the final goal. Reinforcement is contingent (dependent) upon the new, refined behavior.

Reinforcers may be tangible such as gumdrops, money, prizes, or hugs, or they may be social such as praise, laughter, or cheers. Reinforcement may also be given to oneself, such self-reinforcement is called *internal reinforcement.* The athlete who practices for long periods of time or the student who works alone on a research project may be motivated as much by self-defined feelings of achievement as by external rewards. Success is reinforcing. For the behavioral theorist, the analysis of adolescent behavior is focused on what form reinforcers take in adolescent culture. Different individuals are motivated by different reinforcers. Praise for work well done may work well for one adolescent but not at all for another. Further, positive and negative reinforcers sometimes have a way of getting confused.

A friend of mine tells a story of a young teacher who, during the course of a lesson, began asking students questions about information they were expected to know. When the teacher called on one particular student, he responded with a horrified gasp and whine. Not wanting to upset the student unduly, the teacher went on to another student. The next time the teacher called on the student the reaction was the same, perhaps even more terrified. By the end of the week, the student responded with virtual hysteria when asked a question. In behavioral terms the student had learned that he could rid himself of an unpleasant circumstance (answering the teacher's question) by putting on this act. The teacher, on the other hand, was learning to avoid the unpleasant situation altogether. One of the interesting things about avoidance learning is that it has a way of becoming self-reinforcing. If you manage to avoid an unpleasant experience, you find that pleasant.

The teacher in this case soon recognized that the problem had gotten out of hand. She was advised to go back to the classroom with a new strategy. This time when she asked the student the question, the reaction was the same, the student went into his act. The teacher, however, waited until the student calmed down and said, "Let me rephrase the question." The student started in again, but the teacher continued to wait. When the student began to quiet down again, the teacher said, "Perhaps you would like a different question," with the clear implication that sooner or later he was going to have to answer a question. After some time (the teacher reported it felt like an eternity), the student did answer the question, whereupon the teacher thanked him and went on.

This episode illustrates the next important characteristic of the behaviorist model: One eliminates behavior through extinction rather than punishment. In *extinction* either no positive reinforcement is given or the unpleasant stimulus is not removed following a behavior. In punishment, on the other hand, something unpleasant is introduced *following* the behavior.

The behavior is ineffective. *Punishment*, in contrast, involves either the removal of something positive or the presentation of something negative following the undesired behavior. By and large, behaviorists do not see punishment as a preferred method of behavior control. Unless punishment occurs within a context in which the learner understands what is acceptable behavior and recognizes that a reward is likely for preferred behavior, it is likely to be ineffective. Further, at the same time a student is receiving punishment from a teacher or coach, he or she may gain prestige points among peers. Punishment may be effective in limited settings, but it should be used with caution. Also, while from a purely behavioral point of view, extinction may take its form in the failure to remove an unpleasant stimulus, the human learner may interpret such actions as punishment. Even in the situation described above, the teacher must be sensitive not to carry it too far.

Although reinforcers or rewards are important concepts in the study of human behavior, they do not stand alone. It does not follow that if we reinforce someone for behaving as we wish, that they will automatically fall into line. Human behavior is too complex and external reinforcers are only one element in a complex psychological environment. Nonetheless, reinforcement principles are valuable tools in dealing with human behavior.

More recently, behaviorally-oriented psychologists have become more accepting of the "cognitive" dimension of human behavior and adapt their theory to account for other aspects of human thought. Principles of reinforcement theory should be seen by the person working with young people as one set of techniques that may be effective, especially in learning new skills. Excessive use of extrinsic reinforcers, however, may lead to a diminished motive to learn (McKeachie, 1976). While learning does depend on adequate feedback and reinforcement, there are limits. If overdone, extrinsic reinforcement is ineffective and perhaps detrimental to performance.

Cognitive Views

Cognitive development theorists draw mainly on the writings of the late Jean Piaget and his followers. Piaget, whose theory will be given greater attention in Chapter 6, proposes that beginning in infancy the human being progresses through a regular series of patterns of thinking and problem solving. Of primary concern for students of the psychology of adolescence is the shift from what Piaget refers to as concrete operational thought to formal operational thought.

According to cognitive developmental theory, adolescence is dominated by a radical shift in one's ability to think and to solve problems. In the words of Heinz Werner (1958): "Whenever development occurs, it proceeds from a state of relative globality and lack of differentiation to a state of increasing differentiation, articulation and hierarchical integration" (p. 126). As adolescents mature cognitively their views, of themselves and their relationship to and with their world, change qualitatively and quantitatively. At early levels of cognitive maturity, the child's or adolescent's views are rigid, concrete, and egocentric. Their perceptions of their own roles and the roles of others are self-centered. They tend to see people as good or bad. Things are right or wrong. There is no room or tolerance for ambiguity. They favor the opinions of those who are powerful and hold high status solely because of their status. At higher levels of conceptual maturity, views are more flexible with refined differentiation among and within concepts. Individuals are likely to use abstract descriptors in characterizing their world. They not only recognize ambiguity, they are more tolerant of it and expect it.

During childhood and earlier levels of cognitive maturity, thinking is restricted by the child's need to have concrete representations of a problem before it can be solved. Problem-solving strategies are not very systematic, and the child is not capable of speculating about what might be if the environment were suddenly altered. Thinking is primarily categorical, and the child finds "exceptions to the rule" hard to consider.

During adolescence most young people experience a profound shift in their ability to think about the world. Rather than being tied to concrete reality, the adolescent's conceptual world is expanded to include abstract reality and abstract possibility. Problem-solving strategies become sophisticated and efficient, based on the ability to formulate hypotheses and to test those hypotheses. Rather than being incapable of handling ambiguities or exceptions to rules, the adolescent may become fascinated by them. They may become argumentative solely for the sake of testing out the limits of their new abilities. An adolescent may spend considerable mental energy playing with a concept as though it were an intellectual toy. A 14-year-old girl once spent 45 minutes explaining to me that there could be no such thing as "nothing," because as soon as we consider "nothing" it becomes "something," and "nothing" ceases to exist. Adolescents may also "think about thinking" or question the nature of reality and existence. This new ability dominates their interaction with their environment.

Because of their newfound ability to consider what *might* be, adolescents, especially late adolescents, are often highly idealistic. They are likely to see a utopian, idealized world as a real possibility and to be frustrated that others, especially adults, do not see the world in a similar fashion. Adolescents may see the adult world as cynical, too committed to the status quo, and insensitive to the needs of humanity. Not surprisingly, discussions between adolescents with this view and adults whom the adolescent regards as irrelevant (for example, their parents) are often explosive. This idealism is, however, an expected outgrowth of the substantial, new intellectual powers of the adolescent.

DEMOGRAPHIC VIEWS OF ADOLESCENCE

A variety of economic and social forces are currently operating on the population of the United States in ways that may result in a major alteration of the country's demographic makeup. Demography is the statistical study of the distribution of people in a population. In looking at the demography of adolescence we find that, as a group, adolescents continue to account for less and less of the total U.S. population.

During the period of the 1960s and 1970s the proportion of the U.S. population that were teens swelled as a result of the "Baby Boom" that followed the second world war. Beginning in the years of the "Great Depression" and continuing through the second world war, birth rates among American women declined. The change in fertility prompted a psychologist of the time to write "It is expected that by 1950, there will be at least 2 million fewer boys and girls in the second decade of life than in 1940—an absolute decrease in this age group for the first time in our history. Moreover, the decrease will continue" (Frank, 1944, p. 7). The projection of a decline by 1950 was a safe bet since those children had already been born. The projection of a continued decline beyond 1950 was more problematic. Frank could not have foreseen the increase in births that was to come. In the years 1945 to 1964, children were born in astonishing numbers. By 1958, the first of the Baby Boomers entered their teen years. The last of the Baby Boomers entered their teen years in 1977. In attempts to respond to this larger population, communities were forced to build new schools and colleges were required to expand. Now many of those buildings stand empty because of smaller enrollments.

In 1970, 52.5 million school-aged (5 to 17 years) children and adolescents accounted for 25.6 percent of the total U.S. population. By 1980, the number of school-aged children and adolescents decreased to 47.2 million or 20.8 percent of the total U.S. population. Keeping in mind the caution that Frank (1944) once made a similar projection, the downward trend is expected to continue through 1990 when the group will shrink to 45.1 million, a decline in size of nearly 7 million in 20 years. While there is expected to be a small increase by the year 2000, the downward trend is expected to continue well into the next century (Bureau of Census, 1983).

Not only is the size of the child and adolescent population changing (see Table 1–1), its composition is also being altered. Increasingly, the child and adolescent population will be made up of those who are currently described as minorities. Among 10 to 19 year olds, for example, there were an estimated 3.3 million Hispanics in 1985. By

Table 1–1 Size of Adolescent and Youth Population in the United States: 1980 to 2000

	1980		*1990*		*2000*	
Age Group	*Number*	*Percent*	*Number*	*Percent*	*Number*	*Percent*
10–14	18,241	8.1	16,776	6.7	19,518	7.3
15–19	21,161	9.3	16,894	6.8	18,887	7.1
20–24	21,312	9.4	18,352	7.4	16,910	6.3

Source: U.S. Bureau of Census (1983) Provisional projections of the population of states. *Current Population Reports,* Series P-25, No. 937. Washington, D.C.: U.S. Department of Commerce.

the year 2000 there are expected to be 5.4 million, an increase of 64 percent (Exter, 1978). Also, young people in this age group are more and more likely to live in poverty (Children's Defense Fund, 1986).

This changing demography will not only affect the schools, it will have a significant impact on other parts of the economy as well. Employers in service industries that depend on the continuous supply of inexpensive labor provided by adolescents are already finding it difficult to maintain adequate staffs in some geographic areas. As the diminished teen population enters the adult years, there will be similar shortages in a variety of occupational categories. On the other hand, an increased job pool coupled with a diminished pool of job applicants should result in a reduction of the youth unemployment rate.

Irrespective of its diminished size, the teen population constitutes a powerful economic force. It is estimated that the total discretionary income of U.S. teens exceeds $50 billion (Guber, 1987). The various industries linked to records and music for adolescents alone account for several billion dollars in spending each year.

DEVELOPMENTAL GOALS

Some writers follow the lead of Robert Havighurst (1948, revised 1972), who suggests that adolescence can be defined by a set of *developmental tasks* that must be completed in preparation for adulthood. Havighurst, like Erickson, felt that each of the developmental tasks of childhood is a basis for the later developmental tasks of adulthood. Some tasks, such as those associated with interpersonal relations, become increasingly complex as a person moves through life. Other tasks—for example, certain psychomotor skills—may be associated with a given period of development. All tasks, however, fit into a lifelong process of psychological and social development.

In their attempt to establish a new body image, adolescents may spend a good deal of time just studying themselves. (© Margaret Thompson)

One of the tasks adolescents must learn is how to channel their aggression and rapidly developing physical strength into productive and socially acceptable behavior. (© Margaret W. Nelson)

By the end of adolescence the young adult should have achieved certain goals, including adult physical and sexual status, a personal identity, financial and psychological independence from parents, mature sexual relationships, and some career goals. The demands of each problem are often not clearly defined, and the form that they take may differ among adolescents. As a simple example, the career goals of lower-income adolescents and those of adolescents from wealthy families are likely to be quite different. Nonetheless, both sets of adolescents need to have a workable set of career goals with which to enter adulthood.

1. *The adolescent must adjust to a new body image.* At no other time since birth does an individual undergo such rapid and profound physical change as during early adolescence. Preadolescence and early adolescence are marked by rapid growth in height and weight as well as the emergence and accentuation of sexual features. No longer does the young person look like a child. Rather, the young adolescent starts to display features of adult physical and sexual maturity. The result is that the adolescent must reconcile this new image seen in the mirror with the self-image of a child. This radical change in the adolescent's physical self may at times be the source of personal anxiety and a fear of being different. It is during this period of development that young adolescents often complain to their physicians about being too tall or too short or too developed or not developed enough.

2. *The adolescent must adapt to increased cognitive powers.* In addition to a sudden spurt in physical growth, adolescents experience a sudden increase in their intellectual abilities. As they mature intellectually, adolescents are able to think not only about more things but also about their world with a new level of awareness. Prior to adolescence, children's thoughts are dominated by a need to have a concrete example for any problem they try to solve. The preadolescent is not able to solve problems that involve abstrac-

tions. Around the middle of the adolescent transition, young people find themselves able to think about problems on a whole new level. Inhelder and Piaget (1958) refer to this transition in thinking as the shift from concrete operational thought to formal operational thought. Beyond an improved ability to solve problems, the shift to formal thinking may also be accompanied by a fascination with this newfound intellectual prowess. It is common, for example, for adolescents to "think about thinking" or have "ideas about ideas." These new abilities, which include the ability to ask the question "What if?" often lead adolescents to commit themselves to concepts of utopia or to idealistic political and social movements. As Piaget (1967) notes, this idealism may lead the adolescent to be impatient with adults who are seen as unwilling, unable, or unmotivated to correct social wrongs. Adults, on the other hand, we are no longer enamored of this intellectual ability, may lose patience with such "cognitive wanderings."

3. *The adolescent must adjust to increased cognitive demands in school.* Adults tend to see high school as a place where adolescents can prepare for adult roles. Courses of study are created with the view that they help the students acquire adult roles. In some cases the relevance to adult roles is quite direct. In others the relevance is indirect— that is, the courses train students in modes of thinking about problems. Often, perhaps too often, the responsibility of the high school is interpreted with the understanding that adolescents will pursue additional training in college. School curricula are often dominated by an assumed need to meet the academic demands that are to come. Even vocational training in high school is often influenced by the assumption that students will get additional vocational skill training beyond high school. High school curricula becomes increasingly difficult and often more abstract, irrespective of whether students have made the transition to formal operational thought. Not all adolescents make the intellectual transition at the same rate; students who have not completed the transition may find adjusting to demands for abstract thought difficult or impossible.

4. *The adolescent must expand his or her verbal repertoire.* As adolescents mature intellectually and adjust to increased demands for academic and social competence, they must also acquire language skills for relating to more complex problems and tasks. Their limited language of childhood is no longer adequate. Often this language development lags behind intellectual growth, and adolescents are able to think at levels well above those reflected in their language. Elkind (1967) refers to this inarticulate behavior as "pseudostupidity." Adolescents may *appear* incompetent because of their inability to express themselves meaningfully, but they may be far more capable than their language suggests.

5. *The adolescent must develop a personal sense of identity.* Erik Erikson (1959, 1968, among others) conceives of adolescence as a distinct period separating childhood from early adulthood. During adolescence individuals must begin to recognize their own uniqueness and form personal identities. This new identity is a synthesis and reorganization of previous identifications with parents, adults, and other authoirity figures. The individual integrates previous experience, including resolution of early developmental crises, into a personal conception of "Who am I?" and "What is my role in life?" At the point at which an individual identity is reformulated, the adolescent may suffer a crisis of identity.

During this period, peer groups serve an important purpose. Because adolescents no longer find their childhood identities adequate but, have not yet formed their adult identities fully, they need a setting within which they can experiment with alternate roles. Peer groups provide that setting. But, there is a price that they must pay for this privilege: conformity to the demands of the group. As adolescents' identities take form, they become less dependent on their peer group and assume more responsibility for their own behavior. This does not mean, however, that identity formation stops after adolescence; complete identity formation is a lifelong evolutionary process. But adolescence seems to be central to the reorganization of a dependent-child identity into a responsible-adult identity.

6. *The adolescent must estabish adult vocational goals.* As part of the adolescent's process of establishing a personal identity, he or she must also develop some plan for achieving an adult vocational role. Adolescents need to identify, at least on a preliminary basis, what they plan to do as adults and how they plan to achieve their goals. As part of making these decisions, adolescents need to develop a realistic idea of their resources, both psychological and economic, for achieving their goals. This process requires that adolescents evaluate their strengths and weaknesses realistically as well as determine what social, psychological, and economic barriers might need to be overcome to achieve certain goals.

7. *The adolescent must establish emotional and psychological independence from his parents.* Perhaps one of the more stressful developmental goals of adolescence is the need to establish psychological and emotional separation from parents. To adequately create a personal identity, adolescents may still wish to keep the secure, dependent relationships of childhood. The adolescent may thus vacillate between the desire for dependence and the need for independence. The need to assert one's individuality and adult independence may take the form of hostility and lack of cooperation with parents or other authority figures. The parents' dilemmas are when to exert control, how much control to exert, and when to release control. That balance between control and release changes with time and circumstances. Eventually this need for psychological separation from one's parents is replaced by an adult relationship with them, which includes respect and appreciation but not dependence.

8. *The adolescent must develop stable and productive peer relationships, including heterosexual relationships.* Although peer interaction is not unique to adolescence, peer interaction seems to hit a peak of importance during early and middle adolescence. The degree to which an adolescent is able to make friends and have an accepting peer group is a major indicator of how well the adolescent will successfully adjust in other areas of social and psychological development (Hartup, 1977). Peer groups serve an important role in the socialization of adolescents to adulthood. Rather than being a negative force, peers often provide standards against which adolescents may compare and evaluate themselves. Peers expose fellow adolescents to alternative values, attitudes, and behaviors and offer a protective setting within which the individual adolescent can evaluate current values and establish psychological independence from parents. Ultimately, however, the adolescent must also establish psychological independence from peers. Early heterosexual friendships set the stage for later intimate and mature relationships.

9. *The adolescent must learn to manage his or her own sexuality.* With their increased physical and sexual maturity, adolescents need to incorporate into their personal

identity a set of attitudes about what it means to be male or female, as well as a set of values about their own sexual behavior.

Although traditional sex role stereotypes may be appropriate and perhaps damaging to adequate psychological development, adolescents must recognize their own femininity or masculinity as an integral component of their self-concept. Contemporary media are much more openly sexual than in previous generations. Society as a whole tends to have a much more permissive attitude about premature sexual activity. Thus, as McCreary-Juhasz (1975) suggests, the responsibility for deciding whether or not to be sexually active has shifted from society to the individual. If an individual decides to engage in sexual intercourse, then another set of decisions regarding contraception, as well as children and possibly marriage, must be made. Premature commitment may interfere with the satisfactory resolution of other developmental tasks. In addition to a sexual identity, which may or may not include sexual intercourse, adolescents must establish some concept of their masculinity or feminity.

10. *The adolescent must adopt an effective value system.* During adolescence, as individuals develop increasingly complex knowledge systems, they also adopt an integrated set of values or morals. Early in moral development the child is provided with a structured set of rules of what is right and wrong, what is acceptable and unacceptable. Some of those values and attitudes are readily verbalized, whereas others are intrinsic but less well recognized. Eventually the set of values that is provided by parents and society may come into conflict with values expressed by peers and other segments of society. To reconcile such differences, the adolescent restructures all those beliefs into a personal ideology. As adolescents progress from concrete to formal thought, their awareness and ability to abstract expands as they begin to consider various alternatives and ideas and as they hypothesize what would happen in an idealized world.

11. *The adolescent must develop increased impulse control, or behavioral maturity.* As the individual moves from early to late adolescence, hedonic, self-serving behavior is replaced by mature, socially appropriate behavior. Early adolescence may be marked by a high degree of impulsiveness and "acting out," especially among young boys. Many of those behaviors that appear to adults to be irrational are results of a failure to control that impulsiveness. Gradually adolescents develop a set of self-controls through which they learn what behavior is acceptable and what is not. In working with disturbed adolescents, I often encounter the diagnosis "Unsocialized Aggressive Reaction of Adolescence." At first the label struck me as odd and actually a bit amusing. I asked myself whether there were *socialized* aggressive reactions. The more I thought about it, the more I realized that indeed there are socially acceptable aggressive reactions. Being aggressive in socially approved manners, such as on a football field or in other competitive settings, is acceptable. Being aggressive in ways that are disapproved, however, may lead to trouble. Some psychologists expect some socially unacceptable aggression, maybe even some delinquency, among most adolescents, as part of the process of establishing self-control is trying the limits of what is acceptable. As socialization toward adulthood moves along, adolescents find that some of society's rules are ill-defined and may even be incompatible with their own ideas. Gradually, however, adolescents replace "unsocialized" behavior, first with "socialized" behavior and eventually with behavior intended for the general good of society.

It may go without saying that these developmental goals are not independent of one another. An adolescent does not tackle them one at a time. As one goal is advanced it may have an effect on the advancement of the other goals. Similarly, life goals or developmental tasks do not suddenly cease after adolescence.

Many of the developmental changes that are described within this textbook follow a common thread. There is a regular progression that may be seen in adolescents' intellectual, social, and emotional growth. There is a shift from a rather undifferentiated, self-centered view of one's world to a more complex, highly abstract view of the world. In Piaget's terms this shift is seen in the transition from concrete to formal thought (Chapter 6). In David Hunt's view there is a similar growth in social development (Chapter 7), and Lawrence Kohlberg's theory of moral development follows a similar pattern (Chapter 12), as does an adolescent's view of self (Chapter 3), vocational goals (Chapter 8), and relationships with parents (Chapter 9) and peers (Chapter 10). It would appear, then, that at least on some level there is a general trend of movement toward the satisfaction of developmental goals during adolescence that coincides with cognitive maturity.

We need to be cautious, however, before we jump to the conclusion that we now have a general theory of adolescence. The state of the field is not yet at that point. If anything, what this trend represents is the author's biases and an attempt to offer a general structure within which you the reader may read this text.

Further, although early-, middle-, and late-adolescents clearly differ in their ability to interact with their world, it does not automatically follow that all young people progress in the same, orderly fashion so that at some magic age, say 21, they are suddenly fully functioning adults who have satisfied all developmental goals and have no growth left before them. As Lipsitz (1977) warns, there is a danger in labeling adolescence as a "transitional" period because it implies that adolescence is unique in that sense. Although there are transitions associated with the period of life we call adolescence, there are likewise transitions related to early adulthood, middle adulthood, and old age.

SELF-CONCEPT

An overriding assumption upon which this text is based is that the central developmental task that unites all the others is that the young person must develop a new sense of self with which to enter adulthood. In dealing with the idea of the adolescent's emerging sense of self, we need to distinguish between self-concept and self-esteem. One's self-concept is a composite of an individual's beliefs about who she or he is or is not. Self-esteem, on the other hand, relates to the overall value the individual holds toward the elements of his or her self-concept.

Morris Rosenberg (1965, 1975) offers a useful way of thinking about the structure of one's self-concept. While Rosenberg's ideas will be developed more fully in Chapter 3, it is worth mentioning here that Rosenberg suggests one's self-concept is built on three major divisions, the *extant* self, the *desired* self, and the *presenting* self. The extant self is the current array on self-views. For the individual it serves as the answer to the question: "Who am I?" The desired self, on the other hand, reflects what the

---

VIGNETTE 1–2
FERRIS BUELLER'S GUIDE TO DITCHING

Images we have of adolescents and adolescence are frequently drawn from films and books. One recent film that has the earmarks of becoming a longtime "camp" film is "Ferris Bueller's Day Off." The film follows the exploits of a young man who proceeds to con his parents, his friends, and society as he ditches school for the day. The film was sufficiently popular that a book was made based on John Hughes' screenplay. Presented below is Ferris' monologue on the subtleties of cutting school and not getting caught.

Excerpted from: Strasser, Todd (1986). *Ferris Bueller's Day Off* (based on John Hughes Screenplay) New York: Signet Books, pp. 22–23.

Cut and Don't Get Caught: The Fine Points of Ditching by Ferris Bueller.

As he soaped up in the shower he imagined himself standing at a podium before a huge crowd of kids: I'd like to thank you all for cutting school and coming to hear me today. As you know, the topic of my talk will be ditching. You might be interested to know that I have just come from Harvard, where I gave an intensive three-month seminar on the subject that was so effective no one showed up on the last day.

Many of you probably think it's a waste of time to come to a lecture about ditching, right? You're probably asking yourself, What's the big deal? If you want to ditch, you just ditch, right?

Wrong. Ditching is a complicated activity. It must be approached in an organized way, especially if you plan to make a career of it.

For instance, one very serious danger in playing sick is that if you do it often enough and well enough, it's possible to believe your own act. I know people who get so psyched up for their act that it takes them most of the day just to feel well again!

And then there's the boredom factor. Many people ditch and feel great for about an hour. Then they realize that they have nothing to do but eat and watch TV. I myself have ditched and gotten so bored that I did homework!

So the most important preparation you can do for a day of ditching is make a plan. Otherwise you're just gonna sit around worrying about what to do. And what do you need that grief for? Especially when the whole point is to take it easy, cut loose, and enjoy it.

That concludes my lecture for today. Go out and have a good time, but don't forget to bring a note from your parents to school tomorrow. Remember, the day after you graduate you will forget everything you ever learned in high school, but forgery is a skill that lasts a lifetime. Thank you.

---

individual would like to be like. The desired self results from the adolescent's answer to the question: "Who would I like to be?" or "What would I like to be?" The presenting self is a temporary status that the individual assumes for the purpose of achieving progress toward the desired self. Your role as "student" is not a permanent part of your self-concept. It serves a necessary role in achieving some goal, for example, to become a counselor, a youth minister, a teacher, and so forth.

Self-esteem may be defined by the discrepancy between the extant self and the desired self. But, it is not simply a matter that a large difference between the two represents a negative self-image or low self-esteem. While this is so, it may also be true that a very small difference or no difference between the two also indicates low self-esteem. A person with a positive sense of self and positive self-esteem is usually described as having reasonable goals and standards of excellence. One whose extant and desired selves are the same might be thought of as having no goals, hence, low self-esteem. The person with positive feelings of self-esteem has moderate goals that are achievable but which also represent a challenge. If the goals are too distant and unachievable, the adolescent is likely to see himself or herself as a "loser," unable to succeed. The professional who works with adolescents should have as her or his goal the establishment of a firm sense of adolescent self-esteem and a positive sense of self among adolescents.

INDIVIDUAL DIFFERENCES

A common theme throughout this text is that the practitioner must be responsive to the differing characteristics of adolescents. Perhaps at no other time in development can such heterogeneity among individual's in a group be seen as in early and middle adolescents. To encourage the pratitioner to be responsive to individual differences is no small request. As will be seen in subsequent chapters, adolescents differ on a large variety of dimensions—physical, social, and psychological—and on three different levels:

1. Most obviously, because there is such a progression from concrete to abstract thinking or from undifferentiation to complex differentiation of one's world, it is important for adults working with adolescents to recognize that wide differences *among age groups* may exist. The social responsibility, intellectual behaviors, and value judgments that we can reasonably expect from a college sophomore are quite different from those we expect from a high school freshman.

2. *Within age groups* there may be large differences among individuals. These differences may be related to disparities in stages of development that individuals have achieved or to dissimilarities in social or personal style. In a typical class of high school seniors there may be a group operating on the more advanced levels of conceptual and social development, whereas others are operating at the level expected of the average sixth grader. On the other hand, among those who are operating at the level of formal operational thinking, there may be wide variability in the manner in which individuals apply those abilities in solving problems.

3. There are additional differences *within individuals*. Too often, we expect individuals to behave with equal maturity in all settings. For example, we may expect a boy or girl who is physically mature early to act with a corresponding social maturity. Adolescents may operate with different levels of social maturity given the familiarity of the setting, how tired or refreshed they feel, how near their friends are, and so on.

Individual differences should be viewed in light of how they affect the way in which particular adolescents respond to their environment. The problem of responding to individual differences is increased by the fact that one environment may be beneficial for one group of adolescents, whereas the same setting may be not only *not* beneficial but actually harmful for others. On the other hand, another environment may have just the reverse effect. The role of the practitioner becomes one of optimizing the match between the personal characteristics of adolescents and their environments to facilitate some outcome. Given this role, the practitioner may operate on any or all of the three elements in the setting: the individual, the environment, or the desired outcomes.

Remedial Intervention.   In remedial intervention the adolescent is presumed to have a deficit that needs to be raised to an acceptable, functional level. If, for example, an adolescent's academic achievement suffers because of low reading ability, the intervention is most obviously to raise the reading level. However, the instructional procedures for accomplishing this end are different for teens than for primary-school learners. One remediational approach may not be effective for all, even when the desired outcomes are essentially the same.

In a different case, a physician or nurse may recognize that an adolescent's chronic stomach problems are not a result of something inherently wrong with the stomach but the result of a mouthful of decayed teeth. The intervention in such a case is more clear: the practitioner arranges, either through parents or a welfare agency, to have the adolescent's teeth cleaned and filled, bringing the adolescent's oral hygiene up to an acceptable, normative level of good health.

Compensatory Intervention.   In a compensatory model the individual's predisposition is taken as a given, one that is perhaps unchangeable. The athlete with weakened knee ligaments wears a brace or support to compensate for the deficiency. Some school-related problems may be reduced if a nearsighted student is provided with glasses. The intent in the compensatory model is not to alter individuals but rather to provide individuals with external devices or compensatory skills that allow them to interact more satisfactorily with their environment.

In both the remedial and compensatory frameworks the indiviudal is seen as needing change or aid. In some circumstances, however, a practitioner may feel it more appropriate to establish different environments in order to facilitate the desired outcome.

Capitalization Strategy.   In the third strategy for individualization, a practitioner capitalizes on some trait of the adolescent that has benefited by one treatment as compared to another. In one case an individual with trait X performs better under treatment 1 than under treatment 2. In contrast, individuals with trait Y perform better under treatment 2 than under treatment 1.

French (1958) reports a study in which learners who were group oriented were compared to learners who were success oriented. French looked at the performance of these two kinds of learners when feedback was task related versus group related. When success-oriented learners were given task-related feedback, especially with respect to individual achievement, they performed much better than when given feedback of how the group was getting along together. Group-oriented learners responded just the opposite; they did not want to be singled out.

The capitalization model is based on the premise that *different treatments* have *different effects* with *different people.* The object is to maximize the effectiveness of a treatment, be it educational, physical, medical, or psychological, by matching the treatment to the strengths of the individual.

Use of individualized treatment does not imply that the practitioner needs to create an infinite set of treatment modes. Individualization may mean selection of a treatment from a limited number of alternatives or it may mean variation within a specific treatment modality. Consider the following two cases: Both Arthur and Bill had epilepsy. Epileptic seizures may be effectively controlled through alternative drugs. The short-term goal in both cases was similar; control of the seizures. Both Arthur and Bill were given the same anticonvulsant drug. Bill very quickly showed an allergic reaction to the drug. The intervention strategy was therefore altered and a different drug was used. Arthur, on the other hand, was not allergic to the drug, but the normal dosage sent him reeling. It was simply too strong. Lessening the dosage accomplished the goal. In both cases the goal was the same, but the practitioner altered the treatment to meet the individual characteristics of each patient. Furthermore, the progress toward that specific goal was documented, so that subsequent practitioners and others in the treatment team were aware of the progress and modifications in the treatment plan.

Individualization implies professional selection and application of treatment modes, given a knowledge of individual predispositions. The decision-making process must be continuous as new information is made available. Often that information is unavailable until a treatment is attempted. Although the medical analogy of an allergic reaction may seem obvious, other noncompatible reactions may be seen in educational, psychological, or social interventions. In such cases the treatment program should be modified.

SUMMARY

Adolescence is a period of development bridging childhood and adulthood. During adolescence individual adolescents establish a unique identity with which they enter adulthood. This identity is a composite of the satisfactory completion of a set of developmental goals. Adolescence is not simply an upward extension of childhood, nor is it a downward extension of adulthood. The adolescent must adjust to a unique set of physical, psychological, and social demands of adolescence.Adolescents do not act randomly or irrationally anymore than adults do. Although their ground rules vary, adolescents act purposefully in order to handle normal developmental stress.

The text presumes that the central developmental task of adolescence that unites all the others is that the young person develop a new sense of self with which to enter adulthood. Those who work with adolescents should strive to foster a positive sense of self among them.

Adolescence is marked by wide variability among individuals in maturational status, social background, and psychological predispositions. The practitioner who works with adolescents should be prepared to offer multiple modes of treatment or instruction. Decisions as to the most appropriate form of intervention depend on the degree of flexibility available in defining acceptable outcomes and the variety of appropriate paths to those outcomes.

THE STUDY
OF ADOLESCENTS
IN LABORATORY
2 AND NATURAL SETTINGS

Our knowledge and understanding of adolescent growth and development is largely the result of research studies that differ in format and question but which have as a common element that the group of interest is adolescents. Unlike some areas in the physical sciences, the study of adolescent development is not guided by a single clear-cut theory. Rather, a variety of theories are tested—some with direct relevance to adolescence, some only indirectly related. Just as the theoretical stances among researchers differ, their methods of research may also vary.

There are three purposes of this chapter. The first purpose is to review basic elements of research design as they relate to the study of human and adolescent development. Because it is an overview, the more advanced student, who has already been introduced to this information elsewhere may prefer to skip this chapter or to skim it for review. The second purpose is to offer guidelines for evaluating research studies, and the third is to provide some guidance on where you might begin a research project. Frequently, students are asked to write a paper or to conduct a study as part of their course requirements. If you are unfamiliar with the area of human development in general, and adolescent development in particular, you might feel in a bit of a quandary about where to begin.

RESEARCH METHODS

Research is the systematic analysis of a question through the planned collection, analysis, and interpretation of data. An investigator who wishes to study adolescent behavior and development must start with a clearly stated problem. Usually the problem can be expressed as a question regarding the relationship between two or more variables—for example, "What is the impact of early versus late maturation on self-esteem?" or "What is the relationship of chronic alcohol abuse among early-adolescents to their social adjustment?" Although the statement of the problem appears, on the surface, to be relatively straightforward, it is at this point that many investigators falter. Kerlinger (1973) points out, "It is not always possible for a researcher to formulate his problem simply, clearly, and completely. He may often have only a general, diffuse, even confused notion of the problem" (p. 16). It is the single most common flaw in research proposals.

A problem statement reflects an expected relationship between an *independent variable* and a *dependent variable*. The independent variable is that variable over which the researcher has direct or indirect control. If a researcher were to study the impact of peer counseling experiences on self-esteem of adolescents, the researcher would randomly assign subjects to either an experimental condition which was given the peer counseling experience or to a control condition which was not. The independent variable of peer counseling experience is thus "controlled" by the researcher. In a question regarding effects of early versus late maturation on self-esteem, the independent variable is early and late maturation which the researcher "controls" by selecting adolescents who fit into one or the other category. Self-esteem, the outcome in both of these example studies, is the dependent variable.

The manner in which the researcher defines the independent and dependent variables may also have an impact on the outcome of the study and its interpretation. How early is "early" maturation? What is meant by self-esteem? The researcher is obligated to offer an *operational definition*. An operational definition provides a clear statement in observable terms as to what constitutes the independent and dependent variables. It is at this second point that the next most common research error occurs. The researcher may fail to adequately define his or her treatment or outcome variable. The careless researcher may measure the wrong thing.

After stating the problem, the researcher should attempt to incorporate the question within a broader theoretical structure and to relate it to previous research. In the process of delineating the relationship of the question to a broader theoretical and research context, the researcher formulates a specific set of testable hypotheses.

Once the hypotheses are formulated, the researcher must select from the many alternative research designs and methodologies the one that seems most relevant to the question. A wide variety of research methods are available to the researcher (see, for example, Campbell & Stanley, 1966; Cook & Campbell, 1979; Festinger & Katz, 1953; Kerlinger, 1973; Webb et al., 1966). However, the principal distinction made in most reviews of research methods is between experimental and nonexperimental research. Both broad categories are then broken down further on the basis of specific designs or methodologies. Although experimental research is clearly the most precise mode of research and allows the researcher the strongest support for a theory, it is often too contrived to ask important questions. In cases in which such a degree of control is not feasible, a nonexperimental approach may be preferable.

The choice of one research design or another should be guided by the question and the hypotheses to be tested, not the opposite. Trying to force a question into a design is the wrong approach unless the researcher is trying to assess the usefulness of certain research designs for developmental psychological questions. The complexity of research designs will increase as the researcher tries to gather evidence to several intersecting questions at the same time. As the number of independent and dependent variables increases, so does the complexity of the research design and the analyses needed to study the problem. Nonetheless, even as the complexity of the design increases, the attributes underlying sound experimentation remain stable. This does not mean that complex designs are better designs. Some of the most exciting studies are the simplest. It is not the design that makes or breaks a research study, it is the theory. The most sophisticated research design is worthless in the absence of solid theory.

Cattell (1966) identified six dimensions which underlie all forms of experimentation:

1. *The number of observed or measured variables in an experiment.* In the simplest of experiments, this dimension of research design is reduced to assessing the impact of a single independent variable on a single dependent variable. A researcher may, however, choose to manipulate a set of multiple independent variables and observe their effects on multiple dependent variables.

2. *The presence or absence of manipulation.* Traditionally, there has been an implicit, if not explicit, assumption that to be a "real" experiment, the researcher must have direct control over independent variables through manipulation. In developmental research we often do not have that luxury. We simply cannot create early or late maturers. Experimentation thus often implies indirect control of independent variables. Cattell prefers to refer to independent variables as "defined" conditions instead of "controlled" conditions.

3. *The presence or absence of time sequence between measures.* The measurement of an outcome measure may occur at the same time as the mesurement of the independent variable or it may be delayed. Thus, self-esteem might be measured during the period when young pepole are advanced or delayed in physical maturation or the measure of the dependent variable increases, time permits all sorts of other experiences to "contaminate" the relationship.

4. *The degree of situational control.* In a laboratory experiment, the researcher has a great deal of situational control. Alternative, contaminating sources of effect are controlled or "held constant." The advantage of the tightly controlled experiment, is that the researcher is able to gather information about the research question in the absence of excessive extraneous sources of error. The disadvantage of the laboratory study is that the highly controlled setting may not parallel real life. As a researcher moves outside the controlled setting of the laboratory, into classrooms, institutions, or uncontrolled natural settings, the clarity of the relationship between independent and dependent variables becomes muddied. The choice of one research design over another results in tradeoffs. One research design does not serve all needs.

5. *The choice of variables to be considered in the experiment.* Researchers must make some choices about which variables will be included in the study. One simply cannot study everything. Further, the researcher must select from among multiple, possible variations on a given variable.

6. *The choice of subjects for the experiment*. Research subjects are those individuals who agree to participate in a study. While a researcher may want to study all high school students who consume alcohol, the task would be too great. Hence some decisions must be made about who will and who will not be asked to particpate. This decision is important since the wrong choice might lead to unwanted bias in the research design.

Experimental Research

The most narrowly defined research designs, and the most restricted and controlled are traditional, orthodox experiments. Campbell and Stanley (1966) define experimentation as "research in which variables are manipulated and their effect on other variables observed." The definition reflects a more traditional view of experimental methods that presumes the researcher has direct control over the application of a specific set of experimental conditions to samples of research subjects who have been randomly assigned to those conditions.

In one sense or another, an experiment is a systematic study of the impact of an independent variable, or a set of independent variables, on a dependent variable or a set of dependent variables.

In the true experimental tudy, a researcher attempts to measure the impact of some independent variable over which he or she has direct control on some dependent variable. For example, if a person were to study the question, "What are the effects of marijuana on driving ability?" marijuana use would be the independent variable and driving ability would be the dependent variable. In this case, a specific amount of marijuana might be provided to a randomly selected *experimental* group, and nothing would be given to another randomly selected *control* group. Each group would then drive in a simulation machine. If differences were found in driving performance between those who had smoked marijuana and those who had not, we would conclude that marijuana smoking affects driving performance.

Certainly such a study would be an oversimplified test of the question of whether marijuana smoking affects behavior. However, another researcher could build on the study by adding more controls and asking additional questions. For example, perhaps just *thinking* you are smoking marijuana alters your behavior. What would happen if larger doses or better grades of marijuana were used? Although the complexity of the question increases, the basic design remains the same. That is, individuals are randomly assigned to treatment groups, and after the experimental or control conditions have been applied, all are given the same outcome test.

Randomization is very important to experimental design. It is a way of increasing the chances that the groups are similar at the start. In random assignment, every individual has an equal chance of being assigned to any one of the experimental groups. This is done to reduce the chances of one group having some characteristics in common that would put them at an unfair advantage over another group.

An essential characteristic of the experimental design is that the experimenter tries in every way possible to ensure that all variables other than the variable of interest are controlled or equalized. By doing this, any differences among the groups on the dependent variable are considered to be *caused* by the different treatments.

At the conclusion of the orthodox experiment, a researcher offers a statistical comparison between the groups. Usually, the statistical test involves comparing the *average* performance of subjects in one group to the *average* performance of subjects in the other. If the scores of the subjects in the compared groups are sufficiently different, the researcher may report the differences to be "statistically significant." This means that the odds of finding a difference like the one observed by chance alone are small.

Wold (1954) reports an experiment by J. Dietl in 1849 on the treatment of pneumonia. During the mid-nineteenth century, medical treatment was still dominated by the medieval practice of bleeding and the use of purgatives in the treatment of disease. Dietl assigned patients with pneumonia to three groups. The first group was treated with leeches to bleed the patient. The second group was treated with repeated enemas. The third group, a "control" group, received no "medical" treatment but was placed in bed and given fresh air, sunlight, and nourishing food. The results shattered conventional medical wisdom of the time. The first and second "experimental" groups had mortality rates of one in five. His "control" group had a mortality rate of one in 13. The death rate under conventional medical treatment was nearly three times that of the control group. The treatment was more dangerous than the disease.

Not all writers accept the orthodox limits on what constitutes an "experiment." In his definition, Cattell (1966) carefully avoided the restriction of manipulation. Cattell defined an experiment as: "A recording of observations, quantitative or qualitative, made by *defined* and *recorded* operations and in *defined* conditions, followed by examination of data by *appropriate* statistical and mathematical rules, for the existence of significant relations (p. 20, emphasis added)." While Cattell avoids the term manipulation, he does emphasize the need for definition. It is the responsibility of researchers to provide precise operational definitions of all variables under study.

An operational definition provides clear, observable methods for establishing experimental conditions and for measuring outcomes. If a researcher wishes to study the effects of participating in an outdoor camping experience on self-concept, the outdoor camping experience may be operationally defined by describing the experiences that the experimental group will receive compared to a control group. Self-concept might be defined operationally as scores on the Rosenberg (1965) self-concept scale. Note, however, that the Rosenberg scale is not the only self-concept measure available. Another researcher might select the Offer (1982) Self-Image Questionnaire or the Coopersmith (1967) Self-Esteem Inventory, or the Piers-Harris (1964) Self-Concept Scale. Since each instrument measures self-concept in somewhat different ways, it is important to report which measure is used.

According to Campbell (1957) the ideal research design is one that is both internally and externally valid. *Internal validity* refers to the degree to which the described relationship between the independent and dependent variables is justified. Threats to internal validity are found when errors in research design and control jeopardize the truth value of the research study. As internal validity decreases, the confidence with which the researcher can link the independent and dependent variables is lessened. The more precisely restricted and well-controlled the experimental study, the greater the

Children's and adolescents' self-concepts and motives are strongly influenced by the environment of the neighborhood they live in. (*top*—© Frank Siteman MCMLXXX; *bottom*—© Eric Kroll 1978/Taurus Photos)

internal validity. As researchers' control of randomization or application of treatments is reduced, internal validity suffers.

While internal validity refers to the integrity of conclusions within the context of a single study, *external validity* refers to the generality of the results beyond the confines of the specific experiment. The degree to which the sample of subjects to whom the treatments are applied are representative of a larger population of possible subjects and the degree to which experimental conditions parallel other conditions, the greater the generality and the greater the external validity.

Of the two forms of validity, it may be argued that internal validity is the more important. Without it external validity is problematic. It is, however, possible to so precisely and narrowly define experimental conditions in a laboratory study, that generality is valid only to other similar laboratory conditions. In developmental psychological and adolescent research we often do not have the ability to randomize subjects as we wish and our ability to create real-life situations is limited. The result is a tradeoff in internal and external validity.

Quasi-Experimental Research

Campbell and Stanley (1966) and Cook and Campbell (1979) provide a series of alternative research strategies which are meant to maintain internal and external validity within the realisitc constraints felt by most social scientists. The constraints of orthodox experimental research create a serious risk to generalizing results to real-life conditions outside the laboratory. Campbell and Stanley describe a series of "quasi-experimental" designs which approximate true experiments but which respond to realistic constraints facing the researcher who deals with human subjects. Campbell and Stanley point out that the quasi-experimental designs are not meant to replace orthodox experimental designs. Rather, they offer additional choices, especially when randomization of subjects is not possible.

The most common application of quasi-experimental designs is what Campbell and Stanley refer to as the nonequivalent control group design. This design uses intact, nonrandomly selected groups. One group is given an experimental treatment, another is not. Both groups are studied in a parallel manner and measured before and after the treatment. The researcher then attempts to "statistically equate" the two groups on the basis of the first measure and to see if differences are found on the second.

Campbell and Stanley offer additional quasi-experimental designs that go beyond the limits of this chapter. Their monograph, "Experimental and quasi-experimental designs for research," is considered by most social scientific researchers to be "must reading" for the serious student. Many of the designs originally laid out by Campbell and Stanley are refined and clarified in Cook and Campbell's (1979) volume.

Nonexperimental Research

In many cases, especially when the population in which the researcher is interested is adolescents, a true experimental design is logically and ethically impossible. We cannot, for example, randomly assign children to rich or poor families when we want to study the impact of family background on some outcome variable. In nonexperimental studies a researcher usually uses a measure of association called the correlation coefficient.

Although historically the correlation coefficient was a major breakthrough for the social sciences, it has today become a less respected tool, perhaps because of an overreaction to its misuses. The coefficient describes a *relationship* between two variables, ranging from an inverse relationship (negative correlation) through no relationship (zero correlation) to a direct relationship (positive correlation). In any correlation all that is shown is that the scores of two variables tend to correspond in some way. If we have two variables X and Y, and we say that a positive correlation exists between them, then we know that as X scores increase, Y scores also tend to increase. If, on the other hand, we have an inverse relationship between the two variables, as X scores increase, Y scores tend to decrease. Notice that I keep saying "tend to." No cause-and-effect relationship is implied by a correlation coefficient, only a correspondence between sets of scores; that is, a correlation coefficient reflects the amount of common variance, or the extent to which two variables *covary*. For example, suppose you found that there was a negative correlation between self-reported anxiety and performance on the SATs. You might be tempted to conclude that the high anxiety causes the low test performance. However, it could be argued that just the opposite occurred—that is, that low performance on the SAT caused high anxiety. Although correlation coefficients may be used in very strictly defined circumstances to make causal statements (Blalock, 1964), we must be very cautious about such conclusions.

Longitudinal and Cross-Sectional Research

There have traditionally been two primary methodologies for assessing age- or development-related changes. In longitudinal research a group of subjects is identified and studied over a span of several years. In cross-sectional research several groups of subjects, differing in ages, are viewed at one time. Both approaches have advantages and disadvantages, and recently some researchers have combined the two methods into a third methodology, called cohort designs.

In *longitudinal* research an investigator selects a sample of people and follows their development over a period of time. Thus any characteristic of a subgroup that sets it apart from the total sample may be studied to assess cumulative effects. In one of the more famous longitudinal studies of adolescence, H. Jones (1939a, b) and his associates selected a group of children from the Oakland Bay area that they intended to follow through adolescence. Subsequently the Oakland Growth Study was extended to adulthood (M. Jones, 1953, 1965), and still more recently a comprehensive analysis of long-term patterns of personality development has been completed (Block, 1971). Thus in a longitudinal study, stability or instability in patterns of development can be analyzed.

Longitudinal research is not without its problems. First, longitudinal research is exceptionally expensive in both time and money. Sometimes many years may pass before clear results are observed. This passage of time creates another problem. Deaths, moving away, and the simple refusal of subjects to continue participation change the sample over time. In the Oakland Growth Study, for example, Block (1971) managed to study 80 percent of the original sample. However, the 20 percent who were no longer represented may be different in important ways from those who remained in the study. Finally, there is always the problem of 20–20 hindsight. Several years into a longitudinal study, an investigator may regret not having gathered now-important information at an earlier time. This is a problem in all research, but it is particularly frustrating in longitudinal studies.

Cross-sectional designs examine samples of different age groups at one point in time. In contrast to longitudinal studies, the data are collected within a short time span and are available for analysis and synthesis relatively quickly. However, unlike longitudinal research, the investigator has no way of assessing relative developmental status over time, and comparing subjects from one age group to another may not be reasonable. Comparing 10-, 20-, 30-, and 40-year-olds may be misleading, because the four groups represent different generations and different cultural effects (Labouvie, 1976). Today's 20-year-old was an adolescent during the 1970s, whereas the 40-year-old was a teen during the 1950s.

Some of the problems associated with longitudinal and cross-sectional designs are lessened through the use of *cohort* designs. A cohort is a grouping of subjects selected on the basis of some homogeneous characteristics, such as birth (age). Although there are several versions of cohort designs (Labouvie, 1976; Schaie, 1973; Baltes, 1973; Price, 1974), the most practical and widely used is what is called the cross-sequential design (Labouvie, 1976). Thus in the year 1976, we might have selected a 1968 cohort (8-year-olds), who are to be compared to a 1964 cohort (12-year-olds), a 1960 cohort (16-year-olds), and a 1956 cohort (20-year-olds). What makes the cohort design different is that we measure our cohort groups four times at four-year intervals, as shown in Table 2–1. The advantage of the cohort sequential design is that we can assess both developmental and generational effects. Although the cohort designs are still in the process of clarification, they and other new designs (Nesselroade & Baltes, 1978) are offering new insights into the developmental process.

Table 2–1 Age of Cohorts at Time of Testing

	AGE			
Cohort	1976	1980	1984	1988
1968	8	12	16	20
1964	12	16	20	24
1960	16	20	24	28
1956	20	24	28	32

Naturalistic Observation

As Bronfenbrenner (1977) has cogently argued, research in human development needs to maintain a healthy balance between rigor and relevance. The primary difficulty with most research in human development is that in order to maintain a degree of rigor, children and adolescents are asked to respond to unusual tasks in an unnatural setting— the laboratory. Consequently, most behavior reported in research studies is artificial and measured over very short periods of time. Bronfenbrenner calls for increased use of observation in natural settings, guided by some of the same demands for precision and rigor that dominate experimental research.

In the study of human behaviors, we do not have the degree of control that is available in the physical sciences. Ethics preclude the use of experimental treatments that could lead to physical or psychological damage of the subject. Thus we are often

Pranks and some limited delinquency are a normal part of the adolescent transition from childhood to responsible adulthood. (© Joel Gordon 1974)

left with nonexperimental settings from which we must make inferences. Some researchers in human development (for example, Barker, 1965; Altman, 1975) call for an ecology of human behavior—that is, the scientific study of human behavior in its natural surroundings. In using an ecological approach for the study of adolescents, we would need to specify carefully the observable elements of a person's environment.

Suppose you were to try to identify the impact of an environment on some behavior of a target adolescent under a variety of settings. The adolescent's behavior may differ when in school, at church, at home, at a drive-in theater, and so on. Thus, when speaking of a person interacting with his or her environment, we must specify *which* environment.

Bronfenbrenner suggests that an *ecosystem* (the composite of environmental forces affecting an individual) can be broken down into at least four levels of influence on the behavior of a person at a given point in time. The first level, the immediate environment, is called a *microsystem*. You are reading this text in a specific setting, perhaps a dormitory room. That room is really a composite of stimuli that affect you. The air may be stuffy or pleasant, the radio may be playing, the view from your window may be attractive. Your reaction to these components of your enviornment may aid or hinder your studying behavior (Rothkopf, 1968). Further, the radio in the background may serve to help you study but may have the opposite effect on your roommate.

At another level, Bronfenbrenner proposes you operate within a *mesosystem*. Not only is your present behavior affected by your immediate environment, you are affected by your friends' attitudes about studying, the "atmosphere" of the college at which you are studying, and your parents' attitudes about work in general. Although this part of your ecosystem is less tangible, it does nonetheless have an impact on your present studying behavior. Your peers, for example, do not have to be physically present to influence you. Elements of your mesosystem help define the roles you specify for yourself.

At a still more remote level, you operate in an *exosystem,* which is composed of formal and informal agencies of society that help shape our attitudes and behavior. These agencies may also shape the character of the elements of our mesosystem. The mass media and the government are examples of agencies in our exosystem. The effect of such agencies, though remote or less direct, is real and continuous.

At the most remote level of influence is what Bronfenbrenner calls the *macrosystem,* which includes general societal ideologies. The system of government, current social values, ethnic or national heritage, and educational models influence attitudes and behaviors at a general level. The macrosystem gives organization and meaning to the roles defined by the other levels of our ecosystem.

Using naturalistic observation requires that the observer be well schooled in the category system to be used. The researcher must be able to demonstrate that, given a coding scheme, a variety of observers would agree, at some reasonable level, on what is being observed. Naturalistic observation, if it is done well, may be the most demanding of research methodologies.

VIGNETTE 2–1

OF ADOLESCENT CULTURES AND SUBCULTURES

Although the Maroni River Caribs described in the text choose to convey some of their cultural values through an initiation rite, global society as a whole uses a variety of techniques to convey what is valued. Often values are seen in the writing and art that a culture produces. From the most elaborate literature and ornate artwork to the furtive scribblings on walls, people try to communicate the ideas and values of their society. Graffiti, although it is not usually considered as a primary source of literary enlightenment, is nonetheless often artistic, humorous, and reflective of current social and political forces. Graffiti is certainly not new. Archaeologists have found graffiti on walls of long-buried cities. In this short piece, Anthony M. Deiulio of the State University of New York at Brockport suggests that graffiti is a valuable source of information about the values and attitudes of today's youth. What values do you see reflected in graffiti in your locale?

Source: Excerpted from Anthony M. Deiulio, "Of Adolescent Cultures and Subcultures," *Educational Leadership* (April 1978), pp. 517–220. Reprinted with permission of the Association for Supervision and Curriculum Development and Anthony M. Deiulio. Copyright © 1978 by the Association for Supervision and Curriculum Development. All rights reserved.

Graffiti have been with us since prehistoric times. The Oxford English Dictionary defines a graffito as, "A drawing or writing scratched on a wall or other surface; as at Pompeii or Rome." It mirrors the world of its own day, and it throws a broad beam of light on the preoccupations and fears, dreams and desires, feelings and hopes of the people whom the social scientists quantify and computerize. So too with the graffiti of adolescents. Graffiti gives adolescents a certain satisfaction also, for through it they can vent their hostilities, express their fantasies, communicate their triumphs, declare their rebellion, and promote their propaganda.

CHARACTERISTICS OF ADOLESCENT GRAFFITI

Certain characteristics of the phenomenon of adolescent graffiti, based on a number of long-term research studies, should be noted:

- *It is universal.* The sprays, scrawls, and scratches appear in all the world's teenage cultures. According to recent reports from Moscow, the handwriting is on the wall even in Russia with its long-time reputation as a graffiti-free society.
- *It is costly.* The New York City Transit Authority recently spent $4 millilon to clean its 6,200 subway cars of spray paint graffiti. In San Francisco, secondary students were to be granted cash incentives by the Board of Education if they could reduce the graffiti in their schools. And in some states, laws have been passed making parents financially responsible for the graffiti their children paint on buildings, rest rooms, and other property.
- *It can take several forms.* Usually graffiti appear as statements, single words, or pictures, but often can include various symbols to which certain meanings are understood or have been attached.
- *It is difficult to differentiate graffiti on the basis of sex.* Graffiti written by girls— that found in the girls' lavatories in churches and schools, for example—is as strong, political, trite, or sexual as that written by boys. One slight difference: girls' graffiti may sometimes show faint signs of the traditional romanticism of the girl-loves-boy theme. One other possible distinction, according to a report by the Council of British Ceramic and Sanitary Manufacturers, is that the quality of art work is higher in the ladies' ''loos'' than they found in the gents' lavatories.
- *It is usually transitory.* Despite those found in the excavations of Pompeii, most do not last a very long time. A custodian's paintbrush, a teacher's washcloth, or a plasterer's trowel are all impending threats to the longevity of these inscriptions.
- *It is not all pornographic.* The correlation between pornography and graffiti is not as high as many would like to believe. In fact, in some of the long-term collections, one can see the increasing seriousness of purpose and the larger issues being dealt with as opposed to the mere epithets, obscene statements, and pornographic invitations one finds among the earlier evidence.

Interviews

Often, especially during the early phases of a research program, researchers find valuable information through interviews of individuals or groups. Unlike structured experiments the research interview often uncovers information that might otherwise go undetected. The disadvantage of the interview is that the researcher amasses an enormous amount of information that must be organized and interpreted. Also, particularly in group interviews, one person's views may dominate and give a false impression of the importance of a given idea. Good interviewing takes practice.

The concept underlying interviewing as a research method is fairly straightforward. The researcher identifies a group of individuals who share some common experience. In our own research, for example, we were interested in studying the problems of adolescents who have insulin-dependent diabetes mellitus. We then proceeded to interview several young people with this illness to gain their perspectives.

If you decide to try to interview adolescents, it is useful to keep a few guidelines in mind. First, decide in advance what you want to accomplish in an interview. What are your objectives? While some benefits may be gained through unstructured observations (Lincoln & Guba, 1985), I find that the new researcher does much better with a clear sense of direction and focus. Further, having a focus often puts the person being interviewed at ease. This may be a problem in dealing with adolescents who are often self-conscious and an interview may be a bit anxiety provoking.

Be prepared for the interview. Have preliminary questions written in advance. While an interviewer may not wish to "script" the interview, it is helpful to have a dozen or so questions ready. The newer you are at interviewing, the more questions you should have ready. Whenever possible, try to get some knowledge about the person you intend to interview. Sometimes referring to the adolescent's interests or accomplishments helps put them at ease. Establish an appointment for the interview. When dealing with adolescents it is wise to confirm the appointment on the day before the interview since they are apt to forget.

When you conduct the interview maintain a cordial, relaxed but professional attitude. Tell the person whom you are to interview the purpose of the interview and try to make him or her feel at ease. Try not to come across like a "snoop." Most important, when you conduct an interview the purpose is to let the subject talk. You want to hear what he or she has to say, not the opposite. Ask your question and then allow the person to respond. Allow time for the person to answer. This may involve periods of silence while the person decides what to say. Always treat the person with respect and do not make flip jokes in response to his or her answers.

Once a person has answered your initial question probe the answer for more detail. Ask the subject to clarify or expand on some point he or she has made. Toward the end of the interview it is worthwhile to provide an open-ended question such as "Is there some question I might have asked that I did not? Is there some information about this problem that I am missing?"

Once the interview is over it is useful to reassure the person that his or her answers will be treated with confidentiality (particularly if their answers contain sensitive information). It is sometimes useful to permit the subject to ask you questions about what your purpose is now that he or she has participated in your study.

Observer Interference

In the scientific study of adolescents, a researcher has to be aware that the behavior observed or measured may not be totally natural. The fact that someone is observing or measuring another person's behavior is *obtrusive*—that is, measuring and observing behavior alters it (Webb, Campbell, Schwartz & Sechrist, 1966). For example, suppose you are driving along and suddenly see a state police car in your rearview mirror.

Some cultures, such as the San Carlos Apaches of Arizona, have a formal "rite of passage" to mark the achievement of sexual maturity. (Martin Etter/Anthro-Photo)

Irrespective of whether you were speeding or not, you are likely to monitor your speed and become much more aware of your driving behavior. In much the same way, a subject in a psychological experiment is aware of being watched and does not want to "act badly." Actually any of three elements in an experiment can alter the natural behavior being studied: (1) the person being observed or measured; (2) the observer or the instrument; or (3) the demand of the task. Although the intrusiveness of observers or testing situations diminishes over time, we suspect that the impact is never totally eliminated.

A person participating in an experiment typically knows it. (Ethics preclude imposing experimental treatments without the subjects knowing about it.) Thus we are apt to see what might be called a guinea-pig effect (Webb et al., 1966). When people realize that they are part of an experiment, very often they will try to figure out what the experimenter is "trying to prove." Once they determine this, correctly or incorrectly, they are likely to start playing roles. Most often the roles assumed by the subjects are intended to be helpful to the researcher. Every so often, however, a subject will assume a role that is meant to be disruptive. In either case, the results are altered.

An additional source of error from a person being observed is called a *response set*. People often respond to a test with patterns that have little to do with what is supposedly being measured. Most people have filled out attitude surveys with statements like "Cats are nice animals," and five alternatives: strongly agree, agree, uncertain, disagree, strongly disagree. Some people are reluctant to mark either extreme even though they may despise cats. Alternately, some people are most apt to *strongly* agree or disagree with nearly everything. A third group has a tendency to mark uncertain very often. A researcher's interpretation of the attitudes of such individuals will therefore be clouded by factors other than those supposedly being measured.

The researcher may unknowingly bias the results. Perhaps one of the cleverest demonstrations of obtrusiveness in experimental research was by Robert Rosenthal. The phenomenon has become known as the Rosenthal effect. Rosenthal demonstrated that an experimenter enters a laboratory with some advance knowledge of how the results should come out. The net result is that the experimenter may unwittingly convey expectations to the subject and thereby bias the outcome. In Rosenthal's classic study, students in a psychology rat lab were given rats and were told that their rat was either a genetically superior or inferior rat. Actually, the assignment of rats to students was random. Nonetheless, the learning performance of the two sets of rats was in accord with what would be expected of the two "genetic groupings." Apparently the students' expectations influenced the rats' behavior.

Finally, the task itself or the setting may be obtrusive. When you walk into a church, a temple, or a library, your behavior differs from your behavior in a football stadium, a sorority or fraternity house, or a tavern. In effect, your surroundings dictate appropriate and inappropriate behavior. Likewise, as you enter a medical or psychological laboratory your behavior changes. You take stock of the behavior that is appropriate and act as expected, or in ways that run counter to what is expected, depending on your personality.

THE ETHICS OF RESEARCH WITH ADOLESCENTS

The history of research with children and adolescents includes several studies in which an investigator has placed the importance of the research question ahead of the rights of the individual who served as the *subject* of study. Research subjects have been deceived and manipulated in the name of science in ways that could possibly lead to their physical or psychological harm with little or no apparent regard on the researcher's part for the rights of the people involved.

Although such studies make up a minority of research, their existence has motivated many professional societies and government agencies to take a strong stand on such procedures. Their position is that an individual who agrees to participate in a study should not, as a result of the study, be subject to any physical or psychological harm.

Physical harm is, of course, easier to define than psychological harm. Psychological stress and anxiety may occur as a result of some experimental manipulation, and an investigator must try to assess whether the stress is a necessary outcome of the study, and, if so, whether the study is necessary. As an example, in the "classic" Watson and Raynor (1920) study of Albert, an infant was placed in a room with a white rat. Initially Albert liked the rat. However, every time Albert approached the rat or the rat approached Albert, the experimenter struck a loud gong. In a short time Albert was terrified by the rat as well as by other objects that reminded him of the original source of the fear. Although Watson and Raynor claimed to have deconditioned Albert from his fear, did they have the right to submit the child to the study in the first place?

Because of the risks of psychological (or even physical) harm to children and adolescents who participate in research studies, attempts have been made to clarify the rights people have when serving as research subjects. Organizations such as the Society for Research in Child Development, the American Psychological Association, the American Pediatric Association and the American Educational Research Association provide guidelines for the ethical use of children and adolescents as research subjects. Any college or university in which faculty or students engage in research using human subjects is mandated to have a human subjects committee.

When adolescents are asked to take part in a research study, they must be told what is to happen and what they are expected to do before they agree to participate. They must also be told if there are any risks they may face by agreeing to take part in the study. Risks include any physical or psychological discomfort they may feel during or after the study. Once they have been informed, the research subjects must sign a written agreement that: (1) they understand what is being asked of them and what is going to happen, (2) they are participating voluntarily, and (3) that they can stop participating at any time. This *informed consent* is required for any study in which humans are the research subjects. But, when the research subjects are children or adolescents, this requirement may present some problems.

Because younger adolescents are often unable to understand complex directions, the description must be offered in clear and simple terms. This is not always easy. The researcher must describe the demands and risks of the study without biasing the behavior of the adolescent subjects. While the requirement is oftentimes inconvenient, an honest review of the procedures and the general purpose of the study is usually sufficient.

A more practical problem arises when deciding whether one needs to get the adolescent's parents' informed consent too. Since adolescents are often still legally minors, it may be necessary. The question of whether or not to require informed consent is one which troubles many colleges' human subjects review committees. In some cases the question is answered by whether the state has defined young people as legally "emancipated" or independent of their parents. Usually this is set at age 18. College students, even when they are financially dependent upon their parents, are usually considered to be independent. Teen parents are also often described as legally independent. In those cases, no parental consent is needed. On the other hand, research involving adolescents still living at home whose privacy is being invaded or who might be "at risk" for physical or psychological harm must require both the adolescent's and his or her parents' informed consent.

Holder (1981) suggests that in cases when the need for parental approval might infringe upon the adolescent's rights of privacy, that the need for parental informed consent might not be asked. This might occur in a study of adolescents who have had an abortion. The girl may have had the operation without her parents' knowledge. To ask parental permission to talk to their daughter about her abortion would violate the adolescent's right to privacy.

Holder (1981) also argues that when information gathered is not particularly sensitive that parental permission may not be required. Many, however, disagree as to what questions are or are not sensitive. In any case, one should get the opinion of an independent review committee. If parental permission is required then the same demands for clear, simple descriptions of the purpose, procedures and risks must be provided. Parental permission must be given in writing.

Often in studies using adolescents, information regarding school achievement or school performance may be useful. Such information is protected by law as confidentail, and it is not generally available unless written consent is obtained from both the adolescent and the parents.

Any data that is collected from an adolescent subject must be held in confidence. Although an investigator may and should provide a summary of general results of the study, individual data should not be made available. In rare circumstances, information may surface during a study that you, as a researcher, see as an indicator of serious risk to the adolescent subjects. If that occurs, you may wish to get guidance from your professor as to how to handle such information.

Most universities and colleges now have a review committee to evaluate whether research violates the rights of a human subject. Members of such a committee might be consulted early in the development of a research problem to see what guidelines might be followed. Ultimately, however, the responsibility for ensuring that the rights of the adolescent subjects are preserved rests with the researcher. You should evaluate any research study that you might pursue in light of the adolescent's rights to privacy and freedom from physical or psychological harm.

WHERE TO BEGIN

When students in a course such as this are asked to write a term paper or conduct research, they often rightfully complain that they are just becoming familiar with the area and that they are at a loss as to where to begin beyond the index at the end of this book. How do you go about finding information about adolescents when you've just begun to learn about the area? A wide variety of disciplines directly or indirectly study adolescents. Where do you begin? Fortunately most libraries have indexes that abstract journals and books in specific areas. Also, most disciplines have regular publications that provide a current review of the relevant literature on a specific topic. Presented below is a limited selection of such resources that you may find helpful in pursuing a topic in adolescent behavior and development.

Probably the first index that you should study is the *Child Development Abstracts and Bibliography*. It is published three times a year by the Society for Research in Child Development and indexes journals and books that focus on children's (including adolescent's) behavior and development. Other indexes that are less *specifically* related to child and adolescent development but that have references to studies in adolescence are *Psychological Abstracts, Sociological Abstracts, Current Index to Journals in Education (CIJE), Language Behavior Abstracts, Index Medicus,* and *Education Index.*

Leading researchers and writers on a specific topic in child or adolescent development are often asked to write reviews of current literature and provide an overview of current thought. *The Annual Review of Psychology* has an update on research in developmental psychology every other year. However, that review is usually limited in value for those interested in adolescence. Volumes such as the *Review of Child Development Research, Advances in Child Development and Behavior, Review of Research in Education, Yearbooks of the National Society for the Study of Education* (especially 1976 and 1982) or Wolman's (1982) *Handbook of Developmental Psychology* contain useful and current summaries of research in specific areas. Of particular help for the more advanced student are the two-volume *Carmichael's Manual of Child Psychology* (Mussen, 1970) and the more recent five-volume revision (Mussen, 1983), as well as Adelson's (1980) *Handbook of Adolescent Psychology.* Those compilations provide excellent summaries by some of the leading authorities in the areas of child and adolescent development.

As students, your abilities to read and react to research studies may vary considerably. Some readers will already have read many research articles and feel comfortable with the task. Others may not feel quite so comfortable reading journal articles. They do not know how. The information, especially the statistical information, may seem overpowering. I encourage my students not to get too worried about the adequacy of the statistics until they are further along in their studies. The ability to critique an article statistically comes with time. For the student who is unfamiliar with reading journal articles, I suggest the following basic questions you may ask when reviewing an article:

1. Does the author clearly state the research question and the hypotheses to be tested? You should be able to identify with reasonable ease the problem to which the researcher is attending.

2. Is the study worth including in your review? This doesn't mean that all research studies need to be profound—few are. Rather, you, as a person evaluating research, must decide whether the study is worth including in *your* review.

3. Is the research designed to answer the question? Unfortunately, many studies use designs and procedures that are not necessarily the best for, or even appropriate to, the question asked. Quite often, research studies need to be so controlled that they lose the element of reality that exists outside the laboratory.

4. How well does the study control other variables? In the elementary study we described earlier in this chapter, the answer was, "Not too well." One must be careful, however, not to get carried away with looking for other variables. An investigator simply cannot control everything. Rather, it is necessary to look at questions covered by series of studies that complement each other. Also, hindsight is often much better than foresight; the investigator, too, may now recognize the same limitations.

5. Is the sample of subjects for the study appropriate? Sometimes reseachers make mistakes in their selection of people, which in turn casts doubt on the degree to which we can

generalize to the population as a whole. If the subjects in our study were all heavy users of marijuana, can we say anything about nonusers? Very often a number of questions arise about randomization, an important control procedure.

6. Do the conclusions follow from the results? Are the author's conclusions and generalizations justified on the basis of the reported study?

7. Finally—for those with enough expertise—is the statistical analysis appropriate? Are the data and results presented accurately and in an understandable form?

SUMMARY

The student of adolescent behavior and development will quickly find that the quantity of research in adolescence is much smaller than for infancy or preschool children. But, the range of research designs is still quite large. The choice of research design should be guided by the research question the investigator wishes to pursue. The degree to which the research design fails to meet the researchers needs may result in results that are not interpretable. In the view of Campbell (1957), the optimal research design is one that is both internally and externally valid. The more precisely a researcher is able to define his or her independent variables, sampling procedures, and dependent variables, the more likely the researcher will be able to see the limits to internal and external validity. As researchers deal with the complexities of research with adolescents, they are often likely to make sacrifices of internal validity to maintain some degree of reality.

A well-formulated research design has as its base a well-formulated research question. A clear statement of the research question permits the researcher to specify the population to be studied, the alternative treatment conditions to be constructed, how they are to be applied, how outcomes are to be measured, and how data are to be best analyzed. It is in the definition of the conditions that Cattell focuses his attention in defining what makes up an experiment. Without clear definitions, researchers are likely to have unclear results.

The choice of a research design should flow from the question asked. The best questions are not always the most complex. If a research design becomes too complex, the questions can easily get out of hand. Further, the most sophisticated of research designs is only as good as the theory behind it. As new students of adolescent development your initial research efforts should be modest. Start with a clear, simple question.

Beyond design issues, research with adolescents is constrained by the need to deal with ethical issues. Any data from adolescents must be gathered under conditions in which the participant has agreed to participate, after being informed of the nature of the study and what is expected of them. In many cases, informed consent must also be gotten from the adolescent's parents. Any subject should have the right to refuse to participate and to stop participating at any time. All data gathered during a research study should be treated as confidential.

SELF-CONCEPT AND AFFECTIVE GROWTH

3

Oft times nothing profits more than self-esteem,
grounded on just and right, well managed.
Milton, *Paradise Lost*

Self-love, my liege, is not so vile a sin
As self-neglecting
Shakespeare, *King Henry V*

A central theme throughout this text is: During the adolescent years, young people must restructure their image of who they are, and of what they see as their role in life. It is not simply a matter of concluding that they are no longer children and that they are now more like adults. It is, instead, a matter of working through their own answers to questions like "Who am I?," "What do I value?," "What is my role in life?," "What do I want to become?" Adolescents' new self-concepts that emerge out of the process of asking these questions, result in a personal sense of uniqueness, a new sense of self. This new definition of who they are brings together their perceptions of their own physical beings, their capabilities, their sexuality, their occupational plans and goals, their value systems, and their feelings of psychological separation from their parents.

As central as the construct of self-concept is to the adolescent transition, it is at the same time an elusive target to study. Psychologists who study self-concept have had notorious trouble in converging on a common definition (Wylie, 1974). Confusion persists from failure to distinguish between self-concept and self-esteem, self-image and self-worth, ideal self, self-regard, self-blame, self-satisfaction, and others.

In our focus on adolescent self-concept and self-esteem, self-concept is thought of as a multifaceted assessment of one's attributes while self-esteem is a global evaluation of what that self-concept implies. Our self-concept is an accumulation of our perceptions about our physical, social, educational, and psychological self-images. Self-concept pulls together a broad range of more specific images of ourself with respect to certain situations, to specific tasks. In a way, our self-concept is our honest statement of who we think we are. It pulls together our various self-images. It results from our looking at ourselves as objects. When we conclude, "I am a well-organized person," or "I am uncomfortable in crowds," or "I am basically a shy person," we are reflecting on how we see ourselves. Our self-concept may change given different tasks. In a group of close friends, you may see yourself as at ease and friendly. In a large crowd of strangers you may see yourself as socially inept, unable to make the simplest introduction of yourself to others. Which view is correct? Both are. Each represents your assessment of who you are in each situation. That self-assessment, however, dictates our behavior. If we see ourselves as socially inept, we will behave in accord with that image. If we see ourselves as outgoing and comfortable with people, we will behave in accord with that image.

Offer (Offer, Ostrov, & Howard, 1981, 1982, 1984) defines self-image (which we will view as comparable to self-concept) as a composite of five primary self-views. These primary self-views are in turn made up of one to three subviews. According to Offer, the adolescent's self-image is made up first by a psychological self in which the

The interactions of young people with their grandparents and other senior citizens encourage a sense of the continuity of life. (Chris Brown/Stock, Boston)

adolescent evaluates personal impulse control, mood, and body image. It is secondly, made up of a social self in which the adolescent evaluates personal social relations, morals, and vocational and educational goals. The third and fourth dimensions of Offer's scheme include the adolescent's sexual self and familial self. The last dimension of self-image is what Offer et al. describe as a coping self which is made up of the adolescent's sense of mastery of his or her personal external world, of psychopathology, and of superior adjustment. Taken as a whole, these dimensions make up the adolescent's self-concept.

Self-esteem, on the other hand, relates to the net evaluation one gives to his or her self-concept. Coopersmith defines self-esteem as "The evaluation which the individual makes and customarily maintains with regard to himself; it expresses an attitude of approval or disapproval, and indicates the extent to which the individual believes himself to be capable, significant, successful, and worthy. In short, self-esteem is a *personal* judgment of worthiness" (Coopersmith, 1967, pp. 4–5). Self-concept and self-esteem are not always easily distinguished. Professionals will regularly describe a person as having a "good self-concept" or a "bad self-concept" when they might more accurately be referring to "positive self-esteem" or "negative self-esteem." Further, even when assessing self-concept, we find that individuals use adjectives and self-descriptors that are affectively loaded. Adjectives such as attractive, self-assured, and helpful have positive connotations and, when they are used, reflect positive self-esteem. Other adjectives, such as insecure, sloppy, dumb, clumsy, and ugly have negative connotations and reflect negative self-esteem. Thus, while in our dealings with self-concept and self-esteem, we will try to view them separately, in practice they are not always easily distinguishable.

Morris Rosenberg (1965, 1975, 1979) offers a three-faceted view of adolescent self-concept that is worth attention. Self-concept, in Rosenberg's view, is a composite of all of a person's thoughts and feelings with reference to oneself as an object. It is an accumulation of all the beliefs and attitudes a person has regarding personal strengths, weaknesses, physical traits, associations, and so forth. Rosenberg further proposes that one's self-concept has an *Extant Self,* a *Desired Self,* and a *Presenting Self.* The Extant Self is a person's view of him- or herself as it exists right now; it is our present self-concept. Our present self-concept comes in response to the question, "Who am I?" The Desired Self is a person's view of those traits he or she would like to possess; it is our preferred self-concept. Our preferred self-concept comes in response to the question, "What would I like to be?" The Presenting Self is the image that one presents to others; it is our public self-concept. Our public self-concept comes in response to the question, "How do others see me?" Our public self is not always the same as our private or current self-concept.

Our extant self, or our current, real self-concept is made up of our various social roles, psychological traits, and physical attributes. It not only includes a physical description of ourselves and an assessment of psychological and social strengths and weaknesses, it includes our memberships in certain social groups, to the extent that those memberships are important to our definition of who we are. Our membership in social clubs, religious groups, service groups, and honorary societies serves an important function in our assessment of who we are. Also, we use social labels to describe categories which have status. We describe ourselves as "author," "athlete," "bachelor," "class president," . . . Some aspects of our self-concept are more central and important to our overall sense of who we are. Thus, our self-concept is organized with the more central features of our self-concept in dominant roles. Rosenberg also suggests that our self-concept contains *ego extensions*. Ego extensions are people or groups who exist outside ourselves but whose success or failure affects our sense of pride or shame. We have a sense of ownership of these ego extensions. A college student or alumnus who follows a particular sports team closely and whose emotional highs and lows are affected by the success or failure of the team, show their commitment to an ego extension. Note that the ego extension's success or failure may have little or no dependence on the behavior of the individual. In other cases the social and emotional links between a person and an ego extension may be quite close. Parents, for example, have strong emotional bonds with their children and their children's behavior affects the parents feelings of self-worth.

Our preferred self parallels our current self. In juxtaposition to the features of our current self are a comparable set of features indicating how we would like to see ourselves. If a person sees himself as disorganized and wishes he were organized, we see a discrepancy between the two. On the other hand, another person sees herself as sociable and is content with that self-image, little or no discrepancy exists between the current and preferred self-image. One might assume (as some researchers have) that as the overall discrepancy between the current and preferred self-concept increases, one's self-esteem diminishes. Rosenberg leaves the question of self-esteem to others. However, to an extent the discrepancy model appears valid. A very large gap between how one sees him- or herself and what that person would like to be would imply negative self-esteem. But what about the person who shows no discrepancy at all? Is that an indication of positive self-esteem? No difference between the current and preferred self-concepts might also indicate low self-esteem since the person displays no goals for growth. People with positive self-esteem not only are accepting of their current self and view themselves positively, they also have goals for personal growth. These goals are, however, moderate and reasonable. Hence, in a discrepancy model, positive self-esteem may be more accurately reflected in a moderate discrepancy between the current, perceived self and the desired self.

Recently, Markus and Narius (1987) offer additional insights into the importance of what they call "possible selves." In their description, possible selves include not only those images of self that a person would like to become but images of self that the person would *not* like to become. As such these possible selves motivate and shape one's behavior. A student studies, in part, to achieve some job or degree. A student may also study to avoid being labeled as a failure.

Our public self-concept, the view we present to others is not always how we really see ourselves. We have elements of our self-concept that we keep private because some current setting does not allow us to display them or because to display those parts of ourselves might set us up for ridicule and rejection. Young adolescents are often pressured to verbalize values that are not really part of their own belief system. John is an eighth-grade student from a lower-income neighborhood. On a test of general academic ability, John scores quite high. Yet, he is currently grouped with low achievers. He is something of an anomaly in the group since the work is easy for him. When asked, however, John has no desire to go back into regular classes. In a conversation with John, it was clear that he too was aware of the discrepancy. His answer to the question of why he wanted to stay in a class of low achievers when he could succeed in a regular class revealed his insight. "Out there, if I do o.k. in class, my friends call me a 'brown-nose.' Here, I can do o.k. and nobody bothers me. I can even help some of the other kids. Out there I can't act like it's (learning) too easy or they think I'm a freak." John's public self protects his real self-concept.

In some cases, our presenting self is a role that we take on for a short time or for an extended time in an effort to achieve some element of our desired self. While in college, we call ourselves "students." Yet, we intend "student " only as a temporary part of our self-concept in our progress toward some longer range goal.

The structure and content of our self-concept also changes as we mature. Our self-concept, like other aspects of our conceptual structure becomes increasingly complex and interconnected as we mature (Kegan, 1982; Kegan, Noam & Rogers, 1982; Loevinger, 1976). As children move into adolescence and as adolescents move toward adulthood, their answers to questions about who they are become more multifaceted and tends to include abstract as well as concrete attributes. Early adolescents and preadolescents, given the question "Who am I?" will respond with a list of physical features and things they like (Montemayor & Eisen, 1977). A typical nine-year-old boy, for example, answered:

> My name is Bruce C. I have brown eyes. I have brown hair. I have brown eyebrows. I am nine years old. I love! sports. I have seven people in my family. I live on 1923 P. Dr. I am going to be 10 in September. I'm a boy. I have an uncle that is almost 7 feet tall. My school is P. My teacher is Mrs. V. I play Hockey! I am almost the smartest boy in the class. I *love*! food. I love fresh air. I *love* School. (p. 317)

Notice that the nine-year-old's answer consists almost completely of concrete attributes. By early adolescence, responses to the same question are still mostly concrete characteristics, but gradually reports begin to include references to interpersonal characteristics or abstract categories. One 11-year-old girl wrote:

> My name is A. I'm a human being. I'm a girl. I'm a truthful person. I'm not pretty. I do so-so in my studies. I'm a very good cellist. I'm a very good pianist. I'm a little bit tall for my age. I like several boys. I like several girls. I'm old-fashioned. I play tennis. I am a *very* good swimmer. I try to be helpful. I'm always ready to be friends with anybody. Mostly I'm well-liked by some girls and boys. I love sports and music. I don't know if I'm liked by boys or not. (pp. 317–318)

Although there are still many references to concrete characteristics, the girl also compares herself with respect to others and labels herself with such abstract terms as truthful, old-fashioned, and helpful; she also provides some assessment of her personality. By late adolescence, responses to the question are much more likely to include references to personal style. Concrete attributes, although while still there, are not emphasized. A 17-year-old girl wrote:

> I am a human being. I am a girl. I am an individual. I don't know who I am. I am a Pisces. I am a moody person. I am an indecisive person. I am an ambitious person.

I am a very curious person. I am a confused person. I am not an individual. I am a loner. I am an American (God help me). I am a Democrat. I am a liberal person. I am a radical. I am a conservative. I am a pseudo-liberal. I am an atheist. I am not a classifiable person (i.e.—I don't want to be). (p. 318)

The shifts in the structure of the adolescent self-concept are not sharp . Dusek and Flaherty (1981) found that self-concept develops smoothly and continuously over the adolescent years. One's self-concept, may, however, be temporarily or permanently altered by the occurrence of significant social and psychological crises during its unfolding. A variety of research studies show that significant life events and crises may disrupt the physical and psychological well-being of adolescents and adults (Rabkin & Struening, 1976).

Beginning with Holmes and Rahe's (1967) meausres of stressful life events among adults and Coddington's (1972a, 1972b) studies with children, and more recently Johnson and McCutcheon's (1980) studies with children and adolescents, negative life events such as divorce, a death in the family, or a move are seen as possible contributors to physical and psychological distress (Healy & Stewart, 1984). Johnson and McCutcheon (1980) add an important distinction not found in the earlier studies that life events are not always negative and stressful. They may be positive and have beneficial effects on one's feelings of adequacy and self-worth. Further, the same life event (for example, moving or changing schools) may be negative for one adolescent but positive for another and neutral for still another. The value of the event depends on the adolescent's perception of it. Nonetheless, the occurrence of major life events and the ability of the adolescent to manage them represent major contributors to the young person's feelings of self-worth. The more adequately a young person deals with stressful transitions, the better his or her sense of self-esteem. Conversely, if a young person fares badly, self-esteem will suffer. At the same time, the net self-esteem adolescents hold entering transitions or crises will determine, in part, their ability to cope with the stress. The two interact.

Our self-esteem does not operate independently of our other developmental; needs. Maslow (1954) notes that before people have positive feelings of self-esteem, of success and respect, their basic needs must be satisfied. That is, they must have their physical needs met, they must feel a sense of security, and they need a sense of "belongingness," they need to be loved and accepted. Without satisfaction of these basic needs, self-esteem is an illusion. Likewise, without self-esteem, achieving self-actualization, the highest level of Maslow's model of personal growth, would be impossible.

Further, our self-concepts and our self-esteem grow out of our experiences. From our earliest interactions as babies to our last experiences as older adults, our self-concepts are in a state of continuous evolution. Perhaps more than any other contemporary psychologist, Erik Erikson has helped us undersand this concept of an evolving self, especially as it relates to the adolescent years. Erikson's "Eight stages" of human development, described in this chapter (see Figure 3–1) have met with great public and professional interest. Erikson's concept of an "identity crisis" has found its way into today's general language.

	1	2	3	4	5	6	7	8
VIII								INTEGRITY VERSUS DESPAIR
VII							GENERATIVITY VERSUS STAGNATION	
VI						INTIMACY VERSUS ISOLATION		
V	Temporal Perspective versus Time Confusion	Self-Certainty versus Self-Concious	Role Experimentation versus Role Fixation	Apprenticeship versus Work Paralysis	IDENTITY VERSUS IDENTITY CONFUSION	Sexual Polarization versus Bisexual Confusion	Leader- and Followership versus Authority Confusion.	Ideological Commitment versus Confusion of Values
IV				INDUSTRY VERSUS INFERIORITY	Task Identification versus Sense of Futility			
III			INITIATIVE VERSUS GUILT		Anticipation of Roles versus Role Inhibition			
II		AUTONOMY VERSUS SHAME, DOUBT			Will to Be Oneself versus Self-Doubt			
I	TRUST VERSUS MISTRUST				Mutual Recognition versus Autiatic Isolation			

Figure 3–1 Erikson's eight stages of man and related personal conflicts. *Source:* Reproduced from *Identity, Youth and Crisis* by Erik H. Erikson, with the permission of W. W. Norton & Company, Inc. Copyright © 1968 by W. W. Norton & Company, Inc.

ERIK ERIKSON

Erikson was a student of both Sigmund and Anna Freud. Although Erikson was influenced by Freud, and his theory of personality has its roots in Freudian theory, Erikson shifted the focus from a set of inborn sexual motivations to social and environmental influences. A person's personality is the result of how well one's social environment meets that person's needs at each in a series of stages of development. Like Piaget, Erikson believes the sequence of stages is genetically determined but that their form is environmentally determined.

Erikson's (1959, 1968) writings have been immensely popular, and his psychological analysis of Mahatma Gandhi's militant nonviolence, *Gandhi's Truth* (1969), was awarded a Pulitzer Prize and the National Book Award for philosophy and religion. Likewise his psychological history of Martin Luther, *Young Man Luther* (1968) makes fascinating reading and, as much as any of his other writings, gives the reader a picture of the dynamics of his theory.

Erik Erikson sees adolescence as a distinct period of development, separating yet bridging childhood and adulthood. Although Erikson focuses on the process of ego identity formation during adolescence, he sees ego formation as progressing throughout life.

In Erikson's view, a person develops a sense of identity as a result of working through a set of psychological and social tasks. The process of developing a sense of identity or a sense of self is a lifelong task. Although the stress associated with identity development in adolescence is of great importance, it must be seen as but one conflict in a series of conflicts that an individual must face throughout life. Thus, although the identity conflict of adolescence may be stormy, so might other developmental conflicts.

1. *Trust versus mistrust.* Like Freud, Erikson sees infancy as the first stage of personality development. During infancy the individual must develop a sense of *trust.* Parents provide affection and warmth and satisfy basic needs. Erikson feels that we never fully satisfy all our needs, but the infant from a healthy environment learns that others can be trusted. In contrast, infants who are raised in an environment of neglect and abuse, lacking in nurturance or love, develop a general attitude of *mistrust* of others.

2. *Autonomy versus shame and doubt.* In early childhood, about ages one to three, the child faces the second task. During this period the child must develop an initial sense of *autonomy,* or self-control. Children during this stage establish themselves as individuals and demonstrate that they can do things on their own. They are clearly still dependent upon their parents, but they begin to see themselves as individuals in their own right. During this stage parents need to exercise enough firm control to protect the child from harm but allow the child to explore new areas independently. Failure to achieve a sense of autonomy of personal adequacy because belittling parents or overprotective parents do not allow experimentation during this period leads to a sense of *shame* and *doubt* about one's own abilities.

3. *Initiative versus guilt.* During preschool years, ages three to five, children begin to play with thoughts and are curious and imaginative. Through their imagination children test the limits of reality and fantasy. Their control over their own bodies is increased, and much of what they learn is through imitation of parents and other important adults. In a positive setting children develop a sense of *initiative* in which exploration and questioning are accepted parts of their identity. In nonconducive environments, in which parents are overly strict and discourage spontaneity, children develop a sense of *guilt.*

4. *Industry versus inferiority.* School-age children, about six to 11 years, are intent upon developing a sense of duty and accomplishment, or what Erikson calls a sense of *industry.* Children begin to set aside the fantasy and play of preschool and prefer to work with real things. During this period children develop social know-how and academic skills. Much of their thoughts are directed at clearly differentiating the real and the unreal. Children reach out to try new tasks and are increasingly competitive. Failures or mistakes, by themselves, should not be discouraged because they form the

base for future learning. Repeated and excessive failure, however, may lead to a sense of *inferiority*. When children meet with repeated failure, they develop a self-image in which they see themselves as inadequate to take part in the working world.

5. *Identity versus identity diffusion.* During adolescence the previous elements of an individual's self-image are reassessed and reformulated into an image that includes what role the adolescent anticipates as an adult. The adolescent develops a sense of *personal identity.* Whereas adolescents at this period of development are likely to express a need for freedom from authority, especially parents' authority, they conform highly to the authority of the peer group. The peer group, rather than being a negative force, offers a protective setting that is alien to the adult world and allows the adolescent to experiment with alternative life roles and value systems.

This general reformulation of personal identity takes place during the *identity crisis,* in which the adolescent actively breaks down and restructures the organization of his or her personality. The very complex and important nature of the decision-making process makes the period of transformation one of intense conflict. The adolescent may thus alternate between actively exploring new roles and stepping away from decision making.

In settings that provide too little structure for selection of alternative roles and values, the adolescent may be unable to decide on an alternative. In this case the adolescent has no clear personal identity and may suffer *role diffusion.* In the long run this alternative may be especially disruptive for the adolescent. Among disturbed and severely depressed adolescents, self-descriptions often include phrases such as "I'm nothing, a loser." Alternatively, the adolescent may choose a *negative identity.* In working with delinquent youths, one gets the impression, for example, that being "delinquent" is better than being nothing at all. Assuming the identity of delinquent offers a set of roles and values that give some direction to an adolescent's life, even though that direction is in opposition to the preferences of society.

Marcia (1966, 1980) has been able to measure differences among four states of transition in the movement toward identity achievement. When parents provide too little freedom for exploration of alternative roles, the adolescent may experience *identity foreclosure.* That is, the adolescent accepts as a personal identity a set of roles and values that have been specified by someone else. An adolescent boy who is expected to be a doctor or lawyer just like his father and grandfather before him may not see much room for divergence. Likewise, an adolescent girl who is led to expect a singular role as housewife and mother may not experience conflict, because no alternatives are seen as reasonable. Young people, both males and females, in a state of identity foreclosure tend to be dogmatic and willing to submit to authority. They lack self-directiveness (Marcia, 1980).

At the next level of development of a personal identity, Marcia sees *identity diffusion,* during which adolescents lack commitment to a set of values and goals. Their behavior is impulsive and self-centered.

Prior to achieving a functioning identity, adolescents enter a period of *moratorium,* during which they are actively in the identity crisis. Among the principle struggles that seem to be prevalent during this phase is the struggle to see oneself as free from parents and authority (Marcia, 1980).

Identity achievement occurs among those adolescents who have actually gone through the restructuring and decision-making process. Those who do achieve a sense of personal identity have a stronger sense of self-directedness and a feeling of satisfaction about personal beliefs and goals. In contrast, those adolescents in states of identity diffusion or moratorium are less likely to value or recognize their distinctiveness. In making the transition to an achieved identity, adolescents may need help in identifying their own strengths and limits and in recognizing their uniqueness and value as human beings. Counseling also requires aiding the adolescent in exploring and recognizing role and value choices. Ultimately, however, counselors need to ensure that the adolescents' decision-making activities are conducted in an atmosphere that is not restricted by arbitrary standards of what is and is not acceptable. On the other hand, neither should the process be conducted within a completely unstructured context.

Some cautions should be stated about the process as seen by Marcia, because it is not clear that the process of identity formation among females is comparable to that among males. Socialization toward adult identity formation is not the same, and it is not unlikely that the process of identity formation similarly differs. Identity foreclosure, for example, seems to have less negative impact among females than males.

Just as identity formation does not begin at adolescence, neither does it end with adolescence. An individual's sense of personal identity is continuously refined throughout life. But, just as the way the adolescent resolves the conflicts preceding identity formation—especially its immediate precursor, the strugle to achieve a sense of industry—affects the identity crisis, so does the adolescent's achievement of a sense of identity have an impact on subsequent conflicts. It has an especially strong relationship to the struggle to achieve a sense of intimacy in young adulthood.

6. *Intimacy versus isolation.* Following adolescence the young adult must establish a sense of *intimacy* with another person. Beyond the immediate, sexual intimacy which Erikson sees as essential to a relationship, there is a more general level of intimacy in which the individual's sense of identity becomes fused with the identity of another

Although adolescents need strong peer relationships, they also need time to be alone. (Photograph by John Pitken)

person. Close personal relationships with people of both sexes lead to a general feeling of acceptability in society. Failure to achieve a clear personal identity during adolescence interferes with establishing close relationships with others. If a young woman, for example, is unsure of who she is, then it is not possible for her to be open enough with another person to reveal herself enough to establish an intimate relationship. Failure to establish close intimate relationships leads to a sense of *isolation.*

7. *Generativity versus stagnation.* During middle adulthood a person develops a sense of *generativity,* which refers not only to parental status but also to a productive and creative role in the service of others. Generativity means feeling that what one does benefits successive generations. Failure to master this task leads to *stagnation* and self-indulgence.

8. *Integrity versus despair.* Finally, during old age, the individual needs to develop a sense of *integrity,* a sense of accomplishment and a feeling that one's life was worthwhile, that there was meaning to one's life. A feeling of integrity can emerge only when in retrospect an elderly man, for example, feels that he has been productive in work and in parenthood and that what he has done was of benefit to others. This does not mean that he looks back over his life "through rose-colored glasses." He sees his hardships and sufferings as a normal part of life, outweighed by the sense of accomplishment. Failure to develop this feeling leads to a sense of *despair.*

VIGNETTE 3–1
THE FIT IN THE CHOIR

The identity crisis is the keystone of Erikson's theory of personality development. Whether or not adolescents establish an adequate sense of personal identity is critical to their psychosocial adjustment during adult years. The process of answering the question "Who am I?" may be associated with some periods of considerable inner turmoil and rebellion. Such seems to have been the case with Martin Luther, who as a young Augustinian monk wrestled with the question of who or what he was and was not. Erikson studies the life of Luther as an archetypic example of a person going through the stages of personal development. The result of that study was his Young Man Luther. *Presented below is an abridged description of Luther's identity crisis, as represented in "the fit in the choir."*

Source: Reprinted from *Young Man Luther* by Erik H. Erikson, with the permission of W. W. Norton & Company, Inc. Copyright © 1958, 1962 by Erik H. Erikson.

Three of young Luther's contemporaries (none of them a later follower of his) report that sometime during his early or middle twenties, he suddenly fell to the ground in the choir of the monastery at Erfurt, "raved" like one possessed, and roared with the voice of a bull: "*Ich bin's nit! Ich bin's nit!*" or "*Non sum! Non sum!*" The German version is best translated with "It isn't me!" the Latin one with "I am *not!*"

It would be interesting to know whether at this moment Martin roared in Latin or in German; but the reporters agree only on the occasion which upset him so deeply: the reading of Christ's *ejecto a surdo et muto daemonio*—Christ's cure of a man possessed by a *dumb spirit.* This can only refer to Mark 9:17: "And one of the multitude answered and said, Master, I have brought unto thee my son, which hath a dumb spirit." The chroniclers considered that young Luther was possessed by demons—the religious and psychiatric borderline case of the middle ages—and that he showed himself possessed even as he tried most loudly to deny it. "I am *not*," would then be the childlike protestation of somebody who has been called a name or has been characterized with loathsome adjectives: here, dumb, mute, possessed.

. . . [Luther's] days in the monastery were darkened by a suspicion, which Martin's father expressed loudly on the occasion of the young priest's first Mass, that the thunderstorm had really been the voice of a *Gespenst,* a ghost; thus Luther's vow was on the borderline of both pathology and demonology. Luther remained sensitive to this paternal suspicion, and continued to argue with himself and with his father long after his father had no other choice than to acknowledge his son as a spiritual leader and Europe's religious strong man. But in his twenties Martin was still a sorely troubled young man, not at all able to express either what inspired or what bothered him; his greatest worldly burden was certainly the fact that his father had only most reluctantly, and after much cursing, given his consent (which was legally dispensable, anyway) to the son's religious career.

It must have occurred to the reader that the story of the fit in the choir attracted me originally because I suspected that the words "I am *not*!" revealed the fit to be part of a most severe identity crisis—a crisis in which the young monk felt obliged to protest what he was *not* (possessed, sick, sinful) perhaps in order to break through to what he was or was to be. I will now state what remains of my suspicion, and what I indend to make of it.

If we approach the episode from the psychiatric viewpoint, we can recognize in the described attack (and also in a variety of symptomatic scruples and anxieties to which Martin was subject at the time) an intrinsic ambivalence, an inner two-facedness, such as we find in all neurotic symptoms. The attack could be said to deny in its verbal part ("I am not") what Martin's father had said, namely, that his son was perhaps possessed rather than holy; but it also proves the father's point by its very occurrence in front of the same congregation who had previously heard the father express his anger and apprehension. The fit, then, is both unconscious obedience to the father and implied rebellion against the monastery; the words uttered both deny the father's assertion, and confirm the vow which Martin had made in that first known anxiety attack during a thunderstorm at the age of twenty-one, when he had exclaimed, "I want to be a monk." We find the young monk, then, at the crossroads of obedience to his father—an obedience of extraordinary tenacity and deviousness—and to the monastic vows which at the time he was straining to obey almost to the point of absurdity.

MEASURING SELF-WORTH

Several measures of self-concept and self-esteem are available for the practicing professional. But, one should use some caution in selecting a measure of self-concept. The available measures vary considerably in reliability and validity (Wylie, 1974) and different measures reflect quite different views of the character of self-concept and self-esteem.

Among the more widely used scales that offer a global assessment of self-concept or self-esteem are the Rosenberg (1965) Self-Esteem Scale and the Coopersmith (1967) Self-Esteem Inventory. Measures that provide assessments on multiple self-concepts include the (Piers, 1969) Children's Self-Concept Scale and the Offer (Offer, Ostrow & Howard, 1982) Self-Image Questionnaire for Adolescents.

One popular technique used by many researchers and practitioners to assess a discrepancy between current self and desired self is to have adolescents scan a checklist of several adjectives (Gough, 1960) and mark those adjectives that they think describe themselves. The adolescents are then given a second copy of the list and are asked to check those adjectives that describe the way they would like to be seen. The closer the perceived self is to the ideal self, the stronger or more positive the individual's feelings of self-worth. If the two sets of adjectives are very divergent, then we can assume that the adolescent has lower feelings of self-worth. What a person sees and what he or she would like to see are too different.

As Winston Churchill (1948) recalled the time when England was entering war with Germany and he was about to be named Prime Minister, he wrote "By the afternoon, I became aware that I might be called to take the lead. The prospect neither excited nor alarmed me. I thought it would be by far the best plan." At first glance, Churchill's statement might seem arrogant. It is not. Rather, it is an accurate reflection of his self-concept. Further, it suggests another important role of self-concept; that self-concept establishes expectations for ourselves. If we see ourselves as capable, we behave accordingly. If we see ourselves as incapable, we also behave accordingly. When an adolescent says with conviction, "I could never be a good student," he or she has already established a serious stumbling block to success. Being a good student is not compatible with her or his self image. On the other hand, positive feelings of self-worth should not be confused with conceit. An adolescent who has positive feelings of self-worth is more likely to be at ease in stressful settings. However, as a society, we discourage individuals from saying, "I like myself" or "I am a really super person." We are encouraged to be humble and a bit self-effacing. For adolescents the pressures to conform to this demand are added to their own questions of whether they are worth much. A practioner cannot help but be impressed to hear so many statements from young people like "I'm ugly," "I'm dumb," or "My feet are too big." It is often difficult to get early- or middle-adolescents to express their strengths.

In identifying an adolescent's self-concept, it does not matter whether the adolescent's self-perceptions are accurate from your or anyone else's point of view. The self-perception is the "reality" that dominates the adolescent's life. The anorexic girl who sees herself as fat even though she is emaciated has, as an integral part of her self-concept, the perception that she is somehow less than desirable. Likewise, the boy who sees himself as stupid even though teachers see him as potentially bright has, as an integral part of his self-image, the feeling that he lacks competence. Both will interact with others in ways that reflect that feeling, rather than in ways that reflect external reality.

The role of a practitioner working with a youngster with a misperceived self-attribute is not to confront the adolescent with the "truth." Most of us have seen a discouraged teacher look at a girl like the one described and say, "You have the brains to do well. Why don't you apply yourself?" That the technique is not effective is probably best shown in the expression on the girl's face after hearing this. The practitioner who wishes to alter this adolescent's self-image to a more realistic self-appraisal needs to do so gradually. The practitioner should also realize that it may not be possible to change an adolescent's self-image totally.

FACTORS AFFECTING SELF-ESTEEM

The ability of an adolescent to satisfactorily work through the process of establishing a new sense of self and the type of self-image that emerges from the conflict differs as a result of any number of factors. The environment in which lower-income black adolescents develop a personal sense of identity is obviously much different than the environment of an upper-class, white adolescent.Further, the number of social and educational options available to the two groups are widely separated. Their freedom to consider alternate life-styles is simply not the same. Thus they will emerge from adolescence with very different self-images.

One study of affluent youths found, for example, that for a while they have to learn to live with an extraordinary number of choices. They grow up with the knowlege that they have the ability and the resources to do whatever they please. It is an attitude that stays with them throughout life (Coles, 1977).

Lower-income youths do not see life as providing nearly as wide a range of choices. Adolescents from an inner-city, lower-income neighborhood or a poor rural farm do not see themselves as having many options. Their freedom to experiment is limited by lack of financial resources. Also, adolescents from lower-income families are less likely to see themselves as having much say in the control of their lives.

Middle-income adolescents fall somewhere between these extremes. Although their opportunities for choice are broader than for their lower-income peers, they have fewer options than the more affluent adolescents do. In each case, self-concept and identity are influenced by their families' level of income.

Not only the family but also the neighborhood from which an adolescent comes have an impact on self-perceptions. Adolescents who come from professional families are more likely to expect to go to college than those from blue-collar families. However, adolescents from blue-collar families are more likely to plan on college as the average family income of the neighborhood increases, and adolescents from professional families are less likely to plan on college as the average family income of the neighborhood decreases (Wilson, 1959).

Other factors also affect adolescent self-concept and feelings of self-worth. As adolescents' value systems differ from the majority of their neighborhood peers, the lower their feelings of confidence and self-worth. Youths from Catholic families who are raised in predominantly non-Catholic neighborhoods have lower self-esteem than those who grow up in predominantly Catholic neighborhoods. Similar patterns are found for Protestant and Jewish adolescents (Rosenberg, 1975). Apparently the discomfort of finding oneself with values or a relevant social-status variable that is different from that of the majority of peers is unsettling enough to lead many adolescents to question those values and therefore their own value.

Rosenberg (1965) also found that low self-esteem in adolescents was associated with parental indifference. That is, whereas positive, supportive interactions with parents were most associated with positive feelings of self-worth, low self-worth was not conversely related to negative, nonsupportive interactions. Rather, parental indifference or lack of parent-adolescent interactions seemed to lead to diminished feelings of self-esteem. Adolescents interpret their parents' lack of response as a lack of caring. In another study adolescents with low self-esteem viewed communication with their parents as nonconstructive (Flora, 1978). Family warmth and nurturance and active involvement of parents with their children are regularly demonstrated to be benefically related to positive self-esteem and to social adjustment of the children (Baumrind & Black, 1967; Coopersmith, 1967; Piers & Harris, 1964; Rosenberg & Simmons, 1972). Conversely, family discord and hostility are related to lower self-esteem and more maladjustment (Rutter, 1980; Bishop & Ingersoll, 1984).

SELF-ESTEEM AND SOCIAL ADJUSTMENT

Whether or not adolescents are able to accept the strengths and limits of others is directly related to their ability to accept their own strengths and limits. Self-acceptance is basic to general social acceptance. Failure to accept yourself decreases the chances of others accepting you. Conversely, acceptance by others may increase your acceptance of yourself. The two processes complement each other. When adolescents view themselves as different from their peers, they are likely to be seen the same way by peers and, because of that, be separated from them (Goslin, 1962). A healthy personality and positive feelings of self-worth are fundamental to positive social adjustment.

SHYNESS

An important reflection of a person's feelings of self-worth is the way in which he or she interacts with others. It is not uncommon for people to feel uncertainty or anxiety about meeting new people or entering new situations. For some, however, the prospect of entering a group of unknown (or even known) people is a source of considerable physical and psychological discomfort. The thought of having to meet someone new might bring on perspiration, a pounding heart, a queezy stomach, and clammy hands. They may wander the halls of a building trying to get up the courage to enter an office to which they must go for an interview. When asked why they feel so threatened by social settings, they will often tell you that they fear making a foolish mistake and being thought of negatively by others. We all know such people and we may even describe them as "painfully shy" as if we recognize the torment they experience. But, every so often, someone will tell us that they too are shy and we are taken by surprise since those people seem so at ease. This situation is frequently the case among public personalities who are forced to be congenial and outgoing but who, in private, are shy. People such as Carol Burnett, Johnny Carson, and Phil Donahue describe themselves as basically shy.

Shyness is not unusual. When adults are asked if they are shy, two out of five

Warm, caring, supportive parents play an important role in the development of positive self-esteem. (© Margaret Thompson)

will answer "Yes." If adults are asked if they have ever thought of themselves as a shy person, nearly all say they have. For some who answer that they are shy, their shyness is overwhelming and socially debilitating. For others who answer that they are shy, however, their shyness causes vague discomfort and hesitance. The latter group is able to function well and it is this group that we are often surprised to hear is shy.

The psychologist who is most associated with the psychological study of shyness and its treatment is Philip Zimbardo. Zimbardo (1977; Zimbardo & Radl, 1982) has established a continuing program of study on shyness and has established a shyness clinic in which participants develop skills for dealing with their shyness. Zimbardo finds that the group that shows the highest proportion of people who rate themselves as shy is young adolescents, especially girls. Nearly two-thirds of early adolescents see themselves as shy. Shy teenage girls are more likely to view themselves as less intelligent, less attractive, and generally more negative. Shyness and lowered self-esteem are related.

Zimbardo and Radl (1982) attributed the increased rate of shyness at early adolescence to self-consciousness about the various physical, psychological, and social changes young people experience. Young adolescents are acutely aware of peers and feel strong personal pressure to be acceptable. At the same time, they are increasingly aware of others' thoughts. Zimbardo and Radl (1982) focus on that emerging ability during early adolescence and draw upon the concept of adolescent egocentricism described by Elkind (1967) to account for their increased self-consciousness. Recall from Chapter 1 that Elkind indicates that during adolescence, young people are increasingly able to assume the perspective of others. More importantly, they can now understand that others have thoughts. The egocentric trap is that the young person is likely to assume that everyone thinks like he or she does. Since the young person is concerned with his or her physical, intellectual, and social adequacy, the assumption is that everyone else is likewise so concerned. An adolescent's egocentric view is that everyone else is inordinately concerned with his or her well being. As an extension of this egocentric thinking, the adolescent creates an "imaginary audience" which is critically aware of all she or he is doing. The shy person is afraid that since he or she is self-critical that everyone else shares that view. As a result, shy adolescents are likely to rate themselves as lonely and having a difficult time developing friendships, especially with members of the opposite sex (Ishiyama, 1984). While it may be argued about whether self-esteem affects an adolescent's perception of his or her popularity or the converse is true, a recent study finds more evidence for the first possibility (Bohrnstedt & Felson, 1983).

Dealing with one's shyness is not always easy. Even among those who are able to cover their shyness with an outgoing image may feel anxieties. The public or presenting self and their real extant self are not the same. They may fear that if their real shyness and insecurity were to be discovered they would be thought of as a phony. For the shy boy, asking a girl for a date is torturous. Rejection of any sort for the shy person is seen as confirmation of their inadequacy. Shy people need to learn that shyness is a learned social behavior and that they can unlearn it. Effective methods for dealing with shyness include role playing social settings to practice ways of dealing with people. Since compliments are a source of discomfort, the shy person must learn to accept compliments graciously and to use the opportunity to offer compliments as a way of initiating a social interaction. Too often, shy people and those with lowered self-esteem, engage in negative self-talk. They think about themselves as inept or incompetent. They need to practice using positive self-descriptors. Finally, they need to take social risks by trying to meet new people. It is important to help the shy person set reasonable goals in their transition from a shy, withdrawn person to a more outgoing person. Too lofty goals may result in early failure. For a while shy people will of necessity separate this new outgoing self from their self-view as anxious. Ultimately, however, they should be encouraged to merge the two into a new self-image.

VIGNETTE 3–2
DEAR JULIET

Why would someone write to a person who does not exist? Each year, for example, several letters are sent to the great fictional detective Sherlock Holmes. In the same way, each year literally thousands of letters are sent to Juliet Capulet, that archetypical romantic adolescent. Do they write Juliet as a symbol of eternal love, as one of the letters suggests, or is it that like Ann Landers or Dear Abby the person is basically a stranger? Perhaps as interesting a question is, What kind of person would take the time to respond as "Juliet's secretary?"

Excerpted from Hamblin, Dora Jane (1979) "New career
for Juliet: advice to other lovelorns." *Smithsonian, 10*
(2), 156.

It was right there, on the news-service wire. Marie Osmond, the TV star, was being interviewed in London. She, and not Olivia Newton-John, she told reporters, had been first choice to play the female lead in *Grease*. She had turned it down "on moral grounds" because she wanted her first movie to be "a beautiful, tasteful picture." Well, she was asked, would she turn down a *Romeo and Juliet* film on the same moral grounds? "I don't know," said Marie dubiously. "I haven't read the script."

What Marie Osmond didn't know, besides her Shakespeare, was that Juliet Capulet, while not exactly alive and well in Verona, gets 400 to 500 lovelorn letters a month. Hardly an Ann Landers volume of mail, but enough to need the services of a secretary. She gets letters like this:

Dear Juliet:

I am turning to you because you are the symbol of eternal love. Thus you may be able to understand me. I am Serghej G. of Ljubljana. I am madly in love with a girl, but our parents cause trouble. One night I went out of the house to walk in the fresh snow and wanted to kill myself. Then I thought of you, and all of a sudden my life seemed more beautiful. If you can, write me a word to console me. . . .

Dear Juliet:

I am Jennifer, 14 years old, and I am in love with a boy but I don't know if he loves me. I changed my hair today, before I went to school, and he said "You seem different." Does that mean he loves me? Please reply at once. I found your address in a literature book. . . .

William Shakespeare's "literature book," and the agonies of young love, produce letters in a rainbow of scripts and languages, and some weary *postino* at the Verona post office gathers them up and delivers them to the city hall.

There for the past several months a tall, clear-eyed economics student named Paola Sella has taken them home to answer in her spare time. She has become the unpaid, unofficial "secretary to Juliet," as she signs her replies.

No one in Verona remembers exactly when the letters began to come, but they began to be answered in 1937. That was the year the city council of Verona neatened up a crypt in an abandoned Franciscan convent and installed in it a stone sarcophagus which resembles a watering trough but which had been revered for centuries as "Juliet's tomb."

As custodian of the tomb, the city installed Ettore Solimani, a sober man with the outward bearing of a ferocious shrine guard and the inner soul of a Romeo. In those days many letters were directed to "the tomb of Juliet," and Solimani took it upon himself to answer as many as he could. He wrote slowly, painfully, by hand and almost always in Italian, though occasionally he would find university students to help him with the mysteries of foreign languages. For 40 years he signed himself modestly "*la segretaria di Giulietta.*"

SELF-WORTH AND ACHIEVEMENT

Researchers have found that students' performance in school depends in part on how they feel about themselves (Covington & Beery, 1976). What an adolescent *thinks* about his ability may be more important than his actual level of ability. The more positively individuals feel about their ability to succeed, the more likely they are to exert effort and feel a sense of accomplishment when they finish a task. In the same fashion, the more negatively individuals evaluate their ability to succeed, the more likely they are to avoid tasks in which there is uncertainty of success, the less likely they are to exert effort, and the less likely they are to attribute any success or lack of it to themselves.

Persons with low feelings of self-worth tend to have a high fear of failure and high feelings of failure (Covington & Beery, 1976). Given a task in which they must set goals, those with low self-esteem are likely to set unrealistically difficult or overly easy goals. For example, in a ring-toss game in which students can toss the rings at the goal from any distance they desire, those with low self-esteem stand either right next to the peg or too far away. Those who stand right next to the peg avoid feelings of failure by assuring success. Those who stand too far away insure failure but also provide themselves an excuse. Those with positive self-esteem are more likely to set goals of intermediate difficulty. In the ring-toss game they are more likely to choose a distance that does not ensure success or failure but allows a reasonable chance of success. If, after one set of tries, the players are given the option of moving and trying again, the high self-esteem individuals will use the information from the first try and adjust the distance to make the task more reasonable (or a bit more difficult if the first try was too easy). Those with low self-esteem do not make use of that information.

In achievement-oriented settings like the school, the need to avoid failure may dominate a student's choice of activities and selection of courses. The student may either avoid participation in achievement-related activities altogether or participate just enough to get by but not enough to risk failure. Alternatively, the student may select tasks that are excessively difficult. The "blame" for failure is thus removed from the student and placed on the task (Covington & Beery, 1976).

Those students with high self-esteem, a motivation to achieve, and positive feelings of self-worth are more likely to select moderately difficult tasks and attribute the outcome to their own efforts. Although they do not desire failure, they do not have an overwhelming fear of it. They assume that any achievements are a result of a combination of their own efforts and talent.

The feeling that what one accomplishes results from personal effort and control of the situation is learned. By experience and training we learn to internalize responsibility and control. Further, the pattern is cyclical. Success breeds success and failure breeds failure. The motivation to achieve and successful achievement lead individuals to attribute the success to their own efforts. This builds feelings of pride in accomplishments, which in turn increases the likelihood that the individual will engage in achievement-related behaviors in the future with a willingness to continue to try to achieve.

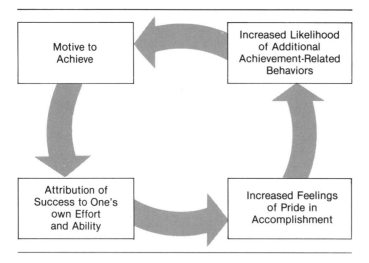

Figure 3-2 The pattern of develop-ment of the achievement motive. *Source:* B. Weiner, "Attribution Theory, Achievement Motivation and the Educational Process," *Review of Educational Research 42,* (1972): 208. Copyright 1972, American Educational Research Association, Washington, D.C.

(See Figure 3-2.) Externalization of control, or assuming that what happens results from luck or from control by outsiders, is also learned. Adolescents who are low in the motive to achieve also see themselves as largely controlled rather than in control of themselves. They are not only more likely to feel that effort is not a primary-characteristic of success but also that lack of success is equated with lack of ability (Weiner, 1972).

Minority adolescents and adolescents from lower-income families are very likely to display this attitude (Katz, 1967). They come from homes and neighborhoods that not only do not reinforce the attitude that what people do is a result of their efforts but instead reinforce the opposite. Middle-class youths, on the other hand, have been instructed that to have ability and fail to put out an effort is immoral; one is morally obligated to use one's talents (Weiner, 1972).

In classrooms, when the teacher expects students to do well and the students fail, the teacher is more likely to attribute the failure to lack of effort or lack of motiva-tion (Weiner & Kukla, 1970). Students low in achievement motivation are apt to report, "I failed because I'm dumb." Teachers are apt to answer, "You failed because you did not try." The highly achievement-oriented teacher implies by this response that the student does have sufficient ability (Weiner & Kukla, 1970). Similarly teachers give more praise and less punishment to students who are seen as exerting effort (Lanzetta & Hannah, 1969).

THE LOCUS OF CONTROL

People with a positive self-image usually feel in control of their own lives. They feel that what they do makes a difference in whether they achieve some outcome. On the other hand, individuals with a negative self-image are apt to feel that what happens to them is mostly the result of luck or fate. The tendency of people to attribute their success or lack of it to themselves or to luck has been labeled as the *locus of control* (Rotter, 1966).

Depending on their past experience, adolescents differ in their tendencies to see themselves as in control of their own lives. Teens from lower-income families and lower-income neighborhoods are less likely to feel such internal control. Rather, low-income adolescents are more likely to see their life as controlled by others. They see that they have little control over their livelihood. An adolescent who views major events as the result of luck, fate, or the whim of people in power, is said to have an external locus of control. Those who see such events as in their own control are internally motivated or have an internal locus of control. When asked how one gets into the college of one's choice, the externally motivated youth is likely to be convinced that it is all a matter of who you know. The internally motivated youth is likely to attribute such an outcome to individual effort or personal ability. Although it may be argued that the external perception is correct in some cases and probably correct in more cases if you are poor, the perception reflects a general attitude about who is in control.

Some studies show that, on the average, boys are more likely than girls to be internally motivated. In the same fashion, girls are less likely to picture themselves as leaders or as academically successful or as successful in traditionally made-dominated areas. One author described this tendency as a "fear of success" (Horner, 1970). When asked to consider the story of a woman who was at the top of her medical school class,

Success not only breeds more success but also leads to improved feelings of self-worth.
(© Bill Stanton/Magnum Photos, Inc.)

a majority of women college students reported that the woman felt anxious and guilty and that success would lead to unpleasant consequences, such as loss of feminity or social rejection (Horner, 1970; Hoffman, 1974). The same projection of anxiety and guilt was not seen when the person being considered was male rather than female (Feather & Raphelson, 1974).

Among preadolescent and adolescent students it has been found that both boys and girls show a tendency to avoid success in the middle school years. By late high school, however, boys show an increased motive to succeed, whereas girls show an increased motive to avoid success (Romer, 1975). Further, the motive to avoid success was more noticeable among girls in coed schools than noncoed schools. The early dominance of a motive to avoid success may be related to typical peer pressure not to be "too brainy." The very strong needs of early-adolescents to be acceptable and accepted have a strong influence on willingness to be noncompetitive, and female achievement in male domains is discouraged. Thus if a young girl is successfully competing against her male peers, she receives negative feedback from friends and adults. Eventually she learns to avoid those settings in which she might succeed because they are anxiety provoking. She also learns to associate success with a loss of feminity. As an alternative, women may identify affiliation or getting along with others as a "safe" form of success (Bardwick & Douvan, 1971). More recently researchers have found that, rather than fearing success, women desire success but fear society's reactions toward women who compete against men and succeed (Tresemer, 1974; Olsen & Willemsen, 1978).

SEX-ROLE IDENTITY

An intergral part of the adolescent's self-concept is his or her sexual or gender identity. As part of their emerging personal identity, individuals need to incorporate those bodily features that make them male or female. To say that an individual needs to establish a sexual identity does not automatically imply that the identity incorporates society's traditional stereotypes of maleness and femaleness.

Western society identifies one well-defined set of personal attributes that are valued in men and a separate set for women. Autonomy, independence, dominance, aggression, and the inhibition of emotion are seen as valued traits in males, whereas females are expected to be warm, nurturant, passive, dependent, and emotional (Sears, Maccoby & Levin, 1957). Occupational roles requiring administrative responsibility and strength are classified as "masculine" jobs, whereas roles of caring for others and being passive are "feminine."

Knowledge and internalization of sex-roles appears to occur early in a child's development. Preschool boys and girls are aware of social roles that are traditionally assigned to men and women (Williams, 1977; Romer, 1981) and by first and second grade, children readily project maleness and femaleness to occupations (Siegal, 1976). There is little reason to believe that gender roles are genetically determined, instead, they are more likely to be socially induced. Young children model the same sexed parent and society reinforces behaviors that conform to traditional stereotypes and fails to reinforce, or tries to eliminate behaviors that do not. Children learn quickly that some behaviors are acceptable for girls but not boys and others are acceptable for boys but not girls. By late childhood and early adolescence, these "rules of behavior" are crystallized into rigid schema of maleness versus femaleness (Bush et al., 1977). To some adults, this rigid sexism is unsettling. However, Kohlberg (1967) notes that there is an expected and necessary developmental stage during which young people maintain a rigid adherence to society's definitions of sex-roles. After that period of rigidity, young people are able to reevaluate and recognize ambiguities in role definitions and to tolerate multiple views. It may be necessary for young people to incorporate stereotypes before they can evaluate and modify them as they move to a level of independent thinking.

Society responds with approval when adolescents act in ways that conform to expectations and with disapproval when they do not. When asked to indicate what qualities among females make for a good student, junior high school teachers list the following (Sadker & Sadker, 1974, p. 58):

appreciative	sensitive
calm	dependable
conscientious	efficient
considerate	mature
cooperative	obliging
mannerly	thorough
poised	

On the other hand, those same teachers expect a good male student to be (p. 58):

active	energetic
adventurous	enterprising
aggressive	frank
assertive	independent
curious	inventive

These preferences parallel the traditional stereotypes of males and females and probably serve to influence how the teacher reacts to the adventurous, energetic girl or the appreciative, sensitive boy. It is not unlikely that these expected behaviors also generalize to subject matter areas. Thus girls are not expected to do well in math and science, whereas boys are. Conversely boys are not expected to do well in the arts or reading. Further, it is likely that curricula and textbooks are structured to preserve these expectations (Saario, Jacklin & Tuttle, 1973). The adolescent boy or girl who deviates from these unwritten gender codes may be the subject of suspicion.

Not only do teachers have different expectations of male and female students, they often respond differently to the same behaviors from males and females (Dweck & Bush, 1976). High school and college women claim that their in-class contributions are less likely to be taken seriously than those of their male peers (O'Brien, 1976).

Although considerable attention has been focused on the inappropriateness of many traditional sex-role stereotypes, there is no reason to presume that society has relinquished them. Indeed, during adolescence, rather than ignoring sex roles, contemporary youths are very much concerned with being "masculine" or "feminine." As suggested before, some solidification of sex roles may be a necessary prerequisite to progression to higher levels of socialization. On the other hand, unilateral, unquestioning acceptance of traditional gender roles may disrupt the normal unfolding of an individual's personal identity.

DEVELOPING SELF-WORTH

In your role as practitioner, you will encounter many adolescents with negative feelings about themselves. As part of your dealings with these adolescents, you may try to nurture positive feelings of self-worth and a better self-image. Although there is no easy formula for accomplishing this goal, some guidelines may be useful:

1. *Help the adolescent learn to set goals.* Adolescents with low self-esteem typically set unrealistically high or low goals for themselves. As a person working with such adolescents, you will want to help them establish a realistic set of long-range and short-term goals. Further, it will be necessary to determine when the goals are achieved and what reward the adolescent may expect for completing the goals. You should state these goals and the plans for achieving them clearly and record them as an Individualized Treatment Plan (ITP).

2. *Guide the adolescent toward a realistic assessment of strengths and weaknesses.* For goals to be reasonable, they must be within reach but not overly easy. To be able to set goals, adolescents must recognize where they are starting from. Goals should capitalize on strengths and either compensate for or try to eliminate weaknesses. Evaluation of strengths and weakness should not be made by the practitioner and provided to the adolescent. The adolescent needs to exert honest effort in self-evaluation. The practitioner serves to augment and guide this process.

3. *Accept adolescents as individuals.* If adolescents with low feelings of self-worth are to accept themselves as individuals, then those who work with them must similarly recognize their individuality. Adolescents have special needs not only because of their developmental status but also because of their unique personal backgrounds.

4. *Encourage the adolescent to become involved and active.* Adolescents with low self-worth will often avoid participating in activities because they are afraid of failure. As a part of the ITP, specify plans for social activity and rewards for participation. Because participation with others has been avoided, it may be necessary to increase demands for social interaction gradually.

5. *Listen to what the adolescent tells you.* Your conversations with adolescents will be filled with seemingly irrelevant wanderings. In the course of those wanderings, however, the adolescent may make vague reference to a problem with the hope that you will pursue it. To verbalize a problem openly may be too difficult for an adolescent with low self-worth. An offhand reference may be the adolescent's way of providing an opening for further discussion of a problem area without being too vulnerable.

6. *Encourage the adolescent to speak positively.* In talking with adolescents with low self-esteem, you will quickly see that the majority of their statements are negative. One strategy for change is to encourage the individuals to talk about themselves and about events in positive terms. One counselor tells his adolescent clients to stand in front

of the mirror each morning and privately tell themselves, "I am the most important person in the world to me today." Because this is foreign to them, they look at him as though he were kidding. When he explains that he is not and that he would like them to try it for a week, they usually reluctantly agree. After a week they often come back and say, "Hey! That's not bad. It's really a nice way to start the day!"

7. *Include the adolescent in the decision-making process.* As decisions and goals are established, adolescents must see themselves as trusted and able to be part of that process. If the rebellion or maladaptive behavior that brought an adolescent to you results in part from a feeling that his parents will not allow him any decisions, it is critical that you do not replace one authoritarian relationship with another. For some adolescents the ability and willingness to participate may be greater than for others, but the opportunity must be there. Further, their role should be documented in the ITP. In some ways this may look like a contractual arrangement between the client and counselor—and in many ways it is.

8. *Allow the adolescent to make mistakes.* It is unreasonable to expect perfection. Many adolescents who come for counseling complain that they feel their parents expect them to be perfect, that they cannot make a mistake. Often an older brother or sister did very well, and the parents, teachers, and administrators all expect the same of them. Their feelings of self-worth suffer because they do not see themselves as perfect.

As a corollary to allowing adolescents to make mistakes, you may find it necessary to *allow the adolescent to save face.* Oriental cultures place a great emphasis on allowing a person to save face when he or she is humiliated. In a counseling role you may find that, especially during early interviews, you wil have to ensure that the adolescent has the chance to avoid embarrassment over a mistake. Once rapport and trust are established this will become less necessary.

9. *Expect failures.* Although this does not sound terribly positive, it is realistic. As a counselor you should not become complacent when you make some progress with a client; it is still possible to have everything seem to fall apart. Such experiences are disheartening but common. For adolescents with lowered self-worth, however, failure may serve to confirm what they have believed all along—that is, that they are losers. As a counselor you should be ready and willing to start over at some previous point in the progress. Remember, the client may have been establishing a low self-concept for fourteen years before coming to you.

10. *Be an effective model.* Much of what can be gained in the counselor-client relationship occurs because the adolescent sees how someone with positive feelings of self-worth acts. This does not mean that the counselor is a mindless Pollyanna. However, the counselor should exemplify the behaviors that adolescents see as desired.

SUMMARY

In Chapter 1, I concluded by saying that the central development task of adolescence is the establishment of a new sense of self with which a young person enters adulthood. This new sense of self unites the divergent developmental tasks which help to define the adolescent transition. A positive sense of self serves as a base for future positive growth. A negative sense of self interferes with growth; it estabishes internal barriers since success and acceptability are incompatible with a negative self-view. Most people have a mixture of positive and negative views of themselves. The typical adolescent might thus view himself or herself positively in one setting and negatively in another.

Our self-concepts are not single, all encompassing views of oneself. Rather a self-concept is a composite of several views of oneself. How we see ourselves is a function of what we think we are now as well as what we would like to be. Our self-concept also includes temporary definitions of who we are that serve to protect our self-esteem or to achieve our desired self. There is, thus, a degree of fluidity to our self-concept. It changes as we mature and as we have a broader range of experience. Like any inferred concept, self-esteem is difficult to define and assess. The manner in which practitioners try to measure an adolescent's self-concept or self-esteem will depend on their orientation and purpose. For purposes of this chapter, self-concept refers to an organized set of beliefs an individual holds about himself or herself. Self-worth or self-esteem refers to the value that the individual places on those beliefs.

Adolescents who have positive feelings of self-worth have a realistic appraisal of their strengths and weaknesses. They are more likely to be active, to initiate activities, to follow through even after meeting with some failure, and to attribute success to their own efforts and talents.

Adolescents who have negative feelings of self-worth are often oversensitive to criticism. Because they view themselves as inadequate, they take criticism as rejection. They are less likely to engage in activities, and, if they do, their participation is affected by fear or failure.

During adolescence the individual's self-concept is consolidated into a personal identity. It is with this identity of "Who am I?" that the adolescent enters adulthood. Failure to resolve the conflict of identity formation adequately may result in a diffused, unclear identity or the acceptance of a negative identity.

Early- and middle-adolescents place great importance on what others think. This concern is heightened by adolescents' assumption that an invisible audience is excessively concerned with everything that they do. For adolescents with low self-esteem, this concern may be nearly overpowering. They are convinced that others view them as losers and do not like them. To avoid the hurt of rejection, adolescents with low self-esteem may respond by maintaining a mask of hostility, contempt, or mistrust of others. If others see the hostility as unpleasant and avoid them, their feelings of inadequacy are reinforced.

Still others respond to their fears of unacceptability and rejection by feelings of shyness. For many young people, shyness is a source of considerable psychological pain. Like so many other problem behaviors described in this text, shyness has the character of a vicious circle. The shy person feels incapable of dealing with social situations. When he or she attempts to initiate social encounters, the attempts are often halting and not terribly comfortable. Anything that goes wrong (in reality or in the shy person's view) serves to reinforce the person's negative sense of self, this in turn leads to greater hesitance to initate social encounters.

In the case of the shy person, it is not clear whether shyness leads to lowered self-esteem or whether low self-esteem leads to shyness. It may not matter. What matters is that the individual be provided skills to deal with the problem behavior since it is the behavior itself that continues to reinforce those negative self-feelings. As feelings of competence emerge, self-esteem will improve.

The development of a positive self-concept may be the most important task of adolescence. Likewise, it may be the most important concept for you, as a practitioner, to keep in mind.

4 | PHYSICAL GROWTH AND DEVELOPMENT

As young people enter adolescence, they are faced with a range of changes in their physical being. During early adolescence, at a time when young people often express an intense desire to not be different, one finds wide variations in physical appearance. If you were to enter a typical classroom of sixth-, seventh-, or eighth-grade students you would find wide differences in levels of physical maturity. Some youngsters would already be well into adult physical status while others would still appear very much like young children. Yet, within a short time, some of those who now look childlike will undergo a rapid and radical transformation of their physical selves.

Early adolescence is a period of major physical growth and change. Only during infancy and prenatal development did the child experience comparable radical and extensive physical changes. During infancy, however, the child was not burdened with the social value of the physical transition. During adolescence, the shift from childlike physique to adultlike physique has considerable social and psychological value. Thus, while the radical shift in physical appearance and physical status has an important biological function, the same shift has profound influence on young adolescents' self-concepts. Puberty marks an important developmental transition. The result of adolescents' intensified interest in their physical selves often takes its form in an increased awareness of their bodies and a preoccupation with one's own image in the mirror. Sometimes, much to the annoyance of other members of the adolescents' families, they may spend more time in the bathroom primping.

The general name applied to this period of change is *puberty*. Puberty is the stage of physical development in which an individual begins to show secondary sexual characteristics such as pubic hair, breasts, and widened hips in girls, or facial hair, pubic

Concern with physical appearance takes on a new level of importance in adolescence, and teenagers may spend much time simply "primping." (© Kit Hedman/Jeroboam, Inc.)

hair, and lowered voice in boys. The name *puberty* comes from the Latin word "pubescere" which means "To be covered with hair" (Katchadorian, 1977). Primary sexual features also mature to their adult function. Strictly speaking, puberty ends when sexual maturation or the ability to reproduce is achieved, even though growth may continue beyond that point. What actually triggers puberty is not clear, but the primary glands in the process are the hypothalamus and the pituitary, which control the release of *human growth hormone* (HGH), the gonadotropins, and other hormones.

Prior to puberty, growth in height is stable, averaging about five to six centimeters (two and a half inches) per year. At about age 11 or 12 for girls and 13 or 14 for boys, there is a sudden increase in output of HGH leading to a growth spurt of eight to nine centimeters per year. Once an individual has passed through this growth spurt, further gains in height are small, and by age 17 or 18 in girls and 18 or 19 in boys most adolescents reach adult stature (Tanner, 1970; Katchadorian, 1977). (See Figure 4-1.) During this transition there is an increase in weight for both boys and girls. However, the source of the increased weight differs. Girls show an increasingly greater proportion of body fat, whereas boys show rapid increases in lean body mass (Forbes, 1976).

Further, while we focus on the very visible *external* changes of early adolescence, the biological "clock" has initiated *internal, hormonal* changes three to four years in advance of the visible growth spurt (Money, 1980).

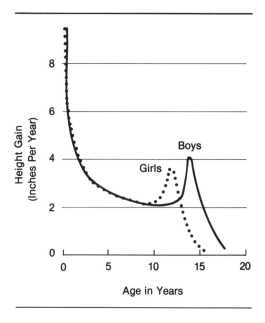

Figure 4–1 Average rates of growth. *Source:* Redrawn from Tanner, Whitehouse, and Takaishi, "Standards from Birth to Maturity for Height, Weight, Height Velocity and Weight Velocity: British Children," *Archives of Diseases of Childhood* 41 (1966): 466. Reprinted by permission.

In accommodation to the increased size, not only does the skeleton become bigger, its character also changes. During childhood and puberty, the structure of the bones and joints become more adultlike. The bones become hardened through calcification and these stages of skeletal maturation can be categorized through X-ray techniques. As with evidence from growth spurt data, skeletal age ratings indicate that females mature earlier than males (Roche, Roberts & Hammill, 1976).

Further, there are other structural changes in the proportionality of the young person's body. Before puberty, and during the growth spurt, growth is greater in the long bones. The young preadolescents may look like they are "all legs." After the major growth spurt of puberty, growth occurs primarily in the trunk of the body. As an indication of the differential growth pattern, if one compares simple standing height to what is called sitting height, an interesting relationship is found. Sitting height is measured while the person is seated in a standard sized chair. It is, thus, a measure of trunk length. In early to middle childhood, the ratio of sitting height to standing height decreases regularly because the legs grow faster than the trunk (Tanner, 1970, 1978). After puberty, there is an increase in the ratio indicating faster trunk growth. It is during the period of rapid spinal growth that structural weaknesses may be revealed. In particular, it is during this period that the adolescent may be diagnosed as having *scoliosis,* a bending of the spine to the side.

Not only do we see a shift in the vertical proportions of the adolescents' bodies, there is a change in the ratio of shoulder to hip width. Before puberty, the ratio of shoulder to hip width is roughly the same for boys and girls. With puberty, girls experience a widening of hips relative to shoulders while boys experience a widening of shoulders relative to hips (Tanner, 1978; Faust, 1977).

There is a common sense idea that these periods of rapid physical growth at puberty result in awkwardness among adolescents. This idea is based on a sense that skeletal growth and muscular growth are "out of sync." Actually, research evidence does not support that conclusion (Carron & Bailey, 1974; Faust, 1977; Malina, 1980; Tanner, 1970). Research evidence shows that muscular strength increases in proportion to skeletal size and shows its peak growth about a year after the growth spurt (Carron & Bailey, 1974; Tanner, 1970). While there may be normal asynchronies within individual growth patterns (Eichorn, 1975), there is no overwhelming evidence of a period of physically based awkwardness. If awkwardness does occur, it may be more a function of self-consciousness than of physical discordance. Further, adults may view normal motoric development of the early adolescent as somehow not in synchrony with "someone his size." That is, adults may have expectations of physical capabilities that are not realistic (Petersen & Taylor, 1980).

HEIGHT, WEIGHT, AND PROPORTIONALITY

Height is a relatively reliable indicator of physical status during preadolescence and early adolescence. Between infancy and puberty, boys and girls will, on the average, grow at the same rate (see Figure 4–1). At puberty, the young person experiences a sudden, rapid acceleration in growth. For girls, the typical age for this growth spurt is about 10, for boys, about 12. It must be remembered, however, that wide variability exists around these averages. Some will experience their growth spurt earlier, some later. Those who experience an early growth spurt are also likely to grow more during their period of peak growth than either normal or late maturers. Early differences in height between early and late maturers dissipate by adulthood (Tanner, 1987).

Because norms and standards for height and weight are often useful to practitioners who are involved with young people, the most recent height and weight norms for school-age children and youths compiled by the National Center for Health Statistics (Hamil et al., 1977) are reproduced as Figures 4–2 and 4–3. To find the relative standing of a boy or girl with respect to the national distribution, merely find the point of intersection of the person's age and height (or weight). The curved lines represent percentile ranks—that is, the percentage of the total population that is shorter (or lighter) at that specific height (or weight) for each age group. A boy of 14 who is five feet five inches tall lies somewhere between the fiftieth and twenty-fifth percentiles, which means that he is taller than at least 25 percent of 14-year-old boys but shorter than at least 50 percent.

Today's youths are taller than those in previous generations. If you were to compare the average heights of youths in 1902 (see Baldwin, 1916) to current norms for children and youths, you would find that from ages six to 15, today's boys range from 7.9 to 12.9 cm. (centimeters—about three to five inches) taller than their 1902 peers. Girls are, on the average, between 4.7 and 12.4 cm. (about two to five inches) taller than their 1902 peers for the same age groups. At ages 17 and 18, or at approximately adult height, the differences level out and males are about 5.2 cm. (about two inches) taller and females 3.7 cm. (one and a half inches) taller than their 1902 counterparts. In the 1890s, less than 5 percent of young men were over six feet tall (Gallagher, 1960).

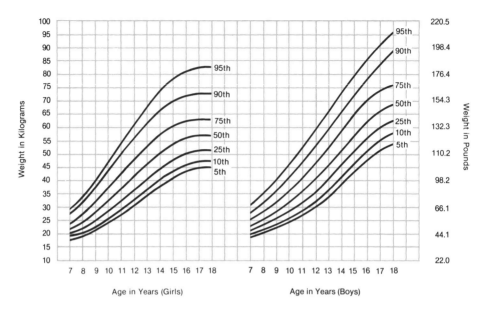

Figure 4–2 Weight gain by percentiles. *Source:* Adapted from National Center for Health Statistics, Department of Health, Education and Welfare, *Vital and Health Statistics* (Washington, D.C.: U.S. Government Printing Office, 1977): 60–61.

Today more than that percentage of 15-year-olds and nearly 25 percent of 18-year-olds exceed six feet (Hamil et al., 1977). This trend toward ever-taller generations, however, seems to be tapering off.

Figure 4–3 Height gain by percentiles. *Source:* Adapted from National Center for Health Statistics, Department of Health, Education and Welfare, *Vital and Health Statistics* (Washington, D.C.: U.S. Government Printing Office, 1977): 58–59.

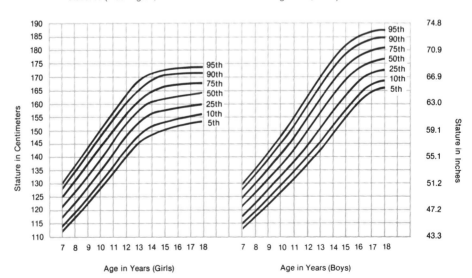

CHANGES IN FEMALES

For girls, puberty is marked by an increase in the size of their genitals, the appearance of pubic hair, and the growth of breasts. Both pubic hair development and breast development progress in predictable patterns and are sometimes used to chart the course of pubertal development. Pubic hair begins to appear during the early phases of puberty. It is first seen as downy, unpigmented hair. The hair gradually becomes darker and courser until it approaches adult quantity and texture. Breasts also develop in a progression from an early "bud" stage to adult size and appearance (Tanner, 1962, 1970, 1978). The predominantly feminine physical traits result from increased estrogen production relative to androgen production.

About midway through the pubertal transition, young girls experience a single physical change that is often seen as marking the onset of adult maturity. That is, girls begin to menstruate. *Menarche,* or first menses, is sometimes equated with full adult sexual status but the onset of menstruation does not automatically mean a young girl is fertile. There may be a period of one to two years following menarche when a young girl remains naturally sterile. Menarche typically occurs after the growth spurt and seems to be tied to a minimum percent of body fat (Frisch & McArthur, 1974; Frisch, Revelle & Cook, 1973). Because menarche occurs shortly after the growth spurt, girls who experience menarche early tend to be taller during the early teen years but height differences between early and later maturing girls even out during adulthood (Faust, 1977; Frisch & Revelle, 1970; Tanner, 1978). Young females who experience continued lower levels of body fat because of diet or significant exercise are apt to have delayed menarche or disruption of menses. Intense physical training appears to delay menarche proportionate to the number of years a young girl exercises before menarche (Frisch et al., 1981).

Beyond its physical role, menarche and menstruation may have an impact on feelings of self-worth. Historically, menstruation has been tied to myth and taboo. In biblical writings, the menstrual woman was described as "unclean" (Leviticus: 15:9). It is still often the object of fanciful notions, especially among teen males. Among young girls, the occurrence or nonoccurrence of menarche may represent some perceived status among peers. The menstruating young girl must also incorprate new health care behaviors in relation to the occurrence of menstruation and incorporate all the changes into their physical and sexual self-image.

Because of the range of adjustments a young girl must make to menarche and menstruation, it is not surprising that many postmenarcheal girls have negative feelings about menstruation (Whisnant & Zegans, 1975; Clarke & Ruble, 1978). Younger girls may have difficulty understanding and internalizing the process of menstruation. They used words like "scared," "upset," and "ashamed" to describe their feelings about their first menstrual experience (Whisnant & Zegans, 1975). Other researchers, however, found more ambivalence and confusion about menarche but no particular trauma (Ruble & Brooks-Gunn, 1982). Still other studies indicate that young girls' feelings regarding menstruation are influenced by the symptoms they typcially experience during menses (Brooks-Gunn & Ruble, 1982; Grief & Ulman, 1982).

In any case, irrespective of whether parents have talked to their daughter about menstruation before her first period (a large proportion of parents do not), the occurrence

Adolescence is a period of development marked by great individual differences in growth and appearance. (Photograph by Laimute E. Druskis)

of menarche may be stressful, especially for early maturers whose peers have not also had their first menses. Thus parents and teachers should be prepared to be empathetic with a young girl who is upset by the event of menarche.

The average age of menarche in the United States is currently about 12.77 years, with 80 percent of girls having their first menses between ages 11.0 and 14.0 (MacMahon, 1973). Nevertheless, it is not uncommon to find girls having their menarche in the fourth or fifth grades. Further, like height, age of menarche has been shifting for the last several generations. The average age of menarche in 1870 was 16.5 years. By 1930, the average age of menarche had dropped to 14.5, and by 1950, it was 13.5. Given a 1970s estimate approaching 12.5, the age of menarche has been dropping one year every 20 years. The best guess is that the change in age of menarche, as in height, is due to improved nutrition (Tanner, 1970). (One can project this trend to illogical extremes: carrying the trend backward to the year 100 would put the average age of menarche at 110, and projecting it into the future would anticipate girls in the year 2230 having their first menses *in utero*.) The trend, however, cannot continue indefinitely in both directions. In fact, there is recent evidence that it is leveling off in several parts of the world (Katchadorian, 1977).

The impact of the trend toward earlier sexual maturity must be recognized, especially in the social institutions most directly responsible to today's youths. Given a stable rate of sexual intercourse among teenagers across generations, the drop in the age of menarche and, as a result, the age of fertility, would lead to a net increase in teenage pregnancies. Given an increase in rate of unprotected sexual intercourse among contemporary teenagers, the likelihood of teenage pregnancies is even greater.

CHANGES IN MALES

For boys pubescence—arriving at puberty—is marked by increased sensitivity of the testes to pressure, as well as a reddening and changes of texture of the scrotum. Testes increase to as much as seven times their prepubescent size (Barnes, 1975). The size of the penis and scrotum also increase, and pubic hair appears. As with girls, boys' initial pubic hair is downy and unpigmented. It begins to grow at the base of the penis and gradually gets darker and coarser, spreading upward along the trunk and downward along the thighs. Boys will also begin to show facial hair and a slight recession of the hair line. Their voices deepen by as much as an octave or more.

For boys, first ejaculation is not as significant an event as first menses is for girls. Its appearance does not lead to a significant change in life style. Like menarche, however, it serves as an important marker in the adolescent transition. First ejaculation usually occurs during masturbation or as a nocturnal emission. Like menarche, first ejaculation is apparently occurring at earlier ages. Unlike menses, ejaculation does not occur without some psychosexual input (Eskin, 1977). Full adult sexual potency is not reached at first emission, but some degree of potency is present early, and that potency increases steadily (Steen & Price, 1977).

For both boys and girls, puberty brings an increase in axillary (armpit) sweating and axillary hair. Systolic blood pressure and heart rate increase to adult levels. One curious difference in development between adolescent males and females is seen in patterns of hemoglobin concentration in the blood. Boys show a steady increase in hemoglobin percentage, whereas the value remains quite constant in girls. Also, among black girls, not only is the average percentage stable across adolescence, it is well below the average for whites. Using typical norms, the values for black girls are hazardously close to anemia (Heald et al., 1974). It is not clear, however, whether the lower homoglobin level indicates a tendency toward anemia among black girls or whether it represents a basic metabolic difference.

SEX MATURITY RATINGS

At any age within the adolescent years, wide differences in level of physical maturation may be seen among boys and girls (see Figure 4-4). It is sometimes useful for practitioners and researchers to be able to document the physical maturity of an adolescent. The most accurate way of defining physical maturity is probably through X-rays of the wrist which are then compared to standards of *Bone Age.* This approach is impractical on a widespread basis.

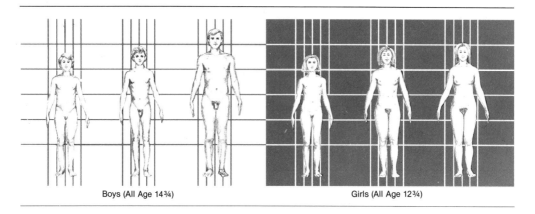

Boys (All Age 14¾)   Girls (All Age 12¾)

Figure 4–4 Different degrees of pubertal development. *Source:* J. M. Tanner, "Growth and Endocrinology of the Adolescent," in L. J. Gardner, ed., *Endocrine and Genetic Diseases of Childhood* (Philadelphia: Saunders, 1969). Reprinted by permission.

Alternatively, sexual maturation can be described in terms of the progression of secondary sexual characteristics. As secondary sexual characteristics become more adultlike, the adolescent is rated as sexually more mature. Tanner (1962) has described the transition in sexual maturity in five stages described in Table 4–1. The progression of these *Sex Maturity Ratings* is reliably related to the occurrence of other indices of physical maturation (Thornburg & Aras, 1986).

Practically, it is not feasible for someone other than a physician to use the Tanner stages since they require a physical examination of the adolescent. Fortunately, however, adolescents can estimate their own levels of sexual maturity using a set of line drawings developed by Duke (Duke, Litt & Gross, 1980; Brooks-Gunn & Warren, 1985). When Sex Maturity Rating measures are used, relative status in physical and sexual maturity is found to be related to self-concept and self-esteem (Susman et al., 1985; Brack, Orr & Ingersoll, in press). As young people move into the adolescent transition, they are

Table 4–1 Tanner's Sex Maturity Ratings for Boys and Girls

	BOYS		
Stage	*Pubic Hair*	*Penis*	*Testes*
1	None	Preadolescent	Preadolescent
2	Sparse, slight pigmentation	Slightly enlarged	Scrotum enlarged, pink, texture changed
3	Begins to darken and curl, small amount	Longer	Larger
4	Coarse and curly, adultlike but less in quantity	Longer and larger in breadth	Larger, scrotum darkens
5	Adult distribution	Adult	Adult

Table 4–1   Tanner's Sex Maturity Ratings for Boys and Girls (continued)

	GIRLS	
Stage	Pubic Hair	Breasts
1	None, preadolescent	Preadolescent
2	Sparse, slight pigmentation, along labia	Slight enlargement of breast and papilla, diameter of areolar increases
3	Begins to darken and curl, small amount	Breast and areolar enlarged
4	Coarse and curly, adultlike but less in quantity	Areolar and papilla form a secondary mound
5	Adult distribution	Mature adult breast contour

Adapted from: Tanner, J. M. (1962) *Growth at adolescence.* (2nd. ed.). Oxford, England: Blackwell Scientific Publications.

frequently unsure about their physical self-image. The uncertainty may show itself in excessive modesty and a reluctance to take showers in school. Physical education teachers will regularly tell of youngsters who either refuse to shower and go back to class sweaty or try or take showers with a bathing suit on. As Petersen and Crockett (1985) state, however, pubertal status must be viewed within a broader context of social and psychological factors which also affect self-esteem.

CHEEVERWOOD

©1985, Washington Post Writers Group, reprinted with permission.

PSYCHOLOGICAL CORRELATES OF PHYSICAL GROWTH

Children and adolescents feel a variety of pressures not to be different from the physical norm. The extent to which an individual is different or does not fit the mold of most of his or her peers, because of gaps in maturation or physical handicaps, may lead parents, peers, and teachers to expect the adolescent to behave in ways that are thought to be related to those physical characteristics. That is, the fact that an individual is tall or short, heavy or thin, physically mature or immature, may lead others to expect that person to act like tall, short, fat, or skinny people. When peers and others see differences as undesirable, a young person may suffer ridicule or be excluded from social activities. On the other hand, when they regard the difference as desirable, positive reactions may occur; for example, one may be chosen as a leader. Adolescents who are different from the norm, or who view themselves as different from the norm, may fear being left out by peers or being singled out as odd. Those fears may, in turn, interfere with the adolescent's development of personal feelings of self-worth.

Although most people are anxious to one extent or another about their physical appearance, that worry may become particulary troublesome during puberty and adolescence. As Dwyer and Mayer (1969) note, demands by peers for physical sameness are greatest during adolescence, the period in which we see the greatest differences in development. Additionally, just the rapid physical growth and development alone associated with puberty and adolescence are likely to produce anxiety over body image.

Somatotypes

Historically the best-known advocate of relationships between body type and personality was William Sheldon (for example, 1944). Sheldon classified physiques into three *somatotypes* and suggested that each body type was associated with a set of personality characteristics. Endomorphs are large torsoed, short, and fat, and were said to be outgoing, jovial, gregarious, and sociable. Mesomorphs are muscular and were said to be callous, noisy, assertive, and vigorous. Ectomorphs are tall and lean, and were said to be restrained, inhibited, neurotic, and shy. Sheldon saw the relationship between physique and personality as a direct one. That is, a woman was nervous and shy *because* she was an ectomorph. Although several writers have pointed out that Sheldon's original idea was unsound (see, for example, Hammond, 1957; Humphrey, 1957), a number of studies have shown stable relationships between somatotype, or physique, and behavioral patterns. Davidson, McInnes, and Parnell (1957), for example, showed that physique and certain psychiatric characteristics were related among children. Ectomorphic boys were, for example, more likely to be anxious and to score higher on a variety of measures of psychological stress or maladjustment.

You should be very cautious, however, in concluding that physique *causes* psychosocial adjustment. If a relationship does exist it is probably because of a form of social causality. Society has a set of cultural stereotypes for body types and personalities. A mesomorph is *expected* to be a leader and aggressive. These expectancies are communicated early in life and can be found even among preschool children (Staffieri, 1967). By the time boys or girls reach adolescence they easily identify cultural stereotypes relating physique to personality and will attribute those stereotypes to themselves in accordance with their self-perceptions (Sugarman & Haroonian, 1964). That is, mesomorphs learn to behave like mesomorphs are *supposed* to behave. Further, there is some evidence that among junior high school students physique is related to classroom behavior and popularity (Hanley, 1951).

Although not a study of adolescents, Walker's (1962) study of the relationship between physique and school adjustment among nursery school children is relevant. Walker had photographs of nude preschool boys rated for the three dimensions of somatotype. He then had the teachers of those children rate their performance and adjustment in school. Recognizing that other factors might intervene between physique and behavior, Walker was nonetheless able to show regular relationships between teachers' ratings of a student's behavior and that student's physique. Walker found, for example, that endomorphic boys were rated as more assertive and revengeful, whereas mesomorphic boys were more apt to be labeled as easily angered or quarrelsome. Teachers were also more likely to rate the mesomorphic boys as leaders in play, ambitious, daring, chance taking, energetic, and self-confident. In general the teachers felt the mesomorphic boys were more "boyish." Ectomorphic boys, on the other hand, were more likely to be labeled as neurotic or timid. Although we cannot automatically assume that teachers' ratings and students' behaviors necessarily match, Walker's study gives us valuable evidence that there is a relationship between teachers' perceptions of a student's behavior and the physique of the student.

Staffieri (1967) had boys aged four to 10 rate silhouettes of endomorphic, meso-morphic, and ectomorphic boys on a variety of psychological and social traits. The results of his study indicated that even the youngest boys had well-established social stereotypes for body types that they did not hesitate to attribute to the silhouettes. They typically rated endomorphs as socially offensive and delinquent, mesomorphs as aggressive, out-going, assertive, and leaders, and ectomorphs as introverted or neurotic, nervous, retir-ing, and shy. Later Staffieri (1972) showed that slightly older boys not only have the same stereotypes but also clearly prefer to look like the mesomorph.

I often ask students and teachers in my classes to associate silhouettes of endo-morphic, mesomorphic, and ectomorphic youths with a set of adjectives. They are told to choose the silhouette that is most likely to show a given trait. The results of that demonstration seldom vary. The same stereotypes that Staffieri found with preschoolers are found with undergraduate and graduate students and teachers. They attribute almost every negative social trait to the endomorph and attribute qualities of leadership and assertiveness to the mesomorph. They label ectomorphs as timid and studious.

In other studies physical attractiveness has been shown to be related to both perceived popularity and real demonstration of socially desirable behavior (Cavior & Dokecki, 1973; Kleck, Richardson & Ronald, 1974). Physical height is also associated with positive and negative expectancies.

The point of all this is that, whether or not Sheldon was correct in his assump-tion that somatotypes cause personality, society has very strong stereotypes associated with given body builds and may selectively reinforce behaviors that conform to expec-tancies and thereby shape a personality to match a body type. When there is a mismatch between the behavioral predispositions of a young person and the behavioral expectan-cies of a person in power (for example, a teacher), conflict may arise.

Early and Late Maturation

Discrepancies between one's own level of maturation and one's perceived ideal level of maturation may be a source of considerable anxiety. In the Oakland Growth Study, very early and very late maturers showed differential patterns of psychosocial adjustment that persisted into adulthood. Jones (1957) followed the status of early and late maturing adolescent boys from a earlier (Jones & Bayley, 1950) study. In the first study early maturers had substantial growth advantages over their late maturing cohorts. But by adulthood those earlier height and weight differences had been eliminated. However, differences remained between the two groups in psychosocial skills. The early maturers rated higher in general social ability including leadership and respnsibility. Late maturers scored higher on indices of maladjustment and a need to be directed by others. Later Jones (1965) reported that early maturers are more likely to make a positive impression when meeting people for the first time. Other investigators (Tobin-Richards, Boxer & Petersen, 1983; Petersen & Crockett, 1985; Duncan, Ritter & Dornbusch, 1985) have similarly found that self-images of early maturing boys were more favorable and that they do better academically. Early maturing girls on the other hand are more negative about themselves. On the other hand, there are some studies which show no such differences in self-esteem related to timing of puberty (Simmons & Blyth, 1987; Simmons, 1987).

In the case of the early maturer, the effects of the discrepancy may be either positive or negative. Early maturers, especially young girls who show very advanced physical development as compared to their age mates, may be tempted to identify with older youths, who may not reciprocate. On the other hand, teachers may see the precocious physical development as indicative of general advanced maturity and treat early maturers as if they were older by delegating more responsibility to them. Peers also respond differently to the early maturer. One study (Faust, 1960) showed that among sixth-grade girls, for example, a girl was more likely to be accepted if her level of physical development conformed to the rest of the class. The early maturing girl was rated lower in prestige. By junior high school, however, advanced physical development was an asset, and the early maturer had higher prestige.

Late maturers may suffer considerable anxiety associated with their body image. They do not show any outward signs of physical maturity. For example, late maturing boys do not have pubic hair or larger genitals, whereas late maturing girls lack pubic hair or noticeable breasts. Late maturers may be the object of teasing or ridicule, or they may *feel* that they are the object of ridicule. Thus the shower after gym may be a very threatening and anxiety-provoking experience.

The problem of late maturers developing a positive self-image is exaggerated in the case of the person with a hypoactive (underactive) pituitary gland. Normally the pituitary secretes sufficient HGH, human growth hormone, which stimulates two or more inches of growth per year until early adolescence, when there is a sharp increase in HGH output. In the person who has a hypoactive pituitary, the body fails to generate sufficient quantities of HGH and gonadotropins to initiate the prepubescent growth spurt and the appearance of secondary sex characteristics. The result is that these individuals are considerably shorter than their peers, and, more distressing, they fail to *look* grown up. Their physical development, *as perceived by others and by themselves,* is considerably younger than their chronological age. Because of this, others may expect that such individuals are also socially and intellectually immature.

Consider, for example, the following case of a young 20-year-old man who suffered from a hypoactive pituitary (Money, 1973). His physical size and appearance were a source of considerable stress. His self-worth suffered considerably especially as it derived from the way others treated him. Potential employers, for example, assumed he was too juvenile to be responsibly employed. Further, his physical retardation had generalized to his sexual development, and although some sexual maturation had occurred, it was not very advanced. Again his self-image suffered. He wanted to be thought of and treated as an adult, but his peers, employers, and society as a whole viewed him as a child.

In the case of the hypoactive pituitary patient, hormonal injections can effect some improvement. For most late maturers, the problem is solved by time. Physicians, counselors, and school personnel, however, should be aware of the psychological stress that either the very early or very late maturer may experience. Physical education personnel should be particularly alert to the hazards of emphasizing those skills that place late maturers in a position where they cannot compete and thus become the focus of harassment from peers. Likewise, although most schools are sensitive to the need for privacy among young girls, especially in shower facilities, that privacy is not often afforded to young boys. For the late maturer whose physical and sexual development is delayed, the situation may be equally embarrassing.

Physical Attractiveness

Society has a strong positive bias toward "good looks." Beauty and physical attractiveness are highly valued traits in our society. Our choice of friends, associates, lovers, and spouses is strongly influenced by their and our physical attractiveness. When university freshmen were randomly paired in a "computer dance," their attitudes toward

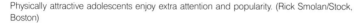

Physically attractive adolescents enjoy extra attention and popularity. (Rick Smolan/Stock, Boston)

their dates were largely determined by the date's physical attractiveness. Each person was asked to rate his or her date on a variety of characteristics. The more attractive the date, the more he or she was liked and the more likely the respondent wanted to date that partner again (Walster et al., 1966). Personality, intelligence, and social skills were viewed as insignificant. Further, Berscheid & Dion (1971) found that more physically attractive people expect to date more physically attractive partners.

Physical attractiveness is such a powerful factor in our interpersonal behavior that we have developed a bias that can be phrased "What is beautiful is good" (Dion, Berscheid & Walster, 1972). That is, we automatically project a variety of positive attributes onto physically attractive people. Byrne (1971) found that when students are asked to rate strangers solely on the basis of a photograph, attractive females are rated as more intelligent and moral. Good-looking men and women are assumed to be more socially adept, more likely to achieve high-prestige occupations, and happier and better adjusted than their unattractive counterparts (Dion & Berscheid, 1974). The only area in which attractive people rate less well than their unattractive counterparts is as potential parents.

In another study male students were asked to complete the California Personality Inventory. They then received evaluative feedback on their performance from either an attractive or unattractive female graduate student. The male students were most pleased when the attractive female gave positive feedback and least pleased when she gave negative feedback. Whether the unattractive female gave positive or negative feedback made little difference (Sigal & Aronson, 1969). In a later study the males were given the chance to volunteer to help the female experimenter in another setting. Irrespective of whether the attractive female gave positive or negative feedback, the males wanted to help (Sigal & Michela, 1976). Apparently it made no difference that she had just given them negative feedback on their performance on a personality inventory; it was more important to the males to be close to her so that they might change her opinion.

Consistently, attractive people are favored along a variety of dimensions, whereas unattractive people are seen as less desirable. Not only do peers respond this way, but so also do professionals interacting with attractive and unattractive clients or students. It is not surprising, then, that young people want to be seen as attractive. Further, youths and society are inundated with images of what it means to be physically attractive and what physically attractive persons like to do. One has only to watch television commercials to see the simple (but erroneous) logic that people use, that is, "Beautiful people use this product. If I use the product, then I will be beautiful."

Advertisers capitalize on this basic belief by repeatedly assuring the teenage public that their product will lead to popularity, happiness, desirability, and success. One indication of the size of the teen cosmetic market is the fact that the annual market for acne preparations alone is in excess of $110 million. Whether or not the idea is valid, advertisements emphasize the message that "Attractive people have it made."

Obesity

Among the variety of problems associated with body type and psychological adjustment, obesity holds a position of considerable current interest. Even the American government has warned that American society is, on the whole, overweight. Among adolescents, the common estimate is that upwards to 30 percent of young people are obese (Colletti & Brownell, 1982; Maloney & Klykylo, 1983). The weight control industry has become big business with considerable profit being made by catering to the desires of people who want to lose weight. Media advertising is a curious mix of encouragements to gorge oneself with high-calorie junk foods and to sign up for various weight-reduction plans.

Many physicians are concerned that excess weight is troublesome for more than aesthetic reasons. Obesity has repeatedly been linked to a variety of medical anomalies, including hypertension, cardiovascular disease, myocardial failure, and diabetes, as well as premature death. Some evidence has been found that adult women who have been obese since adolescence run an increased risk of uterine cancer (Blitzer, Blitzer & Rimm, 1976). Obesity is also associated with a general pattern of psychological distress. The combined effects of physical stress and social expectancies associated with obesity, reviewed earlier, could well lead to generalized anxieties and negative self-image, which in turn lead to inadequate social adjustment, including school adjustment.

Obese students are self-conscious about their body image and blame their body image for causing their interpersonal problems. When given open-ended questions about social interaction, obese girls will give many more weight-related responses than their normal counterparts (Canning & Mayer, 1967). Obese individuals often report hating their body, and they attribute past and present unhappiness to their physical appearance (McQueen, 1973). They are also likely to rate themselves as aggressive, socially isolated, self-conscious, hostile, phobic, and fearful (Crisp et al., 1970; Wunderlich & Johnson, 1973).

Obese adolescents are the object of considerable negative prejudice. They are often seen by peers and adults as morally, socially, and physically impaired (Allon, 1982). In one set of studies, preadolescent children were shown a series of six drawings. The drawings included a normal child, a child wearing a leg brace, a child in a wheelchair, a child with a hand missing, a child with a facial disfigurement, and a child who was grossly obese. The children were asked to order the pictures from the most to the least liked. In seven of eight groups of children, the picture of the obese child was ranked last (Richardson et al., 1961; Goodman et al., 1963). Even among adult social groups with high rates of obesity, the obese child was rated least likeable (Maddox, Bach & Lieberman, 1968). Further, obese adolescents appear to experience prejudice in admission to prestigious colleges (Canning & Mayer, 1967).

Categorizing someone as obese is not simply a matter of saying that a person is overweight, although a fairly common criterion for obesity is being more than 20 percent heavier than the average weight for their height. Such a criterion by itself may be misleading, however. For example, two men who are both six feet tall and weight 215 pounds may be judged very differently if one is a football player whose weight is mostly muscle mass, whereas the other's weight is primarily body fat. What we need for a judgment is an index of body fat.

To obtain a truly accurate index of body fat is very difficult and expensive. Some contend that the use of skinfold thickness measured by a set of calipers offers a quick and reliable estimate of body fat. Selzer and Mayer (1965) suggest that the tricep skinfold, which is measured about midway on the upper arm, is the easiest and best single indicator of body fat. Before puberty, body-fat and lean-body-mass percentages are about the same for boys and girls. Following puberty, girls show a more rapid increase in body fat. Once the pattern stabilizes, accumulations of body fat are 2 to 3 percent higher for girls than boys. For adolescents the cutoff points for identifying obesity in girls are up to 12 millimeters thicker than for boys because of this difference. Although skinfold criteria are not without problems, they are much better than measures that depend on a ratio of height to weight. The early identification of the obese child remains, however, an important problem, because the obese child is the precursor of the obese adolescent, who is in turn the precursor of the obese adult. The longer one is obese, the more difficult it is to lose the extra weight.

Treatment of obesity has been and remains a difficult problem. Weight reduction for the chronically obese adolescent is very difficult. It is not sufficient to assume that the cause of obesity is excessive eating and that reduction of calories will lead to weight loss. Although excess calories are the predominant cause of obesity, with less than 5 percent of the cases "glandular" (Barnes & Berger, 1975), it is not sufficient to assume that reduction of caloric intake will automatically lead to weight loss. Treatment is not that simple. Obesity for the 95 percent who do not have glandular problems is not the same and therefore cannot be treated the same way. Because there are a wide variety of factors that motivate the obese adolescent, one treatment is not going to work well for all.

Some recent research indicates that obese children and adolescents develop more adipose (fat) cells than their normal weight peers. Further, those adipose cells remain in the body even after considerable weight is lost. It is as though the cells shrink but remain ready to expand again. Those who lose great amounts of weight have fat cells that are similar to normal weight people who have experienced famine or starvation. Thus, the common complaint of many chronically overweight people that even eating "normal" portions causes them to gain weight may have some truth.

It is not, however, simply the amount of food that the obese individual eats but the type of food and the patterns of eating that contribute to the problem. Obese individuals not only eat more, they eat more, more often (Leon & Roth, 1977). Further, as Schachter and Rodin (1975) suggest, chronically obese people are more likely to view themselves as unable to control their own behavior. They feel controlled by their environment. They are relatively insensitive to internal cues of hunger and satiation and more sensitive to external cues such as the sight, smell, or taste of food or even of activities associated with food (Schachter, Goodman & Gordon, 1968). When they try to diet, they thus have difficulty depending on internal cues to assist them (Rodin, 1981).

Any program of weight reduction must combine dietary restriction with some alteration of eating habits. Thus some investigators have proposed that behavior modification techniques are most appropriate. In some way the therapist must shape new eating behaviors that will lead not only to weight reduction but also to maintenance of the weight loss (Leon, 1976). Therein lies the frustration of most weight-reduction programs. Although some programs are successful in helping obese individuals to lose weight, they often fail to help their clients maintain that weight loss for any period of time. A program

VIGNETTE 4–1
EATING OUT OF CONTROL

A young woman once explained to me that her eating problem had begun when she wanted to lose a little weight. She was, in her words, a bit "poochy" and wanted to try out for her high school cheerleading team. But, after losing fifteen pounds, she just could not seem to stop. By the end of her senior year in college she was still trying to break a cycle of binge eating and starving that had become part of her life. Her self-concept and feelings of self-worth had suffered badly. In recent years, public attention has focused on the problems of young people, particularly young women, who become obsessed with being thin. The obsession, carried to an extreme, may lead to death.

Source: Bayer, A. E. (1984) Eating out of control:
Anorexia and bulimia in adolescents. *Children Index, 13*
(6), 7–11.

Just five more laps around the track and then I'll get home,'' Kim S. thought to herself. She was down to 82 pounds now, but she just had to lose another two. It was a routine day. A half piece of toast (no crust and no butter) and a diet soft drink for breakfast. Salad (no dressing) for lunch. Gymnastics class after school and then jogging.

"Perhaps I'll make a chocolate cake, or cupcakes, for tonight's family dessert. But I'll have to tell Mom I just ate. I'm not hungry. I'll eat later." But for Kim there was no "later." Her heart had stopped on the next lap.

The N.'s worry about Becky. She too jogs a lot and avoids eating with the family. Mrs. N. still buys only small quantities of food, and hides the breakfast cereal for Mr. N. and the other children. With the weekly support group meeting for the N.'s, and Becky's therapy, there are more encouraging signs since the crisis when Becky was hospitalized for hypokalemia (low potassium) and cardiac arrhythmia. There are no more family arguments about food and eating. Becky still binges on large quantities of food—and purges by vomiting—but the incidents are becoming less frequent. There is more time for the normal social life of a teenager. Becky is recovering.

The stories of Kim and Becky are no longer foreign to many of us. They parallel the traumas of many young people and their families today, including those of singers Karen Carpenter and Cherry Boone O'Neill.

These are cases of adolescent eating disorders. Kim had primary anorexia nervosa, while Becky suffers from a form of bulimia. Anorexia is characterized by a dramatic weight loss from continuous self-starvation or from severe self-imposed dieting. Bulimia is characterized by binging and purging, usually be self-induced vomiting or by using laxatives, accompanied by frequent weight fluctuations rather than profound, continuous weight loss. Both anorectics and bulimics share a preoccupation with food and an irrational fear of being fat. In about half the cases, anorectics develop bulimic episodes in the course of their illness. Some bulimics will also occasionally adopt anorectic patterns. These cases are sometimes referred to as bulimarexia.

Anorexia and bulimia can have serious health consequences. Hospitalization, as in Becky's case is often required, and deaths like Kim's and Karen Carpenter's are, sadly, too frequent.

of weight reduction should include an attempt to divorce eating from other activities—for example, watching television. A therapist may encourage the obese patient to eat only at the kitchen table and only at certain times of the day. An obese client should be trained to eat more slowly and to be able to leave food on the plate. The individual should also be given alternative behaviors to cope with emotional stress, boredom, and fatigue (Barnes & Berger, 1975). Obviously certain foods should not be available, and a reasonable dietary regimen should be followed. Crash and fad diets can be temporarily rewarding in the psychological benefit of rapid weight loss, but they run the risk of physiological damage that may have very serious ramifications. Further, crash dieting does not attend to the behavior patterns that led to the weight problem in the first place.

Anorexia Nervosa and Bulimia

In contrast to obesity, practitioners report two additional problems related to eating. In a society that places heavy emphasis on leanness and equates excessive leanness with beauty and sexual attractiveness, it is not altogether surprising that we are seeing an increase in psychological profiles related to obsessive concerns with being thin. Currently, two patterns of behavior are causing especial concern. The first, *anorexia nervosa,* is potentially the more troublesome since in an attempt to maintain thinness, a young person may starve her- or himself to death. The second, *bulimia,* or binge-purge syndrome is not usually seen as life threatening but can cause major harm to the physiological makeup of the young person who depends on the technique. Both patterns of behavior are associated with seriously low self-esteem. It is a mistake however, to think that these *eating disorders* are new. Cases of women starving themselves in religious ecstasy or described in romantic literature have been reported for centuries (Brumberg, 1985).

Roughly translated, anorexia nervosa means "nervous loss of appetite," but that is a misnomer. More realistically, anorexic patients seem to have a food phobia, just as claustrophobics have a fear of enclosed spaces. An anorexic patient, although hungry, typically either refrains from eating or, if she eats, induces vomiting following a meal or uses laxatives excessively. Anorexia should not be thought of, however, as just being underweight or overzealous in dieting. In some cases anorexic patients become so emaciated that permanent physical harm results; some may actually starve themselves to death. In the past few years, the number of cases seen by physicians has skyrocketed until now roughly one girl in 300 suffers from this disease.

The anorexic may actually view herself as fat. Their physical self-image is distorted. In case studies of anorexics, they sometimes explain that they started by trying to lose just a few pounds but once started could not stop. The American Psychiatric Association (1980) describes anorexia as an "eating disorder" in which the young person:

1. Has an intense fear of becoming obese, which does not become less intense as the person loses weight.
2. Has a disturbed body image, that is she or he feels fat even though emaciated.
3. Loses at least 25 percent of original body weight, or if the individual is under 18-years-old, the weight loss added to the normally expected weight gain combine to make the 25 percent.

4. Refuses to maintain a body weight over a minimal weight for her or his age and height.
5. Has no known physical illness that would account for the weight loss.

Because the anorexic's body fat percent is so low, they often cease having menses. As the disease progresses they may develop a downy hair which covers their body, their circulation is impaired and their extremities develop a bluish cast.

Anorexia seems particularly prevalent in middle class homes. One may wonder why. Bruche (1978) uses the image of the "Golden Cage" to describe the plight of anorexic girls. That is, those who are born to wealth and privilege feel "burdened by the task of living up to such specialness (p. 39)." These young people feel self-imposed and other-imposed pressures to conform to images of success and beauty. Because they are born into a privileged life, they feel an additional obligation. They feel intense demands to be "perfect."

While anorexia is primarily a problem among females, there is a small minority of anorexics who are male. The usual percentage figure given to indicate the proportion of male anorexics is 5 to 10 percent. That figure may be underestimated since traditional literature on anorexia has focused on cessation of menses and psychoanalytic images of "fear of oral pregnancy" (Anderson & Mickalide, 1983). Both criteria eliminate males. The key element appears to be self-induced starvation with or without self-induced vomiting. Hence, males are capable of engaging in the same self-destructive behaviors.

Bulimia, or the binge-purge syndrome, shares some elements in common with anorexia, but is not typically as extreme in its effect. Bulimics have periods of uncontrollable urges to eat (often during times of stress). During those eating binges, they gorge themselves with enormous amounts of food. Once they binge on the food, they feel guilt and remorse. They then induce vomiting to purge themselves of the food. As a group, they tend to have low self-esteem since the binge-purge cycle takes on the character of a habit and they report feeling unable to control it.

For a period, bulimia was seen as simply another form of anorexia nervosa but that view has changed (Schlesier-Stroop, 1984; Yudkoviz, 1983). The American Psychiatric Association (1980) describes a bulimic as a person who:

1. Has recurring episodes of binge eating in which they eat large amounts of food in a relatively short (less than two hours) period of time.
2. Has at least three of the following:
   a. Consumes easily eaten, high caloric food during the binge.
   b. They try to keep their binge secret.
   c. They stop the binge when they feel abdominal pain, fall asleep, are interrupted by others, or induce vomiting.
   d. They have repeatedly attempted to lose weight by severely restrictive diets, self-induced vomiting, or the use of purgatives.
   e. They have frequent fluctuations of weight of 10 or more pounds due to alternating periods of binging and fasting.
3. Are aware that their eating pattern is abnormal and fear not being able to stop the behavior.

4. Are depressed and feel very negative about themselves after their eating binges.

5. The bulimic episodes are not due to anorexia or a known physical disorder.

Bulimia is much more prevalent than anorexia. In one study of high school girls (Van-Thorne & Vogel, 1985) roughly one in eight were classified as probably bulimic. Younger girls in the school were more likely than the older girls to be bulimic. Like the anorexic, the bulimic tends to be obsessed with being "perfect." But, while the anorexic is obsessed with being excessively thin, the bulimic is motivated by a fear of being fat.

Both anorexia and bulimia are difficult to treat. Those programs of treatment that have had apparent success have usually been a combination of group therapy combined with some form of behavior-modification therapy. In the behavior-modification approach, it is the behavior itself that is seen as the problem and alternative behaviors need to be encouraged to replace the problem behavior. In the case of anorexia, the behavioral regimen may be more constrained, but for both groups, the therapist

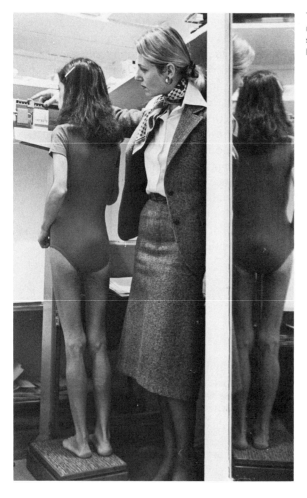

This girl's appearance is typical of that of the growing number of American adolescents, mostly females, who suffer from anorexia nervosa. (Neal Boenzi/NYT Pictures)

establishes a series of behavioral contracts. It is, however, important for young people dealing with anorexia and bulimia to deal with their feelings and concerns within the context of a support group. In cases with which I am familiar, the young people repeatedly find such groups most helpful since they had felt no one else could understand their personal frustration in dealing with their problem.

Perhaps the more difficult forces that the anorexic and bulimic must face are social pressures to be thin. In advertising and media, being thin to the point of gauntness is portrayed as the main criterion for beauty and desirability. As an indication that societal pressures influence young people's views of their ideal body image, consider a study of health attitudes of young people in their body image. They were asked first whether they thought they were thinner than most of their peers, about the same size as their peers, or heavier than most of their peers. They were then asked whether they would prefer to be heavier or lighter or to stay about the same as they were. As you can see in Table 4–2, girls reported overwhelmingly that they wanted to be thinner than they were, and boys reported that they wanted to be heavier than they were. Even among those girls who rated themselves as thinner than most, over half reported that they wanted to be thinner still. Cultural stereotypes of desirable body styles seem to have a profound effect on adolescents' personal image.

Table 4–2 Reported Self-Perception and Desired Body Size Among Adolescents Aged Twelve to Seventeen*

Self-Perceptions	WANT TO BE:			
	Thinner	The Same	Heavier	Total
Thinner than Most	Boys 1.4	24.5	74.5	17.9
	Girls 7.9	36.2	55.9	9.0
About the same as Most	Boys 10.7	70.2	19.2	69.7
	Girls 41.6	53.9	4.6	63.0
Heavier than Most	Boys 68.3	26.9	4.8	12.4
	Girls 93.7	6.0	0.4	28.0
Totals	Boys 17.9	55.0	27.1	
	Girls 48.4	40.8	10.8	

Source: National Center for Health Statistics, Department of Health, Education and Welfare, *Vital and Health Statistics* (Washington, D.C.: U.S. Government Printing Office, 1975): 7.

*Adapted from Scanlon, 1975.

Acne

Among the more common problems facing adolescents is the appearance of blackheads and whiteheads, or *acne*. Acne vulgaris, the form of acne most common among teens, is usually a minor ailment requiring minimal medical intervention. The most effective treatment is time. Only in severe cases may radical intervention, such as cosmetic surgery, be required, but this is rare. Because acne is common, there may be a tendency on the part of teachers, counselors, and physicians to view it as unimportant

Although this is a relatively severe case of acne, evenless-serious cases may cause anxiety in adolescents.

unless it becomes severe. However, as Reisner (1975) warns, the psychological stress that a young person may suffer from fear of rejection of exclusion may be more important than the physical marring of the complexion. Schachter (1972) studied young people with and without acne and found that although there is no overall difference in the number of activities participated in by the two groups, acne sufferers enjoyed the activities less.

Because acne is associated with a variety of old wives' tales relating it to increased sexuality or masturbation, the adolescent who has acne may suffer unwarranted feelings of guilt. Most probably, acne is simply the result of increased androgen output (Gallagher, 1960) or a genetic propensity. The fact that acne is usually more severe in boys gives this theory some credence. Although girls are more likely to display signs of acne earlier—for example, 38 percent of 12-year-old girls versus 21 percent of 14-year-old boys report acne—the trend reverses by age 14, and by age 17, 68 percent of boys versus 53 percent of girls report acne (Scanlon, 1975). Further, although girls are more likely to consult a dermatologist for treatment, boys usually suffer more severe cases of acne.

Acne vulgaris is different from other forms of acne and should not be confused with acne that is a result of drugs, both legal and illegal. Blackheads and pimples in acne vulgaris result from increased activity of the sebaceous, or oil-producing, glands located beneath the skin. If the oil in a pilosebaceous duct is exposed to the air, it will oxidize and become a blackhead. If, on the other hand, the oil is not exposed to the air, if a layer of skin covers the duct, the result is a whitehead.

Although many caring parents nag their teenagers about diet as a cause of acne, there is no objective evidence to support this. Even chocolate, unless the individual is allergic to it, is not a culprit. A well-balanced diet, although beneficial to one's general well-being, does not seem terribly important in the control of acne. Parents should be advised against making unreasonable and unnecessary dietary restrictions that might prevent acne-suffering adolescents from participating with peers at a time when they fear being excluded because of their acne.

SUMMARY

The general name given to the physical changes which transform a child into a young adult is puberty. Puberty is not a single event but a set of events that make up the process of becoming a sexually mature adult. Besides growing in height and weight, adolescents begin to grow pubic and armpit hair, have lowered voices, and show those secondary sexual characteristics that help differentiate masculine and feminine body types. Strictly speaking, puberty ends when the adolescent reaches adult sexual maturity, but, the starting and finishing points of puberty are not so easily marked. The boundaries of puberty are unclear.

In less developed cultures, signs of puberty such as first menstruation or the appearance of pubic hair serve as signs that a young person is ready to assume an adult role. Rites of passage or initiation rites in such cultures are often tied to those signs. In our culture, puberty does not serve a comparable point of demarcation. There is no clearly defined point to which one can point and say a young boy or girl is clearly an adult. However, as young boys and girls begin to show signs of puberty, adults expect them to behave more like adults. At the same time, young people recognize that the physical changes of puberty are underway and begin to question who they are. They see the signs of physical maturation as reflecting their move toward adult physical, social, and psychological status.

Adolescents must also deal with social pressures to conform to societal stereotypes of what is physically attractive or unattractive. To the degree that young people see themselves as not conforming to these societal demands, their self-esteem suffers. Combined with normal feelings of adolescent egocentrism, young people expect that their overwhelming concern with their physical acceptability is shared by everyone. Adolescence is thus often a period of anxieties about one's body image.

For some, concerns over body image become so much of an obsession that they use behaviors that are potentially self-destructive in an attempt to maintain physical attractiveness. In cases of anorexia nervosa and bulimia, the adolescent's focus is on body size, particularly thinness. Resorting to extreme behaviors to maintain low body weight or to lose weight, however, runs the risk of causing irreparable damage to one's body.

It is not surprising that some writers, especially those with a medical orientation, focus on the physical transition of adolescence as the central source of change. The large number of adolescent patients seen by physicians who report concerns about physical and sexual maturity reinforce this view. Further, the radical changes associated with puberty are so profound that they demand attention. However, it is a mistake to assume that adolescence is little more than a physical transition. Adolescents must adjust to a variety of intellectual, social and psychological changes in addition to the physical changes. The new sense of self may take on more importance during some parts of the adolescent transition and less important during others. The adolescent's physical self must be incorporated into his or her broader sense of self.

5 DRUGS AND ALCOHOL

Twenty-five years ago, the use of illegal drugs by adolescents was not common. What drug use that did occur was limited to a small group of alienated and disaffected young people. In the period beginning in the mid-1960s and continuing through the 1970s, use of illegal drugs spread quickly, and to many adult observers, seemed to have gotten totally out of control. Not only were disaffected and alienated youths experimenting with mind-altering drugs, but a wide range of young people from all social classes were doing so. Drug use was also occurring with increasing frequency in the middle school grades and was even occurring in elementary schools.

On the surface, it would seem that a problem of such proportions would have led to a national campaign to deal with drug use and abuse in the schools. In some ways it has. Millions of dollars have been spent on programs of drug and alcohol education. However, that drug and alcohol education programs that have occurred have been largely ineffective (Hanson, 1980). Attempts by schools to respond to the problem are often disorganized and uncertain. Also, parents, educators, and politicians are typically reluctant to admit the problem is real. They choose, instead, to ignore the problem of drugs in a vague hope that the problem will disappear by itself. School administrators may seem to prefer to ignore alcohol and drug related behavior rather than to deal with the legal and social complexities of adolescent drug use. Drug and alcohol use among contemporary adolescents remain major physical and psychological health problems.

PATTERNS OF DRUG USE

How widespread is the use of drugs and alcohol? The answer to that question depends in large part on how the question is phrased. If we ask a person "Have you ever used marijuana?" we may get a different anwer than if we ask that same person "Have you used marijuana in the past year?" We may get a still different answer if we ask that person about use during the past month or about daily use. We would naturally expect that "ever used" rates would be higher than "past year" rates which would, in turn, be higher than "past month" rates. For the past several years, researchers at the Institute for Social Research at the University of Michigan have asked a national sample of high school seniors to describe their drug use patterns and their drug attitudes. These researchers (Lloyd Johnston, Patrick O'Malley, and Jerald Bachman) thus provide data and comparisons for various levels of drug experience over the many years of their study.

The most recent of these annual studies tells us that drug use among high school students has peaked and is in a slow process of decline (Johnston, O'Malley & Bachman, 1987). Use of a wide variety of drugs seems to have peaked during the period 1979 to 1980 but have declined in the years since. Whether or not this decline will continue is not clear. Data from the Johnston et al. report were used in generating Table 5-1. While their report offers more elaborate summaries of data beginning in 1975 and continuing yearly, Table 5-1 offers a glimpse of the major changes in drug use over a 12-year span.

Children learn attitudes about drugs from their parents, especially from their parents' *behavior.*
(© Elizabeth Crews)

Table 5–1 Trends in Drug Use Among American High School Seniors: 1975, 1980, and 1986

	EVER USED			USED IN THE PAST YEAR			USED IN THE PAST MONTH			USED DAILY FOR THE PAST MONTH		
	1975	1980	1986	1975	1980	1986	1975	1980	1986	1975	1980	1986
Marijuana/ Hashish	47.3	60.3	50.9	40.0	48.8	38.8	27.1	33.7	23.4	6.0	9.1	4.0
Inhalents*	10.3	11.9	15.9	3.0	4.6	6.1	0.9	1.4	2.5	0.0	0.1	0.2
Hallucinogens	16.3	13.3	9.7	11.2	9.3	6.0	4.7	3.7	2.5	0.1	0.1	0.1
Cocaine	9.0	15.7	16.9	5.6	12.3	12.7	1.9	5.2	6.2	0.1	0.2	0.4
"Crack"						4.1						
Heroin	2.2	1.1	1.1	1.0	0.5	0.5	0.4	0.2	0.2	0.1	0.0	0.0
Stimulants	22.3	26.4	23.4	16.2	20.8	13.4	8.5	12.1	5.5	0.5	0.7	0.3
Sedatives	18.2	14.9	10.4	11.7	10.3	5.2	5.4	4.8	2.2	0.3	0.2	0.1
Tranquilizers	17.0	15.2	10.9	10.6	8.7	5.8	4.1	3.1	2.1	0.1	0.1	0.0
Alcohol	90.4	93.2	91.3	84.8	87.9	84.5	68.2	72.0	65.3	5.7	6.9	4.8
Cigarettes	73.6	71.0	67.6	na	na	na	36.7	30.5	29.6	26.9	21.3	18.7

*Not asked until 1976, hence, the "1975" value is really 1976.

na: Not asked.

Source: Johnston, L. D. O'Malley, P. M. & Bachman, J. G. (1987) *National Trends in Drug Use and Related Factors Among American High School Students and Young Adults, 1975–1986.* Washington, D.C.: National Institute on Drug Abuse.

Look, for a moment, at the use rates of marijuana and alcohol. In 1975, 47.3 percent of high school seniors admitted ever using marijuana and 90.4 percent to ever using alcohol. In 1980 the comparable percentages were 60.3 for marijuana and 93.2 for alcohol. Thus, there was a marked increase in the percent of high school seniors who had ever tried marijuana (+ 13.0 percent) and a small change (+ 2.8 percent) in the percent who had ever used alcohol. By 1986, the percent of seniors who had ever tried one of these two drugs shifted downward to 50.9 percent for marijuana (a drop of 9.4 percent) and 91.3 percent for alcohol (no real change). When, however, we view the question with respect to yearly or monthly use, marijuana use has shown an even sharper decline in the past five years (about 10 percent). Alcohol use, particularly use in the past month, also declined.

In the earlier edition of this text (Ingersoll, 1982), I noted that if we looked at the daily use of drugs, marijuana use in 1977 outpaced alcohol use among high school students by a fairly significant degree. In 1986, however, daily marijuana use has tapered off and now holds no advantage over daily alcohol use. Fears that marijuana might emerge as the major drug of choice in the next generation seem to have been unfounded.

The one major category of illegal drugs that showed substantial and consistent gains over the course of the Johnston et al. studies was cocaine. In the most recent report, however, cocaine use appears to be tapering. Use of stimulants which was marked by increases until recently has begun to decline. Cigarette smoking, on the other hand, has shown a regular decline in popularity. Use of sedatives, tranquilizers, heroin and hallucinogens remains restricted to irregular use among a small minority of teens. There has, however, also been an increase in the overall percent of high school seniors who report having used some illegal drug besides marijuana.

In one study (Wong & Allen, 1976) in which teens were asked to rate drugs in terms of perceived danger and also to indicate which drugs they used, an intriguing pattern was found. This pattern is shown in Figure 5-1. Those drugs that adolescents saw as most dangerous were the ones they used least. Those drugs that they saw as less dangerous were the ones they used more frequently. There were two notable exceptions. Alcohol which teens saw as somewhat dangerous continued to be widely used. Marijuana, which teens saw as a relatively harmless drug was not as widely used as might be expected.

Beyond diminished use patterns, adolescents' attitudes toward drugs and the use of drugs appear to becoming more conservative. The Johnston et al. studies show that disapproval of regular use of drugs is now widespread among high school seniors. While disapproval has long been associated with those drugs adolescents saw as posing a "great risk" to health, now that disapproval is also being directed at those drugs seen as posing less of a health threat.

With fair regularity, adolescent boys are more likely to use drugs and alcohol than adolescent girls. The only exceptions to that pattern are in the use of stimulants which is equal across sexes and in smoking which is somewhat higher among high school girls (Johnston et al., 1984).

Students are more likely to use drugs if they see their peers using drugs (Kandel, 1973, 1978; Jessor & Jessor, 1977; Chassin, Presson, Sherman, Corty & Olshavsky, 1981; Huba & Bentler, 1980). Peer approval and peer support are important in both initial and continued use of drugs. Family support and closeness work against drug use (Jessor & Jessor, 1977; Kandel, 1973, 1978) as does religious commitment. Where family support systems break down, the teen is likely to look to peer groups for structure. Chronic use

Figure 5–1 Ratings by high school students of the use and dangerousness of various drugs. *Source:* M. R. Wong & T. Allen (1976) "A three-dimensional structure of drug attitudes." *Journal of Drug Education, 6,* 1987. Reprinted by permission of Baywood Publishing Company, Inc.

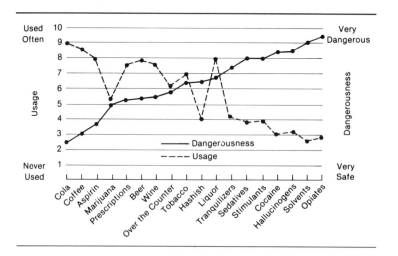

of drugs is often related directly to unstable and erratic family environments. The more stable and supportive the family the less likely the student will try drugs, and, if tried, the less likely the adolescent will continue using them (Blum, 1972).

Jessor (1979), Jessor & Jessor (1977), Jessor, Chase & Donovan (1980) and others (Hundleby, Carpenter, Ross & Mercer, 1982) have made the important connection between regular drug and alcohol use and other problem behaviors. Those adolescent who are regular drug users also tend to have higher rates of delinquency, lower educational performance, higher rates of school absenteeism and dropping out, earlier sexual activity, and a lack of social responsiveness.

We will discuss four general classes of drugs in this chapter. *Stimulants* are drugs that excite or stimulate the central nervous system. Use of stimulants, or uppers, is associated with increased levels of activity and the ability to go without sleep for extended periods of time. Amphetamines, cocaine, and even caffeine are all stimulants. *Depressants,* on the other hand, slow down or depress central nervous system activity. Use of depressants, or downers, is associated with feelings of drunkenness or intoxication. Barbiturates, sedatives, alcohol, and methylqualone (quaaludes) are all depressants. *Hallucinogens* are drugs that alter an individual's perception of reality by altering perceptions or by inducing hallucinations. Lysergic acid diethylamide (LSD), marijuana, hashish, and psilocybin are all classified as hallucinogens. *Opiates* are drugs that are synthetic or natural derivatives of opium. Officially, opiates are medically designated to reduce pain; however, they also have hallucinogenic qualities and promote feelings of euphoria.

By and large, drug use among teens is concentrated within a few types of drugs. Use of other drugs may occur in sporadic fashion, but it does not usually last long. What is curious is that the most widely used drug, alcohol, is often viewed with the least alarm by adults.

DRUG USE AND ABUSE

The question of when we can call drug *use* drug *abuse* is not an easy one to answer. In the strictest sense, any use of an illegal drug can be called abuse because the user has broken the law. Such a definition is not very useful. Experimental use of drugs, although it might reasonably be discouraged, often goes no further than experimentation, and no long-term or short-term, negative impact occurs. Although we cannot consider all drug use to be drug abuse, clearly certain kinds of use create problems for the individual and society. I will define *abuse* for purposes of this chapter as any drug use that interferes with an individual's performance at school, home, or work, or in society.

Drug dependence may take two forms—*physical dependence* and *psychological dependence.* Physical dependence occurs when an individual's biological balance is altered and the drug is needed to avoid serious withdrawal symptoms. Psychological dependence occurs when an individual has a preoccupation with the altered states of consciousness brought on by drugs or feels unable to cope with stress in the absence of drugs. Not all drugs lead to physical dependence, but all drugs may lead to psychological dependence. Not all drug abusers are drug dependent.

Dr. Joseph Zabik, a researcher in alcoholism and pharmacology at Purdue University, describes the progression toward drug dependence in the following manner (personal interview): Initially an individual may experiment with a drug out of curiosity or to be part of the crowd. An adolescent who continues to use the drug regularly over an extended period of time develops a tolerance to the drug. That is, at first a small dose creates the desired state of mind. Gradually, however, larger and larger amounts of the drug are required to achieve the same impact. Individuals who continue to use these increased dosages may develop a physical or psychological dependence on the drug. Although some drugs have no known physically addictive characteristics, all may have psychologically addictive characteristics. Dependence is most obvious when an adolescent goes through a period of withdrawal, in which the drug of dependence is no longer available. Withdrawal symptoms may be mild—including minor physical discomfort and anxiety or irritability—or, in cases of strong dependence on certain drugs, it may be *very* stressful, with severe pain and paranoid hallucinations. Although while not all drug users develop a physical or psychological dependence, it is, nonetheless, a very real possibility. The common notion that addicts were once "experimenters" has a good deal of truth in it.

Keniston (1968) describes three groups of drug users on college campuses: tasters, seekers, and heads. By far the largest group are those he calls *tasters*. Tasters' use of drugs is usually casual or experimental. The second group are called *seekers*. Their use of drugs is occasional but regular. They try to achieve heightened awareness, relief from boredom or depression, or just "an experience." Finally, the most regular users of drugs are the *heads*. They are a small but highly visible miniority who use drugs with frequent regularity. As Keniston says, however, even heads are not necessarily drug addicted, although addicted youths would fall into this category. The important point is that, even with the general upswing in drug use, the percent of regular drug users among the college population is relatively small and varies with the type of college campus and the section of the country.

Macdonald (1982, 1984) has suggested that the process of moving toward abuse of drugs can be described in a series of stages ranging from early familiarity and experimental use to later serious abusive behavior. At first, adolescents are aware of alcohol and drugs but are not motivated to try them. At some point, however, young people are faced with a decision to try or to decline some drug (usually alcohol or marijuana). In the absence of strong family support, positive self-esteem, a commitment to religious values which preclude drugs, or a peer group which will support a decision to decline, young people are unlikely to resist pressures to use drugs. The more adolescents see their peers as "doing drugs" the more likely they are to try drugs themselves (Kandel, 1973, 1978). The less family support and the greater the family conflict, the more likely they are to enter the process of experimentation (Hendin, Pollinger, Ullman & Carr, 1981). The stronger the commitment to a set of religious values, the less likely they are to try or to continue to use drugs (Jessor & Jessor, 1977).

Macdonald describes the first phase of drug use as *Learning the Mood Swing*. Use of drugs during this phase is largely recreational and is probably a function of a need to be accepted by the peer group. Friends and peers may actively encourage each other's participation in the use of some drug. Drug users may have strong feelings of ambivalence about the use of drugs during this level. They may want to explore the mood alterations and to be part of the group but fear the consequences of getting caught. Their fears of addiction are probably not strong since they see their use as slight and are convinced it could never happen to them. Pressuring one another to participate offers the security of the group and the sense that "everybody is doing it." The young person who resists participating may be coaxed with promises that "It will make you feel good" or that "Everybody does it." If a young person continues to resist, the peer group may then resort to threats of exclusion and to labeling the nonparticipant as a "nerd" or a "geek" or some other equally offensive term. Claims that drugs will make the adolescent "feel good" may be given credence by advertisements which depict drugs giving instant relief from pain and pressure. Adolescents' popular heroes may openly advertise that they are drug users. The message often comes through to young people, look at those people who use drugs and how successful they are. Young people may easily interpret these messages to say that they are *expected* to use drugs. Sometimes these external pressures are combined with personal curiosity about the mood swings with drugs.

During the next phase of the process, Macdonald suggests that the adolescents' motivations shift to *Seeking the Mood Swing.* Use increases and the young people are increasingly apt to use drugs as a way of dealing with stress. They may use alcohol or marijuana to help them relax for a test or to escape from "hassles." They are also more likely to expand their repertoire of drugs to include stronger drugs. Use of drugs at this level is increasingly polydrug use. That is, the adolescent uses many different drugs and may mix them in a given session. As use increases and attention becomes more focused on achieving altered mood states, behavior changes and academic problems begin to appear. In a real sense, the increased need to experience these mood alterations represents the early stages of psychological addiction.

At some point, the adolescent who uses drugs regularly runs the risk of moving into deeper involvement with drugs. At the next level of involvement, the adolescent drug user's motivations shift to a *Preoccupation with Mood Swings.* While authors differ in their definition of how much drug use constitutes drug abuse, nearly all would agree that this level of drug involvement is abusive. Drug use is extended beyond "recreational" drugs and psychological addiction is firmly established. Depending on the drug being used, initial stages of physical addiction may also be found. To support the use of drugs, which by now has become an expensive habit, adolescents at this level of involvement may sell drugs to friends to get money. Cost of maintaining the habit continues to increase. Macdonald also notes the personality of adolescents at this third level of drug involvement appears developmentally arrested at an earlier stage.

At the last stage of drug involvement, the user is increasingly motivated to use drugs to avoid the discomfort and pain of withdrawal. Macdonald calls this phase "*Doing Drugs to Feel O.K.*" He could as easily have called it "Doing drugs to avoid feeling bad." Failure to maintain levels of the addicted chemical in the person's system now leads to pain and illness. More drugs are needed merely to survive. Tolerance levels to various drugs are high and the ability to achieve altered mood states associated with early use patterns may no longer be possible.

ALCOHOL

We can easily argue that drinking alcohol is an American institution. When the Pilgrims set sail for the New World, their cargo included 14 tons of water. It also included 42 tons of beer and 10,000 gallons of wine. The Puritan minister, Cotton Mather, called liquor "The good gift of God" (Critchlow, 1986). Today, alcohol consumption supports a multibillion dollar industry in the United States alone. As a drug, alcohol continues to be the most widely abused substance among adolescents and adults. (The most widely used drug is probably caffeine.)

Alcohol is the most widely used drug among American teens. Among high school seniors, 91 percent report ever having used alcohol and 65 percent report having used it in the past month (Johnston et al., 1987). Rates of alcohol use have declined modestly since 1980, but are roughly equal to those in 1975; a consistent 5 to 6 percent of high school seniors report drinking every day. Among college students, 83 percent classify themselves as drinkers (Engs & Hanson, 1985). Rates of drinking among college students were not related to the minimum drinking age in the college's state (Engs & Hanson, 1986).

Before proceeding, you might want to classify your own drinking behavior on a scale that has been used in several recent studies of alcohol use and abuse (from Rachel et al., 1975):

CATEGORIES OF DRINKERS

Abstainers: Do not drink or drink less than once a year.

Infrequent Drinkers: Drink once a month at most and drink small amounts per typical drinking occasion.

Light Drinkers: Drink once per month at most and drink medium amounts per typical drinking occasion *or* drink no more than 3–4 times per month and drink small amounts per typical drinking occasion.

Moderate Drinkers: Drink at least one a week and small amounts per typical drinking occasion *or* 3–4 times a month and medium amounts per typical drinking occasion *or* no more than once a month and large amounts per typical drinking occasion.

Moderate/Heavy Drinkers: Drink at least once a week and medium amounts per typical drinking occasion *or* 3–4 times a month and large amounts per typical drinking occasion.

Heavy Drinkers: Drink at least once a week and large amounts per typical drinking occasion.

Teenagers' Drinking Patterns

Alcohol remains the number one drug used by teenagers. By the end of high school nearly all have sampled alcohol, and the majority drink with some regularity.

Alcohol remains a highly popular drug among teenagers, many of whom view drinking as a symbol of adult status. (© Susan lapides)

Although most adolescents—like most adult drinkers—drink only occasionally, one in nine is considered to be a problem drinker, but there are an estimated 500,000 teenage alcoholics.

A nationwide survey of junior and senior high school students found that, using the drinking scale previously described, about 11 percent of the students were rated as heavy drinkers. Another 14 percent were moderate-to-heavy drinkers. At the other end of the continuum, 27 percent of the teens described themselves as abstainers. Table 5–2 shows, however, that the choice to drink or to abstain is strongly related to age. While 38 percent of 13-year-olds were abstainers, 20 percent of 18-year-olds were. Conversely, 12 percent of 13-year-olds were moderate-to-heavy drinkers, while 41 percent of 18-year-olds were (Rachel et al., 1975). Among adults, 32 percent are abstainers (Callahan, Cisin & Crossley, 1974).

Among college students, 21 percent classify themselves as heavy drinkers; 32 percent of college males and 13 percent of college females. The highest rate of heavy drinking appear to be found in the freshman and sophomore years (Engs & Hanson, 1985). Heavy drinking is also a serious problem among young enlisted personnel in the military (Burt & Biegel, 1980).

Alcohol, or more accurately, ethanol, is a depressant. The term *depressant* refers to a drug's effect on the brain and the central nervous system, not to the emotion of depression. In small quantities, alcohol may seem to have the opposite effect—that is, energizing a person and reducing inhibitions. The reason for this is that small quantities of alcohol depress brain activity in the area related to emotional arousal. When we drink alcohol, 20 percent is processed immediately from the stomach into the bloodstream.

Table 5-2 Drinking Patterns of Teenagers

Drinking Level	AGE					
	13	14	15	16	17	18
Abstainer	37.8%	27.8%	24.7%	22.6%	17.2%	20.5%
Infrequent	23.6	18.8	14.1	11.2	11.4	6.9
Light	14.4	16.6	17.4	17.1	20.3	15.1
Moderate	12.7	15.4	16.2	17.3	17.5	16.5
Moderate/Heavy	7.3	11.7	16.0	17.4	19.0	20.8
Heavy	4.3	9.7	11.5	14.5	14.6	20.2

Source: J. V. Rachel et al., *A National Study of Adolescent Drinking Behavior, Attitudes and Correlates* (1975). Report to the National Institute on Alcohol Abuse and Alcoholism, Department of Health, Education and Welfare (Washington, D.C.: U.S. Government Printing Office) p. 147.

However, as the level of alcohol in the bloodstream increases, the depressant action of ethanol becomes more profound.

Blood-Alcohol Levels

Blood-alcohol level (BAL) refers to the percent of alcohol found in a person's bloodstream. A BAL of .05 indicates that an individual has .05 parts alcohol to 100 parts blood, or 1 part per 2,000. Although .05 does not sound like much, it is a potential factor in auto accidents, because at that level activity in the front of the brain is slowed down. A BAL of .05 is roughly the blood-alcohol level of an average 160-pound person who has drunk three ounces of whiskey within two hours *after* eating a meal. That same amount of whiskey would affect some 160-pound people more quickly and would have a stronger effect on people weighing less than 160 pounds and on those who have not eaten a meal in the previous two hours. Because teens are likely to weigh less than adults, they are likely to be affected by alcohol more quickly.

A BAL of .10 is usually the legal limit that defines drunkenness. At .10 people become clumsy and awkward, their speech may be slurred, their senses are dulled and distorted, and their ability to do skilled tasks is impaired.

By the time a person reaches a BAL of .20, coordination is severely affected, and the person is likely to stagger and reel. Emotional outbursts involving crying and raging are common. A BAL of .30 is very serious. The ethanol is affecting the deeper parts of the brain, and the person may become confused and disoriented. At BALs of .40 and .50 the inner brain is profoundly affected, and the person will fall into unconsciousness. The depressant activity may lead to stoppage of the heart or lungs and death.

Adolescents are more likely to be adversely affected by alcohol than adults for several reasons:

1. On the average adolescents weigh less than adults; thus comparable amounts of alcohol are less effectively metabolized.

2. Adolescents lack experience with alcohol and have not developed a set of internal standards by which to govern their drinking.
3. Adolescents are more likely to try to demonstrate they can handle alcohol by "chugging."
4. Adolescents lack emotional maturity and are more susceptible to the psychological impact of intoxication.

Why do young people start drinking? Although the answers are not totally clear, it seems that parents, more than peers, seem to be involved in early drinking experiences. The first use of alcohol usually occurs at home with the approval of parents. Thus early in adolescence the parents convey their approval of alcohol consumption, even when later consumption occurs outside the home.

Parents and adolescents often do not view alcohol as a drug. If they do see it as a drug they are likely to think of it as harmless and its use as a natural part of growing up. This attitude is especially true of beer and wine which is seen as somehow not as dangerous as whiskey. But, a 12-ounce can of beer, a 5-ounce glass of wine, and an ounce-and-a-half shot of 86 proof whiskey all contain one-half ounce of alcohol.

Most analyses of variables that lead to continued use of alcohol by adolescents point to the level of parents' use of alcohol as a primary predictor. The more the parents drink the more their offspring are likely to drink (Bracht et al., 1973). Teens regard drinking as an adult activity. It provides a way for them to act like adults, and in fact getting drunk may be a kind of an initiation rite. Adults usually remember that they too drank as teens and therefore view drinking as innocent or as much less of a problem than ''real'' drugs.

"Thank heaven! Maybe now he'll
stay away from pot."

Source: By permission of Bill Mauldin and Wil-Jo Associates, Inc.

Although religious preference and commitment to religious values are predictors of drinking behavior among adolescents, the relationship is not a simple one. Those who are raised in religion in which alcohol consumption is permitted are more likely to drink than those raised in fundamentalist religions; but a curious phenomenon occurs when the second group does drink. Those who have been prohibited and then start drinking often fail to have any degree of control and are more likely to be problem drinkers (Bracht et al., 1973).

Other studies show that peers play a significant role in reinforcing and encouraging drinking among high school students (Jessor & Jessor, 1977) and college students (Rogers, 1970). Peers provide strong pressures not only to drink, but to drink to get drunk. Adolescents are more likely to begin drinking with the express purpose of getting drunk (Brown & Finn, 1982). Much of the social activity involved in teen drinking is directed toward that goal. "Chugging" games in particular speed up the process. Further, teens appear to get drunk on a regular basis more often than adults. Drinking is an important element in the social scene of many groups of adolescents. Since social gatherings usually require travel, authorities are especially concerned about risks associated with drunk drivers. Among college students, 48 percent readily admit to drinking after driving and 45 percent to drinking *while* driving (Engs & Hanson, 1986). While Hanson and Engs (1984) found stability over the years in the drinking behavior of college students, they also found an increased uneasiness about admitting their drinking to others who might disapprove of drinking.

A small but signficant number of adolescents drink to relieve anxiety and tension. The practitioner can play an important role in helping adolescents cope with the internal and external pressures to consume alcohol and with their own attitudes about drinking. To do this, the practitioner should try to determine the motives behind the drinking and to help the adolescent find other means to deal with those motives. In some cases the practitioner may prefer to help the adolescent to control his or her drinking in the settings that usually lead to drunkenness.

MARIJUANA

The major drug of choice besides alcohol (excluding tobacco) among teens is marijuana. Intoxication from the use of marijuana may include feelings of euphoria, relaxed drifting, and of time passing slowly. Early researchers (for example, Halikas, Goodman & Gruze, 1972) wrote that occasional use of marijuana did not seem to cause major problems for otherwise well-functioning individuals. Among many who were youths during the 1970s, there grew a sense that marijuana was relatively harmless and certainly no more dangerous than alcohol.

More recent evidence indicates that marijuana is not as benign as once thought. First, to describe use as "occasional" is ambiguous. Does "occasional use" mean once a week, once a month, or once a year. A user of marijuana may describe her or his use of the drug as "occasional" while a clinician might call it "regular." Second, many of the early writers were dealing with marijuana that was considerably less potent than today's drug. The psychoactive agent in marijuana is called delta-9-tetrahydrocannibinal (delta-9-THC). The street drug of the early and mid-1970s rarely had delta-9-THC concentrations greater than 1 percent. Today, delta-9-THC concentrations of 1 percent and delta-9-THC concentrations of 5 percent are frequent (Petersen, 1984). Third, a decade and a half of research has indicated that chronic marijuana use has serious physical and psychological drawbacks.

Whether or not marijuana is physically addictive remains a subject of debate. While some argue strongly that it is physically addictive, examples of addictive behavior are drawn from groups of marijuana users who are apt to be poly-drug users. There are few who would question the psychologically addictive aspects of marijuana use. Macdonald's (1982, 1984) description of the motive to continue seeking mood alterations is applicable to the individual who uses marijuana on a regular basis.

Arguments for possible physically addictive aspects of marijuana use are not without merit. Unlike moderate levels of alcohol which are metabolized and excreted from one's body within a few hours, delta-9-THC can reside in a person's body for extended periods of time. Delta-9-THC is stored in the body's fat cells and brain cells. Traces of the drug remain and accumulate. The combined result of the psychologically addictive aspects of marijuana and the buildup of delta-9-THC in the person's body is a problem that has been linked to what researchers are calling the *amotivational syndrome* (McGlothlin & West, 1976; Cohen, 1982; Halikas, Weller, Morse & Shapiro, 1982; Mellinger, Somers, Davidson & Manneheim, 1976).

Adolescents who use marijuana with regularity are subject to a loss of motiva-

Smoking "grass" has become widespread, and its use is increasing, even among early-adolescents. (© Eric Kroll/Taurus Photos)

tion. They lack energy and ambition, they are reluctant to work and become more passive and self-focused. This amotivational syndrome interferes with their academic progress, their work, and their family relations. Beyond reduced motivation, there is evidence that regular use of marijuana leads to impaired memory and intellectual functioning (Ferraro, 1980). In experimental studies of the effects of marijuana intoxication on learning and recall, research subjects were less able to remember material learned while they were high on marijuana. Heavy users of marijuana have greater difficulty in maintaining good grades and staying in college (Mellinger et al., 1976), general lowered achievement in high school (Johnston, 1980), and higher rates of absenteeism and of dropping out of school altogether (Kandel, 1975).

Beyond psychological risks associated with regular marijuana use, marijuana has also been linked to reduced sexual functioning and sexual development (Harclerode, 1980; Kolodny, Masters, Kolodner & Toro, 1974; Hembree, Nahas & Huang, 1979). Long-term users of marijuana run increased risks of all the respiratory problems tied to cigarette smoking (Cohen, 1981). Since adolescence is a period of rapid physical growth, risks are particularly significant. Any organ is at risk during periods of rapid growth. Without question, marijuana is a health threat.

Currently, over half of high school seniors report ever having used marijuana (Johnston et al., 1986). But while the percent of students who report ever using marijuana is down from five years earlier, rates of recent and regular use are down even more noticeably. But, despite efforts to legalize marijuana and the fact that many states have tried to deemphasize criminal penalties for possession of small quantities of marijuana, it remains illegal. It is, thus, the most widely used illicit drug. Marijuana use may be seen by some teens as a way to challenge authority and to exert independence (Hays, Winburn & Bloom, 1975).

Peer approval plays a central factor in initial and continued marijuana use (Barrett & James-Cairns, 1980; Jessor & Jessor, 1977; Kandel, 1973, 1978). The more adolescents see their friends using marijuana, the more likely they are to use it themselves. Conversely, when adolescents begin to use marijuana they are likely to search out friends who are also users.

Further, marijuana use, as other drug use, fits into the adolescent's view of her- or himself (Chassin, 1984). The more the adolescent sees marijuana use as a reflection of his or her self-image, the more likely the individual is to use it. Jessor (1979; Jessor & Jessor, 1977; Jessor, Chase & Donovan, 1980) links regular marijuana use with with a broad spectrum of deviant and problem behaviors among adolescents. Those who use marijuana regularly are likely to engage in other socially deviant behaviors. In a study of heavy abusers of marijuana, serious abusers frequently exhibited rebellion against parents and authority along with other behaviors that were described as angry and problematic (Hendin, Pollinger, Ullman & Carr, 1981). Marijuana use is not, however, a major cause of violence (Abel, 1977) but may precipitate violent behavior among those who have a predisposition toward violence.

Users of marijuana tend to rate higher on scales of nonconventionality. They are less likely to feel committed to traditional cultural values and tend to view themselves as nonconformists (Jessor, 1979). In general these nontraditional attitudes tend to prevail across a range of social traditions and values, including sexual morals, religious beliefs, and political beliefs. Users also tend to value and be interested in creativity and novelty more than nonusers. On the other hand, marijuana use is also associated with lower motivation to achieve (Jessor & Jesson, 1977).

One important question that troubles many adults is the relationship of marijuana use to experimentation with other drugs. The evidence is clear that those who have tried marijuana are more likely to try other illegal drugs. The higher the degree of use, the greater the likelihood. However, marijuana is not always the initial drug of experimentation (Blum & Richards, 1979).

TOBACCO

Smoking has been termed the "largest preventable cause of death in America today" (Pinney, 1979). Despite a widespread campaign against smoking, and mounting evidence that chronic cigarette smoking is linked to cancer, heart disease, and emphysema, many young people continue to smoke. Among today's high school seniors, 68 percent have smoked at one time or another (Johnston et al., 1987), and 19 percent admit to daily smoking. Of those who smoke daily, 57 percent began smoking by the ninth grade. Heavy smokers, that is, those who smoke a pack or more a day, are highly likely to have used illicit drugs.

Why do teens begin smoking? Are they oblivious to the dangers of respiratory and heart diseases tied to cigarette smoking? Teens are probably not unaware of the well-publicized evidence that cigarette smoking is dangerous to their health. Most recognize the harmfulness of smoking and disapprove of it. Yet tolerance of smoking seems to increase with age across the adolescent years (Schneider & Vanmastrigt, 1974) and with increased association with those who do smoke.

Parents who smoke provide role models for their children (McAlister, Perry & Maccoby, 1979; Chen & Thompson, 1980). If they approve of smoking by their own behavior, their children are likely to be positively predisposed toward smoking even if the parents explain that they do not like smoking and wish they could stop. It is this predisposition in childhood which serves as a major predictor of the decision to initiate smoking during the teen years. In studies by Chassin and her colleagues (Sherman, Presson, Chassin, Bensenberg, Corty & Olshavsky, 1982), preadolescent children's *expectations* that they would or would not smoke during adolescence were predictors of their actual behavior. The degree to which they saw smoking as part of their projected self-concept was significant.

Lanese, Banks, and Keller (1972) also point to older siblings as prominant in adolescents' decisions to initiate smoking. When older siblings smoke, there is a higher chance that younger siblings will choose to smoke too. This influence is augmented by parent and peer attitude toward smoking.

As with other drug decisions, peers play an important role in adolescents' decisions to start smoking or not (Schneider & Vanmastrigt, 1974; Mettlin, 1976; McAlister et al., 1979; Chen & Thompson, 1980). The more peers see smoking as "cool" or "in," the more likely the individual adolescent is to initiate smoking in order to be acceptable. As the adolescent's peer group is increasingly composed of nonsmokers, however, the more the individual adolescent is capable of maintaining resistance to pressures to begin smoking. Close friends who elect to smoke also influence the individual adolescent's decision. Thus, if one's best friend starts to smoke, then it is more likely that the individual will also begin (Schneider & Vanmastrigt, 1974; Lanese, Bank & Keller, 1972).

Teenage smokers are also likely to admit that smoking is addictive. Over half of those who smoke a half pack or more each day claim to have tried to quit and failed; nearly half would like to quit (Johnston et al., 1987).

Adolescents' refusal to admit they may be at risk for the health hazards of smoking is probably a function of their perceived sense of invulnerability to harm, their lack of time perspective, and their denial of the risks. Chen and Thompson (1980) found nonsmokers to be more knowledgeable about the risks of smoking than smokers. Pederson, Baskerville, and Lefcoe (1981) found that knowledge and attitudes about smoking were negatively related to smoking. The more adolescents know, the less likely they are to smoke. The question arises then whether smokers have never heard the information or whether they deny its existance. For most adolescents, the risks of lung cancer and heart disease appear remote and they typically feel that they can quit at any time they choose. College students often add that smoking helps them concentrate. There is some evidence to suggest that the latter claim is true for heavy smokers.

Of increasing concern is the widespread use of "smokeless tobacco" by adolescent males. Nationally, about 16 percent of boys ages 12 to 17 have used some form of smokeless tobacco. In some rural areas, upwards to 80 percent have. This increased use of smokless tobacco has been accompanied by an increase in oral cancers, especially among young users. Much of the motivation for its use appears to be linked to its assumed "manliness."

DEPRESSANTS

Depressants slow down the activity of the central nervous system. Medically, depressants are used to induce relaxation and sleep; they dull one's senses. As mentioned earlier, alcohol acts as a depressant. In small amounts it serves to relax the person. In larger amounts, it leads to intoxication and drunkenness. Other depressants can generate similar feelings of intoxication. When used in conjunction with alcohol, the results can be deadly.

Barbiturates and Sedative-Hypnotics

Barbiturates and other nonbarbiturate depressants, such as dilantin (Valium), methylqualone (quaaludes, sopors), and others, are medically prescribed as antianxiety or sleep agents. Their effect is to reduce feelings of anxiety, tension, fear, or apprehension, allowing a person to cope more adequately with stress. In larger doses, these drugs lead to an intoxication similar to that of alcohol. It is not uncommon for barbiturates to be used in combination with alcohol.

An adolescent who is using barbiturates may appear drunk but not smell of alcohol. His or her speech may be slurred, coordination impaired, and ability to concentrate on complex problems disrupted. Continued use may lead to distorted perception and heightened anxiety.

Barbiturates are dangerous in high doses, and overdose can lead to death. Regular use of barbiturates leads to increased tolerance plus physical and psychological dependence. Regular users of barbiturates must be withdrawn from the drug slowly; otherwise, the withdrawal symptoms may be too severe.

Barbiturate and tranquilizer use is relatively low among adolescents and is very low among early-adolescents. By late adolescence and young adulthood, however, nonmedical use of sedatives and tranquilizers increases substantially. Among those in the Johnston et al. (1987) study, 2 percent had used sedatives within the past month. Over the period 1975 to 1986, there was steady decline in the rate of nonmedical use of sedatives and tranquilizers.

STIMULANTS

In contrast to depressants, stimulants excite the central nervous system. In small quantities, stimulants increase the level of arousal and help overcome fatigue. They increase the heart rate, raise blood pressure, and suppress appetite. Hence, they are often used in diet pills. The two most commonly used stimulants are caffeine—found in coffee, tea, cola drinks, and chocolate—and nicotine—found in tobacco. Cocaine also acts like a stimulant even though it is often legally described as a narcotic.

Cocaine, once the drug exclusively of the wealthy because of its high price, is now being used by more people, including adolescents. (© Margaret Thompson)

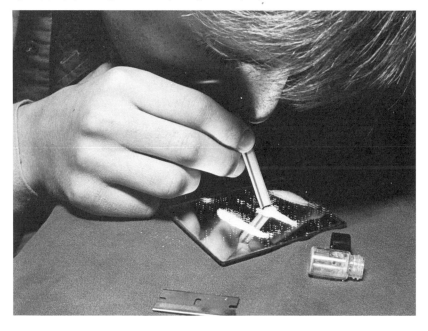

Cocaine

A decade ago, cocaine (coke, snow) was still largely a drug used by a small corps of wealthy drug users. It has long been a popular drug in the entertainment industry. Jazz songs from the 1930s often sang of the glories of "coke." Cocaine is usually taken by "snorting." In 1975, when Johnston and his colleagues initiated their studies of high school seniors, only 9 percent had ever used cocaine. By 1986, 16 percent of the seniors reported ever using the drug and 13 percent had used cocaine in the previous year. If monthly use of cocaine is descriptive of at least moderate and probably regular use of a drug, 6 percent of high school seniors now fall into that category of users of cocaine. Cocaine is clearly a psychologically addictive drug and is probably physically addictive. Cocaine use has many of the same traits as amphetamine use including potentially serious "down" periods following the high.

In recent years, drug enforcement officials have become alarmed at the increased use of "Crack," cocaine which is smoked (Time, 1986). Used in this way the cocaine creates a faster "rush" but also a lower "crash." The particularly problematic issue is that "Crack" seems to be highly addictive and that the addiction occurs quickly. Among the Johnston et al. (1987) seniors, 4 percent had used "Crack" within the past year.

Amphetamines

Early studies of amphetamine and methamphetamine (speed) abuse indicated that they usually occurred in conjunction with barbiturate abuse. Thus, amphetamine and barbiturate use appeared to follow the same patterns. This appears to be no longer true. While sedative use has declined, stimulant use has increased. Johnston et al. suggest that much of the increase may be due to the use of "look alike" drugs intended to mimic amphetamines and of diet pills which contain legally available stimulants.

VIGNETTE 5–1
ALICE IN HORRORLAND

The excerpt below is taken from an anonymous diary of a young girl called Alice. The title of the book, Go Ask Alice, *is drawn from a drug culture rock song, the theme of which was, in turn, reflecting on another Alice. Alice in Wonderland sampled mushrooms and other items which altered her reality. This particular segment of* Go Ask Alice *reveals the young girl's near panic as the effects of drugs now seem out of control. Her altered consciousness was no longer a pleasant trip.*

April 11

Dear Diary,
I don't want to write this down because I really want to blot it out of my mind forever, but I'm so terrified that maybe if I tell you, it won't seem so terrible. Oh Diary,

please help me. I'm scared. I'm so scared that my hands are sticky and I'm actually shaking.

I guess I must have had a flashback because I was sitting on my bed planning my mother's birthday, just thinking about what to get her and how to make it a surprise, when my mind got all mixed up. I can't really explain it, but it seemed to be rolling backwards, like it was rolling in on itself, and there was nothing I could do to stop it. The room got smoky and I thought I was in a head shop. We were all standing around reading the ads for the second hand junk and for every kind of sex deal imaginable. And I started to laugh. I felt great! I was the highest person in the world and I was looking down at everyone and the whole world was in strange angles and shadows.

Then suddenly it all changed into some kind of underground movie. It was slow and lazy and the lighting was really weird. Naked girls were dancing around, making love to statutes. I remember one girl ran her tongue along a statue and he came alive and took her off into the high, blue grass. I couldn't really see what was happening, but he was obviously putting it to her. I felt so sexy I wanted to break wide open and run after them. But the next thing I remember, I was back on the street, panhandling, and we were all shouting at the tourists, "Mighty kind of y'all. I hope you have a nice orgasm with your dog tonight."

Then I felt like I was being smothered and I was up in a glare of revolving lights and beacons. Everything was going around. I was a shooting star, a comet piercing the firmament, blazing through the sky. When I finally got myself together, I was lying on the floor nude.

I still can't believe it. What's happening to me? I was just lying on my bed, planning my mother's birthday, listening to records and bham!

Maybe it wasn't a flashback. Maybe I'm schizo. That often starts in teenagers when they lose contact with reality, doesn't it? Whatever it is, I'm really screwed up. I can't even control my mind. The words I wrote when I was out are just squirming little lines and roads with a lot of rotten crap and symbols in between. Oh, what am I going to do? I need someone to talk to. I really and truly and desperately do. Oh God, please help me. I'm so scared and so cold and so alone. I have only you, Diary. You and me, what a pair.

Later

I've done a few problems in math and even read a few pages. At least I can still read. I memorized a few lines and my mind seems to be functioning pretty well now. I did exercises too and I guess I've got control of my body. But I wish I had someone who knows what's happening and what will happen. But I don't, so I must forget this thing. Forget, forget, forget, and not look back. I'll go ahead with Mom's party. Maybe I can get Tim and Alex to take her to an early movie after school and than I can have a lovely dinner ready on the table when they get home. I'll pretend this has all been a nightmare and forget it. Please God, let me forget it and don't let it happen again. Please, please, please.

By themselves, amphetamines lead to an increased feeling of power and energy. However, the exhilaration and "high" caused by the stimulants may be followed by a "crash," or a period of profound depression. Chronic users may find that they have trouble "getting down" from an amphetamine high. Thus a pattern of "uppers" in the morning and "downers" at night may emerge.

Adolescents who use amphetamines usually experience a loss of appetite and appear nervous and excitable. Physically, the pupils of their eyes are dilated, they perspire heavily, and their hands may tremble. Emotionally, they are talkative and show rapid mood swings and overactions to events. Regular users begin to have feelings of fear and apprehension. In extreme cases these fears become severe and may lead to a psychotic breakdown.

As with barbiturates, tolerance and dependence develop rapidly. Chronic abuse and overdose of amphetamines may lead to *toxic psychosis,* in which the user shows behavior very much like an actively psychotic patient. Severe overdose can cause death.

HALLUCINOGENS

As with alcohol, the use of hallucinogens is not new. Naturally occurring hallucinogens are found in certain mushrooms, weeds, and cacti. Use of hallucinogenic mushrooms and peyote was recorded as early as 1000 B.C. (Schultes & Hoffman, 1979, 1980). Today, literally dozens of hallucinogens are available. Some, such as marijuana, are mild hallucinogens, whereas others, such as LSD or PCP, are stronger and potentially toxic.

LSD and PCP

Probably the most widely known of the synthetic hallucinogens available to today's young pepole is lysergic acid diethylamide (LSD). LSD was first synthesized in 1938, and as early as 1943, it was recognized as a hallucinogen. By the late 1960s, LSD had become widely available and was a matter of increasing public concern. Stories of suicides under LSD trips, chromosomal damage, and psychotic reactions of users led the public to view LSD as a seriously dangerous drug.

In a national survey of drug use (Abelson & Fishburne, 1976), only 5 percent of those between the ages of 12 and 17 report ever having used LSD or another hallucinogen. When asked whether they had used a hallucinogen within the past month, fewer than 1 percent said that they had. In the age group 18 to 25, 17 percent admitted to ever using a hallucinogen and only 1 percent to having used one in the previous month (Ableson & Fishburne, 1976). In the 10-year San Mateo study, use of LSD seemed to hit a peak in the early 1970s and has dropped gradually ever since (Blackford, 1977). In the Johnston et al. (1987) studies, use has shown a steady decline since 1975.

Currently, more attention is being focused on the use of phencyclidine (PCP), or "angel dust." Among American adolescents and youths, the use of PCP is the fastest growing of the potentially dangerous drugs, PCP is used legally as a powerful anesthetic for animals. Its use as an anesthetic for humans was short-lived since patients reported serious psychological disturbances following its use. Regardless, PCP, known as the "peace drug," became a popular drug during the late 1960s. Its use seemed to die off until relatively recently; now it is used much more widely than ever.

In its liquid form PCP is usually sprayed on parsley or oregano to be eaten or smoked. In some cases it has been sprayed on marijuana to make a "super joint." Usually users report that one experience was so unpleasant, they never tried PCP again. However, some users find the anesthetic and hallucinatory effects much more desirable, and PCP becomes a drug of choice. Chronic users may develop physical tolerance for PCP, but it is unclear whether physical dependence occurs. There is little doubt that psychological dependence may develop.

In extreme cases PCP may lead to bizarre hallucinations and behavior. The PCP user may show symptoms that look very much like severe psychosis. At such times, PCP users have been known to display superhuman strength. One indication of the increased level of abuse of PCP is the number of admissions to medical emergency rooms associated with PCP overdose. From 1976 to 1977, there was more than a 100 percent increase in the number of PCP admissions.

INHALANTS

A popular drug use pattern among some adolescents in sniffing glue and using inhalants such as gasoline or aerosols. Chronic inhalant abuse is a problem mainly among young drug users and among the very poor. Inhalants are popular in part because of their ease of availability. A young person can go into any grocery store, buy a tube of airplane glue, get a paper bag, and proceed to get "high." Ease of availability should not, however, be interpreted to mean that such drugs are safe. Death may be caused by suffocation or heart failure. Inhalation of freon, for example, can freeze the air passages.

Among college-age students, use of nitrous oxide (laughing gas) or chloroform seems more popular, when inhalants are used at all. The effects are the same, however, including giddiness and exhilaration. Chronic use of inhalants increases tolerance, and although no apparent physical dependence has been demonstrated, high toxic levels may cause irreparable harm to the liver and kidneys.

HEROIN AND OPIATES

Perhaps the class of drugs most frightening to the general public includes heroin and other opiates. In reality, of all the drugs used by adolescents, heroin is used by only a small percentage. Nonetheless, the physically and psychological addictive properties of opiates makes them a source of special concern.

There are four kinds of opiates. First, there are natural derivatives of opium, such as morphine and codeine. These drugs, originally valued as painkillers, also have mood-altering qualities. In some people the drugs produce a feeling of euphoria. Most people, however, achieve only confusion, disorientation, and nausea. It is not unusual for people who experiment with an opiate not to get the euphoric high of regular users.

Heroin, a synthetic derivative of opium, is transformed by the human body into morphine. As with morphine, tolerance levels and physical dependence develop with continued use. Only 1.2 percent ever used heroin (Johnston et al., 1987) with only .6 percent reporting having used heroin in the previous year. These figures are not intended to minimize the problem of heroin use. For even the small proportion of adolescents who use heroin regularly, it is a serious problem. In major metropolitan areas, heroin use often extends to younger drug users and is justifiably a cause of much concern.

The third category of opiates includes the completely synthesized drugs like methadone, which are often used in the treatment of heroin addiction. The use of methadone, however, does not eliminate the physical drug dependence but instead replaces heroin with a less harmful drug. Further, methadone- and heroin-dependent youths are usually polydrug users and may be dependent on other drugs as well.

The fourth category of opiates is probably the least abused; it includes prescriptive drugs that contain minimal quantities of opiates, such as paregoric or codeine cough syrups.

DRUG AND ALCOHOL EDUCATION

When educators are asked to rate their ability to handle alcohol education, they report a general lack of self-confidence (Milgram, 1974). Teachers involved in drug education often lack credibility among the students, because the students think they know more about drugs than the teachers—and they are probably right. There is a real need for teachers to be aware of such attitudes among the student population. Likewise, teachers must have accurate information about the characteristics of various drugs and the symptoms of chronic abuse.

Because so much attention has been directed toward drug and alcohol use among contemporary adolescents, schools and communities have become increasingly involved in drug and alcohol education programs. Many states now require junior and senior high schools to offer drug education in the standard curriculum. Usually such programs have had as an implicit or explicit goal the reduction or elimination of drug and alcohol use among the students. whether or not abstinence from alcohol or drugs is a reasonable goal is a matter of some debate. There is a general agreement that whenever reduction of drug use has been a goal, drug and alcohol education have been very unsuccessful. Some drug and alcohol education programs have in fact been credited with an *increase* in drug usage among students.

Martin Wong (1976) has described the more generally used models of drug education. Although Wong directs his comments at drug-education programs, they apply equally to alcohol programs, which are often kept separate from drug education.

The *legal-political model* of drug education is oriented around the premise that drugs are immoral and illegal. Laws are made to protect people from immorality and their stiff enforcement is essential. Confusion sometimes exists in these programs over whether drugs are illegal because they are immoral or whether they are immoral because they are illegal. A legal-political model assumes that informing adolescents of the illegality of a drug will serve as a deterrent.

Programs in this category usually invite police authorities or government officials to describe to large groups the criminal prosecution that may follow if the adolescents are caught breaking the law. As a general approach to discourage experimental or casual use of drugs and alcohol, the legal-political model has not been very effective. It lacks credibility with students, in part because they see the laws as unfair. Further, the programs often include questionable information. The result is that a large population of adolescents choose to ignore the law.

The second major "education" approach to drug education consists of scare tactics. The *fear-induction model* uses films and personal accounts of the devastating effects of alcohol and drugs. Any number of horrors are shown, usually in chilling detail, with the assumption that adolescents will agree that drugs are something to avoid. Some adolescents may. However, most are largely unimpressed by this approach, again because it often confuses truth with fiction. Few controls have been placed on the accuracy of information. Students know, for example, that drugs taken in small quantities will not cause the severe withdrawal effects associated with chronic use.

Many of the films in these programs are so full of inaccuracies that students see them as comical. For example, the 1949 film *Reefer Madness* is very popular in campus movie houses. The film depicts a young girl who smokes one "reefer" and immediately falls prey to all forms of humiliation and degradation. Not only do students view the film as funny, they often report that they like to get high on marijuana while watching this film.

Scare tactics can also take the form of warnings. For example, consider this warning about marijuana use issued by the Federal Bureau of Narcotics:

> Under the influence of this drug marijuana, the will is destroyed and all power of directing and controlling thought is lost. . .many violent crimes have been committed by persons under the influence of the drug. Not only is marijuana used by hardened criminals to steel them to commit violent crimes, but it is also being placed in the hands of high school children. . .Its continued use results many times in impotency and insanity (Testimony to the U.S. Senate Subcommittee on Taxation, 1937, reported in Zinberg & Robertson, 1972).

Many schools and agencies prefer to use what Wong calls the *information-processing, rationality model,* in which educators argue with facts. They are convinced that when drug users or potential users learn all the facts about drugs, they will weigh the evidence and conclude that alcohol or drugs is not worth the risk. Although this type of program has an intrinsic appeal, it is based on the premise that the information is convincing and that the students are able to make weighted decisions. Because much of the information is, by its nature, abstract or remote to the adolescents' immediate experience, those assumptions may not be valid. Also, it may not be the attraction of drugs but instead the influence of peers that is the primary cause of drug experimentation and use.

Again, information control is critical with this model. This has been a problem in the past, because much information was misleading. Moreover, there may be an inverse effect. Students may become drug connoisseurs—they know which ones are safer or easier to take, which drugs cause what effects, and so on. This may increase their confidence and their probability of using drugs and alcohol. Information-based drug-education programs often draw upon the testimonials of former addicts to convince young people that the decision to use drugs is a bad one. Although his or her experience makes the former addict an "expert" of sorts, the effectiveness of these speakers in discouraging young people from using drugs has not been encouraging. Students are apparently unconvinced that they can become addicted or that if they become addicted that breaking the habit would be all that difficult.

In some instances, proponents of alcohol and drug education suggest that, rather than dwell on what *not* to do, programs should be geared toward positive adaptive behaviors. In the case of alcohol education, this might include encouraging those who are going to drink to do so responsibly.

As was mentioned earlier, for a variety of reasons adolescents are more vulnerable to the adverse effects of alcohol. Because less than one-third of teens rate themselves as abstainers, it might be appropriate to describe the characteristics of responsible drinking. Dr. Morris Chafetz, who served as the director of the National Institute on Alcoholism and Alcohol Abuse, offers this set of guidelines for adult drinkers that are equally applicable to teen drinkers:

1. *Sip, don't gulp.* Alcohol is processed into the bloodstream almost directly, and drinking large quantities quickly puts more alcohol into the bloodstream. "Chugging," the popular drinking game among high school and college students, can overload the system. There is a safe level of alcohol intake. Individuals who stay within their ability to metabolize alcohol are more likely to remain in control.

2. *Don't drink without eating.* "Never drink on an empty stomach" is an old adage, and, as with many such sayings, it has a grain of truth. Food serves to slow down the metabolism of alcohol. However, the term *food* does not refer to the typical "munchies" of potato chips and pretzels that are usually eaten while drinking. Carbohydrates are of little help in slowing the transfer of alcohol into the bloodstream. High protein or fatty foods, on the other hand, do help to slow down the process. Thus, a cheeseburger and a glass of milk *before* drinking will do much to slow the rate of metabolism.

3. *Don't drink alone.* Drinking alone because of emotional upset can lead to trouble. It is better to have someone to talk to. Also, drinking in groups has a curious effect. If you are part of a group that expects to act drunk, you will probably feel drunk on less alcohol.

4. *Don't drink to prove yourself.* Unfortunately, adolescents, especially boys, regard alcohol consumption in large quantities as part of being an adult. "How much you can hold" is an index of maturity. This is a very difficult idea to combat without sounding too "preachy" to young people.

5. *If you drink, don't drive.* This guideline needs little elaboration. An enormous number of traffic deaths are related to alcohol consumption. The accident rate for drivers with a BAL of .2 is 100 times higher than that of nondrinking drivers.

6. *Don't mix drinks.* Switching drinks may lead to faster intoxication, but it also may lead to nausea. Diluting drinks with water slows down absorption, but carbonated beverages and sweet syrups speed it up. Equally as important, do not mix alcohol

and other drugs. Alcohol interacts with most drugs to make the effect more potent, but the interaction may be deadly.

Does this position say to adolescents, "You are going to drink anyway—so here's how"? Not really. Rather, the position recognizes that experimental and casual use of alcohol is a normal part of the contemporary adolescent scene, and, that being so, we should at least provide guidelines on how to respond intelligently. Indeed we might tie such an approach with attempts to discourage excessive drinking in teens, much in the same way we should discourage excessive drinking in adults.

Whether or not a given pattern of alcohol or drug education is effective depends, first, on the group of adolescents at which it is being aimed and, second, on the goals that are used to determine success. No single approach has been shown to be effective with all students. Each of the approaches described above may be useful for some subgroups of teenagers. Thus, although fear-induction is not a generally effective approach, it may work for some learners.

SUMMARY

Of all the problem areas in the study of adolescent development in contemporary society, few raise as much concern among parents and practitioners as the widespread use of alcohol and drugs among today's young people. Current data about use and abuse of alcohol and drugs among high school seniors has a bit of the character of a "good news-bad news" story. The good news is that drug use has apparently peaked and is now in a period of decline. The bad news is that use of illicit drugs is still widespread and alcohol consumption continues at very high rates.

Primary contributors to the use of drugs and alcohol by adolescents are peers and personal perceptions of drug and alcohol use as adult activities. Peer groups have the capability to bring to bear intense pressure to conform and to use drugs. The more widely drugs are used in an adolescent's peer group, the more likely that individual adolescent is to initiate use of a drug. Conversely, the more an adolescent identifies with a drug free or relatively drug free group the less likely he or she is to initiate drug taking activities. The family and home environment can also have a significant impact on adolescents' decisions to or not to try drugs. Adolescents from homes that are warm and caring, that are supportive and cohesive are much less likely to try drugs, and if they try, are less likely to continue their use. Adolescents from homes which lack cohesion, warmth, and support are likely to turn to peer groups for support and willingly pay the price of conformity.

Media play uncertain roles in adolescents' decisions to use or not to use drugs and alcohol or to smoke. On the one hand, public service announcements are shown which encourage adolescents to say "no" to drugs. But, the effect may be countered by media celebrities who openly advocate use of drugs, alcohol, and smoking.

Drug and alcohol education have not been overly successful. In part, their lack of success may be attributed to poor curricula and in part to unrealistic goals. Any successful program of drug and alcohol education must deal with information about drugs and alcohol in an open and honest manner. But, information about drugs should not be taught without dealing with young people's feelings about drugs and what roles drugs play in their own lives. Drug educators need to help young peole deal with their ambivalent feelings about using drugs. Often young people will admit to curiosity about drugs as well as fear of using drugs and getting caught. They also fear getting addicted to drugs but also fear exclusion from the peer group. Young people need a place to voice those fears. When they do they are often surprised to find that others in the group share their same feelings but were afraid to voice their own opinion for fear of being different. Drug and alcohol education should help young people plan strategies for dealing with pressures to try drugs. Role playing and practice can be beneficial.

Drug and alcohol use remain significant physical and psychological health problems among American youths. Too often communities would rather pretend that the problem does not exist in their home town. If parents admit that there is widespread use of drugs they are often reluctant to admit to the possibility that their own child is involved. Worse still, some parents in an attempt to "help" the social life of their teen child, provide alcohol for their child's party or permit alcohol to be brought in. Again, too many adults see alcohol as harmless and not as a dangerous drug, especially when misused.

INTELLECTUAL
GROWTH
6 AND DEVELOPMENT

Beyond adjusting to the major changes in their physical self, young people must also deal with new abilities to think about their world. The ways in which adolescents think about their world is a function of not only their general intellectual capability but also of their manner of thinking and processing information. Differences among individuals in general intellectual capabilities are often equated with differences in intelligence. This view is, however, misleading. While general intellectual abilities may play an important role in the individual's overall ability to deal with his or her environment, the way in which the person interacts purposefully with his or her environment is really the result of a complex array of personal preferences and cognitive strategies. Adolescence is particularly marked by the emergence of abstract thinking and reasoning skills.

Psychological models of human thinking are described as human *information processing* theories. In an information processing model, the human is seen as taking information into the "system" through a set of sensory mechanisms and registers. These sensory registers transfer information quickly to *short-term memory*. Short-term memory, or immediate memory is, as the name implies, used for storing information temporarily. If information in short-term memory is not used quickly, it is lost. When you have looked up a telephone number and forgotten it by the time you began dialing you have experienced the limits of short term memory. Short-term memory is also limited in size. One can hold only a limited number of pieces of information in short-term memory at a given time. Among adolescents and adults that limit is about seven units. Hence, psychologists often talk about the "magic number 7, plus or minus 2" to describe the limits of short-term memory (Miller, 1956). Some of the limits of short-term memory can be overridden by rehearsing the information and through use of memory devices.

Since short-term memory is temporary, information must be transferred from short-term memory into *long-term memory.* Once information is lodged in long-term memory it is there permanently. Our inability to remember information from long ago is not a result of its disappearance. Instead, it is the failure to recall results from our inability to "find" the information. It is also likely that information held in long-term memory is organized and structured in ways that permit us to access that information when it is needed. When new information is entered into long-term memory, it is incorporated within and related to existing information (Ausubel, 1963, 1967).

The monitoring of the flow of information into and out of short-term and long-term memory is managed by a series of *control processes* (Atkinson & Shiffrin, 1968). These control processes include general intellectual ability as well as internal biases in the individual intellectual system. Individual preferences for patterns of learning, for dealing with information, and for understanding the environment all alter the flow of information within the information processing system. During adolescence, new controls in the flow of information emerge. Adolescents see their world in new ways. They consider new possibilities. They prefer to deal with new forms of questions. Their thinking becomes more adultlike and they are able to deal with abstractions. As adolescents recognize these new talents, they must be integrated into their sense of self as an intelligent being.

Historically, there have been two general ways of looking at intellectual or cognitive growth in adolescence. The first is the more traditional view. It encompasses intellectual growth within the assessment of intellectual ability as measured through formalized testing. The use of standardized tests of intelligence continues to be a focus of controversy, particularly with reference to the use of intelligence tests in selecting people for educational or employment programs. The second draws on more recent theories of cognitive development, especially those which build on the important work of Jean Piaget and Barbel Inhelder. Both approaches are relevant since they reflect the complex nature of cognitive development.

TESTS OF INTELLECTUAL ABILITY

Toward the end of the last century, Alfred Binet and Theodore Simon were commissioned by the French government to develop a test to screen "feeble-minded" students who would benefit from special training. It was felt that without a scientific assessment technique teachers might use such special classes as a way of eliminating troublemakers from the class. It was (and still is) not uncommon for a teacher to refer a rowdy but bright troublemaker and keep a quiet but intellectually retarded student. A more objective procedure was needed. To avoid teacher bias in the selection of students for special classes, Binet developed a screening device known commonly as the intelligence test.

The Binet Test

Binet and Simon studied the behavior of children in a wide variety of problem tasks. Through astute observation Binet and Simon found that the developmental characteristics of certain tasks made them useful in differentiating intellectually retarded or intellectually precocious children from average children. Later, *relative* intellectual status, as measured by the Binet-Simon Test, was indicated by an *Intelligence Quotient* (IQ), or the ratio of a child's *Mental Age* (MA) to his *Chronological Age* (CA) multiplied by 100. Chronological age was simply the age of the child in months, and mental age was the age at which an "average" child scores as the testee did. If, for example, a testee scored as high as an average child of 12 years 3 months, the testee's MA would be 147 months. If that testee was a girl whose CA was 10 years 3 months, or 123 months, her IQ—equal to her MA (147 months) divided by her CA (123 months) times 100—would be 119. In such a case, the girl would be labeled as intellectually above average. If, on the other hand, the same girl was found to have an MA of a child 7 years 6 months, she would be labeled as intellectually below average, with an IQ of 73. If her MA equalled her CA, the result would be an IQ of 100, the index of average intelligence. The ratio is multiplied by 100 solely to remove the decimal. Imagine having an IQ of 1.15.

The Binet tests were adapted for use in America by Lewis Terman and Maude Merrill at Stanford University. The result, the Stanford-Binet, is still one of the two predominant tests of individual intellectual ability. The other test, the Wechsler Intelligence Scale for Children (WISC), and its adult version, the Wechsler Adult Intelligence Scale (WAIS), use a somewhat different testing format, but the intent is the same: a variety of tasks of differing difficulty define a testee's relative intellectual performance. Although many still call the score from such a test an "IQ," that name is not really accurate. For a variety of reasons, the IQ per se was found to be an inadequate index of intellectual performance. The IQ has been replaced by a standardized index that reflects an individual's relative standing within a distribution of people of the same CA. Because the distribution of intelligence-test scores is essentially normal (with a small discrepancy in the lower end of the scale), we are able to tell approximately what percentage of the population lies above or below a given intelligence test score. Figure 6–1 shows the distribution of intelligence-test scores in the population as a whole. A little more than two-thirds of the people tested with the Standford-Binet will have intelligence-test scores between 84 and 116. About 2 percent have scores higher than 132, and about 2 percent have scores lower than 68. Statistically, only one person in 1,000 scores 148 or above, and only one scores 52 or below.

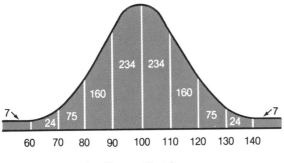

60   70   80   90   100   110   120   130   140

Intelligence-Test Scores

Figure 6–1 Expected distribution of 1,000 scores on a standard test of intelligence.

Group Versus Individual Tests

Although most people have taken some form of intelligence test, they may not have taken an individual test. Rather, they have taken a group test, in which they were given a test booklet and a response sheet to complete, very likely in a large auditorium or classroom. The purpose of a group test is to approximate the scores obtained on individual tests. Group tests are considerably more efficient and less expensive than individual tests, but a practitioner should be very careful about equating the two. The individual examination provides considerably more diagnostic information. An individual test should be administered only by a qualified psychometrist who is able to provide more than a single number, the test score, at the end of the testing session. Sometimes, however, psychometrists do not provide additional information; in those cases the teacher or practitioner should feel free to ask for more information.

What is it that intelligence tests are supposed to measure? I have tried to refrain from equating intelligence with intelligence test scores. However, the famous psychological historian E. G. Boring (1923) is credited with saying that intelligence is what the intelligence test measures. What Boring meant was that we define a psychological trait in terms of the way we measure it. Unfortunately his definition avoids the question of what is being measured and what it means to be intelligent.

VIGNETTE 6–1
A TEST OF INTELLIGENCE

Every so often a popular magazine like Reader's Digest *prints a short test that they claim to be a test of intellectual ability. Whether these tests would stand up under scientific scrutiny is not the question. The tests are challenging and use items that are common to group tests of intelligence. Notice the types of questions that are asked, and as you try to answer the questions, consider how you solve the problems.*

Source: "Are You A Genius?" *Reader's Digest 114*
(April 1979): 96–98. Reprinted by permission of Mensa.

You're smart, but are you brainy enough to qualify for Mensa, the international organization whose only requirement for membership is an I.Q. in the "genius" range? *The Reader's Digest* first asked that question in January 1974 with a quiz similar to the one that follows. Mensa subsequently received over 70,000 letters from Digest readers. Of those hopefuls, over two percent became eligible for membership. To see if *you* belong among the intellectual elite, take this test. Be sure to time yourself; there are bonus points for finishing in less than 15, 20 or 25 minutes.

1. Which of the lower boxes best completes the series on the top?

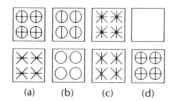

(a)   (b)   (c)   (d)

2. I am a man. If Larry's son is my son's father; what relationship am to Larry?

(a) His grandfather   (d) His grandson
(b) His father   (e) I am Larry
(c) His son   (f) His uncle

3. Which word does not belong in the following group?

(a) Knife   (d) Feather
(b) Swan   (e) Lovely
(c) Smile   (f) Thought

4. Which two shapes below represent mirror images of the same shape?

(a)   (b)   (c)   (d)   (e)

5. What number comes next in this series?

$$9, 16, 25, 36, \ldots$$

6. Complete this analogy with a five-letter word ending with the letter "H." High is to low as sky is to ----H.

7. In the box below, a rule of arithmetic applies across and down the box so that two of the numbers in a line produce the third. What is the missing number?

$$
\begin{array}{ccc}
6 & 2 & 4 \\
2 & ? & 0 \\
4 & 0 & 4
\end{array}
$$

8. Complete this analogy with a seven-letter word ending with the letter "T." Potential is to actual as future is to ------T.

9. In the group below, find the two words whose meanings do not belong with the others.

(a) glue   (d) nail
(b) sieve   (e) string
(c) buzz saw   (f) paper clip

10. Mountain is to land as whirlpool is to:

(a) forest   (d) sky
(b) wet   (e) shower
(c) sea

11. Find the number that logically completes the series:

$$2, 3, 5, 9, 17, \ldots$$

12. Two of the shapes below represent mirror images of the same shape. Which are they?

(a)   (b)   (c)   (d)

13. Statistics indicate that men drivers are involved in more accidents than women drivers. The only conclusion that can certainly be drawn is that:

(a) Male chauvinists are wrong, as usual, about women's abilities.
(b) Men are actually better drivers but drive more frequently.
(c) Men and women drive equally well, but men log more total mileage.
(d) Most truck drivers are men.
(e) There is not enough information to justify a conclusion.

14. In the box below, a rule of arithmetic applies across and down the box so that two of the numbers in a line produce the third. What is the missing number?

6	2	12
4	5	20
24	10	?

15. If $A \times B = 24$, $C \times D = 32$, $B \times D = 48$ and $B \times C = 24$, what does $A \times B \times C \times D$ equal?

(a) 480   (c) 744   (e) 824
(b) 576   (d) 768

16. Which of the four lower sections best completes the series on the top?

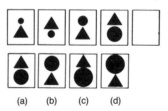

(a)   (b)   (c)   (d)

17. Which word does not belong in this group?

(a) microscope   (b) magnifying glass
(c) microphone   (d) telescope
(e) telegraph

18. Find the two words nearest in meaning to each other.

(a) beam   (d) ray
(b) lump   (e) collection
(c) giggle

19. If Jim turns right *or* left at the stop sign he will run out of gas before he reaches a service station. He has already gone too far past a service station to return before he runs out of gas. He does not see a service station ahead. Only one of the following statement can be positively deduced:

(a) He may run out of gas.
(b) He will run out of gas.
(c) He should not have taken this route.
(d) He is lost.
(e) He should turn right at the stop sign.
(f) He should turn left at the stop sign.

20. Complete the following analogy:

(a) + − 0 are to:

(a) + −0   (c) − + 0 (e) + + 0
(b) 0 + −   (d) 0 − +

ANSWERS

(1) C. Omit the horizontal line in the asterisk, as it was omitted in the circle. (2) C. (3) E. The other words are nouns. (4) D and E. (5) 49; 9 is 3 squared, 16 is 4 squared, 25 is 5 squared, and so on. Also, 9 + 7 = 16, 16 + 9 = 25, 25 + 11 = 36, and so on. (6) Earth. (7) 2. In each vertical and horizontal row, the second number is subtracted from the first. (8) Present. (9) B and C. All the others hold things together. (10) C. A whirlpool is part of the sea as a mountain is part of land. (11) 33. The difference between the numbers is progressively multiplied by 2. (1) B and D. (13) E. (14) 240. (24 × 10 and 12 × 20 both equal 240). (15) 768. It is not necessary to determine the values of A, B, C, D. Simply multiply 24 × 32. (16) D. The ball gets larger in each box, while the triangle remains the same size, and the ball and the triangle keep alternating positions. (17) E. The others are all things that increase images or sounds. (18) A and D are synonyms. (19) A. Just the fact that Jim can't see a service station ahead doesn't mean there isn't one. (20) C. Positive and minus change positions; neutral stays in the same place.

SCORING

Give yourself one point for each correct answer. You receive an additional five points if you finished the test in less than 15 minutes, three points if you finished in less than 20 minutes, and two points if you finished in less than 25 minutes.

If you scored:

- 20–25 points: you are extremely intelligent—a perfect candidate for Mensa.
- 15–19 points: This should put you in the higher percentiles of the population—definitely a Mensa candidate.
- 10–14 points: Nothing to be ashamed of—a most respectable score. You should probably try the complete, standard Mensa test.
- Fewer than 15 points: forget about joining Mensa, but don't stew about it. You may just be having a bad day. Some of the most successful writers, businessmen, artists, and other famous people don't have exceptionally high I.Q.'s either.

What's the verdict? If you think you may be Mensa material, or you'd like to receive membership information, write to Mensa, Dept. D.C. 1701 W. Third St., Brooklyn, N.Y. 11223.

Boring's definition is not terribly satisfying. But, it does reflect a sense that many share, that scores on a test of intelligence are a major indicator of academic or intellectual potential. The definition of "intelligence" sometimes depends upon whom is asked. When "experts" are asked to define intelligence, they are apt to focus on abstract thinking, problem solving and a capacity to acquire knowledge (Snyderman & Rothman, 1987). Lay people, on the other hand, focus more on what might be described as "social intelligence" and on practical problem solving (Sternberg, 1982; Sternberg, Conway, Ketron & Bernstein, 1981). Further, what constitutes intelligent behavior in one culture may not be seen as intelligent in another.

Perhaps the most widely used definition of intelligence is the one offered by Wechsler (1958):

> Intelligence is the aggregate or global capacity of the individual to act purposefully, to think rationally and to deal effectively with his environment. It is global because it is composed of abilities which, though not entirely independent, are qualitatively differentiable. By measurement of these abilities, we ultimately evaluate intelligence. (p. 7)

The assessment of intelligence would thus be accomplished by using a variety of measures intended to evaluate purposeful or adaptive thinking. Intelligence in this sense is seen as a composite of abilities, a general intellectual capacity.

In contrast, some theorists argue that intelligence must be defined in light of specific intellectual abilities. The theorist who paved the way for this point of view was L. L. Thurstone (1938), who proposed that there were seven "primary mental abilities" and that descriptions of intellectual ability should reflect relative standing in all forms of ability rather than in terms of a global ability.

J. P. Guilford extended the logic of the multifactor model of intelligence by proposing that intelligence is described by the intersection of the type of *content* of the problem posed, the *mental operation* required to solve the problem, and the *product,* or type of response demanded. Each dimension of the task was further divided into smaller units. By combining the three dimensions which each set of units. Guilford identified and labeled 120 separate intellectual abilities. He envisioned the "structure" of intellect as a box depicted in Figure 6–2.

Among Guilford's better-known distinctions was the difference between *convergent* and *divergent* thinking. According to Guilford, most educational and psychological tests demand convergent thinking, in which there is a single clearly correct answer to a problem. (For example, What are the first three elements in the periodic chart?) However, very little testing is directed at divergent thinking, which allows and encourages multiple possibilities for the same question. (How many ways can you use a shoe?) Many writers believe that divergent thinking is basic to creative thinking and originality. We will give more attention to creative thinking later in the chapter.

Sternberg (1984) offers a somewhat different view of the structure of intelligence in which intelligence testing should be guided by a three-fold view of intelligence. Intelligence, in his view, is a combined result of internal cognitive processes, abilities to analyze and respond to problems, and abilities to behave intelligently in everyday settings. In Sternberg's view, intelligence involves more than possessing abilities. It includes the individual's abilities to muster those resources to deal with a variety of problem tasks, including common social tasks. Intelligence is not a single, unitary trait. Intelligence is a result of a complex array of abilities. Unlike Guilford, however, Sternberg more realistically accepts the fact that these multiple abilities are highly interrelated.

Figure 6–2 Guilford's structure of the intellect. *Source:* J. P. Guilford. "Three Faces of Intellect," *American Psychologist 14* (1959): 470. Copyright 1959 by the American Psychological Association. Reprinted by permission.

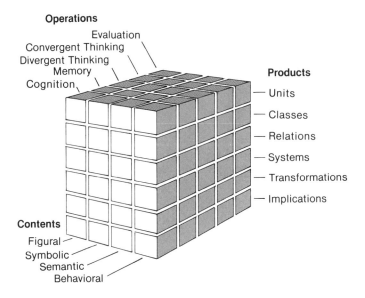

Cultural Bias

Some critics have argued that tests of intelligence are "culturally biased" and are questionable indicators of intellectual abilities, especially for minorities whose language and cultural base may be incompatible with the demands of the test. Such critics point to specific items as discriminatory or racist. One of the items on a WAIS subtest is "Who was Goethe?" It may be argued that this item is biased toward middle- or upper-class youths, who have a greater chance of hearing about Goethe. On the other hand, advocates of intelligence testing argue that the information is generally available and that the bright youth will encounter it regardless of social class. And the bright youth will likely recall it at a later time. Others point to specific items that reflect middle-class value systems. For example, one item from the Stanford-Binet test is "What is the thing to do when you are on you way to school and see that you are in danger of being late?" Although the item is intended to measure "comprehension," knowledge of the correct answer implies adherence to a value system that emphasizes punctuality.

The selection of one or two items from a test of mental ability to demonstrate cultural bias may be misleading. The tests are made up of a variety of items that are meant to sample intelligence across many areas. However, items for an intelligence test are deliberately chosen from those skills and abilities that are favored by the dominant culture. Because the tests are designed to sort those who will do well or poorly in that dominant culture, they are by definition culturally biased.

Culture-Fair Tests

Some test makers have tried to develop culture-fair tests of mental ability—that is, tests that assess intelligence with items that have little or no inherently culture-biased material. Typical items on these tests are mazes or figure problems that are said to require fewer language skills. The logic is that if differences in language based on ethnic background are eliminated, then the cultural bias will also be removed. Tests such as the Culture Fair Intelligence Test (Cattell & Cattell, 1959) and the Raven's Progressive Matrices (Raven, 1960) are said to measure general mental ability without bias stemming from cultural or language differences.

The Growth of Intelligence

Prior to adolescence, scores on intelligence tests are highly variable. The earlier individuals are tested, the less stable are their scores. As children reach adolescence, however, their relative position in the intelligence test distribution begins to stabilize (Bayley, 1965). That is, although intellectual ability may continue to grow during and after adolescence, relative standing in the mental ability distribution will remain about the same. Selective individual cases may show dramatic change in intellectual growth during adolescence, but the overall pattern of cases does not.

As students progress through high school, achievement tests and tests of intellectual ability are more likely to measure abstract knowledge. (Arthur Grace/Stock, Boston)

One popular notion regarding intelligence is that intellectual growth peaks during late adolescence and from that point continually declines through adulthood. This idea has its roots in a study reported by Wechsler (1958). Wechsler reported data taken from a cross-sectional study of intelligence in which the best average performance at the time of testing was shown by testees aged 20 and 21. However, although the data for the 50-year-olds and the 20-year-olds were from the same test, the differences in performance may have resulted from very different experiences. For example, assume that the tests were given in 1950. In 1950 nearly 60 percent of 17-year-olds graduated from high school, whereas in 1920 (when the 47-year-olds were 17) only about 15 percent of 17-year-olds did so (Golladay, 1977). Thus the differences in performance were not necessarily a result of age. The same problem might occur in a contemporary study, because the 20-year-olds of 1950 would be compared with students of the 1970s, who are even more likely to have completed high school. Curiously, though, a national study of youths in the late 1960s found that overall students were scoring somewhat lower on Wechsler tests of intelligence than their 1949 counterparts (Scanlon, 1973).

When data from cross-sectional studies are compared to those from longitudinal studies, very different interpretations emerge. In one study, for example, Owens (1953) retested a group of men who had taken an intelligence test in 1917 as college freshmen. He retested those same men again 10 years later (Owens, 1966). Rather than showing the drop in intellectual performance anticipated by the Wechsler study, Owens's data showed a net increase in performance from age 17 to age 50. The largest gains were in general verbal ability and general reasoning. Performance in numerical ability showed a decline. Bayley (1965) also found a leveling off in intellectual growth after adolescence but did observe a steady increase over adulthood. Further clarification is offered by the study of Schaie and Strother (1968), who found that gain or decline in intellectual abilities, whether reviewed in longitudinal or cross-sectional studies, varies with the type of task used.

Although there is overall stability in patterns of intellectual growth, there are differences among individuals. Some adolescents will show much larger gains during their teen years than others. Those who show the larger increases often show higher levels of curiosity and higher motivation to achieve. Those who show a decrement in performance are more likely to be rated as passive (Kagan et al., 1958).

There is little doubt that the home environment in which a child or adolescent is raised has a significant impact on the development of intelligence. It is unclear, however, how much we are able to alter intellectual growth by programs of intervention. Some studies would lead us to believe that early and intensive intervention has a major impact on socially induced retardation (Heber & Dever, 1970), but the results of those studies are not well documented. Also, there is little research on attempts to alter intellectual development by programs of intervention during adolescence. Studies such as those by Heber indicate, however, that intellectual growth is not unchangeable or irredeemable.

Ethnic Differences

Perhaps the most inflammatory topic associated with the measurement and study of intelligence is the question of ethnic and socioeconomic differences in performance on traditional tests of intelligence. Researchers have repeatedly reported a difference of 10 to 20 intelligence-test points between black and white Americans (Backman, 1972; Jensen, 1969, 1972; Scanlon, 1973). Similar differences are reported between lower-income and middle-income children and youths (Backman, 1972; Herrnstein, 1971; Scanlon, 1973). You should remember that the researchers are reporting *averages*. Because a person is black does not mean that his intelligence is 15 points lower than a white person's. Nor does reporting such differences explain why they occur.

Arthur Jensen (1969, 1972) has proposed that 80 percent of the *variability* in intelligence is determined genetically and, further, that the difference in intellectual performance between whites and blacks is genetically determined. Jensen's arguments are based on (1) the premise that certain psychological characteristics can have genetic components and (2) the fact that differences in racial characteristics are genetic. Herrnstein (1972) offered a slightly modified version of this argument to account for intelligence score differences between lower- and middle-income populations. Herrnstein suggested that the genetic pool for the lower-income population has been depleted over generations as the more intelligent people move vertically through the social class structure and leave the lower-income group a genetically inferior pool.

Not all researchers agree with the genetic hypothesis. A variety of alternative explanations have been offered to explain the differences in performance on tests of intelligence. Some suggest that the differences are the result of bias in the testing situation, nutritional deficiencies, racist characteristics of the test, educational differences, ethnic attitudes, linguistic patterns, or some combination of these (Gordon, 1973). The evidence is simply not conclusively favorable to the genetic hypothesis.

The difference in the distribution of scores on tests of intelligence for ethnic groups has serious educational ramifications. Because the distribution of scores among black children and youths is below that of their white peers, they are six times more likely to be assigned to classes for the retarded (Shuey, 1966) if intelligence tests are used as the primary selection criterion. The problem is not resolved simply by dismissing the intelligence test as irrelevant or racist. Black youths must still be provided with a quality education, and, at this point at least, the characteristics of the predominant educational pattern are not compatible with their needs.

Perhaps the most harmful result of the misunderstanding of group differences in intelligence or achievement is that some people fail to recognize that the differences reflect *averages.* Differences in group means tell us little about the ways in which we are to deal with individual differences within the groups. Because we may find group differences between blacks and whites, males and females, northerners and southerners, or any other groups on an educational or psychological measure, we are not justified in applying different standards to the entire population of people.

PIAGET'S THEORY OF COGNITIVE DEVELOPMENT

An alternate model of intellectual growth and development to that represented by standardized tests of intelligence is the model of conceptual development described by Jean Piaget. To Piaget, it is not enough to say that adolescents score higher on tests of intelligence than younger children simply because they have had more learning and experience. Not only do adolescents know *more*, their knowledge is qualitatively different from children's. In some sense this shift is represented in standard tests of intelligence by a qualitative shift in the types of questions asked as the individual matures. Advanced questions on these tests usually require abstract thinking.

To Piaget, however, the shift in thought was more than just coincidental. The shift from concrete thought to abstract thought is the hallmark of adolescent cognitive development. Piaget referred to the new found intellectual ability of adolescence as *formal operational thinking* and believed it represented the culmination of stages of cognitive develoment that begin in infancy. With the change, the adolescent is able to think beyond the present, to consider the abstract, and to think of alternate possibilities beyond those immediately available.

Piaget's theory of cognitive development (Piaget, 1970; Inhelder & Piaget, 1958) was built on certain assumptions of the nature and purpose of thinking. It is sometimes helpful to know that Piaget was trained as a biologist and that he drew on the basic adaptive principles of homeostasis—the body's tendency to return to stable equilibrium after a disruption—to represent human intellectual adaptability.

The central element in Piaget's theory of conceptual growth is the schema, or mental structure. A schema is a collection of bits of knowledge in an organized pattern that aids in our interpretation of our environment. As collections of knowledge, however,

Cognitive development is a lifelong developmental process. Even young children enjoy solving problems. (© Susan Lapides)

schema are not simply a conglomeration of facts. Rather, schema also contain strategies for analyzing and evaluating information. The backgammon player, for example, possesses not only a knowledge of basic rules of the game, but also flexible, adaptive strategies for playing the game. In the same way mental structures serve to guide our adaptive behavior when we encounter new problems. In Piaget's terms, mental development results from the individuals interacting with and adapting to their environment. Although a strong genetic component of mental development influences the patterns of cognitive growth, intellectual growth is a result of both maturation *and* environment.

The child progresses through the course of developing mental structures by means of experiences that lead to imbalance in mental structures, or in Piaget's terms disequilibrium, and by the adaptive responses necessary to achieve balance or equilibrium. As the child has more adaptive experiences, the mental structures become more complex and more flexible. In adapting to disequilibrium, the individual draws on the processes of *accommodation* and *assimiliation*. That is, when people recognize new information in their environment, their schema are unsettled. To resolve the imbalance, a learner may either alter the cognitive schema to be compatible with the new information (accommodation) or alter the perception to be compatible with already existing mental structures (assimilation).

Consider the following: Jack is an adolescent boy who has been raised in a Protestant household. He was asked by his Roman Catholic girlfriend to go to church with her one Sunday. Jack agreed, though with some anxiety, because he had never been to a Catholic church before and he was unsure about what would happen. The day arrived and Jack escorted his girlfriend to her church. As the service progressed Jack was surprised to find that, although there were differences, there were also common features between his own and his girlfriend's religious services. Finally, the service progressed to a prayer that Jack knew from his own religious training. The prayer is common to Christian religions. Jack joined in and felt reasonably comfortable in participating because, with the exception of the substitution of "trespass" for "debts," the prayer seemed the same. Suddenly, however, Jack realized he was continuing with the prayer as he knew it while everyone else had stopped. Jack was noticeably embarrassed but his girlfriend told him not to worry.

What happened? In Piagetian terms, Jack was presented with a problem to which he needed to respond. As he assessed the problem he found common elements and applied a schema he already possessed. What Jack did not know was that the prayer ending he was familiar with did not occur immediately in the Catholic service. His experience, although momentarily embarrassing, led to an alteration and refinement of his schema. The application of his existing mental structures to the problem is an example of assimilation. The modification of the structure is an example of accommodation.

It is not necessary to actually experience an event to modify a cognitive schema. The act of reading about a problem and someone else's solution may alter your mental structure. That is, you accommodate your schema to incorporate new information by indirect or vicarious experience. By most definitions learning occurs only under conditions of accommodation. It would, however, be misleading for you to infer that all assimilation is bad. In many cases we assimilate new information in an attempt to keep things simple.

This is an important point in Piaget's theory. For accommodation to occur, something must cause disequilibrium in your current schema. As an adaptive learner you try to correct this imbalance. The entire course of cognitive growth is thus marked by a series of problems that cause disequilibrium and by attempts to reestablish equilibrium through assimilation and accommodation.

Stages of Development

According to Piaget, intelligence progresses from infancy to adulthood through an *invariant* sequence of four cognitive stages. To say that we progress through stages of intellectual development means that to reach adult levels of functioning, we must first go through the earlier stages. The order of progression through the stages is invariant: each of us goes through them in the same order although we may go through them at a different rate.

At birth children operate with sensorimotor schema, which are knowledge systems based on sensations gained first by the infant's reflexive or random movements. The infant's world is composed of those things that can be sucked, smelled, seen, or touched. Knowledge of the environment is based on nonverbal responses and is linked to the immediate physical reality. The infant who shakes a rattle associates the physical movement with the noise of the rattle. If you observe babies, you will notice that initially their movements are not well differentiated. They move everything. As they mature, however, their schema become more refined and their behavior more precise. Knowledge, however, remains tied to the immediate physical reality of a setting. In Piaget's terms, if a stimulus is not in the immediate physical environment of an infant, it does not exist for that infant. "Out of sight, out of mind" defines sensorimotor thinking.

At around two years of age, the child begins to use preoperational, or *intuitive,* thought. By this stage children recognize that something exists even when it is not within sight or touch. However, if there is an alteration of the perceptual character of their environment, they presume the object has changed. The prime characteristic of this stage of cognitive development is the formation of images. Children's conception of the world around them is based largely on perceptual images. However, the child also develops language skills during this time. During the next few years children acquire an extraordinary vocabulary and ability to produce syntax. However, their schema are still relatively primitive.

Children at sensorimotor and preoperational levels of thinking are highly *egocentric.* As Piaget used the term, egocentrism refers to the child's assumption that his or her view of reality is the view that everyone shares. The child is unable to conceive of an alternate view of reality. If you ask an 18-month-old girl to show you a picture she has drawn, she is most likely to show you the back of the picture while she looks at the front (Flavell, 1977). The child assumes that if she can see it, so can you.

Egocentrism continues into the intuitive stage of thinking. The world of preoperational children is still perceptually bound. If their perception of an object is altered, they presume the object is altered. In perhaps the best-known task developed by Piaget, equal amounts of liquid are poured into two identical beakers. The liquid from one beaker is then transferred to a tall, thin beaker, and the child is asked whether the amounts are still the same or whether they are different. Preoperational children will answer that they are no longer the same, that the tall, thin beaker has "more." [Wadsworth (1978) describes a variety of such tasks for interested readers.]

As children pass to the next cognitive stage, they no longer respond that the tall, thin beaker has "more." Rather, they will recognize that, although the shape has been altered, the quantity has not. They are able to *conserve* their schema even when what they see changes form. However, they can manipulate schema only with concrete, hands-on referents. They are working with *concrete operational schema.*

Children typically make the transition at around ages six to eight, although some will not make it until somewhat later. During the concrete operational stage the learner is capable of solving problems as long as there is a concrete referent. This does not mean that the concrete operational person lacks flexibility. The individual is able to generalize operations across a wide variety of settings and through various alterations. The concrete operational person, however, *cannot* relate to problems that require abstract referrents. They are unable to handle problems requiring formal, symbolic logic.

During the concrete stage the individual sees the world in literal, concrete terms. Given a problem in which a series of red and white liquids are mixed, the concrete operational child will consistently expect that the result will be pink. If, however, the result of one combination of red (iodine) and white (starch) liquids is blue liquid, the child is now faced with an exception to the rule. A concrete operational child, when asked how this could be, is apt to answer "magic." Their literal system does not have room for qualifiers such as "Red and white liquids *usually* yield pink, *but some* red and white liquids yield other colors."

During adolescence the individual shifts from depending on concrete operational schema to using *formal operational schema*. Formal operational thought represents the final stage of intellectual development in Piaget's terms. The formal operational thinker is able to conceive of problems on an abstract level, can handle propositional logic, and can engage in hypothetical thinking, considering "what might be" or "what would happen if...." Whereas the concrete operational child's thought is dominated by the "real" world, the physical world is only one aspect of the formal operational child's experience. Indeed, Inhelder and Piaget (1958) found that for the formal operational adolescent, "reality is now secondary to possibility." Formal operational thinking permits the adolescent to make hypotheses, to consider radical alterations of their conceptual world, and to think about the implications of those changes.

When faced with a problem situation, concrete operational thinkers need familiar objects or real examples to relate to so that they can use the concrete, tangible properties of the objects to organize their world. Formal operational thinkers, on the other hand, are able to incorporate abstract relationships into the organization of their conceptual

The rapid growth of cognitive abilities during adolescence often leads to heightened interest in new concepts. (Owen Franken/Stock, Boston)

world. They are not tied to the physical reality in their consideration of possibilities. They are also able to use symbols to represent their thoughts.

One 16-year-old girl was intrigued by the fact that while most other materials contract when changing from liquid to solid, water acts in the opposite fashion. That is, as water turns to ice, it expands. The more she thought about this, the more she began to consider the ramifications for the earth if water acted as other materials do. She was able to ask the question "What if water contracted and got more dense when it froze?" By doing so she was able to project how this would change the balance of nature.

This ability to conceive of *what might be* is an essential characteristic of formal operational thought. The formal thinking adolescent is not constrained by reality. Whereas concrete operational thinkers see only concrete reality, formal operational adolescents see reality as but one aspect of the total situation and are capable of assessing or predicting what would happen if reality were altered. Science fiction takes on a new meaning when young people consider alternate realities or alternate universes. Importantly, as adolescents enter formal thinking, they are able to consider possibilities from the perspective of an extended time frame. They are more able to see that events that are separated by time are connected. Even among formally operational adolescents, this ability is not fully developed and they are only marginally able to see that their present behaviors may have an impact on their lives 5, 10, or 15 years hence.

Time references are even more difficult for the concrete operational adolescent. Because young adolescents are restricted to the concrete, their thinking is anchored to the present. Their ability to think of cause-effect relationships over an extended period of time is limited. This inability applies both to historical sequences and futuristic projections. Helping the concrete operational adolescent recognize that antecedents to a historical event may have occurred several years earlier than the event itself is difficult. If seeing relationships between present behavior and future status is hard for the formally operational adolescent, it is nearly a foreign thought to the concrete operational adolescent. Parents, teachers, and counselors often warn a ninth-grader that she or he should study hard and get good grades since those grades will be important in three years when she or he wants to apply to college. Not infrequently, the adult is greeted with a look of cosmic disdain. To the young adolescent, three years may seem like an eternity away. They cannot conceive of the relationship between now and then. It is too remote. Part of the conflict in views of adults and adolescents may result from their very different perspectives of time. For the adults, three years is a very short time and the connectedness of events over such a short time frame is very real.

Adolescents who have reached a level of formal operational thinking are also able to understand the concept of "control." Suppose you ask an adolescent boy if he can demonstrate that water boils at 100° C. (Centigrade). The adolescent dutifully goes to the water faucet, gets a cup or so of water. When the water boils, he removes it and finds that the reading is 101.2° C. (You look over his shoulder to make sure that he does not "round off.") The young person tries again with a second pan of water, but this time he finds that the boiling point is 100.8° C. After five tries, he finds that the average is 100.9° C. He repeats this procedure with river water but finds that the boiling point is 101.4° C.

At this point, the adolescent is faced with a dilemma. The textbook says that water boils at 100° C., but his results do not agree. The reason for the discrepancy is that the young person is not taking into account the other variables that have an impact on the boiling temperature of water. A formal operational youth will recognize the problem and be able to create an experiment to demonstrate that, *other things being equal,* water boils at 100° C. That is, the student would use distilled water and test the boiling point at different levels of air pressure. A concrete operational youth, on the other hand, is unable to solve problems that require control of several variables. In looking at a problem, he is likely to use a trial-and-error approach or focus on the variable that he sees as important, ignoring all others.

Sieglar and Liebert (1975) provide an interesting task that examines thinking style. Please take time now to try to solve the problem. Ideally a tester would set up an electric train with the characteristics described in the problem and let you solve it by trying various combinations of switches. The strategy that you use to solve the problem would be important. Formal thinkers tend to solve the problem systematically, not at random. The most important problem for the formal thinker is not identifying the correct combination but determining *how* it works. Although concrete operational learners may "solve" a formal operational problem, they solve it by using concrete operational means or by trial and error (Herron, 1975, 1977) and are typically unable to explain how or

---

SIEGLAR PROBLEM

Imagine that you are running an electric train that is hooked up to three switches in front of you. Two of the three switches determine how fast the train will go. The way these two important switches are set—down and down, up and down, down and up, or up and up—will determine the speed of the train. The various combinations of positions are given below. Your task is to determine which combination of switches is important and how they work.

Switch 1	Switch 2	Switch 3	Train Goes
Up	Down	Down	Slow
Up	Up	Up	Not at all
Down	Down	Down	Fast
Up	Down	Up	Slow
Down	Up	Up	Slow
Down	Down	Up	Fast
Down	Up	Down	Slow
Up	Up	Down	Not at all

Which switches were important?

1 & 2   2 & 3   1 & 3

The way they worked was:

Source: R. S. Sieglar and R. M. Liebert, "Acquisition of Formal Scientific Reasoning by 10- and 13-Year-Olds: Designing a Factorial Experiment," *Developmental Psychology 11* (1975): 401–402. Copyright 1975 by the American Psychological Association. Reprinted by permission of the publisher and author.

why their solution works. The formal operational thinker can do both and, further, is able to generalize a principle gained from solving the problem to other problems. If you were unable to solve the electric train problem, does that mean that you are not formally operational? Not necessarily. One problem does not assess the total domain of formal thought. Further, people may achieve formal thought in one domain and not in another. It is a mistake to assume that a young person 14- or 15-years-old is consequently thinking on a formal level. It is reasonably clear that not all adolescents achieve formal thinking. Kohlberg and Gilligan (1971) found that only 45 percent of late adolescents were operating at that level, and Blasi and Hoeffel (1974) concluded that less than 50 percent of adolescents achieve formal operational thought. In addition, there is a sizable group of adults who do not display formal thought (Tomlinson-Keasey, 1972; Arlin, 1975).

It is an additional mistake to presume that a person who is formally operational in one area is formally operational in another. The young person who thinks abstractly in areas of math or science may think in concrete terms in history and literature. Another young person may operate in the opposite way. Even within an area we may find ourselves using formal thought in one situation and reverting to concrete thought in another, depending on our mood, the complexity of the situation, or some other factors.

Because adolescents may be operating on a formal level does not mean that they are immune to problems of egocentric thoughts. David Elkind (1967, 1978) notes that young people suffer from a new form of egocentrism. Although adolescents are more capable of understanding another's perception, they are still subject to assuming that the other person's perception is the same as their own. They are able to differentiate between their perceptions and others' perceptions of physical events, but they are less able to separate their perceptions of abstract features. For example, the adolescents assume that other people value certain features or items in the same way they do. They project any uncertainties that they hold about themselves to an *invisible audience* of others who feel the same way about them. Thus, if a young girl is nervous about a birthmark, she may feel that everyone notices it and thinks it (and she) is ugly. She may even refuse to believe that others do not care. Consider yourself. What would happen if you were in a grocery store and knocked over a dozen or so cans of soup. You probably would feel embarrassed, sure that everyone was thinking, "What a klutz!" You look around and find that very few people are paying any attention at all. You have just created a similar invisible audience. In the adolescent this amorphous "they" may have a profound impact. The plea that parents hear, "Everyone is doing it," may be another version of this phenomenon. Beyond the fact that these pleas are attempts to coerce parents into allowing them to conform, adolescents may see this "invisible crowd" as very real. They do not want to be isolated from others ("everyone") as different.

Sometimes adolescent egocentrism takes the form of zealous idealism. In their thoughts about society and a perfect world, adolescents may develop what they see as perfect answers to social injustice. They may be frustrated when they find that not everyone agrees with them or sees the possibility of same perfect reality.

This egocentrism of adolescence leads to a *personal fable.* In a personal fable an adolescent boy, for example, may see himself as unique and somehow immune from harm. In more dangerous cases this personal fable may lead to chance-taking behavior that is sometimes characteristic of young drivers. Basically the attitude reflected in the personal fable is "It can't happen to me!" Of course the adolescent does not have a corner on the personal fable market. Consider smokers who provide excuses for not quitting or auto drivers who fail to use seat belts. Egocentric behavior is seen at all ages, but this behavior emerges most profoundly during adolescence.

INDIVIDUAL DIFFERENCES

Gifted Adolescents

Some young people hold special talents and are described by adults as "gifted." Just what the term "gifted" means is not always clear but it is clear that some young people display exceptional talent at very early ages. Michaelangelo's talent was recognized and nurtured early by Lorenzo de'Medici, who was himself a gifted poet and politician. Albert Einstein wrote out the rudiments of his theory of relativity at the age of 12 in a letter to his uncle. At 15, Mozart had already completed 18 symphonies, two operettas, an opera, and numerous concertos.

Gifted adolescents are individuals who display some exceptional talent or promise in one or more areas, such as the arts, science, math, or leadership. Although the gifted do not necessarily score high on an intelligence test, a large proportion of those labeled as gifted perform well above the average on traditional measures of intelligence (Vernon, Abramson & Vernon, 1977). Not surprisingly, intellectually precocious youths typically excell on Piagetian measures of cognitive development (Keating, 1976). Intelligence, however, should not be the sole criterion by which we identify the gifted.

About 1921, Louis Terman identified 1,500 children whose intelligence test scores were in the range labeled "genius." For every thousand people in the population, only five would perform as well. Whether or not intelligence should serve as the primary characteristic of giftedness these children were certainly unusual. Terman followed the progress of these gifted individuals through their adult years.

In the original sample there were more males than females (857 to 671), and the discrepancy in performance between sexes was more apparent as the children grew older. One way to explain the difference is to suggest that at the time the sample was taken (and even currently) girls were systematically encouraged *not* to display marked intelligence and peer pressure to conform increased with age. In a sense society regards high IQ as better in boys than in girls.

The data from the Terman study are invaluable in dispelling common stereotypes of genius children. As a group the children were taller, heavier, stronger, earlier in arriving at sexual maturity, and more healthy than their average counterparts. Further, the gifted children rated high on what some have called "behavioral" intelligence. They were rated as more trustworthy and more honest (Terman, 1925, 1930).

By their mid-forties, the group had compiled an impressive list of accomplishments. Although Terman is quick to note that many nongeniuses make such achievements, the group was still exceptional. Of the sample, 70 percent finished college and 40 percent earned advanced degrees. The latter group was again disproportionately composed of males. It is also of interest that the death rate, rate of criminal behavior, and rate of alcoholism were very low. Emotional maladjustment was no more rare in the gifted group than in the population as a whole, but women in the sample suffered more than men (Terman & Oden, 1959).

A major study of mathematically and, more recently, verbally precocious youths is not being conducted at Johns Hopkins University (Stanley, Keating & Fox, 1974; Keating, 1976). Among the problems that such studies encounter is the adequate assessment of the gifted. Stanley (1976) reports a case of a sixth-grade girl who scored at the eleventh-grade level on a vocabulary test. She might have scored higher because she got every item on the test correct. Thus Stanley suggests we may need to assess the gifted youth with tests intended for adults.

Many of the intellectually precocious youths identified in the Johns Hopkins study are accelerated into college-level studies early. However, for those whose early college admission is inadvisable or not currently warranted, some curricular intervention is still indicated. Program planning for the intellectually precocious youth is necessary. Fox (1976) notes that, to be effective, individualized intervention requires both adequate assessment of individual strengths and development of programs that capitalize on and nourish those strengths. She suggests that although some educational bureaucracies may be reluctant to create unique educational experiences, the problems of assigning gifted children to advanced classes can be simplified if an individualized treatment plan (ITP) specifies what outcomes can be achieved by such intervention.

As in the Terman studies, the mathematically precocious youngsters are behaviorally more mature than their agemates. Psychologically they are confident and well adjusted, seeing themselves as intelligent, capable, adaptable, logical, honest, and clear thinking. The boys in the study are also more likely to see themselves as sarcastic, opinionated, and cynical (Haier & Denham, 1976). Many educators have negative attitudes toward the gifted, seeing them as argumentative, opinionated, and impatient. However, they are also likely to see the gifted as alert, clear thinking, and intelligent (Haier & Solano, 1976). Teachers who are unfamiliar with gifted children seem to hold more negative attitudes that those who are familiar with some.

Creativity

Educators are increasingly interested in the domain of creativity. This is in part a response to increased dissatisfaction with standard tests of intelligence and a feeling among many that creative learners are neglected in the schools. However, those who have tried to give a clear definition of creativity have found it even more difficult to define than intelligence. Wallach and Wing (1970) have gone so far as to suggest that we cannot explain what has happened with other psychological models of thinking. Crockenberg (1972) adds that we know relatively little about the antecedents to the creative process, especially among children and adolescents, and that measures of creativity lack validity.

Most conceptions of creativity are built in one way or another on the premise that creative individuals show a high level of flexibility in their thinking (Cattell, 1971). Creative people seem to be able to change direction or perspective in thought with ease

Adolescence may be a period of increased creative activity as the young person becomes capable of conceiving of new, untested patterns. (Jean-Claude Lejeune/Stock, Boston)

and view a problem or creative domain from multiple points equally well. They tend to think about problems from other than conventional positions. Most investigators concur with E. Paul Torrance (1966, 1972) that flexibility is the ability to "break mental sets." A mental set occurs when our pattern for thinking interferes with our solving a problem.

If you see the pattern of nine dots in Figure 6–3 as a square with implicit boundaries, you will have difficulty solving the problem. The ease with which you can "break set" reflects general flexibility in thought. The converse of flexibility is rigidity of thought or resistance to changing thought.

Torrance (1966) adds two more attributes of the creative person. In addition

Figure 6–3   Creativity problem.

•   •   •

•   •   •   **Problem:** Connect these nine points using four straight lines without lifting your pencil from the
•   •   •   paper and without retracing any line.

to flexibility, creative people tend to generate many ideas (fluency) and many unique and unusual ideas (originality). Some speculate that the ability to "break set" may be critical in the development of creativity. I would argue, however, that, irrespective of whether flexibility of thought leads to creative results, the ability to "break set" is a worthy educational goal in and of itself. To make "creativity" a criterion for school success may be equally as fallacious as making IQ gain a criterion for head-start programs. However, it may be more realistic to try to foster some behavior (for example, flexibility) that is related to creativity. Torrance has suggested that the teacher or parent who wishes to encourage creativity must create an environment that fosters positive feelings about flexible thinking. Torrance gives guidelines to foster those attitudes:

1. *Value creative thinking.* The adolescent should see that the parent or teacher values and appreciates creative thinking.
2. *Make children more sensitive to environmental stimuli.* To be fluent and flexible, the adolescent must have a wide range of responses available and must have skills to observe a wide variety of characteristics. By teaching adolescents to be sensitive to variations and changes in their surroundings, you also increase their ability to consider alternative aspects of a situation.
3. *Encourage manipulation of objects and ideas.* Adolescence is a time when young people normally engage in mental games and play with thoughts. Instructors need to encourage this tendency.
4. *Teach the adolescent how to evaluate each idea systematically.* As an individual begins to develop divergent thinking abilities, the patterns of intellectual thinking may be unorganized and unsystematic. Sometimes concept flexibility can be encouraged through the use of heuristic techniques. A *heuristic* is a systematic procedure that serves as an aid to problem solving and originality, such as brainstorming, synectics, and so on.
5. *Develop a tolerance of new ideas.* Adolescents and children tend to be intolerant of uncertainty. Tolerance of ambiguity and uncertainty is fundamental to originality. Often such tolerance involves holding off judgment about the value of ideas. Sometimes what initially strikes you as a widely silly idea may develop into an original and creative solution to a problem. (It may also remain a silly idea.)
6. *Beware of forging a set pattern.* Creative and original thinking is hindered when people think there is *one* right way to go about solving a problem. Once again, to be flexible means to be able to "break set," to be able to think about a problem in alternative modes.
7. *Develop a creative classroom atmosphere.* Part of the learning process involves seeing how creative people act. Teachers should practice considering alternatives, withholding judgment on unusual ideas, and maintaining a tolerant attitude about uncertain areas, if adolescents are expected to behave similarly. (Practice what you preach!)

Whether creative or exceptional academically talented youths have any more adjustment problems than their more average peers is not clear. In the original Terman studies, the impression was given that exceptional children and adolescents had better social adjustment than their average peers. More recent data (Van Tassel-Baska, 1985), indicate that academically talented adolescents recognize their own unusual intellectual capabilities. It should not be seen as a sign of arrogance that academically talented adolescents recognize their gift. It is a legitimate part of their self-concept. On the other hand, because these gifted adolescents recognize their talent, they may also have internal and external pressures for perfection and excellence.

VIGNETTE 6–2
THE BAROMETER STORY

This story of the experience of one science student who grew tired of answering questions in the same old way brings up a variety of issues. Not only does the vignette relate to the confrontation between an obviously bright student and the "system." It raises more general questions about the dependence on convergent thinking as the dominant mode of testing. Although we are tempted to leap to the defense of this student, who is obviously able, the problem of how to adequately assess their students still remains for most teachers. How might you have handled this situation?

Source: Alexander Calandra, "The Barometer Story,"
Current Science: Science and Math Weekly, Bulletin
no. 14 (January 6, 1974). Special permission granted by
Current Science, published by Xerox Education Publications, © 1974, Xerox Corp.

Some time ago, I received a call from a colleague who asked if I would be the referee on the grading on an examination question. It seemed that he was about to give a student a zero for his answer to a physics question, while the student claimed he should receive a perfect score and would do so if the system were not set up against the student. The instructor and the student agreed to submit this to an impartial arbiter, and I was selected.

THE BAROMETER PROBLEM

I went to my colleague's office and read the examination question, which was, "Show how it is possible to determine the height of a tall building with the aid of a barometer."

The student's answer was, "Take the barometer to the top of the building, attach a long rope to it, lower the barometer to the street, and then bring it up, measuring the length of the rope. The length of the rope is the height of the buiding."

Now, this is a very interesting answer, but should the student get credit for it? I pointed out that the student really had a strong case for full credit, since he had answered the question completely and correctly. On the other hand. if full credit were given, it could well contribute to a high grade for the student in his physics course.

A high grade is supposed to certify that the student knows some physics, but the answer to the question did not confirm this. With this in mind, I suggested that the student have another try at answering the question. I was not surprised that my colleague agreed to this, but I was surprised that the student did.

Acting in terms of the agreement, I gave the student six minutes to answer the question, with the warning that the answer should show some knowledge of physics. At the end of five minutes, he had not written anything. I asked if he wished to give up, since I had another class to take care of, but he said no, he was not giving up. He had many answers to this problem; he was just thinking of the best one. I excused myself for interrupting him, and asked him to please go on. In the next minute, he dashed off his answer, which was:

"Take the barometer to the top of the building and lean over the edge of the roof. Drop the barometer, timing its fall with a stopwatch. Then, using the formula $S = \frac{1}{2}at^2$, calculate the height of the building.''

At this point, I asked my colleague if he would give up. He conceded and I gave the student almost full credit. In leaving my colleague's office, I recalled that the student said he had other answers to the problem, so I asked him what they were.

"Oh, yes," said the student, "There are many ways of getting the height of a tall building with the aid of a barometer. For example, you could take the barometer out on a sunny day and measure the height of the barometer, the length of its shadow, and the length of the shadow of the building, and by the use of a simple proportion, determine the height of the building."

"Fine," I said. "And the others?"

"Yes," said the student. "There is a very basic measurement method that you will like. In this method, you use the stairs. As you climb the stairs, you mark off the length of the barometer along the wall. You then count the number of marks, and this will give you the height of the building in barometer units. A very direct method.

"Of course, if you want a more sophisticated method, you can tie the barometer to the end of a string, swing it as a pendulum, and determine the value of 'g' at the street level and then at the top of the building. From the difference between the two values of 'g,' the height of the building can, in principle, be calculated."

Finally he concluded, "If you don't limit me to physics solutions to this problem, there are many other answers, such as taking the barometer to the basement and knocking on the superintendent's door. When the superintendent answers, you speak to him as follows: 'Dear Mr. Superintendent, here I have a very fine barometer. If you will tell be the height of this building, I will give you this barometer."

At this point, I asked the student if he really didn't know the answer to the problem. He admitted that he did, but that he was so fed up with college instructors trying to teach him how to think and to use critical thinking, instead of showing him the structure of the subject matter, that he decided to take off on what he regarded as mostly a sham. . . .

If academically talented youngsters see themselves as exceptionally capable in intellectual areas, those same young people may fail to exude the same confidence in their self-perceived social and physical abilities. Indeed, academically talented students are prone to voice concerns about their social and physical selves as not exceptional (Van Tassel-Baska, 1985). Whether those concerns about their physical and social selves were any more problematic than the average peers was not clear. But, professionals cannot dismiss the possibility that these fears might interfere with the fostering of talent.

Programs for talented adolescents should provide the opportunity for counseling to reconcile feelings of uncertainty emerging from their own recognition that their talents may not be uniformly high in all areas. In counseling intellectually precocious adolescents, care must be taken to insure that the youths themselves have an active role in the generation of problem solutions. They are likely to rebel against solutions they see as totally external. In all cases, group experiences are useful in allowing talented youngsters the opportunity to share ways of dealing with the frustrations that arise from possessing exceptional talent.

Mental Retardation

Retarded adolescents, like their gifted counterparts, are identified by their relative position in the normal distribution of intellectual functioning. Their performance is, however, significantly below average, and diagnoses may range from mild to serious impairment. Definitions of degree of mental retardation may include cutoff points on standardized tests of intelligence such as those in Table 6-1 offered by the American Association of Mental Retardation (Grossman, 1983). In their guidelines, you will note that the ranges are not exact. A test of intelligence does not stand alone and the score, the IQ, is an estimation. Decisions related to assignment of categories of retardation also must include assessments of other adaptive behaviors.

Table 6-1 Levels of Retardation By Intelligence Test Range

Term	Range
Mild Mental Retardation	50–55 to Approximately 70
Moderate Mental Retardation	35–40 to 50–55
Severe Mental Retardation	20–25 to 35–40
Profound Mental Retardation	Below 20–25

Source: Grossman, H. J. (ed.) (1983) Classification in mental retardation. Washington, D.C.: American Association of Mental Retardation.

Mentally retarded adolescents are individuals whose cognitive development has not kept pace with peers of their own age (Zigler, 1969). This formulation would characterize intellectually superior adolescents as those whose pace of cognitive development has exceeded their age peers'. As Zigler notes, this formulation implies that both types of exceptional individuals (excluding those with organically caused retardation) fall within the expected *normal* range of variability of the distribution of intelligence scores.

Mental retardation results from several factors, including metabolic and genetic disorders, birth traumas, malnutrition, drug and alcohol use by mothers during pregnancy, brain injury, and social stress. About three-fourths of all cases of mental retardation occur with no clearly identified organic cause and are associated with economically and educationally deprived backgrounds.

Often the problem of the retarded learner must be viewed beyond the confines of the individual. It is not uncommon for parents and families of severely handicapped children to feel resentment toward the child, who may be disruptive to the family. In some areas groups of parents with retarded children meet to exchange ideas and provide emotional support.

MAINSTREAMING

Until recently, schools have responded to the educational needs by separating developmentally disabled students and assigning them to special education clases. Under examination, however, these classes had (and continue to have) some very visible features. First, they were composed mainly of boys and second, they were composed mainly of minorities. Special education continues to be a target of criticism, especially when the sole or primary instrument for assignment is the standardized intelligence test.

Under Public Law 94–142, handicapped students of all kinds are reentering the mainstream. PL 94–142 demands that handicapped youths be provided with the "least restrictive environment" necessary to meet their needs. In most cases the least restrictive environment is interpreted to be the normal classroom, either in lieu of or in coordination with special classrooms. In some cases of profound handicap, the least restrictive environment may turn out to be a total special environment.

The general term for providing least restrictive environments is *mainstreaming*. As Caster (1975) indicates, mainstreaming does not mean that teachers of traditional classes are going to be responsible for providing specialized training for dozens of severely handicapped youths. Rather, the complete educational system must attempt to meet the educational needs of handicapped youths, part of which is their need to interact with nonhandicapped peers.

The core feature of PL 94–142 is the individualized education plan (IEP). An IEP is a statement compiled by an instructional team identifying:

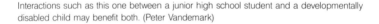

Interactions such as this one between a junior high school student and a developmentally disabled child may benefit both. (Peter Vandemark)

1. the current level of a handicapped student's performance;
2. specific long-term and short-term educational needs of the learner;
3. specific strategies and resources for meeting those needs;
4. target dates for initiating and completing the services;
5. a program of participation in the regular classroom; and
6. appropriate behavioral criteria for assessing progress (Pasanella & Volkmor, 1977).

Parents of handicapped learners are expected to participate in the planning process, and the planning team must ensure that the handicapped students' individual rights are not violated. The law further requires the team to review each IEP annually and submit a written report of the individual's progress toward the IEP goals.

In many ways PL 94–142 is going to require an alteration of the thinking and planning of teachers, principals, and other school personnel. To ensure that schools (and states) conform to the demands of PL 94–142, the bill includes a provision that failure to comply leads to termination of federal funds.

Cochrane and Westling (1977) provide guidelines for implementing mainstreaming in the schools. School personnel must be made more aware of the characteristics of mildly handicapped children and adolescents. This can be accomplished through in-service training or additional course work. Because special education teachers have been trained specifically for working with the handicapped, they may be used both as roving aids and as instructors of school personnel. Nonhandicapped adolescents in the school need to be educated about the needs of handicapped students. Too often, the mainstreamed adolescent may face exclusion or taunting by normal peers (Gottlieb & Budoff, 1973; Gottlieb, Semmel & Veldman, 1978). Schools should avail themselves of community resources to supplement the skills and resources available internally.

SUMMARY

A cognitive developmental view of children's and adolescent's thinking has broad generality. We have already encountered evidence in Chapter 3 that the child's and adolescent's sense of self is affected by their level of cognitive development. Hence, not only do adolescents need to incorporate their new intellectual abilities into their sense of self, their new cognitive abilities affect the manner in which their self-view is organized. The relationship is reciprocal. The shift from concrete to formal operational thinking is also reflected in the entire range of the young person's social thinking. In later chapters, parallel cognitive development is seen in social thinking, moral judgments, vocational choice, and perceptions of others.

Recall that earlier in this chapter it was noted that from an information processing view, one's behavior is a function of the way in which the individual processes information. If the flow of information within the individual is restricted by a concrete, self-centered view of reality, thinking and behavior are similarly restricted. In studies of political behavior, for example, Adelson (1980) found that in early adolescence, concepts of government and law are self-oriented and concrete. Even when presented with abstract concepts, the young adolescent will concretize the issue. On the other hand, as the flow of information within the individual is increasingly affected by formal operational thinking, the adolescent is able to deal with abstractions, ambiguity, and a decentered view. Thinking and behavior are comparably freed.

From a cognitive developmental view, instigation of change in cognitive schema is caused by the generation of imbalance or cognitive conflict in the intellectual system of the individual. Facilitating growth is thus possible by managing the adolescent's environment in ways that create dissonance or disequilibrium. But, initiation of imbalance must be within the limits of the individual's abilities to tolerate ambiguity and uncertainty.

7 | ADOLESCENTS AND THE SCHOOLS

Nearly a century ago, Albert Marble (1894) stated his assumptions for an ideal city school system. Marble said, "Widespread intelligence [knowledge and understanding] is essential in a free republic; and, therefore, public school education should be universal, obligatory and free. These propositions are taken for granted in outlining an ideal city school system. (p. 154)" When Marble wrote these ideals at the end of the nineteenth century, education was neither obligatory nor universal. Only a minority of young people attended any form of secondary school.

As we move toward the twenty-first century, many of the problems facing Marble and his contemporaries persist. Urban educators continue to struggle with widespread cultural diversity among their students and with the problems of educating the urban poor. Rural educators struggle with a changing economic structure which causes shifts in traditional rural roles. When Marble focused on urban schools, he was concerned with a minority of the American population. While the industrial revolution was in full swing, the nation was still predominantly rural and the concept of suburbia was still in the future. It is unlikely that Marble could have foreseen the staggering shift in national demographics that was to occur in the next 90 years. By 1940, 52.6 percent of the American population lived in urban areas and by 1980 the figure had risen to 74.8 pecent.

Beyond the shift in pure numbers, the profile of the American high school student has also changed. Increasingly, the population of American schools is composed of minority students. In many urban schools, Blacks and Hispanics now comprise the predominant student population. If current trends continue, by the middle of the next century, Hispanics will become the largest minority population.

What roles do schools serve given this rapidly changing demography? In society's view, schools are usually seen as serving young people by teaching them basic skills and "lore" which will help them become productive members of society. Thus, choices of curricula are often linked to their relevance for success as an educated person. One's view, then, of what makes for an educated person sets the stage for whether he or she sees schools as being successful or unsuccessful. Modern schools, particularly modern high schools have been the target of a variety of social critics on the premise that in their current structure, they fail to prepare young people for life in a contemporary technologic and pluralistic society (Coleman, 1975; Cusick, 1983; Boyer, 1983; Sizer, 1984; National Commission on Excellence in Education, 1983).

While schools provide an academic and vocational function, it would be short-sighted to neglect the social and psychological function they play (Sarason & Klaber, 1985). A large part of the adolescent's social life is built around school-related activities. It is a place where friendships are made and nurtured. It is a place where young people experiment with social roles and develop new aspects to their sense of self.

What constitutes the legitimate domain of schools and what role schools should assume are, therefore, continuing issues in modern society. Should schools concern themselves with the adolescent's mental health, sexuality, drug education, and vocational training? Should schools stick to the basics? If academics are to be the sole concern of schools, what curricula should be retained and which should be eliminated? Should certain books and materials be eliminated from the schools because they are offensive to one or another group? What should be the role of the teacher, the principal, and the counselor? The answer to each of these questions will depend on to whom the ques-

The high school dropout may suffer feelings of alienation because of lessened ability to get a useful job. (Owen Franken/Stock, Boston)

tion is addressed. The result is that the general picture one gets of contemporary schools is confusing and certainly not complimentary.

ACHIEVEMENT

The most obvious role of schools is to teach students in standard areas of achievement. The effectiveness of schools in meeting this challenge has been the focus of a variety of critics. Repeatedly, American students fare badly when their levels of achievement are compared with those of students from other countries. In studies of the National Assessment of Educational Progress (NAEP), results have been found that indicate a generalized lowering of achievement in science, math, and writing. In the report, *A Nation at Risk,* the National Commission on Excellence in Education (1983) described the situation as a "Rising tide of mediocrity." They went on to note "If an unfriendly foreign power had attempted to impose on America the mediocre educational performance that exists today, we might well have viewed it as an act of war." In a similar manner, a National Science Foundation study (National Science Board, 1983) stated that "Far too many emerge from a Nation's elementary and secondary schools with inadequate grounding in mathematics, science, and technology."

Further, concern is often expressed that overall achievement is declining. Among the more widely targeted topics in declining academic achievement is the general decline in performance on the Scholastic Aptitude Test (SATs). From 1952 to 1963, performance on the SATs remained fairly constant. However, from 1963 through the mid-1980s average performance declined steadily. Not only was the overall average performance reduced, but the number of students scoring over 700 also declined. In the past few years, there has been a modest recovery, but overall performance remains below earlier levels.

Perhaps more unsettling than poorer SAT performance is the evidence of widespread illiteracy among some groups of American youths. Consider the case of Peter Doe.

The case involved a suit filed by a young man against the San Francisco, California, Unified School District. According to laywers for Peter Doe (a fictitious name), school records indicated that Peter's measured intelligence was in the average range. He had maintained an above-C grade point average through elementary, junior, and senior high school. Further, Peter had not been retained at any grade level nor had there been any apparent consideration of retaining him. Peter's mother had repeatedly been told by school officials that Peter needed no remedial instruction. However, upon graduation from high school, Peter was unable to read well enough to fill out a job application or to follow directions printed on other forms. Peter was functionally illiterate (Abel, 1974).

The Peter Doe case is probably unusual for a variety of reasons, but it raises the question of how often students complete 12 years of schooling without achieving some basic level of competence. One wonders how such a student could go from year to year with no intervention or how his mother could fail to see that a real problem existed, irrespective of the feedback from school officials. But more than that, consider the implications of completing high school and being unable to read well enough to fill out a job application. What employment is available to a person like Peter Doe? Should we hold schools responsible to guarantee some basic level of competence? If a school fails to bring a student to this basic competence, can the school be held legally responsible?

The Peter Doe case also raises the question of how widespread the problem of illiteracy is among today's adolescents. Definitions of illiteracy vary, but most studies estimate that the number of young people who are functionally illiterate is considerable. In one study illiteracy was defined as being able to read no higher than the level of a beginning fourth grader. Using that criterion, researchers found that 4.8 percent, or about one in 20 American youths between 12 and 17 years of age were illiterate (Vogt, 1973). This translates into more than one million young people, not including those over 18 who cannot read well enough to handle their basic needs.

Further study of the problem of illiteracy shows that boys are more likely than girls to be illiterate. Minority and lower-income adolescents are much more likely to be rated as illiterate than white, middle-class youths. To what degree these differences can be blamed on early school experiences versus the failure of high schools to remediate reading problems is not a meaningful question. *Both* elementary and secondary schools need to reassess their teaching procedures if any significant change is to occur.

In addition to being disturbed about deteriorating reading achievement, the American public and the professional community are becoming increasingly alarmed by lowered levels of general academic achievement among today's children and youth.

VIGNETTE 7–1
BOOK BANNERS

The scene was not Nazi Germany in the 1930s but the United States in the past decade. Crowds of people were throwing "objectionable" books into a bonfire—books like 1984, Catcher in the Rye, *and* Tom Sawyer. *In Hammond, Indiana activists had the* American Heritage Dictionary *removed from the school library for containing "objectionable" language. Throughout the country groups organize to exclude literature that fails to conform to their own political, religious or social agenda. Many point to these activities and argue that such censorship violates the fundamental human rights guaranteed in the First Amendment to the U.S. Constitution. On the other hand, procensorship groups argue that, as concerned parents, they have the right and responsibility to review materials made available to or required of their children. Where do you stand on this issue? Does one set of "rights" override another set of "rights?" Consider the recent case in Tennessee in which parents brought against the use of a specific textbook series on the premise that it violated their own religious beliefs.*

Excerpted from: Sitomer, Curtis J. (1986) "Tennessee textbook ruling fuels religion-in-schools controversy." *Christian Science Monitor,* October 27.

The continuing controversy over the role of religion in American public education has been importantly fueled with a federal court ruling in Tennessee.

After weeks of testimony, a verdict was entered in favor of fundamentalist parents and students who contended that textbooks selected by a local school board contained themes offensive to their religious beliefs.

Many observers say the Tennessee decision will have broad implications for other cases around the nation involving the content of school textbooks.

US District Court Judge Thomas G. Hull's decision in the Tennessee case leaned heavily on the free-exercise-of-religious clause of the First Amendment to the Constitution. "In forcing the plaintiff-students to read from the Holt series [Holt, Rinehart & Winston texts], the defendants have burdened the plaintiffs' right to free exercise of their religion," Judge Hull wrote in a 27-page opinion.

Hull ruled that the students could not be disciplined for refusing to participate in reading classes using the opposed books, but he did not require the school district to provide alternative reading materials. He suggested that the students could be taught reading at home.

The ruling will be appealed to a US Sixth Circuit Court of Appeals in Cincinnati. And analysts says it may eventually reach the Supreme Court. "[Such cases] are all part of the same pattern to condemn the schools for attempting to indoctrinate children with godless concepts" says John Buchanan, chairman of People for the American Way, a group that entered the Tennessee case on behalf of the school board.

Mr. Buchanan, an ordained Southern Baptist minister and a former Republican congressman from Alabama, sees these cases as attempts to censor secular materials in the classroom and provide alternative texts that are flavored with denominational religious viewpoints.

He believes that the so-called Religious Right—including evangelists Pat Robertson and Jerry Falwell—have taken unfair advantage of public concerns over violence in the schools and drug abuse to "condemn schools and courts" and promote a "religious agenda."

But Sally Reed, chairman of the National Council for Better Education, a conservative citizens group, applauds the Tennessee ruling.

"It sends a clear message that parents' rights are not secondary to states' rights," Mrs. Reed says. "Hopefully, it will now give parents the incentive to take on local school districts. . . . Parents have too long been trusting of school districts."

"And the National Education Association and People for the American Way have abused this trust," she adds. "That's the reason we have seen such growth of home schooling and private schools."

"The real issue is local control. Each school must reflect community standards and values," Reed stresses.

Robert L. Maddox, executive director of Americans United for Separation of Church and State, is disturbed by the Tennessee case, because he feels that the fundamental parents have "bought hook, line, and sinker" the arguments against "secular humanist" being advanced by the Religious Right.

He praises Judge Hull, however, for being "sensitive" to some First Amendment concerns by refusing to mandate an alternative religion-cloaked curriculum for those who objected to the Holt texts.

At the same time schools are criticized for failing to train students in traditional basics, they are simultaneously under pressure to train those students in "new" basics. Beyond traditional curricula, schools are being asked to assume responsibility for sex and drug education. Also, schools are under pressure to make students "computer literate" without any clear consensus about what computer literacy means.

Source: Reprinted by permission of The Denver Post.

EFFECTIVE SCHOOLS

While reports of lowered achievement tempt us to be critical of all schools, it is clear that many schools and many teachers are doing good jobs. One approach that has been suggested is to study intensively those schools and teachers who are capable and effective and determine what it is that they do that is different from their less effective counterparts.

Effective Schools are defined as those in which students generally perform above average on standard measures of achievement. Of particular interest in such studies are those schools with large populations of economically poor students. Such schools would be expected to have lower achievement, but not all of them do (Edmonds, 1983). In one review Purkey and Smith (1983) identify some key features of effective schools. First, the principal plays an important leadership role in setting the tone for the entire school. Second, the teaching staff is stable and regularly given more training; good teachers yield achieving students. Teachers made maximum use of available time. Third, curriculum was well-specified and fit together as a whole. Fourth, parents were encouraged to be active in school activities. Fifth, achievement and excellence was recognized on a schoolwide basis with ceremonies and awards.

TEACHER ROLES

What makes for good teachers of adolescents? We have all had instructors whom we thought were really excellent. We have also had some that were not. The problem is, we might not all agree on which teachers were which. You probably have had the experience of having friends tell you what a great teacher X is, only to find out that you and the teacher have a personality conflict. Over the past several years, researchers have tried to isolate those traits which differentiate good from poor teachers.

Rosenshine and Berliner (1978) have shown that there is a consistent and direct relationship between the amount of time in which students are "academically engaged" and their subsequent levels of achievement. Thus, teachers who are able to maintain higher, consistent levels of time-on-task among students are likely to be the ones with higher overall levels of student achievement. Just how, then, do good teachers keep their students academically engaged?

Those teachers who are most effective are also good classroom managers. Their classrooms run smoothly and disruptions are at a minimum. Good teachers seem to know when to allow some minor off-task behavior to go without intervention but when to intervene before minor disruptions become major disruptions. Effective classroom teachers are clearly in control of the flow the classroom. Control, in this sense, however, should not be confused with arbitrary and rigid control. As Tjosvold (1980) points out,

The increased cognitive abilities associated with adolescence are tied to increased academic demands. (© Elizabeth Crews)

an excessively, autocratic controlling orientation leads to student alienation and resentment which, in turn, results in a lack of cooperation between student and teacher.

Effective teachers establish reasonable limits which are seen as necessary for the classroom to function. Students need and expect teachers to set ground rules. These ground rules are established early and the first few weeks require considerable effort on the part of the teacher to insure that the rules are followed (Emmer, Evertson & Anderson, 1979). This is not, however, a way of saying "The teacher needs to show the students who is boss." Rules are few, concise, and clearly written with desired student behaviors stated. Effective teachers tend to focus more on compliance with the rules and reinforce those positive behaviors verbally and nonverbally.

Effective teachers monitor students for signs of potential disruption (Ingersoll & Goss, 1981). As off-task behavior approaches a point where it is potentially disruptive, the effective teacher intervenes at a level appropriate to the student behavior. The timing and the accuracy of intervention are essential if the intervention is to be effective (Kounin, 1970).

Effective teachers have a sense of *pacing* (Brophy, 1986; Kounin, 1970; Arlin, 1979). Instruction moves at a steady pace. Little time is spent on procedural details because students know what is expected; they know the routines (Yinger, 1979, 1980). Transitions from topic to topic are smooth and instructional momentum is maintained. Less effective teachers seem to stumble as they shift between tasks; student attention wanes and time is spent trying to reestablish that momentum. One study of high school classrooms found them to be inordinately inefficient along the dimension of smooth procedures and transitions (Cusick, Martin & Palonsky, 1976). Students spend a total of three hours a day on procedural and maintenance tasks or waiting for others to complete those tasks.

Teacher questioning and information giving in effective classrooms are balanced. Most important, students are actively involved in the process of learning (Brophy, 1986). Level of instruction and level of questions are varied. That is, not all instruction is at a factual level. Instruction includes facts and higher level manipulation of facts.

Students View Good Teaching

The characteristics of good teaching which were just described are drawn from researchers who spend considerable time in classrooms observing the teaching process. They are "experts." In our own studies, we asked a different group of experts to tell us about good and poor teachers (Ingersoll & Strigari, 1983; Goss, 1984). The experts we asked were middle and high school students. While their answers were not always as sophisticated as researchers', they were still very informative. Compare the traits identified by researchers with this more straightforward description by an eighth-grade girl and an eighth-grade boy:

> The most important thing in teaching is that you practice what you teach and not always yell at the students like it is their fault or something.

> The most important thing in teaching is that you teach kids stuff and make then learn.

Or, consider these answers by some tenth-graders:

> The teacher has to be understanding and really make the classroom foremost. Teachers do not understand kids and the class is absolutely awful. The teacher has to do different things, not always the same procedure. If the teacher is fun and nice but still teaches and makes the kids learn, the kids will like him or her and make better grades. There aren't enough teachers who are like that.

> It is important that the teacher show me exactly how to do something and make it stick so I will always remember how to do it.

While some students' answers may lack precision, they point to some important elements. Students report that they are more likely to cooperate with teachers when they see the teacher as in charge or in authority (Goss, 1984). When students see teachers as not in charge, as not possessing authority, they feel justified in disrupting the class. In a study of junior high school students (Metz, 1978), disruption was likely when there was a mismatch in teacher behavior and students' expectations of teacher behavior. Disruption, however, differed in lower track and upper track classes. In lower track classes, testing the teacher's authority was focused on behavioral disruption, testing the teacher's ability to keep order. In higher tract classes, student challenges to teacher authority were focused on the teacher's mastery or lack of mastery of the content matter.

COMPETENCY-BASED EDUCATION

Partly in reaction to cases like that of Peter Doe and partly in recognition that a substantial number of college freshmen lack basic skills, there has been a movement toward identifying the minimum competencies necessary to complete high school satisfactorily. By mid-1978, two-thirds of the states had initiated mandates for minimal competency standards, and others are likely to follow suit in the near future.

In principle, the concept of competency-based education (CBE) is straightforward. Every learner should have a specific set of skills and concepts, in order to be certified as having graduated from high school. This set of outcomes would be understood to be minimal levels of performance for which a high school diploma or certificate would be awarded. Students who are below that level would not be certified until they achieved those basic competencies.

In practice, however, a variety of problems with the CBE approach have yet to be worked out (Brickell, 1978):

1. It is obvious that assessing competence at the end of high school is too late to allow for any meaningful remediation. Minimal levels of competence must also be identified at the elementary and middle school levels.
2. There is a lack of consensus on which skills are "minimal." For example, if the traditional basic skills of reading and math are used, how do we address other content areas, such as art, history, home economics, and so forth. There are also what might be termed "life skills," or knowledge necessary to get along in society. The question of which

competencies are minimal has probably caused more difficulty that any other. To include competencies from all areas, however, might result in an unmanageable number of minimal competencies.

3. It is not totally clear how to test for minimal achievement. If we use paper-and-pencil tests of the type used in most schools and by the NAEP, we may be unfairly discriminating against those who have poor test-taking skills. If we test in "real life" settings on the job, the costs become prohibitive. we are also left with the question of what constitutes minimal acceptable levels of performance. Can one set of minimal standards be fair or meaningful to all groups? If the same minimal standards were applied to all schools, we might find the standards too low for some and too high for others. On the other hand, such information might provide evidence by which *schools* could be judged for their level of "competency."

4. Finally, what is the school's obligation to those who fail to reach a minimal competency level?

The problems of CBE are numerous and unlikely to be solved overnight. It does appear at this time, however, that CBE is here to stay. Ultimately, it will be a poisitive step forward. But in the interim, schools and states will have to wrestle with many problems.

RESTRUCTURING THE SCHOOLS

In a report of a Presidential Commission on Youth entitled *Youth: Transition to Adulthood* (Coleman, 1975), James Coleman and his associates argue that schools are not capitalizing on the physical and creative energies of today's youths. In an attempt to become more efficient, schools have also become sterile and impersonal. The amount of time youths spend in school has increased, but the time is filled with curricula that have little relevance to the real world. This in turn has led to increased alienation of students including, but not limited to, school dropouts. What Coleman proposes is a radical change in the structure of American schooling with the goal of merging youths into society earlier. The Commission recommended the following changes in the structure of schooling:

1. *Reduce the size of the schools.* Smaller schools would facilitate the development of interpersonal relationships. Coleman and his colleagues say that large consolidated schools are impersonal. Their bureaucratic structure leads to an atmosphere akin to large university campuses. Smaller units would also reduce teacher specialization. Teaching would by necessity become interdisciplinary. On the other hand, large school districts are economically able to provide a broader spectrum of alternatives. Dividing large campuses into smaller units, the commission believes, offers the student the benefit of both worlds.

2. *Provide apprenticeship work experiences early.* The current structure of schools restricts interaction with adults and the "real world." Because instruction is isolated within the context of the classroom, its practicality is seldom seen. To change this, students could alternate between work and study. They would spend one-half of the school day in formal classes and the remaining half in an apprentice role on a job.

3. *Increase responsible participation by youths in the community*. The commission concluded that schools systematically reduce the decision-making responsibility of students. To be prepared to function in an adult community, students should have experience in meaningful responsibility beyond the very limited roles usually available in the schools. One might, for example, create internship roles in head-start agencies, political parties, election campaigns, or peer-counseling programs.

4. *Reexamine legal constraints on young people.* Laws aimed at the youth labor market were originally enacted to reduce economic exploitation of the young and their subjection to harsh working conditions. Those same restrictions ultimately limit the employment options available to young people. The current laws also protect the adult labor market from an influx of competitive, cheap labor. The commission proposed that the government provide tax or economic incentives for youth training programs.

5. *Introduce a voucher system.* Schools should allow young people the right to greater flexibility in job opportunities and provide for increased self-responsibility. The idea is to provide each young person a voucher equivalent to the average cost of a four-year college education. The young person could then cash the voucher in on any accredited training program. Such a system presumes a degree of maturity (or clarity of purpose) in young people, a presumption that may not be valid. Many college juniors and seniors are still unsure of their long-term career goals.

6. *Allow greater flexibility in completion of degree requirements.* Youths should be allowed greater latitude in leaving and reentering school. They should be able to leave school for a year or two, gain work experience, then reenter school, and complete their education with no penalty. Although college students can and do make use of such an option, similar fluidity among high school students is discouraged, directly or indirectly.

All in all, the overriding conclusion of the Coleman Commission was that the schools should be responsible for creating an environment that motivates students to learn, providing interesting and relevant curricula, increasing the options available to the students, and allowing increased responsible decision making among students.

Although few educators would argue with the general recommendations offered by the Coleman Commission, not all agree with the specific proposals that it offered. The report has met with hostile reaction from a variety of critics, including a former president of the National Education Association (Wise, 1974). The alternatives advocated in the report are built on presumptions about the workaday world that may not be totally accurate. It is not clear, for example, how the quality of apprenticeship training on the scale implied by the report would be monitored and controlled. Such a program would certainly require widespread government intervention to an even greater degree than is currently felt. Further, the report fails to differentiate between those students for whom the current system is unsatisfactory and those for whom the system works well.

Ebel (1972) argues for an alternative but more traditional view of the responsibility of the schools. In Ebel's view schools should help students acquire basic knowledge and competence that will be useful in later life. Knowledge is not, however, equated with pieces of information, but with those intellectual concepts that emerge out of using and applying the information. Intellectual skills and general ability to solve problems should emerge from knowledge acquisition. Also, Ebel feels that the schools should give up other roles that interfere with its primary function of developing intellectual skills. He points, for example, to the legal requirement to keep young people in school until some minimum age, usually 16. This makes the schools custodial institutions for delinquents and others who resent being there. Further, Ebel feels that schools should not be expected to provide interpersonal counseling, drug and alcohol education, and other extras that detract from its primary role.

In either view, Coleman's or Ebel's, there is clear dissatisfaction with the current structure of schooling. The nature and structure of schooling needs to be reevalulated in light of the needs of the wide variety of students served by the schools.

"Either this is a great moment, or we had better set some minimum standards for graduation from high school!"

MIDDLE SCHOOLS

Within recent years, many school systems have reassessed their traditional grade structure for young students in the preadolescent and early adolescent years. Increasingly, school authorities recognize that the emotional, social, and phychological needs of early adolescents differ from those of the high school student and also differ from those of the elementary school student. Those students in grades 6 through 8, for example, are not yet full-blown adolescents nor are they still little children (see Thornburg, 1981); yet, sometimes they act like both and leave educators, as well as other professionals, in a quandary about how to cope with them.

The standard structure of the "Junior High School" seemed to imply, even through its name, that the school's role was one of introducing students to the independent world of the "Senior High School." Hence, the classroom organization and structure of the curriculum paralleled the high school. Junior high was an apprenticeship for senior high.

More recently, that view has been reassessed. Since preadolescents and early adolescents are in a period of transition from childhood to adolescence, perhaps the structure of schooling should be more in keeping with their developmental stage. One author (Eichorn, 1966), even proposes the introduction of the term *transescent* to describe the group.

Recall from Chapter 1 that the developmental tasks of adolescence do not take on equal importance throughout the adolescent years, some in the middle adolescent years, and some in the later adolescent years. Early adolescents are more concerned with their new sense of a physical self, with new peer relations that include the first, tentative interactions with members of the opposite sex, with their first struggles to assert themselves as independent from parents yet not wanting to let go of the secure bonds of childhood, and their first glimmerings of more advanced thinking abilities.

One structure that has been proposed for the preadolescent and early adolescent years is the *Middle School* (see Johnson, 1980). The middle school is not simply a reworked junior high school with a new grade configuration. At their best, middle schools combine elements of the dependent, nurturant, secure structure of elementary schools with the more independent, complex structures of the high school. The intent is to provide a more gradual transition for the student.

Conceptually, the purpose of the middle school makes good sense. The structure of schooling should be fitted to the cognitive-social developmental level of the students. Failure to do so may result in failure and frustration and ultimately to alienation from the school structure which is intended to help students.

Epstein (1978) has advanced the hypothesis that periods of brain growth and stabilization are correlated with other elements of cognitive maturation. While Epstein admits to great variability in actual levels of brain and cognitive maturation among middle schoolers, he proposes that curricula, especially middle school curricula, be restructured. According to Epstein, novel information should be introduced during periods of rapid brain growth, but presentation too early may disrupt later learning. In Epstein's view, the middle school should emphasize relearning of factual material. While Epstein's theory and research have come under criticism (Marsh, 1985), he does focus on the need to match curricula and instructional design to the developmental status of the learner. Failure to match learner characteristics and learning environment can disrupt the educational progress of students.

VIGNETTE 7–2
TEACHING AMERICAN STUDENTS TO THINK

Critics of American public education regularly point out that beyond the decline in American students' basic skills abilities, a morie serious decline is seen in their ability to solve problems. While educators, at all levels from elementary school to graduate school, profess to emphasize students' abilities to think, they often focus on factual recall. Students will regularly study for tests with the premise that must be able to repeat from rote memory what the instructor wants to hear; creativity or thinking is too dangerous because one might not get a good grade. How can we reform the American educational system? Can we retain a positive attitude toward learning basic skills and at the same time encourage critical thinking?

Excerpted from: Marquand, Robert (1986) "Teaching American Students to Think." *Christian Science Monitor,* Feb. 28.

Johnny and Jenny may know a lot of facts about the Declaration of Independence, what with more emphasis being given in American classrooms to basics like history, math, and reading. But they are less able to ask significant questions about it than students were a generation ago, according to a number of educators.

Today's students are not learning as well how to identify unstated assumptions. They know less about what it means to infer, to extrapolate, to build an argument, to form and defend an opinion, to see implications. They are, in short, not learning enough about thinking critically, these educators say.

Though it has built slowly over the past few years, the drive to teach "critical thinking"—also referred to as "creative," "effective," or "skillful" thinking—is beginning to be felt in the educational mainstream.

"Many youngsters these days look at you blankly when you ask them to *support* a fact or an opinion," says Sydelle Seiger-Ehrenberg, a thinking-skills instructor at the Institute for Curriculum and Instruction, a 30-year-old Ohio firm that trains teachers in how to develop critical-thinking skills among students. She says students often feel that "because something is called an opinion, it must have intrinsic merit."

"In what is called an 'information society,'" says Jay McTighe of the Maryland Department of Education, students and citizens need to develop critical interpretive abilities so as not to be "swamped by information" or unduly swayed by misleading political arguments. "Job fields are changing so quickly," he adds, "that thinking is [also] the skill you bring to a job."

There are dozens of approaches to teaching critical thinking. The basic need, educators say, is to get students to start questioning the statements made by teacher or textbook. A central tenet: Students should learn to engage in an internal dialogue with what they're studying—analyze it from different points of view, make it their own.

Many of the thinking skills—for example, analysis, synthesis, and evaluation—are taken directly from standard logic and philosophy courses and are developed in a number of ways, including interactive group or class discussions, writing exercises, and techniques in self-questioning.

Ron Brandt, editor of Educational Leadership, says concern about critical thinking marks "a shift in the notion of what education is." For several years, he says, schools have been providing an "intellectual education" for a minority and "vocational skills for the rest of us." The teaching of critical thinking is starting to cut across such barriers.

In the past five years nearly 2,000 scholarly articles have been written about critical thnking and the ways it is being taught in kindergarten, elementary and secondary schools, and colleges throughout the United States. Schools in about 30 states now have critical-thinking skills programs. And California requires that critical thinking be taught in its schools from Grade 6 through college.

Learning what it takes to ask intelligent questions strikes some people as so obvious a skill that it hardly need be taught in school. It is simple, say the teachers of critical thinking courses. Good thinkers have done it throughout the ages. However, many current students aren't exercising this native ability.

There are a variety of reasons students aren't picking up thinking skills naturally, say educators. One of the causes is social. "We don't talk as much to each other," says Ms. Seigler-Ehrenberg. "Families don't talk around the table. Kids are off watching TV or taking karate lessons. It's not easy to establish thinking models under those conditions."

But much of the blame has also been placed on the public schools. In "A Place Called School," acknowledged to be one of the best of the recent studies on public education, author John Goodlad notes that, while parents perceive "intellectual development" to be the central purpose of schooling, the average school devotes less than 1 percent of class time to the interactive discussion that helps students hone such skills. It's impossible to do that, says one teacher, when in history, for example, you must get to the Civil War by January and the Vietnam war by June.

Students' writing ability—long a testing ground for such thinking skills as rigor, clarity, and organization—are also at a low ebb.

In 1960, for example, 80 percent of the freshmen at the University of California at Irvine passed a basic composition test. In 1984, 80 percent failed the same test. Carol Booth Olson, head of the Irvine program, says that students may be proficient at "rote exercises" and memorization—but they have "declined drastically in their ability to see the symbolic or universal."

"If we are ever going to do anything but build monuments to the great books, kids are going to have to learn higher-order cognitive skills," says Eugene Garver, who holds a chair in critical thinking at St. John's University in Minnesota. Students, he says, need to go beyond the fact that in the Lincoln-Douglas debates, Douglas was for slavery and Lincoln was against it. Both men used the Declaration of Independence to back their arguments. And it takes cultivated thinking skills to recognize the virtues and fallacies, he says. "Unfortunately the Lincoln-Douglas debates is different from learning simplistic formulas for detecting phony advertising appeals."

MATCHING ENVIRONMENTS

The degree to which a school environment or atmosphere meets the individual needs of learners has an impact not only on higher academic performance but also on the personal satisfaction of students and their feelings of personal adequacy (Pervin, 1968). In school settings in which teachers fail to respond to the personal characteristics of learners, those learners demonstrate lowered performance and diminished feelings of personal adequacy.

Thelen (1967) has argued that classrooms should be organized so that there is an optimal match between learner and teacher characteristics. Thelen had teachers in junior and senior high school classrooms identify the types of students they felt benefited from their classes. He then had students rate the type of teacher from whom they felt they learned best. Thelen then created classes by matching students and teachers by their preferences. Other classes were established through ordinary procedures. The more teachable the students, in terms of the teachers' preferences, the better the outcomes for both students and teachers.

A variety of personal characteristics may interact with environmental features that lead to improved or impaired performance. Among the more promising work on generating matched learner-learning environment models in education is David Hunt's (1971, 1975; Hunt & Sullivan, 1974). Hunt describes the development of conceptual styles, combining Piaget's theory and his own earlier work in personality development (Harvey, Hunt & Schroder, 1961).

Hunt outlines three general stages of conceptual style that are not dependent on age—as are Piaget's levels of cognitive development and Kohlberg's levels of moral development (see Chapter 12)—but that tend to develop across adolescence. Learners at Stage A are described as unsocialized, egoistic, and hedonic. Learners at this stage are motivated by what is personally gratifying. Stage A thinking dominates among preadolescents and early adolescents. When asked to respond to the statement "What I think about rules," they give such answers as:

> I do not like them. They are no fun!
>
> Sixth-grade boy

> Rules sometimes can be a real trip! You are expected a lot of times to do things that don't even make any sense! Rules run you. I hate being ran (sic) around. Why can't we enjoy ourselves more? The reason is because of a lot of bummer rules!
>
> Twelfth-grade boy

Hunt describes learners at Stage A as impulsive and intolerant of ambiguity, with little self-control. Notice that even a twelfth-grader may still be at this stage. The optimal environment for Stage A learners is highly structured with emphasis on concrete examples and clear, immediate reinforcement for correct responses. Table 7–1 describes the learning styles and matching learning environments for Hunt's three cognitive stages.

The network of concepts that Stage A learners apply to the solution of problems lacks complexity. It is simple and categorical. In Figure 7–1, which describes the developmental matching model, Hunt tries to depict the low level of cognitive complexity of Stage A learners by the use of a simple, two-branched schema.

Stage B learners are highly socialized and depend on authority figures for guidance. Thinking among Stage B learners tends to consist of either/or, right/wrong categorical thinking and a high degree of conformity. Stage B conceptual development is associated with middle adolescence. When asked to respond to the statement "What I think about rules," they answer with such responses as

> I think rules are good. If we didn't have them, we wouldn't have a proper school, or know how to do anything.
>
> Sixth-grade girl

Table 7–1   Characteristics of Cognitive Style Groups

	Expected Characteristics of Stage Group	*Observed Characteristics of Classroom Group*
Stage A	Egocentric, very negative, impulsive, low tolerance for frustration	"Noisy, poorly disciplined, inattentive." "Easily confused, less self-control than others."
Stage B	Concerned with rules, dependent on authority, categorical thinking	"Orderly, quiet, attentive." "Questions asked to impress teacher." "Do not have faith in their convictions."
Stage C	Independent, inquiring, self-assertive, more alternatives available	"Did not rely on teacher's directions." "Interested in finding out information." "Stand up for their convictions."

Source: Adapted from D. E. Hunt, "Matching Models in Education: The Coordination of Teaching Methods with Student Characteristics." *(Toronto: Ontario Institute for Studies in Education, 1971), p. 30.*

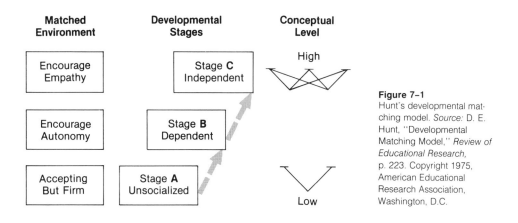

Figure 7–1
Hunt's developmental matching model. *Source:* D. E. Hunt, "Developmental Matching Model," *Review of Educational Research,* p. 223. Copyright 1975, American Educational Research Association, Washington, D.C.

You have to have them. But if you have them they should be used not for just a few but on all people that function with them.

Twelfth-grade boy

Hunt describes learners at Stage B as orderly and concerned with rules. The optimal environment for Stage B learners is moderately structured. Teachers should encourage independent thinking within relatively well-defined problem areas rather than assigning very unstructured tasks. Teachers of these learners do well to capitalize on their competitive tendencies.

Hunt describes learners at Stage C as autonomous thinkers who prefer working independently and maintain a high tolerance of ambiguity and uncertainty. Given the question about rules, Stage C learners may respond:

I think they have a place in society, or in the world, but many of them become oppressive and tend to restrict people from reacting in a natural way. I think this is bad. But they are good in school many times to keep order. In communities are all right too, if they are made for the good of the people.

Twelfth-grade girl

I think rules are necessary but shouldn't be taken to extremes. A lot of people brake (sic) rules, but there are so many that you can't help it. If I had my way I'd live without them, but someone will always take advantage of a good thing.

Twelfth-grade boy

Hunt describes the optimal environment for Stage C learners as open with low structure and a wide variety of alternatives. Problem-based, discovery learning is best suited to Stage C learners, because they are self-motivated and prefer to work on their own. The network of concepts that Stage C learners apply to the solution of problems is highly complex. It is organized with many interrelations and qualifications. In Figure 7–1, the complexity of the conceptual level of Stage C learners is contrasted with that of Stage A learners by the use of multiple, interrelated schema with multiple branches.

Like Piaget's theory of cognitive development, Hunt's model is based on the presumption that the modes of cognitive style develop in sequential stages. To reach Stage C, learners must progress through Stages A and B. The teachers's or counselor's role becomes one of identifying the matching environment that best aids progress. If an environment is not optimal, the result is poorer performance. Hence, although an open environment with little structure is optimal for Stage C learners, when Stage A learners are placed in unstructured tasks, they are overwhelmed with the ambiguity and uncertainty. The result is frustration and poor performance. The opposite, however, does not seem to occur. Stage C learners are able to function quite well in highly structured tasks. They seem flexible enough to operate in most environments. If there are differences in the performance of Stage C learners in structured versus unstructured environments, they appear to be found in the students' attitudes toward the tasks. Thus, although they perform well on highly structured tasks, such as programmed instruction, they find them boring.

ACADEMIC MERIT VERSUS SOCIAL CLASS

A long-standing controversy in the study of educational attainment is whether the primary variable underlying success in social status or academic ability (Rehberg & Rosenthal, 1978). One view claims that schools serve primarily to reinforce and solidify already existing social status in society. Success results not from any ability or motivation but from social class-related variables. Success for those of low social status is unlikely. The opposing view is that the American schools are based primarily on a model in which ability, not social status, is the variable of importance. Although able students from higher-income families may have greater long-range chances for further education and higher occupational status, the schools promote and encourage attainment among all students, irrespective of social status.

A longitudinal study of high school students found that, on the whole, contemporary schools respond more to ability than to social class. As early as ninth grade, assignment to the academic or college-bound curriculum had little to do with the social status of the student. Rather, ability and how the students perceived their parents' attitudes toward educational achievement were most important. Students from upwardly mobile families or low social status families who are motivated to achieve are not stifled by a rigidly stratified school system. School counselors, who might be expected to be influenced by social status if schools were so oriented, paid little attention to social status variables in their academic counseling. Advice or counseling was influenced more by academic ability (Rehberg & Rosenthal, 1978).

Another study showed that both academic ability and social status were significant contributors to status attainment 15 years after high school. For males, however, academic ability had more impact than social class background. For females, social status variables seemed more important in long-range attainment. The only area in which ability, seemed to play a more important role among women was in feelings of self-worth (Alexander & Eckland, 1975).

The impact of teachers and counselors in encouraging lower-income students cannot be overstressed. Often lower-income and minority students view the schools as hostile and unresponsive to their needs. Teachers and counselors must be aware of these

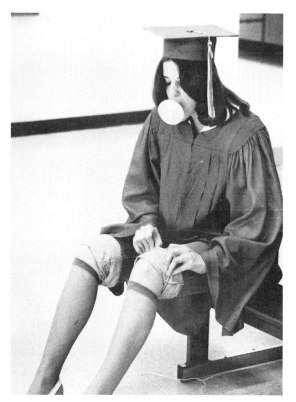

Adolescents are likely to exhibit an incongruous mixture of formality and casualness, maturity and immaturity. (Jim Richardson/Black Star)

feelings and convey a positive attitude toward these students and their potential for success. Often adults in high-prestige occupations who come from lower-income backgrounds will report that two or three teachers or counselors really seemed to have faith in them and conveyed that attitude.

DROPOUTS

It is common for adults to warn young people that education is their key to future vocational and social success. Yet, despite that well-meant advice, many young people either fail to heed the warning or simply do not believe it; they "drop out" before completing high school. For a variety of reasons, they prefer to take their chances without a high school diploma than to continue on.

Because of widely different definitions of "dropouts," actual rates of dropouts are not clear. The most often quoted value is that 20.1 percent of high school students (1 in 5) will drop out before graduation (Caliste, 1984). Rates among urban schools often exceed 50 percent (Maurer, 1982), that is, more drop out than graduate. Among ethnic minorities, rates sometimes run as high as 60 to 70 percent. Some students simply stop attending classes but never inform school authorities of their decision, thus, actual dropout rates may be higher.

When people think of the "typical dropout," they may draw upon a stereotype of someone who is failing academically and who is probably unable to complete high school work. While dropouts usually perform less well in traditional academic areas than those who stay in school, research studies of dropouts do not support that stereotype that they are unable. Most dropouts are intellectually capable of completing high school (Friedman, 1984). In one study, 40 percent of the dropouts had been enrolled in a college preparatory curriculum and only 17 percent had actually been failing (Grant, 1984).

Most dropouts report that they would have stayed in school if teachers had paid more attention to them and if they had been treated more as humans than as inmates. In a survey of students who had dropped out of the Denver Public Schools, less than 5 percent answered that a teacher had encouraged them to stay in school. Other studies (for example, Ekstrom, Goertz, Pollock & Rock, 1986), support the view that dropouts are more likely to be alienated from school.

On the other hand, research studies do indicate that the less capable student is at risk for dropping out of school. Often the less capable dropout is reading at or below the seventh-grade reading level. They experience continuing frustration with an academic curriculum that becomes more and more remote. Schooling becomes an experience to be avoided since it represents repeated and regular failure.

As Gold and Petronio (1980) note, poor academic performance by a student strains the relationship between the teachers and the student. It also strains the relationship between the academically less able student and higher achieving peers. This psychological separation leads to frustration, alienation, and lowered feelings of self-worth, at least with respect to schooling. This sense of frustration, in turn, results in behavior problems, delinquency, and rebellion (Elliott & Voss, 1974). It is not altogether surprising then that students who find schools to be a place of discomfort and failure should prefer to drop out.

This concept that the aversiveness of school leads to delinquency and rebellion is supported by research. Lower-income youths who ultimately dropped out of school did indeed show very high rates of delinquent behavior. Their delinquent behavior escalated steadily until they dropped out of school. Once they dropped out of school their delinquent behavior declined steadily until, of all groups studied, they had the lowest rates of delinquency (Elliott, 1966; Elliott & Voss, 1974). Among other groups of boys who graduated from high school, there was no similar immediate decrease in delinquent behavior after completing high school. When these students do drop out, they may gain a sense of competence through marriage or a job, their self-esteem improves and, thus, their delinquency rate often drops (Jensen & Rojek, 1980).

In a very real sense, dropouts represent an index of failure of the current educational system. While the current structure meets the needs of many, if not most of its students, it is largely unresponsive to the needs of a significant number of others. Currently, the group that is less well served is disproportionately composed of poor and minority students. As the nation's profile changes and minorities account for larger and larger proportions of the school population, there is a serious risk that schools are becoming less responsive.

Failure to deal adequately with the dropout issue is serious. School dropouts are at a disadvantage in the labor market and are usually limited to unskilled and semi-skilled positions. They are more likely to be among the unemployed (Bachman, Green & Wirtanen, 1971), and to earn less in their lifetime. High school graduates can expect to earn 48 percent more wages in their lifetime than dropouts, college graduates can expect to earn 98 percent more (U.S. Bureau of the Census, 1978).

High school graduates are at an advantage in other ways as well. They are more likely to rate themselves as more socially acceptable, self-confident, and mature (Combs & Cooley, 1968). Further, school dropouts are more likely to marry earlier, have more children, have more marital problems and to die earlier (U.S. Bureau of the Census, 1978).

Traditionally, the school dropout has been seen as an academic failure who is, in turn, doomed to a life of economic and social failure. The traditional view is an overstatement of fact, but it does reflect the greater likelihood that the dropout will continue to experience problems in society. In this sense, dropping out of school is not the *cause* of future problems, rather it is symptomatic of a more general set of problems. To be responsive to the needs of the potential dropout, schools must consider attractive and valuable alternatives. In particular, schools should consider alternatives which focus on vocational development.

The scope of the dropout problem motivated the members of the Urban Superintendents Network (1987) to identify six strategies for intervention. First, intervention efforts should be made early in students' educational careers. Efforts at the secondary level may be too little and too late. Second, school leaders should make efforts to create a positive school climate in which discipline and good student-teacher relationships are fostered. Third, school systems should advocate high standards for students *and* teachers. Fourth, efforts should be made to recruit teachers with strong academic credentials.

Fifth, school systems should create a broad range of instructional programs aimed at the divergent needs of students. Sixth, school systems should foster collaborative efforts with community agencies.

There is an additional group of dropouts who have recently come under study. Not only do high school students drop out but there is a group of college students who drop out. Among college dropouts, like high school dropouts, the reasons for discontinuing go beyond simply having poor grades (Bean, 1985; Bean & Metzner, 1985). Beyond academic performance, the degree to which students see the institution as providing a comfortable "fit" to their needs plays an important role. The more likely a student is to have a personal commitment to the institution, the more the student feels he or she belongs, the less likely the student will dropout.

SUMMARY

A variety of national assessments of the American educational process have found the system, in general, short of the ideal. Middle schools and high schools have come under particularly stinging criticism. While clamors for educational reform are not new, they seem to be taking on a new urgency. While much criticism can be focused on the educational "system" the site of most school learning is the classroom.

An instructor is responsible for establishing conditions that facilitate learning among students. Learning in the classroom is neither automatic nor inevitable. An instructor who wishes to achieve specific outcomes must ensure that conditions are appropriate for learning to take place. Although some learning may occur in unorganized, unplanned instruction, there is no guarantee that what is learned is productive or beneficial.

Instruction may be provided by a classroom teacher, or by a computer, a teaching machine, a film, a text, and so on; the same principle holds. Effective instruction demands organization to achieve outcomes, which must be specified in advance. The instructor must have a clear understanding of the structure of the material and the characteristics of the learners, in advance. This does not mean that instruction is teacher-centered, autocratic monologues that lead the student in lock-step fashion. Even so-called open classrooms, when they are effective, have structure. The structure, however, differs.

Alternative suggestions have been made concerning alterations to the school "system." Proposals include a focus on competency-based education. Competency-based education offers the advantage of giving the schools, the students, and the community a clearer picture of what is reasonably expected of learners.

Competency-based education, by itself, is not enough. Schools must become more responsive to the different needs of their students. Students' educational needs shift as they mature. During early levels of cognitive social maturity, young people view their world in simple, concrete terms. They need greater structure and emotional support. As students mature cognitively and socially they are more able to manage in less structured environments. Indeed, among more cognitively advanced students, less structure is likely to be preferred. One caution, however, should be restated from Chapter 6. Not all students are operating at a common level of cognitive social maturity and a given student may operate on a more advanced level on one domain and on a less mature level in another.

Failure to adapt school enviroinments to the needs of students may result in feelings of alienation and isolation. In some instances, schools may be required to provide alternative learning environments for particular groups of students.

CHOOSING
8 A VOCATION

Prior to the industrial revolution of the late eighteenth century, young men and women began their adult vocational roles as early as 12 or 14 years old. Adolescents had little, if any, input into the decision-making process, because their vocational roles were largely dictated by their parents. When they reached an age at which parents and the local community expected them to start learning a trade, adolescents were assigned an apprenticeship. In some cases this apprenticeship role was as simple as working with the father at his trade or, in the case of girls, assuming increasingly responsible roles around the home by working with the mother. In each case the adolescents' adult roles were assumed to be the same as their parents'. In urban areas a young boy might be apprenticed to a master craftsman. The agreement might be formalized in a written contract specifying that the boy would serve as an indentured servant for a given period of time, and in return the craftsman would provide room and board and train the young man in his trade (Kett, 1977).

By their late teens, young people were already well established in the working world. Even those who practiced law and medicine might be doing so by the age of 21. Incidentally, those professions did not require a college degree—about the only profession that did at that time was ministry (Kett, 1977).

With the onset of the industrial centers and the need for large, cheap labor forces, the picture of youth employment changed somewhat. Although fewer youths were employed as apprentices, a large contingent of this new work force was young men still in their early teens. Young boys were hired to provide unskilled, manual labor in the mills or the mines. Once again, however, even this early occupation was assumed to approximate their adult vocational role. They learned their trades on the job. As the industrial revolution progressed and the need for cheap labor exceeded the available number of young boys and immigrants, young girls also began to work in the mills. The need for cheap labor persists; the industry that currently makes use of youth labor most generally is the fast-food business. As Kett comments, only in commercials are the workers in fast-food restaurants over 21.

As the strength of labor unions increased, and as social agencies became alarmed at the general exploitation of children and youths in industry, laws were enacted to restrict the employment of young people. By the 1930s, when the Great Depression was at its worst, jobs were so valuable that youth labor laws became even more restrictive and young people were forced into extended schooling (Borow, 1976). Thus the traditional apprenticeship and the introduction of young people into the labor market have been largely eliminated. The rationale has been, of course, that the additional schooling will better prepare young people for entering the labor market as adults.

Several writers agree with the President's Commission on Youth (Coleman, 1975) that there is a need to reevaluate both youth labor laws and the structure of education as it relates to future career opportunities. As you will recall, the Coleman group advocated restructuring the schools to allow academic approval of apprenticeship roles. At present the structure of most schools often hinders the progression of youth toward skilled trades.

The Carnegie Commission (Boyer, 1983), in contrast, suggested that high schools offer a single "mainline" curriculum. The mainline curriculum would have adequate flexibility to permit the choice of electives appropriate to either advanced education or to entering adult vocations. Both reports agreed that the current structure of high school curricula are inadequate and perhaps dysfunctional.

But even the apprenticeship model may be shortsighted if it fails to orient the adolescent toward the future. If we prepare adolescents for the workaday world as we see it today, we may be preparing them for obsolescence. We expect that as today's young people move through their adult years, they will make several significant job changes during their work lives. Further, many currently standard jobs will cease to exist or be radically redefined. Just as there is no longer a job for the "coalman" on a railroad train, other jobs will disappear or be eliminated in the next 20 years.

Consider dentistry as a field. In the 1950s leaders in the field committed themselves to a program of research which would reduce the need for dental services through a program of preventive dentistry (in a sense making themselves obsolete). While dentists have not become totally obsolete, our children benefit by experiencing considerably fewer dental problems. Our children's children will enjoy even more refined dental care. As a result, the future job market for dentists is expected to diminish and the role of the dentist in the year 2000 will be substantially altered.

On the other hand, our efforts to anticipate the future may be impaired by the limits of our vision. In the hurry to make the current generation of youths "computer literate," many failed to recognize that computer literacy 10 years from now will not be defined in the same way it is today. Our most effective strategy in vocational counseling may, therefore, be to train youths to be responsive and flexible. "Technological literacy" and "information literacy" may be more important skills (Naisbitt, 1982).

The purpose of this chapter is to provide an overview of the process contem-

Federal laws now prohibit the exploitation of children like this young coal miner from the early part of this century, but adolescents still form a large segment of the "cheap" labor force, especially in "fast food" restaurants. (*left*—Lewis W. Hine, George Eastman House; *below*—© Susan Lapides)

porary adolescents go through in their selection of an adult vocational role and the factors that influence their decision. We will also look at the general picture of youth employment today.

VOCATIONAL CHOICE

In Chapters 1 and 3, I noted that an essential part of one's personal identity is the vocational role she or he chooses. Preparation for adult vocational roles is described as a primary developmental task (Havighurst, 1972). Others point to achieving vocational independence as the culmination of adolescence. Greenberger (1984) identified the development of a work orientation as a central element in establishing autonomy. Certainly, an adult's vocational self is an important element in his or her identity. In the same fashion, the adolescent's answer to the question "What are you going to be when you grow up?" represents an essential element in the process of establishing one's personal identity. Choice of a vocational path is, at the same time, a reflection of the individual's self-concept. Yet, adolescents must often make choices in a context of poor information regarding vocational choices, distorted pictures of the present and future job markets, and lack of adequate career counseling which permits young people to be focused yet maintain some element of flexibility.

The nature of that selection process depends on both general developmental characteristics of the adolescent and the realities of the working world. Further, those "realities" are constantly changing. Borow (1976) for example, has noted that in the years since the Second World War advances in technology continue to alter worker productivity. The purchasing power and standard of living for the average American has never been higher. Currently, however, vocational choice among young people is as likely to be influenced by what young people see as a necessary basis for a personally acceptable standard as by desires for material wealth. Increasingly, young Americans are entering large industrial organizations that are complex, highly structured, and impersonal. Decisions about how one's job will be done are often made at levels remote from the individual worker. Vocational choice is thus likely to be influenced not only by the realities of the working world but by one's own perceptions of and attitudes toward various choices.

Attitudes Toward Vocations

The occupations young people aspire to are related to how they see the job fulfilling basic needs. However, those needs shift in priority as a young person matures, and they continue to be altered at different stages in life. In one study, male and female students in the eighth, tenth, and twelfth grades were asked to tell what they valued in their future careers. The two most important characteristics were the same for both boys and girls across all levels: job satisfaction and personal interest in the job. Beyond that, however, boys were more likely to value salary and achievement of personal goals, whereas girls were more likely to value the chance to make personal contacts and the ability to help others. Both boys and girls rated whether a job is in demand and the opportunity for future advancement low in importance. Older boys and girls were both more likely to rank the relationship of an occupation to one's family life as highly important (Gribbons & Lohnes, 1965). Whether the same ordering would be found among high school students now, 25 years later, may be questioned. However, the point is that the perception of what is valued in future vocations shifts with age and differs among groups as well as among individuals.

Vocational goals are also influenced by the level of prestige that is associated with various occupations. Studies have repeatedly shown that certain occupations are ranked as highly prestigious, whereas others are ranked very low. Table 8–1 shows the top, middle, and bottom rankings of 90 occupations used in one study (Hodge, Siegal & Rossi, 1964). When prestige rankings are compared over long periods of time, there is a high degree of stability in relative standing (Hodge et al., 1964; Hakel et al., 1967). High-prestige occupations remain high and low-prestige occupations remain low. Further, the relative ranking of professions is stable across races and sexes (Braun & Bayer, 1973) as well as across national boundaries (Inkeles & Rossi, 1956; Mitchell, 1964).

Table 8–1 Level of Prestige of Certain Occupations

Top 10 (1 to 10)	Middle 10 (41 to 50)	Low 11* (81 to 90)
U.S.Supreme Court Justice	Owner-operator, Print shop	Restaurant waiter
Physician	Trained machinist	Taxi Driver
Nuclear Physicist	Farm owner and operator	Janitor
Scientist	Undertaker	Bartender
Government Scientist	Welfare worker, City	Clothes Presser in Laundry
State Governor	Newspaper columnist	Soda Fountain Clerk
Cabinet Member, Federal Government	Policeman	Sharecropper
College Professor	Reporter, Daily Paper	Garbage collector
U.S. Congressman	Radio announcer	Street sweeper
	Bookkeeper	Shoe shiner
		*Two were tied at 81.

Source: Reprinted from "Occupational Prestige in the United States, 1925–63," by R. W. Hodge, P. M. Siegal, and P. H. Rossi, *American Journal of Sociology, 70* (1964): 290–291, by permission oif the University of Chicago Press.

Sex Roles

Perhaps in no other area has the problem of sex-role stereotypes been addressed more fully than in the world of work. Historically women have been barred from a variety of occupations because of their sex. Even with many of the sexual barriers removed, women are still vastly underrepresented in some job categories and overrepresented in others. As was indicated in the previous chapter, sex-role stereotypes describe expected personality characteristics of men and women solely on the basis of their sex. Women were therefore expected to assume nurturant and passive roles with little opportunity to exert leadership and control.

Attitudes about women in the working world are changing; however, the changes in attitudes are not universal. There are some who, on the basis of their own personal and religious convictions, believe that the nurturant role should be the role of women.

Adolescents, like adults, are more likely to aspire to the high-prestige job of the physician than to that of the sanitation worker. (*top*—© Paul Fortin/Picture Group; *bottom*—Charles Gatewood)

The degree to which attitudes among adolescents about work roles for men and women are changing is not totally clear. One study (Mitchell, 1977) found that most adolescent girls from the Midwest still expected to pursue only those careers that have been traditionally open to women, such as clerical work, teaching, and nursing. They were aware that a broader range of possible occupations existed. But if they did consider a male-dominated occupation, it was usually a high-prestige or glamorous job, such as doctor, lawyer, or airplane pilot.

A nationwide study of high school seniors found that although some young people still feel that a wife should not work at all and should assume total responsibility for child care, most thought that wives should work either part- or full-time and that responsibilities for child care should be shared. Males tended to be a little more traditional in their views, but the differences in expectations were minor (Herzog, Bachman & Johnston, 1979).

Although many of the barriers to full employment of women have been eliminated, full equality is still to come. Many of the obstacles that remain are more subtle. For example, if a young woman chooses to enter the field of psychology, it is almost always presumed that she will pursue a career as a clinical psychologist rather than as a research or industrial psychologist. Such barriers, or at least stumbling blocks, are primarily attitudinal, not only in terms of men's attitudes toward women colleagues but also women's attitudes toward themselves. In one review of psychological barriers to occupational aspirations among women, O'Leary (1974) found that many of the attitudinal differences that might be expected on the basis of a traditional stereotyped view of women were not found. O'Leary reported that attitudinal problems were found in the areas of self-esteem, self-confidence, and role conflict. The last conflict results when what society traditionally expects from women is incompatible with expectations of an occupational role. O'Leary noted that part of the difficulty may lie in the lack of a clearly visible variety of women role models who demonstrate success at handling those demands.

Vocational Aptitudes

Much of the traditional research activity in vocational development has involved using aptitude tests to match individuals to the occupations most suited to their values or interests. Alternatively, similar instruments may be used to screen job applicants to see who is most suited for a given task.

VIGNETTE 8–1
THE BOXER

While each development task of adolescence is important to the individual's overall sense of self, the development of a vocational self-image takes on centrality as the young person strives to be an adult. It is through having a job, through earning a living, that real adult independence occurs. Students who read this text are probably using education as the primary vehicle through which adult vocational independence is being gained. For young men and women from poor neighborhoods, that luxury may be out of reach. How then do they establish vocational independence. Presented below is the story of one young man, Mario Munoz. He has chosen boxing as his route to success.

Excerpted from: McQuay, David (1986) "Mario Munoz"
Denver Post, April 6.

Mario Munoz wears exhaustion on his face after sparring four tough rounds against an opponent who already has turned professional. Munoz has boxed since he was 12 years old and hopes to get his chance in the '88 Olympics.

Inside the Rude Park Community Center, while others swim or play in a pickup basketball game, 17-year-old, 139-pound Mario Munoz hits a punching bag until it fades into a blur. Grunts come from another boxer pummeling a body bag, and the coaches bark advice at two others sparring in the ring. A few teenage girls sit and eye the brown young men. A wide-eyed little boy stands next to Mario, watching him punch the bag until it flutters into something wild and dreamlike, a hummingbird of leather.

As relentlessly as he assaults that bag, Mario Munoz's handshake is soft and polite. He's a nice kid from the projects, where he lives with his mother and girlfriend and sisters and nieces. He doesn't drink, he doesn't smoke; he goes to school and works part time, but most of all he boxes. Those fists have won 130 of 150 amateur fights. They've taken him to New York and Havana and Romania. Five or six days a week he goes to the gym noisy with girltalk and boytalk and he works out. He's in the local

Golden Gloves tournament in Denver this week; if he wins he goes to the regionals in Great Falls, Mont., and then to the nationals. Then there's the Olympics in '88, and maybe the pros.

American boxing has always attracted kids from poor and tough neighborhoods. Generations ago, the Irish-Americans, Italian-Americans and Jewish-Americans fought their way to the top. Then, as those groups assimilated into the middle class, blacks began commanding the sport. Blacks still dominate boxing, but the rankings of the small and medium weight categories have become peppered with Spanish names.

This is oversimplifying the changing ethics complexion of the sport, and we'll leave the theories to the sociologists. But the attraction of boxing to underprivileged young men such as Mario Munoz probably has more to do with defending oneself against young toughs, with being practical, than it does with lashing out symbolically at poverty and prejudice.

Ask Mario what he has learned from boxing, and he says with the wisdom of a Zen master: "I've learned to control my temper."

He was born in Juarez, Mexico, and moved across the border to El Paso, Texas, when he was small. He doesn't talk much about his father, who drank and got into bar-room fights. "Most of us have a grudge against him," he says.

The family moved to Denver, the parents divorced, and Mario begain getting into fights at school. "In my first year in junior high, I got into three fights in a row. I would get suspended, come back and get into anohter fight."

A kid would mouth off at him, and Mario would duke it out. "You've got to defend yourself. If it happens to you once, it'll happen to you again. Guys who start fights know who to pick on. They pick on the weak ones."

He started fighting at Rude's at 12, and he started getting pretty good a couple of year later. A 25-year-old man foolishly wanted to spar with him, and Mario sent him home with a concussion. He stopped getting into fights at school. Until recently his grades at West High were good. "I'm not doing as well in school as I used to because I've been traveling so much," Mario says. Now he is getting C's and D's. "Since I've been traveling so much, school's a little bit harder."

There is more fun at the gym, where a brotherhood of young Hispanics hangs out. Staying clean and working out at Rude's, there is a pride of fighting for a club that has won the state title many times. Mario has a lot of fans.

"Hey, Mario," a guy says, horsing around outside. He has lifted a buddy's leg up and is making him hop around. "What ya doing, writing an autobiography?"

"Mario, I was looking for you," a girl coos with a smile. Mario's pretty girlfriend, Lupe Chavez, walks up a little later and tells him she's going to a friend's house. She kisses him. Things are not so bad: He's young, strong, handsome, it's a beautiful day at the rec center, and he thinks he's going to win the Golden Gloves next week.

Most adolescents have experience at one time or another with one of a variety of vocational interest inventories. The two most commonly used versions have been and remain the Kuder Occupational Survey (Kuder & Diamond, 1979) and the Strong Vocational Interest Blank (1943, 1955). In the typical survey, testees are asked to indicate their likes, dislikes, and values. For example, the *Kuder Occupational Interest Survey* (Kuder & Diamond, 1979) is intended for use with high school and college students. Students are asked to react to a series of 100 items, each item tells of three activities. The student is asked to tell which of the three he or she most prefers and which is least preferred. The goal of the test is to develop a profile of the student's interests and to identify possible occupations that are consistent with the student's interest pattern. A counselor may use the information to explore career options with the student. Counselors must expand their views, however, beyond the limited occupations included in the analysis provided by the authors of the instrument. There is simply no instrument that could deal with all occupations.

Alternatively, an adolescent may be tested to determine particular areas of strength or weakness that make him or her suited for certain occupations but less suited for others. An adolescent who shows high verbal or high numerical aptitude but low aptitude in tasks that require dexterity and coordination would be encouraged to set career goals that build on the strengths and minimize the weaknesses.

That aptitudes influence one's success or failure in a given occupation is intuitively obvious. Further a person goes through a degree of automatic selectivity in recognizing his or her own strengths and weaknesses. The adolescent with poor math and spatial skills is not likely to have mechanical engineering as an occupational goal. Just how an individual develops this self-awareness and focuses in on career goals are a concern of a number of theorists, who have tried to make some order of the process.

THEORIES OF VOCATIONAL CHOICE AND DEVELOPMENT

Several attempts have been made to identify the process that adolescents go through in understanding the role of a career in their life and selecting a specific vocation. One view sees career development more broadly in light of the place of person's career holds in reference to more general personal adjustment and growth. The other view focuses attention on the selection of a specific set of vocational goals and plans to achieve those goals.

As with other characteristics of social and psychological growth during adolescence, vocational awareness becomes increasingly complex as young people approach adulthood. Thus it is necessary to account for both the breadth of awareness of alternative vocational roles paired with the increasing precision with which adolescents specify their expected vocational roles.

Ginsberg's Theory

Eli Ginsberg and his associates (1951) offered one of the first formulations of a theory of vocational choice. Their research focused on four variables that they saw as influencing adolescents' adult vocational *choice*. The first, the *reality factor,* includes economic, social, and environmental pressures that limit available options. As adolescents mature, they are increasingly likely to make compromises in career goals as a result of their recognition of these realities. The second factor, *education,* influences career development primarily in terms of its preparation for adult career choice. The higher the quality of education, the more options an individual has available. The last two factors, *emotional characteristics* and *personal values,* influence adolescents' career choice by their impact on the range of choices that are comfortable for the individual.

In Ginsberg's view vocational choice develops gradually from about age 11 to about age 24. It does not occur suddenly or rapidly. Instead, adolescents progress through stages of increasingly realistic goal statements.

Ginsberg suggests that at the earliest level, up to about 11-years-old, preadolescents' concepts of future occupational roles are largely based in *fantasy.* During that stage children imagine themselves in attractive adult roles with little regard to abilities or opportunity. The fantasy stage is, however, important because it creates a readiness to address the task of vocational choice during adolescence.

From age 11 to about 18, adolescents create *tentative* vocational goals that are altered as they progress toward a mature choice. Initially, tentative vocational goals are dominated by adolescents' interests—that is, what they like or dislike. Gradually, adolescents' choices are also influenced by their self-perceived abilities and their assessment of their potential for achieving certain goals. Finally, tentative goals are influenced by adolescents' value systems.

In late adolescence, individuals move into a stage where they make increasingly specific, realistic choices. This *realistic* stage of career choice is further broken into an *exploratory* phase, in which individuals try to implement career choices. As the individual

An important part of the preparation for adult vocational roles is the acquisition of skills related to those roles. (© Billy E. Barnes)

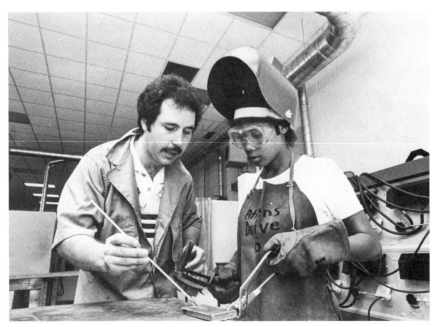

enters a job or college training, the goal *crystallizes* and, gradually, as the goals become clearer and more stable, they become *specific*.

The importance of the Ginsberg approach is that it recognizes the fluid nature of career choice during adolescence and begins to show that the adolescent's concept of career goals changes not only specifically but qualitatively with maturity. It also focuses attention on the decision-making characteristics of vocational choice, the need to compromise choices with a recognition of reality, and the need to capitalize on those characteristics that are likely to lead to success. However, Ginsberg's description of the process is more accurately seen as representing the way vocational growth *should* be in the mature and healthy individual. Where psychological and social variables inhibit normal maturation, young people do not experience such smooth transitions. More recent writers (especially, Jepsen, 1984) have focused on the commonality of the vocational choice maturational process as paralleling other cognitive-social developmental processes. Hence, complexity of self-views with respect to vocational goals may be expected to expand and become more refined in conjunction with other cognitive social processes.

Further, there is a normal expected period of indecision in young people's process of making vocational choices (Crites, 1981) and also in their choices of academic majors in college (Titley & Titley, 1980). Rather than being a negative, this period of indecision may reflect a healthy evaluation of alternatives. But, while some degree of indecision is normal and healthy, significant indecision may reflect other psychological problems including low self-esteem and high social anxiety (Fuqua & Hartman, 1985).

Super's Theory

Perhaps no other writer has had as much impact on our understanding of vocational development as Donald Super (1953, 1957; Super et al., 1963). Super combines aspects of developmental psychology and self-concept theory into a theory of vocational *development*. Vocational development includes both vocational choice and the orderly progression of the individual's view of himself and his relationship to a chosen vocation. Rather than focus on the process of occupational choice, Super focuses on career vocational development. In Super's view, the selection of an occupation is an attempt by the individual to fulfill his or her sense of self. The vocational expressions of one's sense of self shift as the individual matures.

Super sees adolescence as a critical period in which individuals restructure their image of themselves. One's vocational goals and how one rates those goals in light of their indication of personal self-worth are important elements in one's total self-esteem. For example, two people choose truck driving as a possible occupation. One person sees it as "really exciting. I love the freedom of being on the road." The second sees the same job as one that "I can get because I am not able enough to do anything else." The values that they place on the occupation and therefore themselves are different. The more positive a person's feeling of adequacy, the more likely he or she is to have positive attitudes about a chosen occupation. Because the adolescent with a positive self-image is likely to have a valid assessment of personal strengths and weaknesses, the career choice is also likely to conform to pressures of reality. However, "reality" is also viewed as subject to change.

Like Ginsberg, Super sees vocational development progressing in a continuous, forward moving, orderly fashion through adolescence and into adulthood. However, Super more clearly specifies that vocational development continues through adult years. Super identifies five stages in the process of lifelong vocational development, beginning with *growth* (birth to early adolescence), *exploration* (early adolescence to young adulthood), *establishment* of a career (young adulthood to middle age), *maintenance* of a career (middle age to old age), and *decline* (old age). These stages are further broken down into more specific, associated tasks.

During the exploration phase of adolescence, the young person must *crystallize* a vocational preference. By this, Super means that the adolescents' self-image gradually takes form as vocational options are evaluated. Eventually the adolescent makes some tentative choices. Next the adolescent must *specify* the choice. During late adolescence one is expected to convert general vocational goals into more specific occupational choices and to make a commitment. At that point the individual may recognize that additional training is necessary to achieve the more specific choice or that an entry job is a necessary step in achieving the goal. It is then the task of the late adolescent to *implement* that choice. That is, the young person actively attempts to initiate the necessary sequence of events to achieve the specific goal.

During the establishment stage of early adulthood, when the young person has entered into the beginning stages of a career, he or she is then expected to stabilize and adjust to his or her role within the chosen vocation.

There may be during this stage a continued period of trial. That is, the individual may find that the initial concept of the job was unrealistic or that the specific employer was not compatible with personal values. Thus there may be some shifting in roles and positions. Gradually, however, this trial period is replaced by a commitment to a vocation and a desire to advance and improve.

Super's theory differs from Ginsberg's in that it contends that vocational development is a lifelong task extending beyond adolescence and young adulthood. In addition, Super calls attention to the fact that vocational development, although important in and of itself, is part of the more general process of self-concept development and must be viewed from this broader perspective.

Holland's Theory

An alternative approach to vocational choice is found in John Holland's (1959, 1973) writings. Holland's approach is based on the assumption that choice of vocation is influenced primarily by the personality of the individual making the choice. His research has led him to conclude that there are six basic modal personality types related to vocational choice. The relationship among the six is seen in Figure 8–1.

Holland defines the *realistic* person as one who favors occupations built around objective, concrete tasks. Realistic people prefer jobs that require physical strength and manipulation of the environment, such as agriculture or technical occupations. People with this orientation avoid tasks which require verbal or interpersonal skills. *Social* people on the other hand, are particularly drawn to interpersonal tasks and seek close personal

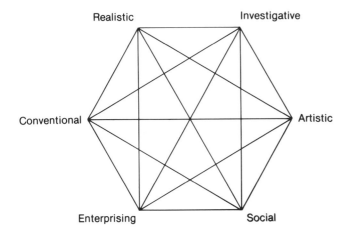

Realistic   Investigative

Conventional   Artistic

Enterprising   Social

Figure 8–1 Holland's hexagonal model.
Source: ACT Research Report No. 29: J.
L. Holland et al., An Empirical Occupation
Classification Derived from a Theory of
Personality and Intended for Practice and
Research, (Iowa City, Ia.: The American
College Testing Program, 1969).
Reproduced with permission.

relationships. They typically assume roles in counseling or religion and are frequently seen as leaders.

Holland defines the *investigative* person as one who prefers to work with abstractions and avoids tasks requiring physical strength and dexterity. Like their realistic counterparts, however, they tend to feel discomfort in interpersonal settings. People with an investigative orientation are often drawn to scholarly or scientific roles. The realistic person is inclined to act while the investigative person is inclined to think. The *enterprising* person is one who possesses a high level of self-confidence and is self-assertive. They tend to be highly verbal and choose occupations in which they can accumulate recognition and power. Where the investigative person likes to manipulate ideas, the enterprising person prefers to manipulate people and to dominate others.

Holland defines the *artistic* person as one who prefers dealing with tasks that are low in structure and permit freedom of expression. They tend to be drawn to careers in the creative arts, music, or drama. The *conventional* person, in contrast, is drawn to settings with high structure and clearly defined roles. They feel most comfortable when someone with authority and status assumes responsibility for decision making. They tend to choose occupations that lead to social approval but that are not likely to demand originality of thought. Clerical positions with accounting tasks that have clearly correct, acceptable answers are preferred by conventional individuals.

Holland goes on to say that one's choice of vocation is influenced by one's personality because each occupational environment has characteristics that correspond to the attributes of the personality types. Thus an individual gravitates to a work environment that provides the best fit with his or her personality.

Very rarely does an individual fall perfectly into one of the six categories. Rather, each individual has some combination of traits with certain facets more pronounced than others.

Holland's theory reflects a sophisticated extension of the traditional model in vocational counseling in which a counselor attempts to guide individuals in career exploration on the basis of a personality or interest profile. However, in addition to the clearly applied character of such a model, Holland also provides evidence that the selection process is not capricious but predictable in light of individual preference.

Some Limits on Vocational Theories

Although each of the three theories described in this chapter, and other theories not covered, offer a perspective on vocational choice and development, they are not without problems. Osipow (1983) has shown that all the theories are based primarily on data on white males and that the validity of the models for describing vocational choice and career development among women and minorities is open to question. Further, the inherent danger in the misuse of models such as Holland's is that such categories will lead to oversimplified personality-occupational stereotypes.

With specific reference to Holland's approach, Osipow warns that there is a risk of assuming too much stability in human traits. The problem of instability of traits over time is especially relevant in dealing with adolescents. One's sense of self and one's interests and motivations change on the basis of experience and maturation. Hence, the links between current and future interests cannot be seen as invariant. Holland's model must be seen as solely an advisory model.

YOUTH EMPLOYMENT AND UNEMPLOYMENT

A significant proportion of adolescents work either part- or full-time. Among students ages 16 years to 17 years, 41 percent were also working. On the average in 1985, teenagers who worked had an average income of about $1,800 (Wetzel, 1987). The proportion

The early vocational fantasies of children are often influenced by people in jobs that children see as exciting, such as those of police officers and fire fighters. (© Beryl Goldberg)

of young people, both males and females, who enter the labor market during their teen years continues to rise dramatically. Most teen employment remains in the service industries.

Irrespective of their increased numbers and their importance to the service economy, teen workers remain most vulnerable to economic uncertainties. Young workers lack seniority and are typically employed in unskilled or semiskilled roles, hence, they are most vulnerable to job loss. While the number of teen workers has increased, so has the rate of teen unemployment (see Table 8–2). Unemployment rates among teens are 2.7 times the rate for working adults. As may be seen in Table 8–2, unemployment rates among minority youths are consistently higher than among white youths. Further, when a ratio of minority to white unemployment rates is created, it is seen that the risk of unemployment among minority youths is increasing (Wetzel, 1987).

Table 8–2   Unemployment Rates of Youths By Race: 1955–1986 (Percent of Labor Force Unemployed)

Year	White	Black and Others	Ratio of Black to White
1955	7.9	13.8	1.75
1960	10.2	17.9	1.75
1965	9.2	16.9	1.84
1970	9.9	19.4	1.96
1975	14.5	27.6	1.90
1980	12.0	26.4	2.20
1986	11.1	26.6	2.40

Source: Wetzel, J. R. (1987) *American youth: A statistical snapshot.* Washington, D.C.: William T. Grant Foundation.

Despite the figures in Table 8–2, the actual rate of youth unemployment is not altogether clear. Because of the way unemployment rates are computed, youth unemployment rates are very subject to error. Employment statistics are based *only* on those who are out of work *and* are looking for work. High school and college students who are looking for part-time employment are included in the figures, but school dropouts who are unemployed but who, in their frustration, have given up looking for work are not included. Even the rates of students who are employed or seeking part-time employment are not all the same. Those attending a two-year college, for example, are much more likely to work while going to school than those attending a four-year college.

A variety of factors serve to keep unemployment rates among youths high. The combination of restrictive child labor laws, compulsory education laws and minimum wage laws effectively eliminate a large proportion of potential youth laborers from the market (Haisch, 1964). Additionally, young workers lack a skilled trade and are less capable of competing for those openings that occur. Employers are sometimes reticent to hire young laborers since the costs of training may be high and the employers fear that young workers are more prone to stay in one job for a limited time. For minority youths, these same factors operate but the minority youth also experiences limits linked to a variety of sociopolitical variables, some tied to poverty, some to institutional racism (Morse, 1981). Labor unions, for example, have repeatedly restricted entry of minorities into apprenticeship programs (Cogan, 1982).

When chronic unemployment is additionally tied to dropping out of school, a vicious cycle begins in which the young person lacks training and qualifications yet is eliminated from getting the needed training because he or she is unqualified. Levine (1979) outlines a series of stages through which typical young job seekers progress as they leave school and begin to search for a job. First the young job seekers feel a sense of *optimism*. They are hopeful and expect to find doors open. Repeated closed doors and refusals, however, lead the young job seekers to develop feelings of *ambiguity*. They begin to be less confident of their own capability and their self-esteem begins to suffer. As the period of ambiguity becomes prolonged, they become increasingly bored and frustrated. They may feel parental or adult pressures to be employed as well as internal pressures for their own feelings of competence. If the process continues too long, the result may be *despair* and apathy. Since rates of chronic unemployment are highest among minority youths, it is not altogether surprising that nonwhite youths are considerably more pessimistic than white youths about their chances of future employment (Gallup, 1979).

The picture is not, however, totally bleak. From 1980 to 1990, there will be a drop of nearly 20 percent in the total number of 16- to 24-year-olds in the national labor market. Thus, if the number of positions available to youths remain relatively stable, then there will be an automatic decline in the youth unemployment rate. The drop, however, will not likely represent a significant change in the principal problems of youth employment, especially early access to the skilled labor market.

VIGNETTE 8–2
SHOULD TEENS WORK?

Here's the good news: You've gotten a part-time job after school. Here's the bad news: They want you to work at exactly the time when you are involved in track. Working while you are going to school has its pros and cons. Its pros include having cash to spend during your spare time. The cons include less spare time. Should young people work while they are still in school? Does the work experience prepare them for adulthood? Does it deprive them of chance to experience the fun of youth? Does work interfere with their studies? Presented below is a synopsis of Steinberg and Greenberger's When Teenagers Work. *Do you think the conclusions are fair?*

Excerpted from Myers, Jim (1986) "All Work and No Play—or Studies?" *USA Today*, October 3.

Penny Shumake, a 16-year-old high school junior, is a typical smiling face behind the counter at McDonald's.

The St. Petersburg, Fla., teen is working 25 hours a week to make $201 payments of a red '86 Camaro.

Like most USA high schoolers—and their parents—she thinks she's doing the right thing: holding an after-school and weekend job that teaches her to be responsible and manage money. "I'm learning what it's going to be like when I get out of high school," Shumake says.

A new study on teen employment says she may be wrong, too much part-time work is doing our high school students more harm than good.

The authors, two developmental psychologists, say students who spend long hours flipping burgers or bagging groceries frequently see their grades drop, develop unrealistic views about money, and are more likely to be involved in delinquency and drug use.

Their study questions cherished assumptions of the work ethic. And working teens—particularly those from middle- and upper-income families—have become the national norm.

More teens work during the school year in the USA than in any industrialized nation—6.5 million 16- to 19-year-olds. Entire industries—fast food and convenience stores among them—thrive on low-cost teen labor; some also thrive on the $40 billion teens spend each year.

But common, too, are stories about kids dozing off in math class.

Felix Murray, an 18-year-old senior in Dunedin, Fla., fell a term behind working until midnight at a supermarket. Says Murray: "I was sleeping in school." Now he has a job that ends at 9 p.m.

Michael Wilson, a 17-year-old senior in Washington, D.C., says his grades dropped from Bs to Cs, when he started working 25 hours a week at a Hechlinger Co. home improvement center. "My mother said if my grades didn't go up, I'd have to quit the job. So I made myself do my homework." He's using the money to help at home and save for college.

Are they on the wrong path? Authors Laurence Steinberg and Ellen Greenberger, in their new book, *When Teenagers Work,* say even idleness may be a safer route to adulthood than too much afterschool work.

Their study of 530 teens in Orange County, Calif.—a vast, predominantly white suburb of Los Angeles—concludes that jobs don't necessarily teach good work habits: "We find high rates of deviant behavior at work—stealing from the employer, vandalizing property, lying about the hours worked, calling in sick when they're not or working while drunk or stoned," Says Steinberg, a professor at the University of Wisconsin.

The book says most trouble comes when students work more than 15 to 20 hours a week, the USA average for teen employees. Says Steinberg: "The more time kids work, the worse off they are."

Entering the Job Market

Most teens have had a part-time job while in high school or college, but the time at which they leave school and attempt to find full-time employment still represents a major transition in their life. Achieving financial self-sufficiency represents the final stage of establishing independence from parents. Although true financial independence may not occur immediately, the path is set. Further, full employment represents a principal element in one's personal identity. Finally, the first job seemingly plays some part in a person's long-term career goal.

Given all these characteristics, it would seem likely that young people would devote a great deal of time and thought to deciding about their first job. Actually, most young people select their first job after school in a very haphazard fashion (Singell, 1966; Orstein, 1975). Young people give little thought to the decision, and most simply take what is available. There is a certain pragmatic reality that any job may be better than none. But, although the first job may not bear *directly* on long-term career goals, the first job is related to later likelihood of unemployment and the level of wages one will earn (Stephanson, 1978).

The value of working while still in high school seems to be mixed. On the one hand, early work experience may provide a young person with a sense of the realities of the workaday world. High school work experiences, even when they are largely unskilled positions, may place the young job seeker in a more advantageous position when he or she enters the adult labor market. Some work experience on an application or resume may be viewed more favorably than no work experience at all. On the other hand, research evidence indicates that those students who work more than a few hours a week are likely to have lower grades and more negative attitudes about work in general. They spend less time with their family and their ability to participate in school related social or academic activities is restricted. Those who worked full-time or nearly full-time jobs while attending school had higher rates of cigarette, alcohol, and drug use (Steinberg, Greenberg & Vaux, 1982; Greenberger & Steinberg, 1986).

Attitudes and Work

Perhaps the function that early employment serves is to improve an adolescent's vocational self-concept. Some have argued that the individual adolescent's attitudes about self and work may be the most important factors in career achievement (Coleman, 1975; Jepsen, 1985). Work values held by young people during their high school years are related to post high school vocational choice and to adult job satisfaction (Jepsen, 1985). When work related attitudes are positive, the adolescent has less difficulty in adapting to the demands of the workaday world. When those attitudes are negative, the adolescent becomes alienated and views career opportunities as out of reach and therefore not worth striving for.

There is a higher likelihood of negative attitudes about self and work among poor black and poor white youths. In reviewing the difficulties reported by managers of manpower agencies who had extensive experience with disadvantage youth, Kalachek (1969) found the principal problem to be one of attitude. Repeatedly counselors found young clients "alienated, discouraged, immature, lacking self-esteem and not conversant with accepted middle-class work values" (p. 7). On the other hand, high school youths who are internally motivated, who see career gains and rewards as resulting from their own initiative, experience higher rates of employment success and less unemployment than those who are externally motivated (Andrisani, 1978). As practitioners, therefore, the most beneficial intervention you may attempt in improving adolescents' career opportunities is to operate on their self-images. Changes in self-concept and self-esteem among minority and lower-income youths may do more to diminish employment disadvantages than any other factor.

It should, however, be emphasized that most young people do not have negative attitudes about work and employment. Indeed, their attitudes overall are strikingly similar to older workers' (Andrisani, 1978). If there are differences in attitudes, they lie in adolescents' perceptions that career development is *less central* to what constitutes personal fulfillment or personal satisfaction. Today's youths view work as more than simply a means to accumulate money and material goods. Instead, they see a career as having value only if it leads to personal growth and fulfillment. Youths are also likely to feel that their careers should not displace other intrinsically valued roles in their personal lives, such as their family or personal well-being. Overall, adolescents view a career as essential for personal growth and fulfillment but not primary (Havighurst & Gottlieb, 1975).

VOCATIONAL COUNSELING

A central component in the establishment of a personal identity is setting adult vocational goals and expectations. Adolescents need to identify, at least generally, what occupational role they expect to play as adults and to determine some alternative paths toward those goals. Of course, setting vocational goals with high school students should be pursued with the clear undestanding by both counselor and client that those goals may be altered with experience. Even among college freshmen, one in eight expects to change the major field of study or the career choice by graduation (Austin, 1981). In reality, the number who end up in other than their expected career as stated in their freshman year is probably considerably greater than 12 percent.

The professional community does not regard guidance toward vocational decision making as very effective (Ryan, 1978). Guidance efforts either have not been systematic or have been based on limited and sometimes inaccurate information.

Career education and guidance should involve experiences that unveil alternative adult work roles and outline the necessary steps for their achievement. Career guidance must also help adolescents to specify their goals and realistically assess their own economic, psychological, and social resources. The counselor should first aid the adolescent to identify his or her strengths, weaknesses, and needs. Unrealistic career goals may do more damage than good to the adolescent's self-esteem. Again, it might be expected that those with low self-esteem might set unrealistically high or low goals. Given a set of alternate career goals, the counselor and adolescent must then map out the educational and economic demands for achieving those goals.

Counselors and schools have a major responsibility to establish career guidance as a continuing process during the high school years. Ryan (1978) has provided a curriculum scheme in which the career guidance process is shifted from career opportunity awareness in grade nine to career preparation in grades 11 and 12. Note that the curriculum emphasizes different aspects of the vocational decision-making process depending on the grade level. A more appropriate guide for counselors might be the level of individual social development, because eleventh-graders are not all at the same point in their emotional or affective development and would not all benefit from the same experiences. Nonetheless, the principal point of the model is accurate: The progression of decision making must be increasingly complex to meet the needs of adolescents as they get closer to adult vocational roles.

Finally, counselors should encourage adolescents to have a backup strategy if their primary occupational choice becomes inaccessible. Economic and social forces may change over time, and those forces may impinge upon an individual's progress toward some goal. The question "What if it does not work out? Then what?" must realistically be faced. The most clear, if overused, example is the exceptional athlete who plans on a career as a professional athlete. These adolescents need to understand that the number of opportunities for professional athletic careers is severely limited, and although it may be a goal worth pursuing, a backup strategy is advisable.

Counselors record progress toward the establishment of vocational goals in the form of individualized plans. Any advancement toward or alteration of goals and skills are thus readily accessible and observable to both counselor and adolescent. The plan specifies short-term and long-term goals, and it can include the achievement or failure to achieve any of those goals. Because progress toward career goals usually takes time, the guidance plan has the advantage of providing evidence, over a long time span, of gain that the adolescent may not have been aware of.

SUMMARY

Although adolescents' decisions regarding careers are an important part of the identity formation process, those decisions are not isolated from other decisions and processes inherent in the transition to adulthood. Neither is career development confined to adolescent development. It is a lifelong process. Educators and counselors should be aware that premature closure on a career choice may interfere with the adolescent's search for a personal identity by cutting off the exploration of alternative roles too soon. Conversely, prolonging the decision too long may result in a failure to achieve a stable identity before entering adulthood.

Career decisions during adolescence, although setting the stage for adult career development, should not be seen as forever unchangeable. Indeed, only a minority of high school seniors will be employed in jobs resembling their expected occupation. The development of a concept of oneself in an occupation is a continuous process. As adolescents mature conceptually and socially, their concepts of the role of work in their lives and their working roles become more complex. Further, those perceptions are balanced by an improved perception of reality. If self-esteem is low, those perceptions become distorted, and expectations become unrealistically high or low.

Career choice is an important element in identity formation. Schools should provide educational and guidance experiences that facilitate that process. Career development experiences should provide opportunities for adolescents to develop positive attitudes toward themselves and work, to acquire knowledge of alternative occupational roles, and to develop skills basic to the decision-making process. Career decisions should be considered an integral part of the adolescent's emerging self-concept. The types of career goals adolescents set are likely to reflect personality predispositions as well as general feelings of personal adequacy. In addition to acquiring the more general skills and abilities related to vocational choice, adolescents should be encouraged to develop needed job entry skills.

To be maximally responsive to career development needs during adolescence, schools may need some restructuring. Most schools are currently organized with college as the primary post-high school role toward which a student is oriented. To respond to career-oriented needs may require alternative experiences not now a part of the usual curriculum. This does not imply that we totally reject the current educational structure—it obviously works quite well for many students. It does not, however, work for all. Education that builds on experiences like apprenticeship may be more directly relevant to the long-term development of vocational skills.

9 | PARENTS AND ADOLESCENTS

When I was a boy of fourteen my father was so ignorant
I could hardly stand to have the old man around. But,
when I got to be twenty-one I was astonished at how
much he had learned in seven years.

Mark Twain

If there is a specifically turbulent part of adolescence, it is probably associated with adolescents' needs to establish psychological independence from their parents. Their dependent relationship of childhood must be altered as they near the independent status needed in adulthood. During this shift parents and adolescents are often at odds with one another. Parents still see the need to exert control over their children, whom they regard dependent and immature. Adolescents feel treated "like a child" and prefer to think of themselves as adults, worthy of adult trust and adult responsibilities. Some joke that adolescence *is* a period of storm and stress—*for the parents*.

Parents, when faced with this transition, may find themselves talking to a daughter or son who is suddenly argumentative and hostile. The teenager, on the other hand, views the parents as old-fashioned and, as Mark Twain puts it, ignorant. The problem for the adolescent is, in part, that the dependent relationship of childhood that is being abandoned is secure and they are not sure of the value of adult independence. For the adolescent both alternatives are thus attractive: although adult independence is enticing, the dependent relationship of childhood is secure. Parents may recognize intellectually that their adolescent must become independent in order to move out of the house and into adult maturity, but they may still relish the dependent relationship that their child has with them.

During late childhood and preadolescence, parents often see their child as cooperative and cheerful. Children see their parents in an idealized fashion: their mothers and fathers always right and all knowing. The child is thus motivated to cooperate and in general looks to parents and authority figures for guidance. Parents serve their children by providing for their basic needs and offering a secure home environment. Both parents and children become increasingly secure within this relationship.

As teens begin to see themselves as individuals and start to prepare for adult roles, then it becomes necessary for them to leave the dependent role of childhood behind. They strive to achieve emotional and psychological inidependence, particularly from parents. Adolescents' need to free themselves or, as Ausubel (Ausubel, Montemayor & Svajian, 1977) describes it, emancipate themselves from their parents and childhood, may also be a source of fear and anxiety. The dependence of childhood is certain. The independence of adulthood is uncertain.

In their struggle to establish themselves as independent, adolescents may resort to a variety of maneuvers, including passive resistance, open hostility, or both. They may refuse to participate in activities with the family or to cooperate with parents, Arguments with parents may take the form, ''You just don't understand,'' or ''I'm the only one who can't do that.'' Parents at this point may become distressed that their adolescent is causing a major disruption in the household and may fear that this new behavior reflects the way the adolescent is going to go through life. In more tumultuous transitions, parents may become mutually hostile toward the adolescent.

College may offer a setting in which the adolescent finalizes emotional and psychological separation from parents. (© Frank Siteman MCMLXXX)

Sometimes the adolescent *does* seriously disrupt the family, and the family may need professional help. In family counseling it is not uncommon to find that the parents are divided on issues concerning their adolescent and that the adolescent has seemingly tried to foster that division by pitting the parents against each other. In counseling families who have problems with their adolescents, it is very important not to take sides too quickly. The "fault" for the disruption rarely falls in one place.

Whether or not the emancipation process is tumultuous for a given family may depend in large part on the patterns of family interaction during childhood. If the transition is anticipated and if parents provide opportunities for increased responsibility, self-management, and independence throughout childhood and early and middle adolescence, then the need for greater independence during late adolescence will not be as sharply defined. The transition is less likely to be rocky. In families in which the teenager is not allowed to participate in the decision-making process, the transition may be more stormy.

The transition to adult independence is not a sudden one, and parents should not feel that they must "lose control" overnight. The adolescent's need to remain *dependent* dissipates gradually but continuously. Likewise, parents need to decrease the degree of control they exert over the adolescent and increase their expectations of self-control steadily. By late adolescence the shift to adult independence and responsibility should be nearly complete.

Establishing emotional and psychological independence from one's parents does not necessarily require physical separation. But some during late adolescence may need the added physical distance (such as being away at school) to solidify their psychological independence and form an identity with which to enter adulthood. Historically this was accomplished by sending the youth to another family to live and work as an apprentice. At the end of the apprenticeship, the adolescent was financially and psychologically independent of his parents (Kett, 1977). Among contemporary adolescents that same process must be achieved while the young person is still financially dependent on his parent.

Other adults in positions of authority should also recognize that, as part of adolescents' emancipation efforts, they too may be the object of rebellion or hostility. They too must be responsive to the differing needs for dependence and independence within and among groups of adolescents.

When the struggle for emotional independence takes its form in hostility, belligerence, and perhaps some mild delinquency, the conflict may be very stressful for both parents and adolescents. Adolescents pleading not to be treated as children may act very childish. Parents driven to distraction may feel angry and resentful, which in turn leads to feelings of guilt. Further, many professionals unwittingly place a heavy guilt burden on many caring parents by emphasizing the impact of neglectful or abusive parenting on psychological maladjustment. If parents see their adolescent as sullen, argumentative, and hostile, they are likely to blame themselves and try to determine what they did wrong. We need to reassure parents that the resistance and antagonism of middle adolescence are not necessarily their fault. We need to encourage parents to develop new modes of communication with their adolescents. On the other hand, parents should not presume that because the motive to establish emotional independence is a normal part of the adolescent transition, they should be benignly tolerant of their adolescent's outbursts. A balance that includes respect for the rights and needs of both the adolescent *and* the rest of the family needs to be achieved.

PARENTING STYLES

The general pattern of parents' interaction with their children and adolescents has an impact on the psychological and social development of their offspring. In their attempts to socialize their children, parents interact in ways that can be characterized, first, in terms of the degree of parental control they exert, and, second, in terms of the emotional support they provide (Thomas et al., 1974; Becker, 1964). The words *parental control* should not be confused with "overrestrictiveness." Parents who exercise firm control over their children may be just as warm and supportive as some who exert little control. Conversely, parents who use little control may be just as cold and rejecting as some high-control parents. Becker (1964) sees the relationship between these two dimensions of parenting style in the form shown in Figure 9–1.

Baumrind (1968) describes four types of parenting styles that coincide roughly with the four combinations of control and support seen in Becker's diagram (Thomas et al., 1974). *Permissive* parents provide high emotional support but exert little parental control. Adolescents from permissive homes have the right to make their own decisions even if the decisions are in basic conflict with the parents' wishes. Baumrind suggests that the permissive style is associated with development of creative thinking, because the children are allowed and encouraged to try out a variety of ideas and life-styles. On the other hand, Baumrind also points out that although the parents may assume a permissive stance in a caring fashion, the child or adolescent may interpret their behavior as uncaring. The lack of assertive parental input may lead the adolescent to feel that the parents do not care what happens and may further result in feelings of insecurity.

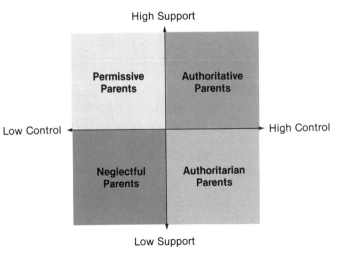

Figure 9–1 Becker's model of parenting styles. *Source:* Reprinted by permission of the publisher, from *Family Socialization and the Adolescent* by Darwin L. Thomas, Viktor Gecas, Andrew Weigert, Elizabeth Rooney (Lexington, Mass.: Lexington Books, 1974).

Authoritarian parents provide low emotional support but high control. Authoritarian parents maintain absolute authority over what the child is to do, permitting little or no choice for the child. This type of parental style is often associated with adolescent delinquency, high aggression, low self-esteem, and low religiosity in the offspring (Thomas et al., 1974). Because adolescents from authoritarian homes are not allowed any input into decision making (even when decisions concern them), they may develop feelings of worthlessness. They feel incapable of making decisions. Adolescents from authoritarian homes will sometimes replace the parental decision maker with another equally autocratic substitute, who provides an attractive alternative. In some cases this decision maker may be a religious leader or it may be a peer group.

Authoritative parents also provide high control, but control is paired with warmth and strong emotional support. The authoritative parenting style is labeled by some researchers as democratic, although that label may be misleading. Although a child or adolescent has input in the decision-making process within the family, the final responsibility for decisions rests with the parents, who can overrule the child or children. As Baumrind notes, however, the balance of control and release of control in the authoritative household may need to shift during the adolescent transition to provide for an increased degree of independent decision making by the adolescent. Authoritative families tend to produce dependent and conforming offspring who do not engage in divergent or creative thinking, but there is some research to the contrary. Goertzel and Goertzel (1962), in a study of eminent and creative people, found that they often came from structured families with opinionated parents, However, even convergent thinking, perhaps more common among children of authoritative parents, is paired with high feelings of positive self-esteem and religiosity during adolescence and adulthood.

Baumrind's distinction between authoritative and authoritarian parents is a particularly important one: although both types of parents depend on high control, they differ in the amount of emotional support that accompanies their high control. The implicit assumption in the Baumrind position, as in others, is that discipline and control—when used firmly, fairly, and consistently in the context of a warm, supportive family environment—are positive components in effective childrearing.

Finally, Baumrind describes a subset of parents who are low in control and low in emotional support, whom she labels *neglectful.* Parents in such families see their children as burdens and essentially leave them to their own devices. As a result, children from these homes suffer lowered self-esteem and have poor social interaction skills (Thomas et al., 1974).

Elder's (1963) research led to a similar sorting of family interaction patterns, but Elder's analysis was concentrated more on the dynamics of interchange regarding the decision-making process, especially as that process had reference to the adolescent in the home. In those families that Elder described as *autocratic,* adolescents have no say at all in the decision-making process, even when the decisions directly affect them. The entire decision-making process rested with the parents, usually with one parent. In *authoritarian* families, adolescents have some input, but the authority and decisions were firmly fixed in the parents. *Democratic* families allow and encourage input from their adolescents regarding the decision-making process, but the ultimate authority for decision making still resides with the parents. *Equalitarian* parents, on the other hand, not only encourage input but also consider every member of the family as having an equal voice in family decision making. *Permissive* parents, as in Baumrind's description, prefer to let their adolescents exercise their own judgment in most or all major decisions. The permissive parent may help the adolescent by discussing a problem, but the decision-making responsibility ultimately rests with the adolescent. *Laissez faire* parents not only expect adolescents to be responsible for their own decisions, they also maintain a hands-off policy in the decision-making process. The adolescents are on their own. Finally, the *ignoring* parent, like the neglecting parent described previously, leaves adolescents to their own devices. The parents impose no constraints because they do not attend to the adolescent's needs or care about the adolescent's needs. Notice that in Elder's scheme the shifts in parenting styles are somewhat subtle from one level to the next. Although warmth and caring are not immediately prominent as a sorting dimension, they are implicit.

In a somewhat different approach Minuchin (1974, 1985) and Olson (Olson, Sprenkle & Russell, 1979; Barnes & Olson, 1985) focus on dimensions of family adaptability and cohesion. *Cohesion* is described as the degree to which a family "sticks together;" it also represents the degree to which family members are expected to think alike. The interesting thing about this model is that it suggests either extreme of the cohesion dimension is unhealthy. At one extreme a family can be so cohesive that family members become *enmeshed,* they lose any individuality. At the other extreme family members can become so *disengaged* that they offer each other no support. *Adaptability* refers to the degree to which a family is able to respond to stress. Adaptability ranges from overreactive and *chaotic* families to seriously nonresponsive and *rigid* families. Along both dimensions, moderation is seen as reflecting the most healthy family setting. As family patterns reflect extremes on these dimensions, the risk of maladaptive behavior in the children increases.

A strong social support system is essential for positive adjustment of all family members (Bronfenbrenner, 1979; Garbarino, 1982). Parental warmth and strong social support result in improved self-esteem among the children. On the other hand, children and adolescents from families marked by hostility and weak support systems have lowered self-esteem (Bishop & Ingersoll, 1984; Rutter, 1978; Whitehead, 1979). In some cases, family environments are so disruptive that when asthmatic and diabetic children are removed, their conditions improve (Minuchin, 1974).

Although such classifications are useful and important, you, as a reader, should be cautioned that not all parents can be neatly placed into little boxes. By splitting the descriptions into high and low control or high and low support, we ignore those parents who lie the middle range, whose styles may or may not have effects that fall between the extremes. It is not enough to split the difference. Also, parents use a variety of styles depending on their mood, their health, the problem area, the child, and so on. The typologies do, however, provide useful guidelines for classifying parenting styles. Moreover, they set the stage for demonstrating that the style with which parents interact with their children does have an effect on their children's social and psychological development.

PARENTING STYLE AND PERSONALITY DEVELOPMENT

The patterns in which parents exercise control and provide emotional support have a significant impact on the personality development of their children and adolescents. Although it is difficult to provide clear categories of family environments, the general concensus seems to be that children raised in warm, supportive families with firm but fair control are least likely to be identified as maladjusted during adolescence and adulthood. Children from cold, rejecting families that depend on harsh and often erratic control, are more likely to show problems in social and emotional adjustment.

Aggression and delinquency have repeatedly been related to the atmosphere in the home. Aggressive individuals are more likely to come from homes in which parents depend on severe and excessive physical punishment for discipline and control (Sears, Maccoby & Levin, 1957; Bandura & Walters, 1959). Adolescents with psychiatric disorders are similarly more likely to come from homes with a higher degree of instability (Rutter, 1983).

A variety of factors influence the preferred parenting style within a given family. In a cross-cultural study of parent-child relationships, it was found that the degree to which parents emphasize "compliant" values (obedience, nurturance, responsibility to

Contrary to the popular image of mutual antagonism, most adolescents and their parents have generally positive feelings for each other. (Jean Shapiro)

others) or "assertive" values (achievement, independence, self-reliance) was related to the economic stability of the culture (Barry, Bacon & Child, 1957). As technology and economics provide greater ease of satisfying basic needs, then families are more likely to emphasize achievement-oriented behaviors. As cooperation among families becomes necessary for survival, then compliant behaviors are encouraged. However, when the economy is below some minimal subsistence level, cooperation among families is not reasonable. The result may be increased antisocial aggression and self-reliance.

Kohn (1977) has suggested that in our culture, white-collar, middle-income families tend to transmit values of self-reliance, achievement, and creative thinking, which are more in line with the traditional orientation of schools. Blue-collar families, on the other hand, have a different perception of social reality and are more likely to emphasize conformity to authority, dependence on others, and nonacademic achievement. White-collar parents are, for example, more likely to discipline their children on the basis of their interpretation of the children's motives, whereas blue-collar parents are more likely to respond solely to the behavior (Gecas & Nye, 1974).

Larger families are more likely than small families to depend on firm, authoritarian control (Holtzman & Moore, 1965). Older children in large families are, however, more likely to assume adult roles earlier. They often assume surrogate or "associate" parent roles in the care of younger brothers and sisters. Such parenting roles are more likely to be placed on older daughters than sons, because the role is largely a nurturant one. Because of this, the pursuit of independence and the establishment of a personal identity may be more difficult for girls than boys in large families. Girls from large families are more likely to be aware of family tension than boys, at least in the Holtzman study. They are also more likely than their small family counterparts to report family tension. Additionally, Holtzman found that the amount of tension reported in a family was negatively related to the amount of stress reported among adolescents. Large family size, low income, and little education are not *by themselves* significant contributors to tension and aggression within the family (Farrington, 1978). The impact of the total ecology of the family must be considered. Stress is related to a combination of factors.

In another important study by Glen Elder (1974), women and men who were adolescents during the Great Depression were studied as adults to see what impact that major economic upheaval had on their personality development. Elder found that the impact of the depression was mixed and was related to the social status and stability of the family prior to the catastrophe. Boys from middle-class families who suffered serious financial setbacks during the depression showed better psychological health and stronger drive as adults than boys who came from middle-class families who did not suffer a similar calamity. Boys from families that suffered financial setbacks achieved levels of educational achievement comparable to their more fortunate peers, but by age 38 to 40 they were actually employed in higher-status positions.

In contrast, the opposite seemed true for lower-class and working-class boys. Financial disaster had a very negative effect. Boys from working-class families who experienced financial setbacks were less likely than their peers who did not suffer setbacks to continue their education, and as adults they were employed in lower-status occupations.

Among girls from middle-class families, those who suffered financial setbacks were expected to assume household roles while their mothers went to work to help support the family. As adults they had less education and were more likely to prefer homemaking than their nondeprived counterparts. In general they had a much stronger commitment to traditional family life values. There was also some evidence that they, as with the males, had better psychological health as adults.

THE GENERATION GAP

A generally popular opinion holds that today's adolescents and youths are inalterably opposed to the attitudes and values expressed by their parents' generation and, conversely, that parents are antagonistic to adolescents' peers, who are viewed as antisocial or antiestablishment. This so-called generation gap leads to inevitable conflicts and hostility between parents and teenagers, because neither side understands the other.

The concept of a generation gap has been widely accepted by the popular media and by such notable social scientists as Margaret Mead (1969) and Theodore Roszak (1969). However, researchers who have attempted to demonstrate a general discontinuity in values and attitudes between the generations have not found any major rift. In fact, rather than discord, there seems to be a good deal of harmony between adolescents and their parents about what is valued (Douvan & Adelson, 1966; Feuer, 1969; Thomas, 1974; Yankelovitch, 1974).

One study asked parents and their teenagers to tell how they felt about "teenagers in general" and "adults in general," both from their own perspective and what they thought the others' perspective would be. That is, parents filled out the questionnaire from their own point of view and also from what they thought their teenager's point of view was. The teens were asked to do the opposite. The results indicated that both parents and teenagers had favorable views of adolescents. Parents, however, overestimated the ratings that teenagers would give themselves, and teenagers underestimated the ratings that parents would give to them (Hess & Goldblatt, 1957). The discrepancy was not so much in the real views but in the expected views.

In their study of conflicts between parents and youths over value structures, Douvan and Adelson (1966) found no major differences. Indeed they concluded:

> Parent-peer conflicts are less severe and general than they are reported to be. Some discrepancy of values is sure to be found since the two generations differ in perspectives, but for the most part, we believe, core values are shared by parents and peers, and conficts center on peripheral or token issues. (p. 84)

Like the notion of storm and stress during adolescence, the idea of the generation gap may be the outcome of people projecting the behavior of a minority of adolescents onto the whole, and it may be reinforced by the emancipation efforts of middle adolescence. Baumrind (1975) suggests that the alienated, antiauthoritarian stance pictured in the generation gap is more likely to result in families whose parenting styles are either highly restrictive or very permissive. Keniston (1965) describes parents of alienated youths as themselves unfulfilled and trying to achieve fulfillment through their offspring.

Whether adolescents have positive or negative attitudes about their parents, and whether they accept their parents' ideals as valid, depend to a large degree on whether they see their parents as caring, responsible, and reliable (Smith, 1970, 1976). By way of contrast, delinquent youths often describe their parents as inconsistent, unstable, and unreliable (Becker, 1964). As teenagers see their parents as less competent, they are more likely to see their peers as an attractive alternative. In a sense adolescents from unstable homes are "pushed" to their peers by parents who fail to provide adequate role models.

For the most part, however, the generation gap does not exist. Although we can observe some attitudinal differences between generations, depending on what questions we ask (Thomas, 1974; Chand, Crider & Wiltis, 1975), we find no evidence of a massive rejection of parental ideals. Thus the adolescent may *behave* as though rejecting the parents' values, but inwardly there may be little difference in opinion.

PARENT-YOUTH CONFLICT

What then do we make of the parent-teen conflicts that are so typical in descriptions by both parents and adolescents? The arguments and tensions that often dominate family interactions are not figments of someone's imagination. The conflicts and arguments are real. But, rather than reflecting an outright rejection of parental values, the conflicts are part of the natural establishment of the adolescent's personal identity.

Recent research evidence confirms that even among families with well adjusted adolescents there exists some normal challenge to parental authority (Steinberg, 1987a; Steinberg & Silverberg, 1986). This within family tension and confict may serve an important function in affirming the adolescent's need for autonomy which is, in turn, a primary attribute of psychological maturity (Greenberger, 1984).

At one level parents understand the need for adolescents to establish autonomy. Parents assume that as adolescents mature they will take on more responsibility for their own behavior. Yet, even with parental recognition of the need for adolescent autonomy, adolescents complain that their parents refuse to give them any responsibility and treat them like children. Parents, on the other hand, complain that they wish their teenagers *would* act responsibly and cooperate with the rest of the family. Both sides of the conflict usually include some truth and some fiction. Parents are often reluctant to give too much responsibility to adolescents, because they fear negative consequences. Teenagers may want additional responsibility, but they also want to enjoy the irresponsibility and freedom of childhood. Elkind (1984) adds an additional concern that in contemporary western culture there is pressure for very early psychological separation from parents and that young people are being coerced into adult roles for which they are unprepared.

The parent's task is to provide the teenager with the chance to assume an increasingly responsible role in the family. This may be established in the form of contractual agreements—for example, "If you want the keys to the car, then you will mow the lawn." In other more general cases, adolescents should be expected to maintain a regimen of responsibilty for their own affairs.

Adolescent reluctance to cooperate with parents or adult authorities should not automatically be interpreted as *refusal* to cooperate. A hostile, uncooperative stance may be necessary to protect the adolescent's feelings of self-worth by implying a rejection of a dependent relationship. If the parent's demands are in opposition to the peer group's desires, a lack of cooperation may serve to assert individuality. As the desires of parents and peers become increasingly incompatible, the chances for an explosive confrontation increase. Even still, the reluctance and hostility may be coping behaviors necessary to address the conflict. When parents assert control in opposition to peers, they often provide the adolescent with a workable rationalization for not participating with those peers: "I *have* to go with my parents," or "I can't do it. My *parents* won't let me."

The teen may really prefer to have the parent exercise control in these periods of conflict. Remember that at this point the adolescent vacillates between a desire for independent adult status and a need to maintain the secure, dependent status of a child. Thus, although their outward verbalizations are hostile and belligerent, adolescents may really want their parents to enforce control and assume responsibility.

One bewildered mother related an incident in which her 14-year-old daughter wanted to go with some friends on an unchaperoned weekend camping trip. The parents said no, they did not think it was a wise idea. After a highly argumentative and tearful session, their daughter called her friends to tell them, in caustic tones, "My parents won't let me go." Both parents expected a moody and hostile weekend. Instead, as their daughter hung up the telephone, she suddenly changed her mood and said, "Thanks, Mom and Dad," and calmly walked to her room. Her parents were baffled.

In fact, the daughter in this case may not have wanted to participate in the weekend, but she had not yet gained sufficient self-confidence to resist her peers. When her parents took responsibility for the decision, she was relieved of the problem of explaining herself to her peers.

Responsible parenthood implies, as Baumrind suggests, an authoritative role. But parents must achieve a delicate balance between controlling and releasing control of the adolescent. It is clear that part of the socialization process of adolescents approaching adulthood is their increased acceptance of adult responsibility. The balance, therefore, between control and release of control changes from early to middle to late adolescence. By late adolescence the transition to independence and release of control should be nearly complete, although strong emotional ties may still persist (Ausubel et al., 1977).

THE STRUGLE FOR AUTONOMY

Ausubel (Ausubel, Montemayor & Svajian, 1977) focuses on adolescents' autonomy from their parents as the critical variable that defines the end of adolescence. Freud (1917) saw the struggle to establish independence and autonomy from parents as central to the development of a strong ego in adolescence. Establishing autonomy, however, was expected to be a painful process. It was expected that in attempts to separate themselves, adolescents would resort to rebellion, lack of cooperation and outright hostility. Later,

Caring for younger siblings develops a sense of family and responsibility. (© Christopher Brown/Picture Group)

using a sociological perspective, Davis (1940) outlined the same expected conflict between parents and their adolescents.

Taken to an extreme, recognition of adolescents' struggles for autonomy might seem to validate the concept of a generation gap. However, the focus on the generation gap fails to recognize that the adolescent, while striving for autonomy, may not automatically want to relinquish dependence. On the other hand, the emergence of family conflict over issues of control and responsibility are a result of this struggle.

At the same time adolescents are struggling with their attempts to "break away," their parents are similarly trying to "let go." Parents recognize that to be adults their children must be able to operate on their own. Yet, the dependent relationship between parent and child is two-way. Hence, releasing the apron strings may also be a painful process.

Since society as well as parents expects the process of establishing independence to be complete as a person enters adulthood, psychological maturity is sometimes equated with autonomy (Greenberger, 1984). Parents and society expect that as adolescents mature they will become self-reliant and assume responsibility for their own behavior. Yet, research evidence (Steinberg & Silverberg, 1986) suggests that the transition from dependence to autonomy is not as simply defined as some think. Rather than moving from dependence on parents to autonomy, adolescents are more likely to shift to dependence on peers. Autonomy from peers grows as young people value peer acceptance less (Cohen, 1980).

As indicated earlier, David Elkind (1984) has expressed concern that the process of moving toward adult autonomy has been speeded up too much. He documents several case studies of young people who are forced into the adult world at an early age. They wear adult clothes, are expected to act like adults, and are given adult responsibilities. The problem is that these young people are not socially mature enough to handle the stress. The result of too much freedom too fast is often for these young people to resort to alcohol and drugs and even suicide.

Similar concerns are sometimes raised regarding the growing number of "latchkey" children and adolescents who come home to an empty house. As the number of children living in single parent or dual career homes increases, more children and adolescents are being left to take care of themselves while parents work. The benefits or detriments of this arrangement are still a matter of debate. One study (Long & Long, 1984) was initiated after the authors encountered an increasing number of former latchkey children in therapy. The Longs found increased levels of fear, boredom, social isolation, and resentment toward parents combined with lowered feelings of self-worth. On the other hand, not all evidence has been negative. In one study of latchkey and non-latchkey children, no differences were found on measures of social functioning (Rodman, Pratto & Nelson, 1985).

SINGLE PARENT FAMILIES

During the 1970s, the nation's divorce rate in the United States increased rapidly, raising cries of alarm that the traditional family was in danger of disappearing. However, the increase in divorce rates has not been stopped or slowed (Norton & Moorman, 1986) and the overwhelming majority of children live in two-parent families. Nonetheless, it is estimated that a child born this year has a 50 percent chance of experiencing a family divorce by age 16 (Bumpass, 1984) and a 60 percent chance of spending at least one year in the home of a single parent (Norton & Glick, 1986). If a mother remarries, half of those children will experience a second divorce (Bumpass, 1984). Divorce and dissolution of the family is a major source of stress for young people. Not infrequently, they feel to blame for the divorce and their self-esteem suffers. Further, when one or the other parent remarries, they must readjust to their new roles with stepparents and perhaps stepsiblings.

In the past "broken homes" have been a convenient and ready target to blame for a variety of social and psychological maladjustments, especially delinquency. Even today, if we were to look at the backgrounds of teens who are in juvenile homes, it might seem that an extraordinary number come from broken or disrupted homes. We need to be cautious, however, not to jump to conclusions too quickly. It may be that juveniles who come from broken homes are more likely to become delinquent, *or* it may be that delinquents who come from broken homes are more likely to end up in penal institutions. Although divorce and broken homes are convenient scapegoats, there is little evidence to indicate that divorce will, by itself, produce delinquent children (Herzog & Sudia, 1973).

The effects of divorce, separation, or remarriage on children are more directly related to the emotional atmosphere of the family before, during, and after the crisis than the event itself. Marital hostility, either in intact or separated families, is a much more pervasively negative factor (Bishop & Ingersoll, 1984; O'Leary, 1984; Oltmanns, Broderick & O'Leary, 1977). Conversely, a positive, nurturant family environment contributes to adolescent self-esteem as well as adolescents' abilities to cope with stressful life events (Johnson, 1986).

Saying, however, that divorce and separation is not inherently a cause of delinquency or maladjustment, does not imply that divorce is not a painful transition for adolescents. In one study, almost without exception, adolescents who underwent divorce said it was emotionally painful (Wallerstein & Kelly, 1980). Further, in comments of some of my students who are now young adults, the emotional pain of divorce lasts for several years.

In counseling divorced, separated, or remarried parents and their children, a common set of problems seem to emerge that hinder the adjustment of children and youths in those families:

1. A turf problem is typically associated with custody of the children following separation. The whole question of who will now be responsible for the children is often the focal point of argument and misunderstanding.

2. Parents are often hesitant to discuss the coming separation with the children until it occurs or is imminent. Life between the parents up to the separation becomes a form of peaceful (or not so peaceful) coexistence, in which the parents assume that their children have no idea of what is happening. This attitude and behavior may have serious effects on the emotional well-being of the children. At certain levels of cognitive development, children may understand the concept of legal separation only superficially; they may fear that the parents may not only divorce each other but divorce the children as well.

3. Children and adolescents may misunderstand the causes of a separation and/or divorce and feel that they are somehow to blame. The children must be assured that they are not the cause of the divorce and, once again, that the parents are divorcing each other and not the children. Parents need to explain to the children that they still love them and will continue to see them, even if they are not living together as a family.

Parents in families undergoing separation should encourage their children and adolescents to talk about their feelings about the crisis. Very often it is helpful to explain that most people, children and adults, suffer and feel depression when faced with such a crisis. That depression may take other forms besides despair and sadness—for example, apathy and lack of motivation to do schoolwork or to spend time with others. It may also be helpful to have a support group of other young people in similar circumstances. Such a group helps its members see that their feelings and fears are not unique and provides examples of the ways in which others have tried to solve their problems. This type of group can be particularly important because the suffering of the

Economic and family demands on children who grow up in poor, single-parent families may lessen their chances of experiencing the "luxury" of an identity crisis. (Bob Adelman/Magnum Photos, Inc.)

child or adolescent is often compounded by the fact that the parents—also undergoing an emotional crisis—simply do not have the time or energy or psychological resources to respond to their hurting children.

It is important, in the period following divorce, to encourage the parent who does not have primary custody to maintain contact with the children and adolescents. Too often the parent who is not living with the children feels that it would be better to disappear from the scene and not to interfere. That attitude, however, is not a realistic reaction to the problems involved. The physical separation of the parent may lead to the children feeling guilty and anxious. They may feel that they are at fault in some way. Although fathers are being granted custody more frequently, the father is still the parent most likely to be separated from the children. As you will see, absence of the father leads to specific kinds of problems. In either case, however, I cannot overstate the importance of the separated parent maintaining contact and communication with the offspring following the crisis.

Rather than single-parenthood, the family factor that is most likely to be associated with maladjustment and delinquency is a lack of stability and support at home. Sometimes the family is more stable *after* a divorce than before it. It may be the extra burden of single-parenthood added to an already unstable and stressful situation that contributes to the overall pattern of maladjustment among troubled youths.

That is not to say that the absence of a father or mother from the home does not create problems. There is some evidence that in father-absent homes, both boys and girls have difficulty establishing an adequate gender identity. Lacking a male role model, boys in fatherless homes may choose the mother or peers as their model. When boys select their peers as their role model, they may assume a stereotyped masculine, or *macho* role (Hannerz, 1969).

The effects of father absence on personal development depend on the reason for the absence and the age of the child when the absence begins. One study of adolescent girls found that girls from fatherless homes felt less secure around male peers and adult males than those from father-present homes. Girls whose father was absent because of divorce were more likely to try to gain the attention of adult males and females. Girls whose father had died, on the other hand, showed considerable anxiety in the presence of a male interviewer (Heatherington, 1972). Girls who were daughters of divorced parents were also more likely to marry earlier and to select marital partners who had a pattern of social maladjustment (Heatherington, Cox & Cox, 1982).

At some point children of single parents may face an additional adjustment problem. If one or both of the parents decides to remarry, the children may need to learn to live with a new stepparent and perhaps stepbrothers and stepsisters. The adolescent who may have assumed increased responsibility in the absence of one of the parents may now be asked to give up that responsible role.

The displacement is additionallly traumatic if the young person has assumed the role of a surrogate partner with shared roles in family decision making. Also, a young person who is fond of the new stepparent may suffer loyalty conflicts at remarriage. The young person may feel caught in the middle of obligations to both parents and in fact may hold on to some fantasies of reconciliation. These fantasies are eogcentric in the sense that adolescents may feel that their behavior controls whether the parents reunite—if they can change, the parents will be reconciled. Remarriage, of course, puts a strain on those fantasies. (The fantasies are not unlike those of abused children, described in the next section, who feel that they have control over their parents' behavior and that, if they can alter their own behavior, the parent will stop being abusive.)

ABUSIVE PARENTS

While the great majority of parents respond to their children in a positive, loving fashion, any discussion of parenting must be tempered by the reality that some do not. A minority of parents physically, emotionally, or sexually abuse their children and adolescents. Child abuse is an emotion-laden issue but defining abuse is not easy. Although extremes of abuse are clear, not all instances of abuse are easily recognized.

Physical abuse occurs when a parent, adult, or caretaker inflicts physical injury on a child. In some cases injuries may be sufficiently traumatic to require medical care or hospitalization of the child. Hence, it is often the physician, the nurse, or the physical education teacher who is the first to see evidence of abuse. Anyone who deals with child abuse on a regular basis becomes aware of the sadistic lengths to which some parents will go. In extreme cases, the injuries may result in the death of the child. Most cases of physical abuse, however, are not severe enough to result in hospitalization. Thus, most cases of physical abuse go unreported. While most media attention to physical abuse is directed at abuse of infants and young children, parental beatings of adolescents that lead to hospitalization are not unheard of. Some evidence suggests that the incidence of physical abuse increases as a child moves into adolescence (Paperny & Deisher, 1983) since behavior problems which are most often antecendent to physical abuse (Kadushin & Martin, 1981) also increase. One study (Garbarino, Sebes & Schellenbach, 1984), reports that in 47 percent of reported cases of abuse, the victims are adolescents.

Psychological or emotional abuse is defined as verbal or psychological behaviors by a parent, adult, or caretaker which lead to lowered feelings of self-worth (see Hart & Brassard, 1987). Most of us have experiences in which someone has said or done something that caused us great psychological pain—made us feel worthless. Some children and adolescents live with continuous berating and verbal abuse. There is currently no agreed upon definition of psychological abuse. Yet, among those who deal with adolescents and children in clinical settings, there is no question that psychological abuse is real.

Families in which physical and emotional abuse are found tend to be unstable. Abusive parents are unhappy and isolated, lack social support, and are uncertain about security of family finances (Kadushin & Martin, 1981; Smith, 1984). In their review of abuse, Garbarino and Gilliam (1980) conclude that maltreating families are more likely to favor use of physical and psychological coercion, are not adaptable, are more hostile, and operate at lower levels of cognitive functioning. Additionally, abusive families more often have a stepparent (Garbarino et al., 1984).

While no social class is immune to child abuse, cases of physical abuse are more frequent among lower income families where stress from financial uncertainty is heightened (Kadushin & Margin, 1981; Pelton, 1978; Smith, 1984). For the same reasons, and the increased risks of isolation and behavioral immaturity, abuse is more likely among very young parents. When compounded by resentments of an unplanned, unwanted pregnancy and termination of normal, social relationships of adolescence, teen parents are ill-equipped for the stresses of parenthood.

Research evidence also suggests that unattractive or deformed children, mentally retarded and emotionally disturbed children are more likely to be abused (Elmer & Gregg, 1967; Smith, 1984). Any trait that makes the child less lovable increases its chances of being abused (Martin, 1976). Sometimes, the abused child has the misfortune of reminding the abusive parent of the other parent who is resented or disliked. In many cases, abusing parents describe their own parents as having treated them in the same way (Solomon, 1973; Steele & Pollock, 1968). People tend to "parent" their children in much the same way that they were themselves "parented." When a parent is abusive, succeeding generations are more likely to perpetuate the cycle.

Most physical abuse grows out of usually acceptable disciplinary behaviors in which the parent responds, then overresponds, to perceived or real child misconduct (Gill, 1970). In cultural groups where harsh, physical punishment is sanctioned, abuse is more likely. It is, in part, our tendency to focus on severely abused children who need medical care that leads us to not attend to a wider range of parental behaviors which are also abusive but do not require medical care and therefore go unreported. Even in cases of clear abuse, presentation of evidence which will be acceptable in a court of law is difficult. In some instances, it seems the wrong person is punished.

John, a 14-year-old boy, threatened to kill his father after his father had hit him with a belt buckle hard enough to draw blood. John was placed on probation by the courts. After several instances of running away, following similar beatings, John was assigned by the courts to an adolescent psychiatric unit. John's father was not punished.

Sexual abuse occurs when an adult sexually victimizes a child or adolescent; it includes incest, rape, molestation, and exploitation through pornography. Sexual abuse most commonly takes the form of an adult male having sexual relations with a child or adolescent boy or girl. Cases in which a female adult sexually exploits a male child are rarer. In a study of college students, Finkelhor (1979) found that 19.2 percent (about one in five) of females and 8.6 percent (about one in 12) of males reported having been sexually victimized as children. In the great majority of cases, the sexually abusive adult is not a stranger but a member of the immediate or close family or a family friend.

Reports of incest increase as young people enter early adolescence. The increased reports may reflect an actual increase or they may result from children's increased awareness of the social stigma of sexual victimization.

Jane, a 15-year-old, was brought to the attention of a child-welfare agency by her older sister. Jane had been forced to have sexual intercourse with their stepfather several times over the previous six months. The stepfather had also been having sexual relations with the older sister until she had left home and was also sexually active with a younger, 12-year-old sister. The two younger girls were removed from the home and placed in a foster home. In the meantime, the mother and stepfather blamed the three girls for causing all the trouble. "Besides," the stepfather argued, "it ain't nobody's damn business what I do with my daughters."

Many children and adolescents, however, are reluctant to report the sexual victimization since they may blame themselves for the behavior. It is not uncommon for the perpetrator to foster that belief. A major task in the counseling of sexually (and physically) abused children and adolescents (even as adults), is to help them understand that the abuse was not their fault.

Finkelhor (1980) lists eight factors related to sexual victimization of children:

1. Living in a family with a stepfather
2. Having lived for some time without the mother
3. Not being close to the mother
4. Having a mother who never finished high school
5. Having a sexually punitive mother
6. Having no physical affection from the father
7. Living in a family with a poverty level income
8. Having two or fewer friends

As more of these eight factors are present, the risks for sexual victimization of young girls increase. Sexually victimized children and adolescents lack the physical scars of the battered child. Nonetheless, self-esteem suffers badly.

One study followed the development of abused children in 50 abusive families

(Elmer, 1967; Elmer & Gregg, 1967). Of those who had suffered physical abuse leading to broken bones, only 10 percent recovered fully. The remainder retained physical, mental, and emotional scars that seemed to become increasingly serious as the child approached adolescence.

Currently public agencies are demanding legislation providing them greater power in responding to cases of physical and sexual abuse. Treatment of abusive parents, however, is exceedingly difficult and varies with the type of abusers and the reasons for their abusive behavior.

In dealing with abused children and adolescents it is important to restate that only a small minority of actual cases are reported. Not all cases require medical treatment, and when they do not, reporting depends on the victim. Further, while social agencies are likely to respond with pity for the small child who is abused, they sometimes seem less willing to deal with the abused adolescent. Notice, for example, that even though abused adolescents account for 47 percent of reported cases, nearly all of the public service announcements on child abuse depict small children. The message is almost that adolescents are not abused.

Prosecution of sexual abuse is difficult. Verbal statements by children in prelegal interviews are often compromised by well-meaning but incompetent interviewers. Further, courts are typically reluctant to equate incest with forcible rape (Sgroi, 1982).

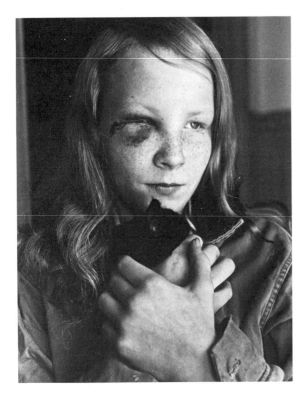

An unpleasant reality is that some children and adolescents are subject to physical or sexual abuse. (© Eugene Richards/Magnum Photos, Inc.)

DING-BAT JUDGES AND CHILD ABUSE

Those who work with services for abused children are not infrequently frustrated by the courts' reluctance to intervene in family affairs. Most judges and juvenile referees are sensitive to the problems of abuse and try to resolve such problems in ways that meet the demands of the legal system yet protect the rights of the child. At the same time, judges are obligated to follow rules of presentation of evidence and to assure the rights of the accused. Abuse cases also raise questions about the right of the courts to invade the sanctity of the home. In their attempts to not insert the courts in the home, and in their protection of the rights of defendants, it sometimes seems that the real loser in the process is the abused child. Every so often, however, a case comes along that makes concerned citizens wonder about the wisdom of the "system." In the following news column, Mike Royko, the Chicago-based writer, expresses his indignation over the handling of one case of child-abuse.

The 1-year-old child was in terrible shape when her grandmother brought her into Cook County Hospital.

Her arms were broken in three separate places. Her face and jaw were bruised. She had a concussion. There were burn marks on her arms. Hundreds of what appeared to be pinch marks covered her abdomen.

She was in shock, her blood count was dangerously low and she was having trouble breathing.

She was rushed into surgery. When they opened her belly, they found bleeding. Her liver had lacerations. Her pancreas was bruised and bleeding. She had 10 centimeters of dead bowel.

After surgery, she was put into the intensive care unit. That's when doctors discovered the old fractures of both arms that were beginning to heal.

The doctors reported their findings to the Illinois Department of Children and Family Services, which investigates suspected cases of child abuse.

A case worker went to the family's home on Chicago's South Side and asked the young mother and the grandmother what had happened to the child.

They were hostile, defensive, and they refused to concede that anybody had done the baby harm. Nothing had happened. The baby just go sick.

When they came to the hospital, the case worker tried again, talking to them separately, hoping they'd be honest. Again they refused.

But somebody at the hospital picked up a clue. The baby has a 3-year-old brother, and the boy told a doctor the mother has a boyfriend, a fellow named Calvin. He said Calvin sometimes hit, choked and pinched him.

The mother finally admitted that when she had left the house for a few hours, taking her son with her, she had left the baby in the care of the boyfriend.

Doctors noticed something else. When the mother visited the baby in the hospital, Calvin came along. At the sight of him, the baby became hysterical, screaming and thrashing. Calvin was ordered to stay away from the hospital.

There was enough evidence of child abuse for the DCFS to take the case to Cook County Juvenile Court and ask for temporary custody of the child.

As a doctor said: "There was no question that the baby had been abused. From all the medical records, and just looking at her, it was obvious."

A doctor testified and told about the broken bones, both old and new, the facial bruises, and burn marks, the bleeding.

Then the mother and grandmother testified. Amazingly, they said that nothing had happened to the baby while it was home.

Then how, the mother was asked, did the child suffer such terrible and extensive injuries?

She and the grandmother offered a remarkable theory. They said that if the baby was injured, it must have somehow happened while she was in the hospital.

After the lengthy testimony about the child's condition, everybody turned to Judge Ronald Davis to hear his ruling.

According to those who were in the courtroom, Judge Davis said that, yes, it did appear that there was an "injurious environment" in the child's home.

But, he said, there did not appear to be an "urgent or immediate danger."

So, he refused to give temporary custody of the child to the state agency.

Or, put another way, he said the child should be returned to her mother.

And in a few days, that's exactly what will happen. A source at the hospital says: "She's getting better. Her teeth are budding out now. She was starved at home, didn't get enough calcium. She's still missing part of her bowel, but her two broken arms are mending. Her liver has been sewn up. And her concussion is gone. She's coming along nicely.

"But we can't keep her here for more than another week or two. Then we have to return her to her mother. We don't want to do that, but we have no choice."

They have no choice because of Judge Davis' ruling that there was no "immediate danger" in the very place where the child wound up looking like she had been run over by a truck.

When asked to explain his ruling, Judge Davis said:

"Juvenile proceedings are confidential. We are not allowed to discuss them. We're not permitted to discuss them under the law."

Well, that law doesn't prevent me from discussing such cases.

And if Judge Davis's superiors happen to read this, maybe they would like to discuss why somebody like Judge Davis is dealing with the lives of children.

Can't they find a nice, harmless parking ticket court for him?

SUMMARY

One of the primary elements in developing an individual identity during adolescence is the establishment of emotional and psychological independence from parents. The emancipation process may cause greater or lesser stress, depending on the patterns of parent-child interaction that have been established during early and middle childhood. Parents need to recognize that adolescents are attracted not only by the independence of adulthood but also by the secure relationship of childhood dependence. The task for parents, then, is to gradually shift responsibility from themselves to the adolescent. The moves toward independence are best facilitated in warm, supportive family environments in which structure and control are regularly replaced with demands for self-reliance.

Often practitioners who talk with parents about their teenagers, especially during those times when parent-adolescent communication is strained, will find that parents feel guilty about their anger toward their adolescents. Resenting your own children is something that society says a ''really caring'' parent would never do. That attitude is indeed unfortunate, because we can all feel anger at someone we care for. Parents, however, often feel that their relationships with their children are somehow different. For example, when an infant screams all night, night after night, depriving one or both parents of needed sleep, the parents soon begin to resent the disruption. However, they also begin to feel guilty about resenting this ''innocent child.'' The same thing holds for many parents of adolescents. If an adolescent uses hostility and lack of cooperation as mechanisms for establishing independence, the parents may start to have guilt feelings over their anger and resentment about these disruptions to the entire household. In addition, parents hear directly and indirectly that if their child has ''problems,'' it is the parents' fault. Once again the parent may harbor considerable guilt.

Parents cannot ignore the needs of their adolescents to establish emotional independence. But neither should they ignore the needs of the remainder of the family while they attempt to facilitate the transition. Parents need to increase their demands for self-reliant and responsible behavior within and outside the family setting.

As current trends in marriage, divorce and remarriage continue, more and more adolescents will have complex family histories. Some will live with both parents, some with a single parent, some with a parent and stepparent. As family configurations shift, adolescents must adjust to new styles of parental control and family interaction. It is little wonder, then, that such family transitions as divorce and remarriage are major stressful life events for young people.

Finally, a discussion of the role of parents in relation to adolescents must deal with the issues of abuse and neglect. Most parents struggle to raise their children in the best possible environment. An unfortunate minority inflict physical and psychological injury on their children. Cases of physical abuse are more common as loneliness, isolation, and stress dominate family interactions. Cases of sexual abuse increase under conditions of a stepfather living in the home or as closeness to the mother is strained. Counseling physically and sexually abused adolescents requires a great deal of sensitivity to deal with their conflicting feelings of guilt, anger, and humiliation.

10 | FRIENDS AND PEERS

One issue on which there is general consensus among those who work with, study, or raise adolescents, is the strong impact of the peer group on adolescent behavior. The need to "get along with" peers, be accepted by the group, and not be seen as different, may seem at times to totally dominate the adolescent's thoughts and actions. Few writers, however, would argue that this influence is automatically or necessarily negative. Indeed, peers and friends play a vital, positive role in developing social skills during adolescence.

If the impact of peers is negative at times, that impact is far outweighed by the ramifications of being excluded from the peer group. Failure to establish workable social ties with peers is a major predictor of social and emotional maladjustment during adolescence and adulthood (Hartup, 1983).

The relationships that adolescents establish with friends and peers, especially during early and middle adolescence, play an important role in aiding the adolescent to establish the social skills and feelings of personal competence that are necessary for adult functioning. As the adolescent works toward establishing a sense of personal identity and independence from family influences, peers and friends provide emotional support and a sense of security while the adolescent experiments with new roles. Thus the peer group serves as a kind of a buffer, providing a middle ground between the childish, dependent relationship with parents and adult independence. Among peers, adolescents are more free to experiment with alternate value systems and identities (Erikson, 1968). Friends and peers offer feedback on the acceptability or unacceptability of the experimental systems. In addition, they provide an adolescent with an interim identity as "one of the group." As the interim group identity is replaced by a personal identity, the need to conform to the demands of the peer group lessens.

Friends provide the most immediate source of peer influence. (© Frank Siteman MCMLXXX)

Up to this point, I have used the terms *friends* and *peers* in sequence. The terms are not, however, interchangeable. The term *friendship* refers to close personal commitments among a small group of people with whom the adolescent is able to share feelings, plans, fears, and fantasies. Typically we think of friendship as a relationship that exists between two people. Of all peers, friends are the least demanding of rigid conformity.

A small cluster of friends who closely identify with each other is called a *clique*. Cliques tend to be small groups of individuals who share common values and a common sense of purpose. In most cases a clique is usually homogeneous in terms of age and sex, and it is usually composed of individuals who live near each other and are of similar social standing.

Peers is a more general term referring both to close friends and to a broader, less clearly definable body of age mates or social mates who share common experience. At another level, more remote from the individual adolescent than the clique, is what we call a *crowd* (Coleman, 1980). A peer crowd is a conglomeration of cliques, larger and more diverse than cliques. As adolescents move into middle and late adolescence, crowds are made up of both sexes (Dunphy, 1963, 1969). The crowd sets up a dogmatic code of dress, language, and rules for acceptable behavior. The crowd is not nearly as sympathetic to the needs or feelings of the individual as the clique or a friend. Also, because the crowd lacks any clear boundaries, it may be most frightening to those adolescents who lack self-assurance. The demands from this group are less immediate than from the clique, but allegiance to the group may require some sacrifice of individuality.

Less clear and more remote, but apparently very powerful, peer influences come from an invisible "they" who are all wearing the latest fashion fad or who are all allowed by their parents to stay out late. This amorphous "they" is much like the invisible audience that the adolescent feels is preoccupied with his well-being (Elkind, 1967, 1978). In some cases the adolescent may even assume a defensive and protective posture for "them."

THE FUNCTION OF PEER GROUPS

Peers and friends seem to serve four areas of adolescents' personal development (Wagner, 1971):

1. Adolescents learn how to interact with others through peer groups. We are social beings and our ability to get along with others and be accepted by others is critical to adequate personal adjustment. Failure to develop these social skills is an antecedent to a variety of adolescent and adult mental health problems.
2. Peer groups provide a setting within which adolescents can establish and clarify their moral standards and value systems. Part of the process of establishing an adult ego identity is the exploration and evaluation of alternate value systems beyond their parents'. Peer groups thus offer a safe, supportive group within which to experiment with these systems.
3. At times of emotional stress, especially family-related stress, the peer group may offer emotional support.
4. The peer group serves an instructing and advising function. Adolescents are told what is "in" and what is not. Similarly, peers serve as a sounding board for questions and attitudes on sex, drugs, and social behavior.

As Johnson (1981a) suggests, adults are often ready to assume that peer groups effects are inherently unhealthy and bothersome. While it is true that peer influence is a major element in adolescents' decisions to participate in antisocial or troublesome behavior, peer influences also provide beneficial social support. Peers and friends serve an important function for adolescents' feelings of self-worth, particularly with reference to feelings of belonging and acceptability. Early adolescents' concerns about their value and worth are tied to their fears of being left out. Belonging and being acceptable are central to their self-esteem and being a member of a group eases those fears. The cost of belonging (conformity) is not seen by young adolescents as especially large. They are sufficiently unsure of themselves that they welcome the chance to depend upon others for guidance. Peers provide guidelines on expected dress codes, school performance, social behavior, and who is "In" or "Out." Part of the price of belonging to one group is the exclusion of other groups.

Recalling Rosenberg's (1965, 1979) description of the adolescent self-concept, peer groups may thus serve as a central extended self. The success or failure of the group reflects the success or failure of the individual. Rosenberg (also Cooley, 1902) argues that peers offer a "looking glass" self in which self-evaluation results from the sensed evaluation of others. To the extent that peers (and significant adults) give feedback that indicates acceptance and approval, one's own self-evaluation is positive. To the extent that peers (and significant adults) give feedback that indicates disapproval and rejection, one's own self-evaluation is negative.

With respect to the second of these functions, the peer group is often seen as replacing the parent. Although this may be true in part, adolescents do not turn to peers rather than parents in all cases. Whether adolescents turn to peers or to parents for guidance and support depends primarily on the quality of interaction between the adolescent and the parents at home. When the peer quality of parent-adolescent interaction is low, the attraction of the peer groups for guidance is high, and consequently, dependence on peers and susceptibility to their demands also increase (Iacovetta, 1975). When adolescents regard the peer group as more stable, more supportive, and thus a more attractive alternative than parents, its influence increases. Conversely, when they see their parents as trusting and trustworthy, parental influence remains strong.

Even in those cases in which interactions with parents are positive, the desire for peer acceptance and approval is a powerful motive for the emerging adolescent. Some degree of conformity to the peer group is not only to be expected but is also a necessary part of the price young people have to pay to be accepted by the group. Adolescents may yield to demands for conformity ranging from common hair styles, clothes, and language, to pressures for some delinquent or antisocial behavior.

If peer groups do have a clearly identified influence that is distinct from parents it is in the area of negative, antisocial behaviors. There is ample research evidence that indicates adolescents' willingness to engage in behaviors that are potentially self-injurious or that potentially cause injury to others is directly related to the likelihood that their friends engage in the same behaviors (Siman, 1977; Kandel, 1978; Jessor & Jessor, 1977; Kazdin, 1987). The more likely an individual adolescent's friends approve of and engage in an antisocial or risk-taking behavior, the more likely the adolescent will also engage in that same behavior. This relationship has been shown to exist in drug and alcohol abuse (Bachman, O'Malley & Johnston, 1980; Jessor & Jessor, 1977; Kandel, 1978), sexuality (Jessor & Jessor, 1977; Sach, Keller & Hinkle, 1984), school dropouts (Rumberger, 1987), and delinquent behavior (Gold & Petronio, 1980; Kazdin, 1987). As peer demands for conformity include delinquent behavior, there are also strong social pressures to protect the group by not "squealing" or "ratting" on the others if one is caught. Both conformity to the group and demands to protect the group are solidified by the threat of exclusion. That is, the adolescent who does not comply may be left out. because the adolescent—especially the younger adolescent—has a high fear of loss of acceptance, of unacceptability and exclusion, the threat is very effective.

Those same variables that promote the negative aspects of peer influences can be used to promote positive adolescent behavior as well. Johnson (1981a, 1981b) suggests that adults should manipulate the same attributes of cooperation and competition which serve to hold the group together to foster more positive academic attitudes and to learn social competence. That is, peer pressure can be transformed into a positive force rather than remain a negative. Focusing peer group identity on a task that has social value, such as public service, serves to reflect on the group's, and therefore the individual's identity (Yarchesi & Mahon, 1984). Counseling adolescents who feel lonely and isolated may involve encouraging them to "get involved." However, since many of these who are isolated have low self-esteem and lack the social skills needed for initiating new social roles, some structure may be required to get the individual started.

In recent years, there has been some movement toward capitalizing on peer influences in a more positive fashion by focusing peer pressure on positive, rather than negative behaviors. Of particular interest has been the emergence of peer counseling techniques for crisis intervention. In peer counseling, young people are trained to be sensitive listeners with appropriate feedback skills (Varenhorst, 1974). Peer counselors are often able to communicate to another adolescent an element of empathy that is less accepted from an adult. For peer counseling to be effective, however, teen counselors need training and support. They are not "little psychologists." In cases where the presenting problem may involve potentially serious consequences (for example, suicide), teen counselors have provided important intermediate roles in suicide prevention and drug counseling (Hamburg, 1980; Kalafat & Schulman, 1982; Varenhorst, 1974).

VIGNETTE 10–1
NIGGER

Dick Gregory, known initially for his comedy and later for his social activism, grew up in St. Louis in a home that he described as "Not poor, just broke." On the surface, Gregory's chances of breaking free of the cycle of poverty were not all that good. Gregory learned early, however, that his talent for humor and his athletic abilities provided him status. Presented below is a description of his discovery of his athletic talent and how it affected him. As you read Dick Gregory's recollection of his youth, consider how status, or the lack of it, affects one's sense of self-esteem.

Excerpted from: Gregory, Dick (1964) *Nigger.* New York:
E. P. Dutton Publishers. Copyright 1964 by Dick
Gregory Enterprises, Inc. Reprinted by permission, all
rights reserved.

I felt a lot better going back to high school that year, wearing new clothes, feeling clean on the outside. When I heard that the track team got to take showers every evening after practice, I asked the coach if I could join. Sumner had the best Negro track team in the state and a brilliant coach, Lamar Smith.

"You run before?"

"Sure, coach, I do a lot of running."

"Where?"

"Around the neighborhood."

He shook his head. "We've given out all the lockers and uniforms for this year."

"All I want to do is take a shower in the afternoon."

He looked me over and kind of smiled. "All right. But you'll have to bring your own sweat suit. And stay off the track and out of my boys' way."

That's how I started in sports. Sumner had a fine athletic field. While the team ran inside the field, around the track, I ran outside, around a city block.

Every day when school let out at three o'clock, I'd get into an old pair of sneakers and a T-shirt and gym shorts and run around that block. In the beginning, I'd just run for an hour, then go and take a hot shower. and then one day two girls walked by and one of them said, "What's he think he's doing ?" And the other one said: "Oh, he must be training for the big races." I just kept running that day, around and around the block, until every time I hit the pavement pain shot up my leg and a needle went into my side, and I kept going around and around until I was numb and I didn't feel anything any more. Suddenly, it was dark and the track team had all left. I could hardly walk home my feet hurt so much, but I couldn't wait until the next day to get out there again. Maybe I couldn't run as fast as the other guys, but I could run longer, longer than anybody in all of the city of St. Louis. And then everybody would know who I was.

I kept running all that fall and all that winter, sometimes through the snow, until everybody in school knew who I was, the guy who never took a rest from three o'clock until six o'clock. I don't think I ever would have finished high school without running. It was something that kept me going from day to day, a reason to get up in the morning, to sit through classes with the Helene Tuckers and the doctors' sons who knew all the answers and read books at home, to look forward to going a little faster and a little longer at three o'clock. And I felt so good when I ran, all by myself like a room of my own. I could think anything I wanted while I ran and talk to myself and sometimes I'd write stories on "My Favorite Daddy" and "What I'd Buy with a Million Dollars," and I could figure out why people did certain things and why certain things happened. Nobody would point to me and say I was poor or crazy; they'd just look at me with admiration and say: "He's training." I never got hungry while I was running even though we never ate breakfast at home and I didn't always have money for lunch. I never was cold or hot or ashamed of my clothes. I was proud of my body that kept going around and around and never had to take a rest.

THE STRUCTURE OF PEER GROUPS

Dunphy (1963, 1969) offers an important analysis and description of the nature of peer group organization among young people as they move through adolescence. Figure 10–1 shows the basics of this model. In preadolescence children tend to form same-age, same-sex cliques. These cliques are isolated from each other and operate roughly parallel to each other. As Dunphy (1969) notes, this age is sometimes called the "gang-age." But *gangs,* as the term is used here, does not refer to stable and formally organized youth gangs such as those found in urban areas. The gang has a common purpose only in the play activity it consumes. Early in this stage, the children may identify themselves as a "club," with secret passwords and special meeting places. Because the group is organized around play, it is not terribly stable, and it has no need to function in conjunction with other gangs.

Dunphy's early stages of group formation parallel Sullivan's (1953) idea of a "chumship" stage. Chumship is a special friendship with a same-sexed peer. During

Figure 10–1   Stages of group development in adolescence. *Source:* D. C. Dunphy (1963) "The Social Structure of Urban Adolescent Peer Groups," *Sociometry 26,* 61. Reprinted by permission of the American Sociological Association.

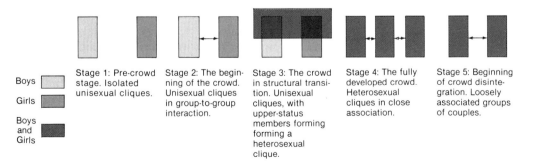

Boys ☐

Girls ▨

Boys and Girls ■

Stage 1: Pre-crowd stage. Isolated unisexual cliques.

Stage 2: The beginning of the crowd. Unisexual cliques in group-to-group interaction.

Stage 3: The crowd in structural transition. Unisexual cliques, with upper-status members forming forming a heterosexual clique.

Stage 4: The fully developed crowd. Heterosexual cliques in close association.

Stage 5: Beginning of crowd disintegration. Loosely associated groups of couples.

Cliques offer a sense of belonging but often at the price of conformity. (Tyrone Hall/Stock, Boston)

preadolescence and early adolescence, same-sexed friendships are intense and form a basis for trying out gender specific roles. Boys will often engage in aggressive play and challenges. It is common to see two junior high school boys hitting each others arms in an attempt to make each other flinch.

At around age 12, there is a change in the nature and function of the peer group. As Horrocks (1976) points out, during this time young people commonly talk about themselves with reference to "our crowd" or "our group." The clique in this sense has attained a certain integrity that makes it unique from other cliques. These cliques are largely unisexual, same-age groups, and the members usually come from similar social backgrounds and have similar values and interests. Unlike childhood gangs, these cliques are more stable and function in conjunction with or in relation to other cliques. This interaction of cliques sets the stage for the emergence of the crowd. This "near-crowd," however, is still primarily unisexual.

During middle adolescence the increasing awareness of one's sexuality and the need to interact with young people of the opposite sex lead to another alteration of the structure of cliques. As the leaders of the cliques begin to interact with opposite-sex cliques, the pattern of organization becomes heterosexual, incorporating both boy and girl cliques. The emergence of the heterosexual crowd is in part necessitated by the onset of dating. As the male/female group becomes more firmly established, heterosexual cliques may emerge. The clique is still, however, largely homogeneous and close-knit.

During late adolescence the nature of the crowd becomes multidimensional, with heterosexual cliques operating in a highly interdependent manner. Membership in a clique is now based on patterns of heterosexual interaction. Gradually these patterns become even more stable as "steady" boy-girl couples join with other similar couples to form a loose association.

THE FORMATION OF PEER GROUPS

Peer groups do not form randomly. The old adage "Birds of a feather flock together" has some basis in reality when it describes adolescent peer group formation. Adolescents are likely to gravitate toward others who share similar values, who come from similar backgrounds, who are at about the same level of intellectual and social maturity, and who have similar interests (Douvan & Adelson, 1966; Kandel, 1978a, b). Usually preadolescents and early-adolescents form friendships with those who live nearby or, sometimes, with schoolmates. As a young person moves into high school, the school becomes increasingly the focal point for peer group activities (Coleman, 1961). Still the groups are formed selectively.

By middle adolescence friendships are increasingly based on common value systems. Not uncommonly, the central core of values of a peer group are more similar than dissimilar to parents' value systems. Common interests, hobbies, or even common choice of college have little to do with the choice of friends (Newcomb, 1966). Among girls there is a clearer transition in the factors that lead to the establishment of friendships as they move from early to middle adolescence. As personal maturity increases, the value that girls give to common value systems likewise increases, as well as their ability to explain the basis for forming friendships. Among boys, however, the transition was less well identified, and the boys were less clear in their explanations for the reasons their friendships were formed. That study also observed that friendships among girls were of shorter duration (Douvan & Adelson, 1966).

Living close to one another is an important aspect in the formation of groups, especially during preadolescence and early adolescence. But proximity does not cease to be a factor even during late adolescence. In a small college dormitory, residents are more likely to establish friendships with those on the same floor than with people on the next floor (Newcomb, 1966). Further, formal social groupings such as fraternities and sororities, which tend to draw individuals with similar values and social backgrounds, foster and solidify friendships by a common identifiable label and closeness in living arrangements.

In Eder's (1985) study of social groupings of middle school girls, selection of group membership was dominated by physical attractiveness and social position of parents. As adolescent girls moved through the eighth-grade, their concern about academic achievement diminished while concern for social status increased. Differences in status attributed to membership in one or another clique increased with the size of the school. That is, the psychological "distance" from the highest to the lowest status groups was greater in larger schools. At the beginning of the school year, there appeared to be some fluidity in the structure of the cliques as individuals moved up or down on the social ladder. Once the cliques reached their capacity level, however, nonmember girls were turned away, ignored, and snubbed. The psychological pain for those who wanted to be a part of a higher status social group but were rejected resulted in considerable loss of self-esteem.

Emphasizing the commonality factor in the formation of peer groups does not imply that peer groups are simply a gathering of individuals who think alike or that peer groups have no influence on behavior or developing values. However, it does imply that the effects of peer groups on value formation, though important, may be overstated. The peer group may influence the individual, but the individual also influences the group. Further, the values of the group are typically not widely divergent from what the individual holds in the first place.

AGE AND PEER GROUPS

As with aspects of personal and emotional development described in earlier chapters, the pattern of interpersonal development shows a shift not only in the form of the peer groups (Dunphy, 1963, 1969) but also in the functions and value that the adolescent attributes to friends and peers. As young people move through adolescence, they perceive that the roles played by peers and friends change from rather self-serving, nonmutual relationships during early adolescence to complex, mutual relationships during late adolescence (Douvan & Adelson, 1966).

During early adolescence young people do not appear to make any firm, lasting commitment to friends. Rather than seeing a friend as someone with whom one may share feelings, they see a friend as someone with whom you do things (Coleman, 1980). Early-adolescents fail to perceive any real reciprocal, mutually beneficial role of friendship.

By middle adolescence teens are more likely to see friendships as based on security and trust. They regard a friend as someone with whom they can share a confidence and

Dating may provide a degree of status among peer-group members. (© Frank Siteman MCMLXXX)

who will be loyal even when they are not around (Douvan & Adelson, 1966; Coleman, 1980). The relationship among friends may still be rigid, because the need for trust and the anxiety over breach of trust or rejection keep the relationship uncertain.

As peer groups and friendships become more stable, the adolescent learns to place trust in other members of the group who, likewise, begin to trust one another. The sharing of secrets and fantasies serves as part of the testing process in establishing this trust. As group concensus of values and attitudes is achieved, individual adolescents place increased trust in the group judgment of what is acceptable and what is unacceptable (Newcomb, 1966).

As young people approach middle adolescence, their anxieties over rejection by peers increase and, likewise, so does their motive to conform. Figure 10-2 shows the results of one study of conformity among adolescent groups (Costanzo & Shaw, 1966). Notice that the tendency to conform to peer pressure increases dramatically during early and middle adolescence and then begins to taper off by late adolescence. The often-reported observation of eighth- and ninth-grade teachers that conformity to the group seems to be the dominant value in the lives of their students is not far from the truth. For middle school or junior high school students, acceptability by the group is paramount.

In another study, researchers found that early-adolescents were more likely to value friendships based on common activities, whether the friend was seen as a source of excitement or whether the friend lived nearby. Among adolescents in the age range associated with the shift from early to middle adolescence, there is an increase in the use of terms that refer to loyalty, admiration, and helping in the description of friendship.

During late adolescence young people see friendships less restrictive and less formal. They are more relaxed with less fear of a breach of trust or rejection. These mutually benefiting relationships are increasingly heterosexual and increasingly oriented toward a sense of adult intimacy.

You can also see in Figure 10-2 that girls were consistently more likely to conform than boys at all age levels. Girls are also more able than boys to articulate what constitutes good friendship (Douvan & Adelson, 1966).

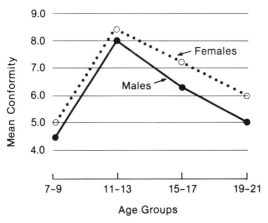

Figure 10-2 Conformity among adolescent groups. *Source:* P. R. Costanzo and M. E. Shaw, "Conformity As a Function of Age Level," *Child Development* 37 (1966): 973. Copyright © 1966 by the Society for Research in Child Development, Inc. Reprinted by permission.

The peer crowd has varying degrees of influence on the adolescent's need to conform.
(Courtesy, Waltham High School, Waltham, Massachusetts. Photograph by Peter Vandemark)

There is, indeed, a consistent tendency for girls to place greater importance on friendships than boys (Coleman, 1980). Gold and Douvan (1969) suggest that this divergence reflects differences in patterns of socialization. Boys are encouraged early to be independent and self-reliant, whereas dependence is more likely to be fostered in girls.

PEERS AND ACHIEVEMENT

High school students currently and traditionally have displayed something of an anti-intellectual attitude. To be overly bright or to achieve too easily is seen not only as not positive but instead may be rated by peers as clearly negative. Classmates prefer the "competent plodder" to the highly intelligent, creative student (Liberty et al., 1963).

In a major analysis of high school students' attitudes, Coleman (1961) found that being intelligent was not valued nearly as much as being popular. In reporting what they felt were the most important characteristics of the "leading crowd" in high school, students felt that having a "good personality" and "being friendly" far outweighed any strivings for academic excellence.

Coleman concluded that adult society segregates adolescents into their own institutions and cuts them off from interacting with adults. Adolescents are thus forced to establish their own subculture, with its own rules and values. In that subculture, status among boys is tied to car ownership, athletic accomplishments, and extracurricular activities, whereas girls value social success, physical beauty, and nicer clothes. Neither sex sees academic success as important.

Other studies reinforce the view that academic success is not only *not* a prized attribute among high school students, but rather it may be a negative trait (Tannenbaum, 1962). Bright students may suffer conflicts between their ability and desire to achieve and their desire to be accepted. Although boys seem more able to reconcile those opposing needs and to strive toward higher achievement as they progress through adolescence, girls are apparently less able to resolve the conflict (Douvan & Adelson, 1966). Once again, it is possible that this difference results from the difference in general values transmitted to boys and girls by society as a whole. Girls, who are expected to be socially adept, may define success or achievement in those terms rather than through academic achievement (Bardwick & Douvan, 1971).

It is a bit unfair to point to the peer group as the primary source of the anti-intellectual attitude. We can easily argue that society devalues academic achievement in high school students and that peers merely reinforce that attitude. One has only to look, for example, at the newspaper coverage given to a National Merit Scholar versus a star athlete.

We need to note once again that friendships do not form at random. In large part, friends have highly similar educational expectations and goals (Duncan, Featherman & Duncan, 1972). Further, they are considerably alike in their actual levels of academic performance (Kandel, 1978a).

In a more general view research demonstrates that the level of a student's educational aspirations is influenced by the overall pattern of educational aspirations of those around him. In the results of of one study (see Table 10–1), both the occupational level of the father and the general socioeconomic level of the school had an influence on college aspirations (Wilson, 1959). A critical review of the impact of school peers on educational aspirations concluded that lower-income students who attend predominantly middle-class high schools are more likely to have higher educational aspirations because of the general level of school expectations. On the other hand, those same lower-income students are also likely to compare their performance to that of their middle-class peers and assess their own ability as low (Bain & Anderson, 1974). It is not simply enough

Table 10–1 Percentages Wishing To Go To College

Father's Occupation	NEIGHBORHOOD SCHOOL GROUP		
	Upper White-Collar	Lower White-Collar	Industrial
Professional	93	77	64
White-Collar	79	59	46
Self-Employed	79	66	35
Manual	59	44	33
Overall	80	57	38

Source: A. B. Wilson, "Residential Segregation of Social Classes and Aspirations of High School Boys," *American Sociological Review, 24* (1959): 839. Reprinted with permission of the author and the American Sociological Association.

to improve a student's motives. We must also provide the academic skills and behaviors necessary for success.

ADOLESCENT SOCIETY

One popular notion is that in some way adolescents are a social entity unto themselves, independent from and alien to adult society. The idea is not terribly different from the supposed generation gap discussed in the last chapter, but it goes beyond simply a difference in values.

The concept was given considerable credence by the publication of James Coleman's important study *The Adolescent Society* (1961). In that volume Coleman puts forth the view that because adolescents are neither children nor adults, adult society is unsure how to respond to them. Thus, historically, adolescents have been systematically isolated from both children and adults. To accomplish this end, society has created unique social institutions (for example, high schools, YMCAs, and so on) that are presumed to prepare adolescents for adult responsibility. In reality the institutions are often unrelated to adult roles and are seen by young people as irrelevant. Adults put adolescents into a social "holding pattern" until they are old enough and mature enough to be absorbed into adult society.

Because adolescents are cut off from adults and adult society, they are forced to turn to their peers for a set of values, for social support, and for learning social skills. Adolescents develop their own society complete with its own moral code, language, and fashions. The hallmark of this adolescent society is conformity to these behavioral codes. Peers enforce conformity to the adolescent society norms by including or excluding individuals as members of "the group." When young people are accepted as members of a group, they are expected to be loyal to the group and to reject adult society and any form of adult responsibility.

Although Coleman's description of an adolescent society has a certain intuitive appeal, not all writers agree that it exists in as extreme a form as originally thought. Adolescents do not form an anti-intellectual, antiestablishment population that conforms blindly to the wishes of peers (Weiner, 1976). Some researchers (for example, Douvan & Adelson, 1966) are concerned that adolescents do *not* have a significant period of separation from adults, that adolescents merge into the adult system of values too early and thereby miss out on a normal developmental progression. If adolescents are conforming, it is to the adult society, because they seem to buy into that system without question. Some differences in attitudes are certain to separate parents and teens, but the existence of a so-called "adolescent society" may be an overstatement of fact.

As with most arguments of this kind, the truth probably falls somewhere between the extremes. Today's adolescents are drawn to the support and acceptance of their peers. But rather than being forced to accept an entirely new set of values, adolescents tend to seek out friends who have values similar to their own. The result is an alliance with a peer group that may at times be in opposition to adult values, but which has, in balance, values very like those of adult society.

VIGNETTE 10–2
THE REAL DUNGEON MASTER

Peers and friends play important roles in socializing children and adolescents toward adulthood. When we play games we learn rules and cooperation. We learn strategies and we see how we and our friends deal with success or failure. Over the past several years, Dungeons and Dragons *has been a popular pastime for many young people. Supporters of the game call it innovative and creative. Its detractors have been less complimentary. Religious fundamentalists describe it as demonic. Presented below is a story based on an interview with the ultimate dungeon master, the creator of the game. How do you evaluate his views of the game?*

Excerpted from: Fisher, Kathleen (1984) "Game helps youth pass from magic to maturity." *APA Monitor,* 15, (No. 12).

When Gary Geigex was a mere tot his mind was filled with a mixture of the fantastic and the cerebral. At night his Swiss father would sit beside his bed and weave elaborate tales of wizened old men with magic rings and gold hidden under rocks. During the day he would play chess and read whatever he could get his hands on.

That childhood of Tom Sawyer and toy soldiers grew into a career. In 1974, Geigex created *Dungeons & Dragons,* a medieval adventure game that fits somewhere between *Monopoly* and improvisational theater and has itself assumed mythical proportions.

Cults have built up around it. Teen suicides have been blamed on it. Religious fundamentalists have claimed that when they burn it, it screams.

While not many adolescents can turn a passion for fantasy into a livelihood, Geigex believes that many have a need to act out in play the transition from the dependency of youth to the independence of adulthood.

Geigex is a former insurance underwriter, not a mental health professional. But child psychiatrists sound a similar theme.

"The symbols in the game represent development toward maturity," he explained. "When you start out, you have no power that will help you deal successfully with the environment. You gradually earn that power.

"There are no winners. You can go on gaining more powers because the game only ends when the players have had enough. And that's usually about the time they discover drinking and girls."

Adults usually aren't comfortable with the game, he said.

"Adults may be willing to role play. But players don't so much role play as role assume; you might reveal more than you care to expose. Adults have some preconceived ideas about games that are hard to let go. They don't understand something that doesn't have pieces and boards and other conventions we're used to."

The basic *Dungeons & Dragons* game involves little more than a book delineating some broad rules of play, to be coupled with the participants' imagination. It evolved from Geigex's adult avocation of weekend tabletop war games. One weekend in 1968 he decided to hide "a great, ugly troll" under a bridge and attack the medieval soldiers with a fire-breathing dragon. Fellow players loved the innovation, and participation, which had been declining, soon tripled.

In 1972, he produced a 50-page manual spelling out some of the basic concepts which was distributed among pen pals.

The next year he and associates founded Dungeons & Dragons Enterprises with $1,000. They have since sold 2½ million copies of the basic game.

Although two avid players have commited suicide, the link seems tenuous. One youth, a prodigy who entered college in his early teens, disappeared on what a private detective described as a "real life" game of *Dungeons & Dragons*. "That's no more possible than playing real life Monopoly," Geigex said. The youth was found on his way to another state to visit his father, but killed himself two years later.

"If you calculate man-years of play, I imagine suicide is higher among who play bridge," Geigex said.

In fact, he suggested, many of those who play the game are former introverts who are "lionized and become extroverts within this narrow realm."

Educators have praised the game, he went on, because it encourages imagination, fosters understanding of real problems and even statistical probability. "I've based it on linear equations and bell curves."

And more than with most games, he said, *Dungeons & Dragons* calls for cooperation. If the characters marshal their complementary strengths—spiritual, physical, magical—they can obtain gold and other profit. If they begin to bicker, they will likely be devoured by dragons.

Geigex believes that competitiveness is instinctive but can be diverted into acceptable channels. He said he stopped playing chess because he found it too competitive.

"I just don't have the killer instinct. It can be very intellectually destructive. I would find my hands shaking from the adrenalin flow.

"I think *Dungeons & Dragons* is weighted toward a moral and ethical world view. I don't know how anyone can get upset about a game where the goal is to kill a big purple worm, a demon or a dragon."

Some religious fundamentalists—the ones that say the game screams when they burn it—say the game is evil because it even refers to demons, he said. "They are more concerned because the game encourages children to think for themselves and not to accept what's told them as gospel."

SOCIAL COGNITION

As adolescents move from early, rigid, and concrete conceptual systems to later, flexible, and more abstract conceptual systems, their perceptions of objects and persons in their psychological environment are similarly altered. These qualitative shifts in thinking extend to their perceptions of siblings (Bigner, 1974), self (Montemayor & Eisen, 1977), peers (Scarlett, Press & Crockett, 1971), teachers (Ingersoll & Strigari, 1983), government (Gallatin, 1979), and interpersonal relationships (Gollin, 1958; Livesley & Bromley, 1973; Peevers & Secord, 1973; Selman, 1980).

The progression of maturation of such concepts follows predictable developmental patterns. During early formation of concepts, they are poorly integrated in the individual's overall conceptual systems. Elements are separated into rigid, nonoverlapping categories. Judgments are absolute and egocentric. Objects and persons are compartmentalized in either-or fashion; multiple classification, the recognition that an object or person may assume many roles, is restricted. As adolescents become more facile in manipulating and integrating their psychological environment, they are increasingly capable and likely to see the elements of their conceptual network as interrelated and interdependent. At the same time, however, the elements do not converge into an undifferentiated whole. Both integration and differentiation occur. As adolescents' conceptual structures become more mature, adolescents also become more tolerant of ambiguity and the possibility of alternative visions of reality than their own.

When early adolescent conceptions of others are called *egocentric,* egocentrism refers to an inability of the individual to distinguish himself or herself from others; other people and objects are simply extensions of the self. In earlier childhood, egocentrism is so complete that children are incapable of taking another's point of view; "I see it this way, therefore, you see it the same way." To function at a more mature level, adolescents must *decenter.* That is, they must be capable to understand and appreciate another's point of view. As Elkind (1967) has pointed out, however, adolescents' improved thinking abilities may result in a new form of egocentrism in which an adolescent presumes that "Since I think this way, everybody thinks this way."

The power of the "invisible audience" during the adolescent years represents an important extension of egocentric thinking into the arena of peer relationships. The adolescent's sense that "Everyone is watching me" is more egocentric than real. Yet, the insecurity generated by the adolescent's beliefs about the invisible audience is very real and it may lead to conformity to standards that exist only in the adolescent's own mind. Young people conform to what they *think* everybody wants without an accurate understanding of what peers actually expect. As Lapsley (1985; Lapsley et al., 1986) cautions, adolescent egocentrism may be less of an issue of limited formal operational thinking as one of limited interpersonal skills.

Like other aspects of cognitive development, interpersonal understanding progresses in a stagewise sequence. Robert Selman (1980) divides the progression of interpersonal understanding into five distinct levels.

At the lowest level (Level 0) of Selman's model, children are unable to attribute any perceptions or thoughts to other people. They are completely egocentric. Friendship is based on physical closeness and the degree to which the child's friend makes the child happy. For the most part, friendships are temporary and unstable. Leadership within a group of peers is based upon physical superiority, the one who is able to coerce others is the leader. When faced with problems, children at the lowest level react physically and impulsively with no real thought to the ramifications of their behavior.

The next level of interpersonal understanding (Level 1), is the most frequent mode of elementary school children. Those at Level 1 are able to understand that other people view the same object differently than they. At this level, however, children are still operating at an early, concrete operational level. Awareness of others' perspectives is limited to concrete objects, hence, they are still mainly self-oriented. Close friendships are still not well-developed, friendships still serve an egocentric function. Friends are described as those with whom you play games and if they do not want to play games they are no longer friends.

In later childhood and early adolescence, youngsters are expected to move into the next level of interpersonal understanding (Level 2). At Level 2, individuals still respond in a concrete operational fashion, but they are able to think of relationships with friends beyond immediate needs. Friendship may become valued for the sake of the relationship itself. Friendship behavior becomes reciprocal. Friends take turns, they make deals, they depend on a sense of fair play.

In middle or later adolescence, Selman expects young people to move into a level of mutual collaboration (Level 3). At Level 3 the individual is able to reconcile one's own needs and the needs of others. Not only does the adolescent recognize that he or she has multiple emotions, but that others also have multiple emotions and that those emotions may differ from one's own. At the same time, friendships take on a new intensity. It is as though friends become part of oneself at a new level. Members of the group become highly interdependent.

At the most advanced level of interpersonal understanding (Level 4), the individual is aware of the complex nature of social interaction. Allocation of authority and leadership is based on democratic processes in which one is selected for the perceived benefit to the group. Leaders are valued for being able to bring and to hold the group together.

POPULARITY AND SOCIAL COMPETENCE

The degree to which an individual adolescent is successful at establishing friendships or being seen as a desriable friend depends on a variety of factors. As Chapter 4 indicated, one of the important elements in being viewed as popular or unpopular is physical attractiveness. The more physically attractive an individual, the more likely he or she is to be seen as a person with whom others want to be associated. Other factors that lead to popularity or lack of it include social status, social skills, and personality attributes.

Consider the case of Dan. Dan is a 14-year-old boy who was referred for counseling after several episodes of "antisocial behavior" in the schools. During the counseling setting Dan complains that nobody likes him. As the counselor obtains more information, it seems that Dan is right—nobody does like him. Students seldom choose him to be part of a team, and they rebel about working with him. Even teachers see Dan as "a bit obnoxious." Students are less gentle and refer to Dan as a "nurd" or a "creep."

On the opposite side of the spectrum, consider Bill. Bill is seen by students and teachers alike as a leader. Bill is not especially athletic, but he is able to hold his own and is a welcomed member of a team in a "pick-up" game. He is also likely to be elected to some student political offices and is seen simply as a really important and popular person.

Dan and Bill represent the extremes in popularity: Dan, severely lacking in popularity, and Bill, having popularity to spare. Most adolescents fall between these extremes, and their popularity may range from high to low. In a typical classroom of adolescents, we can expect that individual popularity will be spread across the entire spectrum of "stars" who are highly popular to "isolates" who have few or no friends.

Although peer acceptance is not in and of itself the all-important determinant of behavior, the lack of peer interaction may lead to long-term difficulty in personal adjustment. The degree to which an adolescent or child is accepted by peers is highly predictive of social adjustment. Thus practitioners should be alert to problems or changes in the social acceptability of individual adolescents.

One method of measuring social prestige is the *sociogram*. A sociogram is a relatively simple assessment technique in which each person in the large group is asked a series of questions regarding choice of peers. Questions may include "Name two people in the class you would like to work with on a project," or "Name two people in the class with whom you would *not* want to work." The results of the sociogram can be plotted in a figure in which each choice is represented by an arrow. (See Figure 10–3.) *Sociometric status* is reflected by the number of arrows pointing to each individual. Sociometric stars are the leaders and are most popular, as indicated by the number of times they are chosen. In Figure 10–3, Bill is chosen by seven of the 12 boys in the room. Fred, however, is chosen by none. Bill is a sociometric *star*, whereas Fred is a sociometric *isolate*. Further, because Jack, Carl, and Ike choose each other and no one else, they can be labeled as a *clique*.

An adolescent's sociometric status stays fairly constant across different settings and over time. Like intelligence test scores and achievement level, the later in personal development the measure is taken, the higher the stability. Also, the extremes of social status are more stable than the middle range. That is, those students who are stars in one setting are likely to be stars in others. One curious problem that this can create, however, occurs when a large group of stars converge into a single setting. For example, a freshman class at a prestigious college may include many young people who were leaders and stars in high school and who must now complete with one another for high status. For some this turns out to be a serious problem in adjusting to college life.

Figure 10–3 An example of a sociogram.

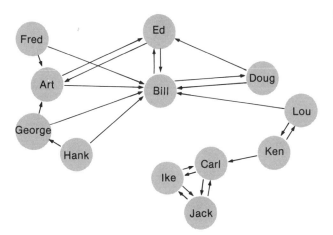

The consistency over different social settings, over different measures, and different ages suggests a generalized indication of social acceptability (Moreno, 1953). Sociometric results obtained from students are directly related to teachers' and adults' impressions of social acceptance. Sociometric status is also related to social and personal adjustment. Adolescents with high prestige show patterns of general positive feelings of self-esteem, whereas adolescent social isolates show very low feelings of self-worth. The isolate also comes across as socially inept. Social isolates seem to lack behavioral know-how.

Children and adolescents who are socially isolated are a matter of considerable concern. Ample evidence exists to show that, as a group, social isolates are more likely to drop out of school before graduation, to engage in delinquent or antisocial behavior, and to show significant mental health problems as an adult (Hartup, 1983). It is not just that these young people are left out of peer groups (neglected), they are actively rejected by peers (French & Waas, 1985). Peer neglected children and adolescents are much less likely to show evidence of maladjustment than those who are rejected. Peer rejected adolescents are more likely to be aggressive loners (Dodge, 1983). The consequences of peer rejection may be more severe than low academic achievement.

Recent studies of the social behavior of children and adolescents as it relates to social acceptance indicates that those who are least socially acceptable tend also to be least socially competent (Dodge, Pettit, McClaskey & Brown, 1986). *Social competence,* the ability of an individual to behave in ways that are skilled and effective, is fundamental to good psychological health. Conversely, social incompetence is a major predictor of psychopathology. Those who are socially adept and aware are more likely

"Hanging out" and being seen by others is part of the process of maintaining adolescent social status. (Photograph by Shirley Zeiberg)

to receive positive feedback from peers and adults. Those who are socially inept are more likely to be shunned and avoided.

Social competence, like social cognition, is a developmentally related characteristic (Eisenberg & Harris, 1984). As one matures cognitively, the ability to anlayze and respond to complex social settings also matures. McFall and Dodge (1982) suggest that the individual's social competence is dependent upon first, the ability to decode the setting. That is, the individual must be able to accurately identify the critical cues in a social setting. Second, the individual must decide which, from among many alternative behaviors, is the most effective and appropriate response. Third, the individual must translate that decision into an actual, smooth behavior. In the latter case knowing what to do and being able to do it may not be the same. Anxiety, inexperience, or emotions may interfere. At the same time, the individual receives feedback from others in the social setting to indicate how adequate or appropriate the response was (Dodge et al., 1986).

One approach to treating the social competence deficit felt by social isolates might be to train them in social skills (Oden & Asher, 1977; Cartledge & Milburn, 1980). Much as shyness can be modified through training in social skills, other forms of social inadequacy can likewise be modified through appropriate training.

A typical program of intervention involves providing the isolate with a fellow student who serves as a model and reinforces the isolate for socially appropriate behavior. In one study an isolate was paired with a peer model. Whenever the isolate behaved in socially approved fashion, the model would provide the isolate with a token. The token incidentally had no value beyond the fact that it represented recognition of achievement. Over time the number of inappropriate behaviors decreased, whereas socially appropriate behavior increased. Further, the number of appropriate behaviors continued to increase after the formal intervention program was terminated. Apparently the isolate learned the very effective strategy of modeling with alternative roles.

SUMMARY

On the whole, peers complement rather than oppose the socializing influences of parents and society. Although peers may have divergent attitudes on some negative social behaviors, there is considerable harmony in attitudes of parents and peers. When family ties are weak and counterproductive, adolescents are more likely to depend on peers for support and approval. Conversely, when family ties are strong and parent-adolescent interactions are productive, adolescents are less likely to turn to peers in times of stress.

Although traditional social and pscyhological theories have sometimes stressed the pervasiveness of peer influences and the existence of a separately functioning adolescent society, that emphasis may have been overstated. There is a great deal of commonality in attitudes among peers who cluster together. On the other hand, the impact of peers, especially with respect to negative behaviors, should not be underemphasized. Peers and friends have an impact that is neither as great as some would believe nor as weak as others might prefer. In general peers provide a positive environment within which the individual adolescent is able to develop a personal sense of identity.

We can see perhaps the most profound impact of peers in those young people who are deprived of peer influences through social isolation. The absence of adequate social interaction during childhood and adolescence leads to social maladjustment during adulthood. Establishing appropriate interpersonal bonds during adolescence is a necessary prerequisite to developing feelings of intimacy as young adults.

ADOLESCENT SEXUAL BEHAVIOR

11 AND ATTITUDES

As young people enter adolescence, they are faced with a new sense of their sexuality. Prior to puberty, they may have been aware that they were boys or girls, but their maleness or femaleness was not very salient. As young people progress through puberty, however, their sexuality becomes more noticeable. Socially and biologically, they become more adultlike and their sexual self becomes more focal. Adolescents must deal with their emerging sexuality in at least two ways. First, they must decide which, if any, gender roles they are willing to internalize. As noted earlier in the text, many young people, at least temporarily, choose to accept very stereotyped male and female roles. Others elect to accept more balanced views of their masculine and feminine selves. The second way in which adolescents must deal with their emerging sexuality is in their sexual behavior with others. Adolescents must learn to manage their sexual behavior. Failure to do so may result in problems that alter their lives radically.

The scientific study of adolescent sexual behavior is fraught with problems. In one review, Diepold and Young (1979) summarized and evaluated most of the existing studies of adolescent sexual behavior and concluded that our actual knowledge of normal adolescent sexual activity is disappointingly limited. Further, they contended that much of what we believed about a major sexual revolution during the 1960s was based on undocumented speculation by the mass media. What research has been done suffers from problems that force us to be skeptical about what we think we know. As Diepold and Young argue, the problems in studying human sexual behavior are difficult enough, but when the humans in question are adolescents, the problems are even more complex.

As an example, Robert Sorensen (1973) compiled what was expected to be a major analysis of adolescent sexual attitudes and behavior, *Adolescent Sexuality in Con-*

temporary America. The study, however, has not met with general acceptance. Among the reasons why reviewers are skeptical of his results is evidence that the youths who Sorensen interviewed were probably not typical (see, for example, Bell, Broderick & Goldsmith, 1973). Sorensen started his research by identifying a national sample of 839 teens who were scientifically selected to be representative of all teens in the United States. To Sorensen's credit, he observed the ethical requirement of requesting the parents' permission to interview the teenagers (some studies have not). Only 508 of the parents agreed. Of these, only 393 of their teenagers agreed to respond to his questionnaire (which was almost 40 pages long). Thus only 47 percent of the original sample ultimately participated in his study. Very serious questions remain over whether the 53 percent who would not or could not participate had attitudes and behaviors similar to the 47 percent who did. It has been shown, for example, that in the Kinsey studies (Kinsey et al., 1953) women volunteer participants were on the average higher in self-esteem and sexually more active (Maslow & Sakoda, 1952). Thus those who did participate in Sorensen's study may not be truly representative of all American teens. Nonetheless, Sorensen's study is not without merit.

Beyond the problems of generalizability of those studied, problems sometimes arise in the study of sexuality in adolescents and children due to the way in which questions about sexual behavior and attitudes are asked. Some questions may yield ambiguous responses. For example, 74 percent of Sorensen's young people answered "false" to this statement: "My parents and I sometimes talk about sex but it makes them very uncomfortable." What does "false" mean? That they never talk to their parents? That they often talk? That their parents don't feel uncomfortable? Using "proper" language may also lead to problems. In another study, Vener and Stewart (1974) reported that many preadolescents answered that they had engaged in sexual intercourse. When interviewers questioned further, they discovered that the youngsters thought that sexual intercourse was talking to someone of the opposite sex.

With these caveats in mind, let us turn our attention to adolescent sexuality.

MASTURBATION

Most professionals recognize that masturbation, or as it is sometimes called autoeroticism, is a normal sexual activity among adolescents. Many young people, however, still report guilt feelings about the behavior. Their feelings of guilt and anxiety about masturbation may arise from religious condemnations of the practice or from fears based on myths about the results of masturbation. A variety of religions disapprove masturbation. Gregory (1968) suggests that those sanctions can be traced to the middle ages when "The Church condemned all forms of sexual indulgence other than genital intercourse between husband and wife with the express purpose of having children. Masturbation became regarded as evil and perverse, and was frequently referred to as 'self-abuse'" (p. 505). Masturbation is also falsely linked to a number of negative effects. It will not, however, lead to insanity, sterility, shortness of stature, or acne.

What information is available about masturbation among adolescents tells us

Many people express worry over the high sexual suggestiveness of advertisements aimed at adolescents. (Photograph by Anita Duncan)

that by late adolescence virtually all males and the majority of females have engaged in masturbation (Kinsey et al., 1948, 1953). In a later study, Haas (1979) found among adolescent males, 75 percent of 15 to 16 year olds and 80 percent of 17 to 18 year olds reported they masturbated. Among adolescent girls the percentages were 52 and 59 respectively. The great majority of the young people in the Haas study thought there was nothing particularly wrong with masturbation. In a study of German youths, few reported they preferred masturbation to sexual intercourse. Masturbation was an alternative for sexual release when coitus was unavailable, it served as a pleasurable alternative (Sigusch & Schmidt, 1973). For many adolescent boys, it is the way in which they experience their first ejaculation.

When guilt feelings are reported among young people, they are often more from guilt about their sexual fantasies while masturbating than the activity itself. In the Haas (1979) study, 90 percent of the boys and 75 percent of the girls who masturbate reported sexual fantasies during masturbation.

For most young people, masturbation is not a source of professional concern. Masturbation is considered a significant problem only when it becomes compulsive. At that point excessive masturbation may reflect other emotional problems. Some young people, nevertheless, still feel anxiety. Edwards (1983) cautions that in dealing with adolescents who are anxious about their masturbation, counselors should avoid explicitly encouraging the act. Efforts should be made to calm their fears, but it should be recognized that the adolescent who has those fears may be trying to exercise some degree of self-control over a personally troubling behavior. Gaining control may be beneficial to the overall feeling of self-worth.

VIGNETTE 11–1
BABYLAND

Each year one of every 10 teenage girls in the United States become pregnant. Nearly half of these young girls carry the pregnancy to completion. The statistics in themselves are alarming. They represent the base for a continuing cycle of poverty in which teen parents' education and social advantage are limited. Statistics, however, sometimes hide the fact that pregnant teens are people with feelings and hopes. The story below is of a young woman, Tammy, and her mother, W, and their attempts to cope with Tammy's baby and its needs as well as to keep some hope for the future.

Excerpted from: Burling, Stacey (1986) "They call this babyland, teen mom says." *Rocky Mountain News,* Nov. 16.

W was stunned when her 17-year-old daughter, Tammy, announced earlier this year that she was pregnant for the third time.

"I was shocked. I was hurt," W said. She spoke softly and evenly.

"I took her in my arms, and we both cried together.

"I was about the same age, too, when I came up pregnant."

So W did what her own mother had done. She accepted her daughter's mistake, grieved for the pain it would bring her and remembered what her mother told her 17 years ago: "Well, you made your bed hard to sleep in."

W knows now how her mother must have felt. "I know it hurt her. I didn't really realize how much I hurt her until Tammy came up," she said as she held Tammy's infant son, Demarco, in her lap. Tammy's first two pregnancies ended in miscarriages.

W, 34, a heavy woman in a simple house dress, moves with the tired resignation of a woman much older. Her family—Tammy, Demarco and Tammy's 16-year-old sister, Gladys—lives on $560 a month in welfare and food stamps in low-income housing.

They've got enough to eat, and they've learned not to care much for fashion. The apartment is orderly and clean. A velvet painting of the Last Supper hangs over a dining room table ringed by lime green chairs. The colors clash, but W has made a comfortable place decorated with trinkets and family portraits.

Tammy has gotten used to the middle-age men who kill time with their bottles on the porches across the street, and she talks excitedly about how her street comes alive at night.

The neighborhood is full of young mothers like her.

"They call this babyland," she said, "'cause there ain't nothing over here but babies."

W wanted more than this, and she wants more for her daughters.

"I had (Tammy) at 16 without an education and I don't want her to go through that. I plead with her day by day, "Tammy, won't you get an education?"

"I quit (school) after I got pregnant. I just stopped. . . . After coming up like that and seeing what a scuffle it's been to raise these kids, it's something I wouldn't want her to go through."

She is keenly aware of how her life would be different if she'd wait to have her children. "I think I'd have finished school. I think maybe I'd been working somewhere where I'd have had a living for myself. . . .

"I'm 34 and I never have been married, but I used to think that I would. I looked at other people, how lucky, how blessed they were to get these things, home, marriage, nice things in life, but I just never got around to it. . . I'm an old maid now."

W worked as a security guard until 1980, when she began having seizures. The 16 pills she takes each day to control them make her tired, and she has slept many of her days away.

She blames herself and her illness for Tammy's pregnancy.

"I feel if it wasn't for me coming down sick like I was, I could have been able to take care of them, watch them. . . . It was like I was just out of it."

Now she's trying to keep Tammy from making another mistake—dropping out of school—by watching Demarco while Tammy goes to high school.

Tammy says she must have forgotten to take one of her birth control pills when she conceived Demarco. She didn't want to be pregnant, "It just happened."

She wasn't using any contraception the first time she got pregnant, at 15. The next year, when it happened again, she stopped taking her pills during a separation from Jerry, her on-again-off-again boyfriend of the last five years.

She was five months along with Demarco when she found out she was pregnant once more. Her weight peaked at 104; she never needed maternity clothes.

Demarco was born three weeks early and weighed only 4 pounds, 6 ounces. He has been a sickly infant.

"He been sick since the day he was born," Tammy said. "If he ain't got diarrhea, he got a cold. If he ain't got a cold, he got an ear infection."

Jerry took an interest in his son at first, but Tammy rarely hears from him now. "He acts like it's too hard to take care of the baby," she said. "He don't make that much money on his job."

So, Tammy rises at 6 each morning to care for the boy before she heads for school. She plays with him when she's exhausted. She worries about how to pay for his diapers and the expensive formula he eats.

At first, the job seemed too hard.

"Sometimes I would get so mad at him, I could just knock him out," she said, "but I just watched my temper with him."

She's grown more patient, but the responsibilities remain a burden.

"Sometimes I get mad and I say, 'Dang, my life is messed up. I can't take it anymore.' . . . Sometimes I just feel that way because most teen-agers my age be having fun, and now I seem tied down."

Already, she is pulling in her dreams. She once planned to join the Air Force; she abandoned that idea when she learned the military wouldn't provide child care.

"I decided, forget it then. I'd just see if I could get a scholarship to get to college, because I ain't got that kind of money," she said. Tammy, who says she gets As, Bs and Cs in school, now wants to be an architect or a nurse or an artist.

She doesn't want any more children, because she doesn't want her children to suffer the way she has.

"I figure if I have any kids, I want to be married," she said. "I don't want two kids by this dude and this dude. I don't want that. I want all my kids to have the same dad.' Since she doesn't want to marry Jerry, that means no more kids.

She praises her mother but is determined not to repeat her life.

"I want it to be different," she said. "I don't want to follow in her footsteps."

W doesn't think her daughter is strong enough to make it alone.

"I think she'd probably throw herself away because she wouldn't know what to do. That's why I want to be here, so I can be her backbone....I don't want her to give up just completely."

Both Tammy and her mother tell Gladys, a vivacious, worldly girl, about having babies.

"I told her I'd kill her, because I know how it is, and I don't want her to do the same thing," Tammy said.

W isn't sure the lectures will help. She started telling her daughters about babies long before Tammy got pregnant. "I've talked to them about it all the time," she said. "It didn't do too much good."

DATING

Dating serves an important role in the process of developing sexual relationships with others. Dating serves as a mechanism for assessing one's physical and social attractiveness to members of the opposite sex. It is also a preliminary behavior to the establishment of the intimacy of young adulthood. As such, dating provides feedback to one's ability to communicate, to listen, and to share feelings. Because dating is tied to these roles it is sometimes an anxiety provoking task for some young people. Young people may desparately want to ask someone for a date but be petrified that the person may say "No."

Most young people begin dating between the ages of 13 and 15 years old although some date earlier and others begin later. Douvan and Adelson (1966) reported that by age 14, 19 percent of girls were dating; by age 16, 72 percent; by age 18, 91 percent. There is a minority of adolescents who do not date at all during their high school years. The percent who do not date at all, however, has declined from the early 1960s (Kopecky, 1974). Girls are more likely to date than boys and more likely to begin dating earlier (Spreadbury, 1982).

Dating plays a role in building the self-concept of the adolescent. It offers a way for the young person to gain feedback on her or his acceptabiity to those of the opposite sex. Satisfactory dating affirms the adolescent's sense of acceptabiity. Unsatisfactory dating may lead the adolescent to question her or his acceptability and result in lowered self-esteem. Dating may also build or lower self-esteem because it is linked to status among peers. Having dates tells others that you are acceptable and attractive. There is some evidence that suggests very early dating does not benefit young adolescents' self-esteem. When combined with other major life events such as changing schools and entering puberty, dating may be stressful and lead to lowered self-esteem (Simmons, Blyth, Van Cleave & Bush, 1979). Conversely, a very late start to dating may also be harmful to self-esteem. A study of older adolescents found that for males with minimal dating experience, adjustment scores were lowered (Himadi, Ackowitz, Hinton & Perl, 1980). Comparable lowered adjustment scores were not found for older adolescent females.

Early dates usually involve going to movies or to get something to eat. Most boys and girls say that they hold hands and perhaps kiss on their first date; few report going any further (Spreadbury, 1982). As dating continues, especially dating with one partner, petting and sexual experimentation become more likely. In several studies, kissing and light petting were nearly as common as dating and were thought to serve to enhance feelings of sexual adequacy (Sorensen, 1973; Vener & Stewart, 1974; Vener et al., 1972). In those same studies, genital petting was much less common, but by age 17, 59 percent of females and 62 percent of males reported genital petting as compared to 71 percent of both sexes reporting light petting (Vener & Stewart, 1973). According to King and his colleages (1977), genital petting is very common among college students.

Dating may also raise new conflicts with parents. Parents may try to protect their child by establishing limits that, to the child, appear unreasonable. Parents may also experience discomfort over their child 's choice of dates. Dating may thus become enmeshed in the adolescents' struggle for emotional independence from parents.

SEXUAL ATTITUDES

Whether or not there has been a sexual revolution, there has very certainly been a major shift in sexual attitudes among the young. In one study, sexual attitudes were assessed on similar groups over a period of 10 years (King, Balswick & Robinson, 1977). The results showed a significant liberalization of sexual attitudes, especially among college women. Table 11-1 presents an example of the change in attitudes. Note that in 1965, 35 percent of the male respondents and 56 percent of the female respondents felt that a promiscuous man was immoral. In 1975, only 19.5 percent of the males and 30.1 percent of the females felt the same way. When the same question was asked about a woman

Table 11-1 Sexual Attitudes of College Students

Statement		Males	Females
1. I feel that premarital sexual	1965	33	70
intercourse is immoral.	1970	14	34
	1975	19.5	20.7
2. A man who has had sexual	1965	35	56
intercourse with a great	1970	15	22
many women is immoral.	1975	19.5	30.1
3 A woman who has had sexual	1965	42	91
intercourse with a great	1970	33	54
many men is immoral.	1975	28.5	41

Source: K. King, J. O. Balswick, and I. E. Robinson, "Sexual Revolution Among College Females," *Journal of Marriage and the Family, 39* (1977): 457. Copyrighted 1977 by the National Council on Family Relations. Reprinted by permission.

who had multiple sexual partners, 42 percent of the males and 91 percent of the females in 1965 felt that such a woman was immoral. In 1975, 28.5 percent of the males and 41 percent of the females responded similarly. We can observe at least two trends in these results. First, there was a substantial liberalization of attitudes over that time period for both males and females. Second, although the double standard, which allows greater sexual latitude for males, is greatly diminished, it has not altogether vanished. Both sexes were more likely to assess the woman who had sexual intercourse with multiple partners as immoral than they were to judge the man for similar behavior.

Although college students are more likely than their noncollege counterparts to have liberal sexual attitudes, the noncollege population is becoming increasingly tolerant of premarital sexual activity. Yankelovitch (1974) finds about a four-year lag in attitudes between college youths and their noncollege peers. In 1969, for example, Yankelovitch found that 57 percent of noncollege and 34 percent of college youths felt that premarital sexual relations were morally wrong. By 1973, 34 percent of the noncollege youths felt the same way. In 1969, 72 percent of noncollege youths felt that sexual relations between consenting homosexuals were morally wrong, whereas only 43 percent of the college youths felt that way. By 1973, 47 percent of the noncollege youths held that attitude.

Although there has been a general trend in liberalization of sexual attitudes among youths, we should remember that wide diversity within and between age groups. Younger teens, on the whole, are more conservative in their attitudes and behavior. Likewise, the more religious a person is, the more likely he or she is to hold more conservative sexual values. As Table 11–1 showed, although much of the sexual double standard has dissipated, it has not been totally eliminated, and females still report more guilt feelings after premarital coitus than males (Schalmo & Levin, 1974).

Recently, Konopka (1983) found adolescent girls to be more tolerant of sexual behavior among peers than previous generations.

A radical shift in sexual attitudes is not automatically accompanied by a similar shift in sexual behavior. We can trace a major alteration in sexual attitudes among youths from 1950 to the 1980s, but the increase in rates of premarital coitus has not been nearly as profound. Indeed the sexual revolution of the 1960s was apparently nonexistent (Conger, 1975). Some shift in behavior has been observed during the 1970s. Nonetheless, worries of a promiscuous generation may be largely unfounded.

PREMARITAL COITUS

In Sorensen's (1973), by the age of 15, 44 percent of males and 30 percent of females were nonvirgins. By age 17, 59 percent of males and 45 percent of females have experienced premarital coitus. These rates were not terribly different for males in the Kinsey studies (Kinsey et al., 1948), but they were substantially higher than the rates for females in those early studies (Kinsey et al., 1953). Thus one might conclude that if a sexual revolution took place at all, it was among women. Other studies reported somewhat lower rates of nonvirginity than Sorensen (Vener, Stewart & Hagen, 1972; Saghir & Robins, 1973), but the trends were still the same. On the average, males were much more likely to be sexually active during early teen years, but by later teen years the differences between the sexes were less. Of interest in the Sorensen study was his evidence that even among sexually active teens, the preference was for serial, monogamist relationships. That is, a sexually active teen had intercourse with only one partner, to whom he or she had a strong emotional commitment. When that relationship ended, the females tended to be sexually inactive until another monogamistic relationship developed.

Perhaps the most informative studies on premarital sexual intercourse among American youths are those conducted by Zelnik and Kantner (1972, 1977, 1980). In 1971, Zelnik and Kantner interviewed a national sample of unmarried women between 15 and 19 years about their sexual behavior. They repeated that study in 1976, covering areas like sexual history and contraceptive use. The principal finding reported by Zelnik and Kantner (1977) was that between 1971 and 1976, there was a 30 percent increase in the proportion of never-married teenage women who had engaged in sexual intercourse. By age 19, 55 percent of never-married women have experienced coitus.

Zelnik and Kantner (1980) again repeated their study in 1979 and found a continued increase in the proportion of never-married teenage women who had engaged in sexual intercourse. In 1971, 30 percent of 15 to 19 year old girls were nonvirgins, by 1976 the figure had risen to 43 percent and by 1979 to 50 percent. By age 19, 69 percent of the teen women in their study had been sexually active. In a sample of males ranging from 17 to 21, Zelnik and Kantner found 70 percent reported having sexual intercourse. As may be seen in Table 11–2, the data show higher overall rates of premarital sexual

Adolescence is marked by heightened awareness of sexuality and sexual feelings. (© Charles Gatewood)

Table 11–2 Percent of Never-Married Women Aged 15–19 Who Ever Had Sexual Intercourse by Age and Race (1971 and 1979)

Age	1979			1971			PERCENT INCREASE 1971–1979		
	Total	White	Black	Total	White	Black	Total	White	Black
15	22.5	18.3	41.4	14.4	11.3	31.2	56.3	62.0	32.7
16	37.8	35.4	50.4	20.9	17.0	44.4	80.9	108.2	13.5
17	48.5	44.1	73.3	26.1	20.2	58.9	85.8	118.3	41.4
18	56.9	52.6	76.3	39.7	35.6	60.2	43.3	47.8	26.7
19	69.0	64.9	88.5	46.4	40.7	73.3	48.7	59.5	13.0
All	46.0	42.3	64.8	27.6	23.2	52.4	66.6	82.3	23.7

Source: M.Zelnik and J. F. Kantner (1980). Sexual activity, contraceptive use and pregnancy among metropolitan area teenagers. *Family Planning Perspectives, 12,* p. 231.

intercourse among black teens. But, the major increases in sexual activity from 1971 to 1979 were among white teens at all ages.

Although Zelnik and Kantner's data show a general increase in sexual intercourse among unmarried teenage women, the data do not imply increased promiscuity per se. Nearly half of the sexually experienced girls reported no sexual intercourse in the month prior to the interview. This was an increase from 39.6 percent in 1971. However, the percent of unmarried females who reported sexual intercourse six or more times in the prior month had also increased, from 12.8 percent in 1971 to 15.3 percent in 1976.

What variables lead a young person to choose to be or not to be sexually active? Data continue to show that religious commitment is negatively related to the decision. The more committed and active an adolescent is to her or his religion, the less permissive she or he is apt to be (Jessor & Jessor, 1975; Sorensen, 1973; McCabe & Collins, 1983; Schultz, Bohrnstedt, Borgatta & Evans, 1977). Peers also play a role in the adolescent's decision. The role seems less one of direct pressure as one of implied approval. If adolescents believe their friends to be sexually active they are more likely to engage in sexual experimentation themselves (Collins, 1974; Sach, Keller & Hinkle, 1984; Schultz et al., 1977). For both males and females, as the number of close friends who are thought to be sexually active increases, so does the risk of sexual intercourse in the person interviewed. There is an alternative explanation that those who plan to be sexually active tend to associate with each other. This possibility is given some credence since religiously committed adolescents have fewer friends who are thought to be sexually active (Schulz et al., 1977).

For most teen boys and girls the decision to have their first sexual intercourse is unplanned. It is a spur-of-the-moment decision. Only 17 percent of females and 25 percent of males say they had planned for the event (Zelnik & Shah, 1983). Those who have no plans for their first (or subsequent) experience with sexual intercourse, for whom the act is "spontaneous," are unlikely to use contraception. The failure to plan, and to use contraception, is a primary factor in the 1.1 million pregnancies among teen women each year. For girls, their first sexual partner is usually two to three years older than she. For boys, their first sexual partner is usually six months younger than he. For both boys and girls, they were usually dating their first partner on a steady basis.

The typical media image would have us believe that first premarital intercourse occurs in a parked car or in a hideaway motel. Actually, 79 percent of the sexually experienced girls in Zelnik and Kantner's (1977) study reported that their first coitus occurred either in their partner's home, their home, or a friend's home. Likewise, 86 percent of the incidences of most recent sexual intercourse (excluding those women who report only one coital experience) were in a home, either the partner's, her own, or a friend's. As Zelnik and Kantner (1977) concluded:

> The partner's home is the most likely place for the most recent intercourse to have occurred regardless of the girl's age at the time. The girl's home becomes increasingly important as the locale for her most recent intercourse as her age increases. Thus, for four out of five sexually experienced unmarried females who have had more than one encounter with sex, the choice seems to lie in the answer to "My place or your place," with his place having the edge. (p. 60)

Sexual intercourse may have mixed effects on adolescent self-esteem. Bell and Chasten (1970) report that among college women, their first sexual experience may lead to lowered self-esteem. In the case of one young women who talked to me, she felt trapped between wanting to demonstrate her commitment to her boyfriend and her fears of rejection and disapproval if her parents knew.

Not all premarital coitus is mutually consenting. In a study of college women, Koos and Oros (1982) found that 33 percent of the women reported they had "Been in a situation where a man became so sexually aroused that you felt it was useless to stop him even though you did not want to have sexual intercourse." In the same study 6 percent reported they had been raped. Writers in the area of adolescent sexual behavior are becoming more alert to a phenomenon called "Date Rape."

TEENAGE PREGNANCY

Along with the increase in the percent of adolescents who are sexually active, there has been an increase in the number of teen pregnancies. From 1960 to 1975, there was a decline in the proportion of infants conceived and delivered out of wedlock for all groups of women over 20 years of age. However, during that same time period, such births among teenage mothers increased by 50 percent. Among very young mothers, the proportion of births out of wedlock was 85 percent. In numbers, there were 92,000 out-of-wedlock births to teenage mothers in 1960. By 1975, the number had risen to 223,500 (Baldwin, 1978).

As noted earlier, there are currently an estimated 1.1 million pregnancies to teenage women between the ages of 15 and 19. There are an additional 30,000 pregnancies to teens who have not yet had their 15th birthday (Guttmacher Institute, 1981). Each year, one in 10 teenage women between the ages of 15 and 19 years old becomes pregnant. Not only has the overall number of teen pregnancies increased, the proportion of sexually active teens who become pregnant has also increased (Zelnik & Kantner, 1980). In recently released data by the Guttmacher Institute comparing several western industrialized countries, the United States ranked highest in teen pregnancies with a rate of 96 pregnancies per 1,000 girls in the 15 to 19 age range. The second highest was found in England and Wales at 45 per 1,000. Canada's rate was 44, France's was 43, Sweden's was 35, and the Netherland's was 14. The teen pregnancy rate in the United States is twice its nearest comparison nation (Jones et al., 1985). For teens 14-years-old, the United States had a pregnancy rate of five per 1,000. Canada was the only other country with a pregnancy rate of one or more for that age group.

Not only is the pregnancy rate among American teens on the increase, there has been an upward turn in the number of teen mothers who are experiencing second and more pregnancies. Of teen mothers, 17 percent are pregnant within one year of the birth of their first baby (Ford, 1983). These trends in teen pregnancies are viewed with alarm by a variety of professionals and social service agencies because both the teen mother and her child are considered to be medically, socially, psychologically and educationally "at risk." They are the single most likely group to need continued governmental financial assistance in the form of Aid to Families of Dependent Children. Among teen-aged girls who drop out of school, one in four does so because of pregnancy.

Because of the teen mother's age and because she is unlikely to seek out good prenatal care, especially in the important first trimester, the fetus is at increased risk for developmentally related problems resulting in impaired nutrition and inadequate health related behaviors. If the teen mother is also using drugs or alcohol, risks to the fetus are increased.

Because the teen mother has an increased tendency toward premature labor, the likelihood of a high risk, low birthweight (less than 2,500 grams, or 5½ pounds) baby is also increased. Low-birthweight infants display a high rate of early childhood anomalies and are disproportionately represented in the population of mental retardates (Camp, Burgess, Morgan & Malpiede, 1984; Pasamanick & Knobloch, 1961; Werner & Smith, 1977). However, once again, many of those risks are greatly reduced by positive hospital and home environments. There is some evidence that very young parents of low-birthweight infants are more likely to be physically abusive to the child (Elmer, 1967; Smith, 1975).

Teenage pregnancies also increase the likelihood of economic strain from interrupted education and limited employability of the mother. Some schools are encouraging teen mothers to complete their education by providing day care and special classes, but many schools still expel teenage mothers on a premise of morality. Such action increases the likelihood of both mother and child needing financial aid from welfare agencies.

For the great majority of teens these pregnancies are neither planned for nor wanted. Only a minority, about one in five, planned to or wanted to become pregnant (Zelnik & Kantner, 1980). Those who intend to become pregnant may see pregnancy as a means of establishing emotional independence from their parents through a new social bond with the father of the child or with the child itself. These young girls often have a poor self-image relating to their ability to become an independent adult in the absence of such a major event. It is not uncommon for a young pregnant teenage girl

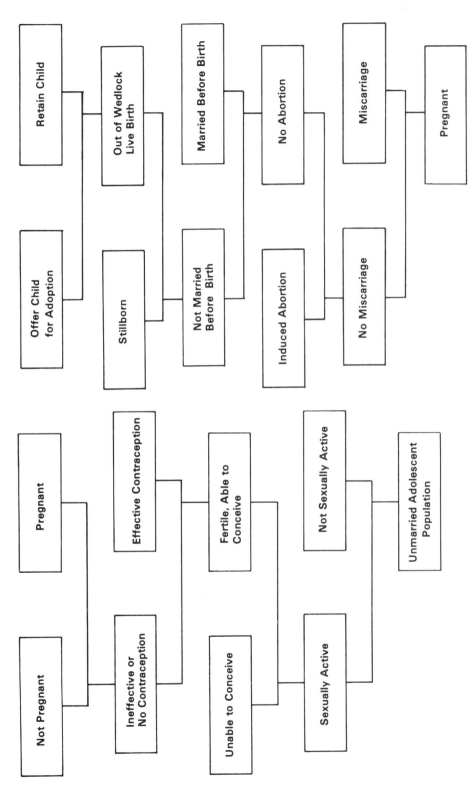

Figure 11–1 Steps toward unwed adolescent parenthood. *Source:* Adapted from K. Davis and J. Blake, "Social Structure and Fertility: An Analytic Framework," *Economic Development and Cultural Change 4* (1956): 211, by permission of The University of Chicago Press. Copyright © 1956.

to say that she is happy about the pregnancy because she "Wants someone to love her back." The failure of the child-parent to recognize that the baby will be demanding and probably not provide the needed emotional support has the ingredients of tragedy. Since the teen's social support system from peers is likely to be cut off or sharply curtailed, their feelings of isolation and alienation are likely to increase rather than diminish. While the focus of these risk factors has been on the teen mother, teen pregnancies also disrupt the educational and vocational growth opportunities for the young fathers.

Why has the rate of teen pregnancies continued to increase even though effective contraception is widely available? What will become of these teen pregnancies? Will young women elect to carry their pregnancies to full term or to terminate the pregnancy prior to the baby's birth? Davis and Blake (1956) and later Cutright (1971) offer a general scheme that describes the path toward out-of-wedlock births among teenage girls. That pattern has been adapted as Figure 11–1. The path toward the birth of a child to a teen mother may be seen as being in three stages: (1) voluntary and involuntary controls over conception; (2) voluntary and involuntary controls over gestation; and (3) legitimization of out-of-wedlock conceptions prior to marriage (Cutright, 1971). For purposes of our discussion, an additional choice point is added to the scheme as defined by the earlier authors. That is, does the young mother choose to keep the baby or to release it for adoption?

Controls Over Conception

It is self-evident that the path toward adolescent pregnancy must begin with an adolescent couple engaged in sexual intercourse. Except in involuntary cases such as rape or incest, most instances of premarital coitus are voluntary. If young people choose to be sexually active, do they also choose to take responsibility for their behavior and to prevent an unwanted pregnancy? If conception is precluded because the boy or girl is infertile at the time of sexual intercourse or if effective contraception is used, the path toward teen pregnancies is terminated. If, however, neither condition is met the risk of teen pregnancy is high.

If the teen woman is not fertile, not able to conceive at the time of sexual intercourse, or if the male is not able to impregnate, pregnancy is averted. The male or female may not be fertile for a variety of reasons. As mentioned in Chapter 4, a young woman who has passed her menarche is not necessarily fertile; there is an average one- to two-year period of natural adolescent sterility following menarch. However, as Cutright (1972) has argued, the drop in age of the onset of menarche has had a significant effect on the rate of teenage pregnancies. If we assume an average year and a half period of natural adolescent sterility following menarche and an average age of onset of menarche of 12.5, about 50 percent of today's adolescent girls are fertile by the age of 14 and 95 percent by age 17. By way of comparison, in 1870, when the average age of menarche was 16.5, less than 1 percent of girls were fertile by 14 years old and only 50 percent by age 18. Thus, solely on the basis of increased proportion of fertile adolescent girls, we can expect a rise in the rate of teenage pregnancies. Tie this with an increased rate of premarital coitus, and you can begin to see the makings of a very serious problem.

A woman may not be fertile simply because it is not the correct time in her ovulatory cycle. However, using that factor as a method of contraception during teenage years may be a poor method, because her cycle may not have become stable enough to become reliable. Rhythm, as a form of contraception, depends not only on stable patterns of the release of ova during the menstrual cycle but also on understanding when pregnancy is most likely to occur. In Zelnik and Kantner's (1977) study, one-quarter of white teenage women and three-fifths of black teenage women who claimed to use rhythm as a form of birth control incorrectly specified the time of greatest risk. As Zelnik and Kantner (1977) note, "Rhythm is not highly regarded as an effective method of contraception, particularly when its use is combined with incorrect knowledge about the timing of ovulation" (p. 63). Having attended sex-education classes did not significantly improve the girls' knowledge of the ovulatory cycle.

A disturbingly large proportion of sexually active adolescents report little or no use of contraception (Sorensen, 1973; Zelnik & Kantner, 1977, 1980). When asked why they don't use contraception, adolescents report that they feel that contraception would debase the love relationship, or that contraceptives were unavailable, or that using contraceptives would be admitting that they need them. Most, however, don't use contraceptives because they do not think they will get pregnant (Shah, Zelnik & Kantner, 1975; Sorensen, 1973). One team of writer describes this attitude as a form of adolescent egocentrism, reflecting a sense of omnipotence (Cvetkovich et al., 1975). Others add that these behaviors conform to adolescents' tendencies to engage in chance taking behavior and their sense of invulnerability.

It does not appear that knowlege of effective contraception will, by itself, lead to the use of contraceptives. Knowing about contraception appears to have little relation to its use (Olson & Robbins, 1982). Most sexually active adolescents are informed. Why then do they risk pregnancy and sexually transmitted diseases by not using contraceptives? A sizable proportion of sexually active women feel that effective contraception is hard to obtain (Olson & Robbins, 1982). Further, when high school and college females were asked to rate the safety of various contraceptive methods, irrespective of effectiveness, a majority of high school women and three-fourths of the college women saw the pill as dangerous. Condoms, foam and diaphrams were seen as safe.

Younger adolescents are more likely to report never using contraception (Zelnik, 1980) and only rarely is contraception used during first sexual intercourse (Kantner, 1983). Indeed there seems to be a two-year lag between first sexual intercourse and the start of contracepting (Akpon, Akpon & Davis, 1976).

Zelnik and Kantner's study noted some increase in the numbers who reported having used contraception. If they use contraception at all, adolescents seem to be using more effective forms and using them with greater regularity. This may be a result of the greater availability of oral contraceptives; in 1971, only 27 percent of contracepting unmarried females aged 15 to 19 reported use of the pill, whereas 59 percent did so in 1976. Also, use of intrauterine devices (IUDs) nearly doubled among teenage women during those five years, whereas the use of withdrawal and condoms decreased. Although adolescent males often carry a condom in their wallet, mostly as a status symbol, over three-quarters of those who do reported not having used one during their last occasion of sexual intercourse (Arnold, 1972). Zelnik and Kantner also reported an increase in the number of women who claimed to use rhythm as a method of contraception, although the authors argued that the increase might be attributed to improved questioning procedures. Irrespective of the increased use of effective forms of contraception, Zelnik and Kantner reported no substantial decrease in the percent of never-married, sexually active females who never use contraception. If couples use effective contraception, they block the path toward teen pregnancy. However, regular contraceptive use among teens remains low and haphazard. Although it is possible that a fertile, adolescent female can repeatedly engage in unprotected sexual intercourse and not become pregnant, such fortune presses the limits of Murphy's Law: If something bad can happen, it will.

Controls Over Gestation

For a variety of reasons related to the health of the mother or the status of the developing fetus, a pregnancy may terminate quickly in the form of a spontaneous miscarriage. Among teen mothers, about 13 percent of pregnancies end in miscarriage (Baldwin & Cain, 1980; Dreyfoos, 1982).

If an adolescent girl does not spontaneously abort, she may then opt for an induced abortion. Prior to 1973, legal abortion was an option only in rare circumstances; thus many young women resorted to illegal abortions, which too often resulted in the mother's death. Since the 1973 decision by the U.S. Supreme Court allowing legal therapeutic abortions, the rate of abortions among teens and nonteens has risen steadily. By 1976, one-third of all abortions were for women under 20 years of age. Among girls under 15, abortions outnumbered live births, and among those 15 to 17, the number of legal abortions was about two-thirds the number of live births (Burnham, 1982). Of the 1.1 million teen pregenancies in 1978, about 150,000 resulted in miscarriages and 419,000 were terminated by induced abortions. By 1980, nearly one-half million women 19 years and younger obtained a legal abortion. Abortions to teen mothers again accounted for 30 percent of all abortions nationally. When women in the age group 20 to 24 years are added, the combined groups accounted for two-thirds of all abortions (Henshaw & O'Reilly, 1983).

Among pregnant teens, 41 percent of pregnancies are now terminated through induced abortions; that proportion has risen significantly from 29 percent in 1974. From 1974 to 1980, the absolute number of teen pregnancies increased 46 percent while the number of abortions increased 63 percent (Henshaw & O'Reilly, 1983).

Abortion attitudes among the population as a whole have become more permissive over the past two decades. In 1965, 73 percent of American adults felt abortion was justified if the mother's health was in danger, in 1980, 90 percent felt that way. In 1965, only 15 percent felt abortion was justified if the woman was unmarried and did not wish to marry the father. By 1980, the rate of agreement to that question had risen to 48 percent and 41 percent felt abortion for any reason was justified (Grandberg & Grandberg, 1980).

Lost in most discussions of abortion is the male in the couple. There is a stereotype that the male disappears at the first mention of pregnancy and has no feelings about the pregnancy at all. While that stereotype may be true in far too many cases, in recent research by Shostak, McLouth and Seng (1984), many men were found to feel much stress and anxiety about the choices of abortion. They reported pain and anger

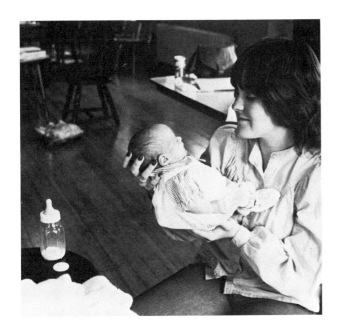

An increasing number of adolescent mothers are choosing to keep their babies. (Courtesy, Family Service Association of Greater Boston, South Shore Center. Photograph © Susan Lapides)

that their feelings were ignored by the women. In another study, the emotional reaction of the woman was influenced by the degree of emotional commitment she felt to the father. The stronger the loving relationship between the girl and the boy the more likely the teen girl will have negative emotional reactions and reject the decision to abort the fetus (Robbins, 1984).

Whether the teen girl chooses to abort or not to abort the fetus depends on a variety of factors including family support, religious commitment, and personality variables. Girls, for example, with high external locus of control are more likely to delay a decision on whether to abort the pregnancy until later in the term than those with an internal locus of control (Dixon, Strano & Willingham, 1984).

Actually, we know little about the psychological ramifications of an abortion on the mother. Adler (1975) reports that younger women are more likely to report guilt or depression following a therapeutic abortion. If the young woman comes from a background that views abortion as reprehensible for religious or moral reasons, she is more likely to report negative emotions. In any case, clinical counseling should be available both before and after an abortion to aid a young woman who opts for this alternative to adjust to those feelings. Because post abortion counseling may not be offered by abortion clinics that are not staffed for that service, the responsibility such for counseling may fall on other agencies.

Marriage

Many young people elect to marry before the birth of the baby. Reasons for this choice are often rooted in culture and religion. About one-third of all teen pregnancies

Not all adolescents choose heterosexual relationships; increasingly, gay couples are making their preferences public. (Rose Skytta/Jeroboam, Inc.)

conceived out-of-wedlock now result in teen marriages before the birth of the child (Zelnik & Kantner, 1980) although that percentage has dropped from over 50 percent in 1964 (Kovar, 1979). Another 9 percent marry after the birth of the child. Teen marriages are notoriously unstable (Bishop & Lynn, 1984). Sixty to 70 percent are terminated within the first six years and the younger the person the more unstable the marriage. If the bride is between 14- and 17-years-old, the risk of failure of the marriage is twice that of couples in which the bride is 18 or 19 and three times that of couples in which the bride is between 20 and 24 (Spanier & Glick, 1981). The reasons for the instability are not totally clear, but certainly stress from early responsibility as parents, reduced income, restricted social support systems, and emotional immaturity play important roles. Among those marriages that survive, those couples that were married as teens report higher rates of marital dissatisfaction, lower level of income, less satisfaction with their standard of living, and more tension (Lee, 1977).

The choice of marriage in most cases of teen pregnancies appears to make a bad situation worse. Early marriage disrupts education and career growth for both the teen husband and wife. Further, these young couples are more likely to have additional children within a short time after the birth of their first child causing more complications in the stability of the home. Perhaps because of these factors, professionals are more likely to discourage teens from marriage. Perhaps because of changing cultural norms, the proportion of teen women who choose to marry before or after the birth of the child continues to decline.

Delivery of the Baby

This year an estimated 531,000 teen women will carry their pregnancy to full term. The risks of premature birth and infant mortality are significantly higher for the younger mothers. The infant mortality rate for babies born to mothers under 15 years of age is more than double that of infants to women over 20 years. For mothers in the age range of 15 to 19 years, the infant mortality rate is nearly half again the rate for women over 20 (Chilman, 1983).

Keeping the Baby

If the teen couple chooses not to marry before the birth of the child or after the birth of the child, the teen mother is then faced with a decision to keep custody of the child or to relinquish it for adoption. It is now estimated that 90 percent of all teen mothers who give birth to a baby out-of-wedlock choose to retain custody of the child (Guttmacher Institute, 1976).

In Figure 11-2 you can see that, although the number of illegitimate births grew steadily from 1960 to 1970 and has remained at a high level despite the availability of legal abortions, the number of adopted children did not keep pace and in fact shows a decline since 1970 (Baldwin, 1976).

Figure 11–2   Illegitimate births and adoptions in the United States. *Source:* Gordon S. Bonham, "Who Adopts: The Relationship of Adoption and Social-Demographic Characteristics of Women," Table 1, *Journal of Marriage and the Family 39* (May 1977): 298. Reprinted by permission of the author.

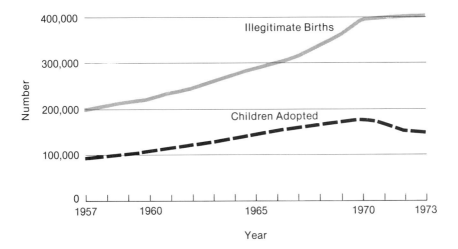

Often these young mothers are simply unaware of the care this newborn will require. They are assuredly unaware of the stresses of normal parenthood which are made more difficult by their lack of emotional maturity. Not infrequently the mother of the teen has a major voice in the decision to keep the baby (Leynes, 1980). Even with the support of their own mothers, these teen mothers who choose to keep their infants may become economically or psychologically unprepared for the task of child rearing.

Far too often the mother and child, or as the Reverend Jesse Jackson (1977) describes them, the child and child, return

> to homes where, because their mothers are immature, unprepared, too poorly educated to find meaningful employment, these children of children will experience enormous family insecurity and, all too often, be condemned to lives of material and mental poverty, physical and psychic deprivation. (p. C7)

I want to make one final point on out-of-wedlock births. As Stickle and Ma (1975) point out, although many may deny it, people often view early pregnancy and illegitimacy as "racial" problems. It is true that illegitimacy rates are 8.5 times higher among lower-income blacks than among whites, but the impact of change in illegitimacy rate for blacks on the total illegitimacy rate for the country is negligible. Indeed, for some age groups of blacks, the illegitimacy rate is leveling off or declining. In 1960, the illegitimacy rate for white girls aged 15 to 19 was 6.9 births per 10,000 live births; in 1968, the rate was 9.9, an increase of 43 percent. For nonwhite girls in the same age bracket, the rate in 1960 was 78.5 versus 86.5 in 1968, an increase of 10 percent. During the same period, there was a 22 percent increase in the illegitimacy rate among white women 20 to 22, whereas black women of the same age showed a 25 percent *decrease* (Cutright, 1973). Simply stated, because blacks compose less than 10 percent of the total population, their impact on the overall illegitimacy rate is small. Any major increase in the overall illegitimacy rate is the result of an increase in the rate among whites.

HOMOSEXUAL BEHAVIOR

As a normal part of adolescents' attempts to clarify their sexual self-identity, many young boys and girls report homosexual feelings or experiences. It is not unusual, for example, for young adolescent or preadolescent boys to engage in group or mutual masturbation; such events are transitory and harmless. But if adults discover the activity and label the boys as homosexual, their unwarranted reaction might lead to unpleasant consequences. The event may be called a homosexual experience, but there is no evidence to suggest that such activity leads to adult homosexual preferences. Practitioners should bear in mind that a real difference exists between homosexual encounters and homosexual preference. Applying the label "homosexual" to a young person who is in the process of forming his or her sexual identity might act as a self-fulfilling prophesy. Many youths who are not homosexual may wonder if they are because of their past homosexual experiences; an adult who reacts by labeling them as homosexual may serve to confirm erroneously what they fear.

Elias and Gebhard (1969) report that 52 percent of males and 34 percent of females engage in sexual play with members of the same sex before puberty. Among males, 27 percent report a homosexual experience that led to orgasm during early adolescence, and 38 percent report similar experiences during late adolescence (Kinsey et al., 1948). Although homosexual encounters leading to orgasm are much less common among adolescent girls (Kinsey et al., 1953), homosexual encounters still occur.

Most adolescent homosexual acts are transitory and do not indicate a true homosexual preference, but the fact remains that some young people may opt for a homosexual preference. To do so, one runs the risk of strong negative social sanction, including social exclusion or rejection, even by parents. A recent survey found that although 68 percent of those questioned said what consenting adults do in private is their own business, 60 percent opposed laws that would permit homosexual acts (Hooker & Chance, 1975). In Sorensen's (1973) study, 75 percent of the adolescents felt that male or female homosexuality was disgusting, and 59 percent felt that we should have laws against homosexuality. Thus, although many gay groups plead for equal rights and encourage homosexuals to "come out of the closet," many homosexuals fear social disapproval and keep their preference silent. The question of whether a homosexual can or should be "cured" or whether he or she should be helped to adapt to living as a homosexual in a heterosexual society should be decided by the person involved. In many cases, counseling should include not only the homosexual youth but also his or her parents, because the parents' acceptance or nonacceptance of their child's homosexual preference may be a source of personal stress.

The reasons why a young person elects a homosexual preference are not clear but some light has been shed on the question by the research of Bell, Weinberg and Hammersmith (1981). Bell and his colleagues found the traditional Freudian notions of over-attachments to mothers had no more relationship to homosexual than to heterosexual choice. What did emerge was evidence that as children and adolescents homosexuals report a greater likelihood to avoid or dislike traditional gender oriented activities. The authors use that evidence and other data to support their conclusion that homosexuality has a strong biological base.

SEXUALLY TRANSMITTED DISEASES

Beyond risks of disrupting one's life because of an unplanned and unwanted pregnancy, sexually active adolescents must face an increased risk of contracting a *sexually transmitted disease* (STD) or as they are often called *venereal disease* (VD). Currently, much attention is being directed at the spread of the deadly *Acquired Immune Deficiency Syndrome* or AIDS. While concern is justified, society cannot ignore the continued epidemic status of other, also serious STDs. *Gonorrhea,* for example, ranks only behind the common cold as the nation's most prevalent communicable disease (Centers for Disease Control, 1985); gonorrhea is four times as prevalent as chicken pox.

The most common factor related to the risk of contracting one of the STDs described in this chapter is unprotected sexual intercourse with multiple partners. The most effective protection against the spread of STDs is restraint. In the absence of restraint, sexually active adolescents should be encouraged to use barrier contraceptives (condoms) as an effective preventative to the spread of STDs.

Anyone who suspects that he or she has been infected with a form of VD should contact a physician or VD clinic immediately. The longer a person delays, the more serious the problem becomes. Most often a clinic will request the names of all the other sexual partners of an infected person. This procedure appears on the surface as an infringement of a person's right to privacy. However, its purpose is to reduce the pool of VD bacteria and the chance of "ping-pong" infection—that is, the infection being passed back and forth. The best treatment is obviously prevention. Condoms offer a reasonable barrier to the transmission of VD, but the use of condoms has diminished. In fact, some points to that drop in use of condoms as one of the major causes of the increase in VD.

Syphilis

Syphilis (or "bad blood," "pox," "siff,") is transmitted by an infected carrier during acts of sexual intercourse, including coitus and anal or oral-genital intercourse. In very rare cases, syphilis may be transmitted by kissing. Because of the close intermixing of the male homosexual population, the risk of syphilis is 10 times greater for them than for their heterosexual counterparts (Stern & MacKenzie, 1975). For both males and females, syphilis is most prevalent in the 20- to 24-year-old range, coordinate with the peak years of nonmarital sexual activity. Reported cases of syphilis are more common among males, but because women are more likely to show no symptoms, underreporting is greater among females.

A person who has contracted syphilis from an infected partner may display signs of the first stage of the disease, known as *primary syphilis*, within 10 to 90 days after sexual contact. During this stage, a pimple-like sore called a *chancre* forms at the place where the bacteria initially entered the body. In males the chancre usually appears on the penis and is readily noticeable, but the chancre may also form on the mouth or rectum. In females the chancre may appear on the inside wall of the vagina; however, it may be far enough up on the walls of the vagina to go unnoticed. On the other hand, the chancre may not appear at all; hence the most obvious sign of syphilis may not be of help in some cases. Although syphilis can be detected by a blood test during the primary stage, unless a girl suspects infection, she has little reason to seek out such a test.

Because the symptoms of syphilis are not always detected, especially among women, the infection may not be discovered until it has moved into its secondary stage. The symptoms of *secondary syphilis* occur anywhere from six weeks to six months after the contraction of the disease and may show up as rashes or sores on other parts of the body, including the soles of the feet or the palms of the hand. The lesions of these rashes are highly infectious. Other symptoms of secondary syphilis are loss of hair, loss of eyebrows, headaches, sore throat, and loss of appetite. Except for the loss of hair and eyebrows, symptoms of secondary syphilis can be (and are) mistaken for a viral infection or flu. As with primary syphilis, the disease is insidious, because the symptoms are not obvious, and, in some cases, disappear so quickly that they cause no alarm or fail to appear at all.

Untreated syphilis moves into a so-called *latent stage*, which lasts between five and 20 years. Actually, syphilis is anything but latent during this period. During this stage syphilitic bacteria attack and destroy healthy tissue and invade the central nervous system and the heart. Although a blood test can detect syphilis during its latency stage, most people do not suffer enough discomfort to warrant a test. Undetected, the disease progresses toward its final stage, *general paresis*, or *tertiary syphilis*, which is manifested by rapid, physical deterioration and eventual death.

A pregnant syphilitic woman has a high probability of transmitting her infection to the fetus, leading to brain damage, birth deformities, or death of the fetus. Fortunately, blood tests on pregnant women have led to the lowest rate of congenital syphilis since 1973 (Centers for Disease Control, 1977).

Of the 28,607 cases of syphilis reported in the United States during 1984, 11,446 (40 percent) were to young people in the age range 10 to 24. Of cases of syphilis among women, 54 percent were to young people in that age group (Centers for Disease Control, 1985). It is not a disease of older people.

Gonorrhea

Like syphilis, gonorrhea ("clap," "morning drip," "the dose") is transmitted during an act of sexual intercourse. A single contact by a male with an infected female involves a 22 percent risk of infection (Stern & MacKenzie, 1975). The gonococcus bacteria incubate on the inside skin of the ureter in males and on the inner wall of the vagina in females. Growth is particularly favored in females during menstruation. Unlike syphilis, no effective blood test is currently available for detection of gonorrhea, although some tests, as well as a vaccine, may be in the offing (Kolata, 1976). Treatment of gonorrhea with antibiotics is usually effective; however, a new strain of gonococcus, which resists all forms of penicillin treatment, has emerged (Centers for Disease Control, 1977).

A male who has contracted gonorrhea from an infected partner may begin to show signs of the disease within two to six days, although in some instances the signs do not show up for a month, and in 10 percent of males there are no symptoms at all. Signs of gonorrhea in the male include a pus discharge from the penis and a burning sensation during urination. Most women show *no* symptoms except a slight vaginal discharge and a minor burning sensation, which can easily be misinterpreted as a urinary or bladder infection. Nonetheless, the Centers for Disease Control (1977) estimates that each day, 5,750 girls will be absent from school because of gonorrhea.

In the current gonorrhea epidemic, the greatest increase in occurrence has been among older adolescent females (Bell & Hein, 1984). The prevalence of gonorrhea among young people in the age range of 10 to 24 is even more marked than syphilis. Of 878,556 cases of gonorrhea reported in 1984, 547,835 (or 62 percent) were in young people in that age range (Centers for Disease Control, 1985). Between one and two out of every 100 people in the age range of 15 to 24 is infected with gonorrhea. Both gonorrhea and syphilis are, incidentally, underreported.

Chlamydia

Another, less well-known sexually transmitted disease is called *Chlamydia Trachomatis.* It is the cause of more than half of the cases of *Nongonococcal Urethritis* (NGU) in men and of *pelvic inflammatory disease* in women. Untreated, chlamydia can lead to chronic urinary infections and sterility. It is thought to be the single most common cause of sterility among women each year. In pregnant women, there is a high risk of transmitting the chlamydia infection to the infant during delivery resulting in increased risk of respiratory illnesses (Babin, 1986). Like other STDs, chlamydia is often asymptomatic, especially among females.

In one study of sexually active, urban high school girls, one-third tested positive for chlamydia (D. Orr, personal communication). In another study of sexually active adolescents in the Baltimore area (Chacko & Lovchik, 1984), 35 percent of males, 27 percent of pregnant females, and 23 percent of nonpregnant females tested positive for chlamydia. Further, among a sample of college women (McCormack, Rosner, McComb, Evrard & Zinner, 1985), 5 percent tested positive.

Since its symptoms are similar to gonorrhea, chlamydia is sometimes overlooked when an individual is being treated for gonorrhea; yet, 40 percent of those with gonorrhea also have chlamydia. Some estimates suggest that chlamydia and NGU are three times as prevalent as gonorrhea and is now the nation's most common STD (Oriel, 1977).

Herpes Virus, Type II

Less generally known but increasingly a concern among those who treat and study VD is herpes simplex virus, type II. Herpes viruses are a class of viruses associated with such maladies as chicken pox, shingles, cold sores, and so on. One strain of herpes, however, is transmitted primarily through sexual contact. A person with genital herpes may suffer blisterlike sores, general fatigue, swelling and inflammation of the eyes, and difficulty in urination. The number of visits for treatment of genital herpes nears 500,000 each year compared with 250,000 per year in 1980 and 50,000 in 1970 (Centers for Disease Control, 1985). Or, as is sometimes the case with gonorrhea and syphilis, one may not know one has genital herpes. Among women, genital herpes may be related to cervical cancer and does lead to high miscarriage rates. A fetus carried to full term by a mother who had a herpes infection during her pregnancy runs a high risk of being born dead or of suffering brain damage. At present, no generally recognized cure is available for genital herpes; the herpes sufferer has the condition indefinitely.

AIDS

In 1982, the editors of Time Magazine emblazoned their cover with a bright red "H" suggesting that Herpes had made it the new "Scarlet Letter." Just a few years later, the letter "A" would regain its literary place, but its referrent might now be to *Acquired Immune Deficiency Syndrome* or AIDS. AIDS has been likened to the Black (Bubonic) Plague that ravaged Medieval Europe. At the start of 1986, 19,000 cases of AIDS had been diagnosed in the United States; of these, 9,000 had died and another 9,000 were expected to die that year. By 1991, it is projected that the number of diagnosed cases of AIDS will reach 196,000 and 125,000 of these will have died (Public Health Service, 1986).

The virus identified as the cause of AIDS has been labeled HTLV-III (Human T-Cell Lymphotropic Virus, Type III) or HIV (Human Immunodeficiency Virus). The virus invades and alters the genetic structure of T-Cells which are central to the immune system. The result is that the individual becomes incapable of fighting off disease; he or she is then susceptible to a wide variety of potentially fatal infections (Lawrence, 1985).

AIDS was first detected because of a sudden increase in the number of cases of Kaposi's sarcoma (a rare form of skin cancer) among male homosexuals.

The HIV virus can be transmitted through infected blood transfusions, by way of tainted syringes, and through sexual intercourse. Casual contact is considered a very unlikely means of transmission of the disease. Because HIV can be transferred through blood transfusions, hemophiliacs were particularly at risk for contracting AIDS. The development of a test for presence of HIV has reduced that risk. AIDS is increasingly a problem among intravenous drug users who may share tainted syringes. AIDS currently remains most widely found among the male homosexual population. In some urban settings, 80 percent of male homosexuals tested for presence of HIV tested positive. It was, for a time, presumed that AIDS would remain primarily a sexually transmitted disease among male homosexuals. Recent studies, however, of Haiti and Africa indicate that women are also susceptible to AIDS. Of the 1,400 cases of women with AIDS in the United States as of 1986, half were not intravenous drug users.

SEX EDUCATION

Much of the information in this chapter points toward the need for adequate sex education. The question is not really whether there should be sex education but where, how, and by whom it should be taught. Ideally parents should provide training and information about sex and sexuality. However, many parents are either ill equipped by lack of correct knowledge themselves or they are hampered by discomfort over discussing sex with their children. In Sorensen's (1973) study, parents were not a primary source of sex information. Only 16 percent of his interviewees reported that they often asked their parents for advice about sexual matters, and 23 percent felt that their parents got very uncomfortable talking to them about sex. One approach, therefore, might be an indirect one in which parents are trained to educate their own children.

Often, perhaps too often, the onus of sex education falls on the schools. The public sees the schools, as agents of society, as the vehicle for imparting knowledge in a variety of domains beyond the traditional curricula. Unfortunately, many segments of society also mistrust the schools; thus the likelihood of a general, well-conceived program of sex education is greatly reduced. Nonetheless, it is in the schools that some degree of control over the quality of sex education may be available.

Any program of sex education should be directed, first, at the self-perceived needs of those for whom the program is primarily intended. Some form of needs assessment is therefore a prerequisite for any successful program. In one such assessment (McCreary-Juhasz, 1975), teens reported needs in the domains of self-understanding and the physical and emotional changes that they were experiencing but did not understand and therefore found frightening. The content of a curriculum in sex education should also be based on needs defined by other sources, for example, experts and pretests on basic knowledge. Further, curriculum must respond to the differing cognitive levels and social backgrounds of the students, both within and between grade levels.

In a recent study by the prestigious National Academy of Science (1986), a distinguished panel of scientists concluded that sex education at the secondary level should be expanded to include school-based clinics which would offer ready access to effective contraceptives.

Critics of sex education often argue that informing children of sexuality should be the parents' responsibility. While the validity of this proposition would be hard to challenge, parents are not always well-equipped to handle the responsibility. In studies of how young people receive their sex information, boys are less likely than girls to receive information about sexuality from their parents and teachers. Chilman (1983) speculates that the reason for this disparity is that society sees the female as in more need of protection and at more jeopardy from the lack of information. Nonetheless, both boys and girls often deal with confused misinformation about their own and each others' sexuality.

Effective sex education should include its own form of the three R's: Responsibility, Respect and Restraint. Young people must understand that misuse of our sexuality has the risk of dire consequences. An unwanted pregnancy or venereal disease may have ramifications which last long after the fun and excitement of a sexual encounter are over. We have a responsibility to manage our sexuality wisely. If a young person decides to be sexually active, then they must act responsibly about that decision and its possible ramifications.

Young people need also to respect the sexual rights of others. Males need to understand the sexual rights of females and to respect their right to say "no." Females must also understand and respect the sexual rights of males and their right to say "no." No one should be coerced into sexual behavior that she or he does not want. Further, young people need to be prepared to deal with sexual coercion should it occur.

Young people should also be encouraged to practice restraint. The decision to be sexually active should not be taken lightly. Young males and females need to know that they have a right *not* to be sexually active. A decision to be sexually active may be terribly difficult to undo and may lead to feelings of guilt and lowered self-esteem.

By saying that young people should be encouraged to practice restraint, I am not advocating a harsh, autocratic litany of horrors bestowed on those who break the rules. I can conceive of no worse method of sex education. Such narrow views are as offensive as so-called "value-less" programs. Rather sex education should be open and honest. Sex educators should try to help adolescents recognize that rules about sexual behavior are for the protection of ourselves and of society. The should also be willing to deal with the risks and responsibilities of decisions to be sexually active.

A successful program of sex education must fit the community within which it occurs. Innumerable sex education curricula have died before they began simply because the schools failed to gain community support. Although people who object to sex education are popularly portrayed as ignorant and reactionary, the fact remains that the schools serve the community and must recognize the differing attitudes within that community. In many cases, objections to the curricula can be appeased. Curriculum developers should realize that a good deal of fear is associated with relinquishing responsibility for sex education to the schools. Because sexuality and morality are so closely tied in many people's minds, some fear that the schools are going to provide moral training counter to the family's values. The limited available evidence suggests that those worries may be unfounded. The amount of *formal* sex education to which an adolescent is exposed does not appear to be related to increased premarital sexual activity, although *informal* sex education from peers does (Spanier, 1976). The validity or invalidity of such attitudes is almost irrelevant. The attitudes exist and any program of sex education must contend with them. In some cases many of the fears may be allayed by educating the parents before instituting the program in the schools. Nonetheless, topics such as homosexuality, abortion, and contraception, necessary in any comprehensive program of sex education, are likely to draw adverse reactions.

An additional question remains: Who should teach a course in sex education? Far too often the person selected is one who the principal thinks *should* be able to teach about sex—for example, a physical education teacher or a biology teacher. That person may be a good choice in some cases, but it does not always hold true. Any effective program of sex education requires that the instructor be able to reach to the students with factual information, be able to elicit responses from students about their sexual concerns, and allow the students to unravel their own solutions without imposing his or her own value system. McCreary-Juhasz (1975) concludes:

> The adult best equipped to help the adolescent is one who: (1) is aware of the stages of heterosexual development through which the normal child passes from infancy to adolescence; (2) is cognizant of the pressures placed on individuals in a changing society; (3) recognizes the influence of the family and adults upon the child; (4) is himself secure about his own sexuality; and (5) is burdened with a minimum of problems related to interpersonal relations. (p. 345)

SUMMARY

Earlier in this chapter, it was noted that each year 1.1 million teenage girls become pregnant. That is, one girl in 10. This translates into 3,000 pregnancies each day, two every minute. Each day, 3,000 more teenage girls face a pregnancy they neither want nor are prepared for. Ninety of those girls will not have yet reached their fifteenth birthday. Of the 3,000 new pregnancies, 420 will end in miscarriage, 1,230 will be terminated through an induced abortion. Of the remaining, 1,350 that result in a live birth to a teenage mother, 378 of the young women will marry before the birth of their child. Of the 972 live births to unmarried teenage girls, only 49 will be offered for adoption. The remaining 923 will retain custody of their babies. These young, single mothers truncate their education and career growth opportunities. Further, because of their unwillingness to get adequate medical care in the important first trimester of pregnancy, the baby is at risk for a variety of psychological, physical, and educational problems. Of those who choose to marry, most marriages will end in divorce within six years.

The scope of teenage pregnancy represents a national crisis. When it is tied to the skyrocketing rate of venereal disease, we are faced with a problem of monumental proportions. A psychiatrist friend once explained to me that he was convinced that 95 percent of all adolescent thinking was sexual in nature—and he was not totally sure that it was not 100 percent. Whether he was unduly influenced by his most frequent clients, or whether he was exaggerating a bit to make a point, his comment describes the importance of sexuality in adolescent behavior and thought. Chapter 3 pointed out that our sexual identity is an intrinsic part of the personal identity with which we enter adult life.

The adolescent's need to clarify what it means to be male or female is influenced not only by the alternation in body image but also by the emergence of sexual motives and the adult ability to respond sexually and to conceive children.

The past 20 years have witnessed a steady and significant change in sexual attitudes among teens and young adults. Both male and females are considerably more liberal in their views of what is acceptable sexual behavior. Those attidues become more liberal as the adolescent get older and reaches young adulthood. As a result, much of the traditional sexual double standard, which approved and encouraged premarital sexual intercourse for boys but disapproved of the same behavior for girls, has lessened. However, the double standard has not totally disappeared, although some adolescents believe that premarital sexual intercourse is all right for girls but only if love is involved. The change in sexual attitudes during the 1960s was followed by a change in sexual behavior during the 1970s. The percent of unmarried teenage girls—especially younger adolescents—who are sexually experienced has increased dramatically.

The changes in sexual behavior are not without risk. Adolescent pregnancy may be among our more serious continuing health problems, because the results of early pregnancy often lead to mothers and infants who are medically, psychologically, and socially "at risk." Likewise, increases in unprotected sexual intercourse have led to an increase in venereal disease to the point where syphilis and gonorrhea are at epidemic proportions.

Suggesting that the answer to problems with adolescent sexuality lies in comprehensive programs of sex education may be overly optimistic. Because sexuality is so intrinsically tied to religious and family value systems, it is likely that any program of sex education that responds to the needs of the students is certain to upset some groups of adults. And because parents are ultimately responsible for the well-being of their children, educators have a responsibility to include all groups in decision making regarding sex education curricula. Ultimately, this may mean that they must first educate the parents.

Any program of sex education should focus on young people's responsible management of their own sexuality, their rights and needs to respect the sexual rights of others, and that restraint is an acceptable alternative to too-early sexual commitment.

12 DEVELOPING A VALUE SYSTEM

As adolescents develop more complex knowledge systems through formal operational thought, they also develop more complex value systems As a result of their ability to consider abstractions, they are also able to question the validity of ideas that they had previously not questioned. For example, one 14-year-old girl wrote:

> Is there a God? It puzzles me. Some people say there is and some say there is not. There is no real proof. If we have never seen God or heard God or anything, how do we know he's there?

Too often such questions are met with adult fear and uncertainty. This girl's questions did not warn that she was rejecting all her parent's values; rather the questions were part of a general reorganization of her value system. Questioning values is not only a normal part of moral development, it may also be necessary if a person's moral ideology is to be internalized.

Part of the personal sense of identity that an adolescent brings to adulthood is a value system or moral ideology. As with other characteristics of the emerging identity, adolescents must be able to explore and evaluate alternate value systems. At times during this process, the values of parents and society may come into conflict with values expressed by peers. During these periods adolescents may outwardly appear to be hostile and alienated. However, as noted earlier, the general value structure of adolescents remains more like their parents' than unlike it (Adelson, 1979). Eventually adolescents merge appropriate aspects of alternative systems with the value system they learn from their parents. Only in rare instances do adolescents replace the value system of early adolescence with a completely new value system during late adolescence.

Three psychological models of moral development reflect the three major theoretical orientations in human development. In the psychoanalytic conception, moral development is incorporated within the broader context of individual ego development. Moral structures result from the resolution of ego conflict and adolescent's struggle to achieve independence from parents. Social learning theorists, on the other hand, see moral development as the result of social reinforcement. Morality results from what one has been taught to believe. Finally, in the cognitive developmental view, moral development is seen as a step-by-step progression through a set of moral structures, which are increasingly abstract and which reflect the general morality of an individual.

THE PSYCHOANALYTIC VIEW

Although it is somewhat fashionable for nonpsychoanalytically trained writers to dismiss psychoanalytic theory, Freudian or neo-Freudian perspectives on moral development offer some insights into the character of the adolescent transition. Basically, psychoanalytic theory proposes that an individual's moral structures emerge from anxieties over conflict between an ideal moral code and a perceived reality. Adolescents develop a personal morality by resolving these conflicts. One such conflict is between the adolescent's need to establish emotional independence from parents and the desire to retain the secure, dependent relationship of childhood.

In the more traditional view, moral development is a continuous series of moves to balance the impact of the emerging superego (conscience). The superego began to take form following the resolution of the Oedipus conflict for boys and the Electra complex for girls, in which a child dealt with incestuous feelings toward the opposite-sex parent. In Freudian terms this conflict is the first in a series of struggles by which an individual gradually internalizes societal norms. In the case of a male, the boy wishes to marry and possess his mother. This leads to jealousy of the father who the child recognizes is sexually intimate with the mother. Eventually, however, this jealousy is replaced by fear of reprisal from the father and by guilt, because the boy recognizes both his incestuous feeling and his jealousy of his father. The boy may fear rejection or castration by his father, whom the boy sees as also jealous but more powerful. The way in which those Oedipal strivings are resolved sets the stage for moral development during adolescence, when the parents are forced into another role.

Following the resolution of the Oedipal conflict, the child starts to internalize the controls and guidelines that the parents establish. Indeed, the child becomes dogmatic in conceptions of right and wrong, good and bad, normal and abnormal. By preadolescence the perceived righteousness of the parents leads the child to idealize them and presume that they can do no wrong, that they are perfect. Unfortunately for the child (and the parents), the parents are soon recognized as imperfect. The child begins to see the parents' flaws and mistakes. Thus the child faces the first conflict of adolescence: their idealized model (the parents) is seen as both perfect and imperfect.

Adolescents' recognition of parental imperfections gradually leads to attempts to reject the parents as an ideal standard. The conflict increases through adolescence as a young person still tries to maintain the perception of an idealized parent and desires to be just like them and dependent on them. At the same time the adolescent wants to reject the parents and achieve independence. The yearning to reject the parents leads to anger and resentment, which in turn lead to guilt and frustration.

Peter Blos (1952, 1972) suggests that when the adolescent's demands for perfection in the parents are not met, the adolescent suffers disillusionment. In a sense the adolescent is left with two alternatives: alter the ideal or alter the perception of the parent. Blos suggests that the ideals are so firmly established that altering or modifying them is nearly impossible. Thus adolescents must change their perception of the parent. The internalized ideals of childhood are consolidated into what Blos (1972) describes as an *ego ideal,* or the "externalization of the lost parental ideal" (p. 51). As they see their parents as increasingly divergent from the ego ideal, adolescents have a greater need to reject the parents. But to reject your parents is to reject a large part of yourself.

Moral development during adolescence thus becomes a progressive struggle to establish "new absolutes" or perfections intended to replace the parents. When adolescents are in the throes of this moral upheaval, they are particularly vulnerable to arbitrary moral systems. An alternative system, especially a religious or social system, may be adopted intact to replace the parental ego ideal. Sudden conversion experiences are examples of this phenomenon.

THE SOCIAL LEARNING (BEHAVIORAL) VIEW

Social learning theorists (for example, Bandura & McDonald, 1963; Bandura & Walters, 1963) see moral behavior as the result of learning much the same as other types of learning. The moral values you display result from your expectation of what will lead to reinforcement. In this case, reinforcement typically takes the form of social approval—that is, people will tell you what a good (and acceptable) person you are. The social learning theorist is talking of social reinforcement not only in the mainstream moral culture but also in alternative cultures. Those people with whom you wish to associate establish norms of acceptable behavior, which they selectively reinforce. In the social learning theorists' view, even the nonconformist yields to group expectations to achieve acceptance and reinforcement.

The learning of socially appropriate or acceptable behaviors starts early in life. Consider the value *sharing.* Parents encourage their very young children to share toys with friends or siblings. Sharing is not an innate virtue—if anything, children often embarrass their parents by refusing to share with children of visiting friends. When children balk at sharing, the parents usually encourage them to do so and if they give in, provide verbal approval and perhaps a hug or two. Over several trials, the child recognizes that sharing leads to social approval, and the behavior of sharing is gradually shaped. (Children sometimes overgeneralize the sharing principle and offer to share a half-eaten, sticky lollipop with their parents or the family pet.) Similar reinforcement is applied to other values. On the other hand, parents and adults try to eliminate socially undesirable behaviors through disapproval or withdrawal of approval. Eventually children develop a body of values; that is, they know which behaviors lead to social approval and which to social disapproval.

Modeling

People also learn socially appropriate behavior indirectly through modeling and imitation. When we enter an unfamiliar setting, we try to get some cues from those around us as to how we are expected to act. If you have ever gone to a formal dinner or banquet, you may have felt ill at ease with the array of dishes and silverware in front of you. Unless you have had some training in the etiquette appropriate to such occasions, you may wonder where to start. If you are like me, you would look at someone who seems to know what to do—perhaps the host or hostess—and model your own behavior after that person's. Your modeling, or imitating, is a highly adaptive response. Further, in cognitive terms, you begin to establish a schema for other similar settings.

In the same fashion children and youths model older adolescents in an attempt to learn the "rules of the game." One of the intervention strategies for social isolates capitalizes on the ability to monitor and model another's behavior to develop social skills.

Modeling and Television

In some instances the process of modeling may be the cause of some concern. Although the examples described above encourage socially approved behavior, the same modeling may be used for socially disapproved behavior. Specifically, society is becom-

Adolescents often become committed to idealistic causes. (© Susan Lapides)

ing increasingly concerned with the potential for youths modeling violent behavior depicted on television and other media.

VIGNETTE 12–1
CHILDREN OF WAR

What is it like to a child growing up in a culture of war? What is the effect of living with the constant awareness that an enemy might kill you or a member of your family? Roger Rosenberg asked this question and proceeded to interview children in places like Beirut, Israel, and Belfast, as well as refugee children from Cambodia and Vietnam. The result is a book called Children of War *which is fascinating and, at times, chilling. Surely living in an environment where murder and mayhem are a "normal" part of life would have an effect on children's moral structures. The excerpt presented below is taken from an interview of two Israeli youths. It could as easily have been Irish, Palestinian, or Cambodian children. How do you react to their sense of morality?*

Excerpted from: Rosenthal, Roger (1983) *Children of War,* Garden City, New York: Anchor Press/Doubleday.

Dror and Nimrod, both ten, are the best of friends and share a bedroom in the kibbutz. Dror wears glasses and looks professorial. Nimrod has a dreamer's face. His brown bangs are cut evenly like a monk's over a pair of eyes the same shade of brown. The boys' room is spare, full of sunlight, and, like most boys' rooms, ridiculous. On the wall hang pictures of two white kittens, a deer, Popeye and Olive Oyl, and an El Al jet. The boys have done some pictures of their own. Dror displays a drawing of Begin and Anwar Sadat, both saying in a balloon above their heads, "Peace is going to come." Nimrod presents a drawing of Indian tepees. Why Indians?

"After the Jews they are the people I love most." He talks in a smoky whisper. "First, because the white men came and made them suffer, and they didn't deserve that. Second, I love how brave they are. I sympathize with them." Asked if his sympathies go toward all oppressed peoples, he says, "if they are innocent and are not against us."

Asked specifically about the Palestinians, he answers that he is still trying to make up his mind about which side is right: "Recently, when there was the shelling of Qiryat Shemona, and they showed the damage done by the Israeli planes in Lebanon, I looked at this and I said: 'Despite everything, I feel sorry that this is happening, happening by people to people. It is not like some animal is doing this.' When we first heard that there was retaliation, all the kids, me included, jumped up and cheered. Later I thought, What good is this revenge?"

Dror adds that he and his friends think a good deal about the children in Lebanon. "I feel terrible for them. They don't have as good shelters as we." He often wonders if they have the same toys and games. "If peace should ever happen, perhaps it would be possible to play with them."

Asked if there is such a thing as a good war, both boys say yes. "Among kids there are good wars. Take the other day. We found a big crate on the lawn, and we played king of the mountain with it. That was a good war." They recreate their excitement, recalling the game. They are asked if they see an analogy between playing king of the mountain and an adult war over territory. Dror says that playing with that crate reminded him of a war. "Even a game can wind up in real tears." They will not speculate whether such games lead to grown-ups' wars. Instead, they describe a different war game of their own, which they play with the children in another building of the kibbutz. They use military tactics. They take prisoners. The game is played according to the strictest rules.

"But the big kids break the rules!" They work up a protest on the spot and encourage each other's indignation. "They lose control! They tie our arms and legs to trees!" When it is suggested that real wars are often won by those who break the rules, Dror confesses that he occasionally breaks the rules himself, but that he feels bad about it. Nimrod says, "I will only break a rule when I'm in danger."

Viewing television or movies and listening to the radio or to music are significant sources of relaxation. Many authorities, however, are concerned that the content of media messages shapes the values of those who listen and watch. They fear that as media portray sexual and violent images as the "norm," that children and adolescents will become hardened to moral and ethical responsibilities for their own behavior. They fear that media promote amoral hedonism. Most attention to the issue of the impact of media on values has been focused on television. Nonetheless, others have also become concerned about the content of popular music, especially images portrayed in rock lyrics and, more recently, rock videos.

Watching television is primarily a passive activity. Rather than actively engaging in play, children and adolescents enjoy creative play vicariously; the television characters enjoy life for the children (Winn, 1977). Concern about this aspect of television has been voiced because active play fosters vocabulary development, impulse control, understanding others' points of view, and role exploration (Piaget, 1967; Singer & Singer, 1976). On the other hand, television may stimulate ideas for pretending or make-believe play among children and adolescents. Television may also provide models of acceptable social behavior, including how to dress, and how to communicate with others. Effects of media may be positive as well as negative. That is, if media have the potential to affect behavior and values negatively as is often claimed, they must also be able to affect behavior and values positively (Greenfield, 1984; Rushton, 1982). Indeed, studies of the impact of television on *prosocial* or socially desirable behavior have shown positive effects of television on developing interracial cooperation (Gorn, Goldberg & Kanungo, 1976), affection (Fryear & Thelen, 1969), friendliness (O'Connor, 1969), and self-control (Wolf, 1973; Wolf & Cheyne, 1972) among children. Although similar studies among adolescents are infrequent, Moriarty and McCabe (1977) in a study of Canadian youths found televised messages could encourage prosocial attitudes and behaviors in team sports.

While some attention has been directed at the role of television in developing prosocial behavior, the larger concern appears to be its effects on antisocial behavior and violence. Repeatedly, studies of the content of television shows, including Saturday morning cartoons, have shown that violence is a frequent and pervasive theme. Studies of the effects of viewing violence on television have not always shown direct ties between viewing televised violence and being violent oneself. Studies do, however, show that some young people are particularly prone to the suggestion that violence is a way of dealing with problems.

Under what circumstances does violence on television incite violence in viewers? In one case, four days following the airing of the television film *Born Innocent,* in which a young girl in a juvenile home is forcibly "raped" by other inmates with a broom handle, three girls and a boy similarly "raped" a nine-year-old girl with a beer bottle. In another case, a young man named Ronnie Zamora, on trial for murder, used as a defense that he had been driven insane by overexposure to violence on television. In still another case, television stations have been asked to refrain from airing the film "Doomsday Flight," because it depicts a skyjacking that occurs frequently every time the film is shown.

For modeling of a televised or filmed behavior to occur, the viewer must see the model in the film as attractive and as achieving some reward for the violent behavior. It is unwise to infer that television violence "causes" violent behavior in the viewer; however, some individuals are clearly more susceptible to suggestion than others.

A British study conceded that repeated, continuous exposure to violence on television does lead to increased violence among delinquent boys (Belson, 1978). In other studies, consistent relationships were found between the amount of televised violence adolescents watched and their aggressive behavior. These results were found for both boys and girls (Eron & Huesmann, 1980; Hartnagel, Teevan & McIntyre, 1975; Huesmann, Lagerspetz & Eron, 1984). On the other hand, in a study by Milavsky and his colleagues at the National Broadcasting Company (Milavsky, Kessler, Stipp & Rubens, 1982) suggests that the link between televised violence and aggressive behavior is a short-term rather than a long-term outcome. While televised violence may increase the chances of short-term aggression following exposure, evidence was not found for a long-term alteration of personality.

Another concern expressed by some researchers is that frequent and continuous televised violence may lead to a lack of responsivity to violence or a reduced sense of concern for victims. If a person watches too much televised violence, is there a chance that she or he will become cynical or callous about violence? In one set of studies (Zillman, 1982), male college students were shown hard-core pornography for long periods of time. Much of the films depicted women in roles where men were sexually violent and the women aroused. After watching these films, the research subjects acted as a jury in a mock rape trial. Those who had been subjected to the intensive viewing of pornography were less likely to find the rapist guilty than those who had not been exposed to the pornography. Whether the results of such studies can be attributed solely to imitation, or to reduced inhibitions toward violence, is unclear. The results are, however, provocative.

THE COGNITIVE DEVELOPMENTAL VIEW

The third model of moral development is the cognitive developmental theory. This model was first outlined by Jean Piaget in his classic volume *The Moral Judgment of the Child* (1932). As with most aspects of cognitive developmental theory, the foundations were laid out by Piaget. The cognitive developmental view of moral development, however, has been refined to its current more well-known version by Lawrence Kohlberg (1964,

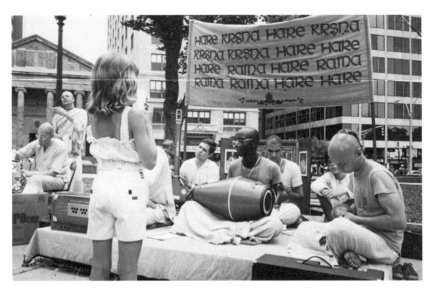

As part of their search for a personal value system, some adolescents explore alternative value structures. (© Susan Lapides)

1958; Kohlberg & Gilligan, 1971). The cognitive model differs from previous models in that it is oriented toward the intellectual structures that an individual child or adolescent uses in determining moral behavior. Further, the cognitive model is a maturational model. Just as adolescents' intellectual structures change from preoperational to concrete operational to formal operational structures, the quality of moral structures changes as the individual matures, to permit more complex moral judgments concerning the surrounding world. In contrast to the behavioral view, the essential ingredients in moral development in the cognitive view are not moral behaviors but moral judgments (Kohlberg, 1964). Moral judgments precede moral behaviors but do not always lead to them. That is, an individual may analyze a situation and make a moral judgment, but then behave in a way that is not in accord with that judgment.

In Piaget's view moral development moves from other-oriented moral judgments (heteronomous) to self-oriented moral judgments (autonomous). Early in cognitive development moral judgments are based on an understanding of what parents or those in authority see as moral. The moral structures are not based on any inherent understanding of morality but on a set of external demands to conform to what is right and acceptable. Moral structures in this early stage of moral development are oriented toward obedience to authority and are seen as rigid and inalterable.

As children mature, Piaget claimed that their moral structures become more flexible and internally defined (autonomous). Right and wrong are defined in light of a more general moral sense. In Piaget's terms, this second level of moral reasoning is a natural outgrowth of intellectual maturation, and in an environment that permits social growth, the child will normally make the transition to this level of moral thinking.

While Piaget's model provided a general theoretical scheme for viewing shifts in moral judgments, it failed to discriminate adequately among the qualitative changes in moral judgment that occur between the morality of childhood and the more sophisticated morality of late adolescence and adulthood. Lawrence Kohlberg (1964) reworked and extended Piaget's initial idea into a more complete model of moral development. Kohlberg's model is currently the more widely recognized and is having the more profound impact on social thought.

Kohlberg uses a clinical interview procedure similar to the technique originally used by Piaget. The child or adolescent reads or is told a story built around an ethical dilemma. (See Vignette 12–2.) After hearing the story, the person is asked to respond to a specific question about the story. No matter what answer the adolescent gives, the interviewer probes the boundaries of the answer to determine why the person answered as he or she did and what level of judgment he or she used. Eventually the interviewer analyzes the testee's responses in light of a set of criteria that classify the answers into Kohlberg's stages of moral development.

VIGNETTE 12–2
KOHLBERG'S MORAL DILEMMA

Presented below is an example of a moral dilemma used to attempt to measure an individual's level of moral development. Note that, regardless of the "answer" given to the first question, the interviewer asks the person to elaborate on the answer. Beyond the value of this method for assessing moral development, it is useful on a more general level as an interviewing and teaching technique. If you decide to administer the problem to a friend, you need to explain that this is part of a set of problems that is used by psychologists to assess moral reasoning. There are no right or wrong answers to these dilemmas. Rather, the questions are intended to press the limits of moral beliefs. You should allow the person to feel free not to participate. What my own students often find is that they expect everyone to answer the questions as they would, or they think they know how a friend will answer. If you use this structured interview technique, assess its value in more general terms for your role as a professional practitioner working with adolescents or others.

Source: Extracted from Lawrence Kohlberg, "Stories, Stage Descriptions, and Example Answers," Harvard University Project on Moral Development. Reprinted by permission of the author.

In Europe, a woman was near death from a special kind of cancer. There was one drug that the doctors thought might save her. It was a form of radium that a druggist in the same town had recently discovered. The drug was expensive to make, but the druggist was charging ten times what the drug cost him to make. He paid $200 for the radium and charged $2,000 for a small dose of the drug. The sick woman's husband, Heinz, went to everyone he knew to borrow the money, but he could only get together about $1,000, which is half of what it cost. He told the druggist that his wife was dying and asked him to sell it cheaper or let him pay later. But the druggist said, "No, I discovered the drug and I'm going to make money from it." So Heinz got desparate and broke into the man's store to steal the drug for his wife.

1. Should Heinz have done that? Was it actually wrong or right? Why?
2. Is it a husband's duty to steal the drug for his wife if he can get it no other way? Would a good husband do it?

3. Did the druggist have the right to charge that much when there was no law actually setting a limit to the price? Why?

Answer questions 4(a) and (b) only if you think Heinz should steal the drug.

4. (a) If the husband does not feel very close or affectionate to his wife, should he still steal the drug?
   (b) Suppose it wasn't Heinz's wife who was dying of cancer but it was Heinz's best friend. His friend didn't have any money and there was no one in his family willing to steal the drug. Should Heinz steal the drug for his friend in that case? Why?

Answer questions 5(a) and (b) only if you think Heinz should not steal the drug.

5. (a) Would you steal the drug to save your wife's life?
   (b) If you were dying of cancer but were strong enough, would you steal the drug to save our own life?
6. Heinz broke into the store and stole the drug and gave it to his wife. He was caught and brought before the judge. Should the judge send Heinz to jail for stealing or should he let him go free? Why?

Stages of Moral Development

Kohlberg describes moral development as moving regularly through six stages, from a basically hedonic, egocentric morality to a principled morality based on respect for the dignity of human beings. In stage 1, the *punishment-obedience orientation,* moral judgment is motivated by a desire to avoid punishment or possible unpleasant consequences. Adolescents may avoid sexual intercourse because of a fear of pregnancy or a fear of "getting caught." Stage 1 judgments are not oriented toward the inherent morality of an event; rather, decisions are based on the fear of possibly unpleasant consequence if those in power are offended. Conversely, stage 1 morality justifies nearly any behavior as long as threat of punishment is removed or is not a possibility.

Later in childhood, moral judgments shift toward a slightly higher level. In stage 2, the *instrumental-relativist orientation,* moral judgments are directed not at avoiding punishment but at gaining favor or a material outcome. Stage 2 might be called the "What's-in-it-for-me?" level of morality. An adolescent's primary motivation is the satisfaction of pesonal, social, or physical needs. Stage 2 individuals, like their stage 1 counterparts, are not bothered by shoplifting, joyriding, cheating on income taxes, or fixing traffic tickets—as long as they do not get caught. When they interact with others, their moral judgments are based on a trade-off model. Any service or favor that a stage 2 adolescent does for another person is done with the expectation of payoff. Loyalty, gratitude, and a sense of justice are outside the realm of their thought. In Kohlberg's model, both stages 1 and 2 represent *preconventional* levels of moral judgment. In neither case do adolescents think of the rightness or wrongness of an act. Rather they are motivated toward serving themselves. Morality has little role in their lives.

Stage 3 morality, the *good-boy/nice-girl orientation,* represents a significant shift in moral thinking, because it reflects the first sense of morality of behavior. Adolescents at this level of moral development judge morality in light of the basic moral standards of society. Their interpretation of those standards, however, is rigid and inflexible. They are not motivated by the expectation of immediate payoff but instead by the expectation that what they do is *approved* by society. Being "nice," helping others, doing "what is right" are important at this stage. Adolescents at this level respond to problems in terms of fixed, literal interpretations of rules. Things are right or they are wrong. There is little ambivalence. Their commitment to authority and to others for approval, however, may create conflicts. In their desire to conform to those in control for approval, they may be forced to choose between pleasing either the crowd or the adult authorities. Decisions are influenced by the immediacy of the approving group. The nearer the peer crowd, the parents, or the authorities, the more effect they have. The individual has, however, begun to internalize the conventional morality of the dominant society and for the first time responds to the morality of a situation.

Toward early adolescence many individuals make a somewhat subtle shift in moral structures. At stage 4, the *law and order orientation,* individuals still respond in categorical right-wrong fashion, but they also recognize that moral beliefs require a context that assures social order. Both stage 3 and stage 4 morality reflect what Kohlberg calls *conventional* morality. By this Kohlberg means that the individual has internalized the conventions, the explicit values, of a society. Adolescents at the conventional level of development have a strong orientation toward authority figures. These authorities may be traditional authority institutions; however, because an individual claims to reject traditional institutions does not automatically imply that he or she is operating above or below a conventional level. Rather, the person may be oriented toward an alternate figure or authority system that offers another set of "absolutes."

During late adolescence or during adulthood, some individuals progress to a level of moral development that Kohlberg refers to as *postconventional,* or *principled morality.* At stage 5, the *social contract orientation,* individuals see morality in terms of individual rights and agree to the general standards provided by society. Stage 5 people have not only internalized these values but have also evaluated them in terms of some logical standards. Because of this, Stage 5 people are more likely to see exceptions to rules and to assess morality in relative terms. They no longer see values as absolutes.

A very few individuals achieve the highest level of postconventional thought. At stage 6, the *universal ethical principle orientation,* individuals view morality in terms of a fundamental respect for human beings based on general ethical principles. For some at stage 6 (for example, Thomas Aquinas, Martin Luther King, Malcolm X, or Mahatma Gandhi), the ethical scheme may conflict with the predominant, conventional moral structures of their society.

Consider, if you will, how those at preconventional and postconventional levels of moral development would respond to a discussion of the 55-mile-per-hour speed limit. Those at a preconventional level would say they go 55 mph only if there is a police officer in the area. They may even describe elaborate devices that they use to avoid getting caught speeding. Those at a conventional level respond first and foremost that the 55 mph limit is the law and that they believe those who tell them that it saves gasoline. Those at a postconventional level may also respond further, that there is a good reason for the law because it has led to a reduction in traffic deaths. Their motivation to maintain the speed limit is the knowledge that their behavior affects the lives of others.

It does not follow that a person who is at a postconventional level of cognitive development will always behave in a manner that reflects that level. Although postconventional individuals are more likely to behave in ways that reflect advanced moral development, they may at times act in purely hedonic, self-gratifying terms.

Consider how you react to a stop sign when there is clearly no one else around at 3 A.M., 8 A.M., 12 noon, and 8 P.M. Most people, including me, react to the stop sign differently at different times of day.

Kohlberg's system is not without its flaws and critics. Several writers have attempted to caution that the cognitive developmental model has its shortfalls. Even Kohlberg (1981) has introduced some modest modifications into his overall system of cognitive moral development. In Kohlberg's revision, preconventional moral thinking is still marked by egocentric thought. Morality is initially defined by obeying authority in order to avoid punishment. At the next level, morality is defined by its instrumental value: either behavior is seen as satisfying one's own needs or, if behavior serves someone else's needs, it has some personal payoff. There is, however, some basic awareness of others' needs.

At the conventional level, thinking is still concrete and conforms to strict versions of morality defined by those in authority. Kohlberg continues to describe the third stage as dominated by doing what is good or nice. Loyalty and trust are valued and rules must be followed strictly. Kohlberg suggests that the person operating at this level is oriented toward a "concrete Golden Rule." That is, morality is understood by putting oneself in another person's shoes, however, morality is not seen on a more global, interpersonal basis. At the fourth stage, moral thinking is increasingly oriented toward preserving the broader social order. Most adolescents and adults operate at these two levels.

Perhaps the major alteration Kohlberg offers in his revision is the introduction of a transitional level of moral thinking between conventional and postconventional thinking. Moral choices during the transition from a conventional to a postconventional level are personal and subjective. One's commitment to a broader social order is partially severed and obligation to rules is selective. In some ways this new level sounds like the instrumental hedonism of stage two. However, the adolescent who moves into this transitional stage is in the process of reformulating views on the relationship of individual and societal morality. Choices of rules and moral guidelines are not, however, guided by a broader set of personal moral principles.

At the postconventional or principled level of moral thinking, the individual is guided by a broader view of social interaction. Basic human rights are valued and what is seen as right are those behaviors which preserve those basic human rights even if the behaviors cause modifications in the rules of the broader social system. At the last stage of moral development, the individual is guided by universal principles of justice and of respect for the dignity of all human beings. These universal principles transcend societies.

Because someone is seen as operating at the highest level of moral development does not, by the way, mean that the person has no faults. Biographies of Martin Luther, Abraham Lincoln, Martin Luther King, Mahatma Gandhi and others who are held up as examples of people operating at the level of universal ethical principles show that each had weaknesses. Their weaknesses do not, however, detract from their forward vision.

Kohlberg's theory of cognitive moral development has also been criticized on a variety of methodological grounds, but perhaps the most interesting of criticisms has come from one of his former students, Carol Gilligan (1982). In many of Kohlberg's studies the sample of people studied were all male. When male and female samples were studied, the results sometimes indicated that females lagged behind males in levels of moral development (for example, Holstein, 1976; Haan, Langer & Kohlberg, 1976). As Walker (1984) notes, there has been a historical tradition in psychology to suggest that women are morally inferior to men dating at least to Sigmund Freud's writings (1927). Gilligan argues that the reason for the lag is *not* because the female subjects were morally less mature, rather, dominant moral themes for females are stated in "A different voice."

In Gilligan's view, males are socialized at an early age to be "separated," to be individuals. Justice at the higher levels of Kohlberg's model implies individualization of views. Females, on the other hand, are socialized to be "connected," to be members of the group, and to nurture the group. When answers reflect this type of reasoning, then women are more likely to be rated lower on Kohlberg's scale. In this view, then, Kohlberg's scale is seen as sexually biased. Gilligan is quick to point out that "connectedness" and "separatedness" should not be seen as equated with "femaleness" and "maleness." Connectedness-separatedness is a continuum and that males often have feelings of connectedness and females of separatedness. What differs is the degree of commitment to each end of the continuum.

On the other hand, Walker (1984) recently provided an extensive review of sex differences in levels of moral development and found that the issue of sex differences in moral development is vastly overstated. Walker's analysis found no evidence for widespread, systematic bias in Kohlberg's stages of moral development.

The Universality of Moral Development

Kohlberg believes there is a *universality* in moral development—not in specific mores or values but in the sequential development of increasingly complex moral structures from preconventional through conventional to postconventional thought. Kohlberg supports this premise with data from several cultures. You can see in Figure 12–1 that in early adolescence, stage 1 and 2 morality dominate in both the United States and Taiwan. By middle adolescence the emergence of conventional thinking is evident. You can infer the degree to which conventional or postconventional thinking is differentially encouraged or fostered within the two societies.

Kohlberg's model of moral development bears strong resemblance to David Hunt's model of conceptual development, described in Chapter 7. Hunt's model is more broadly defined than Kohlberg's; however, many of the essential characteristics of a step-by-step developmental model are the same. For example, to achieve a level of

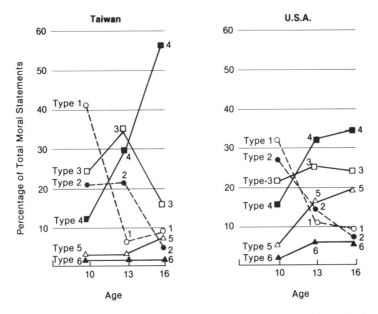

Figure 12–1 Levels of moral judgment in Taiwan and the United States. *Source:* Reprinted from "Moral Education in the Schools: A Developmental View," *School Review 74* (1966): 10, by L. Kohlberg, by permission of the University of Chicago Press. Copyright ©1966.

postconventional thought, a person *must* first go through the levels of preconventional and conventional thought. As with other progressions, we assume that an individual does not fall back to lower levels of development.

You might infer from some of Kohlberg's writings that a person is clearly at one stage of development or another. It is more likely that moral development, as with other domains of cognitive development, is fluid, and a person may be in multiple levels of development depending on the environmental conditions and the ethical issues involved (Rest, Davison & Robbins, 1978).

While Kohlberg's stages of moral development are invariantly ordered, it does not follow that all adolescents will progress evenly through those stages, even within the same culture. A variety of social variables, including intelligence (Hanks, 1985), education, social prestige, and family patterns of communication enter into the picture (Walker, 1983; Bush, Walsh & Rothman, 1981; Colby, Kohlberg, Gibbs & Lieberman, 1983). Kohlberg argues that moral development is fostered where social and emotional experiences involve responsibility and decision making.

Moral Development and Moral Behavior

Although the behavioral theorists tend to view the issues of moral behaviors without looking at the level of moral judgments, and cognitive theorists seem similarly disinclined to view the impact of levels of judgment on behavior, some research has crossed this artificial division. Quite obviously, the two theories are not independent.

As early as the classic Hartshorne and May *Studies in Deceit* (1928), evidence has shown that commitment to a set of moral values is related to behavior in other settings that require a moral choice. In a reanalysis of that data, Burton (1963) found that consistency between moral values and moral behavior increased with age across adolescence. Similarly, Bloom (1964) found that as personal maturity, including a commitment to a set of values, increased, impulsiveness decreased. The links between cognitive-social development and social behavior are not clear but low levels of cognitive-social development during early adolescence are associated with higher rates of disruption. As disruptive students mature in their social judgments, their disruptive behavior diminishes (Geiger & Turiel, 1983).

In a major study of the relationship between the level of moral judgment and behavior among college students and Peace Corps volunteers, those who displayed postconventional, principled moral judgments were more likely to be politically active, to live independently, and to describe themselves as idealistic (Haan, Smith & Block, 1968). Those students at the conventional level of moral development were unlikely to be politically committed and were more likely to describe themselves as ambitious. Young people at the conventional level of moral development were less likely than either their preconventional or postconventional peers to have conflict with their parents. Youths at the postconventional level of development were more likely to rate themselves as not religious, but they were also more likely to have been raised in nonreligious families.

POLITICAL CONCEPTS

Like their developing concepts of morality, children's and adolescents' concepts of the political system and social order progress regularly with increased cognitive maturity. Like other cognitive developmental shifts, concepts of the political system proceed from rather global, simplistic, concrete, self-centered, and undifferentiated views to complex, abstract, highly differentiated, and multifocal views (Adelson, 1979, 1983; Gallatin, 1979). At early levels, the government is seen in rigid authoritarian structures: "Government keeps us in line...Stops people from doing wrong...makes people do what is right" (p. 158). Responsibility is vested in the authority which *makes* people behave.

At early levels of political cognition, adolescents fail to differentiate between symbols of authority and the government or strucure which is represented. Weinstein (1957) asked children and young adolescents about their feelings concerning their national flag. Flags were seen, not as symbols, but as something akin to religious relics. Damaging the flag was not a *symbolic* insult, it was a real, physical damage to their country. Among older children there was, however, at least a beginning sense of the arbitrariness of the symbol-country link. One child said, "If I lived in a different country and liked the way things were I probably would like their flag best." Further, during the preadolescent years, children operate with what might be called a "patriotic filter" (Cooper, 1965). They reject any negative images of their homeland. Views of other countries take on the we-they character (Cooper, 1965; Lambert & Klineberg, 1967).

As adolescents move toward a middle level of political awareness, they are increasingly likely to view the government in a cooperative relationship with its people, but solutions to major problems are simplistic. During mature stages of political conceptions, adolescents are aware of the interdependent nature of society; they have a broader world-view.

Beyond the increasing complexity of thought, the shift in political concepts and political idealism is not infrequently accompanied by social-political activism. Adolescence is a period of intense political idealism. Student activism is frequently the stimulus which heightens social awareness of moral and social issues. Youth protest must be credited, for example, with the national reexamination of its stance toward involvement in Vietnam in the 1970s, the move toward racial equality in the 1960s, and the focus on politics of South Africa in the 1980s.

While much of the focus of youth activism is usually on college campuses, political activism and youth protest may also be seen among the high school levels. However, in the high school years, activists are more likely to be a minority. As Coleman (1961) and Musgrove (1965) suggest, younger adolescents are less likely to "rock the boat." Beyond their tendency to not question authority, they tend to exert most energies toward conforming to peers.

ADOLESCENT PREJUDICE

More than 40 years ago, Gunnar Myrdal (1944) wrote in his *An American Dilemma,* that while the American ideal proclaims "All men are created equal," American society was rife with examples of inequality. A decade later, the U.S. Supreme Court, in a landmark decision *Brown versus the Board of Education of Topeka Kansas,* maintained the racial segregation in American public schools was unconstitutional and that institutional segregation be eliminated with all deliberate speed. Beyond its immediate goal of eliminating inequalities in educational opportunity for minority and majority children and youths, there was a sense among advocates of desegregation that as interracial contact increased, racial prejudice would decrease (Pettigrew, 1967; Schofield & Sager, 1983).

Four decades after Myrdal's grim evaluation and three decades after the U.S. Supreme Court's mandate, communities and courts continue to deal with issues of institutional and personal racism. Racism and anti-Semitism are far from eliminated. As with society as a whole, adolescents are faced with moral decisions about how they relate to people of different races and religious values.

From a psychological view, there is an inherent sense that prejudiced people think differently than nonprejudiced people (Allport, 1954). Prejudice is a learned response in which the individual maintains an unfavorable ethnic attitude about some targeted group. While one might reasonably argue that prejudice may be a positive attitude, that view does not conform with our common sense meaning of the term.

Most psychological writers agree that ethnic attitudes are made of up three elements: cognitions, emotions, and response tendencies (Allport, 1954; Ehrlich,1973; Harding, Proshansky, Kutner & Chein, 1969; Westie, 1964). These three elements interact with each other and result in either positive or negative predispositions toward a targeted group. The degree to which those attitudes are transformed into actual behaviors which serve to demean and segregate a targeted group is discrimination.

Cognitions in ethnic attitudes are beliefs an individual holds about the targeted group. Those beliefs are often stereotypic and are generalized to all members of the targeted group. The validity or invalidity of the stereotypes is not always easily distinguished by the prejudiced person. The beliefs are important, however, since they form filters through which information about the targeted group is sorted.

Cognitions are tied to affective or emotional values of the group. Stereotypes may or may not be emotionally loaded. If one believes, for example, that "All blacks have rhythm" but has neither positive nor negative associations with that belief, it serves mainly, to filter new information. If that belief is tied to negative feelings about black people, then any real or imagined association with "black rhythms" may be open to attack. Early reactions to rhythm and blues music were often vaguely disguised attacks on "black music." As the child learns beliefs about that targeted group, she or he also learns feelings about the group.

The third part of an ethnic attitude learned by the chld is a set of response tendencies. Not only does the child acquire beliefs and feelings, he or she also learns how one behaves toward members of the target group. It is often believed that prejudiced people behave in a prejudiced manner. But prejudicial beliefs are not always good predictors of prejudicial behavior. The more socialized an individual, the more likely he or she is attuned to acceptable versus unacceptable behavior. When a neo-Nazi group paints swastikas on the side of a Jewish Temple, our sense of the link between attitudes and behavior is confirmed. But, when a young person is taught to mistrust members of the target group but to treat them civilly, the more benevolent behavior may mask the underlying prejudice.

In the earliest psychological study of adolescent prejudice, Minard (1931) presented high school students with a series of social problem situations involving ethnic groups. Students were asked what they felt was the "right thing to do" and then were asked what they actually would do. With reference to the ideal behavior, that is, the right thing to do, Minard found diminishing prejudice across grade levels. But when questioned about real behavior, adolescents were apparently more likely to show prejudice as they moved into the higher grades. Recent data drawn from elementary, junior, and senior high school students undergoing court-ordered desegregation (Ingersoll, Pugh, Harris & Heid, 1985) shows an increased negative interracial attitude among white high school students, especially males. Black students were not likely to show more negative attitudes.

During the 1960s, Charles Glock and his associates (Glock, Wuthnow, Piliavin & Spencer, 1975) gathered ethnic attitudinal data from adolescents in three northeastern communities. The primary focus of the study was to assess anti-Semitic sentiments among non-Jewish white and black high school students. To a lesser degree, the study was also directed toward anti-black attitudes among non-Jewish white adolescents. The study suffers a serious conceptual shortfall in its failure to assess ethnic attitudes of Jewish adolescents. There is no compelling evidence to show that any ethnic group is immune to the development of prejudice.

Glock found widespread anti-Semitism among non-Jewish adolescents. A majority thought Jews to be "conceited," "vain," "selfish," "sly," "bossy," "unfriendly," and "powerful." A substantial minority felt Jews were "gaudy," "immoral," "pushy," and "troublemakers." Non-Jewish white adolescents also showed considerable anti-black sentiments, describing blacks as "troublemakers," "gaudy," "immoral," "sloppy," "vain," "quitters," and "untrustworthy." The only positive traits consistently attributed to black students were "athletic" and "having school spirit." While there are several cautions that may be made about the Glock studies, they do point to widespread acceptance of negative ethnic stereotypes by today's young people.

Since, as adolescents mature they are increasingly able to differentiate their own egocentric concepts and perceptions from the concepts and perceptions of others, one might expect a diminishing of prejudice during late adolescence (Ingersoll, 1984; Grinder, 1985). To date, however, no real evidence exists to show this to be true. What limited evidence does exist shows more narrow attitudes as students move through the high school years. Perhaps if these same students were followed into their young adult years, or were sorted into those who were and those who were not operating at advanced levels of cognitive maturity, such trends would be found.

RELIGION AND ADOLESCENTS

There has long been interest in the attitudes of young people toward religion. The earliest studies of the psychology of religion focused on adolescence as a time of intense religious awakening. Starbuck, one of the first writers in the psychology of religion, went as far as to conclude, "If conversion has not occurred before twenty, the chances are small that it will ever be experienced" (1899, p. 28). Other early psychologists, including G. Stanley Hall and William James, were similarly convinced that adolescence was a critical period in religious development. Hall, for example, pointed to historical evidence that the religious fervor of the saints reached a peak during adolescence. Although we would question today the type of evidence that some of those early investigators used, we must still recognize the depth of concern about religion and spirituality among adolescence. Young people often develop strong commitment to or strong opposition to institutional churches and/or religion. As with other aspects of personal development, looking at religious or moral development in isolation from the lifelong process of acquiring a sense of values may be misleading. Actually, the process of religious development is a lifelong process, and as with other conceptual schemes, it is subject to shifts throughout life.

Currently, there is a renewed interest in the topic. The rekindling of evangelical movements among college-age and high school students, and the attraction that a variety of cults holds for many young people, have brought the question into the public eye once more.

Most explanations as to why adolescence is such a critical period in the development of more permanent religious attitudes have focused on two factors. On one hand, many see the adolescent religious concern in the context of the identity crisis. The adolescent's need to internalize a personal system of values is a part of the more general striving

Some religions select early adolescence as the time for formal initiation into the adult community; the Jewish Bar Mitzvah is an example of such a ceremony. (Paul S. Conklin)

to establish a personal identity. Alternatively, some focus on the intellectual transition of adolescence and put the changes in religious beliefs within the broader perspective of general cognitive development.

Identity Development

Because an important element in developing a personal sense of identity is the internalizing of a personal value system, some writers see the characteristic interest in religion as a part of the general identity-formation process. Adolescents need to establish a firm, internalized concept of what is right and wrong, what is acceptable and unacceptable. Further, they wrestle with the question that most religions address: "What am I to do with my life?" "How did life begin?" "What is my responsibility to my fellow human beings?" "Is this all there is to life?"

As adolescents work through these issues they are brought to other questions about their relationship with a divine Being or about whether there is a God at all. It is important for adolescents to clarify and answer these questions in a personal fashion in order for subsequent, personal, moral development to occur.

In a similar view, Ruth Strang (1957) saw the development of a set of religious beliefs as part of the establishment of adolescents' feelings of self-worth. Teens' feelings of adequacy and self-worth may be inferred from the way they think God views them. Adolescents with negative self-worth see themselves as unworthy of God's love, or as being punished, or as unacceptable to those around them because of past sins.

Those with positive self-worth are more likely to see themselves as loved by God, to see God as a help in times of stress, and to see God as a source of strength and courage in general.

Intellectual Development

The second view of adolescents' relationship to religion focuses on Piaget's stages of intellectual development and Kohlberg's stages of moral development. Religious conviction is part of the general pattern of cognitive moral development. As Piaget (1967) explains, middle and late adolescence is a time when emerging formal thought leads to intense idealism. As abstract thought develops, adolescents are able to consider utopian schemes and are impatient with what they see as a lack of adult or church responsiveness to pressing social problems.

As adolescents shift from concrete to formal thought, their ideas about the teachings of their faith follow the same progression. Just as they think about science and math on abstract levels, they also examine their religious beliefs on the same level. The simplistic beliefs of childhood are replaced by internal and personal understandings of the same concept (Kuhlen & Arnold, 1944). Concepts of God become more abstract and less literal. There is also evidence that they become less dogmatic and rigid. Note, for example in Table 12–1 that there is a regular decrease in concrete beliefs and a regular increase in abstract beliefs and in questioning from ages 12 to 18.

Religious educators and clergy often find adolescents very hard to work with. When adolescents are not totally unresponsive, they ask endless questions about the meaning of life, immortality or the lack of it, the existence of God, and the value or truth of the religion in which they have been raised. Their emerging idealism may lead to confusion and anger about seeming inconsistencies between church doctrine and social policy. As they read history, they may become distressed at the politicization of religions and the justification of persecution of minorities by dominant religions. Too often those in charge regard such questions or concerns as indications of an emerging atheism, and they feel compelled to cut the question off with a dogmatic "truth." More than likely the young person who asks a knotty question does not really expect an answer. In the course of trying to clarify values, those questions naturally emerge. Rather than closing the questions off, adults should encourage them and allow the adolescent to expand on the question—and why it is a question.

Stages in Faith Development

To try to separate the development of a religious identity from religious cognitive development may be misleading. The views of Erikson, Piaget, and Kohlberg are not antagonistic to each other but are complementary. James W. Fowler (1976, 1981) has combined the approaches into a series of stages of faith development. According to Fowler's six stages of development of faith concepts, an individual's scheme of faith progresses from simple, narrowly defined concepts of faith to highly complex, multifaceted concepts. Like Kohlberg's conception, these stages are sequential—that is, to

Table 12–1   Changes in Adolescents' Religious Beliefs

Statement	Age:	"BELIEVE"			"WONDER ABOUT"		
		12	15	18	12	15	18
God is a strange power working for good, rather than a person.		46	49	57	20	14	15
God is someone who watches you to see that you behave yourself, and who punishes you if you are not good.		70	49	33	11	13	18
I know there is a God.		94	80	79	2	14	16
Catholics, Jews and Protestants are equally good.		67	79	86	24	11	7
There is a heaven.		82	78	74	13	16	20
Only good people go to heaven.		72	45	33	13	27	34
Hell is a place where you are punished for your sins on earth.		70	49	35	13	27	34
Heaven is here on earth.		12	13	14	18	28	32
People who go to church are better than people who do not go to church.		46	26	15	17	21	11
Young people should belong to the same church as their parents.		77	56	43	10	11	11
The main reason for going to church is to worship God.		88	80	79	4	7	6
It is not necessary to attend church to be a Christian.		42	62	67	18	15	8
Only our soul lives after death.		72	63	61	18	25	31
Good people say prayers regularly.		78	57	47	13	13	27
Prayers are answered.		76	69	65	21	25	27
Prayers are a source of help in times of trouble.		74	80	83	15	10	9
Prayers are to make up for something that you have done that is wrong.		47	24	21	18	17	9
Every word in the Bible is true.		79	51	34	15	31	43
It is sinful to doubt the Bible.		62	42	27	20	26	28

Source: R. G. Kuhlen and M. Arnold, "Age Differences in Religious Beliefs and Problems in Adolescence," *Journal of Genetic Psychology* 65 (1944): 293.

reach the higher levels of development implies progression through the lower levels. Table 12–2 presents the stages and their position relative to the stages of development defined by Piaget, Kohlberg, and Erikson.

Stage 1: Intuitive-Projective Faith.   The lowest level of development is based on an intuitive and imitative knowledge of faith. Beliefs are focused primarily on an omniscient but magical God. The child sees such natural phenomena as lightning, thunder, and northern lights as rewards or punishment for their own behavior; for example, "God made the sun shine for my birthday," or "Why did God make me sick on the day I was to go to the dance?" The child's conception is highly egocentric. As adults, we are not immune to stage 1 feelings. When we are driving to an appointment and are in danger of being late, and every traffic light is green, we are likely to think something like "I must have done something right," implying that some magical power has caused the lights to be green as a favor to us.

Table 12–2   Expected Parallels Among Developmental Theories

Piaget (Cognitive)	Kohlberg (Moral)	Fowler (Faith)	Erikson (Psychosocial)
(0–2)—Sensory-Motor		0—Undifferentiated	1—Trust versus Mistrust
(2–6)—Intuitive or Prelogical [Preoperational]	0—The good is what I want and like	1—Intuitive-Projective	2—Autonomy versus Shame and Doubt 3—Initiative versus Guilt
(7–11)—Concrete Operations	1—Punishment and obedience orientation		
	2—Instrumental hedonism and concrete reciprocity	2—Mythic-Literal	4—Industry versus Inferiority
(12–)—Formal Operations	3—Orientation to interpersonal relations of mutuality	3—Synthetic-Conventional	5—Identity versus Role-Confusion
(Piagetian stages are taken to be necessary but not sufficient for corresponding stages of moral and faith development	4—Maintenance of social order, fixed rules and authority	4—Individuating-Reflexive	6—Intimacy versus Isolation
	5—Social contract, utilitarian, law-making perspective	5—Paradoxical-Consolidative	7—Generativity versus Stagnation
	6—Universal ethical principle orientation	6—Universalizing	7—Integrity versus Despair

Source: Reprinted from ''Stages in Faith: The Structural-Development Approach'' by James W. Fowler, pp. 188–189, in *Values and Moral Development,* ed. by T. C. Hennessy. © 1976 by The Missionary Society of St. Paul the Apostle in the State of New York. Used by permission of Paulist Press.

Stage 2: Mythic-Literal Faith.   The next stage, most common to childhood and preadolescence, is a faith dominated by a literal acceptance of the dogma of a religion and a strict adherence to the concreteness of its symbols. That is, the child regards the symbol as important not because it *represents* something but because it has concrete reality. Not uncommonly, this concrete reality may also acquire stage 1, magical characteristics, as in a good-luck charm. Rules and guidelines are inviolable and absolute. Once again, adherence to the rules leads to rewards by God, disobedience to punishment.

Stage 3: Synthetic-Conventional Faith.   At stage 3, faith provides a social structure within which to handle the complexities of daily living. Religious rules are interpreted rigidly, and members of the faith community are all expected to adhere to the rules. The strict interpretation is often extended to imply, sometimes implicitly and sometimes explicitly, that the rules are the *only* true ones.

Stage 4: Individuating-Reflexive Faith.   During late adolescence young people find themselves in a struggle between loyalty to the community and a quest for individuality, between concrete objectivity and abstract subjectivity, between feeling obligated to serve others and a desiring to fulfill themselves. Those struggles may and do generalize to the adolescents' relationship to religion. Stage 4 requires a personalizing of religion and a recognition of personal responsibility to a faith community.

Stage 5: Paradoxical-Consolidative Faith. During this later stage of faith development, individuals recognize and appreciate the integrity and validity of positions other than their own. Recognizing the value of other faith forms, and exploring their extra dimensions, expands the individual's personal faith develpoment.

Stage 6: Universalizing Faith. The rare person who achieves this level is able to live in harmony with all people. The feeling of oneness does not interfere with the person's sense of individuality, because the oneness with humanity is transcendent.

Older adolescents are considerably less likely than younger adolescents to attend church regularly. This phenomenon is not new and has been recognized for some time (Kuhlen & Allen, 1944). Does this mean that higher levels of cognitive moral development interfere with religious commitment? That is unclear. However, the reluctance to attend church does not necessarily mean an alienation from religion in general or even from the church in particular. Some young people reject institutional religion but maintain a personal set of beliefs that are very much like those of the church they rejected.

Adolescents reject the institutional church because they feel that the conventional church is unresponsive to personal and social needs (Beit-Hallahmi, 1974). They regard church attendance as superficial and uninteresting. Once again, the abstract value of a personal ideology may be incompatible with the more concrete value of attending church because of an imposed rule. As one young person declared, ''God is not dead, the church is dead' (Babin, 1969).

Religiosity. This brings us to the interesting question of what we mean by the term *religious*. Quite clearly, ''being religious'' means something very different to adolescents at different stages of moral or faith development. Dittes (1969) notes that arguments about whether religiousness is observed in steadfast adherence to rules of the institutional church or in a personal knowledge of God can be found in the writings of the Old Testament prophets.

Dittes prefers to distinguish between *consensual* and *committed* religiosity. The distinction (based on earlier work of Allen & Spilka, 1967) is between the type of religious conviction an individual maintains. Consensual religion refers to a commitment to the formal, institutional church and adherence to its formal structure and rules. Committed religion refers to a subjective, personal set of beliefs that may or may not include a commitment to the institutional church.

In most studies reviewed by Dittes, evidence consistently showed that the greater the adherence to a purely consensual religion, the more likely individuals are to profess rigidly and dogmatically the unacceptability of those who adhere to another set of beliefs. As a corollary, their unwillingness to allow diversity and to recognize complexity may lead to antisemitism and racism (Dittes, 1969).

Given the distinction between consensual and committed religiosity, and the findings that older adolescents are more likely to see God or religion in abstractions,

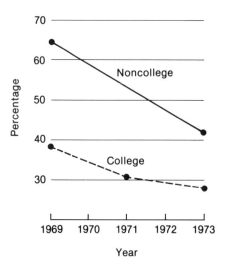

Figure 12-2 Adolescents who see religion as a very important value. *Source:* From *The New Morality: A Profile of American Youth in the 70's,* pp. 14 and 26, by D. Yankelovitch. Copyright © 1974 McGraw-Hill Biook Company. Used with permission of McGraw-Hill Book Company.

it is unclear whether trends such as the one reported by Yankelovitch (1974) in Figure 12–2 refer to a decline in the value placed on religion or a shift toward more committed but less consensual beliefs.

Conversions

Although conversion experiences are not uncommon among adolescents, conversions are not all the same. We can describe at least four different types of experiences, all of which refer to the deepening of a personal commitment to a set of religious beliefs or a supreme being (Glock & Stark, 1965).

By far the most common type of conversion is a *confirming* experience in which some event or series of events serve to confirm what an individual already believed to be true. Adolescents who undergo a confirming experience report no radical shift in their views. Rather, these young people report they have a more general sense of a divine being and that their knowledge intensified.

In recent years the "born again" movement has been given much attention by the popular media. Being "reborn" is an example of what Glock and Stark refer to as a *responsive* experience. In a responsive conversion experience, individuals feel that not only have they come to know God better but also that God has suddenly taken a personal interest in them. This conversion may occur following a perceived "miracle" or some other event that an individual sees as a divine intervention or an answer to prayer. There is a strong bias toward this form of conversion experience among some denominations and a strong bias against it in others. Among Southern Baptists, for example, 93 percent reported a responsive conversion experience, whereas only 26 percent of Roman Catholics and 9 percent of Congregationalists did so.

Two other types of conversion experiences presumably include the former two but are deeper in intensity. In the *ecstatic* experience the relationship between God and the converted person becomes deeply emotional. Individuals report charismatic or ecstatic experiences in which they speak in tongues or have uncontrolled body movements and uncontrolled praising. In certain sects the ecstatic experiences are quite clearly sexual in content and symbol. The last form of conversion experience is the *revelational* experience, in which individuals believe they have achieved such a close relationship with God that he has chosen them to reveal a divine plan or message. They see themselves as prophets.

Whether adolescents experience one or another of these conversion experiences depends on a variety of factors. Because conversion experiences are common to certain denominations, and because historically adolescence has been seen as the prime time for conversions, we have the elements of a self-fulfilling prophesy. That is, adolescents are expected to have conversion experiences, thus they may feel motivated to seek such experiences.

Cults

Any discussion of religion and youths is sure to raise the issue of cults. While parents, teachers, and clergy have long been troubled by splinter religious groups which recruit young people into their fold, the emergence of a new wave of cults in the past two decades has heightened those concerns. Fears that members of cults are "brainwashed" or "programmed" took on new urgency following the mass suicide-murders of Jonestown, Guyanna in 1978. However, not all cults are as radical as the Jonestown group; some may offer fulfillment of members' needs not met through traditional institutional religions. It is noteworthy to remember that at the turn of the century,

People in religious roles frequently play an important part in helping adolescents clarify their value systems. (Peter Vandemark)

Mormonism was described as a cult and that, in its early history, Christianity was thought by the Romans to be a troublesome cult.

What is a cult and how does it differ from a standard religion or even a sect? Religion offers a scheme within which meaning is tied to the existence of a supernatural being or force (Stark & Bainbridge, 1979). As a religion becomes stabilized it also becomes formalized and institutionalized. *Sects* emerge from the parent religion as members become disaffected and want to refine or purify the religion (Johnson, 1963). A sect represents a splintering off, a breaking away from the standard—a reformation. Cults, on the other hand, represent a new way of conceiving the role of the supreme being in members' lives (Stark & Bainbridge, 1979). As sects and cults stand the tests of time they become institutionalized and become among the standards.

Religion serves at least four broad functions for individuals (Meadow & Kahoe, 1984). It serves to meet *egocentric* needs of individuals. That is, religion functions to meet bodily needs and needs of feelings of security and belonging. Religion also serves a *growth* function by fostering a sense of self-worth in the individual which is tied to one's connection to the religion. Religion serves a *social* function by establishing and passing on a code of conduct and ethics. Religion serves a *cognitive* function by offering reasons and answers to the "Why" questions of existence which plague us all. Like standard religions, cults are built around one or more of these functions. In particular, cults often provide a regimented, simplistic code of conduct and a sense of belonging within a closed community. The individual member feels wanted and needed and is provided clear rules which reduce personal anxieties resulting from having to make one's own decisions.

Cults seem particularly attractive to older adolescents and young adults who may feel alienated and isolated. At such a point they may be unsure of the adequacy of their current (and their parents') value system. At these points of disaffection and confusion, a cult member recruits by assuring the young person answers to all lifes questions and a sense of belonging.

Among the groups that continue to receive wide public attention are the Unification Church of Sun Myung Moon (the Moonies), the Divine Light Mission of Maharaj Ji, the Institute for Krishna Consciousness, the Children of God, the Church of Scientology, and the Way. Although these groups are the ones most often headlined, they are by no means the only such groups. If we include splinter Bible or gospel groups, one in 10 Americans are affiliated with fringe religious groups (Zaretsky, 1977).

Criticisms of cults proceed along two lines. First, noncultists suspect that the leaders of the cults are hypocritical and are exploiting cult members to enhance their own personal wealth. Typically, such critics point to the lavish life-style of the Maharaj Ji or the financial power amassed by Sun Myung Moon, while their followers live at near-poverty levels and panhandle to support their church. It was reported, for example, that in its first full year of operation in the United States, the Unification Church cleared $10 million after expenses (Cornwell, 1976). Members of the cults, however, may see that same wealth as evidence of the truth of the leader's message. That is, if the leader has been lying, why has he been so successful?

The second major criticism leveled at cults is that they have "hypnotic" control over their members—that members are programmed and brainwashed. This accusation of mind-control is tied with allegations of kidnapping and deprivation to accomplish the brainwashing. Cults may have training sessions in which members are isolated in groups in which the teachings of the church are learned and memorized. Members may be encouraged to associate with (and marry) only other members of the cult. They may be required to abandon personal wealth and turn it over to the cult.

A number of deprogramming groups have emerged in response. Often these groups resort to precisely the same tactics of which they acuse the cults. That is, kidnapping, isolation, and intensive teaching sessions. In one case, Daniel Eyink, a member of an Ashram in Cincinnati, was abducted by such a group, who had been hired by Eyink's parents. After a rather heated court fight, Eyink's cult was able to gain a court order for Eyink's return.

Those who jutify deprogramming argue that because cult members have been brainwashed and because they are no longer in full control of their faculties, they should not be afforded the civil liberties of "normal" people. The tactic then is to have the cult member ruled "mentally incompetent" by the courts and to have the parents appointed as "conservators." (This maneuver was designed to provide for the care of elderly people who were no longer able to handle their own affairs [Robbins, 1977].) A serious question remains over whether such procedures deprive cult members of their civil liberties.

Finally, although some of the allegations against some cults may be true, there is no reason to assume that all cults operate in the same fashion. Likewise, it is an error to assume that all cult followers are impossible dreamers, unthinking robots, or mental freaks. Zaretsky and Leone (1975) found that, rather than being destructive to the primary moral codes of society, the major groups were very pragmatic and advocated highly moral doctrines.

SUMMARY

As young people develop more complex intellectual and social structures during the adolescent years and young adulthood, they also develop increasingly complex value structures. As with general cognitive-social thought, value structures progress from self-serving visions of morality, through authority-based, external concepts of morality, to complex, pervasive value systems that tolerate ambiguity and uncertainty. These value systems are reflected to general views of justice, faith, politics, and interpersonal relations.

Not everyone will progress to more complex stages of moral development. Like stages of social and ego development described earlier in this text, most adults fail to move beyond the middle levels of cognition. Just as it is a mistake to assume that all adolescents think on a formal operational level, it is similarly a mistake to assume that young people can, and/or prefer to, deal with value issues at a complex level. Indeed, in the context of religious education, Goldman (1964) has cautioned such a presumption may be more harmful than good.

There is little question that values are learned and that young people enter the adolescent years armed with a range of experiences which have established the foundation for the value systems with which they will exit adolescence. Nonetheless, practitioners working with young people can exert strong influence on adolescents' experiences in value formation and refinement.

Kohlberg (1976) maintains that teachers should play an active role in the value formation process of students. By this Kohlberg does not mean that teachers should moralize and coerce students to the teachers' value systems. Rather, teachers should stimulate development of learners' moral structures by discussing moral and ethical dilemmas. To be effective in this mode, teachers should probe the limits of the students' understanding of an ethical conflict and allow the students to evaluate the rightness or wrongness of various alternatives. By opening the discussion of ethical issues, the teacher provides a context in which students can encounter and evaluate positions other than their own. As students face information new to their existing cognitive moral structure, they must respond not simply by assimilating the new information in a verbatim, rote fashion, but also by evaluating the information. Further, they may need to modify the existing schema in order to accommodate the new information. Facilitating moral development in Kohlberg's terms requires a transitional period of disorganization or disequilibrium so that reorganization may take place. Challenging beliefs through questioning, debating or role playing, generates such disharmony, but the teacher should also *provide time for the learner to reorganize* the schema before too much disharmony settles in. This reorganization may take as simple a form as a presentation or a project.

To be effective, instruction in this mode should maintain many of those characteristics of teaching for productive thinking in other domains. That is, it must occur in a positive, constructive setting in which alternative views are not dismissed out of hand. Teachers who engage in these interchanges must recognize that students may not resolve ethical dilemmas in precisely the fashion that those in authority would prefer. In fact, a student may evaluate the dilemma in ways dramatically opposite to what the teacher expects. This does not mean that Kohlberg is calling for total neutrality or moral relativism on the part of the teacher. Indeed, he believes that, as individuals progress through the stages of moral development, they gain broader, more pervasive concepts of right and wrong.

Adolescents' attempts to clarify and internatlize their own value systems will frequently affect their assessment of religious beliefs. Their reactions to religion may range from mild discomfort and uncertainty to radical redefinition of their religious selves. It is not uncommon for young people, particularly during their later adolescent years, to reject institutional religion, temporarily or permanently, in favor of a more personalized belief system. Adolescence may also be a time of intense religious experiences which serve to confirm their religious beliefs.

The struggle with one's value system is, of course, a life-long process. The end of adolescence does not bring with it a permanently resolved set of value structures. Adults working with young people may serve an important role by helping adolescents realize that adults are also dealing with refinement and clarification of their own values.

13 | JUVENILE CRIME

Each year the Federal Bureau of Investigation releases statistics on the number of crimes committed in the United States. Part of the total number of crimes is used to create an annual Crime Index. Repeatedly, when those statistics are studied by age group, young people under the age of 18 commit a disproportionate share of those crimes. In 1984, a total of 1,684,956 crimes were reported which fell into the categories of the Crime Index. Of these, 527,466 or 31.3 percent were committed by young people under the age of 18 (Federal Bureau of Investigation, 1986). Of the Crime Index offenses committed by those under 18, 58 percent were committed by young people ages 15 to 17. Young people under age 18 accounted for 36 percent of all cases of auto theft, 38 percent of cases of burglary, and 42 percent cases of arson. It is estimated that "one in every nine children in the United States—one in every six male children—will be referred to juvenile court in connection with some delinquent act (other than traffic offenses) before his eighteenth birthday" (Caldwell, 1971, p. 3).

Beyond their increased likelihood to commit crime, young people are also more likely to be victims of crime (Department of Justice, 1986). Rates of victimization of teenagers are twice those of adults, 6 percent of teens have been victims of violent crime and 12 percent of theft. Further, risk of victimization is greater during the later teen years (16 to 19 years). Teens were most at risk for victimization at school.

Some argue that the Uniform Crime Index is unfairly biased against crimes that are common to youths and fails to include more "adult" crimes (Jensen & Rojek, 1980). Although the index includes criminal homicide, forcible rape, robbery, aggravated assault, burglary, larceny, and motor vehicle theft, it excludes fraud, embezzlement, counterfeiting, forgery, arson, organized crime, and narcotics traffic. These excluded crimes are committed primarily by adults. The cost to the public of such "white-collar crimes" as consumer fraud and embezzlement far outdistances all the theft-related crimes of the Crime Index (Jensen & Rojek, 1980). Nonetheless, a group that accounts for less than one-quarter of the national population—the youth population—accounts for more than its share of crime. Some writers go so far as to suggest that as the size of the adolescent population diminishes in the next decade, there will be a similar drop in the national crime rate, unemployment, and even venereal disease.

We may reasonably say that the majority of violent crime by adolescents is committed by a small minority of young people, but we must also admit that the great majority of adolescents at one time or another engage in behavior that is delinquent (Gold, 1966; Haney & Gold, 1973). A major study of delinquent behavior among adolescents found that there is a steady increase in the number of delinquent acts among both boys and girls as they move through adolescence. Boys, however, are consistently more likely than girls to admit to having committed serious delinquent acts, and by 18 they are five times as likely to make such admissions. Further the average seriousness of the delinquent behavior increased for boys but did not increase for girls (Gold & Petronio, 1980). Are we saying that anyone who commits a delinquent act is automatically a juvenile delinquent? No. That would be like calling the drug experimenter a drug abuser.

DEFINING DELINQUENCY

According to one definition, "a delinquent act is one that is illegal and one the individual knows is illegal when he commits it" (Haney & Gold, 1973). Notice that this definition, although precise, skirts the issue of defining a delinquent adolescent. Although the majority of adolescents engage in delinquent behavior, most do not get caught and the overwhelming majority feel they have more than a fifty-fifty chance of never getting caught (Haney & Gold, 1973). However, the more often an adolescent engages in delinquent behavior, the more likely he or she is to get caught. It would be only partly a joke to say that "An adolescent becomes a delinquent only when he gets caught."

The label *juvenile delinquent* arises primarily out of a legal process. Because adolescents who are caught in delinquent behavior and are brought before the courts make up only a minority of those who actually engage in delinquent behavior, our general conclusions about juvenile delinquency and juvenile delinquents may be tainted. The judicial processes that operate in society as a whole also operate in the juvenile justice system. Thus, even among the minority of adolescents who are apprehended for delinquent acts, the likelihood of their case being brought to court and their chance of being sent to a juvenile treatment facility differ for males and females, for blacks and whites, and for lower- and middle-income youths. Hence, any conclusions about the general pattern of adolescent delinquent behavior that are based only on the sample that are caught, are suspect.

One of the primary misconceptions about juvenile crime is that the problem is concentrated in urban, lower-income, black ghettos. Although blacks, and especially black girls, are disproportionately represented in juvenile penal institutions, it does not

The number of arrests of youthful offenders, especially for violent crimes, continues at a high level. (© Leonard Freed/Magnum Photos, Inc.)

follow that they are necessarily more delinquent. Indeed the work of Gold (1966) found that neither black males nor black females were more delinquent than their white counterparts. However, because blacks are overrepresented in jails, other factors are apparently operating on the "official" designation of delinquency.

Another myth is that juvenile crime is primarily the activity of established gangs. Gold (1970) also found that most delinquent behavior was *not* well-organized, planned events by a gang. Rather delinquency is more of a "pick up game," much like playground basketball. Matza (1964) similarly concludes that most delinquent behavior is casual, spontaneous, and loosely organized. Gangs, certainly a real problem, may not account for the majority of youth crime.

There is also a widespread misconception that most violent crime is committed by black offenders on white victims. That is not true. In one survey covering 17 cities, 90 percent of the homicides and aggravated assaults, and rapes involved victims and offenders of the same race. Further, in two-thirds of the homicides and aggravated assaults and in three-fifths of the rapes in those cities, the victims were black (Moynihan, 1969).

It is true, however, that most violent crime among youths is concentrated in the city and that it is higher in densely populated lower-income areas. As Moynihan (1969) has stated, the poverty and social isolation of the urban poor and minorities are perhaps the single most serious problem facing America today. The poverty of the urban areas breeds not only crime but chronic unemployment and basic deprivation of human rights.

At least some delinquent behavior results from pressures among peer groups to conform. To be accepted by or acceptable to the group, a young person may find it necessary to engage in delinquent behaviors. One young girl, arrested for shoplifting, explained that her friends "dared" her to do it, and she was afraid that, if she did not, her friends would think that she was "chicken." In many ways, delinquent behavior can serve as an initiation rite to prove worthiness of belonging to a group.

This peer expectation of delinquent behavior is not limited to lower-income inner-city, gang members. The same pressures are found among adolescents from middle-to upper-income families as well as among adolescents from suburban and rural communities. Indeed, in the period 1971 to 1976, the biggest increases in annual crime among youths were in communities with populations less than 25,000 and in rural areas (Alder, Bazemore & Polk, 1980).

While it is true that the majority of young people engage in some behaviors that could be judged delinquent, it is also important to keep in mind that there is a smaller group for whom delinquency and antisocial behavior is a way of life. As early as August Aichorn's (1935) book *Wayward Youth,* it was recognized that there were differences among types of delinquents. For some, antisocial behavior actually reflects the dominant culture within which they live. In those cases, peer and social approval is tied to the individual's willingness to engage in antisocial behavior. Breaking the law is, in this sense, an adaptive behavior which brings prestige, security, and acceptance. Again, most young people engage in some antisocial behaviors. It is when antisocial behavior becomes excessive and the pattern of antisocial behavior begins to interfere with the young person's ability to adapt at home, in school, or in society as a whole, that the problem may require clinical intervention (Kazdin, 1987). Repeated, regular antisocial behavior is not something to be taken lightly. It is an indicator of general poor adjustment and interferes with other aspects of the young person's life; it should not be thought of as just a phase. Antisocial children do not tend to "grow out of it" (Patterson, 1986).

VIGNETTE 13–1
YOUTH TACTICS

In the article reprinted below, you will read the testimony of a fifteen-year-old gang member from New York City before a legislative committee on crime. Beyond the description of the tactics used by one gang of youths in robbing elderly people, you will get a sense of the attitudes of this young man about the act. As you read through this interchange, try to get a feeling fo those attitudes. What does the young person feel about the crime, about the victim, about the courts?

Source: "Youth Tactics. Hold the Old Lady . . . Look for the Money," *National Observer* (April 2, 1977). Reprinted by permission of the *National Observer,* © Dow Jones & Company, Inc., 1977. All rights reserved.

The Select Committee on Crime of the New York State Legislature held hearings in New York City last December on crimes against the elderly. Among the witnesses was a 15-year-old New York youth who acknowledged participating in gang robberies against the elderly. Here are excerpts from his testimony:

Have you ever been arrested for a crime against an old person?

No, but I have been involved in such—such a crime.

And can you tell us how you got into this?

Well, you know, it's like the neighborhood, coming up. When I was young, coming up, things like that was going on, and as we grew older we started hanging around with these people, getting involved with this and that, hear stories about people, you know, as they say, rushing cribs (robbing elderly persons in their apartments or houses), you know, coming off with big money, you know, so I guess you figure—and they was juveniles under 16, you know. If they got busted they came right home, so it wasn't nothing as far as a record is concerned, you know.

I guess, you know, every time you get arrested when you are a juvenile they say you have to be 16 or the record doesn't count. That's what they said, so it didn't matter how many times you got busted as long as you was under 16, that you wouldn't be accounted as you got older. So it was easy money, you know, never went nowhere so long as you was a juvenile. So that's why everybody did it.

Was there a plan and did you get together at any particular time and decide who you were going to rob or take from?

Well, we had a little group, you know, around the neighborhood—it was quite a few, you know, elderly people that we felt had a lot of money that was worth, you know, robbing, so like most of the acts—most of the crimes took place in the summertime, you know, during summer vacation from school, and all the group of boys that was going together would meet outside in the morning, you know, early, around 7:30, 8 o'clock, just stand, you know. There was an old ladies' center around our neighborhood where people used to go, old people used to go, go shopping, come from there, go back and eat, stand there, play checkers and stuff. So most of the gang used to stay down there and wait for them to go to the store or bank or whatever, just follow them home.

When you got into the building what would you do?

Usually one of the persons, one of the gang would get on the elevator with the lady, see what button she pressed. Like, if she pressed the fifth floor, he will press the fourth, and the rest of us would be, you know, in the stairway, and he would holler up what floor and we would all just run up to the floor she's getting off on. As soon as she opened the door, just walk behind, push her on in, get the money,.

And how many people, how many of you would be on a team doing this?

Well, used to be maybe three or four.

Was there an assignment where one person would hold the old person and the other persons would do the searching of the apartment?

Usually the biggest guy, he'll be the one to hold the old lady. One would be a lookout. Whoever else was left, they would look for the money.

Could you tell us how many crimes you have committed against the elderly without getting caught?

I really couldn't say. It's been quite a few.

During the week, in the summertime, about how many would you commit?

Well, I would say out of a day, you know, however many we would try, we didn't make enough money, we would just go and do maybe five or six a day.

Were you taught how to do this when you first started doing it or did you just pick it up?

Well, when I first did it, you know, I really didn't know too much about it. My brother had did it a few times, you know, so he was having money and I wasn't, and he was not that much older than me, so we was in the same group, hanging out with the same people, so I wanted to get down and do it too, so I just went with him one day and I had never done it before. I just went. We carried it off, so after that I thought it was easy. I just kept doing it.

What was your biggest score?

Oh, a couple of thousand, I guess.

Was there ever a time when you got to Family Court on one of your arrests that there was an adjudication where they found you guilty?

Well, it wasn't on the same kind of charge.

It was a different charge?

Yes. You know, I was found guilty but nothing happened.

Did they place you on probation or anything?

Yes, six-month probation.

What was the charge?

Robbery. Armed robbery.

You had a gun?

Toy.

Toy gun?

Yes.

How old were you when you started picking on the elderly?

Well, I started, I guess, when—I would say I was around 12. My first arrest I was 13, so...

Could you tell us what that crime was?

Well, it was armed robbery in a train station.

Did you go to Family Court on that?

Yes.

What happened to you?

Well, they just dismissed the case and put us on probation for six months.

When you rushed a crib and it was an elderly person, did you threaten them that if they testified against you they would be hurt?

Yes, that was part of it.

And you were told to do that by the other fellows?

Right, in order to keep them from, you know, if anything ever happened, in order to keep them from coming to court. Their being old, you know, they might feel their lives would be endangered, so they were scared.

Have you ever hurt anybody?

Not me.

You have seen them hurt?
Yes. Usually the oldest person is doing it, or the biggest. The biggest guy.

TYPES OF DELINQUENTS

As I have stated, not all delinquent crime is done in gangs, and not all delinquent youths are members of gangs. Gibbons (1970) provides a useful set of categories to describe not only the character of delinquent youths with respect to gang membership but also their motives for delinquent acts and their attitude toward society as a whole. As we noted earlier in the text, our general impression of the delinquent coming from a disorganized or hostile family seems to have validity. Close family ties are strongly related to lower rates of delinquency for both boys and girls (Gold & Petronio, 1980). In most of the cases described by Gibbons, delinquents come from homes characterized by inadequate or careless supervision, overstrict and abusive or erratic discipline, and a general lack of family cohesiveness. Gibbon's categories are the following:

1. The *predatory gang delinquent* is the type of youth that fits the stereotyped image of the gang delinquent. He makes his primary association with the gang and is regularly involved in violent delinquent behavior that will show him to be "cool" or "tough." This individual is antisocial and hostile toward society.

2. The *conflict gang delinquent* identifies with a gang and may join in street fights, "rumbles," or "bopping." Typically, however, his association is less well defined. He is cynical about society rather than hostile, and his commitment to the gang varies.

3. The *casual gang delinquent* is less committed to the gang. His association with the gang is loose, and although he joins in gang activities, his participation is primarily for "kicks." Mostly, this youth sees himself as a nondelinquent and his aspirations of getting an education or at least a well-paying job. His parents are typically blue-collar workers who are themselves law abiding and interested in his welfare. Further, his gang "membership" may not be totally of his own choosing.

4. The *casual delinquent, non-gang member* is what has been termed the "hidden delinquent." His delinquent behavior is intermittent, but he is seldom in trouble with police. Neither he nor adults think of him as delinquent. He is generally committed, in the long run, to the goals of society and describes his delinquent behavior as "having fun."

5. The *auto-theft joyrider* steals cars for joyriding and not for profit. This adolescent typically engages in delinquent behavior in a casual, nonplanned fashion. Like the *casual delinquent,* he usually comes from a middle-class family who gives him close supervision and discipline. He does not see himself as delinquent; however, he likes to think of himself as tough.

6. The *heroin user* thinks of himself more as a drug user than a delinquent. His motives for delinquent behavior are to support his habit. He feels harassed by society and typically rejects it.

7. The *overly aggressive delinquent* is not a member of a gang. He is a loner who engages in seemingly irrational senseless assaults on others. His behavior is sometimes described as sociopathic. He may come from any social class, he usually was raised in a hostile and rejecting family, and he has rarely had close relationships with peers.

8. The *female delinquent* is typically not a member of a gang, although female gang membership is becoming more common. Her delinquent behavior is usually not violent. She does not consider herself delinquent and may engage in delinquent behavior out of boredom. She typically comes from a dysfunctional family setting.

9. The *behavior-problem delinquent* is, like the overly aggressive delinquent, a loner. His delinquent acts are seemingly senseless, but overall he has conventional attitudes about society. Once again, the family setting is usually dysfunctional.

As with any set of categories, the Gibbons classification system may be over-simplified in some cases, and other cases may not fit neatly. Nonetheless, it helps to underscore the fact that juvenile delinquency is not a simple problem; it is multifaceted.

CAUSES OF DELINQUENCY

Just what *causes* delinquency is not easily defined. Those adolescents who are labeled by the courts as delinquent have background factors that differ from their nondelinquent peers. They have, for example, more health problems, including accidents, head injuries, and health problems during infancy (Levine, Karniski, Palfrey, Meltzer & Fenton, 1985). In school they are frequently described as having educational or learning deficits, attention problems, and language skill problems. Their early school behaviors include social isolation, acting out, aggression, and withdrawal. Their later school behavior includes poor academic performance, aggressive acting out, repeated truancy, and ultimately complete discontinuance of their education (Kazdin, 1987; Lipsitz, 1977).

Delinquent youths more often come from families living in poverty and which are less emotionally stable. Parents of delinquent youths are less likely to use consistent and fair discipline. Parental supervision is inconsistent and when discipline is applied it is often physically harsh (Glueck & Glueck, 1962; Geismar & Wood, 1986). Recall from Chapter 9 that the more stable the family structure, the more warmth and support, the more likely a young person is to have positive feelings of self-worth. The more unstable the home environment, the more likely the young person will feel alienated and isolated.

The more typical theories of why delinquency occurs involve the breakdown of effective social control as the reason. Generally, when children develop in social or cultural groupings that are well integrated into the mainstream of society, they are socialized by parents, adults, peers, and institutions in those behaviors that are acceptable. Conformity to the mores and values of the dominant society is maintained through use of positive and negative social sanctions. In disenfranchised or segregated subgroups, there is no commitment to that socialization and maintenance process. Children and adolescents from these subcultures feel no allegiance to the conventions of the dominant culture, and their commitment is to the values of the subculture, which may be in opposition to the dominant culture. When this alienation occurs, delinquency and deviance are likely (Weiss, 1977).

When the nonintegration is coupled with poverty, racial and ethnic prejudice, lack of equality in educational and employment opportunities, and family disorganization, the result is—not too surprisingly—frustration and antagonism toward the dominant society. Although youths from these subcultures see and desire the material and social security of middle-class society, they repeatedly are frustrated in their attempts to achieve these goals through legitimate means. Society may assure us of equal opportunity for all, but in reality, most lower-class youths face innumerable stumbling blocks to socially sanctioned success. Ultimately, minority and lower-income youths may recognize that illegitimate means hold the promise of more immediate gratification of their desires. Thus youths learn quickly that because legitimate or socially sanctioned means are not very functional and are at best remote, their better and more immediate recourse is to resort to illegitimate means (Cloward & Ohlin, 1960; Ohlin & Cloward, 1973).

These youths base their hopes that such a route has promise on a variety of immediately available models. The adults—especially young adults—who are close at hand and who have acquired material status may be pimps, pushers, numbers runners, or thieves. They are a symbol that says, in essence, "Look, I got all these good things. You can too. Do what I do!"

In some cases, however, a youth may be unable to achieve desired ends by either legitimate or illegitimate means. Cloward and Ohlin suggest that these cases are "double failures," who may retreat from society to nonfunctional behavior to achieve nonaccepted

False bravado and a desire to establish or maintain a reputation may lead to chance-taking. (Burk Uzzle/Magnum Photos, Inc.)

ends. The drug addict or junkie is a case in point. Cloward and Ohlin note that the addict accounts for a substantial proportion of juvenile crime, but that the motive is not the achievement of traditionally valued outcomes. Rather the motive is maintenance of a drug habit.

Cohen (1955) argues, however, that the limited-opportunities hypothesis fails to account for the senseless crimes of violence that often seem part of the juvenile gang culture. Cohen argues that many such acts are intended not to achieve material gain but rather to establish a reputation, or "rep." Thus what may seem like a senseless, unmotivated act of violence may be an attempt to establish oneself as a "real badass." Beatings of homosexuals by gangs of young teens often fall into this category.

Cohen places his emphasis on establishing a reputation or feeling of power and importance. Adolescents gain status when they are able to excel in the activities that are valued by society. When adolescents live in a subculture with values that are in conflict with the dominant culture, they are oriented toward rewards in their own subculture. In delinquent subcultures, the more daring and brave are put into positions of leadership and are given status according to the degree of danger that is involved in their acts. In New York City, graffiti is a normal, if not pervasive, phenomenon. Often a young artist will leave a trademark in extraordinary places. The more unusual the location and the more danger or skill required in placing the trademark, the more prestige is awarded.

LABELING

An alternative model of delinquency is called the labeling model. In order to follow the argument of the labeling model, suppose you are a judge in a juvenile court. Two cases are brought before you to be decided. Case A involves a 14-year-old boy who was arrested for car theft, joyriding, and drunkenness. He appears before the court well dressed and with a recent haircut. He is quiet and subdued. Both his mother and father are present, and the boy is represented by counsel. Both parents tell you, the judge, that they are horrified and distressed over what has happened. They promise that it will not happen again, that they will restrict the boy's privileges, seek professional counseling, and do whatever else you might suggest.

Case B involves another 14-year-old boy. He, too, has been arrested for car theft, joyriding, and drunkenness. He, however, is not well dressed—his clothes are dirty and disheveled. When the bailiff tries to direct him to the front of the court, the boy yells, "Keep your hands off me, pig!" The boy's mother is there, his father is not. He is not represented by counsel. His mother complains that she had to take the whole morning off to come down to court, and that, in any case, the boy was never any good. His mother goes on to complain that she cannot control him, that he is simply "no good."

What would you do in those two cases? How would you react? You would probably react as most judges do in these cases. You would be influenced by factors other than the offense itself. The boy in case B is more likely to be labeled "delinquent" even though his crime was no different than case A's. Factors such as race, sex, social class, personal appearance, and family background all have an impact on the chances of being labeled "delinquent"—and that label may itself be the cause of later problems.

One study of two groups of adolescents found that the decision to identify a youth as delinquent was related more to social variables than the severity of the crime (Chambliss, 1973). The first group, the "saints," came from middle-class families and at their court appearance were appropriately submissive and respectful. "Roughnecks," on the other hand, tended to be hostile and belligerent toward the authorities. The "saints" were much more likely to be sent home with a warning or probation. Juvenile justice systems are more likely to use status offenses in dealing with blacks and lower-income youths in their decision to presume delinquency (Waugh, 1977).

Labeling a youth as "delinquent" may have the effect of a self-fulfilling prophecy. Underlying the labeling theory is an assumption that if adults and those in authority repeatedly tell a young person that he or she is delinquent, the young person will begin to believe it and act accordingly. The label itself may be the cause of additional deviant behavior (Werthman, 1977). Our self-concept is not independent of others' views of us. In part, our self-concept is the result of the perceptions of others. Those young people engaged in delinquent behavior who depend most on others for affirmation of their identity are most likely to see themselves as delinquent and to internalize that identity (Chassin & Stager, 1984).

A more extreme view of the labeling process argues that the dominant society *creates* deviance by presuming that its own behavior is normal. Any behavior that deviates from its own definition of normal is therefore abnormal. The rules can be used to sort out those groups that do not conform to the norm and to label them as deviant, criminal, or delinquent (Becker, 1969). To the degree that this view is valid, there is a risk that any minority culture, any lower income culture, or any culture outside the mainstream is labeled deviant.

STATUS OFFENSES

There is a set of "crimes" that are illegal only for juveniles. These crimes, called juvenile status offenses, include behaviors that may be undesirable at all ages but are subject to particularly stern negative sanction when seen in juveniles. Behaviors such as truancy, sexual misbehavior, running away, incorrigibility (unruliness), and disobedience to parents or authority are found in various states' legal statutes. Juvenile courts have jurisdiction over truancy in 39 states and the District of Columbia, for example. In all, status offenses account for up to half of the work load of the entire juvenile justice system (National Institute for Juvenile Justice and Delinquency Prevention, 1977).

Whether juvenile courts should have jurisdiction over status offenses is open to question. Arguments that status offenses reflect predelinquent behavior and that intervention will interrupt the progression toward more severe delinquent acts have not been supported by research. Indeed some researchers have concluded just the opposite. That is, a juvenile offender brought before the courts for status offenses is *more* likely to engage in more serious delinquent behavior later (Werthman, 1977). Another argument for court jurisdiction over status offenses may be even more convincing. In a subset of cases of status offenses, the delinquent behavior represents an acting out of frustra-

Graffiti seems to be a nearly universal phenomenon and ranges from personal to political statements. (© Jim Richardson 1981/Black Star)

tions resulting from an abusive or hostile home environment. Without the legal sanction of the courts, the ability to identify such cases would be seriously impaired.

Because these behaviors are status offenses does not, however, mean that they should be ignored. In some cases, engaging in these behaviors may be a masked plea for help (Weiner, 1980). Likewise, some status offenses may make the adolescent vulnerable to exploitation. This is especially the case with runaways. Each year nearly one million adolescents run away, and over half of all runaways are girls (Walker, 1975).

The highest rate of runaways is found among the 14- to 16-year-old group, and girls are more likely than boys to run away. Most adolescents who run away do so because they have personal conflicts at home and at school. Either the adolescent becomes so overwhelmed by the conflict that escape is the only recourse, or the adolescent uses running away as a means for drawing attention to the conflict. In the second case the runaway usually leaves enough clues to assure being readily found.

Not all runaways, however, *choose* to leave home. An unfortunately large percentage of runaways are instead "throwaways," or adolescents who either are directly told to leave by their parents or are coerced out of the house by pressures from the parents. It is estimated that 30 to 60 percent of runaways are actually throwaways (see Vignette 13–2). Not uncommonly, these young people also have a history of physical or sexual abuse by their parents.

Runaways usually suffer a poor self-image and lack interpersonal skills. Typically, they see themselves in conflict with others and are plagued by feelings of self-doubt and anxiety. Although they see themselves as living lives filled with problems, they feel they are victims of fate and are resigned to the idea that their problems will never be solved (Wolk & Brandon, 1977).

Their feelings of low self-worth and lack of security make runaways vulnerable to those who would exploit youths. Too often, runaways are victims of rape or other violent crimes. They may end up working as prostitutes in large cities. New York has so many young prostitutes who come from the Midwest that one area has become known as the "Minnesota Strip." Of the 4,000 young people who contact the shelter home "Under 21" in New York City, 60 percent were engaged in prostitution or pornography (Ritter, 1979).

Runaway youths may seek out assistance from one of the many runaway youth shelters that are found in most cities, or they may choose to make contact with their families through the national runaway youth hotline. Initially, these agencies were established on an informal, local basis by community organizations in response to immediate needs. As the problem of runaways became more widely recognized, more shelters were established with federal funding. Currently runaway shelters provide short-term shelter and counseling for young people who for one reason or another flee from their homes.

One such shelter in Runaway House, a center where young people can receive confidential counseling. To stay in its dormitorylike shelter, runaways must agree to follow rules that prohibit sex, drugs, and alcohol, abide by a curfew, and share responsibilities for cleaning and maintenance. Beyond this the adolescents are expected to try to work on the family problems that led to their running away and attend group and individual counseling. The adolescents have the option of leaving the shelter when they feel ready, usually within three to ten days (Steirlin, 1973).

Although the adolescents in these settings are often ready and even willing to participate in family counseling, the same is not always the case with the parents. When an adolescent runs away from a disruptive or abusive home, the parents may not be willing to admit that they may be part of the problem, preferring to blame their child. For family counseling to be effective, all members must participate.

In some cases the short-term intervention offered by the shelter home is not sufficient. The young person may need longer care. Some may be served by group foster homes, which try to create stable family atmospheres that provide emotional support within relatively well-structured settings. The group foster home operates on the model of a commune, in which each member of the "family" is expected to participate in the upkeep of the home and in decision making. Fundamentally, whether runaways are counseled in a shelter house or a group foster home, the goal is generally to help them to get a better sense of self-worth and to establish a set of personal goals.

VIGNETTE 13–2
SOME ARE THROWAWAYS

Each year about one million young people run away from home. If they remain away from home for an extended period of time, they typically end up in major urban areas. In that environment, there is a good chance that young runaways will be lured into a life of prostitution, crime, or drugs. Some are murdered. Although most runaways are attempting to escape what they see as a hostile home environment, a disturbingly large number of cases can more accurately be called "throwaways." That is, the parents "expel" the adolescent from their own home. You might want to discuss the impact of being a "throwaway" on a teenager's feelings of self-worth and competence.

Source: Excerpted from Julie Raskin and Carolyn Males,
"Not All Run Away—Some Are Throwaways," *Parade*
(August 13, 1978): 4–5. Reprinted with permission of the
authors and the publisher.

Mike, 17, comes from a middle-class family in Philadelphia. Since he turned 16, his father has kicked him out of the house four times. The first time was when Mike lied about an accident he had while driving the family car. His father found out and began pounding the boy with a football helmet, shouting, "Get out of my sight! Leave! Don't come back!"

"I only had one shoe on," Mike remembers. "I went to get the other, but he wouldn't let me. So I stayed at a friend's house for two nights."

Mike was ashamed. "I kept it mostly to myself," he says. He moved in with an aunt and then, after a few weeks, he returned home.

The bad feelings at home continued. Each time his father threw him out, Mike would stay with relatives or friends. When he had finally exhausted all possibilities, he turned to a home for runaways.

Sherry's divorced mother has had a string of boyfriends. In their small New York apartment, 15-year-old Sherry was in the way, so her mother told the child to leave.

She now lives at a runaway house but still misses her mother. "She cries every day," says her counselor there. "She wonders, 'What's wrong with me that my mother doesn't like me?' She has low self-esteem and is self-destructive: 'Why should I care about me since no one else does?'" . . .

Called trashed kids, pushouts, homeless youth, throwouts and throwaways—they have been rejected by their families and told to "get out," often with no money and only the clothes they are wearing.

A throwaway kid could be the child next door. They come from poor, middle-income and wealthy homes, from rural areas, suburbs, and big cities. They are black, white, girls, boys, and as young as 10, although most are between 15 and 18.

Why do parents kick out kids? "In higher income brackets, throwaway youth are usually the products of family split-ups," says Loraine Hutchins, an administrator at National Network of Runaway and Youth Services, a coalition of houses for runaways. For example, in a second marriage, a stepparent may not want to deal with a new spouse's child. If a choice has to be made, the natural parent chooses the new spouse over the child. Or, in a remarriage, a tolerable family situation becomes difficult when a child is born to the new couple and the adolescent "gets in the way." Sexual interest by a stepparent can also play a part. If a woman sees that her new husband is attracted to her daughter, she may get rid of the child. . . .

Leslie Ann and her stepfather did not get along, and her mother sided with her new husband. Feeling betrayed, Leslie Ann rebelled by staying out late, smoking marijuana and flouting family rules. Finally, after she spent a night away from home without permission, her mother called the police. Leslie Ann was placed in a group foster home.

The girl still loves her mother and misses her. Each Sunday, visiting day, she and the other girls dress up and look forward to seeing their families.

The visitors arrive. As her friends laugh and talk with their mothers, fathers, brothers and sisters, Leslie Ann sits alone by the window watching.

Each Sunday it's the same. She sits waiting for the mother who never comes, wondering why she isn't wanted, why she has been thrown away.

SCHOOL VANDALISM AND VIOLENCE

In addition to the serious increases in crimes that compose the Uniform Crime Index, the past 20 years have been marked by a substantial increase in violence and vandalism in the schools. In their 1975 report on school violence and vandalism in the schools, the U.S. Senate Subcommittee on Juvenile Delinquency concluded that the problem had reached crisis proportions (Bayh, 1975). Annual costs for the nation's schools resulting from vandalism now approach $600 million.

Because of the radical increase in incidents of violence in schools, their effectiveness as centers of learning and positive socialization has been jeopardized. Students and teachers operating in a context of fear and intimidation are unlikely to view the schools as a place they want to be. As an example of the range of violent incidents in schools, 30 percent of Boston teachers indicated they had been victimized at school. Among teachers in California, 36 percent indicated they had been attacked in school and 46 percent report they are afraid at work (Speirs, 1986). Students, especially junior high school or middle school students, are at even greater risk of victimization. Further, the person committing the act of violence is very likely another student. Figures on the incidence of school violence are even more disturbing when one considers that students, teachers, and administrators are all reluctant to report assaults. Students fail to report assaults for fear of reprisal. Teachers fail to report assaults not only for fear of reprisal but for fear they will be blamed for failure to maintain control. Principals are reluctant to report school crimes for fear of negative public reaction.

Local gangs have found that they can extort money from fellow students for "protection" or threats of assault. Gangs also use the schools as a place to recruit new members or "auxiliary" members who pay dues. Students decide to join one gang or another well before high school; such decisions may be necessary if they are to pass safely through a gang's "turf" going to or from school (Research for Better Schools, 1976).

The causes of school vandalism and violence are many and complex. However, they are probably similar to those related to other forms of alienation. In some cases the school authorities themselves must share some of the blame. Arbitrary and oppressive rules, teachers who do not care about students, and unfair or capricious enforcement of rules lead to frustration and hostility. Also, many former students who are classified as dropouts are really "pushouts" (Bayh, 1975). Although the procedure is illegal, principals will coerce a "troublemaker" or "undesirable" out of school by threatening to press charges on some offense unless the student "voluntarily" drops out of school. Such a procedure gets around the legal requirements for expelling students.

The school, however, is only one of several factors in the social context that contributes to increased school vandalism and violence. Community values, peer groups, personal values of individual students, and community pride all have an effect.

Currently school systems across the country are employing a variety of methods to combat vandalism. The methods range from pride-in-your-school campaigns to armed guards and police dogs patrolling the schools during off hours. Schools in which vandalism has become a serious problem need to institute policy and program changes that address the problem. Among the immediate measures that might be taken are the following:

1. Teachers and students should be encouraged to report all incidents of school crime.
2. Watchdog community committees should be established to ensure that discipline is fair and consistent. Students should be part of the watchdog committee, with equal standing, because they are as directly affected by violence and vandalism as anyone. They can also provide a positive perspective on the problem.
3. Security and protection of teachers, students, and property must be improved. Often this may require as simple a move as hiring a security guard or installing adequate lighting.

Although increased security measures are useful and most assuredly necessary, they respond only to the immediate problem and fail to address more general issues. Any long-range plan for reversing the pattern of increasing vandalism and violence must involve the whole community. Too often in schools where vandalism is high, the school and local community are at odds.

In one school system, administrators met with local groups to hear their complaints. The principal objection of these groups was that the school administrators and teachers were racist. At first the administration balked and denied that it was so. Eventually, however, an in-service program was developed for principals and teachers, which increased their awareness of not only blatant forms of racism, but also the subtle and equally demeaning kinds. School atmosphere improved and violence declined.

GANGS

The stereotyped image of juvenile crime is frequently linked to the concept of street gangs. This stereotype has been nurtured by the media even in the face of evidence that most delinquent acts are not committed by gangs. Nonetheless, street gangs present a major problem, especially in major urban areas. As a group they tend to be responsible for more violent crimes. Homicides of and by adolescents are most often tied to gangs. In spite of the interest and attention devoted to street gangs, little can be stated with any certainty about their structure. Gang members are typically not willing to be interviewed, and when they are interviewed, one suspects they are telling the interviewer what he or she wants to hear.

This youth gang from the Bronx includes members from several ethnic groups. Notice that some of them are very young. (J. P. Laffont/Sygma)

Yablonsky (1962) describes the gang as a near-group. The members are bound more by loyalty to the group than to each other. Yablonsky found that a gang typically consisted of a core set of four or five members and a cadre of reasonably regular members who come and go as they are needed and as they desire. On the periphery are other members who occasionally join in gang activities but are not consistent in their allegiance. Yablonsky notes that the size of the gang varies with its sense of security. When the gang's territory, or turf, is endangered, the size of the gang may expand, and it may contract when the territory is secure.

Membership in a gang usually follows ethnic boundaries, and this by itself may provide some degree of commonality. Membership may be presumed of any teenager or preteen who happens to live in the neighborhood. Failure to belong may lead to threats or acts of violence. New members may be recruited or "drafted" as the need arises. The gang leader may have primary responsibility for this function. His "rep," or reputation, may depend on this ability to get a recruit, especially a reluctant one, to "join" (Rubington and Weinberg, 1978).

Gangs also offer the member a sense of identity. In Erikson's terms, the self-image might be termed a negative identity, but for the young person, belonging to the group, being accepted as a member of the gang may serve as a central element in his self-concept. In the absence of a stable family or home environment, the gang may become a substitute for both (Kazdin, 1987). The security of belonging leads to status and feelings of self-worth. The survival of the gang and its "rep" become central, extended parts of the individual member's self-concept. On the other hand, identity tied to the gang has a degree of instability. Many gang members do not see gang membership as their primary source of self-esteem, hence, for them gang commitment may be shallow. Nevertheless, even those with marginal commitment are important for the integrity and survival of the gang. Since the gangs are typically limited to youths, age limits the individual's identification. As adolescents enter young adulthood they are likely to leave the gang in favor of jobs or, if they continue in criminal activities to more adult crimes independent of the gang. Yet, in a study of Chicano gangs, Horowitz (1982) found that the level of respect given a "street warrior" was so high in the community that members had no great desire to leave the streets.

For the most part, gang members are male. Early studies of gangs reported few examples of purely female gangs. When females were associated with gang activity, their role was in the form of a "female auxiliary" to the gang. In auxiliary roles, females may be exploited for sexual gratification of gang members, or an individual female might gain status as a result of her sole or primary association with the gang leader. Female gangs and female juvenile crime has, however, increased markedly over the past several years. In the period between 1960 and 1973 the arrest rates for females under 18 years increased 393 percent for violent crimes and 334 percent for property crimes. During the same period violent crime arrests for males under 18 increased 236 percent and property crime arrests increased 82 percent (Giordano, 1978). Giordano found the need to belong and be accepted may be even stronger among members of female gangs than among members of male gangs. Because a gang is female does not imply that its crimes are less violent (Time, 1977):

> Last month Chicago police finally caught a gang of six girls, ages 14 to 17, after they had terrorized elderly people for months. Their latest crime: the brutal beating of a 68-year-old man. "I was amazed," says Police Lieut. Lawrence Forberg. "They were indignant toward their victims, and none of them shed any tears. This is the first time I've encountered young girls this tough." (p. 19).

DELINQUENTS' VIEWS

When you talk with delinquent youths, you quickly realize that they have developed an elaborate code of rationalization (Sykes & Mazda, 1957). The most frequent type of rationalization they provide is a *denial of responsibility*. They listen to what well-meaning social scientists and social workers say and feed back to these professionals exactly what they expect to hear (Sykes & Mazda, 1957). It is most incongruous to listen to a 14-year-old boy who is unable to read and who has been in and out of juvenile detention centers for three years, elaborate on the social consequences of a fatherless home and an abusive environment.

Other common forms of rationalization are *denial of injury* to the victim and *denial of the victim* (Sykes & Mazda, 1957). Adolescents may view shoplifting of goods in a big store as not making any difference. To them, it is very similar to adult white-collar crime or cheating on income tax. In the second case, the delinquents see the victim as getting what he deserves. Thus they insist that the teacher or storekeeper who is assaulted is being punished for resisting the delinquents or treating them poorly. Alternatively, the youths *condemn the condemner;* that is, they point to the hypocrisy of those in power, such as "cops on the take" or the unfairness of the system.

JUVENILE JUSTICE

What happens when a juvenile offender is caught by police and brought before the courts? The justice system as it applies to young people is not always the same as that for adults. There have been many strides forward in the past few years in providing adolescents who appear before the juvenile courts with the same rights of due process as adults. Nevertheless, in a variety of ways, young pepole are not afforded the same rights as adults. This is because the juvenile justice system, although it parallels the criminal justice system, is not technically part of it. Rather, its procedures are more in line with civil courts.

In 1985, there were over 83,000 young people in public and private detention centers for juveniles (U.S. Department of Justice, 1986). Juveniles who are institutionalized are most likely white, but blacks constitute a larger proportion than in society as a whole. Seven of every eight juvenile inmates are male. The great majority of inmates

Detention in Youth Correction Centers is not always the most effective treatment for youthful offenders but is sometimes the only choice available. (© Jay Paris/Picture Group)

are sentenced to a juvenile center for crimes of violence against people or property. There remains a small minority of young people who are sentenced to juvenile centers because of status offenses.

When viewed from a historical view, the juvenile courts system emerged as an attempt to treat children differently from adults and to provide some protection for children from adult exploitation. Prior to the seventeenth or eighteenth century, little value was placed on children. They were seen as little more than chattel and were not infrequently sold as servants or prostitutes. In the eighteenth and nineteenth centuries, societal attitudes changed; children were seen as needing not only education but also protection. In addition to the establishment of child labor laws, social activists pressed for a separate system for treating children and adolescents who broke the law.

Most attention was focused on youthful offenders who were being used by adult criminals. Young people were (as they are today) being lured into prostitution and vice. Juvenile courts were established to "protect" young people from exploitation and to provide alternative intervention to the system that judged and punished adults. The juvenile courts assumed a parental role, ensuring proper moral training, discipline, and punishment (Empey, 1980).

Although the original ideals on which the juvenile justice system was based were admirable, the institutionalization of juvenile justice and its growth became less than ideal. By the 1960s, social scientists were claiming that, rather than protecting young people, juvenile courts were themselves an element contributing to juvenile crime. The question became, "Who protects the children from the courts?"

As the juvenile justice system developed, its jurisdiction extended not only to crimes of violence and exploitation but also to a bevy of status offenses. Further, because it was conceived of as independent from the adult justice system, the same legal code did not necessarily apply in both cases.

Until recently the juvenile court was not required to provide juvenile defendents with the same rights of due process as adult defendents. Only in 1966, after a Supreme Court ruling, were some of these rights—including the right to have a lawyer present at all proceedings—extended to young people. However, many of the legal rights of adults are still for afforded juveniles. For example, juveniles are not guaranteed speedy public hearings or protection from unwarranted searches.

As discussed earlier, the system itself may have become a factor in the increase in juvenile crime. The labeling process resulting from court hearings, in and of itself, is associated with increased rates of crimes among juveniles. If the juvenile offender is sentenced to a term in a penal institution, the situation is worse. The institutions to which juvenile courts are prone to send juvenile offenders are credited with being training grounds for criminals. Increasingly, experts are advocating that courts refrain from intervening in the meting out of punishment to juvenile offenders (see Jensen & Rojek, 1980).

One positive indication that the juvenile justice system is becoming less likely to send juvenile offenders to penal institutions automatically is that the number of juveniles held in custody in juvenile facilities decreased from 1971 to 1975, whereas the number of available facilities increased. A large proportion of this reduction was a result of young people being referred to group foster homes or to private treatment centers.

Further, most public juvenile facilities have tried to change the jail-like atmosphere that has dominated such institutions in the past (U.S. Department of Justice, 1986).

In attempts to provide other choices for treating the juvenile offender, local, state, and federal agencies have offered such programs as alternative educational settings, work with street gangs, youth shelters, and short-term exprinces in jails that are intended only to provide the youthful offender a picture of what life in jail is really like.

One of the common features of chronic juvenile delinquents is their low self-esteem, especially their low academic self-esteem. Some authors (for example, Gold, 1978) suggest that traditional educational settings are not responsive to the unique personal needs of these young people. Hence, some argue for treatment programs built around alternative educational modes.

In one way or another, whether the intervention is an educational system or a community-based program, the juvenile system needs to intervene in a positive fashion early in the process. The juvenile system should become involved at the first sign of delinquent behavior rather than after several events, when the youthful offender is already deemed a habitual offender and a delinquent. In my opinion, the last alternative should be institutionalization, but that should be resorted to only after all other possibilities have failed.

SUMMARY

Without question, the problem of juvenile crime is complex. Although statistics indicate that juvenile crime is rampant, the statistics may present a biased picture. What leads a young person to engage in delinquent acts is unclear. Certainly most young people engage in some behavior that is considered delinquent. Only a minority of them persist in delinquent behavior to the extent that they end up in juvenile courts.

When the various background factors of delinquency are taken together, it may well be argued that delinquency is the result of years of repeated feelings of failure. Over the childhood years, the young, future delinquent is the subject of failure at home, school and in society in general. Just as success breeds success, or at least feelings of success, failure breeds failure and isolation from peers and adults.

Contrary to popular belief, most juvenile crime is not gang crime. Neither is juvenile crime particularly planned; more often juvenile crimes are spur-of-the-moment acts. Peer pressure undoubtedly is an important factor in encouraging of juvenile crime. Youth gangs are not an element in many crimes, but gangs are, nonetheless, a problem of serious concern. Gang crime is often particularly violent. But simply because a young person is a member of a gang does not explain why he or she engages in criminal behavior.

Finally, serious issues surround the treatment of juvenile offenders. Although most people agree that most juvenile delinquents should not be treated in the same way as adult habitual criminals, it remains unclear whether all types of juvenile crime, ranging from status offenses to homicide, should be treated by the same system. At least within the categories of what might be called "lesser crimes," many social scientists are arguing for alternate intervention strategies to those traditionally associated with court referral.

14 MALADJUSTED ADOLESCENTS

TIME PASSES BY
  MINUTE BY MINUTE, HOUR BY HOUR
    AS I SEE MYSELF DIE.
NO ONE AROUND TO RELIEVE MY LONELINESS
  NO ONE AROUND ME WHO CARES.
EACH DAY THAT PASSES
  I SEE NOTHING BUT CONFLICTS.
NO MEANING TO LIFE,
  YET NO MEANING TO DEATH.
I'M LIKE A ROPE IN A TUG-OF-WAR
  ALWAYS BEING PULLED UPON.
CONSTANT ANGER
  BUT ALL INSIDE,
    AS I SEE MYSELF DIE.
NEVER ANY HAPPINESS
  ONLY HOPELESSNESS AND HELPLESSNESS.
SHALL THE DAY ARRIVE SOON
  OR SHALL I SURVIVE?
HOW CAN I LIVE WITH A CONSTANT LIE,
  FOR..., SHE MUST DIE.

Written by a 17-year-old high school student undergoing psychotherapy

National Institute of Mental Health (1986)

Although most young people pass through adolescence without major trouble, a minority do experience serious adjustment problems. The purpose of this chapter is to provide a brief description of the psychopathology of disturbed adolescents and to offer some general guidelines about the counseling process as it relates to adolescents. This chapter is not intended to be an inclusive review of abnormality or psychopathology, the interested reader who wants more in-depth treatment is referred to Weiner (1982) or Reisman (1986). Instead, attention is limited to some of the primary forms of psychological maladjustment seen by practitioners who work with disturbed adolescents. Further, discussions of psychopathology are not strictly limited to this chapter. Disturbances such as anorexia nervosa, bulimia, obesity, and delinquency are frequently included in discussions of maladjustment. In this text, however, those topics are addressed in other chapters.

An immediate problem in a discussion of maladjustment in adolescents is found in the definition of "normality." What is normal behavior and what is not? We can try to define normality by some statistical means. That is, if behavior or performance on some measure falls within some range around the statistical average, it is seen as normal. If the behavior is outside that range, it is abnormal. For example, suppose you were to give the Beck Depression Inventory (Beck & Beamesderfer, 1974) to a young person. There is a range of scores on that test that are considered normal. Those whose scores fall at one extreme, outside the range of normal scores, are labeled "depresssed."

Alternatively, normality may be defined in terms of social or clinical standards. The question of clinical or social normality might be phrased: "Is the young person behaving in ways that alienate or distance him or her from peers or adults?" Kaplan (1974), for example, describes normal adolescents as those who operate effectively within their social setting, who choose and are able to keep friends, who are more oriented toward growth toward adulthood than regression to childhood, who relate sexually in meaningful, durable relationships with members of the opposite sex, who are able to redefine their relationship with their parents in a positive manner, who are able to deal with stress, anxiety and depression reasonably, who elicit positive feelings from adults, and who score within normal bounds on projective psychological tests. In large part, normality from Kaplan's view appears to reflect positive progress on standard developmental tasks of adolescence such as those described in Chapter 1.

Normality or abnormality, tied to social standards of the setting in which the young person operates, is thus defined by the adequacy with which the young person functions. In particular, clinicians who take this view are likely to focus on a young person's coping strategies. That is, we ask "How well does the young person cope with stress?" While there is a certain intuitive atractiveness to this view of normality, there is also a risk. If normality is defined by the group, then delinquency or heavy drinking may be normal. Normality is not always desirable, especially when normality reflects antisocial patterns.

There is ample evidence to indicate that there is a group of young people who are "at risk," and that these young people are apt to engage in risky behaviors in a variety of areas including drugs, sexuality, truancy, and delinquency (Jessor & Jessor, 1977; Donovan & Jessor, 1985). They have an at-risk profile. There are also particular times in the adolescent transition which seem more prone to engaging in at-risk behaviors. The shift into and out of middle school, for example, seems a potentially problematic time (Petersen & Crockett, 1985; Irwin & Millstein, 1986; Simmons & Blyth, 1987).

The use of the term *psychopathology* in describing maladjusted adolescents reflects the influence of the medical field on this area. Just as *pathology* refers to the nature of a disease, psychopathology refers to the psychological or psychiatric character of a disturbance. Likewise, when psychologists or psychiatrists refer to the "premorbid" personality, they are talking about the personality of the patient prior to the illness.

The most prevalent categories of maladjusted youths that practitioners see in clinical settings are what are broadly labeled as behavioral disorders or character disorders. Such youths are not psychotic—that is, they are not suffering severe personality disorganization. They are, however, coping with environmental stress in ways that are considered maladaptive. These maladaptive behaviors may include some delinquency, violence, or other forms of acting out. Of those adolescents who suffer severe personality disorganizations—that is, who are psychotic—the greatest proportion are schizophrenic. Other categories of psychotic disturbances among adolescents, though recorded, are exceedingly rare.

STRESS

At various points in our life, we experience stressful events which cause us distress and concern. The degree to which we are able to cope with stress reflects on our sense of self. If we cope well, we see ourselves in a positive light. If on the other hand, we fail to cope well, our self-esteem suffers; we feel incompetent and worthless. If we experience failure to cope with stress repeatedly, our general sense of worthiness suffers. Young people who exhibit maladjustment will frequently describe home settings and school settings that are continuously stressful. As you listen to them, you may wonder why they are adapting as well as they are.

Not all stress is bad. Stress can be an important motivator. We operate best under moderate stress. Athletes and executives perform best when competing, they are aroused and motivated. Too much stress, however, is not good. It may lead to physical and psychological distress.

Two decades ago, Holmes and Rahe (1967) created what they called the "Social Readjustment Scale." A series of positive and negative life events were rated for their stress value. Holmes and Rahe found that both positive and negative life changes could result in stress to the individual. Others (Kimball, 1982; Rapaport, 1963) have shown that these significant life events disrupt stable patterns of emotional adjustment. Among adolescents, such stressors have been related to their reports of nonorganic chronic pain (Greene, Walker, Hickson & Thompson, 1985), and the progress of chronic diseases (Beautrais, Fergusson & Shannon, 1982; Chase & Jackson, 1981). Coddington (1972) concluded that, on the average, normal children and adolescents experience three or more traditional life events each year. Each transitional life event requires them to make significant social and emotional adjustments. Coddington noted, for example, that shifting from one school to another is a source of stress. Thus, the normal shift from elementary to middle school, from middle to high school, and from high school to work or to college may be stressful.

Johnson and McCutcheon (1980), however, caution that to automatically presume that *all* life events are universally stressful is misleading. Wide individual differences exist. Using, for example, school changes, some adolescents may look forward to the change and see it in a positive light. Not all significant life events affect all adolescents in the same way. The effect of significant life events depends on how important they are to the individual (Healy & Stewart, 1984).

It is, nonetheless, worthwhile to remember that the occurrence of major life transitions is often a source of stress for young people. Their ability to cope with significant life events wil reflect on their own sense of personal self-worth and on their ability to cope with subsequent stresses.

PSYCHOSOMATIC DISTURBANCES

One of the primary components of a personal sense of identity is an acceptable body image. Any aberration from the "normal" body is thus a source of great concern for the adolescent. As a result of this concern, early- and middle-adolescents may be preoccupied with their bodies and bodily functions and may overemphasize any defect that they notice or imagine, however small.

In some instances, adolescents' concern for their bodies may be converted into

Some adolescents suffer marked feelings of depression, despair, and isolation. (© Joel Gordon 1974)

real physical discomfort. Pediatricians often report that they "cure" many adolescents who suffer chronic headaches or stomachaches with placebo sugar pills. The pills do not act directly on the discomfort, but the adolescent thinks they do. The effect is the same: the symptoms disappear.

Adolescents who suffer chronic physical discomfort without a clear biological cause, may have some psychological stress that is taking its form as physical distress. The label *psychosomatic* indicates that there is some impact of the state of mind (the psyche) on our body (the soma). The opposite can also be true. That is, chronic physical disease may lead to an altered self-perception and psychological distress. Adolescents with physical handicaps, diabetes, asthma, or epilepsy may develop self-images in which their physical limitation has influenced their general perception of themselves as adequate. In such cases, the self-perceived physical limit may result in a general negative self-concept. Even youths with minor physical defects may show adjustment problems (Waldrop & Halverson, 1971).

To say that a symptom is psychosomatic does not mean that the symptom is not real. The symptoms do exist and may be very painful. The asthmatic adolescent girl, for example, who responds to anxiety and stress with wheezing and gasping for breath is in real physical distress. For the physician who responds to the emergency of an acute asthmatic attack, the question of whether the underlying cause of the attack is anxiety, allergies, or some combination of the two may seem only mildly relevant. The most important immediate issue is to relieve the distressful symptoms. In the long run, however, adolescents who respond to stress with somatic symptoms may benefit from counseling. Particularly, these young people often benefit from training in relaxation techniques, in which the individual learns to relax rather than become tense in the presence of stress.

In the case of the asthmatic girl, when the wheezing begins, she has learned to respond by trying to relax. (The initial wheezing may itself be highly anxiety provoking, because she associates it with previous attacks. The anxiety leads to heavier wheezing, which in turn leads to greater anxiety, and so on.) Relaxation interrupts the progression of the attack. The wheezing may not totally dissipate, but it also may get no worse. Eventually she begins to feel that she has some control of her body and over the environment. As these feelings become more well defined, she may also develop confidence in her self-control and a better self-image.

Part of the problem associated with psychosomatic symptoms is that they may lead to *secondary gain*. The adolescent may find that the appearance of the symptoms leads to extra attention and care from others, or the symptoms provide a means to avoid some stressful event. The asthmatic girl may, for example, find the anxiety of participating in a physical education class is circumvented by a wheezing attack before class. The wheezing may be an involuntary response to the stress, but it is reinforced when she is excused from the class. She gains something by the symptom that she may then generalize to other stressful events.

The dilemma of what to do as a teacher or therapist in such a situation is not small. Clearly an adolescent may have a physical impairment that puts him at a disadvantage with "nonimpaired" peers. To reinforce nonparticipation, however, may be a disservice. It may be necessary to provide alternative experiences in lieu of or in addition to those with nonimpaired peers.

Obese adolescents do not participate actively in fast-moving games when they are playing with nonobese peers (Bullen, Reed & Mayer, 1964). However, when all participants are obese and no one is especially handicapped, activity in such games increases. Alternatively, we should encourage handicapped youths to participate in activities in which they are not at a disadvantage.

CONDUCT DISORDERS AND ADJUSTMENT REACTIONS

Most young people who are referred for counseling suffer from what are broadly termed *conduct disorders* or *adjustment reactions.* In some sense the coping mechanisms that these young people have developed to deal with stress are either inadequate or inappropriate. Although their behavior is sufficiently unacceptable that they have been brought to the attention of some school or legal authorities, they are not psychotic. The adolescent who suffers from an adjustment reaction may benefit from counseling and therapy in which more appropriate coping behaviors are developed. It is not unusual for those youths who might be considered "delinquent" by one group, to be labeled by another as suffering an adolescent adjustment reaction. Adolescents who fall into this category are usually impulsive, antisocial, and aggressive. Not uncommonly, they come from disorganized and disruptive families. In my experience, there is frequently a background of physical or sexual abuse.

> P was a 16-year-old girl who was referred to a psychiatric treatment facility after several incidents of running away from home. P had been pregnant twice. The first pregnancy had aborted naturally, the second had been aborted therapeutically. P reports that she still does not use contraception although she is still sexually active because, in her words, "I don't give a damn." P was aggressive and attacked attendants three times in the first two weeks at the facility.
> P's first sexual experience was with her father at the age of 8. P's mother reports no knowledge of this, although P contends that she told her mother and that her mother had told her to "shut your dirty mouth." (P also claims that her first pregnancy may have been by her father.) P first ran away from home at age 11. At age 16, after several arrests for running away and after the courts were alerted to the family setting, P was made a ward of the Welfare Department who, in turn, referred P for psychiatric counseling.

Among adolescents who undergo adjustment reactions, girls are more likely to "act out" by running away or through promiscuity. Boys are more apt to act out aggressively, with bullying, robbery, or impulsive violence. *Acting out* is a general term describing the use of unacceptable or unsocialized behaviors in an attempt to respond to built-up frustrations. The behavior is a coping mechanism, but one that is either socially unacceptable or not sanctioned by society.

For some of these young people, being in a safe and supportive, but structured, environment seems to provide them with an opportunity to "get their act together," or develop some behavioral maturity. Basically treatment consists of training these adolescents in behaviors and coping responses that are socially acceptable and in how to channel their aggression into other productive modes.

Treatment programs in institutional settings often involve gradually increasing the amount of freedom with which these adolescents must cope. Part of their difficulty is their inability to handle their anxiety when they are uncertain or when too many alternatives are available. When they become anxious, they strike out. Their inability to deal with uncertainty reflects their general negative self-image. Because they see that they are unable to handle stress, they view themselves as losers and no good. Given freedom they initially seem to try to prove themselves right. One technique, which is sometimes successful, is to gradually increase the number of options available to these young people, rather than to provide too many freedoms too rapidly. If the increase is too great and the adolescent begins to act out, then the treatment is pushed back to an earlier level at which the adolescent experienced success. The critical feature in any treatment program is to train individuals in coping mechanisms and to enhance their feelings of competence through successful use of those behaviors.

A major dilemma in treating these young people arises when they are ready to return to a home environment. If they have not become wards of the court or the welfare department, they may have to be returned to the family. If the family was disruptive to begin with, there may be a rebound effect. That is, the adolescents will return to the treatment facility after a short period of time at home. Although such rebounds are disheartening, they are not always disastrous. Often these failures are opportunities for the adolescents to recognize their own limits; thus they become better prepared to cope with subsequent releases.

Some of these adolescents never make any changes. They seem to thrive on "conning the system." Those who do change must have or acquire a motivation to change. As one young boy said, "I don't want to be a loser all my life."

DEPRESSION

Most people, at one time or another, have periods in which they feel depressed or uncertain. Events seem to be out of control and they see themselves as unable to cope. During such periods, a person may become apathetic, despondent, and withdrawn. For most people, these periods are short-lived. After a period of "feeling down" they progress forward. For some, however, those feelings do not dissipate and become overwhelming. In extreme cases, feelings of despair and despondency may lead to serious thoughts of suicide, actual suicide attempts, a dependence on mood altering drugs, or other significant mental health problems. We label such feelings of despair, despondency, and apathy as depression.

Increasingly, psychological clinics that deal with troubled adolescents are dealing with serious clinical depression, despair and loneliness. *Depression,* in the clinical sense of the term, refers to general feelings of sadness, helplessness, and despair. Those who are depressed may feel out of control or have vague, unclear feelings of dread. The poem reproduced at the start of this chapter mirrors many of these feelings. In many cases depression does not take the form of sadness, but rather presents itself as lethargy, lack of motivation, engery, or apathy, or as insomnia or excessive sleepiness. Among adolescents, depression is linked to poor academic performance, truancy, delinquency and acting out, substance abuse, and alienation from family and peers (Teuting, Koslow & Hirschfield, 1981). Depressed adolescents may fluctuate between periods of indifference and talkativeness, and between sadness and anger and rage; they may also appear over-sensitive to criticism, describe themselves as feeling helpless and out of control, have death wishes, and have seriously poor self-esteem (Mezzich & Mezzich, 1979).

Depression and low self-esteem are regularly tied together. Coopersmith (1967) links low self-esteem with feelings of incompetence, powerlessness, self-rejection, and unworthiness. Beck (1973) affirms this relationship pointing out that depression and low self-esteem share self-dislike, low self-evaluation, self-blame, and self-criticism.

Depression is not easy to identify among early adolescents. Indeed, Lefkowitz and Burton (1978) questioned the existence of childhood depression. More recent writers, however, are likely to argue that not only does depression exist in childhood and early adolescence, but that it is more widespread than previously thought (Cantwell, 1982). Weiner (1980) notes that part of the difficulty in recognizing depression in younger adolescents results from their underdeveloped time perspective. As adults, we tend to dwell on problems or crises. Early adolescents do not. Since their concepts of the future are limited and they have limited abstract ability, they are less likely to be preoccupied with thoughts which reflect adult depression.

This does not mean that early adolescents should be thought of as immune to depression. Instead their depression may be masked by other symptoms, such as fatigue or vague, unspecified illnesses and body problems. As in adults, depression among teens may result in difficulty in concentrating on tasks.

In studies of depression among adolescents (Rutter, Graham, Chadwick & Yule, 1976; Kandel & Davies, 1982), girls regularly scored as more depressed than boys. However, willingness to admit feelings linked to depression may be more socially accept-able among girls than among boys. In a study of the incidence of depression among adolescents, however, Kaplan, Hong and Weinhold (1984) found no sex differences. Kaplan et al. found that 14 percent of their sample were mildly depressed, 7 percent moderately depressed, and 1 percent severely depressed. Further, depression was more common among lower income adolescents than middle or upper income adolescents.

As Chartier and Ranieri (1984) note, there is little question that depression occurs among adolescents. However, it may not be immediately recognized. The depressed adolescent may act out the depression in aggressive or delinquent behavior. Such delin-quency is different from that of the sociopathic adolescent or the habitually delinquent adolescent, because the behavior usually follows traumatic events like divorce or the death of a parent. The delinquent behavior represents a clear-cut change in behavior. As such, it does not fit the expected behavior pattern of the young person.

Among older adolescents, clinical depression follows much the same pattern as in adults. Depression in middle- to late-adolescents often is tied with excessive alcohol or drug use. Once again, like the early-adolescent, depression often follows some traumatic event. Unlike the early-adolescent, however, the older teen's trauma may be more remote or abstract.

I should make one additional point regarding the relationship of depression to a traumatic event. Depression does not always immediately follow the traumatic event that is later seen to be its cause. M was a boy of 15 whose father died suddenly. His mother felt some responsibility to "keep a stiff upper lip" for the children, and so she resisted her desire to submit to her grief. M saw that his mother was trying to be strong, and because he was now the "man of the family," he too suppressed his grief and took over the leadership role. M's mother welcomed him as a source of support. Several months later M's school grades went down dramatically. He began to drink heavily and was involved in some serious delinquent activity. M's depression about the loss of his father came to the surface in counseling. Once M was able to work through the grief, he could move forward in a more positive fashion. The point is, the signs of depression did not appear immediately following his father's death but were delayed several months. The clue to the counselor was the suddenness of the shift in behavior.

SCHIZOPHRENIA

A small minority of maladjusted adolescents are psychotic. That is, they suffer serious and pervasive psychological dysfunction. Among those who are psychotic, the most common psychiatric diagnosis is schizophrenia. Schizophrenia is a commonly misunderstood problem. There is, for example, a popular misconception that a schizophrenic has a "split personality" or "multiple personalities," such as the cases popularized in *Three Faces of Eve* or *Sybil*. Actually the "split," if there is one, reflects the fragmentation of the schizophrenic's thinking. A more typical pattern of schizophrenic thought it depicted in Hannah Green's *I Never Promised You a Rose Garden.*

Schizophrenia is a general category of psychotic behavior involving an individual's inability to distinguish between reality and fantasy.

When schizophrenia was first described by Kraepelin, it was presumed that the disease had its onset during the adolescent years (Weiner, 1980). Indeed Kraepelin's first label for schizophrenia, *dementia praecox* (cf Weiner, 1980), may be roughly translated as precocious or early madness. Later Bleuler (1911, reprinted 1968) introduced the term schizophrenia, the term which persists. While modern understanding of schizophrenia makes it clear that the disease may have its onset considerably later than adolescence, a significant proportion of chronically schizophrenic patients have their first episode before the age of 25.

The inability of schizophrenic youths to distinguish what is real and unreal, especially when they are actively psychotic, results from their thoughts being dominated by distorted perceptions and hallucinations. To the average person, the thought patterns of the schizophrenic have little or no order. The schizophrenic wanders off on irrelevant tangents or in vague or bizarre fantasies. Schizophrenics often believe that they are being controlled or tortured by someone (or something) who has power over their thoughts. Practitioners must be careful, however, about reacting too quickly to the schizophrenic's behavior as "illogical." To the schizophrenic youth, the behavior may be very logical in light of the distorted view of reality.

Planning the treatment of a disturbed youth often takes the form of a team conference that includes the client. (Michael D. Sullivan)

J was a 15-year-old male who was admitted to a psychiatric treatment facility. He was brought to the facility by the police who picked him up after his mother reported that J had threatened to stab his baby brother with a butcher knife. The police officers reported that when they found J, he was alone in an alley screaming obscenities and "gibberish." His mother said that J had "not been himself" for the last year and a half, following the death of his older brother in an automobile accident. His mother reports, 'He had a change in personality. He talked about things that never happened, like talking to B (his dead brother). The last five days he has been very sick. He hasn't eaten and can't sleep. When he threatened the baby, I called the police. J seemed to lose control and ran out of the house. I don't know. One time he likes you, the next he don't. He wants to fight with his dad and me. Wants to burn the house down... He uses drugs, you know. He can hardly go a day without using something. But he suffered terribly when we lost B. It upset him for a long time. And right after that his good friend moved out of town. He doesn't have many other friends."

In his interview J denied having any problems but responded to interview questions with flat affect. While J admitted to using LSD and marijuana in the past year, use was apparently not regular, and he denied any use in the last two months because, "I seemed to worry a lot about it." J stopped going to school 4 months prior to his admission. In J's words, "I quit school. I just took off and left. I don't have anything to work for. I question everything I do. I guess I have a lack of confidence. I have a problem with being down, feeling pretty low, as low as you can go. I thought of kill-ing myself one time, but it was just a thought that ran through my head. . . . I hear people talking about me, calling me a two-faced stupid asshole. Even people on TV talk about me sometimes. . . . I'm worrying, worrying. I'm tired of worrying. I wake up in the morning and worry about what the day is going to bring. . . At night I hear voices, mainly my brother B, but it's only at night. When I wasn't eating, I saw Jesus, but I think it was only in my head. Do you think I'm hopeless?'' J asked the meaning of the words "paranoia" and "schizophrenia," which he said he heard while he was in the emergency room of a local hospital. J reports that since he has been here people on the TV have been calling him a "big drag and a fag and a toad." He denies any homosexual experiences.

J was diagnosed as suffering from an acute episode of schizophrenia. J responded well to drug therapy and psychotherapy, and within a few months was moved to a "middle-way" house before being returned home. In J's case the schizophrenia followed a series of traumatic events. Prior to that episode, J had not shown any evidence of the psychopathology. The prognosis in such cases is usually better than when the disease unfolds as a gradual, increasingly severe disease. In the latter case, the schizophrenic profile may first emerge as the adolescent is gradually isolated from and by peers. As behavior becomes less and less "normal" and as school performance deteriorates, peers and teachers become alienated from the schizophrenic adolescent. The schizophrenic adolescent's behavior may be described as odd or even weird. Too often, these early signs of abnormality are ignored or credited to "normal adolescent variability" (Weiner, 1980). The outlook for the schizophrenic whose onset is slow and gradual is not good.

Weiner (1982) indicates that childhood and adolescent schizophrenia is characterized by disordered thinking, inaccurate perceptions, interpersonal ineptness and inadequate behavioral and emotional controls. Their thinking and perceptions are particularly problematic. They may view their world through a variety of delusions and their thinking may be disrupted by voices or hallucinations. Their speech may reflect their disrupted thought processes. It may become confused and incomprehensible. They may verbalize bizarre thoughts and behave in odd or unusual ways. They may grimace at inappropriate times and put their fingers to their ears as if to block out unwelcome sounds. Their behavior may become increasingly bizarre. They may stare blankly and walk around in a daze. As they progress into a psychotic state they become increasingly uncommunicative. If they are frustrated or upset, their behavior deteriorates, they become overly upset and sometimes aggressive. It is, however, their distorted thinking and perceptions which constitute the primary trait that differentiates the schizophrenic adolescent from other psychotically disturbed adolescents.

VIGNETTE 14–1
THE ATTACK

Working with psychiatrically disturbed adolescents (and patients in general) is an emotionally, and often physically, demanding occupation. It is difficult for many professional and paraprofessional personnel to overcome their own fears of mental illness in order to feel at ease with patients. When we first work with psychiatric patients, we too often expect their behavior to be strange or bizarre. Actually, what we find is that most of the patients' behavior seems relatively normal. When their behavior deteriorates, only in extreme cases does it become bizarre. Most of the unacceptable behaviors do not seem terribly disturbing, and we may be unnerved that we sometimes see stranger behaviors among untreated people. More than that, however, we often see reflections of ourselves in some of our patients—and that realization is a bit unsettling. It is common, for example, for students taking abnormal psychology to suspect that they suffer from every psychological or psychiatric abnormality from brain disease to schizophrenia. Thus when we face those who have been identified as suffering from a disorder, we may have uncertainties and fears about our own ability to handle stress. On the other hand, when we see patients as people who need help, and when we recognize that there are times when all of us have difficulty in coping, we are more likely to make a positive contribution to their improvement. In this passage from Hannah Green's I Never Promised You a Rose Garden, *the patients "gang up" on the attendant who treats them with disdain. What are the young girl's observations as to why one attendant was attacked but another was not, and probably would not, be attacked?*

Source: Excerpted from *I Never Promised You a Rose Garden,* pp. 65–66, by Hannah Green (Joanne Greenberg). Copyright © 1964 by Hannah Green. Reprinted by permission of Holt, Rinehart and Winston, Publishers.

Deborah saw one attendant attacked by the patients night after night. The attackers were always the sickest ones on the ward—out of contact, far from "reality." Yet they always chose to go against the same man. On the day after a fight that had been more violent than usual, there was an inquiry. The battle had become a free-for-all; patients and staff were bruised and bleeding and the ward administrator had to ask everyone questions. Deborah had watched the fight from the floor, hoping that an attendant would trip over her foot, so that she might play a little parody of St. Augustine and say later, "Well, the foot was there, but I didn't make him use it. Free will, after all—free will."

The ward administrator spoke to everyone about the fight. The patients were proud of their lack of involvements; even the mutest and most wild-eyed managed a fine disdain and they purposely thwarted all of the questions.

"How did it start?" the doctor asked Deborah, alone and very important for her moment in the empty dayroom.

"Well . . . Hobbs came down the hall and then there was the fight. It was a good fight, too; not too loud and not too soft. Lucy Martenson's fist intruded into Mr. Hobb's thought processes, and his foot found some of Lee Miller. I had a foot out, too, but nobody used it."

"Now, Deborah," he said earnestly—and she could see the hope in his eyes, something to do with his own success as a doctor if he could get the answer when another might fail—"I want you to tell me . . . Why is it always Hobbs and why never McPherson or Kendon? Is Hobbs rough on the patients without our knowing about it?"

Oh, that hope!—not for her, but for her answer; not for the patients, but for a moment in his private dream when he would say matter-of-factly, "Oh, yes, I handled it."

Deborah knew why it was Hobbs and not McPherson, but she could no more say it than she could be sympathetic to that raw, ambitious hope she saw in the doctor's face. Hobbs was a little brutal sometimes, but it was more than that. He was frightened of the craziness he saw around him because it was an extension of something inside himself. He wanted people to be crazier and more bizarre than they really were so that he could see the line which separated him, his inclinations and random thoughts, and his half wishes, from the full-bloomed, exploded madness of the patients. McPherson, on the other hand, was a strong man, even a happy one. He wanted the patients to be like him, and the closer they got to being like him the better he felt. He kept calling to the similarity between them, never demanding, but subtly, secretly calling, and when a scrap of it came forth, he welcomed it. The patients had merely continued to give each man what he really wanted. There was no injustice done, and Deborah had realized earlier in the day that Hobbs's broken wrist was only keeping him a while longer from winding up on some mental ward as a patient.

She did wish to say this, so she said, "There is no injustice being done." It seemed to the doctor a cryptic statement—with a patient in bed, another with a broken rib, Hobbs's wrist, another with a broken finger, and two nurses having black eyes and bruised faces. . . .

Whether schizophrenia is a genetic or an environmental disease is not totally clear. Studies of identical twins have shown that if one twin has schizophrenia, the co-twin has a 46 percent chance of having it as well. If, however, a fraternal twin has schizophrenia, the risk to the other twin is about 14 percent; the risk for a nontwin sibling is 13 percent (Nicol & Gottesman, 1983). The family histories of schizophrenics are more likely to include relatives who were also diagnosed as schizophrenic (Gunderson, 1974). Those who are genetically at higher risk are more likely to be affected than those who are not.

On the other hand, there is evidence that the family environment of schizophrenic youths may also have an effect. In studies of adopted children who were schizophrenic versus adopted children who were not, it was possible to identify distinct differences in the family interactions of the two groups. Schizophrenic youths often come from parental environments with unclear and disharmonious communication patterns (Singer & Wynne, 1965)

Finally, according to increasing evidence, schizophrenia may be the result of a biochemical imbalance. It appears that the normal metabolism of specific neural chemicals is disrupted in schizophrenics. Rather than being processed into normal by-products, these chemicals are processed into a mescaline-like or LSD-like chemical in schizophrenics. Schizophrenic hallucinations may thus result from an abnormal metabolism of normal body chemicals (Gunderson, 1974; Nicol & Gottesman, 1983).

SUICIDE

The death of a young person is always unnerving; as Zoe Akins says in her play *The Portrait of Tiero,* "Nothing seems so tragic to one who is old as the death of someone who is young and this alone proves that life is a good thing." The death of an adolescent as a result of suicide is even more startling and difficult to understand. Yet the number of adolescents who attempt or commit suicide each year is not small, and by all estimates the number is growing. Suicide currently ranks behind accidents and homicide as the leading cause of death among teens and young adults.

Estimates of rates of suicide among adolescents are very likely low because suicides are underreported. It is not uncommon for a physician to report such a death as "accidental" in order to relieve some of the trauma, grief, and social stigma that the family experiences. A large number of vehicular deaths are suspect, and in some instances so are homicides. Inner-city youths, for example, do not see suicide as a noble way of dying. Thus they may set themselves up to be killed by a rival gang. Actual rates of suicide may be two to three times as high as estimated.

Since the mid-1950s, the rate of teen suicides has more than tripled. It is now the third most common form of death among adolescents. In the period 1970 to 1980, 49,496 young people 15- to 24-years-old committed suicide (Mercy, Tolsma, Smith & Conn, 1984). Each year, about 5,000 young people in that age range commit suicide. The highest suicide rates are among adolescent white males; during the decade of the 1970s the suicide rate among adolescent males continued to increase while the suicide rate among adolescent females remained relatively steady. What has changed for females, however, is their willingness to use firearms and explosives as a means for committing suicide. Of those females who commit suicide, the proportion who now use more violent methods is only slightly less than males.

Adolescent girls are nine times more likely to attempt suicide than boys, but boys are five times more likely to commit suicide than girls. Further, risk of suicide or attempted suicide increases over the adolescent years. That does not mean that younger adolescents are not at risk since over 100,000 children between the ages of 5 and 14 years attempt suicide each year (Holinger, Offer & Simmons, 1982).

Many suicide "attempts" are probably not intended to result in actual suicides. When engaging in suicide attempts, young people are more likely to choose methods that are "low risk" and have a higher likelihood of being halted before death. Nonetheless, suicide attempts should not be dismissed lightly. They are serious indicators of psychological maladjustment. One in 10 who attempt suicide will commit suicide within five years and the majority of those who commit suicide have attempted or threatened suicide in the past (Avery & Winokur, 1978).

Recently, much concern has been focused on the phenomenon of cluster suicides. The phenomenon of cluster suicides was first noticed in the community of Plano, Texas. Following the suicide of one student, seven others in the community similarly committed suicide within a short time. Similar patterns have been seen in Westchester and Putnam Counties in New York where 36 young people committed suicide within a two-year period; in Montgomery County, Maryland 16 committed suicide during the 1983–84 school year; and in Clearwater, Florida there were 30 attempts in 11 months. It is not really clear why these clusters of suicide occur. The communities share some common traits. They are primarily upper-middle class communities with high expectations for academic and social success. Some speculate that the stress of expectations that are continuously very high may lead to a sense of incapability and incompetence among some young people who see suicide as their only escape from failure. As Husain and Vandiver (1984) note, "Some adolescents would rather choose suicide than fail (in academics and vocational success) and fail their parents" (p. 118).

Not infrequently, young people who have attempted suicide will report feelings of fear of "being made fun of" for their self-perceived failures. They have an insecure self-image and are often convinced that no one cares about them and that no one would care if they were gone. Konopka (1983) reproduced this poem from a suicidal 18-year-old-girl:

> Will it make a difference, world,
> When I am gone?
> I think not.
> You will go on, day after day,
>   never giving me a second thought.
> What then do I owe you?
> Who will ever shed a tear for me?

Why does a young person choose to commit suicide? In the late 1800s, the French sociologist Emile Durkheim identified three types of suicidal personalities. Durkheim described suicide as a response to social stress and the motive for suicide as altruisitc, egoistic, or anomic. *Egoistic* suicides occur among those who are not well integrated into society. They have no close family, social, or religious ties. Single adults who live alone and have no family or no family ties tend to have higher suicide rates. *Altruistic* suicides occur among those who are at the other end of the spectrum. These individuals are so integrated into a group or ideology that they are willing to sacrifice themselves for some perceived greater good. The third type of suicide, *anomic,* occurs in response to a sudden, usually sad, change in an individual's life. Anomic individuals are left with a feeling of confusion and alienation, and they feel unable to cope with their altered life.

A variety of factors influence suicides and suicide attempts among young people. Suicide is more prevalent among college students than among their noncollege peers. There are also differences in rates among college campuses. High-prestige campuses have higher rates than campuses of lesser prestige. Whether college students as a group are more suicidal or more prone to attempt suicide than noncollege students, and whether a college environment generates the stress and feelings of alienation that lead to higher rates of suicide, are open questions.

The commonly held belief that a person who commits suicide "has to be crazy" is not true. Psychopathology, although more likely in suicidal patients (Miller, 1975), is not sufficient to explain away suicide. Neither is suicide an irrational, spur-of-the-moment decision. Suicide attempters usually plan and think about their suicide for some time prior to the actual attempt. In one study of suicidal girls, all had been diagnosed as potentially suicidal well before the event (Peck, 1968). Boys in that same study, however, had no such psychiatric history. When a boy decides to commit suicide, he is more likely to be direct and successful. This is so even though adolescent boys are eight times as likely to be referred for counseling. The percentage of girls who are referred for counseling *and* are considered suicide risks is inordinately high. It may be that the behaviors that lead to referral among boys cover a much broader range of issues than suicide is a factor in referred girls. Many practitioners have prepared simple scales for rating suicide potential among clients. One particular useful scale was developed by Aaron Beck of the University of Pennsylvania and is reproduced in Vignette 14–2.

VIGNETTE 14–2
PREDICTING SUICIDE

How do you know when someone is seriously considering suicide? No one has yet come up with a foolproof scheme for identifying the suicidal person. However, several scales have been developed to alert the practitioner to warning signals in a patient's presuicidal behavior. The scale presented here is one such attempt, by Dr. Aaron Beck, a psychiatrist who has written widely about suicide.

Source: A. T. Beck, M. Kovacs, and A. Weissman, "Assessment of Suicidal Intention: The Scale for Suicide Ideation." *Journal of Consulting and Clinical Psychology 47* (1979): 343–52.

Dr. Aaron T. Beck, a University of Pennsylvania School of Medicine psychiatrist who has devoted many years to research and development of suicide potential rating scales, devised this "suicidal ideation scale." It is designed to help the interviewer get an objective overview of a patient's thoughts and emotions about suicide. Says Dr. Beck, "The situations and responses it lists are meant to be guidelines for a very unstructured interview. The physician should cover them all in his questioning, but he shouldn't hew to them at the expense of interreaction with his patient."

The patient responses are presented in increasing order of seriousness—a "0" response is cause for negligible concern, while a "2" is cause for greatest concern. Though Dr. Beck has not as yet set numerical cut-off points for mild, moderate, and severe suicidal risk, he believes a cumulative score of 15 represents a severe risk of suicide.

SCALE FOR SUICIDE IDEATION
(For Ideators)

Name _____ Date _____

		Time of Crisis *Most Severe Point* *of Illness*
Day of *Interview*		

I. Characteristics of Attitude Toward Living/Dying

( )	1. Wish to Live	( )
	0. Moderate to strong	
	1. Weak	
	2. None	
( )	2. Wish to Die	( )
	0. None	
	1. Weak	
	2. Moderate to strong	
( )	3. Reasons for Living/Dying	( )
	0. For living outweigh for dying	
	1. About equal	
	2. For dying outweigh for living	

	Day of Interview		*Time of Crisis* *Most Severe Point* *of Illness*

( )   4. Desire to Make Active Suicide Attempt   ( )
          0. None
          1. Weak
          2. Moderate to strong

( )   5. Passive Suicidal Attempt   ( )
          0. Would take precautions to save life
          1. Would leave life/death to chance (e.g., carelessly crossing a busy street)
          2. Would avoid steps necessary to save or maintain life (e.g., diabetic ceasing to take insulin)

If all four code entries for Items 4 and 5 are "0," skip sections II, III, and IV, and enter "8" ("Not Applicable") in each of the blank code spaces.

II. Characteristics of Suicide Ideation/Wish

( )   6. Time Dimension: Duration   ( )
          0. Brief, fleeting periods
          1. Longer periods
          2. Continuous (chronic), or almost continuous

( )   7. Time Dimension: Frequency   ( )
          0. Rare, occasional
          1. Intermittent
          2. Persistent or continuous

( )   8. Attitude toward Ideation/Wish   ( )
          0. Rejecting
          1. Ambivalent; indifferent
          2. Accepting

( )   9. Control over Suicidal Action/Acting-out Wish   ( )
          0. Has sense of control
          1. Unsure of control
          2. Has no sense of control

( )   10. Deterrents to Active Attempt (e.g., family, religion; possibility of serious injury if unsuccessful; irreversibility)   ( )
          0. Would not attempt suicide because of a deterrent
          1. Some concern about deterrents
          2. Minimal or no concern about deterrents

          (Indicate deterrents, if any: _____

          _____)

( )   11. Reason for Contemplated Attempt   ( )
          0. To manipulate the environment; get attention, revenge
          1. Combination of "0" and "2"
          2. Escape, surcease, solve problems

III. Characteristics of Contemplated Attempt

( )   12. Method: Specificity/Plannig   ( )
          0. Not considered
          1. Considered, but details not worked out
          2. Details worked out/well formulated

( )   13. Method: Availability/Opportunity   ( )

            0. Method not available; no opportunity

            1. Method would take time/effort; opportunity not readily available

            2. (a) Method and opportunity available

                 (b) Future opportunity or availability of method anticipated

( )   14. Sense of "Capability" to Carry out Attempt   ( )

            0. No courage, too weak, afraid, incompetent

            1. Unsure of courage, competence

            2. Sure of competence, courage

( )   15. Expectancy/Anticipation of Actual Attempt   ( )

            0. No

            1. Uncertain, not sure

            2. Yes.

IV. Actualization of Contemplated Attempt

( )   16. Actual Preparation   ( )

            0. None

            1. Partial (e.g., starting to collect pills)

            2. Complete (e.g., had pills, razor, loaded gun)

( )   17. Suicide Note   ( )

            0. None

            1. Started but not completed; only thought about

            2. Completed

( )   18. Final Acts in Anticipation of Death (e.g., insurance, will, gifts)   ( )

            0. None

            1. Thought about or made some arrangements

            2. Made definite plans or completed arrangements

( )   19. Deception/Concealment of Contemplated Attempt (Refers to communication of ideation to interviewing clinician)   ( )

            0. Revealed ideas openly

            1. Held back on revealing

            2. Attempted to deceive, conceal, lie

V. Background Factors

Items 20 and 21 are not included in total score.

( )   20. Previous Suicide Attempts   ( )

            0. None

            1. One

            2. More than one

( )   21. Intent to Die Associated with Last Attempt (if N/A enter "8")   ( )

            0. Low

            1. Moderate; ambivalent, unsure

            2. High

Counseling an adolescent often means counseling the whole family, because it is often the family as a unit, not just the individual, that is troubles. (Peter Vandemark)

Some teens who attempt suicide hold to a strange mythology of death. They sometimes fail to recognize death as a permanent state. A suicidal patient may tell you that he wants to kill himself but does not want to die. In a similar fashion adolescents who attempt suicide in an effort to "get even" with a boyfriend, girlfriend, or parent, often fail to see that they would not be around to "enjoy" the other person's misery. A suicidal girl often envisions a "sleeping beauty" fantasy, in which she sees herself in her coffin and everybody saying how lovely she looks.

Beyond the tragedy of young people taking their own lives, those who commit suicide leave behind an aftermath of guilt and pain. Parents, family, and friends are left to wonder whether they might have done more; whether they might have prevented the death. In one case, a young girl had repeatedly left her diary out and unlocked. Her mother, trying to protect the girl's privacy, refrained from looking at it. Instead, the mother carefully put the diary back in her daughter's room. After the girl committed suicide the mother found that for weeks prior to her daughter's suicide, the young girl had written that she was lonely and had no friends. She was unsure whether she could continue to live that way. The daughter had apparently left the diary out in an attempt to call attention to her need. In the mother's good intentioned respect for her daughter's privacy, she had missed a critical warning. The mother now must deal with the feelings of guilt from her "failure."

COUNSELING ADOLESCENTS

Adolescents may be referred to a counselor either in a school setting or in a private setting that may or may not be affiliated with a professional therapist. In either setting the practitioner's task may range from vocational or educational counseling to behavioral counseling. Although the purposes of vocational and behavioral counseling are quite different, there are some similarities.

This chapter will introduce you, as a future practitioner, to some of the major issues in counseling adolescents; it will not train you as a professional therapist.

As Tramontana and Sherrets (1984) note, however, most of what we know and expect about the counseling and therapeutic process is based on work with adults. When dealing with adolescents in a counseling role, it is always useful to remember that while adolescents are moving toward adulthood, they are not yet at that stage of maturity.

Establishing a counseling relationship with an adolescent requires a working alliance between the practitioner and the client. Meeks (1972) describes it well. The relationship is a "delicate alliance" between an adult counselor and an adolescent client. Although the relationship has some characteristics in common with the counselor-adult relationship, it also has substantial differences because of the unique developmental character of the adolescent client. Many counselors are so uncertain of the nature of that relationship that they avoid adolescent clients.

For many practitioners the prospect of counseling adolescents is a problem best left untouched. The legendary emotionality and obstinacy of adolescent clients are enough to frighten even the most caring of counselors. When the referral problem is behavioral, many practitioners feel uncomfortable about talking frankly about such issues as sexual behavior and drugs with young people. They report that they have difficulty pursuing some areas without seeming to be a prude or a "dirty old man." Often counseling adolescents brings the practitioner face to face with personal unresolved conflicts, which makes the encounter even more stressful. It is, however, possible to establish a professional counseling relationship with adolescents without being too aloof, on the one hand, or so "chummy," on the other, that the professional relationship is hindered.

ASSESSING THE PROBLEM

The initial tasks in establishing a counseling relationship with an adolescent are (1) to identify the problem that has led to the need for counseling, and (2) to determine how aware the adolescent is of the problem. Even in routine counseling provided by schools as part of career education, the counselor must determine the adolescent's entering level of career awareness. In areas of behavioral counseling, it is necessary to determine whether the adolescent sees the behavior as a problem and, if so, how much of a problem. Early in the interview process, the counselor must encourage the adolescent client to define the problem areas specifically.

Meeks (1971) suggests the following six questions as guidelines for assessing the adolescent's level of awareness of a behavioral problem and the potential for successful counseling:

1. *What level of psychosocial development has the adolescent achieved?* If the adolescent has already achieved some degree of behavioral and cognitive maturity, the

treatment process will be quite different than that for those with lower levels of socialization. Adolescents at higher levels of psychosocial development can reasonably be expected to operate more independently in assessing alternative solutions to the problem. Those at lower levels need more structure and direction in the counseling process. Adolescents who are at a formal-operations level are more able to recognize the multiple aspects of the problem that led to counseling.

2. *What kind of relationship did the adolescent have with his parents prior to adolescence?* If the character of parent-child interaction has been positive through childhood, then any shift in that relationship is probably temporary, and the prognosis for repairing that relationship is good. On the other hand, if parent-child communication has been nonproductive prior to adolescence, the chances of creating a positive pattern of interaction now are reduced.

3. *Did some identifiable event lead up to the problem behavior?* If an adolescent began to show problem behaviors following a divorce or a death of a parent, the therapeutic process will differ from that for a problem behavior with a long history. As with the difference between chronic and acute schizophrenia, described earlier in the chapter, delinquent or disruptive behavior suddenly emerging after a crisis has a better prognosis for improvement.

4. *Does the adolescent feel conflict?* If the adolescent shows some concern about the problem and can express that concern, the prognosis for improvement is better than if he or she sees no problem and is hostile and resistant to suggestions that a problem exists. Recognition of the problem may reflect a degree of behavioral maturity.

5. *Is the adolescent able to describe his or her own behavior and feelings with some degree of objectivity?* An adolescent client who is able to clearly recognize and label feelings, emotions, and consequences of behavior is probably at a higher level of behavioral maturity. The client's ability to assess his or her own behavior realistically makes for a more positive therapeutic atmosphere. Conversely, the adolescent who is overly dependent on one or more defenses and is unable to deal with feelings and emotions realistically will need more help and support from the counselor.

6. *Do the parents desire to improve the situation?* Although you would expect most parents to support improved adjustment in their adolescent, a variety of family stresses may work against their support. If the adolescent is acting out as a result of a disruptive home environment, the parents may be unwilling or unable to aid in the therapeutic process, because they fear their own lack of security with each other may be exposed. Cases in which the adolescent sees the parents as concerned and active participants in the counseling process have much better promise.

Finally, Meeks (1971) warns that the counselor should try to determine the adolescent's motives for seeking counseling. Adolescents who initiate counseling on their own are *rare* cases, and self-referral indicates a high level of social maturity. On the other hand, many adolescents who are brought to a counseling setting against their wishes really know they need help but are saving face by projecting the responsibility on someone else. Because an adolescent is coerced by schools, parents, or courts into a counseling relationship does not mean that therapy will not be effective. Referred adolescents do quite well. Neither should the counselor expect some form of verbal agreement from the adolescent to improve. Such an agreement may be beyond the limits of his or her social maturity at the time of referral. Ultimately, however, behavioral contracts, in the form of treatment plans with behavioral goals, are a good way to specify what the therapist, the parents, and the schools mean by acceptable behavior.

RESISTANCE TO TREATMENT

Adolescents are often reluctant to cooperate with parents or adult authorities in general. Thus it is not uncommon for adolescents to resist treatment. However, reluctance to participate in a counseling setting does not mean refusal to participate. The hostile, resistant posture that the adolescent brings to the first few interviews may be necessary to save his self-respect, which has already been badly battered by the fact that he was sent to a "shrink," or a counselor. Although many of the patterns of resistance dissipate over several counseling sessions, the adolescent may employ some common defensive maneuvers to protect his psychological self from harm. These mechanisms are used whenever threatening thoughts or emotions arise (Wolman, 1968). The most commonly used defensive mechanism is *repression*. When unwanted or unacceptable thoughts emerge, they are forced back into the unconscious. Repression may be so effective that the anxiety-provoking thoughts may only reappear in disguised fashion. On the other hand, adolescents may deal with unacceptable thoughts through a process of *sublimation,* in which the thoughts or emotions are transformed and expressed in a socially acceptable fashion.

A very popular defense mechanism among middle-adolescents is *intellectualization.* As they begin to explore their powers of formal thought, they resort to intellectualizing and abstracting stress and viewing it in a detached, unemotional fashion. Similarly, adolescents may resort to elaborate explanations of why they behaved in a certain way. The use of such *rationalization* allows the adolescent to reduce feelings of guilt by means of a plausible explanation for some undesirable behavior. The rationalization does not, however, explain the true motive for the action. Sometimes rather than using the intellect to hide motives, the adolescent blames someone else for the unacceptable behavior. In some cases this *projection* involves blaming luck or fate or forces beyond human control.

When faced with information or knowledge that does not match the adolescent's conception of reality, the adolescent may resort to *isolation* or *denial.* Isolation is used when the adolescent views new, unwanted information as somehow distinct from what is already known. The new information is kept separate under the guise of "That's not the same. It's totally different." In Piagetian terms the adolescent refuses to assimilate or accommodate. Adolescents may use isolation when the new information is *too* new or *too* threatening. When new information requires radical restructuring of one's cognitive structure, it may indeed be necessary to hold the new information in abeyance. Over time the need for isolation may diminish, and we can integrate the information into our existing knowledge. *Denial* is a more severe reaction to unwanted information. Unlike isolation, in which the new information is recognized but kept separate, denial is a refusal to admit the information exists. Behind ignoring the problem and denying its existence is the hope that it will go away. Denial may, however, be a necessary defense when certain information is simply too disruptive and the adolescent cannot cope with it. In such cases individuals may be encouraged to return to the problem later, when their ability to cope is greater.

A common defensive mechanism among younger adolescents is *regression,* in which they resort to behaviors that were acceptable when they were younger but that are no longer appropriate. Regression is a particularly frustrating maneuver to adults, who typically respond by telling the adolescent, "Act your age," or "Grow up!" On the other hand, regression can be useful in creative thinking. The individual may try looking at a problem from the naive, uncluttered perspective of a child. Freud, in fact, described creativity as "regression in the service of the ego."

Part of the general portrait of maladjusted youths is that they tend to rely excessively on one or a small number of defense mechanisms. As with other adolescents with low self-esteem, they tend to view themselves as "losers." When placed in settings that exceed their ability to cope, they must revert to the most convenient defensive maneuver. When faced with a frustration born out of an uncertain setting, they often respond with the limited set of coping mechanisms available to them. Typically, they strike out at someone or something. And also typically, the response of those in authority is to remove or expel the disruptive adolescent.

For the maladjusted adolescent, expulsion from an unpleasant setting may be a source of relief. In behavioral terms, expulsion may be negatively reinforcing to the unwanted behavior. Ther adolescent learns that aggression provides a form of escape from an environment that tests the limits of his ability to cope. Additionally, the action by the authorities may lead to approval by peers. Finally, expulsion may confirm what the adolescent already felt, that he is incapable of succeeding.

Attention-seeking behaviors among adolescents do not, in and of themselves, reflect low self-esteem, or maladaption. "Class clowns" for example tend to rate higher on scales of assertiveness but are also more likely to be seen as leaders and as cheerful. In other dimensions of self-concept, few differences are seen between class clowns and their nonclown peers (Damico & Purkey, 1978). Class clowns, however, tend to view authorities and teachers with less respect than their more conventional peers.

Adolescents' coping behaviors are inextricably tied to their value system. When adolescents face stress, their selection of a given coping maneuver is based in part on which coping behaviors are viewed as acceptable and which are not. As adolescents mature, they are exposed to more value systems and acquire alternative coping strategies. The psychologically healthy adolescent can sample from a variety of coping maneuvers rather than depend solely on one or on a small set of behaviors.

In dealing with adolescents who are experiencing emotional or decisional conflict, the practitioner's role is to help them sort through their options. Although a counselor's value structures would dictate one decision, that counselor's responsibility is to help the adolescent explore not only that point of view but others as well. In the end, the adolescent alone must make a choice among the various options that are available. The adolescent who is coerced into a decision that may lead to feelings of guilt afterward may be less able to cope with subsequent decisional stress. The counselor should orient the adolescent toward a posture of *vigilance,* which involves sorting through available information, assessing its value, and making a decision on the basis of all available information rather than responding impulsively (Janis & Mann, 1976). Once the client has made a decision, the practitioner may then need to help the adolescent cope with the ramifications of that decision.

FAMILY COUNSELING

Many counselors of adolescents with behavior difficulties prefer to view the situation as a family problem rather than an individual problem. Their view is that the behavioral problems that caused the adolescent to be referred for counseling inevitably have some impact on, or result at least in part from, the family dynamics at home. Sometimes those family dynamics precede the adolescent's problem behavior, and sometimes they result from it. In either case, counselors argue, to treat one and not the other is futile.

Not all families, however, are ready to submit themselves to counseling. The parents may react by saying, "The family is fine; it is the adolescent who has the problem." Further, parents may be divided on their perceived need for counseling and the value of it. In such cases, a counselor may choose to identify the adolescent as the client of record and explain to the family that their help is needed in establishing a treatment program for the client.

In the initial interviews with parents and, say, an adolescent son, a counselor may get the message from the parents that their son is a destructive ingrate who disrupts and disturbs the entire family. The boy, on the other hand, may present himself as an oppressed martyr who is badgered by uncaring, ignorant reactionaries. The counselor should not be too eager to take sides—the truth usually falls somewhere between the two versions (Meeks, 1977).

Parental reaction to the referral of their adolescent for counseling may range from guilt and grief to unabashed relief. Almost all parents feel some guilt, and the counselor should be empathetic with their feelings. The guilt may take the form of feelings of failure to be a good parent. Those feelings come from a natural tendency of parents to assume everything their child does is their fault. Moreover, those natural feelings are reinforced by articles and books (such as this one) that point to the connection between inadequate parenting and behavior problems. Because their child has behavioral problems, they assume that they have done something wrong. The counselor must never draw that conclusion without evidence that it is so. There are abundant examples of families in which three children have no problems but one does. How can one family yield such different results? Consider, for example, the case of Jack:

> Jack was a 12-year-old boy who was referred by school officials for counseling and evaluation. His referral sheet described him as habitually truant and a "troublemaker." He was failing most of his courses and was viewed by his teachers and peers as slow. On an individual test of intelligence he was found to be above average in intelligence. Further testing revealed that Jack suffered from *dyslexia,* a learning disability that interferes with learning to read. In other tests of general information, Jack showed considerable knowledge of current events, which he said he learned "just by listening." His acting out was primarily a defense to avoid reading aloud in front of his peers.

Jack's parents were concerned that they had done something wrong in rearing him. They had not had similar problems with his two older brothers or younger sister. They also felt resentment toward Jack's disruptive behavior. Once the problem was adequately diagnosed, both Jack and his parents relaxed a bit and were able to work on a solution. Fortunately for Jack and his family, the counselor recognized the problem as one that was caused by factors other than a "bad home."

Parents may also feel guilty for their resentment and anger toward the adolescent. The parents may rightfully resent the emotional outbursts of their teenage son or daughter, who repeatedly disrupts the family dinner. However, like the new mother who resents losing her sleep to feed an infant, they simultaneously feel guilty for resenting their own child.

In most cases parents are cooperative and motivated to do what will help their child. However, in a minority of cases therapy may turn out to be a matter of helping an adolescent cope with a sick or maladaptive environment. In cases of chronically disruptive adolescents, in which the family is clearly identified as maladaptive, the task for the counselor may be to help the adolescent develop enough positive feelings of self-worth and enough self-reliant behaviors to operate independently of their family.

A problem that occasionally emerges in the treatment of adolescents is an overly dependent relationship between one of the parents and the child. In such a relationship the mother may be totally dependent for support on her teenager, who in turn is totally dependent on the mother. Neither is able to function independently.

> Mary was a 15-year-old girl who was referred for counseling after an attempted suicide. Mary felt at the time that "It was the only way to get free from my Mother!" Every attempt by Mary to assert her own independence from her was met by tears and inferences of some dire illness (usually cancer) by her mother. In group therapy, Mary said that she did not believe her mother had any illness but that she felt terribly guilty about leaving her mother alone.

CONFIDENTIALITY

In counseling adolescents, a practitioner must always wrestle with the issue of confidentiality of information. With adult patients, information revealed to a professional counselor in a clinical setting is considered absolutely confidential and private. When the patient is an adolescent, however, the issue of confidentiality is complicated. Because the adolescent is a minor and still the legal responsibility of the parent, complete confidentiality of information may not be possible, especially as it relates to potentially dangerous behavior. However, to establish a productive relationship, the adolescent must feel reasonably comfortable in divulging information that will not go beyond the confines of the practitioner's office. On the other hand, if the adolescent reveals personal information that the practitioner interprets as possibly harmful to the client's well-being, the counselor may be ethically and legally obligated to relate that information to the parents. Parents are, in the final analysis, directly responsible for the adolescent's welfare.

Early in the counseling process, it may be wise to clarify the limits within which you may reasonably work. You should try to establish a relationship among the parents, the adolescent, and yourself that ensures confidentiality except in those cases in which serious physical or psychological harm may result. If the information involves physical or sexual abuse by the parents, then the issue of confidentiality may be affected by legal statutes. In such instances you may need to serve as an advocate for the adolescent in opposition to the parents. You should, of course, be well informed of your legal position.

In some cases, confidentiality may be strained because informing parents of a serious problem may not appear to be in the best interests of the adolescent. Parental reactions have been known to be counterproductive or even destructive. For example, a pregnant girl may be afraid to inform her parents because of her fear of their reaction. As a counselor, you must try to assess whether her assessment is valid, or whether it is an overdramatization resulting from natural feelings of fear and guilt. You may, in such cases, try to develop a plan through which the adolescent informs her parents in your presence and with your emotional support.

Finally, an adolescent's plea, "Please don't tell my parents," may really be the request, "Please do tell my parents." In such cases it is usually more beneficial for the adolescent to assume the responsibility. As a counselor, you may once again choose to provide your presence and emotional support for the task.

SUMMARY

Early in the text, I pointed out that the common view of adolescence as a period of storm and stress was misleading. Most young people experience the normal stresses of the adolescent years and are able to draw upon their psychological and social resources to cope. Yet, despite evidence of more general adaptability than maladaptability, the view that upheaval is a normal part of adolescence persists. There are still those who, like Anna Freud, believe that the adolescent who *fails* to show any deviance is the one who is abnormal and should be the object of concern. While overly compliant teens may be a source of concern, the average adolescent is not prone to repeated antisocial outbursts. Dismissing chronic, antisocial, or sudden unusual behavior as just a "phase" may be a serious error. Antisocial behavior and sudden changes in behavior are regularly seen as warning signs of more serious problems. Adolescents whose behaviors diverge from the norm sufficiently to draw the attention of practitioners are candidates for intervention. Further, seriously maladaptive behavior during adolescence tends to persist and may be a warning of more serious psychological and social problems during the adult years (Masterson, 1967).

In the context of this chapter we have dealt with some of the complexities of defining "normal" versus "abnormal." Beyond our concerns about *what* is abnormal, using the label "abnormal" or "deviant" may itself be a source of difficulty. If someone is labeled abnormal we may relate differently to the person. Langer and Abelson (1974) conducted a study related to this issue. They showed two groups of clinical psychologists a videotape of a young man talking about his job experiences. The first group of psychologists were told the young man was a "job applicant." The other group was told the young man was a "patient." Both groups were asked to rate the young man for overall psychological adjustment. Those who thought the young man was a

Much positive counseling occurs in less-formal settings with a teacher, coach, or principal. (Peter Vandemark)

"job applicant" described him as "attractive and conventional looking," "fairly open," "candid and innovative," and "upstanding." Those who thought the young man was a "patient" described him as "tight," "defensive," "passive," "considerably hostile," and "despondent." The psychologists filtered and sorted information gained from the videotape to conform to their expectations of "patient" versus "job applicant."

Some young people clearly need help in coping with the stresses of the adolescent transition. Their ability to cope adequately is limited by social and psychological traits. The role of the counselor in dealing with adolescents is one of helping the young person assess the nature of the problem and possible ways of dealing with it. For most practitioners who work with adolescents, the counseling role is short term. A young person comes to someone trusted and shares a concern. Our role in dealing with such a young person is terribly important. If we are empathic listeners and let the young person know we care, that may be all that is needed to help the young person deal with the current crisis. There are, however, some problems such as suicide or serious drug abuse that go beyond our capabilities. As a practitioner, establish a network of referral agencies for this purpose. In cases of serious problems, serve as a facilitator for the young person to link him or her with an appropriate agency.

On an ethical level, counseling adolescents presents some testy issues. For older adolescents who are independent from their parents, confidentiality of information presented to licensed counselors is usually protected by law. The degree to which confidentiality is protected for children and younger adolescents is unclear. However, teachers and other practitioners are not protected under client-counselor privilege.

15 | CONCLUSION

At the outset of this text, I defined adolescence as a period of personal development during which a young person must establish a sense of individual identity and feelings of self-worth which include an alteration of his or her body image, adaptation to more mature intellectual abilities, adjustment to society's demands for behavioral maturity, internalizing a personal value system, and preparing for adult roles. At the core of that definition is my conviction that the adolescent's development of a positive self-concept is central to adjustment during adolescence and to the ease with which one makes the transition into adulthood. In the chapters that followed, I attempted to expand on the basic definition through focusing on more targeted developmental tasks. In this chapter, I would like to pull the separate elements back together.

The adolescent's self-concept is an accumulation of the individual's beliefs and attitudes regarding personal strengths and weaknesses, physical traits, intellectual abilities and talents, friendships, belonging, social abilities, vocational abilities, and so forth. The parts of self-concept converge into a general whole which serves as a definition of one's current or extant self-concept. The adolescent is also presumed to hold a parallel self-concept in which each of the elements is defined in terms of what the adolescent would like to be. This second, desired self, established for the adolescent a template against which the extant self is evaluated. If the two are very far apart, we presume the individual has a negative self-concept or poor self-esteem. On the other hand, if the two are not different at all, we also presume negativity. Positive self-esteem implies room for growth and a sense that the individual has goals and standards of excellence.

In thinking about the developing adolescent it is important to remember that wide differences exist among and within individuals. Adolescence is not a unitary phenomenon in which all individuals are dealing with the same developmental tasks at the same time. At varying times during the adolescent years, young people focus their psychological energies on different aspects of their emerging sense of self. At one time their principal question is "Am I attractive?"; at another "Am I capable?"; at another "Do people like me?"; at still another "What is my role in life?" Yet, all these and other questions seem to revolve around the bigger question "Am I okay?"

THE PHYSICAL SELF

The degree to which we are satisfied with our body plays an important role in our overall self-concept. We scrutinize our physical selves for any flaws, perhaps we think "My nose is too big" or "I am too tall (short)" or "My hair is stringy." The degree to which we are satisfied or dissatisfied with what we see affects our general evaluation of our self-concept. During puberty and early adolescence, young people experience a radical alteration of their physical selves.

In the absence of serious medical problems, it is reasonable to assume that in the normal course of physical development, young people will achieve adult levels of physical and sexual functioning. To the extent that the progression toward adult physical and sexual status is smooth, the adolescent is apt to feel comfortable with his or her physical self. To the extent that the progression is not smooth, puberty is very early or very delayed, or development is uneven and the young person has to deal with being notably different, adjusting to one's new physique may be stressful.

In our culture great value is placed on physical attractiveness. Hence, the degree to which adolescents see themselves as attractive and appealing is related to their self-assessment. Those who are categorized by society as physically undesirable are very likely to have negative self-images. This is particularly the case with obese adolescents. Beyond the medical risks tied to excess weight, adults and peers react to adolescents who are obese with negative labels and stereotypes.

THE COGNITIVE SELF

During the adolescent years, young people are likely to experience major shifts in their abilities to deal with their intellectual world. In thinking back over the developmental character of several of the tasks of adolescence, notice that a general pattern emerges. In early conceptions, whether those concepts are related to vocation, morality, or self, adolescents thoughts are simplistic and concrete. Reality is conceived from an egocentric, self-serving view. As adolescents mature, their views become increasingly complex and abstract. Their reality is decentered and other oriented.

In our own research with adolescents with insulin dependent diabetes mellitus, we find that the level of cognitive social maturity of diabetic adolescents plays a principal role in their ability to care for their disease (Ingersoll, Orr, Herrold & Golden, 1986; Ingersoll et al., 1987). Diabetes is a somewhat unique chronic illness since with adequate control of diet, exercise, and insulin injections a person can avoid long-term complications. However, the regimen of control is not simple. Changes in diet or exercise alter the insulin needs. Being ill with another disease changes the bodies ability to absorb insulin. Failure to maintain good "control" results in the young diabetic experiencing seizures from too much insulin or the build-up of toxins in the bloodstream. Success at managing the illness, on the other hand, results mainly in the avoidance of the negative seizures. Dealing with diabetes is inconvenient, complex, and requires that the adolescent believes that the effect of what is done now may not be seen for 20 or more years. Pulling these elements together and incorporating them into an overall positive view of oneself as a person who has diabetes is not easy. The adolescent at more advanced levels of cognitive social maturity who is able to conceive of multiple causes and who has a more advanced concept of time is simply more able to manage the disease.

THE SOCIAL SELF

Humans are social beings. We gather in social settings and the ease (or difficulty) with which we interact with others affects our evaluation of our self-concept. Further, our social self is the result not only of our perceptions of our ability to relate to others, but of others' reactions to us (Rosenberg, 1979). That is, our self-esteem is a reflection of how society evaluates us. If society and peers view us in a positive light, we are likely to value our selves as positive. If, on the other hand, society sees us as deviant or in a negative light, we have a negative self-concept. The effect of social approval or disapproval on our sense of self is most clearly described in the text with reference to the society's reactions to physical attractiveness or in labeling on delinquent behavior. The effects are, however, more pervasive. Social feedback on our feelings of acceptability as intelligent, capable, talented, or moral also affect our self-concept.

Our social self-concept combines our various social roles and our assessment of their value. During adolescence, young people must redefine a variety of social roles and relationships. They must, for example, redefine their relationship with their parents. They must redefine their roles with peers and their roles as contributors to society as a whole. Further, they must redefine or reconstitute their value systems with which they deal with other members of society.

LIKING OUR SELVES

Our physical, cognitive, and social selves merge to define our total self-concept. The problem for many adolescents (and for many adults) is that when the product is complete, they focus on those elements that are weaknesses rather than strengths. In our culture there is an implied resistance to say "I like myself." To do so seems conceited. Yet, philosophers, theologians, and psychologists alike agree that to be a healthy person, capable of truly caring for others, you must care about yourself first.

IS IT TOUGHER TODAY?

Parents and adults will frequently ask me if I think today's adolescents have a "harder time growing up" than the adults did when they were young. The answer to the question is not easy. In some ways the question implies that adolescence is inherently stormy and stressful and that in some way today's stressors are more profound than before. On the one hand, today's stressors are no more profound than yesterday's. Like yesterday, today's young people must deal with normal tasks such as transitions between schools, learning a skill, managing their sexuality, and becoming psychologically independent of their parents. For most young people these stressors are not overwhelming and they move with a reasonable degree of comfort toward adulthood. For other young people, the stressors are so profound that adolescence does indeed become a period of storm and stress. The same pattern seen for today's youths was seen in their parents' and grandparents' youth. On the other hand, today's young people face a range of stressors that their parents and grandparents did not. They must deal with a greater availability of and freer access to mind-altering drugs. They are exposed to media images which portray sexual license and drug use as the norm. In that sense today's young people do indeed have a more difficult environment within which to grow.

Our roles as professionals dealing with young people is one of helping them deal with both the typical and atypical stressors of adolescence. To the extent that we can facilitate the development of a positive sense of self-worth among those young people with whom we work, we may accomplish more than we sometimes give ourselves credit.

SOME CLOSING THOUGHTS

It was my intention at the outset of this text to introduce to you a body of information about the physical, psychological, emotional, and social development of adolescents. I worked from the assumption that most of you who take a course such as this expect one day to be working with young people. Thus the material that I included reflects my biases about what the professional practitioner should be aware of. There are, however, some leftover thoughts and guidelines that I would like to share with you. These thoughts focus more on my impressions of those who work well with adolescents than on hard data. I believe that you, as future professionals who will work with people, not just adolescents, will find them helpful.

Respect the Integrity of the Adolescent

One of the common problems that I observe in adults communicating with adolescents is that they talk down to teenagers. It is important to keep in mind that the adolescent is striving to be an adult. Teenagers are understandably naive about some topics, but to talk to them as though they are children is demeaning. A good rule of thumb is to give the adolescent the same respect you expect the adolescent to give you. This may be more easily said than done when you are faced with a hostile and belligerent teenager and you rapidly reach the limits of your own tolerance. In such cases it is better to break off the interchange than to react by squelching or "putting down" the adolescent. An intellectual or emotional put-down may temporarily "put the adolescent in his place," but the verbal barb may be tough to remove later. In any relationship, "hitting below the belt" is unfair, but in the delicate alliance between the professional and adolescent, the harm may be irreparable. Further, for the adolescent who is already suffering a damaged or poor self-image, a put-down by someone who matters may be devastating.

Throughout the text, I have repeatedly referred to the importance of aiding the adolescent to develop positive feelings of self-worth. The respect that adolescents have for themselves may be the single most important factor in their psychological and social development. If adolescents see important adults as not respecting them as individuals, then their ability to accept themselves may be jeopardized.

As a professional you must always keep in mind that adolescents vary along any number of dimensions. Not only are there differences among adolescents, but there are also differences within individual adolescents. Their reactions to stress differ as a function of their levels of social and intellectual development, their feelings about themselves at a given point in time, and any number of other factors. As practitioners we must avoid the temptation to categorize an adolescent by age, home background, or educational level, in much the same way that we must avoid racial or sexual stereotypes. Among the more popular stereotypes of adolescence is that it is a tumultuous period of development. Granted, some adolescents *do* experience storm and stress during adolescence, but not all do. For some, the transition is rather pleasant and uneventful. It is important not to overgeneralize in any direction.

Give A Damn

Several years ago Mayor John Lindsay of New York City initiated a campaign to raise the level of pride and concern that the residents of New York had for their city and its people. The program was called "Give a Damn." That phrase is a good motto for your future work with adolescents. Perhaps the most important attitude you can convey to the teens with whom you work is that you care about them and care what happens to them. To know that what happens to them matters to you may be a very important force in their own personal growth.

Do not be afraid to go out on a limb and give of yourself. As practitioners you will have the chance to do some things that go beyond the defined responsibilities of your job. You may be able to provide the extra push that some adolescents need to get themselves straightened around and moving foward. In my own life, a high school guidance counselor made just that kind of difference. My high school performance was less than stellar. When I finished high school, I had no intention of going on for further education and proceeded to get a job working on trucks. My counselor's role was officially finished. However, he saw something in me that I did not see in myself. After a year he not only persuaded me to go on to college, but he also arranged for financial assistance. None of these acts were *necessary*.

Be Patient—Keep A Sense of Humor

Do not expect miracles to happen overnight. Your efforts may not have an immediate impact on the forward progress of an adolescent. Indeed, when we look at progress over short spans of time, we may feel that we are not accomplishing much. However, when we look at the same adolescents over a longer period of time, we may see definite change.

Similarly, we must help adolescents see that growth does not suddenly cease at the end of the teen years. So much literature and conversation about adolescence convinces teens that this is the particularly troublesome period of life. It is as though problems and pimples will magically disappear at the age of 18. Adolescents do not have a corner on the uncertainty market, and their awareness that you, their parents, and other adults also experience stress may help them gain the perspective that all their problems do not have to be, and will not be, solved immediately. As practitioners we can help adolescents specify what their problems are and seek alternative strategies for resolving those problems. (Those same skills, it can be noted, are useful for problem solving at all stages of life.)

Often the tension of a situation can be relieved by recognizing its complete incongruity. In the same vein, many adult-adolescent interactions can be kept from getting stiff if you can maintain a sense of humor.

Do As You Say

What you say, what you do, and how you handle stress are important, not only to you, but also to the teenagers who are watching you. As an adult in a position of authority, you will often be identified by adolescents as a model of how adults should behave. You have a responsibility to serve as a model for whatever behaviors and values you profess. Your choices in your use of language, your control of your temper, and your openness will serve as an image of what a mature person acts like. Athletic coaches have an extraordinary responsibility in this area. Because they work very closely with a small group of individuals, coaches are very likely to develop a close personal bond with the adolescents on their teams. When a coach explains the merits of good sportsmanship and then screams at officials in foul language, there is an obvious discrepancy between what is said and what is done. The adolescent is left with the dilemma of whether to behave according to what he sees or what he hears.

Be Open and Honest

Adults who work with teens sometimes feel obligated to act as if they "have their act completely together." Perfection is a terribly difficult standard to maintain for yourself and for adolescents. Your willingness to admit that you do not have all the answers is not a sign of weakness but a sign of honesty.

Often adolescents will ask practitioners how they feel about certain issues. Adults are sometimes reluctant to share those feelings on the vague fear that they might "convert" the adolescent. In actuality most questions of this form are part of the adolescent's attempts to assess alternative value structures. Your willingness to relate your views also tells the adolescents that you accept them and are able to let them see you as you are.

Do not be afraid to act. Counselors, and even parents, are sometimes reluctant to say, "I think what you are doing is wrong, and I see real problems ahead." If you care, you need to be honest about those feelings. Sometimes you may make mistakes in judgment, but it is better that you make a few mistakes than do nothing.

Be Gentle With Yourself

A line from the poem "Desiderata" says, "Beyond a wholesome discipline, be gentle with yourself." When working with young people, especially troubled youths, practitioners tend to blame themselves for the adolescents' failures. Like parents, practitioners may be tempted to ask what they did wrong or what more they could have done. Sometimes there are answers to these questions, sometimes there are none. As a practitioner you will encounter both successes and failures. Recognize both for what they are, and try not to be overly harsh on yourself when you fail to see success. Also, be patient; the results of your counseling or help may not be immediate.

Remember that as a counselor or a practitioner you are first a human being with human emotions and feelings. There will undoubtedly be times when you will be discouraged and feel inadequate in your role. You may be certain an adolescent is on a sure path to trouble and feel frustrated because you cannot reach him or stop the problem. If you choose to work with maladjusted or delinquent adolescents, the chances of this happening increase greatly. It is normal at such times to wonder whether there was more that you could have done. Maybe there was and maybe there was not. It is important to realize that all counselors experience both failures *and* successes. There is no such thing as the super-counselor who is all things to all people. There will be some adolescents whom, for one reason or another, you will not like. The first time this happens you will inevitably feel guilty, thinking that because you are a professional, you should be above normal interpersonal feelings. That is not so.

Do not expect that as a counselor or practitioner you will always have the ability to say or do just the right thing to guide an adolescent along the way. We see teachers, parents, and doctors on television or in films who seem to know exactly what to say. In the typical scene, the adolescent is in the middle of an immense crisis, and the adult, with calm and dignity, says or does just the right thing to change the adolescent's attitude miraculously and defuse the potentially explosive situation. As I watch those programs I sometimes find myself wishing, "Gosh, I wish I had said that ." Well, I could have, if I had a team of writers handing me my dialogue. As people working with adolescents in the "real world," you will not have a team of writers. However, if you are open and honest, you will do well more often than not.

Be Honest With Yourself

At this point in your career development, you still have many options. As a future practitioner providing services to adolescents, you should realistically ask yourself the question, "Am I going to feel comfortable working with adolescents?" Quite clearly, for many people the answer to that question is no. The field is not for everybody, and there is nothing wrong in admitting that you are not able to serve all kinds of people.

On the other hand, if the answer to the question is yes, be encouraged that there are many ways in which motivated people can have a significant impact on the lives of young people. There is a need for people who work well with troubled youths; and there are also many other options available for working with normal, well-adjusted adolescents who will benefit from the interaction with adults who care about what happens to them. There is a great deal of personal satisfaction to be gained by working with adolescents. If you see yourself in such a role, I wish you well.

REFERENCES

Abel, D. (1974). Can a student sue the schools for educational malpractice? *Harvard Educational Review, 44,* 416–436.

Abel, E. L. (1977). The relationship between cannibis and violence: A review. *Psychological Bulletin, 84,* 193–211.

Abelson, H. I. & Fishburne, P.M. (1976). *Nonmedical use of psychoactive substances: 1975–76 nationwide study among youths and adults. Part 1: Main findings.* Princeton, NJ: Response Analysis.

Adelson, J. (1979). The myth of the generation gap. *Psychology Today, 12* (9), 33–34, 37.

Adelson, J. (Ed.) (1980). *Handbook of adolescent psychology.* New York: John Wiley.

Adelson, J. (1983). The growth of thought in adolescence. *Educational Horizons, 61,* 156–162.

Adler, N. J. (1975). Emotional responses of women following therapeutic abortion. *American Journal of Orthopsychiatry, 45,* 446–454.

Aichorn, A. (1953; reprinted 1963). *Wayward youth* . New York: Viking Press.

Akpon, C. A., Akpon, K. L., & Davis, M. (1976). Prior sexual behavior of teenagers attending rap sessions for the first time. *Family Planning Perspectives, 8,* 203–220.

Alder, C., Bazemore, G., & Polk, K. (1980). Delinquency in nonmetropolitan areas. In D. Shichor & D. H. Kelley (Eds.) *Critical issues in juvenile delinquency.* (pp. 45–62). Lexington, MA: Lexington Books.

Alexander, K. L. & Eckland, B. K. (1975). School experience and status attainment. In S. E. Dragastin & G. H. Elder (Eds.) *Adolescence in the life cycle.* (pp. 171–210). New York: John Wiley.

Allen, R. O. & Spilka, B. (1967). Committed and consensual religion: A specification of the religion-prejudice relationship. *Journal for the Scientific Study of Religion, 6,* 191–206.

Allon, N. (1982). The stigma of overweight. In B. Wolman (Ed.) *Psychological aspects of obesity: A handbook.* New York: Van Nostrand.

Allport, G. W. (1954). *The nature of prejudice.* Cambridge, MA: Addison-Wesley.

Altman, I. (1975). Environmental psychology: At the start of something big. *Contemporary Psychology, 20,* 205–207.

American Psychiatric Association. (1980). *Diagnostic and statistical manual of mental disorders* (3rd ed). Washington, DC: Author.

Anderson, A. E. & Mickalide, B. F. (1983). Anorexia nervosa in the male: An underdiagnosed disorder. *Psychosomatics, 24,* 1066–1075.

Andrisani, P. J. (1978). The establishment of stable and successful employment careers: The role of work attitudes and labor market knowledge: Its measurement and meaning. Washington, DC: U.S. Department of Labor.

Arlin, M. (1979). Teacher transitions can disrupt time flow in classrooms. *American Educational Research Journal, 16,* 42–56.

Arlin, P. K. (1975). Cognitive development in adulthood: A fifth stage? *Developmental Psychology, 11,* 602–606.

Arnold, C. B. (1972). The sexual behavior of inner city adolescent condom users. *Journal of Sex Research, 8,* 298–309.

Atkinson, R. C. & Shiffrin, R. M. (1968). Human memory: A proposed system and its control processes. In K. W. Spence and J. T. Spence (Eds.) *The psychology of learning and motivation: Advances in research and theory.* Vol. 2. New York: Academic Press.

Austin, M. C. (1981). *Three-tier vocational education program: A report of results and approach.* Paper presented at the annual meeting of the American Vocational Association, Atlanta, GA.

Ausubel, D. P. (1963). *The psychology of meaningful verbal learning.* New York: Grune and Stratton.

Ausubel, D. P. (1967). A cognitive-structural theory of school learning. In L. Siegal (Ed.) *Instruction: Some contemporary viewpoints.* (pp. 207–257). San Francisco: Chandler.

Ausubel, D. P., Montemayor, R., & Svajian, P. (1977). *Theory and problems of adolescent development.* New York: Grune and Stratton.

Avery, D. & Winokur, G. (1978). Suicide, attempted suicide and relapse rates in depression. *Archives of General Psychiatry, 35,* 749–753.

Babin, P. (1969). *Adolescents in search of a new church.* New York: Herder and Herder.

Babin, V. (1986). The impact of chlamydia infections on teen mothers and their children. *Journal of School Health, 56,* 17–19.

Bachman, J. G., Green, S., & Wirtanen, I. (1971). *Dropping out—Problem or symptom? Youth in transition,* Vol. 3. Ann Arbor, MI: Institute for School Research.

Bachman, J. G., O'Malley, P. M., & Johnston, L. D. (1980). *Correlates of drug use. Part 1: Selected measures of background, recent experiences, and lifestyle.* (Monitoring the Future Occasional Paper No. 8). Ann Arbor, MI: Institute for Social Research.

Bachman, M. E. (1972). Patterns of mental abilities: Ethnic, socioeconomic and sex differences. *American Educational Research Journal, 9,* 1–12.

Bain, R. K. & Anderson, J. G. (1974). School context and peer influences on educational plans of adolescents. *Review of Educational Research, 44,* 429–445.

Baldwin, W. H. (1976). Adolescent pregnancy and childbearing: Growing concern for Americans. *Population Bulletin, 31* (2).

Baldwin, W. H. (1978). Testimony before the House Select Commitee on Population, Vol. 2. Washington, DC: U.S. Government Printing Office.

Baldwin, W. & Cain, V. (1980). The children of teenage parents. *Family Planning Perspectives, 12,* 34–40.

Baltes, P. B. (1973). Prototypic paradigms and questions in lifespan research on development and aging. *Gerontologist, 13,* 458–467.

Bandura, A. (1964). The stormy decade: Fact or fiction. *Psychology in the Schools, 1,* 224–231.

Bandura, A. (1977). *Social learning theory.* Englewood Cliffs, NJ: Prentice-Hall.

Bandura, A. & McDonald, F. J. (1963). Influence of social reinforcement and the behavior of models in shaping childen's moral judgments. *Journal of Abnormal and Social Psychology, 67,* 274–281.

Bandura, A. & Walters, R. H. (1959). *Adolescent aggression: A study of child-training practices and family interactions.* New York: Ronald Press.

Bardwick, J. M. & Douvan, E. (1971). Ambivalence: The socialization of women. In K. Gornick & B. K. Moran (Eds.) *Women in a sexist society.* New York: Basic Books.

Barker, R. G. (1965). Explorations in ecological psychology. *American Psychology, 20,* 1–14.

Barnes, H. L. & Olson, D. H. (1985). Parent-adolescent communication and the circumplex model. *Child Development, 56,* 438–447.

Barnes, H. V. (1975). Physical growth and development. In H. V. Barnes (Ed.) *The Medical Clinics of North America, 59,* 1305–1317.

Barnes, H. V. & Berger, R. (1975). An approach to the obese adolescent. In H. V. Barnes (Ed.) *The Medical Clinics of North America, 59,* 1305–1317.

Barrett, C. J. & James Cairns, J. (1980). The social network in marijuana using groups. *International Journal of the Addictions, 15,* 677–688.

Barry, H., Bacon, M. K., & Child, I. L. (1957). A cross-cultural survey of some sex differences in socialization. *Journal of Abnormal and Social Psychology, 55,* 327–332.

Baumrind, D. (1968). Authoritarian vs. authoritative control. *Adolescence, 3,* 255–272.

Baumrind, D. (1975). Early socialization and adolescent competence. In S. E. Dragastin & G. H. Elder (Eds.) *Adolescence in the life cycle.* (pp. 117–145). New York: John Wiley.

Baumrind, D. & Black, A. E. (1967). Socialization practices associated with dimensions of competence in preschool boys and girls. *Child Development, 38,* 291–327.

Bayh, B. (Chair). (1975). *Our nation's schools—A report card: "A" in school violence and vandalism.* Report of the U.S. Senate Committee on the Judiciary. Washington, DC: U.S. Government Printing Office.

Bayley, N. (1965). Research in child development: A longitudinal perspective. *Merrill-Palmer Quarterly of Behavior and Development, 11,* 183–208.

Bean, J. P. (1985). Interaction effects based on class level in an exploratory model of college student dropout syndrome. *American Educational Research Journal, 22,* 35–64.

Bean, J. P. & Metzner, B. S. (1985). A conceptual model of nontraditional undergraduate student attrition. *Review of Educational Research, 55,* 485–540.

Beautrais, A. L., Fergusson, D. M., & Shannon, F. T. (1982). Life events and childhood morbidity: A prospective study. *Pediatrics, 70,* 935–939.

Beck, A. T. (1973). *The diagnosis and management of depression.* Philadelphia: University of Pennsylvania Press.

Beck, A. T. & Beamesderfer, A. (1974). Assessment of depression: The Depression Inventory. In Pinchot, D. (Ed.) *Psychological measurements in psychopharmacology: Modern problems in pharmopsychiatry.* Vol. 7. Basel, Switzerland: Karger.

Beck, A. T., Kovacs, M., & Weissman, A. (1979). Assessment of suicidal intention: The scale for suicide ideation. *Journal of Consulting and Clinical Psychology, 47,* 343–352.

Becker, H. (1969). Deviance and the response of others. In D. R. Cressey & D. A. Ward (Eds.) *Delinquency, crime and social process.* New York: Harper & Row.

Becker, W. C. (1964). Consequences of different kinds of parental discipline. In M. L. Hoffman & L. W. Hoffman (Eds.) *Review of child development and research.* Vol. 1. (pp. 169–208). New York: Russell Sage.

Beit-Hallahmi, B. (1974). Self-reported religious concerns of university underclassmen. *Adolescence, 9,* 333–338.

Bell, A. P., Broderick, C. B., & Goldsmith, S. (1973). "Adolescent sexuality in contemporary America": Three reviews. *SIECUS Report, 2*(1), 1, 3, 11, 12.

Bell, A. P., Weinberg, M. S., & Hammersmith, S. K. (1981). *Sexual preference: Its development in men and women.* Bloomington, IN: Indiana University Press.

Bell, R. R. & Chasten, J. B. (1970). Premarital sexual experience among coeds, 1958 and 1968. *Journal of Marriage and the Family, 32,* 81–84.

Bell, T. A. & Hein, K. (1984). Adolescents and sexually transmitted diseases. In K. K. Holmes, R. A. March, P. F. Sparking, & P. J. Weisner (Eds.) *Sexually transmitted diseases.* New York: McGraw-Hill.

Belson, W. (1978). *Television violence and the adolescent boy.* London: Saxon House.

Berscheid, E. & Dion, K. (1971). Physical attractiveness and dating choice: A test of the matching hypothesis. *Journal of Experimental Social Psychology, 7,* 173–189.

Bigner, J. J. (1974). A Wernerian analysis of children's descriptions of siblings. *Child Development, 45,* 317–323.

Bishop, S. M. & Ingersoll, G. M. (1984). Marital conflict and self-concepts of children in intact and separated-parent families. Paper presented at the Biennial Meeting of the Midwest Society for Research in Life-Span Development, Akron: OH.

Bishop, S. M. & Linn, A. G. (1984). Multi-level vulnerability of adolescent marriages: An ecosystem model for clinical assessment and intervention. *Journal of Marriage and the Family, 9,* 271–282.

Blackford, L. (1977). *Summary Report—Student drug use, San Mateo County, Califoirnia.* San Mateo County (CA) Department of Public Welfare.

Blalock, H. M. (1964). *Causal inferences from nonexperimental research.* Chapel Hill, NC: University of North Carolina Press.

Blasi, A. & Hoeffel, E. C. (1974). Adolescence and formal operations. *Human Development, 17,* 344–363.

Bleich, L. (1980). The developmental role of adolescent literature. *Texas Tech Journal of Education, 7,* 39–47.

Bleuler, M. (1968, originally published 1911). *The schizophrenic disorders: Long term patient and family studies.* Trans. Siegfried M. Clemens. New Haven: Yale University Press.

Blitzer, P. H., Blitzer, E. C., & Rimm, A. A. (1976). Association between teenage obesity and cancer in 56,111 women: All cancers and endometrial carcinoma. *Preventative Medicine, 5,* 20–31.

Block, J. (1971). *Lives through time.* Berkeley, CA: Bancroft.

Bloom, B. S. (1964). *Stability and change in human characteristics.* New York: John Wiley.

Blos, P. (1952). *On adolescence.* New York: Free Press.

Blos, P. (1972). The function of the ego ideal in adolescence. *The Psychoanalytic Study of the Child, 27,* 43–97.

Blum, R. H. (1972). *Horatio Alger's children: Role of the family in the origin and prevention of drug risk.* San Francisco: Jossey-Bass.

Blum, R. H. & Richards, L. (1979). Youthful drug use. In R. L. Dupont, A. Goldstein, & J. O'Connell (Eds.) *Handbook on drug abuse.* Washington, DC: National Institute on Drug Abuse.

Bohrnstedt, G. & Felson, R. B. (1983). Explaining the relations among children's actual and perceived performances and self-esteem: A comparison of several causal models. *Journal of Personality and Social Psychology, 45,* 43–56.

Bonham, G. S. (1977). Who adopts: The relationship of adoption and social-demographic characteristics of women. *Journal of Marriage and the Family, 39,* 298.

Boring, E. G. (1923). Intelligence as the tests test it. *New Republic, 35* (June 6), 35–36.

Borow, H. (1976). Career development. In J. F. Adams (Ed.) *Understanding adolescence.* (pp. 489–523). Boston: Allyn and Bacon.

Boyer, E. L. (1983). *High school: A report on secondary education in America.* New York: Harper & Row.

Bracht, G. N., Follingstad, D., Brakash, D., & Berry, K. L. (1973). Deviant drug use in adolescence: A review of psychological correlates. *Psychological Bulletin, 79,* 92–106.

Brack, C. J., Orr, D. P., & Ingersoll, G. M. (1988). Pubertal maturation and adolescent self-esteem. *Journal of Adolescent Health Care, 9,* 280–285.

Braun, J. & Bayer, F. (1973). Social desirability of occupations: Revisited. *Vocational Guidance Quarterly, 21,* 202–205.

Brickell, H. (1978). Seven key notes on minimum competency testing. *Phi Delta Kappan, 59,* 589–592.

Bronfenbrenner, U. (1977). Toward an experimental ecology of human development. *American Psychologist, 32,* 513–531.

Bronfenbrenner, U. (1979). *The ecology of human development: Experiments by nature and design.* Cambridge, MA: Harvard University Press.

Brooks-Gunn, J. & Ruble, D. N. (1982). The development of menstrual-related beliefs during early adolescence. *Child Development, 53,* 1567-1577.

Brooks-Gunn, J. & Warren, M. (1985). Measuring physical status and timing in early adolescence: A developmental perspective. *Journal of Youth and Adolescence, 14,* 149-161.

Brophy, J. (1986). Teacher influences on student achievement. *American Psychologist, 41,* 1069-1077.

Brown, J. K. (1975). Adolescent initiation rites: Recent interpretations. In R. E. Grinder (Ed.) *Studies in adolescence.* (pp. 40-52). New York: Macmillan.

Brown, J. & Finn, P. (1982). Drinking to get drunk: Findings of a survey of junior and senior high school students. *Journal of Alcohol and Drug Education, 27*(3), 13-25.

Bruche, H. (1978). *The golden cage: The enigma of anorexia nervosa.* Cambridge, MA: Harvard University Press.

Brumberg, J. J. (1985). "Fasting girls": reflections on writing the history of anorexia nervosa. In A. B. Smuts & J. W. Hagen (Eds.) Historical research in child development. *Monographs for the Society for Research in Child Development, 50*(4-5, Serial No. 211).

Bullen, B. A., Reed, R. B., & Mayer, J. (1964). Physical activity of obese and nonobese adolescent girls appraised by motion picture sampling. *American Journal of Clinical Nutrition, 14,* 211-223.

Bumpass, L. L. (1984). Children and marital disruption: A replication and update. *Demography, 21,* 71-82.

Burnham, D. (1982). Induced termination of pregnancy: Reporting states, 1979. *NCHS Monthly Vital Statistics, 31*(7), October 25.

Burt, M. R. & Biegel, M. M. (1980). *Worldwide survey of nonmedical drug use and alcohol use among military personnel, 1980.* Bethesda, MD: Burt Associates.

Burton, R. V. (1963). Generality of honesty reconsidered. *Psychological Review, 70,* 481-499.

Bush, D., Simmons, R., Hutchinson, B., & Blyth, D. (1977). Adolescent perception of sex roles in 1968 and 1975. *Public Opinion Quarterly, 4,* 459-474.

Bush, L. Z., Walsh, W. F., & Rothman, G. (1981). Relationship between parental moral judgment and socialization. *Youth and Society, 13,* 91-116.

Byrne, D. (1971). *The attraction paradigm.* New York: Academic Press.

Caldwell, R. G. (1971). *Juvenile delinquency.* New York: Ronald Press.

Caliste, E. R. (1984). The effect of a twelve-week dropout prevention program. *Adolescence, 19,* 649-657.

Callahan, D., Cisin, I. H., & Crossley, H. M. (1974). *American drinking practices: A national study of drinking behavior and attitudes.* Monograph No. 6. New Brunswick, NJ: Rutgers Center on Alcohol Studies.

Camp, B. W., Burgess, D., Morgan, L., & Malpiede, D. (1984). Infants of adolescent mothers. *American Journal of Diseases in Children, 138,* 243-246.

Campbell, D. T. (1957). Factors relevant to the validity of experiments in social settings. *Psychological Bulletin, 54,* 297-312.

Campbell, D. T. & Stanley, J. C. (1966). *Experimental and quasi-experimental designs for research.* Chicago: Rand-McNally.

Canning, D. T. & Mayer, J. (1967). Obesity: An influence on high school performance. *American Journal of Clinical Nutrition, 20,* 352-354.

Cantwell, D. P. (1982). Childhood depression: A review of current research. In B. Lahey and A. Kazdin (Eds.) *Advances in clinical child psychology.* New York: Plenum.

Carron, A. V. & Bailey, D. A. (1974). Strength development in boys from 10 through 16 years. *Monographs of the Society for Research in Child Development, 39*(4).

Cartledge, G. & Milburn, J. F. (1980). *Teaching social skills to children.* Elford, NY: Pergamon Press.

Caster, J. (1975). Share our specialty: What is mainstreaming? *Exceptional Children, 42,* 174.

Cattell, R. B. (1966). The principles of experimental design and analysis in relation to theory building. In R. B. Cattell (Ed.) *Handbook of multivariate experimental psychology.* Chicago: Rand McNally.

Cattell, R. B. (1971). *Abilities: Their structure, growth and action.* Boston: Houghton Mifflin.

Cattell, R. B. & Cattell, A.K.S. (1959). *Handbook for the Culture Fair Intelligence Test.* Champagne, IL: Institute for Personality Testing.

Cavior, N. & Dokecki, P. R. (1973). Physical attractiveness, perceived similarity and academic achievement as potential contributors to interpersonal attraction among adolescents. *Developmental Psychology, 9,* 44–54.

Centers for Disease Control. (1977). *VD fact sheet, 1976.* (33rd ed.) Atlanta, GA: Center for Disease Control.

Centers for Disease Control. (1985). *Sexually transmitted disease (STD) statistics: calendar year 1984.* Atlanta, GA: Center for Disease Control.

Chacko, M. R. & Lovchik, J. C. (1984). Chlamydia trachomatis infection in sexually active adolescents: Prevalence and risk factors. *Pediatrics, 73,* 836–840.

Chambliss, W. (1973). The saints and the roughnecks. *Society, 11* (Nov–Dec), 24–31.

Chand, I. P., Crider, D.M.K., & Wiltis, F. K. (1975). Parent-youth disagreement as perceived by youth: A longitudinal study. *Youth and Society, 6,* 365–375.

Chartier, G. M. & Ranieri, D. J. (1984). Adolescent depression: Concepts, treatments, preventions. In P. Karoly & J. J. Steffen (Eds.) *Adolescent behavior disorders: Foundations and contemporary concerns.* Lexington, MA: Lexington Books.

Chase, H. P. & Jackson, G. G. (1981). Stress and sugar control in children with insulin dependent diabetes mellitus. *Journal of Pediatrics, 98,* 1011–1013.

Chassin, L. (1984). Adolescent substance use and abuse . In P. Karoly and J. J. Steffen (Eds.) *Adolescent behavior disorders: Foundations and contemporary concerns.* Lexington, MA: D. C. Health.

Chassin, L. & Stager, S. F. (1984). Determinants of self-esteem among incarcerated delinquents. *Social Psychology Quarterly, 47,* 382–390.

Chassin, L., Presson, C., Sherman, S. J., Corty, E., & Olshavsky, R. (1981). Self-image and cigarette smoking in adolescence. *Personality and Social Psychology Bulletin, 7,* 670–676.

Chen, T. T. & Thompson, L. A. (1980). A study of smoking behavior and smoking education at the junior high level. *Health Education, 11,* 37–40.

Children's Defense Fund. (1986). *A children's defense budget.* Washington, DC: Author.

Chilman, C. S. (1983). *Adolescent sexuality in a changing society.* New York: Wiley Interscience.

Churchill, W. (1948). *The gathering storm.* Boston: Houghton Mifflin.

Clarke, A. & Ruble, D. N. (1978). Young adolescents' beliefs concerning menstruation. *Child Development, 53,* 1567–1577.

Cloward, R. A. & Ohlin, L. E. (1960). *Delinquency and opportunity: A theory of delinquent gangs.* Glencoe, IL: Free Press.

Cochrane, P. V. & Westling, D. L. (1977). The principal and mainstreaming: Ten suggestions for success. *Educational Leadership, 34,* 506–510.

Coddington, R. D. (1972). The significance of life events as etiologic factors in the diseases of children: I. A survey of professional workers. *Journal of Psychosomatic Research, 16,* 7–18. (a).

Coddington, R. D. (1972). The significance of life events as etiologic factors in the diseases of children: II. A study of a normal population. *Journal of Psychosomatic Research, 16,* 205–213. (b).

Cogan, J. (1982). How black youth fell behind. *Fortune, 105* (June), 102–121.

Cohen, A. (1955). *Delinquent boys.* Glencoe, IL: Free Press.

Cohen, J. (1980). Adolescent independence and adolescent change. *Youth and Society, 12,* 107–124.

Cohen, S. (1981). Adverse effects of marijuana: Selected issues. *Annals of the New York Academy of Science, 362,* 119–124.

Cohen, S. (1982). Cannabis: effects on adolescent motivation. In *Marijuana and youth: Clinical observations on motivation and learning.* Washington, DC: National Institute on Drug Abuse.

Colby, A., Kohlberg, L., Gibbs, J., & Lieberman, M. (1983). A longitudinal study of moral judgment. *Monographs of the Society for Research in Child Development, 48*(1-2, Serial No. 200).

Coleman, J. C. (1980). Friendships and the peer group in adolescence. In J. Adelson (Ed.) *Handbook of adolescent psychology.* (pp. 408-431). New York: John Wiley.

Coleman, J. S. (1961). *The adolescent society.* New York: Free Press.

Coleman, J. S. (1975). *Youth: Transition to adulthood.* Chicago: University of Chicago Press.

Coles, R. (1977). The children of affluence. *Atlantic Monthly, 240,* 52-60.

Colletti, G. & Brownell, K. D. (1982). Obesity. *Progress in behavior modification, 13,* 123-139.

Collins, J. K. (1974). Adolescent dating intimacy: Norms and peer expectations. *Journal of Youth and Adolescence, 3,* 317-328.

Conger, J. J. (1975). Sexual attitudes and behavior among contemporary adolescents. In J. J. Conger (Ed.) *Contemporary issues in adolescent development.* New York: Harper and Row.

Conklin, E. S. (1935). *Principles of adolescent psychology.* New York: Henry Holt and Co.

Cook, T. D. & Campbell, D. T. (1979). *Quasi-experimentation.* Chicago: Rand McNally.

Cooley, C. H. (1902). *Human nature and the social order.* New York: Schocken.

Cooper, P. (1965). The development of the concept of war. *Journal of Peace Research, 2,* 1-17.

Coopersmith, S. (1967). *The antecedents of self-esteem.* San Francisco: Freeman.

Cornwell. G. (1976). How dangerous ae religious cults? *Readers Digest, 108* (Feb.), 96-100.

Costanzo, P. R. & Shaw, M. E. (1966). Conformity as a function of age level. *Child Development, 37,* 967-975.

Covington, M. V. & Beery, R. G. (1976). *Self-worth and school learning.* New York: Holt, Rinehart and Winston.

Crisp, A. H., Douglas, J. W., Ross, J. M., & Tonehill, E. (1970). Some developmental aspects of disorders of weight. *Journal of Psychosomatic Research, 14,* 313-320.

Critchlow, B. (1986). The powers of John Barleycorn: Beliefs about the effects of alcohol on social behavior. *American Psychologist, 41,* 751-764.

Crites, T. J. (1981). Being ''undecided'' might be the best decision they could make. *The School Counselor, 29,* 41-46.

Crockenberg, S. B. (1972). Creativity tests: Boon or boondoggle for education? *Review of Educational Research, 42,* 27-46.

Cusick, P. A. (1983). *The egalitarian ideal and the American high school: Studies of three schools.* New York: Longman.

Cusick, P. A., Martin, W., & Palonsky, S. (1976). Organizational structure and student behavior in secondary schools. *Journal of Curriculum Studies, 18,* 163-169.

Cutright, P. (1971). Illegitimacy in the United States, 1920-1968. In C. F. Westoff and R. Parks (Eds.) *Demographic and social aspects of population growth.* Report of the Commission on Population and the American Future, research reports, Vol. 1. Washington, DC: U.S. Government Printing Office.

Cutright, P. (1972). The teenage sexual revolution. The myth of an abstinate past. *Family Planning Perspectives, 4,* 24-31.

Cvetkovitch, G., Grote, B., Bjorseth, A., & Sarkissian, J. (1975). On the psychology of adolescents' use of contraceptives. *Journal of Sex Research, 11,* 256-270.

Damico, S. B. & Purkey, W. W. (1978). Class clowns: A study of middle-school students. *American Educational Research Journal, 15,* 391-398.

Davidson, M. A., McInnes, R. G., & Parnell, R. W. (1957). The distribution of personality traits in seven-year-old children: A combined psychological, psychiatric and somatotype study. *British Journal of Psychiatry, 27,* 48-61.

Davis, K. (1940). Sociology of parent-youth conflict. *American Sociological Review, 1,* 523-535.

Davis, K. & Blake, J. (1956). Social structure and fertility: An analytic framework. *Development and Cultural Change, 4,* 211.

Demos, J. & Demos,V. (1969). Adolescence in historical perspective. *Journal of Marriage and the Family, 31,* 632-638.

Diepold, J., Jr. & Young, R. D. (1979).   Empirical studies of adolescent sexual behavior: A critical review. *Adolescence, 53,* 45–64.

Dion, K. & Berscheid, E. (1974).   Physical attractiveness and peer perception among children. *Sociometry, 37,* 1–12.

Dion, K., Bescheid, E., & Walster, E. (1972).   What is beautiful is good. *Journal of Personality and Social Psychology, 24,* 285–290.

Dittes, J. E. (1969).   Psychology of religion. In G. Lindsey and E. Aronson (Eds.) *The handbook of social psychology.* (2nd ed), Vol. 5. (pp. 602–659). Reading, MA: Addison-Wesley.

Dixon, P. N., Strano, D. A., & Willingham, W. (1984).   Locus of control and decision to abort. *Psychological Reports, 54,* 547–553.

Dodge, K. A. (1983).   Behavioral antecedents of peer social status. *Child Development, 54,* 1386–1399.

Dodge, K.A., Pettit, G. S., McClaskey, C. L., & Brown, M. M. (1986).   Social competence in children. *Monographs for the Society for Research in Child Development, 51* (2, Serial No. 213).

Dollard, J. & Miller, N. E. (1950).   *Personality and psychotherapy: An analysis in terms of learning, thinking and culture.* New York: McGraw-Hill.

Donovan, J. E. & Jessor, R. (1985).   Structure of problem behavior in adolescence and young adulthood. *Journal of Consulting and Clinical Psychology, 53,* 890–904.

Douvan, E. & Adelson, J. (1966).   *The adolescent experience.* New York: John Wiley.

Dreyfoos, J. (1982).   The epidemiology of adolescent pregnancy: Incidence, outcomes, and interventions. In I. R. Stuart and C. F. Wells (Eds.) *Prengancy in adolescence: Needs, problems and management.* New York: Van Nostrand Reinhold.

Duke, P., Litt, I., & Gross, R. (1980).   Adolescents' self-assessment of sexual maturation. *Pediatrics, 66,* 918–920.

Duncan, O. D., Featherman, D. L., & Duncan, B. (1972).   *Socioeconomic background and achievement.* New York: Seminar Press.

Duncan, P., Ritter, J., & Dornbusch, S. (1985).   The effects of pubertal timing on body image, school behavior, and deviance. *Journal of Youth and Adolescence, 14,* 207–225.

Dunphy, D. C. (1963).   The social structure of urban adolescent peer groups. *Sociometry, 26,* 230–246.

Dunphy, D. C. (1969).   *Cliques, crowds, and gangs.* Melbourne: Cheshire.

Dusek, J.G. & Flaherty, J. F. (1981).   The development of self-concept during the adolescent years. *Monographs of the Society for Research in Child Development, 46*(4, Serial No. 191).

Dweck, C. & Bush, E. (1976).   Sex differences in learned helplessness: Differential debilitation with peer and adult evaluators. *Developmental Psychology, 12,* 147–156.

Dwyer, J. & Mayer, J. (1969).   Effects of variations in physical appearance during adolescence. *Adolescence, 3,* 353–368.

Ebel, R. L. (1972).   What are schools for? *Phi Delta Kappan, 7,* 401–405.

Eder, D. (1985).   The cycle of popularity: Interpersonal relations among female adolescents. *Sociology of Education, 58,* 154–165.

Edmonds, R. R. (1983).   *Search for effective schools: The identification and analysis of city schools that are effective for poor children.* (Final Report). East Lansing, MI: Michigan State Unviersity.

Edwards, D. W. (1983).   Adolescence and masturbation. *Journal of Social Work and Human Sexuality, 1,* 53–57.

Ehrlich, H. J. (1973).   *The social psychology of prejudice.* New York: Wiley-Interscience.

Eichorn, D. H. (1966).   *The middle school.* New York: Center for Applied Research in Education.

Eichorn, D. H. (1975).   Asynchronizations in adolescent development. In S. E. Dragastin & G. H. Elder (Eds.) *Adolescence in the life cycle.* (pp. 81–96). New York: Halstead.

Eisenberg, N. & Harris, J. D. (1984).   Social competence: A developmental perspective. *School Psychology Review, 13,* 278–291.

Ekstrom, R. B., Goertz, M. E., Pollock, J. M., & Rock, D. (1986). Who drops out of school and why? Findings from a national study. *Teachers College Record, 46,* 356–373.

Elder, G. H., Jr. (1963). Parental power legitimization and its effect on the adolescent. *Sociometry, 26,* 50–65.

Elder, G. H., Jr. (1974). *Children of the great depression.* Chicago: University of Chicago Press.

Elias, J. & Gebhard, P. (1969). Sexuality and sexual learning in childhood. *Phi Delta Kappan, 7,* 401–405.

Elkind, D. (1967). Egocentrism in adolescence. *Child Development, 38,* 1025–1034.

Elkind, D. (1978). Understanding the young adolescent. *Adolescence, 49,* 127–134.

Elkind, D. (1984). *All grown up and no place to go: Teenagers in crisis.* Reading, MA: Addison-Wesley.

Elliott, D. S. (1966). Delinquency, school attendance and droupouts. *Social Problems, 13,* 306–318.

Elliott, D. S. & Voss, H. L. (1974). *Delinquency and dropout.* Lexington, MA: D. C. Heath.

Elmer, E. (1967). *Children in jeopardy.* Pittsburgh, PA: University of Pittsburgh Press.

Elmer, E. & Gregg, G. (1967). Developmental characteristics of abused children. *Pediatrics, 40,* 596–602.

Emmer, E. T., Evertson, E. M., & Anderson, L. M. (1979). The first three weeks of class. . . and the rest of the year. Paper presented at the annual meeting of the American Educational Research Association, San Francisco.

Empey, L. T. (1980). Revolution and counter-revolution: Current trends in juvenile justice. In D. Shehor & D. H. Kelley (Eds.) *Critical issues in juvenile delinquency.* (pp. 157–186). Lexington, MA: Lexington Books.

Engs, R. C. & Hanson, D. J. (1985). The drinking patterns of college students: 1983. *Journal of Alcohol and Drug Education, 31,* 65–83.

Engs, R. C. & Hanson, D. J. (1986). Age specific alcohol prohibition and college students drinking problems. *Psychological Reports, 59,* 979–984.

Epstein, H. T. (1978). Growth spurts during brain development: Implications for educational policy and practice. In J. S. Chall and A. F. Mirsky (Eds.) *Education and the brain. Seventy-seventh yearbook of the National Society for the Study of Education, Part 2.* Chicago: University of Chicago Press.

Erikson, E. H. (1959). Identity and the life cycle. *Psychological Issues,* 1 (no. 1).

Erikson, E. H. (1968). *Identity, youth and crisis.* New York: W. W. Norton. (a).

Erikson, E. H. (1968). *Young man Luther.* New York: W. W. Norton. (b).

Erikson, E. H. (1969). *Gandhi's truth.* New York: W. W. Norton.

Eron, L. D. & Huesmann, L. R. (1980). Adolescent aggression and television. *Annals of the New York Academy of Sciences, 347,* 319–331.

Eskin, B. (1977). When do nocturnal emissions begin in adolescence? Does the date coincide with or resemble first menstruation in girls? *Medical Tribune.*

Exter, T. (1987). How many Hispanics? *American Demographics, 9,* 36–39, 67.

Farrington, D. C. (1978). The family background of aggressive youths. In L. A. Hershov, M. Berger, and D. Shaffer (Eds.) *Aggression and anti-social behavior in children and adolescents.* Oxford: Pergammon Press.

Faust. M. S. (1960). Development maturity as a determinant of prestige in adolescent girls. *Child Development, 31,* 173–184.

Faust, M. S. (1977). Somatic development of adolescent girls. *Monographs of the Society for Research in Child Development, 42,* (series no. 169).

Feather, N. & Raphelson, A. (1974). Fear of success in Australian and American student groups: Motive or sex-role stereotype. *Journal of Personality, 42,* 190–201.

Federal Bureau of Investigation. (1986). *Uniform Crime Reports for the United States, 1984.* Washington, DC: Department of Justice.

Ferraro, D. P. (1980). Acute effects of marijuana on human memory and cognition. In R. C. Petersen (Ed.) *Marijuana research findings: 1980.* Washington, DC: National Institute on Drug Abuse.

Festinger, L. & Katz, D. (1953). *Research methods in the social sciences.* New York: Holt, Rinehart and Winston.

Feuer, L. (1969). *The conflict of generations: The character and significance of youth movements.* New York: Basic Books.

Finkelhor, D. (1979). *Sexually victimized children.* New York: Free Press.

Finkelhor, D. (1980). Risk factors in sexual victimization of children. *Child Abuse and Neglect, 4,* 265–273.

Flavell, J. (1977). *Cognitive development.* Englewood Cliffs: Prentice-Hall.

Flora, R. R. (1978). The effect of self-concept upon adolescents' communication with parents. *Journal of School Health, 48,* 100–102.

Forbes, G. B. (1976). Biological implications of the adolescent growth process: Body composition. In J. I. McKigney & H. M. Munroe (Eds.) *Nutrient requirements in adolescence.* (pp. 57–66). Cambridge, MA: M.I.T. Press.

Ford, K. (1983). Second pregnancies among teenage mothers. *Family Planning Perspectives, 15,* 268–272.

Fowler, J. W. (1976). Stages in faith: The structural development perspective. In T. Hennessey (Ed.) *Values and moral development.* (pp. 173–211). New York: Paulist Press.

Fowler, J. W. (1981). *Stages of faith: The psychology of human development and the quest for meaning.* New York: Harper & Row.

Fox, L. H. (1976). Identification and program planning: Models and methods. In D. P. Keating (Ed.) *Intellectual talent: Research and development.* Baltimore, MD: Johns Hopkins University.

Frank, L. K. (1944). Introduction: Adolescence as a period of transition. *Forty-Third Yearbook of the National Society for the Study of Education, Part 1.* (pp. 1–7). Chicago: University of Chicago Press.

French, D. C. & Waas, G. A. (1985). Behavioral problems of peer-neglected and peer-rejected elementary age children: Parent and teacher perspectives. *Child Development, 56,* 246–252.

French. E. G. (1958). Effects of the interaction of motivation and feedback on task performance. In J. W. Atkinson (Ed.) *Motives in fantasy, action, and society.* Princeton, NJ: Van Nostrand.

Freud, A. (1966). *The ego and the mechanisms of defense.* (Rev. ed.) *The writings of Anna Freud.* Vol. 2. New York: International Universities Press.

Freud, S. (1917). Introductory lectures on psychoanalysis. In J. Strachey (Ed.) *The standard edition of the complete psychological works of Sigmund Freud.* Vol. 16. London: Hogarth.

Freud, S. (1927). Some psychological consequences of the anatomical distinction between the sexes. *International Journal of Psycho-Analysis, 8,* 133–142.

Freud, S. (1952). *A general introduction to psychoanalysis.* New York: Washington Square Press.

Freud, S. (1953). Three essays on sexuality. In *Standard edition of the complete psychological works of Sigmund Freud.* Vol. II. London: Hogarth Press.

Friedman, R. R. (1984). Dropouts in school to work transition. *The Urban Review, 6*(1), 25–42.

Frisch, R. F. & McArthur, J. W. (1974). Menstrual cycles: Fatness as a determinant of minimum height for weight necessary for their maintenance or onset. *Science, 185,* 949.

Frisch, R. F. & Revelle, R. (1970). Height and weight at menarche and a hypothesis of critical body weights and adolescent events. *Science, 169,* 397–398.

Frisch, R. F., Revelle, R., & Cook, S. (1973). Components of weight at menarche and the initiation of the adolescent growth spurt in girls—estimated total water, lean body weight and fat. *Human Biology, 45,* 536–559.

Frisch, R. F., Gotz-Welbergen, A. V., McArthur, J. W., Albright, T., Witschi, J., Bullen, B., Birnholz, J., Reed, R. B., & Hermann, H. (1981). Delayed menarche and amenorrhea of college athletes in relation to age and onset of training. *Journal of the American Medical Association, 246,* 1559–1563.

Fryear, J. L. & Thelen, M. H. (1969). Effects of sex of model and sex of observer on the imitation of affectionate behavior. *Developmental Psychology, 1,* 298.

Fuqua, D. R. & Hartman, B. H. (1985). Differential diagnosis and treatment of career indecision. Paper presented at the annual meeting of the American Educational Research Association, Chicago.

Gallagher, J.R. (1960). *Medical care of the adolescent.* New York: Appleton Century Crofts.

Gallatin, J. (1979). Political thinking in adolescence. In J. Adelson (Ed.) *Handbook of adolescent psychology.* (pp. 344–382). New York: John Wiley.

Gallup Opinion Index. (1979). American public leans to pessimism on job outlook in their communities. Report No. 174, 10–12.

Garbarino, J. (1982). *Children and families in the social environment.* New York: Aldine.

Garbarino, J. & Gilliam, G. (1980). *Understanding abusive families.* Lexington, MA: Lexington Books.

Garbarino, J., Sebes, J., & Schellenbach, C. (1984). Families at risk for destructive parent-child relations in adolescence. *Child Development, 55,* 174–183.

Gecas, V. & Nye, F. I. (1974). Sex and class differences in parent-child interaction: A test of Kohn's hypothesis. *Journal of Marriage and the Family, 36,* 742–749.

Geiger, K. M. & Turiel, E. (1983). Disruptive school behavior and concepts of social convention in early adolescence. *Journal of Educational Psychology, 75,* 677–685.

Geismar, L. L. & Wood, K. (1986). *Family and delinquency: Resocializing the young offender.* New York: Human Science Press.

Gibbons, D. C. (1970). *Delinquent behavior.* Englewood Cliffs, NJ: Prentice-Hall.

Gill, D. G. (1970). *Violence against children.* Cambridge, MA: Harvard University Press.

Gilligan, C. (1982). *In a different voice: Psychological theory and women's development.* Cambridge, MA: Harvard University Press.

Ginsberg, E., Ginsberg, S. W., Axelrod, S., & Herman, J. L. (1951). *Occupational choice: An approach to a general theory.* New York: Columbia University Press.

Giordano, P. C. (1978). Girls, guys, and gangs: The changing social context of female delinquency. *Journal of Criminal Law and Criminology, 69,* 126–132.

Glock, C. Y. & Stark, R. (1965). *Religion and society in tension.* Chicago: Rand McNally.

Glock, C. Y., Wuthnow, R., Piliavin, J. A., & Spencer, M. (1975). *Adolescent prejudice.* New York: Harper & Row.

Glueck, S. & Glueck, E. (1962). *Family environment and delinquency.* New York: Harper & Row.

Goertzel, V. & Goertzel, M. G. (1962). *Cradles of eminence.* Boston: Little, Brown.

Gold, M. (1966). Undetected delinquent behavior. *Journal of Research in Crime and Delinquency, 3,* 27–46.

Gold, M. (1970). *Crime in an American city.* Belmont, CA: Wadsworth.

Gold, M. (1978). Scholastic experiences, self-esteem and delinquent behavior: A theory for alienated schools. *Crime and Delinquency, 24,* 290–308.

Gold, M. & Douvan, E. (1969). *Adolescent development.* Boston: Allyn and Bacon.

Gold, M. & Petronio, R. J. (1980). Delinquent behavior in adolescence. In J. Adelson (Ed.) *Handbook of adolescent psychology.* (pp. 495–535). New York: John Wiley.

Goldman, R. (1964). *Religious thinking from childhood to adolescence.* London: Routledge and Kegan-Paul.

Golladay, M. A. (1977). *The condition of education.* National Center for Educational Statistics. Washington, DC: U.S. Government Printing Office.

Gollin, E. S. (1958). Organizational characteristics of social judgment: A developmental investigation. *Journal of Personality, 26,* 139–154.

Goodman, N., Richardson, S. A., Dornbush, S. M. & Hastorf, A. M. (1963). Variant reactions to physical disability. *American Sociological Review, 28,* 429–435.

Gordon, E. W. (1973). Methodological problems and pseudo-issues in the nature-nurture controversy. In R. Cancro (Ed.) *Intelligence: Genetic and environmental influences.* (pp. 240–251). New York: Grune and Stratton.

Gorn, G. J., Goldberg, M. E., & Kanungo, R. N. (1976). The role of educational television in changing the intergroup attitudes of children. *Child Development, 47,* 277–280.

Goslin, D. A. (1962). Accuracy of self-perception and social acceptance. *Sociometry, 5,* 283–296.

Goss, S. S. (1984). Student perceptions and classroom management. Unpublished doctoral dissertation, Indiana University, Bloomington, IN.

Gottlieb, J. & Budoff, M. (1973). Social acceptability of retarded children in nongraded schools differing in architecture. *American Journal of Mental Deficiency, 78,* 15–19.

Gottlieb, J., Semmel, M. I., & Veldman, D. (1978). Correlates of social status among mainstreamed mentally retarded children. *Journal of Educational Psychology, 70,* 396–405.

Gough, H. G. (1960). The Adjective Check List as a personality assessment research technique. *Psychological Reports, 6,* 107–122.

Granberg, D. & Granberg, B. W. (1980). Abortion attitudes 1965–1980: Trends and determinants. *Family Planning Perspectives, 12,* 250–254.

Grant, M. (1984). An opinion on solving the dropout problem, *Thrust, 13*(6), 14–17.

Gregory, I. (1968). *Fundamentals of psychiatry* (second edition). Philadelphia: W. B. Saunders.

Greenberger, E. (1984). Defining psychosocial maturity in adolescence. In P. Karoly, & J. J. Steffen (Eds.) *Adolescent behavior disorders: Foundations and contemporary concerns.* (pp. 3–38). Lexington, MA: Lexington Books.

Greenberger, E. & Steinberg, L. (1986). *When teenagers work: The psychological and social costs of adolescent employment.* New York: Basic Books.

Greene, J. W., Walker, L. S., Hickson, G., & Thompson, J. (1985). Stressful life events and somatic complaints in adolescents. *Pediatrics, 75,* 19–22.

Greenfield, P. M. (1984). *Mind and media: The effects of television, video games, and computers.* Cambridge, MA: Harvard University Press.

Gribbons, W. D. & Lohnes, P. R. (1965). Shifts in adolescents' vocational values. *Personnel and Guidance Journal, 44,* 248–252.

Grief, E. B. & Ulman, K. J. (1982). The psychological impact of menarche on early adolescent females: A review of literature. *Child Development, 53,* 1413–1430.

Grinder, R. (1985). Adolescent prejudice. Paper presented at the annual meeting of the American Educational Research Association, Chicago.

Grossman, H. J. (Ed.) (1983). *Classification in mental retardation.* Washington, DC: American Association of Mental Retardation.

Guber, S. S. (1987). The teenage mind. *American Demographics, 9*(8), 42–44.

Guilford, J. P. (1959). Three faces of intellect. *American Psychologist, 14,* 469–479.

Gunderson, J. C. (1974). Special report: Schizophrenia, 1974. *Schizophrenia Bulletin, 9,* 16–18.

Guttmacher Institute. (1976). *11 million teenagers: What can be done about the epidemic of adolescent pregnancies in the United States?* New York: Alan Guttmacher Institute, Planned Parenthood Federation of America.

Guttmacher Institute. (1981). *Teenage pregnancy: The problem that hasn't gone away.* New York: Alan Guttmacher Institute, Planned Parenthood Federation of America.

Haan, N., Langer, J., & Kohlberg, L. (1976). Family patterns of moral reasoning. *Child Development, 47,* 1204–1206.

Haan, N., Smith, M. B., & Block, J. (1968). Moral reasoning of young adults: Political social behavior, family background and personality correlates. *Journal of Personality and Social Psychology, 10,* 183–201.

Haas, A. (1979). *Teenage sexuality.* New York: Macmillan.

Haier, R. J. & Denham, S. A. (1976). A summary profile of nonintellectual correlates of mathematical precocity in boys and girls. In D. P. Keating (Ed.). *Intellectual talent: Research and development.* Baltimore, MD: Johns Hopkins University.

Haier, R. J. & Solano, C. H. (1976). Educators' stereotypes of mathematically gifted boys. In D. P. Keating (Ed.). *Intellectual talent: Research and development.* Baltimore, MD: Johns Hopkins University.

Haisch, H. M. (1964). Do child labor laws protect youth employment? *Journal of Negro Education, 33,* 182–185.

Hakel, M. D., Hollmann, T.D., & Dunnette, M. D. (1967).   Stability and change in the occupational status of occupations over 21- and 42-year periods. *Personnel and Guidance Journal, 46,* 762–764.

Halikas, J. A., Goodman, D. W., & Gruze, S. B. (1972).   Marijuana use and psychiatric illness. *Archives of General Psychiatry, 27,* 162–165.

Halikas, J. A., Weller, R. A., Morse, C., & Shapiro, T. (1982).   Incidence and characteristics of amotivational syndrome, including associated findings among chronic marijuana users. In *Marijuana and youth: Clinical observations on motivation and learning.* Washington, DC: National Institute on Drug Abuse.

Hall, G. S. (1904).   *Adolescence: Its psychology and its relations to physiology, anthropology, sociology, sex, crime, religion and education.* New York: Appleton.

Hamberg, B. V. (1980).   Peer counseling can identify and help troubled youngsters. *Phi Delta Kappan, 61,* 562–563.

Hamil, P.V.V., Drizd, T. A., Johnson, C. L., Reed, R. B., & Roche, A. F. (1977).   *NCHS growth curves for children birth–18 years.* Vital and Health Statistics. Washington, DC: U.S. Government Printing Office.

Hammond, W. H. (1957).   The status of physical types. *Human Biology, 29,* 223–241.

Haney, B. & Gold, M. (1973).   The delinquent nobody knows. *Psychology Today, 7*(4), 49–51, 55.

Hanks, R. (1985).   Moral reasoning in adolescents: A feature of intelligence or social adjustment. *Journal of Moral Education, 14,* 43–55.

Hanley, C. (1951).   Physique and reputation of junior high school boys. *Child Development, 22,* 247–260.

Hannerz, U. (1969).   *Soulside: Inquiries into ghetto culture.* New York: Columbia University Press.

Hanson, D. J. (1980).   Drug education: Does it work? In F. R. Scarpitti & S. K. Datesman (Eds.). *Drugs and the youth culture.* Sage Annual Reviews of Drugs and Alcohol Abuse, Vol 4. (pp. 251–282.) Beverly Hills, CA: Sage Publications.

Hanson, D. J. & Engs, R. C. (1984).   College students' drinking attitudes: 1970–1982. *Psychological Reports, 54,* 300–302.

Harclerode, J. (1980).   The effects of marijuana on reproduction and development. In R. C. Petersen (Ed.). *Marijuana research findings: 1980.* Washington, DC: National Institute on Drug Abuse.

Harding, J., Proshansky, H., Kutner, B., & Chein, I. (1969).   Prejudice and ethnic relations. In G. Lindsey and E. Aronson (Eds.). *Handbook of Social Psychology,* Vol. 5. Reading, MA: Addison-Wesley.

Hart, S. N. & Brassard, M. (1987).   A major threat to children's mental health: Psychological maltreatment. *American Psychologist, 42,* 160–165.

Hartlage, S., Howard, K. I., & Ostrov, E. (1984).   The mental health professional and the normal adolescent. In D. Offer, E. Ostrov, & K. I. Howard (Eds.). *Patterns of adolescent self-image.* (pp. 29–43). New Directions in Mental Health Services, no. 22. San Francisco: Jossey-Bass.

Hartnagel, T. F., Teevan, J. J. Jr., & McIntyre, J. J. (1975).   Television violence and violent behavior. *Social Forces, 54,* 341–351.

Hartshorne, H. & May, M. A. (1928).   *Studies in deceit: General methods and results.* New York: Macmillan.

Hartup, W. W. (1977).   Peers, play and pathology: A new look at the social behavior of children. *Newsletter of the Society for Research in Child Development.* (fall), 1–3.

Hartup, W. W. (1983).   The peer system. In E. M. Heatherington (Ed.). *Carmichael's manual of child psychology. Vol. 4: Socialization, personality, and social development.* (pp. 275–386). New York: John Wiley.

Harvey, O. J., Hunt, D. E., & Schroeder, H. M. (1961).   *Conceptual systems and personality organization.* New York: John Wiley.

Havighurst, R. J. (1972).   *Developmental tasks and education.* (3rd ed.). New York: David McKay.

Havighurst, R. J. & Gottlieb, D. (1975).   Youth and the meaning of work. In R. J. Havighurst and P. H.Dreyer (Eds.). *Youth* Seventy-fourth Yearbook of the National Society for the Study of Education, pt. 1. (pp. 145–160). Chicago: University of Chicago Press.

Hays, J. R., Winburn, G. M., & Bloom, R. (1975).   Marijuana and the law: What young people say. *Journal of Drug Education, 5,* 37–43.

Heald, F., Levy, P. S., Hamil, P.V.V., & Rowland, M. (1974).   *Hemocrit values of youth 12–17 years.* Vital and Health Statistics, series 11, no. 146. Washington, DC: U.S. Government Printing Office.

Healy, J. M. & Stewart, A. J. (1984).   Adaptations to life changes in adolescence. In P. Karoly & J. J. Stefan (Eds.). *Adolescent behavior disorders: Foundations and contemporary concerns* (pp. 39–60). Lexington, MA: D. C. Heath.

Heatherington, E. M. (1972).   Effects of father absence on personality development in adolescent daughters. *Developmental Psychology, 7,* 313–326.

Heatherington, E. M., Cox, M., & Cox, R. (1982).   Effects of divorce on parents and children. In M. E. Lamb (Ed.). *Nontraditional families.* Hillsdale, NJ: Erlbaum.

Heber, R. F. & Dever, R. B. (1970).   Research on education and habituation of the mentally retarded. In H. C. Haywood (Ed.). *Social-cultural aspects of mental retardation.* New York: Appleton-Century-Crofts.

Hembree, W. C., Nahas, G. G., & Huang, H.F.S. (1979).   Changes in human spermatozoa associated with high dose marijuana smoking. In G. G. Nahas and W.D.M. Paton (Eds.). *Marijuana: Biological effects.* (pp. 429–439). New York: Pergammon Press.

Hendin, H., Pollinger, A., Ullman, R., & Carr, A. C. (1981).   *Adolescent marijuana abusers and their families: NIDA Research Monograph 40.* Washington, DC: National Institute on Drug Abuse.

Hendin, H., Pollinger, A., Ullman, R., & Carr, A.C. (1982).   The functions of marijuana abuse for adolescents. *American Journal of Drug and Alcohol Abuse, 8,* 441–456.

Henshaw, S. K. & O'Reilly, K. (1983).   Characteristics of abortion patients in the United States, 1979 and 1980. *Family Planning Perspectives, 15*(1), 5–16.

Herrnstein, R. (1971).   IQ. *Atlantic Monthly, 228* (Sept.), 43–64.

Herron, J. D. (1975).   Piaget for chemists. *Journal of Chemical Education, 52,* 146–150.

Herron, J. D. (1977).   Piaget applied: Suggestions for inaction. Paper presented at the national meeting of the American Chemical Society.

Herzog, A. R., Bachman, J. G., & Johnston, J. (1979).   Young people look at changing sex roles. *Newsletter of the Institute for Social Research, 7* (Spring), 3–7.

Herzog, E. & Sudia,C. E. (1973).   Children in fatherless families. In B. M. Caldwell and H. N. Riccuiti (Eds.). *Review of child development research.* Vol. 3. Chicago: University of Chicago Press.

Hess, R. D. & Goldblatt, I. (1957).   The status of adolescents in American society: A problem of social identity. *Child Development, 28,* 459–468.

Hilgard, E. R. & Bower, G. H. (1975).   *Theories of learning* (4th ed). Englewood Cliffs, NJ: Prentice-Hall.

Himadi, W. G., Ackowitz, H. M., Hinton, R., & Perl, J. (1980).   Minimal dating and its relation to other social problems and general adjustment. *Behavior Therapy, 11,* 345–352.

Hodge, R. W., Siegal, P. M., & Rossi, P. H. (1964).   Occupational prestige of the United States. 1925–63. *American Journal of Sociology, 70* 286–302.

Hoffman, L. (1974).   Fear of success in males and females: 1965 and 1971. *Journal of Consulting and Clinical Psychology, 42,* 353–358.

Holder, A. R. (1981).   Can teenagers participate in research without parental consent? *IRB: A Review of Human Subjects Research, 3*(2), 5–7.

Holinger, P. C., Offer, D., & Simmons, R. (1982).   Prediction of adolescent suicide: A population model. *American Journal of Psychiatry, 139,* 302–307.

Holland, J. L. (1959).   A theory of vocational choice. *Journal of Counseling Psychology, 6,* 35–45.

Holland, J. L. (1973). *Making vocational choices: A theory of careers.* Englewood Cliffs, NJ: Prentice-Hall.

Holland, J. L., Whitney, D. R., Cole., N. S., & Richards, M. J., Jr. (1969). *An empirical occupational classification derived from a theory of personality and intended for practice and research.* ACT Report No. 29, Iowa City: American College Testing Program.

Holmes, T. H. & Rahe, R. H. (1967). The social readjustment scale. *Journal of Psychosomatic Research, 11,* 213–218.

Holstein, C. B. (1976). Irreversible, stepwise sequence in the development of moral judgment: A longitudinal study of males and females. *Child Development, 47,* 51–61.

Holtzman, W. H. & Moore, B. M. (1965). Family structure and youth attitudes. In M. Sherif and C. W. Sherif (Eds.). *Problems of youth: Transition to adult in a changing world.* Chicago: Aldine.

Hooker, E. & Chance, P. (1975). Facts that liberated the gay community. *Psychology Today, 9*(7), 52–55, 101.

Horner, M. (1970). Femininity and successful achievement: A basic inconsistency. In J. M. Bardwick (Ed.). *Feminine personality and conflict.* Belmont, CA: Brooks/Cole.

Horrocks, J. (1976). *The psychology of adolescence.* Boston: Houghton Mifflin.

Horowitz, R. (1982). Adult delinquent gangs in a Chicano community: Masked intimacy and marginality. *Urban Life, 13,* 3–26.

Huba, G. J. & Bentler, P. M. (1980). The role of peer and adult models for drug taking at different stages of adolescence. *Journal of Youth and Adolescence, 9,* 449–465.

Huesmann, L. R., Lagerspetz, K., & Eron, L. D. (1984). Intervening variables in the TV violence-aggression relation: Evidence from two countries. *Developmental Psychology, 16,* 746–775.

Humphrey, L. G. (1957). Characteristics of type concepts with special reference to Sheldon's typology. *Psychological Bulletin, 54,* 218–228.

Hundleby, J. D., Carpenter, R. A., Ross, R.A.J., & Mercer, G. W. (1982). Adolescent drug use and other behaviors. *Journal of Child Psychiatry, 23,* 61–68.

Hunt, D. E. (1971). *Matching models in education: The coordination of teaching methods with student characteristics.* Toronto, Ontario: Ontario Institute for Studies in Education.

Hunt, D.E. (1975). BPE: A challenge found wanting before it was tried. *Review of Educational Research, 45,* 209–230.

Hunt, D. E. & Sullivan, E. V. (1974). *Between psychology and education.* Hinsdale, IL: Dryden Press.

Husain, S. A. & Vandiver, T. (1984). *Suicide in children and adolescents.* New York: Spectrum.

Iacovetta, R. G. (1975). Adolescent-adult interaction and peer group involvement. *Adolescents, 10,* 327–336.

Ingersoll, G. M. (1982). *Adolescents in school and society.* Lexington, MA: D. C. Heath.

Ingersoll, G. M. (1984). Adolescent prejudice: A psychological view. Paper presented to the Invitational Conference on Problems of Racial and Ethnic Relations Among High School Youth, George Mason University.

Ingersoll, G. M. & Goss, S. S. (1981). *Monitoring classroom behavior.* Bloomington, IN: Center for Teacher Education.

Ingersoll, G. M. & Strigari, A. (1983). Adolescent views teacher. *Educational Horizons, 61,* 183–188.

Ingersoll, G. M., Orr, D. P., Herrold, A. J. & Golden, M. P. (1986). Cognitive maturity and self-management in adolescents with insulin-dependent diabetes mellitus. *Journal of Pediatrics, 108,* 620–623.

Ingersoll, G. M., Orr, D. P., Golden, M. P., Vance, M., Warnhoff, S. A., & Kronz, K. K. (1987). Cognitive maturity, stressful events and metabolic control in adolescents with diabetes. Paper presented at the biennial meeting of the Society for Research in Child Development, Baltimore.

Ingersoll, G. M., Pugh, R. C., Harris, J. J. Jr., & Heid, C. A. (1985). Prejudice in the schools:

A study of interracial attitudes among elementary and secondary students. Paper presented to the annual meeting of the American Educational Research Association, Chicago.

Inhelder, B. & Piaget, J. (1958). *The growth of logical thinking from childhood to adolescence.* New York: Basic Books.

Inkeles, A. & Rossi, P. H. (1956). National comparisons of occupational prestige. *American Journal of Sociology, 61,* 329–399.

Irwin, C. E. & Millstein, S. G. (1986). Biopsychosocial correlates of risk-taking behaviors during adolescence. *Journal of Adolescent Health Care, 7,* 825–965.

Ishiyama, F. I. (1984). Shyness: Anxious social sensitivity and self-isolating behavior. *Adolescence, 19,* 903–911.

Jackson, J. (1977). The pregnancy epidemic. *Washington Post* (March 3), C7.

Janis, I. L. & Mann, L. (1976). Coping with decisional conflict. *American Scientist, 64,* 657–667.

Jensen, A. R. (1969). How much can we boost IQ and scholastic achievement. *Harvard Educational Review, 39,* 1–123.

Jensen, A. R. (1972). *Genetics and education.* New York: Harper and Row.

Jensen, G. F. & Rojek, D. G. (1980). *Delinquency: A sociological view.* Lexington, MA: D. C. Heath.

Jepsen, D. A. (1984). The developmental perspective on vocational behavior: A review of theory and research. In S. D. Brown and R. W. Lent (Eds.). *Handbook of counseling psychology.* New York: John Wiley.

Jepsen, D. A. (1985). Predicting job satisfaction from work values expressed seven years earlier. Paper presented at the annual meeting of the American Educational Research Association, Chicago.

Jessor, R. (1979). Marijuana: A review of recent psychosocial research. In R. L. Dupont, A. Goldstein, & J. O'Connell (Eds.). *Handbook on drug abuse.* Washington, DC: National Institute on Drug Abuse.

Jessor, R., Chase, J. A., & Donovan, J. E. (1980). Psychosocial correlates of marijuana use and problem drinking in a national sample of adolescents. *American Journal of Public Health, 70,* 604–613.

Jessor, S. L. & Jessor, R. (1975). Transition from virginity to non-virginity among youth: a social psychologic study over time. *Developmental Psychology, 11,* 473–484.

Jessor, S. L. & Jessor, R. (1977). *Problem behavior and psychosocial development.* New York: Academic Press.

Johnson, B. (1963). On church and sect. *American Sociological Review, 28,* 539–549.

Johnson, D. W. (1981). Social psychology. In F. Farley & N. Gordon (Eds.). *Psychology and education: the state of the union.* Berkeley, CA: McCutcheon Publishing. (a).

Johnson, D. W. (1981). Student-student interaction: The neglected variable in education. *Educational Researcher, 10*(1), 5–10. (b).

Johnson, J. H. (1986). *Life events as stressors in childhood and adolescence.* Beverly Hills, CA: Sage.

Johnson, J. H. & McCutcheon, S. (1980). Assessing life stress in older children and adolescents: Preliminary findings with the Life Events Checklist. In I. G. Sarason & C. D. Speilberger (Eds.). *Stress and anxiety,* Vol. 7. Washington, DC: Hemisphere Publishing.

Johnson, M. (1980). (Ed.). *Toward adolescence: The middle school years. Seventy-ninth Yearbook of the National Society for the Study of Education, Part 1.* Chicago: University of Chicago Press.

Johnston, L. D. (1980). The daily marijuana user. Paper presented to the National Drug and Alcohol Abuse Conference. Washington, DC: Sept. 18.

Johnston, L.D., O'Malley, P. A., & Bachman, J. G. (1984). *Drugs and American high school students: 1975–1983.* Washington, DC: National Institute on Drug Abuse.

Johnston, L. D., O'Malley, P. A., & Bachman, J. G. (1985). *Drugs and American high school students: 1975–1985.* Washington, DC: National Institute on Drug Abuse.

Johnston, L. D., O'Malley, P. A., & Bachman, J. G. (1987). *National trends in drug use and related factors among American high school students and young adults: 1975-1986.* Washington, DC: National Institute on Drug Abuse.

Jones, E. F., Forrest, J. D., Goldman, N., Henshaw, S. K., Lincoln, R., Rosoff, J. I., Westoff, C. F., & Wulf, D. (1985). Teenage pregnancy in developing countries: Determinants and policy implications. *Family Planning Perspectives, 17,* 53-63.

Jones, H. E. (1939). The adolescent growth study: 1. Principles and methods. *Journal of Consulting Psychology, 3,* 157-159 (a).

Jones, H. E. (1939). The adolescent growth study: 2. Procedures. *Journal of Consulting Psychology, 3,* 170-180. (b).

Jones, M. C. (1957). The later careers of boys who were early or late-maturing. *Child Development, 28,* 113-128.

Jones, M. C. (1965). Psychological correlates of somatic development. *Child Development, 36,* 899-911.

Jones, M. C. & Bayley, N. (1950). Physical maturing among boys as related to behavior. *Journal of Educational Psychology, 41,* 129-133.

Kadushin, A. & Martin, J. A. (1981). *Child abuse—An interactional event.* New York: Columbia University Press.

Kagan, J., Sontag, L. W., Baker, C. T., & Nelson, V. L. (1958). Personality and IQ change. *Journal of Social Psychology, 56,* 261-266.

Kalachek, E. (1969). *The youth labor market.* National Manpower Task Force Policy Papers in Human Resources and Industrial relations, no. 12. Washington, DC: U.S. Government Printing Office.

Kalafat, J. & Schulman, A. (1982). Telephone crisis counseling service. In N. S. Giddan & M. J. Austin (eds.), *Peer counseling and self-help groups on campus.* (pp. 27-42). Springfield, IL: Charles C. Thomas.

Kandel, D. (1973). Adolescent marijuana use: Role of parents and peers. *Science, 181,* 1067-1070.

Kandel, D. (1975). Reaching the hard-to-reach: Illicit drug use among high school absentees. *Addictive Diseases, 1,* 465-480.

Kandel, D. B. (1978). *Longitudinal research on drug use: Empirical findings and methodological issues.* New York: John Wiley.

Kandel, D. B. (1978). Similarity in real-life friendship pairs. *Journal of Personality and Social Psychology, 36,* 306-312. (a).

Kandel, D. B. (1978). Homophily, selection and socialization in adolescent friendships. *American Journal of Sociology, 84,* 427-436. (b).

Kandel, D. B. & Davies, M. (1982). Epidemiology of depressive mood in adolescents: An empirical study. *Archives of General Psychiatry, 39,* 1205-1232.

Kantner, J. (1983). Sex and pregnancy among American adolescents. *Educational Horizons, 61,* 189-194.

Kaplan, A. D. (1974). *Textbook of adolescent psychopathology and treatment.* Springfield, IL: Charles C. Thomas.

Kaplan, S. L., Hong, G. K., & Weinhold, C. (1984). Epidemiology of depressive symptomology in adolescents. *Journal of the American Academy of Child Psychiatry, 23,* 91-98.

Katchadorian, H. A. (1977). *The biology of adolescence.* San Francisco: W. H.Freeman.

Katz, I. (1967). The socialization of academic motivation in minority group children. *Nebraska Symposium on Motivation.* Lincoln, NE: University of Nebraska Press.

Kazdin, A. E. (1987). *Conduct disorders in childhood and adolescence.* Beverly Hills: Sage.

Keating, D. P. (1976). (Ed.). *Intellectual talent: Research and development.* Baltimore, MD: Johns Hopkins University Press.

Kegan, R. E. (1982). *The evolving self.* Cambridge, MA: Harvard University Press.

Kegan, R. E., Noam, G. C., & Rogers, L. (1982). The psychologic of emotion: A neo-Piagetian view. In D. Cicchetti & P. Hesse (Eds.). *Emotional development.* New Directions in Child Development, no. 16. (pp. 105-129). San Francisco: Jossey-Bass.

Keniston, K. (1965). *The uncommitted.* New York: Harcourt, Brace, Jovanovich.

Keniston, K. (1968). Heads and seekers: Drugs on campus, counterculture and American society. *American Scholar, 36,* 97–112.

Keniston, K. (1970). Youth: A "new" stage of life. *American Scholar, 39,* 631–641.

Kerlinger, F. N. (1973). *Foundations for behavioral research.* New York: Holt Rinehart and Winston.

Kett, J. F. (1977). *Rites of passage: Adolescence in America.* New York: Basic Books.

Kimball, C. P. (1982). Stress and psychosomatic illness. *Journal of Psychosomatic Research, 26,* 63–71.

King, K., Balswick, J. O., & Robinson, I. E. (1977). Sexual revolution among college females. *Journal of Marriage and the Family, 39,* 455–459.

Kinsey, A. C., Pomeroy, W. B., & Martin, E. E. (1948). *Sexual behavior in the human male.* Philadelphia: W. B. Saunders.

Kinsey, A. C., Pomeroy, W. B., Martin, E. E., & Gephart, P. H. (1953). *Sexual behavior in the human female.* Philadelphia: W. B. Saunders.

Kleck, R. E., Richardson, S. A., & Ronald, L. (1974). Physical appearance cues and interpersonal attraction in children. *Child Development, 45,* 305–310.

Kloos, P. (1971). *Maroni River Caribs of Surinam.* Atlantic Highlands, NJ: Humanities Press.

Kohlberg, L. (1958). The development of modes of moral thinking and choice in years ten to sixteen. Unpublished doctoral dissertation. University of Chicago.

Kohlberg, L. (1964). Development of moral character and moral ideology. In M. L. Hoffman and L. W. Hoffman (Eds.). *Review of child development research.* vol. 1. (pp. 383–432). New York: Russell Sage Foundation.

Kohlberg, L. (1966). Moral education in the schools: A developmental view. *School Review, 74,* 1–29.

Kohlberg, L. (1967). A cognitive-developmental analysis of children's sex-role concepts and attitudes. In E. E. Maccoby (Ed.). *The development of sex differences.* Stanford, CA: Stanford University Press.

Kohlberg, L. (1981). *Essays on moral development: The philosophy of moral development.* New York: Harper & Row.

Kohlberg, L. & Gilligan, C. (1971). The adolescent as philosopher: The discovery of self in a post-conventional world. *Daedalus, 100,* 1051–1086.

Kohn, M. L. (1977). *Class and conformity: A study in values.* (2nd ed.). Chicago: University of Chicago Press.

Kolata, G. B. (1976). Gonorrhea: More of a problem but less of a mystery. *Science, 192* (Apr 16), 244–247.

Kolodny, R. C., Masters, W. H., Kolodner, R. M., & Toro, G. (1974). Depression of plasma testosterone levels after chronic, intensive marijuana use. *New England Journal of Medicine, 290,* 872–874.

Konopka, G. (1983). Young girls: A portrait of adolescence: II: sexuality. *Child and Youth Services, 6*(3–4), 30–55.

Konopka, G. (1983). Adolescent suicide. *Exceptional Children, 49,* 390–394.

Koos, M. B. & Oros, C. J. (1982). Sexual experiences survey: a research instrument investigating aggression and victimization. *Journal of Consulting and Clinical Psychology, 50,* 455–457.

Kopecky, G. (1974). The dating scene. *Seventeen, 35,* 25.

Kounin, J. S. (1970). *Discipline and group management in classrooms.* New York: Holt, Rinehart and Winston.

Kovar, M. G. (1979). Some indicators of health related behavior among adolescents in the United States. *Public Health Reports, 94,* 109–118.

Kuder, F. & Diamond, E. E. (1979). *Occupational Interest Survey, Form D D., General manual* (second edition). Chicago: Science Research Associates.

Kuhlen, R. G. & Arnold, M. (1944). Age differences in religious beliefs and problems in adolescence. *Journal of Genetic Psychology, 65,* 291–300.

Labouvie, E. W. (1976). Longitudinal designs. In P. M Bentler, D. J. Lettieri, & G. A. Austin (Eds.). *Data analysis strategies and designs for substance abuse research.* Research Issues, no. 13. (pp. 45–60). Washington, DC: National Institute on Drug Abuse, U.S. Government Printing Office.

Lambert, W. E. & Klineberg, O. (1967). *Children's views of foreign people.* New York: Appleton-Century-Crofts.

Lanese, R. R., Banks, F. R., & Keller, M. D. (1972). Smoking behavior in a teenage population: A multivariate conceptual approach. *American Journal of Public Health, 62,* 807–813.

Langer, E. J. & Abelson, R. P. (1974). A patient by any other name . . . clinician group differences in labeling bias. *Journal of Consulting and Clinical Psychology, 42,* 4–9.

Lanzetta, J. T. & Hannah, T. E. (1969). Reinforcing behavior of "naive" trainers. *Journal of Personality and Social Psychology, 11,* 245–252.

Lapsley, D. K. (1985). Elkind on egocentrism. *Developmental Review, 5,* 218–227.

Lapsley, D. K., Milstead, M., Quintana, S. N., Flannery, D., & Buss, R. R. (1986). Adolescent egocentrism and formal operations: Tests of a theoretical assumption, *Developmental Psychology, 22,* 800–807.

Lawrence, J. (1985). The immune system in AIDS. *Science, 253,* 84–93.

Lee, G. R. (1977). Age at marriage and marital satisfaction: A multivariate analysis with implications for marital stability. *Journal of Marriage and the Family, 39,* 493–504.

Leemon, T. A. (1972). *The rites of passage in a student culture.* New York: Teachers College Press.

Lefkowitz, M. M. & Burton, N. (1978). Childhood depression: A critique of the concept. *Psychological Bulletin, 85,* 716–726.

Leon, G. R. (1976). Current directions in the treatment of obesity. *Psychological Bulletin, 83,* 557–578.

Leon, G. R. & Roth, L. (1977). Obesity: Psychological causes, correlations, and speculations. *Psychological Bulletin, 84,* 117–139.

Levine, H.D., Karnisky, W., Palfrey, J. S., Meltzer, L. J., & Fenton, T. (1985). A study of risk factor complexes in early adolescent delinquency. *American Journal of Diseases of Children, 139,* 50–56.

Levine, S. V. (1979). The psychological and social effects of youth unemployment. *Children Today, 8*(6), 6–9.

Leynes, C. (1980). Keep or adopt. *Child Psychiatry and Human Development, 10,* 185.

Liberty, B. E., Jones, H C., & McGuire, J. E. (1963). Agemate perceptions of intelligence, creativity and achievement. *Perceptual and Motor Skills, 16,* 194.

Lincoln, Y. S. & Guba, E. G. (1985). *Naturalistic inquiry.* Beverly Hills, CA: Sage Publications.

Lipsitz, J. (1977). *Growing up forgotten.* Lexington, MA: Lexington Books.

Livesley, W. J. & Bromley, D. B. (1973). *Person perception in childhood and adolescence.* London: Wiley.

Loevinger, J. (1976). *Ego development.* San Francisco: Jossey-Bass.

Long, T. L. & Long, L. (1984). *The handbook for latchkey children and their parents.* New York: Berkeley Books.

Macdonald, D. I. (1982). The relationship of moderate marijuana use and adolescent behavior. In *Marijuana and youth: Clinical observations on motivation and learning.* Washington, DC: National Institute on Drug Abuse.

Macdonald, E. I. (1984). Drugs, drinking, and adolescence. *American Journal of Diseases in Children, 138,* 117–126.

MacMahon, B. (1973). *Age at menarche.* Vital and Health Statistics, Series 11, no. 133. Washington, DC: U.S. Government Printing Office.

Maddox, G. L., Bach, K. W., & Lieberman, U. R. (1968). Overweight as a social deviance and disability. *Journal of Health and Social Behavior, 9,* 287–298.

Malina, R. (1980). Physical activity, growth and functional capacity. In F. Johnston, A. Roche & C. Susanne (Eds.) *Human physical growth and maturation.* New York: Plenum.

Maloney, M. J. & Klykylo, W. M. (1983).   An overview of anorexia, bulimia and obesity in children and adolescents. *Journal of the American Academy of Child Psychiatry, 22,* 99–107.

Marble, A. P. (1894).   City school administration. *Educational Review, 8,* 154–168.

Marcia, J. E. (1966).   Development and validation of ego identity status. *Journal of Personality and Social Psychology, 3,* 551–555.

Marcia, J. E. (1980).   Identity in adolescence. In J. Adelson (Ed.) *Handbook of adolescent psychology.* (pp. 159–187). New York: John Wiley.

Markus, H. & Nurius, D. (1987).   Possible selves. *American Psychologist, 41,* 954–969.

Marsh, R. W. (1985).   Phreoblysis: Real or chimera? *Child Development, 56,* 1059–1061.

Martin, H. (1976).   *The battered child.* Cambridge, MA: Harvard University Press.

Maslow, A. (1954).   *Motivation and personality.* New York: Harper and Row, 1954.

Maslow, A. H. & Sakoda, J. M. (1952).   Volunteer-error in the Kinsey study. *Journal of Abnormal and Social Psychology, 47,* 259–262.

Masterson, J. F. (1967).   The symptomatic adolescent five years later: He didn't grow out of it. *American Journal of Psychiatry, 123,* 1338–1345.

Matza, D. (1964).   *Delinquency and drift.* New York: John Wiley.

Maurer, R. E. (1982).   Dropout prevention: An intervention model for today's high schools. *Phi Delta Kappan, 10,* 470–475.

McAlister, A. L., Perry, C., & Maccoby, N. (1979).   Adolescent smoking: Onset and prevention. *Pediatrics, 63,* 650–658.

McCabe, M. P. & Collins, J. K. (1983).   The sexual and affectional attitudes and experiences of Australian adolescents during dating: The effects of age, church attendance, type of school, and socioeconomic class. *Journal of Sexual Behavior, 12,* 525–539.

McCormack, W. M., Rosner, B., McComb, D. E., Evrard, J. R., & Zinner, S. H. (1985).   Infection with chlamyda trachomatis in female college students. *American Journal of Edipemiology, 121,* 107–115.

McCreary-Juhasz, A. (1975).   Sexual decision-making: The crux of the adolescent problem. In R. E. Grinder (Ed.) *Studies in adolescence.* (pp. 340–351). New York: Macmillan.

McGlothlin, W. H. & West, L. J. (1976).   The marijuana problem: An overview. *American Journal of Psychiatry, 125,* 1126–1134.

McFall, R. M. & Dodge, K. A. (1982).   Self-management and interpersonal skills learning. In P. Karoly & K. H. Kanfer (Eds.) *Self-management and behavior change.* (pp. 353–392). Elmford, NY: Pergammon.

McKeachie, W. J. (1976).   Psychology in America's bicentennial year. *American Psychologist, 31,* 819–833.

McQueen, R. (1973).   The token economy and a target behavior. *Psychological Reports, 32,* 599–602.

Mead, M. (1928).   *Coming of age in Samoa.* New York: Morrow.

Mead, M. (1969).   *Culture and commitment: A study of the generation gap.* New York: Basic Books.

Meadow, M. J. & Kahoe, R. D. (1984).   *The psychology of religion: Religion in individual lives.* New York: Harper & Row.

Meeks, J E. (1971).   *The fragile alliance.* Baltimore: Williams and Wilkins.

Mellinger, G. D., Somers, R. H., Davidson, S. T., & Mannheim., D. I. (1976).   The amotivational syndrome and the college student. *Annals of the New York Academy of Sciences, 282,* 37–55.

Mercy. J. A., Tolsma, D. D., Smith, J. C., & Conn, J. M. (1984).   Patterns of youth suicide in the United States. *Educational Horizons, 64,* 124–127.

Mettlin, C. (1976).   Peer and other influences on smoking behavior. *Journal of School Health, 46,* 529–536.

Metz, M. H. (1978).   Clashes in the classroom: The importance of norms of authority. Paper presented at the annual meeting of the American Educational Research Association, Toronto, Canada.

Messick, A. C. & Messick, J. E. (1979). Symptamology of depression in adolescence. *Journal of Personality Assessment, 43,* 267–275.

Milavsky, J. R., Kesslar, R., Stipp, H., & Rubens, W. S. (1982). Television and aggression: Results of a panel study. In D. Pearl, L. Bouthilet, and J. Lazar (Eds.) *Television and behavior: Vol. 2* (pp. 138–157). Washington, DC: National Institute of Mental Health.

Milgram, G. G. (1974). Alcohol education in the schools perceived by educators and students. *Journal of Alcohol and Drug Education, 20,* 4–12.

Miller, G. A. (1956). The magic number seven, plus or minus two: Some limits on our capacity for processing information. *Psychological Review, 63,* 81–97.

Miller, J. (1975). Suicide in adolescence. *Adolescence, 8,* 11–24.

Minard, R. D. (1931). Race attitudes of Iowa children. *University of Iowa Studies in Character, 4,* No. 2.

Minuchin, S. (1974). *Families and family therapy.* Cambridge, MA: Harvard University Press.

Minuchin, P. (1985). Families and individual development: Provocations from the field of family therapy. *Child Development, 56,* 289–302.

Mitchell, J. C. (1964). The differences in English and American rating of the prestige of occupations. *British Journal of Sociology, 15,* 166–173.

Mitchell, M. (1977). Attitudes of adolescent girls toward vocational education. Final Report. Bloomington, IN: School of Education, Indiana University.

Money, J. (1973). Sex education for normal and hypopituitary patients. In S. Raiti (Ed.) *Advances in human growth hormone research.* Washington, DC: U.S. Government Printing Office.

Money, J. (1980). The future of sex and gender. *Journal of Clinical Child Psychology, 9,* 132–133.

Montemayor, R. & Eisen, M. (1977). The development of self-conceptions from childhood to adolescence. *Developmental Psychology, 13,* 314–319.

Moreno, J. L. (1953). *Who shall survive? Foundations of sociometry, group psychotherapy and sociodrama.* (3rd edition). Beacon, NY: Beacon House.

Moriarty, D. & McCabe, A. E. (1977). Studies of television and youth sport. In *Ontario Royal Commission on Violence in the Communication Industry Report.* Vol. 5. Toronto, Ontario, Canada: Queen's Printer for Canada.

Morse, L. C. (1981). Increasing unemployment and changing labor market expectations among black teenagers. *American Economic Review, 71,* 374–379.

Moynihan, D. P. (1969). *Maximum feasible misunderstandings.* New York: Free Press.

Musgrove, F. (1965). *Youth and the social order.* Bloomington, IN: Indiana University Press.

Mussen, P. J. (Ed.). (1970). *Carmichael's manual of child psychology.* New York: John Wiley.

Mussen, P. J. (Ed.). (1983). *Handbook of child psychology* (Fourth edition). New York: John Wiley.

Myrdal. G. (1944). *An American dilemma.* New York: Harper.

Naisbitt, J. (1982). *Megatrends.* New York: Warner Communications.

National Academy of Sciences, National Research Council. (1986). *Risking the future: adolescent sexuality, pregnancy and child bearing.* Washington, DC: National Academy Press.

National Commission on Excellence in Education. (1983). *A nation at risk: The imperative for educational reform.* Washington, DC: National Institute for Education.

National Institute for Juvenile Justice and Delinquency Prevention. (1977). *Juristiction— status offenses.* Vol. 5. Washington, DC: U.S.Government Printing Office.

National Institute on Mental Health. (1986). *Adolescence and depression.* Bethesda, MD: U.S. Department of Health and Human Services.

National Science Board Commission on Precollege Education in Mathematics, Science and Technology. (1983). *Educating Americans for the 21st century.* Washington, DC: National Science Foundation.

Nesselroade, J. R. & Baltes, P. B. (Eds.). (1978). *Longitudinal research in the study of behavior and development.* New York: Academic Press.

Newcomb, T. M. (1966). The general nature of peer group influence. In T. M. Newcomb & E. K. Wilson (Eds.) *College peer groups.* Chicago: Aldine.

Nicol, S. E. & Gottesman, I. I. (1983). Clues to the genetics and neurobiology of schizophrenia. *American Scientist, 71,* 398–403.

Norton, A. J. & Glick, P. C. (1986). One parent families: A social and economic profile. *Family Relations, 35,* 9–17.

Norton, A. J. & Moorman, J. E. (1986). Marriage and divorce patterns of U.S. women. Paper presented at the annual meeting of the American Educational Research Association, San Francisco.

O'Brien, G. (1976). Male professors found cool to female issues. *AAUP Bulletin,* April.

O'Connor, R. D. (1969). Modification of social withdrawal through symbolic modeling. *Journal of Applied Behavioral Analysis, 2,* 15–22.

Oden, S. & Asher, S. R. (1977). Coaching children for social skills in friendship making. *Child Development, 48,* 495–506.

Offer, D. (1969). *The psychological world of the teen-ager: a study of normal adolescent boys.* New York: Basic Books.

Offer, D. & Offer, J. (1975). *From teenage to young manhood.* New York: Basic Books.

Offer, D., Ostrov, E., & Howard, K. I. (1981). *The adolescent: A psychological self-portrait.* New York: Basic Books.

Offer, D., Ostrov, E., & Howard, K. I. (1982). *The Offer Self-Image Questionnaire for Adolescents: A manual.* (3rd ed.) Chicago: Michael Reese Hospital.

Offer, D., Ostrov, E., & Howard, K. I. (1984). The self-image of normal adolescents. In D. Offer, E. Ostrov, & K. I. Howard (Eds.) *Patterns of adolescent self-image.* (pp. 5–16). New Directions in Mental Health Services, no. 22. San Francisco: Jossey-Bass.

Ohlin, L. & Cloward, R. (1973). The prevention of delinquent subcultures. In M. S. Weinberg & E. Rubington (Eds.) *The solution of social problems.* Glencoe, IL: Free Press.

Oldham, D. G. (1976). Adolescent turmoil: A myth revisited. *Journal of Continuing Education in Psychiatry, 39,* 23–32.

O'Leary, K. D. (1984). Marital discord and children: Problems, strategies, methodologies and results. In A. Doyle, D. Gold, and D. S. Moskowitz (Eds.) *Children in families under stress.* New Directions in Child Development, no. 24. San Francisco: Jossey-Bass.

O'Leary, V. E. (1974). Some attitudinal barriers to occupational aspirations in women. *Psychological Bulletin, 81,* 809–826.

Olsen, N. J. & Willemsen, E. W. (1978). Fear of success: Fact of artifact? *Journal of Psychology, 98,* 65–70.

Olson, D. H., Sprenkle. D. H., & Russell, C. S. (1979). Circumplex model of marital and family systems: I: Cohesion, and adaptability dimensions, family types, and clinical applications. *Family Process, 18,* 3–28.

Olson, L. & Robbins, J. (1982). Psychological barriers to contraceptive use among adolescent women. In I. R. Stuart and C. F. Wells (Eds.) *Pregnancy in adolescence: needs, problems and management.* (pp. 177–194). New York: Van Nostrand Reinhold.

Oltmanns, T. F., Broderick, J. E., & O'Leary, K. D. (1977). Material adjustment and the efficacy of behavior therapy with children. *Journal of Consulting and Clinical Psychology, 45,* 724–729.

Oriel, J. D. (1977). Chlamydia trachomatis infections. *Medical Aspects of Human Sexualtiy, 14,* 58–60.

Orstein, M. D. (1975). *Entry into the American labor force.* New York: Academic Press.

Osipow, S. H. (1983). *Theories of career development.* Englewood Cliffs, NJ: Prentice-Hall.

Owens, W. A. (1953). Age and mental abilities: A longitudinal study. *Genetic Psychology Monographs, 48,* 3–54.

Owens, W. A. (1966). Age and mental abilities: A second follow-up. *Journal of Educational Psychology, 57,* 311–325.

Paperny, D. M. & Deisher, R. W. (1983). Maltreatment of adolescents: The relationship to a predisposition toward violent behavior and delinquency. *Adolescence, 18,* 499–506.

Pasamanick, B. & Knoblock, H. (1961). Epidemiologic studies on the complications of pregnancy and the birth process. In G. Caplan (Ed.) *Prevention of mental disorders in children*. New York: Basic Books.

Pasanella, A. L. & Volkmor, C. B. (1977). *Coming back . . . or never leaving*. Columbus, OH: Charles E. Merrill.

Patterson, G. R. (1986). Performance models for antisocial boys. *American Psychologist, 41,* 432–444.

Peck, M. (1968). Suicide motivations in adolescence. *Adolescence, 3,* 109–118.

Pederson, L. L., Baskerville, J. C., & Lefcoe, N. M. (1981). Multivariate prediction of cigarette smoking among children in grades six, seven, and eight. *Journal of Drug Education, 11,* 191–203.

Peevers, B. H. & Second, P. F. (1973). Developmental changes in attribution of descriptive concepts to persons. *Journal of Personality and Social Psychology, 27,* 57–72.

Pelton, L. (1978). Child abuse and neglect: The myth of classlessness. *American Journal of Orthopsychiatry, 48,* 608–617.

Pervin, L. A. (1968). Performance and satisfaction as a function of individual-environment fit. *Psychological Bulletin, 69,* 56–68.

Petersen, A. C. & Crockett, L. (1985). Pubertal timing and gender effects on adjustment. *Journal of Youth and Adolescence, 14,* 191–205.

Petersen, A. C. & Taylor, B. (1980). The biological approach to adolescence: Biological change and psychological adaptation. In J. Adelson (Ed.) *Handbook of adolescent psychology*. (pp. 117–155). New York: John Wiley.

Petersen, R. C. (1984). Marijuana overview. In M. D. Glantz (Ed.) *Correlates and consequences of marijuana use*. Washington, DC: National Institute on Drug Abuse.

Pettigrew, T. (1967). Social evolution theory: Convergences and applications. In D. Levine (Ed.) *Nebraska Symposium on Motivation, Vol. 15*. Lincoln, NE: University of Nebraska Press.

Piaget, J. (1932). *The moral development of the child*. New York: Free Press (1965).

Piaget, J. (1967). *Six psychological studies*. New York: Random House.

Piaget, J. (1970). Piaget's theory. In P. H. Mussen (Ed.) *Carmichael's manual of child psychology*. (pp. 703–732). New York: John Wiley.

Piers, E. V. (1969). *Manual for the Piers-Harris Children's Self Concept Scale: How I Feel About Myself*. Los Angeles, CA: Western Psychological Services.

Piers, E. V. & Harris, D. B. (1964). Age and other correlates of self-concept in children. *Journal of Educational Psychology, 55,* 91–95.

Pinney, J. M. (1979). The largest, preventable cause of death in the United States. *Public Health Reports, 94,* 107–108.

Price, D. O. (1974). Constructing cohort data from discrepant age intervals and irregular reporting periods. *Social Science Quarterly, 24,* 167–174.

Public Health Service. (1986). *Public Health Service plan for the prevention and control of AIDS for the AIDS virus*. Report of the Coolfront Planning Conference, June 4 to 6.

Purkey, S. C. & Smith, M. S. (1983). Effective schools: A review. *Elementary School Journal, 83,* 427–452.

Rabkin, J. G. & Struening, E. L. (1976). Life events, stress, and illness. *Science, 194,* 1013–1020.

Rachel, J. V., Williams, J. R., Brehm, M. L., Cavanaugh, B., Moore, R. P., & Eckerman, N. C. (1975). *A national study of adolescent drinking behavior, attitudes and correlates*. Washington, DC: National Institute on Alcohol Abuse and Alcoholism.

Rapaport, R. (1963). Normal crises, family structure, and mental health. *Family Process, 2,* 265–276.

Raven, J. (1960). *Guide to Standard Progressive Matrices*. London: H. K. Lewis.

Rehberg, R. A. & Rosenthal, E. R. (1978). *Class and merit in the American high school: An assessment of the revisionist and meritocratic arguments*. New York: Longman.

Reisman, J. M. (Ed.). (1986). *Behavior disorders in infants, children, and adolescents*. New York: Random House.

Reisner, R. M. (1975). Acne vulgaris. In D. C.Garrell (Ed.) *The Pediatrics Clinics of North America, 20*(4), 851–864.

Research for Better Schools (1976). *Planning assistance program to reduce school violence and disruption.* Philadelplhia, PA: (Author).

Rest, J. R., Davison, M. L., & Robbins, S. (1978). Age trends in judging moral issues: A review of cross-sectional, longitudinal, and sequential studies of the Defining Issues Test. *Child Development, 49,* 263–279.

Richardson, S. A, Hastorf, A. H., Goodman, N. & Dornbush, S. M. (1961). Cultural uniformity in reaction to physical disabilities. *American Sociological Review, 26,* 241–247.

Robbins, J. (1977). Even a moonie has civil rights. *Nation, 224* (Mar), 30–32.

Robbins, J. M. (1984). Out of wedlock abortion and delivery: The importance of the male partner. *Social Problems, 31,* 334–350.

Roche, A., Roberts, J., & Hamill, P. (1976). *Skeletal maturity of youths 12–17 years: United States.* Rockville, MD: National Center for Health Statistics (Series 11, No. 160).

Rodin, J. (1981). Current status of the internal-external hypothesis for obesity. *American Psychologist, 36,* 361–372.

Rodman, H., Pratto, D. J., & Nelson, R. S. (1985). Child care arrangements and children's functioning: A comparison of self-care and adult care children. *Developmental Psychology, 21,* 413–418.

Rogers, E. (1970). Group influence on student drinking. In G. L. Maddox (Ed.) *The domestic drug: Drinking among collegians.* New Haven: College and University Press.

Romer, N. (1975). The motive to avoid success and its effect on performance in school age males and females. *Developmental Psychology, 11,* 689–699.

Romer, N. (1981). *The sex-role cycle.* New York: McGraw-Hill.

Rosenberg, M. (1965). *Society and the adolescent self-image.* Princeton: Princeton University Press.

Rosenberg, M. (1975). The dissonent context and the adolescent self-concept. In S. E. Dragastin & G. H. Elder (Eds.) *Adolescence in the life cycle.* (pp. 97–116). New York: Halstead Press.

Rosenberg, M. (1979). *Conceiving the self.* New York: Basic Books.

Rosenberg, M. & Simmons, R. G. (1972). *Black and white self-esteem: The urban school child.* ASA Rose Monograph Series Publication, Washington, DC: American Sociological Association.

Rosenshine, B. V. & Berliner, D. C. (1978). Academic engaged time. *British Journal of Teacher Education, 4,* 3–16.

Roszak, T. (1969). *The making of a counterculture.* New York: Doubleday.

Rothkopf, E. Z. (1968). Two scientific approaches to the management of instruction. In R. M. Gagne & W. J. Gephart (Eds.) *Learning research and school subjects.* (pp. 107–131). Itaska, IL: F. E. Peacock.

Rotter, J B. (1966). Generalized expectancies for internal vs. external control of reinforcement. *Psychological Monographs, 80,* (1, Whole No. 609).

Rubington, E. & Weinberg, H. S. (1978). *Deviance: The interactionist perspective* (3rd. ed.) New York: Mqacmillan.

Ruble, D. M. & Brooks-Gunn, J. (1982). The experience of menarche. *Child Development, 53,* 1557–1566.

Rumberger, R. W. (1987). High school dropouts: A review of issues and evidence. *Review of Educational Research, 57,* 101–121.

Rushton, J. P. (1982). Television and prosocial behavior. In D. Pearl, L. Bouthilet, and J. Lazar (Eds.) *Television and behavior: Vol. 2.* (pp. 248–257). Washington, DC: National Institute of Mental Health.

Rutter, M. (1978). Early sources of competence. In J. S. Bruner and A. Garton (Eds.) *Human growth and development.* Oxford: Clarendon Press.

Rutter, M. (1980). *Changing youth in a changing society.* Cambridge, MA: Harvard University Press.

Rutter, M. (1983). Developmental psychopathology. In E. M. Heatherington (Ed.) *Handbook of child psychology. Vol. 4: Socialization, personality and social development.* New York: John Wiley.

Rutter, M., Graham, P., Chadwick, O.F.D. & Yule, W. (1976). Adolescent turmoil: Fact or fiction? *Journal of Child Psychology and Psychiatry, 17,* 653–686.

Ryan, C. W. (1978). Practical linkages between career guidance and career education. *Viewpoints in Teaching and Learning, 54*(1), 10–19.

Saario, T. N., Jacklin, C. N., & Tuttle, C. K. (1973). Sex-role stereotyping in the schools. *Harvard Educational Review, 43,* 366–416.

Sach, A. R., Keller, J. F., & Hinkle, D. E. (1984). Premarital sexual intercourse: A test of the effects of peer groups, religiosity, and sexual guilt. *Journal of Sex Research, 20,* 168–185.

Sadker, M. & Sadker, D. (1974). Sexism in the schools: An issue for the 70s'. *Journal of the National Association of Women Deans, Administrators and Counselors, 37,* 69–78.

Saghir, R. C. & Robins, E. (1973). *Male and female homosexuality: a comprehensive investigation.* Baltimore: Williams and Wilkins.

Sarason, S. B. & Kalber, M. (1985). The school as a social situation. *Annual Review of Psychology, 36,* 115–140.

Scanlon, J. (1973). *Intellectual status of youths.* Vital and Health Statistics, series 11, no. 128. Washington. DC: U.S. Government Printing Office.

Scanlon, J. (1975). *Self-reported health behavior and attitudes of youths 12–17 years.* Vital and Health Statistics, Series 11, no. 147. Washington, DC: U.S. Government Printing Office.

Scarlett, H. H., Press, A. N., & Crockett, W. H. (1971). Children's descriptions of peers: A Wernerian analysis. *Child Development, 42,* 439–453.

Schachter, S. (1959). *The psychology of affiliation.* Stanford, CA: Stanford University Press.

Schachter, S., Goodman, R., & Gordon, A. (1968). Effects of fear, food deprivation and obesity on eating. *Journal of Personality and Social Psychology, 10,* 91–97.

Schachter, S. & Rodin, J. (1975). *Obese humans and rats.* New York: Academic Press.

Schaie, K. W. (1973). A general model for the study of developmental problems. *Psychological Bulletin. 64,* 92–107.

Schaie, K. W. & Strother, C. R. (1968). A cross-sequential study of age changes in cognitive behavior. *Psychological Bulletin, 70,* 671–680.

Schalmo, G. B. & Levin. B. H. (1974). Presence of the double standard in a college population. *Psychological Reports, 34,* 227–230.

Schlesier-Stroop, B. (1984). Bulimia: A review of the literature, *Psychological Bulletin, 95,* 247–257.

Schneider, F. W. & Vanmastrigt, T. (1974). Adolescent-preadolescent differences in beliefs and attitudes about cigarette smoking. *Journal of Psychology. 87,* 71–81.

Schofield, J. W. & Sager, H. A. (1983). Desegregation, school practices, and student race relations. In C. H. Rossell & W. D. Hawley (Eds.) *The consequences of school desegregation.* (pp. 58–102). Philadelphia: Temple University Press.

Schultes, R. E. & Hofmann, A. (1979). *Plants of the Gods: Origins of hallucinogenic use.* New York: McGraw-Hill.

Schultes, R. E. & Hoffmann, A. (1980). *The botany and chemistry of hallucinogens.* Springfield, IL: C. Thomas.

Schulz, B., Bohrnstedt, G. W., Borgatta, E. F., & Evans, R. R. (1977). Explaining premarital sexual intercourse among college students: A causal model. *Social Forces, 56,* 148–165.

Sears, R. R., Maccoby, E., & Levin, H. (1957). *Patterns of child rearing.* New York: Harper and Row.

Selman, R. L. (1980). *The growth of interpersonal understanding: Developmental and clinical analyses.* New York: Academic Press.

Selzer, C. C. & Mayer. J. (1965). A simple criterion of obesity. *Postgraduate Medicine, 38*(2), a:101–a:107.

Sgroi, S. (1982). *Handbook of clinical intervention in child sexual abuse.* Lexington, MA: Lexington Books.

Shah, F., Zelnik, M., & Kantner, J. F. (1975).   Unprotected intercourse among unwed teenagers. *Family Planning Perspectives, 7*(1), 39–44.

Sheldon, W. H. (1944).   Constitutional factors in personality. In J. McV. Hunt (Ed.) *Personality and behavioral disorders.* New York: Ronald Press.

Sherman, S. J., Presson, C., Chassin, L., Bensenberg, M., Corty. E., & Olshavsky, R. (1982).   Smoking intentions in adolescents: Direct experience and predictability. *Personality and Social Psychology Bulletin, 8,* 376–383.

Shostak, A., McLouth. G., & Seng, L. (1984).   *Men and abortions: lessons, losses, and love.* New York: Praeger.

Shuey, A. M. (1966).   *The testing of Negro intelligence.* (2nd ed). New York: Social Science Press.

Siegal, C.L.F. (1976).   Sex differences in the occupational choices of second graders. *Journal of Vocational Behavior, 3,* 15–19.

Sieglar, R. S. & Liebert, R. M. (1975).   Acquisition of formal scientific reasoning by 10- and 13-year olds: Designing a factorial experiment. *Developmental Psychology, 11,* 401–402.

Sigal, H. & Aronson, E. (1969).   Liking as a function of physical attractiveness and nature of the evaluations. *Journal of Experimental Social Psychology, 5,* 93–100.

Sigal, H. & Michela, J. (1976).   I'll bet you say that to all the girls: Physical attractiveness and reaction to praise. *Journal of Personality. 44.* 611–626.

Sigusch, V. & Schmidt, G. (1973).   Teenage boys and girls in West Germany. *Journal of Sex Research, 9,* 107–123.

Siman, M. L. (1977).   Application of a new model of peer group influence to naturally existing adolescent friendship groups. *Child Development, 48,* 270–274.

Simmons, R. G. & Blyth, D. A. (1987).   *Moving into adolescence: The impact of pubertal change and school context.* New York: Aldene, Hawthorne.

Simmons, R. G., Blyth, D. A., VanCleave, E. F., & Bush, D. M. (1979).   Entry into early adolescence: The impact of school structure, puberty, and early dating on self-esteem. *American Sociological Review, 44,* 948–967.

Singell, L. D. (1966).   Some private and social aspects of the labor mobility of young workers. *The Quarterly Review of Business and Economics, 6*(1).

Singer, J. & Singer, D. G. (1976).   Can TV stimulate imaginative play? *Journal of Communication, 26*(3), 74–80.

Singer, J. J. & Wynne, L. C. (1965).   Thought disorder and family relations of schizophrenics. *Archives of General Psychiatry, 12,* 201–212.

Sizer, T. (1984).   *Horace's compromise: The dilemma of the American high school.* Boston: Houghton Mifflin.

Smith, S. L. (1984).   Significant research in the etiology of child abuse. *Social Casework, 65,* 337–346.

Smith, S. M. (1975).   *The battered child.* London: Butterworths.

Smith, T. E. (1970).   Foundations of parental influence on adolescents. An application of social power theory. *American Sociological Review, 35,* 860–873.

Smith, T.E. (1976).   Push versus pull: Intra-family peer group variables as possible determinants of adolescent orientations toward parents. *Youth and Society, 8,* 5–28.

Snyderman, M. & Rothman, S. (1987).   Survey of expert opinion on intelligence and aptitude testing. *American Psychologist, 42,* 137–144.

Solomon, T. (1973).   History and demography of child abuse . *Pediatrics, 51,* 1152–1156.

Sorensen, R. (1973).   *Adolescent sexuality in contemporary America.* New York: World.

Spanier, G. B. (1976).   Formal and informal sex education as determinants of premarital sexual behavior. *Archives of Sexual Behavior, 5,* 39–67.

Spanier, G. & Glick, P. (1981).   Marital instability in the United States: Some correlates and recent changes. *Family Relations, 30,* 329–338.

Speirs, V. L. (1986).   School safety programs. *NIJ Reports, SNI, 198,* (July). 8–11.

Spreadbury, C. C. (1982).   First date. *Journal of Early Adolescence, 2,* 83–89.

Staffieri, J. R. (1967).   A study of social stereotype and body image in children. *Journal of Personality and Social Psychology, 1,* 101–104.

Staffieri, J. R. (1972).   Body build and behavioral expectancies in young females. *Developmental Psychology, 6,* 125–127.

Stanley, J. C. (1976).   Use of tests to discover talent. In D. P. Keating (Ed.) *Intellectual talent: Research and Development.* Baltimore, MD: Johns Hopkins University Press.

Stanley, J. C., Keating, D. P., & Fox, L. H. (1974).   *Mathematical talent, research and development.* Baltimore, MD: Johns Hopkins University Press.

Starbuck, E. D. (1899).   *The psychology of religion: An empirical study of the growth of religious consciousness.* New York: C. Scribners.

Stark, R. & Bainbridge, W. S. (1979).   Of churches, sects, and cults: Preliminary concepts for a theory of religious movements. *Journal for the Scientific Study of Religion, 18,* 117–133.

Steele, B. F. & Pollock, C. B. (1968).   A psychiatric study of parents who abuse infants and small children. In R. E. Helfer and C. H. Kempe (Eds.) *The battered child.* Chicago: University of Chicago Press.

Steen, E. B. & Price, J. H. (1977).   *Human sex and sexuality.* New York: John Wiley.

Steinberg, L. D. (1987a).   Bound to bicker. *Psychology Today, 21* (9), 36–39.

Steinberg, L. D. (1987b).   Single parents, stepparents and the susceptability of adolescents to antisocial pressure. *Child Development, 58,* 269–275.

Steinberg, L. D., Greenberg, E. & Vaux, A. (1982).   Effects of working on adolescent development. *Developmental Psychology, 18,* 385–395.

Steinberg, L. D. & Silverberg, S. B. (1986).   The vicissitudes of autonomy. *Child Development, 57,* 841–851.

Steirlin, H. (1973).   Family perspective on adolescent runaways. *Archives of General Psychiatry, 29,* 56–62.

Stephanson, S. P., Jr. (1978).   The transition from school to work with job search implications. In *Conference report on youth unemployment: Its measurement and meaning.* Washington, DC: U.S. Department of Labor.

Stern, M. S. & MacKenzie, R. G. (1975).   Venereal disease in adolescents. In H. V. Barnes (Ed.) *Medical clinics of North America, 59,* 1395–1405.

Sternberg, R. J. (1982).   Who's intelligent? *Psychology Today, 16*(4), 34–39.

Sternberg, R. J. (1984).   What should intelligence tests test? Implications of a triarchic theory of intelligence for intelligence testing. *Educational Researcher, 13,* 5–15.

Sternberg, R. J., Conway, B. E., Ketron, J. L., & Bernstein, M. (1981).   People's conceptions of intelligence. *Journal of Personality and Social Psychology, 41,* 37–55.

Stickle, G. & Ma, P. (1975).   Pregnancy in adolescents: Scope of the problem. *Contemporary Obstetrics and Gynecology.* McGraw Hill reprints.

Strang, R. (1957).   *The adolescent views himself.* New York: McGraw-Hill.

Strong, E. K. (1943).   *Vocational interests of men and women.* Stanford, CA: Stanford University Press.

Strong, E. K. (1955).   *Vocational interest 18 years after college.* Minneapolis: University of Minnesota Press.

Sugarman, A. A. & Haroonian, F. (1964).   Body type and sophistication of body concept. *Journal of Personality, 32,* 380–394.

Sullivan, H. S. (1953).   *The interpersonal theory of psychiatry.* New York: W. W. Norton.

Super, D. E. (1953).   A theory of vocational development. *American Psychologist, 8,* 185–190.

Super, D. E. (1957).   *The psychology of careers.* New York: Harper & Row.

Super, D. E., Starshevsky, R., Matlin, H., & Jordaan, J. P. (1963).   *Career development: Self-concept theory.* New York: College Entrance Examination Board.

Susman, E., Inoff-Germain, G., Nottlemann, E., Loriaux, D. L., Cutler, G. B., & Chrousos, G. P. (1985).   Hormones, emotional dispositions, and aggressive attributes in young adolescents. *Child Development, 58,* 1114–1134.

Sykes, G. & Mazda, D. (1957).   Techniques of neutralization: A theory of delinquency. *American Sociological Review, 22,* 664–670.

Tannenbaum, A. J. (1962).   *Adolescent attitudes about academic brilliance.* New York: Columbia University Press.

Tanner, J. M. (1962). *Growth at adolescence.* London: Blackwell.

Tanner, J. M. (1970). Physical growth. In P. Mussen (Ed.) *Carmichael's manual of child psychology.* (pp. 77–156). New York: John Wiley.

Tanner, J. M. (1978). *Fetus into man: Physical growth from conception to maturity.* Cambridge: MA: Harvard University Press.

Tanner, J. M.(1987). Issues and advances in adolescent growth and development. *Journal of Adolescent Health Care, 8,* 470–478.

Tanner, J. M., Whitehouse, R. H., & Tackaishi, M. (1966). Standards from birth to maturity for height, weight, height veloicity and weight velocity: British children. *Archives of Diseases of Childhood, 41,* 454–471, 613–635.

Terman, L. M. (1925). *Mental and physical traits of a thousand gifted children. Genetic studies of genius,* Vol. 1. Stanford, CA: Stanford University Press.

Terman, L. M. (1930). *The promise of youth. Genetic studies of genius.* Vol. 3. Stanford, CA: Stanford University Press.

Terman, L. M. & Oden, M. H. (1959). *The gifted child at midlife. Genetic studies of genius,* Vol. 3. Stanford, CA: Stanford University Press.

Teuting, P., Koslow, S. H., & Hirschfield, R.M.A. (1981). *Science reports: Special report on depression.* Bethesda, MD: National Institute on Mental Health.

Thelen, H. A. (1967). *Classroom grouping for teachability.* New York: John Wiley.

Thomas, D. L., Gecas, V., Weigart, A., & Rooney, E. (1974). *Family socialization and the adolescent.* Lexington, MA: Lexington Books.

Thomas, L. E. (1974). Generational discontinuity in beliefs: An exploration of the generation gap. *Social Issues, 30,* 1–22.

Thornburg, H. D. (1981). Developmental characteristics of middle schoolers and middle school organization. *Contemporary Educatiuon, 52,* 134–138.

Thornburg, H. D. & Aras, Z. (1986). Physical characteristics of developing adolescents. *Journal of Adolescent Research, 1,* 47–78.

Thurstone, L. L. (1938). Primary mental abilities. *Psychological Monographs,* No. 1.

Time. (1977). Cripples in the war zone. *Time Magazine, 110* (July 11), 20.

Time. (1986). Crack. *Time Magazine, 127* (June 2), 16–18.

Titley, R. W. & Titley, B. S. (1980). Initial choice of college major: Are only the "undecided" undecided? *Journal of College Student Personnel, 21,* 293–298.

Tjosvold, D. (1980). Control, conflict and collaboration in the classroom. *Educational Forum, 44,* 195–203.

Tobin-Richards, M., Boxer, A., & Petersen, A. (1983). The psychological significance of pubertal changes, sex differences in perceptions of self during adolescence. In J. Brooks-Gunn & A. Petersen (Eds.) *Girls at puberty: Biological and Psychological perspectives.* (pp. 127–154). New York: Plenum.

Tomlinson-Keasey, C. (1972). Formal operations in females ages 11 to 54 years of age. *Developmental Psychology, 67,* 364.

Torrance, E. P. (1966). *Torrence Tests of Creative Thinking: Directions manual.* Princeton, NJ: Personnel Press.

Torrance, E. P. (1972). Can we teach children to think creatively? *Journal of Creative Behavior, 6,* 114–143.

Tramontana, M. G. & Sherrets, S. D. (1984). Psychotherapy with adolescents: Conceptual, practical and empirical perspectives. In P. Karoly & J. J. Steffen (Eds.) *Adolescent behavior disorders: Foundations and contemporary concerns.* Lexington, MA: Lexington Books.

Tresemer, D. (1974). Fear of success: Popular but unproven. *Psychology Today, 7*(Mar), 82–85.

U.S. Bureau of the Census. (1978). *School enrollment—Social and economic characteristics of students: October, 1978.* Current Population Reports, series P–20, no. 319. Washington, DC: U.S. Government Printing Office.

U.S. Bureau of the Census. (1983). *Provisional projections of the population of states.* Current Population Reports, series P–25, no. 937. Washington, DC: U.S. Government Printing Office.

U.S. Bureau of the Census. (1983). *State population estimates be age and components of change:*

1980 to 2000. Current Population Reports, series P–25, no. 970. Washington, DC: U.S. Government Printing Office.

U.S. Bureau of Justice. (1986). Children in Custody: Public juvenile facilities, 1985. *Department of Justice Statistics Bulletin.* Washington, DC: Author.

Urban Superintendents Network. (1983). *Dealing with dropouts: The Urban Superintendents' call to action.* Washington, DC: Department of Education.

VanTassel-Baska, J. (1985). Profile of precocity: A three-year study of talented adolescents. Paper presented at the annual meeting of the American Educational Research Association. Chicago.

Van Thorne, M. D. & Vogel, F. X. (1985). The presence of bulimia in high school females. *Adolescence, 20,* 45–51.

Varenhorst, B. B. (1974). Training adolescents as per counselors. *Personnel and Guidance Journal, 53,* 271–276.

Vener, A. M. & Stewart, C. S. (1974). Adolescent sexual behavior in Middle-America revisited. *Journal of Marriage and the Family, 36,* 728–735.

Vener, A. M., Stewart, C. S., & Hagen, D. L. (1972). The sexual behavior of adolescents in Middle-America: generational and British-American comparisons. *Journal of Marriage and the Family, 34,* 696–705.

Vernon, P. E., Abramson, G., & Vernon, D. F. (1977). *The psychology and education of gifted children.* Boulder, CO: Westview Press.

Vogt, D. K. (1973). Literacy among youths 12–17 years. *Vital and Health Statistics,* series 11, no. 131. Washington, DC: U.S. Government Printing Office.

Wadsworth, B. J. (1978). *Piaget for the classroom teacher.* New York: Longman.

Wagner, H. (1971). The increasing importance of the peer group during adolescence. *Adolescence, 6,* 53–58.

Waldrop, M. F. & Halverson, C. F., Jr. (1971). Minor physical deficits and hyperactivity in young children. In J. Hellmuth (Ed.) *Exceptional infant.* New York: Bruner/Mazel.

Walker, D. (1975). *Runaway youth: Annotated bibliography and literature overview.* Washington, DC: Department of Health, Education and Welfare.

Walker, L. J. (1983). Social experiences and moral development in adulthood. Paper presented at the Biennial meeting of the Society for Research in Child Development, Detroit.

Walker, L. J. (1984). Sex differences in the development of moral reasoning: A critical review. *Child Development, 55,* 677–691.

Walker, R. N. (1962). Body build and behavior in young children II: Body build and parents' ratings. *Child Development, 34,* 1–23.

Wallach, M. A. & Wing, C. W. (1970). Faulty construction. *Contemporary Psychology, 15,* 3–4.

Wallerstein, J. S. & Kelley, J. B. (1980). *Surviving the break-up: How children actually cope with the divorce.* New York: Basic Books.

Walster, E., Aronson, V., Abrahams, D., & Rottman, L. (1966). Importance of physical attractiveness in dating behavior. *Journal of Personality and Social Psychology, 4,* 508–516.

Watson, J. B. & Raynor, R. (1920). Conditioned emotional responses. *Journal of Experimental Psychology, 3,* 1–14.

Waugh, I. (1977). Labeling theory. In National Institute for Juvenile Justice and Delinquency Prevention. *Preventing delinquency.* Vol. 1. Washington, DC: U.S. Government Printing Office.

Webb, E. B., Campbell, D. T., Schwartz, R. D. & Sechrist, L. (1966). *Unobtrusive measures: Nonreactive research in the social sciences.* Chicago: Rand McNally.

Wechsler, D. (1958). *The measurement and appraisal of adult intelligence.* (4th edition). Baltimore, MD: Williams and Wilkins.

Weiner, B. (1972). Attribution theory, achievement motivation and the educational process. *Review of Educational Research, 42,* 203–216.

Weiner, B. & Kukla, A. (1970). An attribute analysis of achievement motivation. *Journal of Personality and Social Psychology, 15,* 1–20.

Weiner, I. B. (1976). The adolescent and his society. In J. R. Gallagher, F. P. Heald, & D. C. Garell (Eds.) *Medical care of the adolescent.* New York: Appleton-Century-Crofts.

Weiner, I. B. (1980). Psychopathology in adolescence. In J. Adelson (Ed.) *Handbook of adolescent psychology.* New York: John Wiley.

Weinstein, E. E. (1957). Development of the concept of the flag and sense of national identity. *Child Development, 28,* 172–173.

Weiss, I. (1977). Comparative analysis of social breakdown theories of delinquency—the breakdown of adequate social controls. In National Institute for Juvenile Justice and Delinquency Prevention *Preventing delinquency.* Vol. 1. Washington, DC: U.S. Government Printing Office.

Werner, E. & Smith, R. S. (1977). *Kauai's children come of age.* Honolulu: University of Hawaii Press.

Werner, H. J. (1958). Development from an organismic point of view. In D. B. Harris (Ed.) *Concepts of development.* Minneapolis: University of Minnesota Press.

Werthman, C. (1977). Status offenses. In National Institute for Juvenile Justice and Delinquency Prevention. *Preventing delinquency.* Vol. 1. Washington, DC: U.S. Government Printing Office.

Westie, F. R. (1964). Race and ethnic relations. In R. L. Faris (Ed.) *Handbook of modern sociology.* Chicago: Rand McNally.

Wetzel, J. R. (1987). *American youth: A statistical snapshot.* Washington, DC: William T. Grant Foundation.

Whisnant, L. & Zegans, L. (1975). A study of attitudes toward menarche in white, middle-class American adolescent girls. *American Journal of Psychiatry, 132*(8), 809–814.

Whitehead, L. (1979). Sex differences in children's responses to family stress: A re-evaluation. *Journal of Child Psychology and Psychiatry, 20,* 247–254.

Williams, J. (1977). *The psychology of women: Behavior in a biosocial context.* New York: W. W. Norton & Co.

Wilson, A. B. (1959). Residential segregation of social class and aspirations of high school boys. *American Sociological Review, 24,* 836–845.

Winn, M. (1977). *The plug-in drug.* New York: Viking Press.

Wise, H. D. (1974). In defense of teachers. *School Review, 83,* 113–118.

Wold, H. (1954). Causal inference from observational data: A review of ends and means. *Journal of the Royal Statistical Society, 19,* Series A, 28–61.

Wolf, T. M. (1973). Effects of televised modeled verbalizations and behavior on resistance to deviation. *Developmental Psychology, 8,* 51–56.

Wolf, T. M. & Cheyne, J. A. (1972). Persistance of effects of live behavioral, televised behavioral and live verbal models on resistence to deviation. *Child Development, 43,* 1429–1436.

Wolk, S., & Brandon, J. (1977). Runaway adolescents' perceptions of parents and self. *Adolescence, 12,* 175–182.

Wolman, B. B. (1968). *The unconscious mind.* Englewood Cliffs, NJ: Prentice-Hall.

Wolman, B. B. (1982). *Handbook of developmental psychology.* Englewood Cliffs, NJ: Prentice-Hall.

Wong, M. R. (1976). Different strokes: Models of drug abuse education. *Contemporary Educational Psychology 1,* 1–20.

Wong, M. R. & Allen, T. (1976). A three-dimensional structure of drug attitudes. *Journal of Drug Education, 6,* 181–191.

Wunderlich, R. A. & Johnson, W. B. (1973). Some personality correlates of obese persons. *Psychological Reports, 32,* 1267–1277.

Wylie, R. C. (1974. *The self-concept.* Vol. 1. Lincoln, NE: University of Nebraska Press.

Yablonsky, L. (1962). *The violent gang.* New York: Macmillan.

Yankelovitch, D. (1974). *The new morality: A profile of American youth in the 70's.* New York: McGraw-Hill.

Yarchesi, A. & Mahon, N. E. (1984).   Chumship relationships, altruistic behavior and loneliness in early adolescents. *Adolescence, 19,* 914–924.

Yinger, R. (1979).   Routines in teacher planning. *Theory into Practice, 18,* 163–169.

Yinger, R. (1980).   A study of teacher planning. *Elementary School Journal, 80,* 107–127.

Yudkovitz, E. (1983).   Bulimia: Growing awareness of an eating disorder. *Social Work, 54,* 472–478.

Zaretsky, I, I. (1977).   Cult participation in America. *Intellect, 105* (Mar), 299–300.

Zaretsky, I. I. & Leone, M. P. (1975).   *Religious movements in contemporary America.* Princeton, NJ: Princeton University Press.

Zelnik, M. (1980).   Second pregnancies to premarital pregnant teenagers, 1976 and 1971. *Family Planning Perspectives, 12,* 69–76.

Zelnik, M. & Kantner, J. F. (1972).   Sexuality, contraception and pregnancy among young, unwed females in the United States. In C. F. Westoff and R. Parker, Jr. (Eds.) *Commission on population growth and the American future: Demographic and Social aspects of population growth.* Vol. 1. Washington, DC: U.S. Government Printing Office.

Zelnik, M. & Kantner, J. F. (1977).   Sexual and contraceptive experience of young unmarried women in the United States: 1970 and 1976. *Family Planning Perspectives, 9,* 55–71.

Zelnik, M. & Kantner, J. F. (1980).   Sexual activity, contraceptive use and pregnancy among metropolitan-area teenagers: 1971–1979. *Family Planning Perspectives, 12,* 230–237.

Zelnik, M. & Shah, F. K. (1983).   First intercourse among young Americans. *Family Planning Perspectives, 15,* 64–70.

Zigler, E. (1969).   Developmental versus difference theories of mental retardation and the problem of motivation. *American Journal of Mental Deficiency, 73,* 536–556.

Zillman, D. (1982).   Television viewing and arousal. In D. Pearl, L. Bouthilet, & J. Lazar (Eds.) *Television and behavior: Vol. 2.* (pp. 53–67). Washington, DC: National Institute of Mental Health.

Zimbardo, P. G. (1977).   *Shyness: What is it? What to do about it.* New York: Jove Publications.

Zimbardo, P. G. & Radl, S. L. (1982).   *The shy child.* New York: Doubleday & Co.

Zinberg, N E. & Robertson, J. A. (1972).   *Drugs and the public.* New York: Simon and Shuster.

GLOSSARY

abortion The natural or therapeutic expulsion of a fetus.

accommodation Piaget's term for the process of altering existing schema to meet the demands of new information.

achievement In schooling, the attainment of specified levels of knowledge.

achievement motivation Hypothetical motive to excel or to compete against a standard of excellence in an achievement-oriented setting.

achievement tests Standardized instruments designed to assess levels of academic accomplishment in specific or general areas.

acne (acne vulgaris) A common skin problem of adolescence, characterized by an excessive eruption of blackheads and whiteheads.

adaptability A dimension of family interaction related to the degree to which the family is able to respond to change and stress.

addiction Physiological or psychological dependence on a drug.

adolescence A period of personal development during which a young person develops a sense of individual identity and feelings of self-worth, including adaption to an altered body image, improved intellectual ability, demands for behavioral maturity, and preparation for adult roles.

adolescent An individual going through adolescence.

adolescent society A term used by James Coleman to refer to the demands for common language, behavior, values, and dress codes that dominate the youth population.

adolescent transition See adolescence.

affect An individual's feelings or attitudes.

alcohol A depressant drug, called ethanol.

amotivational syndrome A pattern of loss of motivation related to chronic marijuana use.

amphetamines A class of stimulant drugs.

anorexia nervosa A disease, most often occurring in young women, in which the patient loses appetite and excessive amounts of weight. The disease usually has a psychological base and takes the form of a food phobia.

aptitudes   General or specific abilities related to the potential to succeed in some domain.

assimilation   Piaget's term for the act of altering information to meet the existing structure of an individual's schema.

authoritarian parents   Parents who offer little emotional support but exert strong, dogmatic control.

authoritative parents   Parents who offer high emotional support and exert strong control.

barbiturates   A class of depressant drugs.

blood-alcohol level   The percent of alcohol in an individual's bloodstream.

body image   An individual's perception of how adequate his or her body is in relation to some idealized body.

capitalization strategy   A strategy for intervention that takes advantage of the individual's strengths.

career education   An organized set of experiences to introduce a young person to career alternatives and to aid in the development of career goals.

child abuse   The physical or mental injury, sexual abuse, negligent treatment, or mistreatment of a child under the age of eighteen by a person who is responsible for the child's welfare.

chlamydia   A sexually transmitted disease.

cliques   Closely knit groups of peers who typically exclude others from group membership.

cognitive development   Changes in intellectual ability that occur as an individual progresses from infancy through adulthood.

cognitive theory   Psychological theories that emphasize active, purposeful, conceptual thinking.

cohesion   A dimension of family interaction related to the degree to which the family unit functions as a unit.

cohort   A group of persons who share a common experience.

coitus   Sexual intercourse.

compensatory intervention   Intervention strategies that are intended to provide some mechanisms or skills to compensate for the individual's limitations.

concrete operations   Thought processes, especially among elementary-school-age children and young adolescents, that are tied to concrete examples. The third stage of Piaget's theory of cognitive development.

contraception   Use of birth control procedures or devices.

conventional morality   The middle stages of moral development described by Kohlberg. The motive for morality is primarily social approval, and morality is seen in arbitrary concrete terms.

conversion experience   An intellectual and/or emotional religious experience that deepens religious faith.

correlation   A measure of the degree to which two variables are related.

creativity   The ability to offer unique and divergent responses to common events.

cross-sectional research   Developmental research in which differences in age groups are assessed by measuring individuals grouped at different ages.

cultural bias   A test structure that benefits individuals from one group but not another.

defense mechanism   Coping strategies used by an individual to reduce or avoid anxiety.

delinquent behavior   Criminal or illegal activity, typically associated with juvenile offenders.

demography   Statistical analyses of characteristics of a population of people.

denial   A defense mechanism in which unwanted information is ignored. It is a refusal to admit that the information exists.

dependent variable   In an experiment, the outcome variable to be studied.

depressants   Drugs that serve to slow down nervous system activity.

depression   A psychological state of despondency and dejection that may lead to lack of motivation.

desired self   The individual's preferred view of his/her self-concept.

developmental goals   Skills and objectives that need to be attained in order to adapt at one stage of life and prepare for the next.

disequilibrium A state of uncertainty in which an individual's schema fails to account for a perceived reality.

drug abuse The use of any drug that interferes with the normal functioning of an individual at home, work, or school.

early maturation Significantly premature emergence of primary and secondary sexual characteristics.

ecological research The study of human (or animal) behavior in natural, unaltered settings.

ectomorph A body type characterized by leanness.

ego extension An individual or group with whom an individual has close identification, whose success or failure is taken personally.

egocentrism The assumption that one's own view of reality is the only true perspective.

ego ideal An idealized system of moral values.

ejaculation Emission of seminal fluid.

endomorph A body type characterized by excessive fat tissue.

equilibrium A state of balance. In cognitive theory, it refers to a balance achieved between new information and existing schema.

experiment A controlled pattern of observation in which a researcher systematically manipulates one or more characteristics of the environment and records the outcome.

experimenter bias The intentional or unintentional influencing of the results of an experiment to conform to the experimenter's expectations.

extant self The individual's current view of his/her self-concept.

extinction A behavioral term referring to the elimination of behavior by withholding reinforcers.

faith development Changes in religious or faith concepts that occur as an individual matures.

fear of failure A general motive in which an individual's achievement is affected by the degree to which he or she is anxious about not succeeding.

fear of success A hypothetical motive in which achievement is affected by an individual's anxiety about being excluded for being overly successful.

formal operations (formal thinking) Thought patterns that allow for abstract, hypothetico-deductive thinking. Piaget's fourth stage of cognitive development.

functional illiteracy The inability to read well enough to perform the basic skills necessary to get along in society.

gangs Highly structured groups that may be organized around illegal or delinquent activities.

gender roles Expectations of behaviors that are based soley on one's sex.

generation gap A widely held belief in extreme differences in attitudes between adults and adolescents.

genius Exceptional talent and creativity in a given area.

gonorrhea An epidemic venereal disease caused by the bacteria gonococci; treatable with antibiotics.

hallucinogens (psychedelics) Drugs capable of producing alterations in perceptions, such as illusions, hallucinations, and distortions of reality.

herpes simplex virus II A venereal disease caused by the herpes simplex virus. There is no currently available cure.

heterosexuality Sexual behavior involving individuals of the same sex.

homosexuality Sexual behavior between individuals of both sexes.

identity crisis A major reorganization of the adolescent's self-concept, which emerges from a desire to establish oneself as a unique person.

identity foreclosure The avoidance of an identity crisis by the early commitment to an intact identity, usually provided by parents.

identity formation The lifelong process of developing a personal conception of oneself.

identity moratorium The period in which the adolescent delays fixing upon a final identity and experiments with alternative identities.

imaginary audience An element of adolescent egocentrism described by David Elkind, in which the individual assumes a global body of people are concerned with his/her welfare.

independent variables   In an experiment, those variables that are under the direct or indirect control of the researcher.

individualized treatment plan (ITP)   A specific plan of therapy or intervention based on an individual's strengths, weaknesses, and long-term and short-term goals.

informed consent   The act of agreeing to participate in a research study based on a clear understanding of the risks and requirements.

inhalants   A class of psychoactive chemicals that produce intoxication or altered perception when their fumes are inhaled.

intellectualization   A defense mechanism in which unwanted feelings are analyzed in a detached, rational fashion.

intelligence   The general ability to solve problems and to act in a purposeful manner.

intelligence quotient (IQ)   The ratio created by dividing an individual's chronological age (CA) by his or her mental age (MA) and multiplying by 100. No longer in general use but now often used as a generic term to refer to intelligence.

invisible audience   An imaginary group of people that an adolescent feels is watching every move and is concerned with his or her behavior and appearance.

isolation   A defense mechanism in which unwanted information is seen as somehow distinct from what is already known.

juvenile delinquent   A young person who has committed a crime and has been labeled by the courts as a juvenile offender.

late maturation   Significantly delayed emergence of primary and secondary sexual characteristics.

locus of control   The source of an individual's perceived control of events, either internal (self) or external (others).

longitudinal research   Studies of maturation and development in which changes in behavior with age are measured on a single group of people over an extended period of time.

mainstreaming   The integration of handicapped youngsters into regular classrooms.

masturbation   Sexual self-, or autoerotic, stimulation.

maturation   Developmental changes that result from genetic predispositions or age rather than from experience.

menarche   First menses, the onset of menstruation.

menses   The normal expulsion of blood and unused ova during the woman's menstrual cycle.

mental retardation   Impaired intellectual ability ranging from moderate to profound restriction of ability.

modeling   The learning of behaviors by imitation, or copying the behaviors of a significant other person.

moral development   Changes in concepts of morality that occur as an individual matures.

narcotic   Medically, a drug used to inhibit pain; more generally, any illegal drug.

naturalistic observation   Studying and recording behavior as it occurs in the natural environment, without any manipulation or interference by the researcher.

negative identity   The acceptance of socially disapproved identity as one's own.

negative reinforcement   A behavioral term referring to the removal of an aversive stimulus following a desired behavior.

neglectful parents   A parenting style in which parents offer little emotional support and exert little or no control.

nocturnal emission   Ejaculation of semen by the male during sleep; also called a "wet dream."

obesity   Excessive accumulation of body fat.

obtrusiveness   Alteration of normal behavior by the mere presence of an observer, experimenter, or unusual device.

occupational prestige   The general status afforded a given occupational category.

operational definition   The definition of a psychological or social concept by a set of observable measures.

opiates   A general class of drugs derived from real or synthetic opium.

peer counseling   The use of age cohorts in crisis counseling.

peers Individuals who share some common attribute(s), such as age, sex, race, socioeconomic level, and so on.

percentile Relative standing in a population indicating the percentage who score lower than a given point .

permissive parents Parents who offer high emotional support but exert little control.

personal fable A form of adolescent egocentrism described by Elkind, in which the person sees himself or herself as totally unique in thoughts and feelings.

PL 94–142 (Education of all Handicapped Children Act) Federal legislation requiring that all handicapped children be educated in the least restrictive environment.

positive reinforcement A behavioral term referring to the presentation of a pleasant stimulus following a desired behavior.

postconventional morality The advanced states of moral development described by Kohlberg, in which morality is seen in abstract, relativistic, and universal terms.

preconventional morality The early stages of moral development described by Kohlberg, in which motives for morality are primarily defined by self-gratification.

prejudice A learned response in which an individual maintains an unfavorable ethnic attitude about a targeted group.

primary sexual characteristics The genitals, which at puberty reach adult status and are essential for sexual reproduction.

projection A defense mechanisms in which the blame for unacceptable thoughts or behaviors is directed as someone else.

pseudostupidity Apparent but not real inability of adolescents to solve complex problems, in which a discrepancy exists between real knowledge and the ability to display the knowledge.

psychoanalytic theory Theories of personality development rooted in Sigmund Freud's writings. Personality development is seen in light of satisfactory or unsatisfactory resolution of psychosexual stages.

psychopathology Diseases that are psychological in origin and that result in severe distortion of reality.

psychosomatic illness Illness that results when psychological factors influence bodily functions.

puberty The stage of maturation at which an individual becomes physically capable of sexual reproduction.

pubescence The onset of the transition to adult sexual maturity; the coming of puberty.

rationalization A defense mechanism in which the individual offers a plausible explanation to justify otherwise unacceptable behavior.

reception learning The acquisiton of knowledge through meaningful prose.

reinforcement A behavioral term referring to any event that increases the likelihood of the behavior that immediately preceded it being repeated.

religiosity Degree of commitment to a set of religious values.

repression A defense mechanism in which unwanted or unacceptable thoughts are forced back into the unconscious.

rites of passage Initiation ceremonies that mark the entry of a young person into adult status.

role diffusion The failure to achieve a clear personal identity.

schema A collection of bits of knowledge organized into a pattern that aids our interpretation of our environment.

schizophrenia A psychotic disturbance characterized by severe distortion of perceptions of reality, especially the inability to distinguish fact from fantasy.

secondary gain Social or psychological advantages that result from others responding to features of a disease or disability.

secondary sexual characteristics Physical features of maleness or femaleness that emerge at pubescence but that are not essential for sexual reproduction; for example, pubic hair and breasts.

secular trend Changes in physical maturation patterns seen over successive generations.

self-concept The set of attributes an individual uses to describe himself or herself.

self-esteem   The net value or worth than an individual places on the elements of his or her self-concept.

self-fulfilling prophesy   An event occurring because it is *expected* to occur.

self-image   The set of perceptions that an individual has about himself or herself.

sex education   The systematic instruction in the elements of human and nonhuman sexuality.

socialization   The learning of the values, attitudes, and skills of the society within which an individual must function.

socioeconomic status   Relative social status, related to family income, education, and prestige.

sociogram   A technique for measuring the relative popularity of individuals in an existing group.

sociometric status   The relative popularity of an individual in a group.

sociopathy   Chronically using illegal or immoral behavior without any feelings of guilt or concern for the victims.

somatotypes   Body or physique types described by Sheldon, which are associated with specific personality characteristics.

status offenses   Offenses that are defined as illegal only for specific subgroups of society on the basis of some characteristic—for example, age or sex.

stimulants   Drugs that excite or speed up the activity of the central nervous system.

storm and stress   A phrase used by G. Stanley Hall and some other social scientists to describe the tumultuous characteristics of adolescence.

stressful life events   Normal or unusual events in an individual's life which result in anxiety and stress.

sublimation   A defense mechanism in which unacceptable thoughts are disguised and expressed in socially acceptable forms.

syphilis   A sexually transmitted disease caused by spirochetes. It is usually treated effectively with antibiotics.

teenager   A general term, usually used by adults, to refer to an adolescent. The term implies that adolescence is tied to the "teen" years.

tolerance   The increased ability of the body to withstand the effects of a given drug, so that increased doses of the drug are needed to achieve a desired effect.

transescent   A term sometimes aplied to early adolescents in middle schools.

unsocialized aggressive reaction   Impulsive, uncontrolled expression of hostility and aggression. Typically, this impulsiveness dissipates with maturity and improved socialization, in contrast to sociopathy.

vandalism   Willful, malicious destruction of property.

variable   A measurable trait that may have different states or values—for example, sex, achievement, age, race.

variance   The spread of a group of scores around the average score.

venereal disease (VD)   A disease that is transmitted sexually.

vocational development   Changes in concepts of vocational goals that occur as an individual matures.

INDEX OF NAMES

Abel, D., 116
Abel, E., 161
Abelson, H., 122
Abramson, G., 149
Ackowitz, H., 253
Adelson, J., 7, 49, 157, 212, 233, 234, 235, 237, 238, 252, 275, 289
Adler, N., 263
Aichorn, A., 305
Akpon, C., 261
Akpon, K., 261
Alder, C., 305
Alexander, K., 177
Allen, R., 297
Allen, T., 106
Allon, N., 93
Allport, G., 240
Altman, I., 41
Anderson, A., 97
Anderson, J., 237
Anderson, L., 165
Andrisani, P., 200
Aras, Z., 86
Arlin, M., 148
Arlin, P., 166
Arnold, C., 261
Arnold, M., 294
Aronson, E., 92
Asher, S., 245
Atkinson, R., 130
Austin, M., 201
Ausubel, D., 10, 130, 205, 214
Avery, D., 337

Babin, P., 297
Babin, V., 270
Bach, K., 93
Bachman, J., 104, 105, 179, 188, 229
Backman, M., 140
Bacon, M., 211
Bailey, D., 81
Bain, R., 237
Bainbridge, W., 300
Baldwin, B., 81
Baldwin, W., 257, 262, 265
Baltes, P., 40
Balswick, J., 253
Bandura, A., 5, 17, 209, 277
Banks, F., 117, 118
Bardwick, J., 72, 237
Barker, R., 41
Barnes, H. L., 209
Barnes, H. V., 85, 94, 96
Barrett, C., 116
Barry, H., 211
Baskerville, J., 118
Baumrind, D., 65, 205, 206, 212
Bayer, F., 186
Bayh, B., 317
Bayley, N., 89, 138, 140
Bazemore, G., 305
Beamesderfer, A., 325
Bean, J., 180
Beautrais, A., 326
Beck, A., 325, 331, 339
Becker, H., 313
Becker, W., 205

Beery, R., 69
Beit-Hallahmi, B., 297
Bell, A., 248, 267
Bell, R., 257
Bell, T., 269
Belson, W., 281
Bentler, P., 106
Berger, R., 94, 96
Berliner, D., 165
Bernstein, M., 136
Berscheid, E., 92
Biegel, M., 111
Bigner, J., 240
Binet, A., 130, 131
Bishop, S., 65, 209, 217, 264
Black, A., 65
Blackford, L., 122
Blake, J., 259, 260
Blalock, H., 39
Blasi, A., 148
Bleich, L., 7
Bleuler, M., 332
Blitzer, P., 93
Block, J., 39, 289
Bloom, B., 289
Bloom, R., 116
Blos, P., 277
Blum, R., 107, 117
Blyth, D., 90, 252, 326
Bohrnstedt, G., 67, 256
Bonham, G., 265
Borgatta, E., 256
Boring, E., 132, 136

Borow, H., 183, 185
Bower, G., 17
Boxer, A., 90
Boyer, E., 160, 183
Bracht, G., 113, 144
Brack, C., 86
Brandon, J., 314
Brassard, M., 220
Braun, J., 186
Brickell, H., 167
Broderick, J., 217
Bromley, D., 240
Bronfenbrenner, U., 40, 41, 209
Brooks-Gunn, J., 83, 86
Brophy, J., 167
Brown, J., 114
Brown, J. K., 11
Brown, M., 244
Brownell, K., 93
Bruche, H., 97
Brumberg, J., 96
Budoff, M., 157
Bullen, B., 329
Bumpass, L., 216
Burgess, D., 258
Burnham, D., 262
Burt, M., 111
Burton, N., 331
Burton, R., 289
Bush, D., 73
Bush, E., 73
Bush, L., 288
Byrne, D., 92

Cain, V., 262
Caldwell, R., 303
Caliste, E., 178
Callahan, D., 111
Camp, B., 258
Campbell, D., 33, 35, 36, 38, 44, 50
Canning, D., 93
Cantwell, D., 331
Carpenter, R., 107
Carr, A., 108, 116
Carron, A., 81
Cartledge, G., 245
Caster, J., 156
Cattell, A., 138
Cattell, R., 34, 36, 57, 138, 150
Cavior, N., 89
Chacko, M., 270
Chadwick, O., 331
Chambliss, W., 313
Chance, P., 267
Chand, I., 213
Chartier, G., 331
Chase, H., 326
Chase, J., 107, 116
Chassin, L., 106, 116, 117, 313
Chasten, J., 257
Chen, I., 290
Chen, T., 117, 118
Cheyne, J., 280
Child, I., 211
Chilman, C., 272
Churchill, W., 63
Cisin, I., 111
Clarke, A., 83

Cloward, R., 311, 312
Cochrane, P., 157
Coddington, R., 56, 326
Cogan, J., 197
Cohen, A., 312
Cohen, J., 216
Cohen, S., 115, 116
Colby, A., 288
Coleman, J., 227, 231, 232, 234–236
Coleman, J. S., 160, 168, 169, 183,
    200, 233, 236, 238, 290
Cols, R., 64
Colletti, G., 93
Collins, J., 256
Combs, J., 179
Conger, J., 254
Conklin, F., 11, 12
Conn, J., 337
Conway, B., 136
Cook, S., 83
Cook, T., 38
Cooley, C., 228
Cooper, P., 289
Coopersmith, S., 36, 53, 63, 65, 331
Cornwell, G., 300
Corty, E., 106, 117
Costanzo, P., 235
Covington, M., 69
Cox, M., 219
Cox, R., 219
Crider, D., 213
Crisp, A., 93
Critchlow, B., 110
Crites, T., 193
Crockenberg, S., 150
Crockett, L., 87, 90, 326
Crockett, W., 240
Crossley, H., 111
Cusick, P., 160, 166
Cutright, P., 260, 266
Cvetkovitch, G., 261

Damico, S., 346
Davidson, M., 88
Davidson, S., 115
Davies, M., 331
Davis, K., 215, 259, 260
Davis, M., 261
Davison, M., 288
Deisher, R., 220
Demos, J., 4
Demos, V., 4
Denham, S., 150
Dever, R., 140
Diamond, E., 190, 191
Diepold, J., 247
Dion, K., 92
Dittes, J., 297
Dixon, P., 263
Dodge, K., 244, 245
Dokecki, P., 89
Dollard, J., 17
Donovan, J., 107, 116, 325
Dornbusch, S., 90
Douvan, E., 72, 212, 233–238, 252
Dreyfoos, J., 262
Duke, P., 86
Duncan, O., 237

Duncan, P., 90
Dunphy, D., 227, 231, 234
Durkheim, E., 338
Dusek, J., 56
Dweck, C., 73
Dwyer, J., 88

Ebel, R., 169
Eckland, B., 177
Eder, D., 233
Edmonds, R., 164
Edwards, D., 249
Ehrlich, H., 290
Eichorn, D., 171
Eichorn, D. H., 81
Eisen, M., 55, 240
Eisenberg, N., 245
Ekstrom, R., 78
Elder, G., 208, 209, 211
Elias, J., 266
Elkind, D., 24, 66, 148, 213, 216, 227, 241
Elliott, D., 178, 179
Elmer, E., 220, 222, 256
Emmer, E., 165
Empey, L., 322
Engs, R., 110, 114
Epstein, H., 171
Erikson, E., 15, 16, 24, 56–61, 226,
    294, 296
Eron, L., 281
Eskin, B., 85
Evans, R., 256
Evertson, E., 165
Exter, E., 22

Farrington, D., 211
Faust, M., 80, 81, 90
Feather, N., 72
Featherman, D., 237
Fenton, T., 310
Fergusson, D., 326
Ferraro, D., 116
Festinger, L., 33
Feuer, L., 212
Finkelhor, D., 221
Finn, P., 114
Fishburne, P., 122
Flaherty, J., 56
Flavell, J., 144
Flora, R., 65
Forbes, G., 79
Ford, K., 258
Fowler, J., 294–297
Fox, L., 150
Frank, L., 21
French, D., 244
French, E., 30
Freud, A., 5, 15, 57
Freud, S., 13, 14, 57, 214, 276
Friedman, R., 178
Frisch, R., 83
Fryear, J., 280
Fuqua, D., 193

Gallagher, J., 81, 100
Gallatin, J., 240, 289

Garbarino, J., 209, 220
Gebhart, P., 266
Gecas, V., 207, 211
Geiger, K., 289
Geismar, L., 310
Gibbons, D., 309
Gibbs, J., 288
Gill, D., 220
Gilliam, G., 220
Gilligan, C., 148, 282, 287
Ginsberg, E., 191-194
Giordano, P., 320
Glick, P., 216, 264
Glock, C., 291, 292, 298
Glueck, E., 310
Glueck, S., 310
Goertz, M., 178
Goertxel, V., 207
Gold, M., 178, 229, 236, 304, 305,
    309, 323
Goldberg, M., 280
Goldblatt, I., 212
Golden, M., 352
Goldman, R., 301
Golladay, M., 139
Gollin, E., 240
Goodman, D., 114
Goodman, N., 93
Goodman, R., 94
Gordon, E., 141
Gorn, G., 280
Goslin, D., 63
Goss, S., 166, 167
Gottesman, I., 336
Gottlieb, D., 201
Gottlieb, J., 157
Gough, H., 63
Graham, P., 331
Granberg, D., 262
Grant, M., 178
Green, S., 179
Greenberger, E., 185, 199,2 00, 213,
    215
Greene, J., 326
Greenfield, P., 280
Gregg, G., 220, 222
Gregory, I., 248
Gribbons, W., 186
Grief, E., 83
Grinder, R., 292
Gross, R., 86
Grossman, H., 155
Gruze, S., 114
Guba, E., 44
Guber, S., 22
Guilford, J., 136, 137
Gunderson, J., 336
Guttmacher Institute, 265

Haan, N., 287, 289
Haas, A., 249
Haier, R., 150
Haisch, H., 197
Hagen, D., 254
Hakel, M., 186
Halikas, J., 114, 115
Hall, G., 4-6, 292
Halverson, C., 328

Hamburg, B., 230
Hamil, P., 80-82
Hammersmith, S., 267
Hammond, W., 88
Haney, B., 304
Hanks, R., 288
Hanley, C., 88
Hannah, T., 70
Hannerz, U., 219
Hanson, D., 103, 110, 114
Harclerode, J., 116
Harding, J., 290
Haroonian, F., 88
Harris, D., 36, 65
Harris, J., 245, 291
Hart, S., 220
Hartman, B., 193
Hartlage, S., 7
Hartnagel, T., 281
Hartshorne, H., 289
Hartup, W., 25, 226, 244
Harvey, O., 174
Havighurst, R., 22, 185,
    201
Hays, J., 116
Heald, F., 85
Healy, J., 56, 327
Heatherington, E., 219
Heber, R., 140
Heid, C., 291
Hein, K., 269
Hembree, W., 116
Hendin, H., 108, 116
Henshaw, S., 262
Herrnstein, R., 140
Herrold, A., 352
Herron, J., 147
Herzog, A., 188
Herzog, E., 217
Hess, A., 212
Hickson, G., 326
Hilgard, E., 17
Himadi, W., 253
Hinkle, D., 229, 256
Hinton, R., 253
Hirschfield, 331
Hodge, R., 186
Hoeffel, E., 148
Hoffman, L., 71
Hofmann, A., 122
Holder, A., 47, 48
Holinger, P., 337
Holland, J., 194-196
Holmes, T., 56, 326
Holstein, C., 287
Holtzman, W., 211
Hong, G., 331
Hooker, E., 267
Horner, M., 70, 71
Horrocks, J., 232
Horowitz, R., 320
Howard, K., 7, 52, 63
Huang, H., 116
Huba, G., 106
Huesmann, L., 281
Humphrey, L., 88
Hundleby, J., 107
Hunt, D., 27, 174-176, 287
Husain, S., 337

Iacovetta, R., 229
Ingersoll, G., 65, 86, 105, 166, 209,
    217, 240, 291, 292, 352
Inhelder, B., 24, 141, 145
Inkeles, A., 186
Irwin, C., 326
Ishamaya, F., 67

Jacklin, C., 73
Jackson, G., 326
James-Cairns, J., 116
James, W., 292
Janis, I., 374
Jensen, A., 140
Jensen, G., 179, 303, 304, 322
Jensen, D., 200
Jessor, R., 106-108, 114, 116, 117,
    229, 256, 325
Jessor, S., 106-108, 114, 116, 117,
    229, 256, 325
Johnson, B., 300
Johnson, D., 228, 229
Johnson, J., 56, 217, 327
Johnson, M., 171
Johnson, W., 93
Johnston, L., 104, 105, 110, 116-119,
    122, 124, 188, 229
Jones, E., 258
Jones, H., 39
Jones, M., 39, 89, 90

Kadushin, A., 220
Kagan, J., 140
Kahoe, R., 300
Kalachek, E., 200
Kalafat, J., 229
Kandel, D., 106, 108, 116, 229, 233, 331
Kantner, J., 255-258, 261, 262, 264
Kanungo, R., 280
Kaplan, A., 325
Kaplan, S., 331
Karnisky, W., 310
Katchadorian, H., 79, 84
Katz, D., 33
Katz, I., 70
Kazdin, A., 229, 305, 310, 320
Keating, D., 149, 150
Kegan, R., 55
Keller, D., 117, 118
Keller, J., 229, 256
Kelly, J., 217
Keninston, K., 4, 108, 212
Kerlinger, F., 33
Kessler, R., 281
Ketron, J., 136
Kett, J., 12, 182, 205
Kimball, C., 326
King, K., 253
Kinsey, A., 248, 249, 254, 266
Kalber, M., 160
Kleck, R., 89
Klineberg, O., 289
Kloos, P., 11
Klykylo, M., 93
Knobloch, H., 258
Kohnberg, L., 13, 27, 73, 148, 174,
    281-288, 294, 296, 302

Kohn, M., 21
Kolata, G., 269
Kolodner, R., 116
Kolodny, R., 116
Konopka, G., 254, 338
Koos, M., 257
Kopecky, G., 252
Koslow, S., 331
Koiunin, J., 166
Kovar, M., 264
Kuder, F., 190, 191
Kuhlen, R., 294
Kukla, A., 70
Kutner,B., 290

Labouvie, E., 40
Lagerspetz, K., 281
Lambert, W., 289
Lanese, R., 117, 118
Langer, J., 287
Lanzetta, J., 70
Lapsley, D., 241
Lawrence, J., 270
Lee, G., 264
Leemon, T., 12
Lefcoe, N., 118
Lefkowitz, M., 331
Leon, G., 94
Leone, M., 301
Levin, B., 254
Levin, H., 72, 210
Levine, H., 310
Levine, S., 198
Leynes, C., 265
Liberty, B., 236
Lieberman, M., 288
Lieberman, U., 93
Liebert, R., 147
Lincoln, Y., 44
Linn, A., 264
Lipsitz, J., 3, 27, 310
Litt, I., 86
Livesley, W., 240
Loevinger, J., 15, 55
Lohnes, P., 186
Long, L., 216
Long, T., 216
Lovchik, J., 270

Ma, P., 266
Maccoby, E., 72, 210
Maccoby, N., 117
Macdonald, D., 108, 109, 115
MacKenzie, R., 268, 269
MacMahon, B., 84
Maddox, G., 93
Mahon, N., 229
Malina, R., 81
Maloney, M., 93
Malpiede, D., 258
Mann, L., 347
Mannheim, D., 115
Marble, A., 159
Marcia, J., 59, 60
Markus, L., 54
Marsh, R., 171
Martin, H., 220

Martin, J., 220
Martin, W., 166
Maslow, A., 56, 248
Masters, W., 116
Masterson, J., 349
Matza, D., 305
Maurer, R., 178
May, M., 289
Mayer, J., 88, 93, 329
Mazda, D., 320
McAlister, A., 117
McArthur, J., 83
McCabe, A., 280
McCabe, M., 256
McComb, D., 270
McCormack, W., 270
McCreary-Juhasz, A., 25, 271, 273
McCutcheon, S., 56, 327
McDonald, F., 277
McGlothlin, W., 115
McFall, R., 245
McInnes, R., 88
McIntyre, J., 281
McKeachie, W., 19
McLouth, G., 262
McQueen, R., 93
Mead, M., 11, 212
Meadow, M., 300
Meeks, J., 343, 344
Mellinger, G., 115, 116
Mercer, G., 107
Mercy, J., 337
Merrill, M., 130
Mettlin, C., 117
Metz, M., 167
Metzger, L., 310
Metzner, B., 180
Mezzich, A., 331
Mezzich, J., 331
Michela, J., 92
Michalide, B., 97
Milavsky, J., 281
Milburn, J., 245
Milgram, G., 124
Miller, G., 129
Miller, J., 337
Miller, N., 17
Millstein, S., 326
Minard, R., 291
Minuchin, S., 209
Mitchell, J., 186
Mitchell, M., 188
Money, J., 79, 90
Montemayor, R., 11, 55, 205, 214, 240
Moore, B., 211
Moorman, A., 216
Moreno, J., 244
Morgan, L., 258
Moriarty, D., 280
Morse, C., 115
Morse, L., 197
Moynihan, D., 305
Mugrove, F., 290
Mussen, P., 49
Myrdal, G., 290

Nahas, G., 116
Naisbitt, J., 183

Narius, D., 54
Nelson, R., 216
Nesselroade, J., 40
Newcomb, T., 233, 235
Nicol, S., 336
Noam, G., 55
Norton, A., 216
Nye, F., 211

O'Brien, G., 73
O'Connor, R., 280
Oden, M., 150
Oden, S., 245
Offer, D., 6, 7, 36, 52, 53, 63, 337
Offer, J., 7
Ohlin, L., 311, 312
Oldham, D., 7
O'Leary, K., 217
O'Leary, V., 188
Olshavsky, R., 106, 117
Oltmanns, T., 217
Olsen, N., 72
Olson, D., 209
Olson, L., 261
O'Malley, P., 104, 105, 229
Oriel, J., 270
Oros, C., 257
Orr, D., 86, 352
Orstein, M., 199
O'reilly, K., 262
Osipow, S., 196
Ostrov, E., 7
Owens, W., 139

Palfrey, J., 310
Palonsky, S., 166
Paperny, D., 220
Parnell, R., 88
Pasamanick, B., 258
Pasanella, A., 157
Patterson, G., 305
Peck, M., 337
Pederson, L., 118
Peevers, B., 240
Pelton, L., 220
Perl, J., 253
Perry, C., 117
Pervin, L., 173
Petersen, A., 81, 87, 90, 325
Petersen, R., 115
Petronio, R., 178, 229, 304, 309
Pettigrew, T., 290
Piaget, J., 13, 19, 20, 24, 27, 141–146, 174, 175, 281, 282, 288, 294
Pinney, J., 117
Piers, E., 36, 63, 65
Piliavin, J., 292
Polk, K., 305
Pollinger, A., 108, 116
Pollock, C., 220
Pollock, J., 178
Pratto, D., 216
Press, A., 240
Presson, C., 107
Price, D., 40
Price, J., 85

Proshansky, H., 290
Pugh, R., 291
Purkey, S., 164, 346

Rabkin, J., 56
Rachel, J., 110, 112
Radl, S., 66
Rahe, R., 56, 326
Ranieri, D., 331
Rapaport, R., 326
Raphelson, A., 72
Raven, J., 136
Raynor, J., 47
Reed, R., 329
Rehberg, R., 176, 177
Reisman, J., 325
Reisner, R., 100
Rest, J., 288
Revelle, R., 83
Richards, L., 117
Richardson, S., 89, 93
Rimm, A., 93
Ritter, B., 315
Ritter, J., 90
Robbins, J., 301
Robbins, J. M., 261, 263
Robbins, S., 288
Roberts, J., 80
Robertson, J., 124
Robins, E., 254
Robinson, I., 253
Roche, A., 80
Rock, D., 178
Rodin, J., 94
Rodman, H., 216
Rogers, E., 114
Rogers, L., 55
Rojec, G., 179, 303, 304, 322
Romer, N., 72
Ronald, L., 89
Rooney, E., 207
Rosenberg, M., 27, 36, 53, 54, 63–65,
    228, 353
Rothman, G., 288
Rosenshine, B., 165
Rosenthal, E., 176, 177
Rosner, B., 270
Ross, R., 107
Rossi, P., 186
Roszak, T., 292
Roth, L., 94
Rothman, S., 136
Rothkopf, E., 51
Rotter, J., 71
Rubington, E., 319
Rubins, W., 281
Ruble, D., 83
Rumberger, R., 229
Rushton, J., 280
Russell, C., 209
Rutter, M., 65, 209, 210, 331
Ryan, C., 201

Saario, T., 73
Sach, A., 229, 256
Sadker, M., 73
Sager, H., 290

Saghir, R., 254
Sakoda, J., 248
Sarason, S., 160
Scanlon, J., 100, 139, 140
Scarlett, H., 240
Schachter, S., 94, 100
Schaie, K., 40, 140
Schalmo, G., 254
Schellenbach, C., 220
Schlesier-Stroop, B., 97
Schneider, F., 117
Schofield, J., 290
Schroder, H., 174
Schmidt, G., 249
Schulman, A., 230
Schultes, R., 122
Schulz, B., 256
Schwartz, R., 44
Sears, R., 72, 210
Sebes, J., 220
Sechrist, L., 44
Secord, P., 240
Selman, R., 240, 241, 242
Seltzer, C., 93
Semmel, M., 157
Seng, L., 262
Sgroi, S., 222
Shah, F., 256, 261
Shannon, F., 326
Shapiro, T., 115
Shaw, M., 235
Sheldon, W., 88
Sherman, S., 106, 117
Sherrets, S., 343
Shiffrin, R., 130
Shostak, A., 262
Shuey, A., 141
Siegal, C., 72
Siegal, P., 186
Sieglar, R., 147
Sigal, H., 92
Sigusch, V., 249
Silverberg, S., 213, 215
Siman, M., 229
Simon, T., 130, 131
Simmons, R., 65, 90, 252, 326, 337
Singell, L., 199
Singer, D., 280
Singer, J., 280, 336
Sizer, T., 160
Skinner, B., 13, 17
Smith, J. C., 337
Smith, R., 258
Smith, S., 258
Smith, S. M., 164
Smith, T., 213, 220
Snyderman, M., 136
Solano, C., 150
Solomon, T., 220
Somers, R., 115
Sorensen, R., 247, 248, 253, 256, 261,
    267, 271
Spanier, G., 264, 273
Speirs, V., 317
Spencer, M., 292
Spilka, B., 297
Spreadbury, C., 252, 253
Sprenkle, D., 209
Staffieri, J., 88, 89

Stager, S., 313
Stanley, J., 33, 35, 38, 150
Starbuck, E., 292
Stark, R., 298, 300
Steele, B., 220
Steen, E., 85
Steinberg, L., 199, 200, 213, 215
Stephanson, S., 200
Stern, M., 268, 269
Sternberg, R., 136, 137
Stewart, A., 56, 327
Stewart, C., 248, 253, 254
Stickle, G., 266
Stipp, H., 281
Steirlin, H., 315
Strang, R., 293
Strano, D., 263
Strigari, A., 166, 240
Strong, E., 191
Strother, C., 140
Struening, E., 56
Sudia, C., 217
Sugarman, A., 88
Sullivan, H., 174, 231
Super, D., 193, 194
Susman, E., 86
Svajian, P., 11, 205, 214
Sykes, G., 320

Tannenbaum, A., 327
Tanner, J., 79, 80, 81, 83, 86, 87
Taylor, B., 81
Teevan, J., 281
Terman, L., 131, 149, 150, 152
Teuting, P., 331
Thelan, H., 173
Thelen, M., 280
Thomas, D., 207, 208
Thomas, L., 212, 213
Thompson, J., 326
Thompson, L., 117, 118
Thornburg, H., 86, 170
Thurstone, L., 136
Titley, R., 193
Tjosvold, D., 165
Tobin-Richards, M., 90
Tolsma, S., 337
Tomlinson-Keasey, C., 148
Toro, G., 116
Torrence, E., 151, 152
Tramontana, M., 343
Tresemer, D., 72
Turiel, E., 289
Tuttle, C., 73

Ullman, K., 83
Ullman, R., 108, 116

Vandiver, T., 337
VanTassel-Baska, J., 152, 154
VanThorne, M., 98
Varenhorst, B., 229, 230
Vaux, A., 200
Veldman, D., 157
Vener, A., 248, 253, 254
Vernon, D., 149

Vernon, P., 149
Vogel, F., 98
Vogt, D., 162
Volkmar, C., 157
Voss, H., 178, 179

Wadsworth, B., 144
Wagner, H., 228
Waldrop, M., 328
Walker, D., 314
Walker, L., 287, 288
Walker, L. S., 326
Walker, R., 88, 89
Wallach, M., 150
Wallerstein, J., 217
Walsh, W., 288
Walster, E., 92
Walters, R., 210, 277
Warren, M., 86
Watson, J., 13, 17, 47
Waugh, I., 313
Webb, E., 33, 44, 45
Wechsler, D., 131, 136, 139
Weigert, A., 207
Weinberg, M., 267, 319
Weiner, B., 70

Weiner, I., 238, 314, 325, 331, 332, 334
Weinhold, C., 331
Weinstein, E., 289
Weiss, I., 267
Weller, R., 115
Werner, E., 258
Werner, H., 13, 20
Werthman, C., 313
West, L., 115
Westie, F., 290
Westling,D., 157
Wetzel, J., 196, 197
Whisnant, L., 83
Whitehead, L., 209
Willemsen, E., 72
Williams, J., 72
Willingham, W., 263
Wilson, A., 64, 237
Wiltis, F., 213
Winburn, G., 116
Wing, C., 150
Winn, M., 280
Winokur, G., 337
Wirtanen, I., 179
Wise, H., 169
Wold, H.., 36

Wolf, T., 280
Wolk, S., 314
Wolman, B., 49, 345
Wong, M., 106, 124
Wood, K., 310
Wunderlich, R., 93
Wuthnow, R., 292
Wylie, R., 51, 62
Wynne, L., 336

Yablonsky, L., 319
Yankelovitch, D., 212, 254, 298
Yarchesi, A., 229
Yinger, R., 166
Young, R., 247
Yudkovitz, E., 97
Yule, W., 331

Zaretsky, I., 300, 301
Zegans, L., 83
Zelnik, M., 255–258, 261, 262, 264
Zigler,. E., 155
Zillman, D., 281
Zimbardo, P., 66
Zinberg, N., 125

INDEX OF KEY TERMS

Abortion, 262–263
Achievement, 69–70, 161–162, 180, 236–238
Achievement motives, 64, 70–71, 237–238
Acne, 99–101
Acting out, 26, 310, 329–330
Adjustment reaction, 329–330
Adoption, 265
Adolescence:
    cross-cultural views, 11–13
    definitions, 1–4
    historical views, 4–6
    literary images, 7
Adolescent society, 238
Aggression, 208, 210, 280, 281, 310, 329–330
AIDS, 267, 270–271
Alcohol, 105, 106, 110–114
Amotivational syndrome, 115–116
Amphetamines, 106, 120
Anorexia nervosa, 63, 95–99, 325
Antisocial behavior, 306, 309, 325
Anxiety, 7, 11, 249
Apprenticeships, 12, 182–183, 206
Asceticism, 15
Authoritarian parents, 208
Authoritative parents, 208, 209
Autonomy, 25, 204–206, 213, 277

Baby boom, 21
Barbiturates, 118–119
Behavioral maturity, 26

Behavioral theory, 13, 17–19
Blood alcohol levels, 112–114
Body image, 2, 23, 87, 99, 328, 352
Bone age, 80, 85
Bulimia, 95–99, 325

Censorship, 162–163
Child abuse, 219–224
Chlamydia, 269–270
Cigarettes (smoking), 105, 106, 117–118
Classical conditioning, 17
Classroom management, 165–166
Cliques, 227
Cluster suicides, 337
Cocaine, 106, 120
Cognitive developmental theory, 13, 19, 20, 23, 141–149
Cohort, 40
Competency-based education, 167–168
Conceptual styles, 174–176
Concrete operational thinking, 14, 144
Conditioning, 17–19
Conditional stimulus, 17
Conduct disorders, 329–330
Confidentiality, 348–349
Conformity, 234–236
Control group, 35
Contraception, 256, 260–262
Conversion, 298–299
Coping, 325–327, 330
Correlation, 38–39

Counseling, 229, 342–350
Crack, 120
Creativity, 15, 117, 150–152, 208
Crime index, 303–304
Cross-sectional research, 39, 40
Cults, 299
Cultural fair tests, 138

Date rape, 257
Dating, 91, 252–253
Defense mechanisms, 15–16, 345–346
Delinquency, 3, 14, 26, 106, 179, 229, 244, 303–323, 325
Demography, 21, 22, 159
Dependent variable, 33, 34
Depressants, 106, 111, 118–119
Depression, 325, 330–3332
Desegregation, 290
Developmental task, 22–27
Discipline, 165–166, 210, 309
Divorce, 216–219
Double standard, 254
Drinking levels (alcohol), 110–111
Dropouts, 106, 178–179, 229, 317
Drug dependence, 107–110, 229
Drug education, 103, 124–127
Drugs, patterns of ue, 104–107, 110–124

Eating disorders, 95–99
Early adolescence, 3, 327
Early maturation, 34, 89–90

Ecosystems, 41
Egocentrism, 20, 66, 148, 352
Ego extensions, 54
Electra conflict, 14
Effective schools, 164
Emotional abuse, 220
Experimentation, 33-39
    Dimensions of experimental
    research, 34-35
External valildity, 37, 50

Faith development, 294-299
Family adaptability, 209
Family cohesion, 209
Family conflict, 210, 211, 213-216
Father absence, 219
Fear of success, 70-71
Fixation, 16
Formal operational thinking, 28, 141,
    145-149, 275
Fraternity initiations, 12
Friendship, 227, 233, 235, 236

Gangs, 305, 309-310, 317-320
Generation gap, 212-213
Gonorrhea, 267, 269
Gifted adolescents, 149-150
Graffiti, 42-43, 312
Great depression, 21, 211
Growth hormone, 79, 80
Growth spurt, 2, 80-82

Hallucinogens, 105, 106, 122-123
Height, 81-82, 90
Heroin, 105, 123
Herpes virus, 270
Homosexuality, 266-267

Identity crisis, 16, 56, 62
Identity development, 16, 24
Identity foreclosure, 59
Identity moratorium, 59
Illiteracy, 161-162
Imaginary audience, 67
Impulse control, 26
Independence, 25, 204-206, 213, 277
Independent variable, 33, 34
Individualized plans, 31, 74, 150,
    156-157
Information processing, 129
Informed consent, 47
Inhalents, 123
Intelligence, definitions, 132, 136, 137
Intelligence tests, 130-141
Intellectualization, 15
Internal validity, 36, 50
Interviews, 43, 44
Invisible audience, 67, 148-149

Juvenile justice, 313-315, 321-323

Labeling, 312-313
Latchkey, 216

Late maturation, 34, 89, 90
Learning environments, 173-176
Life events, 56, 326-327
Locus of control, 70
Longitudinal research, 39, 40
Long-term memory, 130
LSD, 106, 122-123

Mainstreaming, 1516-157
Mariujuana, 35, 105, 106, 114-117
Marriage, 263-264
Masturbation, 16, 248-249
Menarche, 83-85, 260
Menstruation, 11, 83-85
Mental retardation, 155-157
Middle adolescence, 3
Middle schools, 170-171
Modeling, 278, 279
Moral behavior, 277-279, 280-281,
    288-289
Moral development, 27, 281-289

Naturalistic observation, 40
Negative identity, 59
Ncoturnal emission, 85
Nonexperimental research, 33, 38

Obesity, 92-94, 325, 329
Observer interference, 44-46
Occupational prestige, 186
Oedipal conflict, 14, 276
Operant conditioning, 17-19
Operational definitions, 33, 36

Parent effects, 65, 106, 208-212, 309
Parenting styles, 207-212
PCP, 122-123
Peers, 4, 25, 59, 106, 118, 226-246,
    256, 305, 325
Peer counseling, 229-230
Permissive parenting, 207, 209
Personal fable, 148-149
Petting, 253
Physical abuse, 219-221
Physical attractiveness, 91-92
Physical growth, 2, 78
Physical handicaps, 87, 93
Political thinking, 289-290
Popularity, 66, 91-92, 243-245
Pregnancy, 83, 250-251, 257-260
Prejudice, 290-292, 311
Premarital sex, 254-257
Problem behavior, 325-326, 344
Prostitution, 315
Psychoanalytic theory, 13, 14, 17
Psychopathology, 210, 226, 244, 325,
    326
Psychosexual stages, 15, 16
Psychosocial stages, 15-17, 57-61
Psychosomatic illnesses, 327-329
Puberty, 2, 11, 78-81, 101, 252
Punishment, 19

Quasi-experimentation, 38

Randomization, 35
Regression, 15
Reinforcement, 17-19, 277
Religion, 106, 256, 292-301
Research ethics, 11-13
Risk taking, 311, 325-326
Rites of passage, 11-13
Runaways, 314-315

Schizophrenia, 332-336
School environment, 24, 164
School structure, 160, 168-171
Scoliosis, 80
Sedatives, 105
Secondary gain, 328
Self-concept, 2, 3, 26-29, 51-77,
    76-77, 79, 86, 89-93, 193-194,
    208-212, 216-218,2 20, 234,
    244-245, 252, 257, 293, 331,
    351-354
    development, 55-56
    fostering, 74-75
    measurement, 62-63
    structure, 27-28, 52-53
Self-fulfilling prophesy, 5
Sex education, 271-273
Sex maturity ratings, 85-88
Sex research, 247-248
Sex roles, 26, 72-73, 186-187
Sexual abuse, 221-222
Sexual attitudes, 253-254
Sexual behavior, 26, 106, 229,
    248-249, 254-257
Sexual growth, 78-87
Sexually transmitted diseases, 3, 23,
    261, 267-271, 304
Shoplifting, 306
Short term memory, 129
Shyness, 65-67
Single parents, 216-219
Skeletal age, 19, 80, 85
Skinfold, 93-94
Smokeless tobacco, 118
Smoking, 105, 106, 117-118
Social cognition, 240-242
Social competence, 244-256
Social Darwinism, 4, 5
Social isolation, 244-245
Sociometry, 242-243
Somatotypes, 88-89
Status offenses, 313-314
Stimulants, 119-120, 122
Storm and stress, 2, 4, 5
Stress, 326-327
Suicide, 29, 336-342
Syphilis, 267-269

Teacher roles, 165, 166-167, 176
Television, 278, 279, 280, 281
Time on task, 165
Tobacco (smoking), 105, 106, 117-118
Tranquilizers, 105, 118-119
Transescent, 171

Unsocialized aggressive reaction, 27,
    329-330

Values, 26
Vandalism, 318–318
Venereal diseases, 3, 23, 261, 267–271, 304
Verbal abilities, 24
Vocational aptitudes, 188, 190, 191, 194–196

Vocational counseling, 194–196, 201–202
Vocational development, 3, 5, 27, 186–188, 191–194
Vocational goals, 3, 5, 27, 185–186, 191–192

Weight, 79, 81–82, 90, 92–99

Youth, 4
Youth employment, 22, 196–201
Youth market, 22, 92